AMERICAN POLIT

POLICIES,

and

PRIORITIES

AMERICAN POLITICS, POLICIES, and PRIORITIES

Sixth Edition

ALAN SHANK

State University of New York, Geneseo

WCB Brown & Benchmark
PUBLISHERS

Madison, Wisconsin•Dubuque, Iowa•Indianapolis, Indiana
Melbourne, Australia•Oxford, England

Book Team

Editor *Edgar J. Laube*
Developmental Editor *Roger Wolkoff*
Production Coordinator *Karen L. Nickolas*
Visuals/Design Developmental Consultant *Marilyn A. Phelps*

Brown & Benchmark

A Division of Wm. C. Brown Communications, Inc.

Vice President and General Manager *Thomas E. Doran*
Executive Managing Editor *Ed Bartell*
Executive Editor *Edgar J. Laube*
Director of Marketing *Kathy Law Laube*
National Sales Manager *Eric Ziegler*
Marketing Manager *Kathleen Nietzke*
Advertising Manager *Jodi Rymer*
Managing Editor, Production *Colleen A. Yonda*
Manager of Visuals and Design *Faye M. Schilling*

Production Editorial Manager *Vickie Putman Caughron*
Publishing Services Manager *Karen J. Slaght*
Permissions/Records Manager *Connie Allendorf*

Wm. C. Brown Communications, Inc.

Chairman Emeritus *Wm. C. Brown*
Chairman and Chief Executive Officer *Mark C. Falb*
President and Chief Operating Officer *G. Franklin Lewis*
Corporate Vice President, Operations *Beverly Kolz*
Corporate Vice President, President of WCB Manufacturing *Roger Meyer*

Cover and interior design by Lesiak/Crampton Design Inc

Copyedited by Deanne Gute

Contents

Preface *xi*

SECTION 1 The Foundations of American Government 1

Chapter 1 Democracy and the American Political System 3

Origins of American Democratic Values
1. The Struggle for Democracy • *Benjamin Barber and Patrick Watson* 8

American Political Culture: Values and Dilemmas
2. The American Political Creed • *Lawrence J. R. Herson* 12

Contemporary American Democracy: Criticisms and Observations
3. Democracy in America? • *Lewis H. Lapham* 18

Chapter 2 The Constitution 27

James Wilson and the Constitution
4. Interview with a Founding Father • *Garry Wills* 34

Separation of Powers: Checks and Balances
5. *The Federalist*, Number 51 • *James Madiso*n 41

The Enduring Constitution
6. A Few Parchment Pages Two Hundred Years Later • *Richard B. Morris* 45

Is Constitutional Reform Needed?
7. The World's Most Stable Democracy • *Charlotte Saikowski* 53

Chapter 3 Civil Liberties and Civil Rights 59

Evolution of Constitutional Protections
8. The Bill of Rights: Protector of Minorities and Dissenters • *Norman Dorsen* 73

Protecting Unpopular Political Expression
9. The Flag Burning Controversy • *U.S. Supreme
    Court*   79

Protecting Minorities
10. Constitutional Equality • *Stanley N. Katz*   85

Protections for the Accused: Should They be Changed?
11. When Criminal Rights Go Wrong • *Paul Savoy*   92

Chapter 4   Federalism and Intergovernmental Relations   103

Federalism and the Political Process
12. Federalism and Theory • *Richard H. Leach*   111

**Federal-State Relations: Centralization and
Decentralization**
13. Opening the Third Century of American Federalism:
    Issues and Prospects • *Daniel J. Elazar*   119

Federal Aid to States and Local Governments
14. Lobbying for the Good Old Days
    • *Jonathan Walters*   131

SECTION 2   Political Participation: Influencing
Government   139

Chapter 5   Interest Groups   141

The Danger of Factions
15. *The Federalist*, Number 10 • *James Madison*   149

The Mobilization of Bias
16. The Scope and Bias of the Pressure System
    • *E. E. Schattschneider*   155

Lobbying: Strategies and Tactics
17. Old-Breed and New-Breed Lobbying
    • *Hedrick Smith*   163

Interest Group Campaigning
18. Sarah and James Brady, Target: The Gun Lobby
    • *Wayne King*   170

Chapter 6   Public Opinion, Political Parties, and Campaigns   181

Public Opinion: Polls and Political Survey Research
19. They've Got Your Number • *Charles Kenney*   189

Political Parties: Prospects for Reform

20. Strengthening the National Parties
• *James L. Sundquist*   198

National Parties and the Presidency

21. Choosing Presidential Candidates: Why the Best Man
Doesn't Necessarily Win • *D. Grier
Stephenson, Jr.*   209

Political Parties and the Media

22. The Press, Political Parties, and the Public-Private
Balance in Elections • *Gary R. Orren and
William G. Mayer*   216

Chapter 7   Voting, Elections, and the Media   225

Voting and Non-Voting

23. Remobilizing the American Electorate
• *Curtis B. Gans*   233

Campaign Finance: Political Action Committees

24. Real and Imagined Corruption in Campaign Financing
• *Larry Sabato*   244

Negative Election Ads

25. The Negative 1988 Presidential Campaign
• *Raymond L. Fischer*   253

The Media, Politics, and Elections

26. Can Democracy Survive the Media in the 1990s?
• *Judy Woodruff*   259

SECTION 3   Political Action: The Machinery of
Government   265

Chapter 8   The Presidency   267

Constitutional Foundations

27. The Presidency and Constitutional Development
• *Alan Shank*   274

Presidential Leadership

28. The Presidency and Its Paradoxes
• *Thomas E. Cronin*   281

Persuasion and Influence: Achieving Policy Goals

29. The Art of Presidential Persuasion • *Marcia Lynn
Whicker and Todd W. Areson*   294

Domestic and Foreign Policy Leadership

30. Reconsidering the Two Presidencies • *Duane M. Oldfield and Aaron Wildavsky*   300

Chapter 9   The Executive Branch and the Bureaucracy   309

The White House Staff

31. The Essence of White House Service • *Bradley H. Patterson, Jr.*   317

Managing the Federal Bureaucracy

32. The President and the Bureaucracy: Enemies, Helpmates or Noncontenders? • *Alana Northrop*   326

The Bureaucracy in Action

33. The Census: Why We Can't Count • *James Gleick*   332

Chapter 10   Congress   341

Legislator—Constituency Roles

34. The Rise of the Washington Establishment • *Morris P. Fiorina*   350

The Legislative Process

35. The Longest-Running Game in Town • *Marjorie Hunter and Tom Bloom*   361

Congressional Politics

36. The Changing Textbook Congress • *Kenneth A. Shepsle*   364

Congressional Roles

37. Games Congressmen Play • *John M. Barry*   374

Limiting Congressional Incumbency

38. Twelve is Enough • *Hendrik Hertzberg*   382

Chapter 11   The Supreme Court   389

Judicial Review

39. Marbury v. Madison • *U.S. Supreme Court*   401

Constitutional Interpretation: Original Intention v. Judicial Activism

40. The Supreme Court's Dilemma and Defense • *Raymond Polin*   406

Supreme Court Decision-Making Process

41. Deciding Cases and Writing Opinions
  • *David M. O'Brien*   412

The Abortion Controversy

42. Roe v. Wade • *U.S. Supreme Court*   420

43. Webster v. Reproductive Health Services
  • *U.S. Supreme Court*   426

SECTION 4 The Outputs of Government   435

Chapter 12 Public Policy 437

The Politics of Rich and Poor

44. Reagan's America: A Capital Offense
  • *Kevin P. Phillips*   443

The Persian Gulf War

45. Operation Desert Storm • *Elizabeth Drew*   452

Environmental Protection: An Assessment

46. Earth Day Plus 20, and Counting • *Bil Gilbert*   460

**The Future of American Politics, Policies,
and Priorities**

47. The Politics of the Restive Majority
  • *E. J. Dionne, Jr.*   468

Appendix   *477*
The Declaration of Independence   *477*
The Constitution of the United States   *481*
Index   *499*

Preface

The sixth edition of *American Politics, Policies, and Priorities* explores and analyzes the principal components of the American political system. As author-editor, I have been most pleased with the enthusiastic response of students and instructors who have used my previous five editions in their basic American government courses. My goal for the thoroughly revised and updated sixth edition is similar to earlier editions: to establish a sound basis for understanding the foundations of American government, the ways of influencing government through political participation, the institutional processes of the presidency, bureaucracy, Congress, and the courts, and various aspects of public-policy problems and issues relevant to the contemporary setting.

The forty-seven selected articles in twelve chapters provide a comprehensive overview of American government. This book encourages students and instructors to discuss and debate the controversies in our polity. The various selections include theory and concepts of American politics, as well as examples of actual practices and performances of the system. This is facilitated by chapter introductory paragraphs before each selection, which summarize major points and raise key questions. The introductory paragraphs also tie together preceding and subsequent titles by showing their interrelationships.

The appendix contains the texts of the Declaration of Independence and the Constitution, which can be used as reference materials for Chapter 2, "The Constitution," Chapter 3, "Civil Liberties and Civil Rights," and Chapter 11, "The Supreme Court."

New features of the sixth edition include thirty-nine articles that were not contained in the fifth edition. Chapters 1, 6, 7, 9, and 12 have been completely revised, and the other seven chapters contain substantially revised chapter introductions and new articles. Students and instructors should find Chapter 12, "Public Policy," especially interesting with recent selections on the Persian Gulf War, the environment, the economy, and the future of American politics. The titles of Chapters 6, 7, and 9 have been changed to include more emphasis on public opinion polls, the media, and presidential management of the executive branch.

Additional new features in this edition include:

- The setting for establishing democratic systems and criticisms of contemporary American democracy in Chapter 1.
- Assessments of constitutional stability and change in Chapter 2.
- Analysis of the flag burning controversy in Chapter 3.
- Lobbying styles and case examples of how state and local officials and gun control advocates and opponents pressure government in Chapters 4 and 5.
- Assessments of the role of the media in presidential elections in chapters 6 and 7.
- Importance of the constitutional basis of presidential authority in Chapter 8.
- Evaluating term limits for Congress in Chapter 10.
- Discussion of the abortion debate in Chapter 11.

The materials for the sixth edition were compiled, edited, and revised during the spring and summer months of 1991, a time of increasing public concern over the condition of the national economy, particularly demonstrated in the conflicts between the president and Congress over extending unemployment benefits.

President Bush took credit for improving foreign policy relations with the former Soviet Union and, together with Secretary of State James Baker, arranged for a Middle East conference between Israel and the Arab states. Congress and various Democrats announcing their presidential candidacies were criticizing President Bush for neglecting domestic priorities. While Bush was announcing historic unilateral cuts in the nuclear arsenal, the Senate was heatedly debating the nominations of Clarence Thomas for Supreme Court Justice and Robert Gates for CIA Director. Much speculation took place over whether the Supreme Court would overturn the *Roe v. Wade* abortion decision.

I hope the sixth edition of this book will inspire students of American politics to comprehend the sources of our nation's strengths as well as to identify new approaches to the domestic and foreign policy problems that directly affect our lives. The major objective of this edition is to encourage active participation in the political life of the community, state, and nation. Students need to develop a basis for positive action in dealing with the complex and often frustrating problems we now face.

ACKNOWLEDGMENTS

I wish to acknowledge the support of several people who assisted in developing, organizing, and completing this edition. Roger Wolkoff, project editor at William C. Brown, encouraged completion of the project. In particular, I wish to thank the many reviewers who provided outstanding advice for the book. These included:

Harold Gortner, George Mason University
Sara Ann Grove, Frostburg State University
Rodney Grunes, Centenary College
Frederick Lee, Eastern Michigan University
Edward Portis, Texas A & M University
Richard Sloan, University of Colorado—Boulder
Henry Steck, SUNY Cortland
Grier Stephenson, Franklin & Marshall College

Ken Deutsch, my colleague at Geneseo, provided suggestions for articles in the chapter on the Supreme Court. Jeffrey Koch provided me with helpful materials on political parties and the media. Liz Ancker did an outstanding job of deciphering my handwritten comments and typing the manuscript. The Milne Library at SUNY-Geneseo remains the primary source of locating books and articles for this project.

The Foundations of American Government

CHAPTER 1

Democracy and the American Political System

The first problem of politics is how citizens can keep their rulers from becoming tyrants. In this chapter, popular control of political leaders is investigated by considering the origins and development of democracy, the values and dilemmas of American political culture, and criticisms of contemporary democracy in American government.

In the American political system, the people are considered the ultimate source of authority. Accountability of the rulers is achieved through various delegations of power—through voting, elections, a constitutional order, and a representative government based on separation of powers and checks and balances. These principles have been debated since the Constitutional Convention of 1787, the Civil War of the 1860s, and the New Deal of the 1930s. The issues of legitimate authority and political accountability have frequently divided the nation and resulted in serious conflicts.

Democracy and political accountability affect American foreign and domestic responsibilities in the 1990s. Internationally, the United States has been concerned with the international drug trade and the invasion of Kuwait by Iraq. President Bush mobilized the military in 1989 and 1991 to battle General Noriega in Panama and Saddam Hussein in the Persian Gulf. The demise of communism in Eastern Europe, including the end of the Cold War with the Soviet Union, brought forth new issues of America's role in promoting peaceful economic and political change. On the home front, the political accountability of elected officials is questioned as a consequence of their inability to solve problems: persistently large federal and state budget deficits, the savings and loan bailout, and response to drug abuse, crime control, homelessness, AIDs, education, and the environment.

DIRECT AND INDIRECT DEMOCRACY

What are the origins of American democracy? Most students would cite the Declaration of Independence or the Preamble to the U.S. Constitution. Benjamin Barber and Patrick Watson, in Article 1, tell us that the struggle for democracy has taken place for at least 2,500 years. Democracy began when Greek tribes took control of cities from kings and established self-governing communities.

These self-governing city-states were one of the earliest examples of direct democracy. This is the rule of the many in contrast to the rule of one (autocracy) or the rule of the few (oligarchy or elitism). Direct democracy means that the people influence, participate, and make the decisions that affect their lives. Key components include citizen participation in the community, political equality, respect for law, and direct involvement in governmental affairs. Direct democracy can be found in New England town meetings; in citizen organizations dealing with consumer affairs, energy, and environmental issues; and in voting on ballot referendums. In several states, local voters have direct control over school budgets. Voters have gone to the polls and decided on such diverse issues as property taxes, demands for a nuclear freeze, mandated death penalty, regulations for beverage containers, and restrictions on private ownership of handguns.

Yet indirect or representative democracy is the foundation of our voting system, election laws, and the procedures by which the executive and legislative branches of government function. Representative democracy includes popular control of the policy makers, political equality, political freedom, majority rule, and protection of minority rights. Popular control is based on elections in which voters select representatives who determine public policies. Political equality is voting equality in which most restrictions on adult suffrage have been eliminated and where each vote counts the same in an election. Political freedom is the absence of coercion in voting—ballots must be secret and at least two candidates must compete for each office. Candidates must be free to express their views and to organize their campaigns. Majority rule operates when the decision of the majority prevails in votes taken by the elected representatives. Also, the minority has the right to criticize and oppose majority decisions, although the minority agrees to accept them. Minorities are also given the opportunity to try to become majorities. In a democracy, minority rights usually include freedom of speech, press, assembly, and petition. Minorities can also form opposition parties and run for public office.

Representative democracy has been a part of the political system since the adoption of the Constitution in 1787. It is unique because it is not the predominant form of political organization in the world. Nevertheless, many nations aspire to a representative government. In 1989, a pro-democracy movement began to sweep through China, Eastern Europe, and the Soviet

Union. In China, students demanded free speech and press, and the end of government corruption. In response, the government ordered a brutal suppression of the students in June of 1989. The Soviet Union loosened its grip over Eastern Europe by permitting open elections in Poland, Hungary, and Czechoslovakia. Hungary permitted East Germans to flee to Austria en route to West Germany. In November, the Berlin Wall came down, and later, German reunification took place. Open elections and political opposition developed in the Soviet Union. Soviet Communist rule eased as Mikhail Gorbachev tied glasnost and perestroika to reviving a failed state-controlled economy. In late 1989, one of the last brutal dictators of Eastern Europe, Nicolae Ceausescu of Romania, was shot by a firing squad. By August 1991, a failed coup in the Soviet Union led to the suspension of the Communist party and an enormous shift of power to the republics.

All of these revolutionary events tell us that Barber and Watson are correct in their assessment that the struggle for democracy is alive and well. Eastern Europe and the former Soviet Union are developing new institutions based on the representative democracy model.

AMERICAN POLITICAL CULTURE: VALUES AND BELIEFS

Political culture refers to the fundamental beliefs and values people have about their political system, including how they believe it should operate and how it actually functions. Have any fundamental characteristics of American political life persisted over time? What political values do Americans have? According to Lawrence Herson in Article 2, nine ideals have persisted since the late eighteenth century: liberty, equality, achievement, justice, precedent, respect for the law, right to private property ownership, and localism. Herson argues that the most fundamental value is democracy. Although most Americans agree on the importance of these values, we frequently disagree on their meaning, interpretation, and application.

Americans believe in the rights of individuals to pursue their own self-interest through hard work, making the best use of private opportunities. Those who fail to prosper have only themselves to blame. Government should promote economic self-interest. Society is built around individual persons, and government is obligated to provide them with life, liberty, and the pursuit of happiness. The United States rejected the European style of authoritarianism or collectivism, where the state is supreme over the individual.

Freedom and equality are important values, but they sometimes conflict with each other. Freedom is the absence of governmental restraints on the individual's personal life and economic pursuits. Equality ensures entitlements to social life: the right to vote, equality before the law, and equal opportunity to compete with others for education, employment, and the so-called good life. A problem occurs when advocates of positive freedom (or substantive democracy) argue that governmental action is needed to achieve equality while advocates of individualist freedom complain that increased governmental power necessarily reduces personal liberty.

The debate over democracy in the 1990s is framed by the conflict between individual freedom versus social and economic equality. Reducing the federal government's domestic programs and bureaucracy is a goal of market-oriented conservatives who want less interference with economic self-interest. Liberals argue for positive governmental efforts to promote equal opportunity: aid to education, assistance to the needy, affirmative action programs for women and minorities, and nondiscrimination against minorities through strong civil rights enforcement.

CONTEMPORARY DEMOCRACY: CRITICISMS AND OBSERVATIONS

In 1989 and 1990, many Eastern European countries and the Soviet Union began a pro-democracy movement. Leaders of these countries looked to the United States and the Western European democracies for guidance in achieving several of the democratic values mentioned by Lawrence Herson in Article 2.

What can American government offer to these emerging democracies seeking to establish new political parties, electoral systems, representative institutions, and the rule of law?

Can the pro-democracy movement learn anything from the United States? Two lessons are available from the earliest days of America's development. First, the new democracies need a bill of rights to guarantee civil, political, social, and economic freedoms. Second, there must be opposition political parties to replace the once-dominant communist parties.

American representative democratic institutions may need essential constitutional, party, and electoral reforms as the former Soviet Union and the Eastern European countries do. The struggle for democratic reform is just as applicable in the United States as in emerging democracies for three reasons. First, the American system of constitutional checks and balances produces fragmentation of power, frustrates leadership, saps efficiency and erodes responsibility. Second, our political parties have lost the key functions of recruiting leadership, standing behind it in office and taking responsibility for its performance. Third, our electoral system is dominated by the media and money, a ballot that confuses the voters, the avoidance of substantive issues, and excessive sensationalism and trivialization during campaigns.[1]

Lewis Lapham in Article 3 is very critical of contemporary American democratic practices and representative institutions. Lapham considers democracy as a temperament or spirit of mind. In his view, democracy is freedom of thought and recognition of social problems that need to be addressed. Sadly, Lapham finds most Americans today are apathetic, uninvolved in their government, unaware of even how American government functions. Political campaigns have become a media-oriented buying and selling game by candidates, where television advertisements are predominant. Voting participation has declined alarmingly. Checks and balances don't apply to the president's warmaking powers. Instead of healthy political debate, there are appeals to nonpartisanship in foreign policy and consensus in domestic policy. Finally, a substantial majority of Americans are willing to yield their civil liberties to the police and the bureaucracy to protect themselves against drug abuse and violent crime.

Lapham identifies several reasons why the struggle for democracy continues in the United States. He argues that for democracy to work well, we need more than parades and expressions of patriotism. Citizens need to become better informed and more active and involved. This will help to counterbalance America's drift toward oligarchy or plutocracy, where small wealthy political and economic elites try to dominate the political system.

CONCLUSION: RESPONSIVENESS OF DEMOCRACY TO PEOPLE'S NEEDS

The three themes raised in this chapter—democracy, political culture, and governance—serve to introduce the principal topics for our subsequent discussion of American politics, policies, and priorities. The overall theme of these chapters is whether or not the American government system of representative democracy is responding effectively to the needs of the people.

Chapters 2, 3, and 4 deal with specific foundations of American government found in the Constitution, the Bill of Rights, and the federal system. Here we explore democratic ideals and values as applied to the structural and political relationships between citizens and government, individual freedoms and government authority, and federal-state-local government relationships.

Section II considers the relationships between American citizens and government and, more particularly, how people can become involved in influencing government decisions. Chapter topics deal with interest groups, political parties, campaigns, elections, and the role of the media.

Section III investigates the specific institutions and power relations of the national government, including the presidency, the bureaucracy, Congress, and the Supreme Court. The institutions are considered in terms of how they exercise power and influence as well as how they interact with each other.

We conclude with a discussion of selected public policy issues in Section IV to show how priorities are established in American government and how specific policy debates are affecting people in the 1990s.

NOTE

1. James MacGregor Burns, "U.S., Model for Eastern Europe?" *New York Times*, 8 Feb. 1990, p. A29, col. 1-4.

Origins of American Democratic Values

1

The Struggle for Democracy
Benjamin Barber and Patrick Watson

In 1990, public television offered a remarkable series of programs focusing on how democracy originated, its values, goals, and obstacles encountered over the centuries. In the companion volume, part of which is excerpted below, Barber and Watson explain that democracy is linked to human freedom, self-mastery, discussion, and deliberation. The practitioners of democracy lack consensus on an overall definition and requirements. Why is this so? Barber and Watson also point out that democracy is not neat or well-ordered; it is a "messy form of political life." What accounts for this? All would agree that democracy and tyranny cannot coexist. In view of the revolt against communism in China, the Soviet Union, and Eastern Europe in 1989–91, the struggle for democracy had a real impact on Americans. Perhaps Barber and Watson's introductory essay will help us to reconsider our own freedoms and help us to value them more.

This is the story of the struggle for democracy—of the endless striving for liberty, for justice, and for power that has been the history of peoples everywhere and in all times. It is a struggle as ancient as human will, reflecting our wish to master our own immediate world, to be free of tyranny from without and within.

But if the struggle for democracy is as old as human consciousness, if we can find evidence of natural co-operation and a rudimentary equality among the earliest tribes, the political quest for formal democratic institutions began in earnest only about 2,500 years ago, on a barren, rocky outcropping reaching into the Mediterranean. That was when Greek tribes wrested control of their cities from the rule of kings and blood clans and set up the foundations for communities to govern themselves—eventually creating one of the most splendid civilizations the world has ever seen.

The spirit of that civilization endures today in the established democracies of the West, where citizens struggle to preserve their old freedoms in the face of complacency and bureaucracy, of oppression and terrorism, and where they labour to accommodate those freedoms to new technologies and new economic conditions. Today we may wonder, as puzzled voters, how our one vote can matter when millions are being cast, or whether the choice is really a choice at all if the alternatives are not of our own making. At the same time, we are apt to think that the battle for true citizenship has largely been won, and that democracy is universally recognized as the ideal system of government.

But is that true? And how will democracy fare in the twenty-first century? Can the civic spirit born in Athens in 430 B.C. deal with the microchip? Is the multinational corporation, which defies the very idea of national sovereignty, compatible with the old-fashioned democratic republic? There are many new questions that suggest continuing perils to democracy, even in those advanced countries where the struggle to establish it is over. And in the newer nations of the Third World, the struggle for democracy has just got under way. There, fledgling communities battle against land owners, professional armies, demagogues flushed with unaccustomed powers, crippling old colonial attitudes, and poverty and ignorance. Many people are still hoping to win the first victories of emancipation and equality. . . .

"Freedom," warned the great French philosopher of democracy, Jean Jacques Rousseau, "is a food easy to eat but hard to digest." For democracy is not simply an ideal to be realized once and for all, or a blueprint to be produced and then reproduced around the world. It is not a destination—it is a journey, a road men and women walk that may traverse many different terrains. Achieving freedom in the first instance may not be so difficult, whether it comes suddenly by violence and revolution (as it did in France), or slowly through an accretion of institutions that extend and protect liberty (as it did in England). Preserving, enhancing, and securing it against its myriad and tireless adversaries is much harder. Governments are no less mortal than people. Winston Churchill's jest—"De-

mocracy is the worst form of government in the world—except for all the other forms"—is no joke. It is hard to conceive of a more chaotic design for government than one that invites absolutely everyone to participate in fashioning it. Deference to authority sometimes seems more comfortable than living with the responsibility of freedom.

We found that to tell the story of democracy is also to explore the fundamental human urge towards self-mastery and liberation: the inclination to speak openly, communicate freely, pray according to one's beliefs, dance to one's own tune, think as one pleases—but to do so in the company of other men and women in a spirit of co-operation. There are people who insist that democracy is an acquired skill that depends on very special circumstances: that it must be taught. That what Thomas Hobbes called "the war of all against all" is the human condition: we are born as enemies and pursue only our own interests with zeal; democracy becomes the cautious experiment in co-operation by which we try gingerly to challenge the terrible reality of our natural condition. But Hobbes was writing during the English civil war in the seventeenth century. A hundred years later, Rousseau argued that our natural condition is one of peace and harmony, and that democracy is the way we make our social life reflect our egalitarian nature. And if freedom is won only by artifice and human invention and is not to be found in nature, what are we to make of the early tribal council that made equals of tribesmen, and encouraged participation in council meetings? What does it mean to say—as Thomas Jefferson says in the American Declaration of Independence—that men are free and equal by nature, and that government serves only to guarantee those natural rights? The old argument is between those "idealists," like Rousseau, who think we are born neighbours and those "realists," like Hobbes, who think we are born adversaries. It is when we turn to look at people from the inside that we find both Hobbes and Rousseau are right. As we discovered, the struggle for democracy also turns out to be a struggle within ourselves: it is a tension we see quite clearly in children between the yearning for freedom and the yearning for security, the need to govern ourselves and the need to be taken care of by others, the need to give and the need to take.

When we set out to make the television series and write this book, we deliberately tried not to define democracy in advance: as a result we found it in the most unexpected places, and found it wanting in many places we expected to find it. We watched democracy at work in the schools and in tribes and looked at formal democracy in the legal constitutions of nations, republics and so-called peoples' republics, constitutional monarchies and one-party democracies, American towns and African villages, face-to-face democracies where almost everyone knows everybody else and bureaucratic democracies where the governors are faceless—democracies all, if we take people at their word, however bizarre it may sometimes seem; yet impostors all, if we set our standards too high.

Westerners, it seems, have a rather proprietary attitude to democracy; after all, they claim, political democracy began in the West. And "one-party democracies" or "peoples' democracies" in which a single strongman claims to rule "in the name of the people" do seem to be contradictions in terms. Yet there are reasons to believe that styles of government other than the typical multiparty parliamentary systems *may* qualify as democratic. The one thing we have become sure of is that there is no consensus on what democracy is or what it requires.

Big states using representatives who are elected by the masses often seem to think they own democracy, and countries like the United States, Canada, France, England, and Mexico make of their size a democratic strength. Yet in such remarkable countries as Iceland, New Zealand, Switzerland, Holland, Israel, and Papua New Guinea, democracy and smallness go hand in hand, and in some of these accountability depends more on the participation of citizens than on the conduct of leaders.

Socialists and capitalists argue about which of their rival systems is more "democratic," disagreeing about the meaning of democracy itself at every step. The socialist argues that capitalism nourishes poverty and inequality in the name of freedom. How can "one man, one vote" be meaningful if some are millionaires and others paupers? Capitalists say that in pursuing equality, socialism limits political freedom. Today we find capitalist democracies trying to become more egalitarian in the name of social justice, and we find socialist dictatorships aspiring to more competition and market freedom in the name of *glasnost* and *perestroika*.

Democracy is deeply rooted in talk. It seems to prefer talk to force, deliberation to whim, good reasons to powerful arms, consensus to conflict, peace to war, co-operation to competition. But no sooner do we define democracy as "reasonable discussion" than someone reminds us that it can also mean the politics of conflict as well as the politics of co-operation; or that through the power of today's media, the government of public opinion we call democracy can enthrone whim rather than deliberation.

Democracy is not tidy. It is a rough, obstreperous, messy form of political life. Montesquieu, that thoughtful and ingenious French predecessor of both the French and the American revolutions, observed that where you find an orderly silence, there you will find tyranny. Wherever we find spirited voices raised in debate, where there is tumult and faction and unceasing talk, where men and women muddle their way to provisional solutions for permanent problems—and so clumsily do for themselves what tyrants or bureaucrats might have achieved much more neatly and efficiently for them—there we can feel assured that we are on the precious turf of democracy. Because democracy is finally—more than any other form of government—about people, just plain people. To be democratic is to disagree about what democracy is.

The research, our travels, the making of the television series, and the writing of the book have taken several years. But one unexpected and moving result, for us, was that we emerged from our long immersion anxious about the power of tyranny, we also emerged exhilarated by the power of democracy. Because we found that the struggle for democracy is intensifying in many places around the world, even if it is shrinking in some. Menaced though it often is by complacency, indifference, corruption, and self-centeredness, it has none the less built enormously powerful institutions for the healing of its self-inflicted wounds. And it is propelled into what looks like an expanding and challenging new century by the passionate determination of men, women, and children, who once having eaten of liberty, never forget its taste.

American Political Culture: Values and Dilemmas

2

The American Political Creed
Lawrence J. R. Herson

Barber and Watson offered broad parameters on the meaning of democracy in Article 1. How are democratic values applied to the American political system? In Article 2, Lawrence Herson explains that democracy in America can include ideas of popular consent of the governed, freedom to choose leaders in periodic elections, and maximizing citizen participation in government decisions. Herson identifies several other values of the American political culture, including liberty, equality, achievement, justice, precedent, the rule of law, private property, and localism. Herson argues that equality is "one of our most troublesome values." Why is this the most controversial value in American democracy? In assessing Herson's inventory of values, which of them do you believe most people accept in their daily political life? Which of the values are in conflict with each other? How can these conflicts be resolved?

From Lawrence J. R. Herson, *The Politics of Ideas: Political Theory and American Public Policy*, pp. 18-24 (Copyright © 1984), reissued 1990 by Waveland Press, Inc., Prospect Heights, Illinois. Reprinted with permission from the publisher.

COMPONENTS OF THE POLITICAL CULTURE[1]

The American Political Creed

We begin with a sketch of the political culture as framed by a distinguished European scholar, Gunnar Myrdal. What Myrdal sees as the essence of the political culture will provide a backdrop for the inventory to follow. The occasion for Myrdal's study (begun in 1937 and published in 1942) was an inquiry into race relations in the United States and the wider social patterns of a then almost completely segregated society.[2] For Myrdal, the essence of the American political culture is contained in what he calls the *American Creed,* a profession of ideals so central to American thought ways that they inform and haunt our political life. The American Creed, says Myrdal, speaks to

> the essential dignity of the individual human being, of the fundamental equality of all men, and of certain inalienable rights to freedom, justice, and a fair opportunity.[3]

For practical purposes, the main norms of the creed . . . are centered in the belief in equality and in the right to liberty.[4]

Myrdal is fully aware that these norms may be more the profession of faith than a description of practice. Without using the language of cognitive dissonance and selective perception, he is very much aware that Americans in everyday life are capable of walling off ideals from behavior. (How else can we account for whites' treatment of blacks and other racial minorities?) But even while recognizing most persons' capacity for "compartmentalizing" ideals and actions, Myrdal quotes with approval Vernon Parrington, whom he calls the "great historian of the development of the American mind."[5] Says Parrington:

> The humanitarian idealism of the Declaration [of Independence] has always echoed as a battle cry in the hearts of those who dream of an America dedicated to democratic ends. It cannot be long ignored or repudiated, for sooner or later it returns to

1. The writer is aware of a problem posed by one of his previous propositions: that what we see is shaped by our values. Any list of cultural components will be grounded in personal judgment, but the following list is drawn from a variety of sources. These include: Gunnar Myrdal, *An American Dilemma* [the quotations used herein are taken from the reprint of the 20th anniversary edition (New York: Pantheon Books, 1972)]; Lloyd Free and Hadley Cantril, *The Political Beliefs of Americans: A Study of Public Opinion* (New Brunswick, N.J.: Rutgers University Press, 1967); Gabriel Almond and Sidney Verba, *The Civic Culture* (Boston: Little, Brown, 1965); Donald Devine, *The Political Culture of the U.S.* (Boston: Little, Brown, 1972); Seymour Martin Lipset, *The First New Nation* (Garden City, N.Y.: Doubleday Anchor, 1967); Alexis de Tocqueville, *Democracy in America,* ed. Phillips Bradley (New York: Vintage Books, 1954), two vols.; Vernon Parrington, *Main Currents of American Thought* (New York: Harcourt Brace Jovanovich, 1954); Carl Degler, *Out of Our Past* (New York: Harper, Colophon, 1970); Daniel J. Boorstin, *The Americans* (New York: Vintage Books, 1974); and Perry Miller, *The New England Mind* (Boston: Beacon Press, 1961).

2. Myrdal, *American Dilemma.* Myrdal was chosen to lead the study because of his good reputation as a lawyer, economist, and sociologist, also because he was not an American. As a Swede, he could be presumed to be free of the cognitive screens through which an American might be expected to view the race problem in the United States.

3. Ibid., Vol. 1, p. 4.

4. Ibid., p. 8.

5. Further studies of compartmentalizing are James Prothro and Charles Grigg, "Fundamental Principles of Democracy," *Journal of Politics* 22 (1960); and Lawrence J. R. Herson and C. Richard Hofstetter, "Tolerance, Consensus, and the Democratic Creed: A Contextual Exploration," *Journal of Politics* 37 (1975).

plague the council of practical politics. It is constantly breaking out in fresh revolt.[6]

Parrington, and Myrdal through him, invoke here our notion of the politics of ideas being grounded in an attempt to close the gap between values and practice. Both writers are optimistic as to long-term outcomes. Sooner or later, they suggest, fundamental values will force changes in behavior, for in the final outcome, behavior will bend in the direction of ideals. Needless to say, one observer's optimism may be another's pessimism. Much depends on personal cognitions. For some observers, a review of civil liberties and white-black relations in the past half-century (as we shall see in later discussion) reinforces Myrdal's optimism; others are less sanguine.

Whether one wishes to declare himself an optimist or pessimist, the essence of Myrdal's version of the creed is a political culture that is driven by a sense of obligation to equality and to inalienable rights to justice, freedom, fair opportunity, and liberty. What we shall do now is add to and subtract from Myrdal's list. In constructing our list we will also be aware of its logical and emotional contradictions. Our list will suggest that the politics of ideas also turns on the inconsistencies between particular values—when, for example, equality of opportunity clashes with equality of outcome, or when equality is to be achieved by curtailing liberty.

A Culture Inventory

Liberty.   High on nearly every observer's list of fundamental American values is liberty. The idea (and word) figures prominently in the Declaration of Independence and in the Preamble to the Constitution. Both documents assert that our political system is created in pursuit of liberty, and the Constitution carries our sense of liberty to more precise definition by spelling out some of its details in the first 10 amendments (the Bill of Rights). High on the list of defined liberties, by virtue of placement in the First Amendment, are liberties of speech, press, and religion.

The idea of liberty has at least two dimensions: freedom *to* pursue one's own purposes, and freedom *from* interference with that pursuit. Neither dimension can be given full scope, for it is generally agreed that one person's freedom shall not extend to curtailing another person's pursuit of liberty. (As a Supreme Court justice put the matter, "Your freedom to swing your fist ends where my nose begins!") In addition, it is generally agreed that one person's freedom shall not do harm to what society defines as the collective good (for example, no free speech if that freedom is used to betray military secrets). Thus, much of the politics of liberty is given to drawing boundaries: between freedom for some and resulting harm to others, and between individual freedom and what has been defined as the collective good. The paradox of liberty, as Edmund Burke, the English philosopher and statesman, once observed, is that liberty to be meaningful, must be constrained.

Equality.   Equality as an ideal to be pursued also figures high in an inventory of the political culture. It is, however, one of our most troublesome values. Attempts at definition quickly give rise to argument. Most of these arguments turn on the distinction between equality of condition (or opportunity) and equality of outcome.

All persons, says the Declaration of Independence, are created equal. But does that proposition mean that each person shall be given an equal opportunity to participate in the political process (the same freedom as others to speak, to vote, to run for political office)? Or does equality convey something more? Does it convey an equality of outcome?

---

6. Parrington, *Main Currents*, re-quoted in Myrdal, *American Dilemma*, Vol. 1. p. 6 ff.

For example, does equality carry an obligation to use public funds to pay election expenses for anyone wishing to run for public office so that poverty will be no bar to office holding?

Does equality extend into social and economic realms? And if so, which idea do we support, equality of opportunity or equality of outcome? Equality of opportunity suggests that each person shall be free to make what he or she is able of his or her life—without undue government interference or assistance. Equality of opportunity places the burden of success or failure on the individual. In contrast, equality of outcome carries a sense that government shall take responsibility for making certain that each person receives something that approaches an equal share of life's rewards. Equality of outcome suggests that responsibility for a person's success or failure shall be shared by both the individual and society.

The politics of equality turns (as does the politics of liberty) on the drawing of boundaries: between a sense of individual responsibility and a sense of social responsibility, between contesting definitions of fairness. The politics of equality also makes us aware of the extent to which basic values interconnect. Dimensions of freedom are part of the politics of equality. There is a web of connection between liberty and equality, and both are joined to the value that we list next, achievement.

Achievement. If achievement is defined as striving to do one's best, the definition is given texture by the poet's injunction: "To strive, to seek, to find, and not to yield."[7] Observers of American culture are in considerable agreement that achievement has been one of its central values. One of the most respected of the early observers, the Frenchman Alexis de Tocqueville, wrote:

> The first thing that strikes a traveller in the United States is the innumerable multitude of those who seek to emerge from their original condition. . . . No Americans are devoid of a yearning desire to rise. . . . All are constantly seeking to acquire property, power and reputation.[8]

The contemporary analyst Seymour Martin Lipset agrees, and makes achievement along with equality "America's key values."[9] But in this parity of ranking, Lipset calls attention to one of the points of contention in the present-day politics of achievement: If achievement alone is permitted to drive the engine of politics, it will produce public policy that encourages conditions of inequality, whereas equality, if left to drive the engine, will circumscribe the freedom to achieve. (Crudely put, shall I be encouraged to achieve a high salary by being permitted to keep all that I earn, or shall my enthusiasm for a high salary be dampened by my being required to pay taxes used to assist those whose earnings are less than mine?)

Justice. The value called justice has several dimensions. One dimension leads us to contemplate a system of law (and indeed, an entire society) dedicated to moral ends. But having been led to that contemplation, questions arise as to which moral ends? One moral end supports capital punishment as being consonant with the ethical principle that those who take life shall lose life. Another invocation of moral ends rejects that contention on grounds that justice must serve the fundamental principle of equality, and because the poor tend to be convicted of murder with greater

7. David C. McClelland, *The Achieving Society* (New York: Free Press, 1976), and Alfred Tennyson, "Ulysses." Many see this poem as the quintessence of the Victorian ideal of achievement.

8. Tocqueville, *Democracy,* Vol. 2, p. 256.

9. Lipset, *First New Nation,* p. 2.

frequency than the rich, capital punishment must be set aside until such time as all are truly equal within the law's outcome.[10]

Closely related to this reasoning is a definition of justice that insists that morality at law is to be achieved by treating all offenders alike whatever their social or economic class. And a third dimension of justice (related to both of these) is the proposition that the outcome shall be the same for all persons tried for the same offense, no matter how separated in time or place. This latter dimension, Edmund Cahn insists, lies at the core of justice. Americans, he says, know justice in their bones. They measure it by any departure from the principle of equal treatment.[11]

As previously suggested, it is not easy to assemble a list of basic values in tidy categories. Each value spills into others. This problem of overlapping categories applies particularly to the two values that come next in our list. Each has a connection to justice, but we disengage them from that category because they apply to aspects of our political life that go far beyond the legal process.

Precedent.   The American political culture is much influenced by the idea that past decisions should be followed by present circumstances. The principle precedent is one of the cornerstones of our common law, expressed by the term, *stare decisis,* which, in effect, enjoins us to let previous decisions stand. As principle, *stare decisis* is embedded in several of our previously noted dimensions of justice, but as a more general principle of politics, the idea of precedent helps confer legitimacy on all manner of government actions and decisions.[12] It is thus of considerable utility in explaining both the continuity of public policy and the operation of social learning.

Rule of law.   Another central value of the political culture speaks to the *rule of law.* By that is meant that rulers and the ruled alike are answerable to the law. A king may very well proclaim that he is above the law, but our politics begins with the idea that no person or group is outside the law or beyond its reach.[13] The idea of the rule of law thus reaches outward to embrace the idea of equality.[14]

Private property.   Deep within the political culture is subscription to the idea that private property has an important role to play in human affairs, and that, accordingly, private property is to be given a protected place in dealings between a government and its citizens.[15]

---

10. Bolstering this argument is a trenchant piece of folk wit: Capital punishment means that those without capital are punished.

11. Edmund Cahn, *The Moral Decision* (Bloomington: University of Indiana Press, 1951). The principle of treating all classes of offenders alike, whatever their economic circumstances, has been given practical effect by the Supreme Court's holding (*Gideon v. Wainwright,* 1963) that in felony cases defendants are constitutionally entitled to legal counsel. In contrast to other Fourth Amendment cases in which the Court has been criticized for coddling criminals, the *Gideon* case has been received with widespread approval.

12. Robert Cobb and Charles Elder, in *Participation in American Politics: The Dynamics of Agenda Building* (Baltimore, Md.: Johns Hopkins University Press, 1972), argue that the legitimacy conferred by precedent is critical to creating the public agenda.

13. Part of the public outcry and congressional consideration of the impeachment of President Nixon sprang from accusations that, in the Watergate affair, he and his subordinates had violated the rule of law.

14. As well as precedent and careful attention to the law's procedure.

15. *Federalist Paper* No. 54: "Government is instituted no less for protection of the property, than the persons, of individuals."

Private property is inextricably bound to the value of achievement, for as Tocqueville noted,

> To clear, to till, and to transform the vast uninhabited continent which is his domain, the American requires the daily support of an energetic passion; that passion can only be the love of wealth. . . .[16]

All that the American asks of his government, says Tocqueville, "is not to be disturbed in his toil and to be secure in his earnings."[17] This desire to be secure in one's property found its way into several of the key provisions of the Constitution; and as we review the development of public policy, we shall return over and over again to arguments that commence when majority rule poses a threat to private property.

Localism.   Americans have always had a strong affection for the principle of local government. Thomas Jefferson went so far as to declare that local governments are "the wisest inventions ever devised by the wit of man for the perfect exercise of self government."[18] And the contemporary scholar, Grant McConnell, is moved to say that

> few tenets of American orthodoxy are more important . . . than the belief in small units of social and political organization as the citadels of virtually all the values associated with democracy.[19]

Tocqueville viewed the American colonials' experience with local government as being responsible for the social learning that permitted their descendants to operate the new republic. And the framers of the Constitution crystalized respect for localism by building the new government on the foundation of federalism.

Arguments over localism helped bring forth the Civil War, and a concern for states' rights has agitated our politics ever since. Contemporary manifestations of the arguments over localism are found in such issues as school busing, holding the states to the provisions of the national Bill of Rights with respect to criminal trials, and even establishing a national highway speed limit.

Democracy.   We save for last what may be the most fundamental value of all, subscription to the worthiness of democracy. As with other values in our list, the meaning of democracy has several dimensions. The principal dimension conveys the idea of consent of the governed, but several other meanings can be stacked on top of that idea. We can, for example, further define democracy as requiring that the electorate has freedom to choose its leaders in periodic elections. (Such is the definition we can build by reading the Constitution apart from the Bill of Rights.) Or, in contrast, we can define democracy as requiring as much citizen participation as is possible in every government decision. We can also extend the principle of maximum citizen participation to the decisions of major corporations. (Such is the democracy conveyed by the slogan "participatory democracy" that was so much a part of the reform movement of the 1960s.) Most persons probably take their preferred definition of democracy to be opportunity to choose officers of their government. But whatever the particulars of definition, the culture's central political value remains fairly constant: Democracy is seen as the best and most preferred form of government.

16. Tocqueville, *Democracy,* Vol. 2, p. 248.

17. Ibid., p. 262.

18. Phillip S. Foner, ed., *The Basic Writings of Thomas Jefferson* (New York: John Wiley & Sons, 1944), p. 749.

19. Grant McConnell, *Private Power and Public Purpose* (New York: Vintage Books, 1966), p. 91.

Contemporary American Democracy: Criticisms and Observations

3
Democracy in America?
Lewis H. Lapham

What is the condition of American democracy in the 1990s? According to Lewis Lapham, there is more lip service to democratic ideals than practice. Lapham argues that our country is becoming more of an oligarchy or plutocracy than a democracy. Why? Do you agree or disagree? Lapham refutes four basic goals of American democracy. In the electoral arena, he finds a great deal of voter apathy and failure of elected officials to represent the people. Citizen participation has been submerged by a commercial definition of democracy. Checks and balances do not work in presidential military actions. Finally, the public is willing to yield many of its civil liberties to autocratic powers of the police. Is Lapham correct in his provocative criticisms of contemporary democracy in America? If not, what counterarguments can be made to challenge his views?

Over the course of the last eighteen months, no American politician worth his weight in patriotic sentiment has missed a chance to congratulate one of the lesser nations of the earth on its imitation of the American democracy. Invariably, the tone of the compliment is condescending. The politician presents himself as the smiling host who welcomes into the clean and well-lighted rooms of "the American way of life" the ragged and less fortunate guests, who—sadly and through no fault of their own—had wandered for so many years in ideological darkness.

The orators haven't lacked edifying proofs and instances. First the Chinese students in Tiananmen Square, holding aloft a replica of the Statue of Liberty against the armies of repression. Next the German crowds dancing on the ruin of the Berlin Wall; then the apprentice democrats triumphant in Budapest and Warsaw and Prague; then Gorbachev in Washington, amiably recanting the communist heresy to his new friend in the White House. And always the Americans, saying, in effect, "You see, we were right all along; we were right, and you were wrong, and if you know what's good for you, you will go forth and prosper in a bright new world under the light of an American moon."

At the end of last summer Ronald Reagan was in Berlin, conducting a seminar for the East Germans on the theory and practice of democracy; John Sununu, the White House chief of staff, was in Moscow showing the hierarchs in the Kremlin how to organize the paperwork of a democratic government; a synod of American journalists had gone off to Budapest to teach their Hungarian colleagues how to draft a First Amendment; in Washington the chief correspondent of the *New York Times* was celebrating the crisis in the Persian Gulf as great and glorious proof that the United States had regained its status as the world's first and foremost superpower, that all the dreary talk about American bankruptcy and decline was just so much sniveling, trendy rot.

I listen to the speeches and read the bulletins in the newspapers, and I marvel at my own capacity for the willing suspensions of disbelief. I find myself humming along with the self-congratulatory cant on *Nightline* and *Face the Nation* or beating four-quarter time with the jingoists' chorus in *Newsweek,* and I forget for the moment that we're talking about a country (the United States of America, a.k.a. "the light of hope and reason in a dark and discordant world") in which the spirit of democracy is fast becoming as defunct as the late Buffalo Bill. About a country in which most of the population doesn't take the trouble to vote and would gladly sell its constitutional birthright for a Florida condominium or another twenty days on the corporate expense account. About a country in which the President wages war after consultation with four or five privy councillors and doesn't inform either the Congress or the electorate (a.k.a. "the freest, happiest, and most enlightened people on earth") until the armada has sailed.

Although I know that Jefferson once said that it is never permissible "to despair of the commonwealth," I find myself wondering whether the American experiment with democracy may not have run its course. Not because of the malevolence or cunning of a foreign power (the Russians, the Japanese, the Colombian drug lords, Saddam Hussein, etc.) but because a majority of Americans apparently have come to think of democracy as a matter of consensus and parades, as if it were somehow easy, quiet, orderly, and safe. I keep running across people who speak fondly about what they imagine to be the comforts of autocracy, who long for the assurances of the proverbial man on the white horse likely to do something hard and puritanical about the moral relativism that has made a mess of the cities, the schools, and prime-time television.

If the American system of government at present seems so patently at odds with its constitutional hopes and purposes, it is not because the practice of democracy no longer serves the interests of the presiding oligarchy (which it never did) but because the promise of democracy no longer inspires or exalts the citizenry lucky enough to have been born under its star. It isn't so much that liberty stands at bay but, rather, that it has fallen into disuse, regarded as insufficient by both its enemies and its nominal friends. What is the use of free expression to people so frightened of the future that they prefer the comforts of the authoritative lie? Why insist on the guarantee of so many superfluous civil liberties when everybody already has enough trouble with the interest rates and foreign cars, with too much crime in the streets, too many Mexicans crossing the border, and never enough money to pay the bills? Why bother with the tiresome chore of self-government when the decisions of state can be assigned to the functionaries in Washington, who, if they can be trusted with nothing else, at least have the wit to pretend that they are infallible? President Bush struck the expected pose of omniscience in the course of the 1988 election campaign when he refused to answer a rude question about an American naval blunder in the Persian Gulf (the shooting down of an Iranian airliner) on the ground that he would "never apologize for the United States of America. I don't care what the facts are."

As recently as 1980 I knew a good many people who took a passionate interest in politics, who felt keenly what one of them described as "the ancient republican hostility" to the rule of the self-serving few. They knew the names of their elected representatives, and they were as well-informed on the topics of the day as any government spokesman paid to edit the news. By the end of the decade most of them had abandoned their political enthusiasm as if it were a youthful folly they no longer could afford—like hang gliding or writing neosymbolist verse.

Much of the reason for the shift in attitude I attribute to the exemplary cynicism of the Reagan administration. Here was a government obsequious in its devotion to the purposes of a selfish oligarchy, a regime that cared nothing for the law and prospered for eight years by virtue of its willingness to cheat and steal and lie. And yet, despite its gross and frequent abuses of power, the country made no complaint. The Democratic Party (the nominal party of opposition) uttered not the slightest squeak of an objection. Except for a few journals of small circulation, neither did the media.

During the early years of the administration, even people who recognized the shoddiness of Reagan's motives thought that the country could stand a little encouragement—some gaudy tinsel and loud advertising, a lot of parades, and a steady supply of easy profits. The country had heard enough of Jimmy Carter's sermons, and it was sick of listening to prophecies of the American future that could be so easily confused with a coroner's report. In return for the illusion that the United States

was still first in the world's rankings, the country indulged Reagan in his claptrap economic and geopolitical theories. For a few years it didn't seem to matter that the Laffer curve and the Strategic Defense Initiative had been imported from the land of Oz. What difference did it make as long as the Japanese were willing to lend money and Rambo was victorious in the movies?

But it turned out that the lies did make a difference—the lies and the Reagan administration's relentless grasping of illegal and autocratic privilege. Congress offered itself for sale to the highest bidder, and the political action committees bought so many politicians of both denominations that it was no longer possible to tell the difference between a Republican and a Democrat: Both sides of the aisle owed their allegiance to the same sponsors. Nor was it possible to distinguish between the executive and the legislative functions of government. Any doubts on this score were dissolved in the midden of the Iran-Contra deals. President Reagan and his aides-de-camp on the National Security Council sold weapons to a terrorist regime in Iran in order to finance a terrorist revolt in Nicaragua. The scheme obliged them to make a mockery of the Constitution, dishonor their oaths of office, and seize for themselves the powers of despotism. They did so without a qualm, and the subsequent congressional investigation absolved them of their crimes and confirmed them in their contempt for the law and the American people. The principal conspirators were allowed to depart with no more than a reprimand.

It was this series of events—so obviously and complacently corrupt throughout the whole course of the narrative—that proved even more damaging to the American polity than the ruin of the economy. Justified by a timid Congress and excused by a compliant media, the Reagan administration reduced the

Constitution to a sheaf of commercial paper no more or less worthless than a promissory note signed by Donald Trump or a financial prospectus offering shares in the Wedtech Corporation.

The defeat might be easier to bear if the politicians would quit mouthing the word "democracy." If they were to say instead, "Yes, we are a great nation because we obey the rule of the expedient lie" or, "Yes, believe in our power because we have gerrymandered our politics to serve the interests of wealth," I might find it easier to wave the flag and swell the unison of complacent applause.

But not "democracy." Maybe "plutocracy," or "oligarchy," or even "state capitalism," but not, please God, "a free nation under law" or, as a professor of government put it in an address to a crowd of newly naturalized citizens of Monticello, the "moral and political reasoning [that] is the republic's unique and priceless heritage."

What "moral and political reasoning"? Between which voices of conscience, and where would the heritage be exhibited to public view? On network television? In the United States Senate? In a high school auditorium in Detroit?

Saddam Hussein's invasion of Kuwait presented a fairly prominent occasion for a display of America's moral and political reasoning, but it was a spectacle that nobody wanted to see or hear. The national choir of newspaper columnists banged their cymbals and drums, shouting for the head of the monster of Baghdad. Loudly and without a single exception, the 535 members of Congress declared themselves loyal to the great American truth that had descended into the Arabian desert with the 82nd Airborne Division. The television networks introduced a parade of generals, all of them explicating the texts of glorious war. The few individuals who publicly questioned the wisdom of the President's

policy instantly found themselves classified as subversives, spoilsports, ingrates, and sore thumbs.

The judgment is one with which I am familiar, probably because my own remarks on the state of American politics often have been attacked by more or less the same gang of adjectives. With respect to the argument in progress, I can imagine the rejoinder pronounced by a self-satisfied gentleman in his middle forties, a reader of *Time* magazine and a friend of the American Enterprise Institute. He wears a three-piece suit and speaks slowly and patiently, as if to a foreigner or a prospective suicide. Having done well by the system, he begins by reminding me that I, too, have done well by the system and should show a decent respect for the blessings of property. His voice is as smug as his faith in the American political revelation ("not perfect, of course, but the best system on offer in an imperfect world"). His argument resolves into categorical statements, usually four, presented as facets of a flawless truth. As follows:

1.

The American government is formed by the rule of the ballot box. What other country trusts its destiny to so many free elections?

The statement is true to the extent that it describes a ritual, not a function, of government. Early last spring the Times Mirror Center for the People and the Press conducted a survey of the political attitudes prevailing among a random sampling of citizens between the ages of eighteen and twenty-nine. To nobody's surprise the survey discovered a generation that "knows less, cares less, votes less and is less critical of its leaders and institutions than young people in the past." The available statistics support the impression of widespread political apathy. In this month's election it is expected that as many as 120 million Americans (two thirds of the eligible electorate) will not bother to vote.

The numbers suggest that maybe the people who don't vote have good and sufficient reasons for their abstentions. Vote for what and for whom? For a program of false promises and empty platitudes? For ambitious office seekers distinguished chiefly by their talents for raising money? For a few rich men (i.e., the sixty or seventy senators possessing assets well in excess of $1 million) who can afford to buy a public office as if it were a beach house or a rubber duck?

Since the revision of the campaign finance laws in the late 1970s, most of the candidates don't even take the trouble to court the good opinion of the voters. They speak instead to the PACs, to the lobbyists who can fix the money for campaigns costing as much as $350,000 (for the House of Representatives) and $4 million (for the Senate). The rising cost of political ambition ensures the rising rate of incumbency (47 percent of the present United States Congress were in office in 1980, as opposed to 4 percent of the Supreme Soviet). The sponsors back the safe bets and receive the assurance of safe opinions. (As of last June 30, the incumbent senators up for reelection this month had collected $83.1 million for their campaigns, as opposed to $25.9 million raised on behalf of the insurgents.)

A democracy supposedly derives its strength and character from the diversity of its many voices, but the politicians in the Capitol speak with only one voice, which is the voice of the oligarchy that buys the airline tickets and the television images. Among the company of legislators in Washington or Albany or Sacramento I look in vain for a representation of my own interests or opinions, and I never hear the voice of the scientist, the writer, the athlete, the teacher, the plumber, the police officer, the farmer, the merchant. I hear instead the voice of only one kind of function-ary: a full-time politician, nearly always a lawyer, who spends at least 80 percent of his time raising campaign funds and construes his function as that of a freight-forwarding agent redistributing the national income into venues convenient to his owners and friends.

Maybe it still can be said that the United States is a representative government in the theatrical sense of the word, but if I want to observe the workings of democracy I would be better advised to follow the debate in the Czech Parliament or the Soviet Congress of People's Deputies. The newly enfranchised politicians in Eastern Europe write their own speeches and delight in the passion of words that allows them to seize and shape the course of a new history and a new world. Unlike American voters, voters in the Soviet Union (repeat, the Soviet Union, Russia, the U.S.S.R., the "Evil Empire," the communist prison, etc., etc.) enjoy the right to express the full range of their opinions at the polls. Instead of marking the ballot for a favored candidate, the Soviet voter crosses off the names of the politicians whom he has reason to distrust or despise. He can vote against all the candidates, even an incumbent standing unopposed. Because a Soviet politician must receive an absolute majority, the election isn't valid unless more than half of the electorate votes, which means that in Moscow or Leningrad the citizens can vote for "none of the above," and by doing so they can do what the voters in New York or Los Angeles cannot do—throw the thieves into the street.

2.
Democratic government is self-government, and in America the state is owned and operated by the citizens.

I admire the sentiment, and I am willing to believe that in the good old days before most of what was worth knowing about the mechanics of government disappeared under the seals of classified information, it was still conceivable that the business of the state could be conducted by amateurs. In the early years of the twentieth century it was still possible for anybody passing by the White House to walk through the front door and expect a few words with the president. It's true that the promise of democracy is synonymous with the idea of the citizen. The enterprise requires the collaboration of everybody present, and it fails (or evolves into something else) unless enough people perceive their government as subject rather than object, as animate organism rather than automatic vending machine.

Such an antique or anthropomorphic understanding of politics no longer satisfies the demand for omnipotence or the wish to believe in kings or queens or fairy tales. Ask almost anybody in any street about the nature of American government, and he or she will describe it as something that belongs to somebody else, as a them, not an us. Only advanced students of political science remember how a caucus works, or what is written in the Constitution, or who paves the roads. The active presence of the citizen gives way to the passive absence of the consumer, and citizenship devolves into a function of economics. Every two or four or six years the politicians ask the voters whether they recognize themselves as better or worse off than they were the last time anybody asked. The question is only and always about money, never about the spirit of the laws or the cherished ideals that embody the history of the people. The commercial definition of democracy prompts the politicians to conceive of and advertise the republic as if it were a resort hotel. They promise the voters the rights and comforts owed to them by virtue of their status as America's guests. The subsidiary arguments amount to little more than complaints about the number, quality, and cost of the available

services. The government (a.k.a. the hotel management) preserves its measure of trust in the exact degree that it satisfies the whims of its patrons and meets the public expectation of convenience and style at a fair price. A debased electorate asks of the state what the rich ask of their servants—i.e., "comfort us," "tell us what to do." The wish to be cared for replaces the will to act.

3.

The American democracy guarantees the freedom of its people and the honesty of its government with a system of checks and balances; the division or separation of powers prevents the government from indulging the pleasures of despotism; the two-party system ensures the enactment of just laws vigorously debated and openly arrived at.

It was precisely this principle that the Iran-Contra deals (the trading of weapons for hostages as well as the subsequent reprieves and exonerations) proved null and void. President Reagan usurped the prerogatives of Congress, and Congress made no objection. President Bush exercised the same option with respect to the expedition in the Persian Gulf, and again Congress made no objection, not even when it was discovered that Saudi Arabia had offered to hire the CIA to arrange the overthrow of Saddam Hussein. For the last forty years it has been the practice of the American government to wage a war at the will and discretion of the foreign-policy apparat in Washington—without reference to the wishes or opinions of the broad mass of the American people.

Dean Acheson, secretary of state in the Truman administration, understood as long ago as 1947 that if the government wished to do as it pleased, then it would be necessary to come up with a phrase, slogan, or article of faith that could serve as a pretext for arbitrary decisions. He hit upon the word "nonpartisan." Knowing that the American people might balk at the adventure of the Cold War if they thought that the subject was open to discussion, he explained to his confederates in the State Department that a militant American foreign policy had to be presented as a "nonpartisan issue," that any and all domestic political quarreling about the country's purposes "stopped at the water's edge."

"If we can make them believe that," Acheson said, "we're off to the races."

Among the promoters of the national security state the theory of "nonpartisanship" was accorded the weight of biblical revelation, and for the next two generations it proved invaluable to a succession of presidents bent on waging declared and undeclared wars in Korea, Vietnam, Guatemala, Grenada, Panama, Cambodia, Lebanon, Nicaragua, and the Persian Gulf. President John F. Kennedy elaborated the theory into a doctrine not unlike the divine right of kings. At a press conference in May 1962, Kennedy said, with sublime arrogance: "Most of us are conditioned for many years to have a political viewpoint—Republican or Democratic, liberal, conservative, or moderate. The fact of the matter is that most of the problems . . . that we now face are technical problems, are administrative problems. They are very sophisticated judgments, which do not lend themselves to the great sort of passionate movements which have stirred this country so often in the past. [They] deal with questions which are now beyond the comprehension of most men."

To President Bush the word "nonpartisan" is the alpha and omega of government by administrative decree: a word for all seasons; a word that avoids the embarrassment of forthright political argument; a word with which to send the troops to Saudi Arabia, postpone decisions on the budget, diffuse the blame for the savings and loan swindle. The White House staff takes pride in the techniques of what its operatives refer to as "conflict-avoidance." Speaking to a writer for *The New Republic* in August, one of Bush's senior press agents said, "We don't do [political] fighting in this administration. We do bipartisan compromising."

But in a democracy everything is partisan. Democratic politics is about nothing else except being partisan. The American dialectic assumes argument not only as the normal but as the necessary condition of its continued existence. The structure of the idea resembles a suspension bridge rather than a pyramid or a mosque. Its strength depends on the balance struck between countervailing forces, and the idea collapses unless the stresses oppose one another with equal weight, unless enough people have enough courage to sustain the argument between rich and poor, the government and the governed, city and suburb, presidency and Congress, capital and labor, matter and mind. It is precisely these arguments (i.e., the very stuff and marrow of democracy) that the word "nonpartisan" seeks to annul.

With reference to domestic political arguments, the word "consensus" serves the same purpose as the word "nonpartisan" does in the realm of foreign affairs: It is another sleight of hand that makes possible the perpetual avoidance of any question that might excite the democratic passions of a free people bent on governing themselves. The trick is to say as little as possible in a language so bland that the speaker no longer can be accused of harboring an unpleasant opinion. Adhere firmly to the safe cause and the popular sentiment. Talk about the flag or drugs or crime (never about race or class or justice) and follow the yellow brick road to the wonderful land of "consensus." In place of honest argument among consenting adults the politicians substitute a lullaby for frightened children: the pretense that conflict doesn't really exist, that we have achieved the blessed state in which (because we are all American and therefore content) we no longer need politics. The mere mention of the word "politics" brings with it the odor of something low and rotten and mean.

Confronted with genuinely stubborn and irreconcilable differences (about revising the schedule of Social Security payments, say, or closing down a specific number of the nation's military bases); the politicians assign the difficulty to the law courts, or to a special prosecutor, or to a presidential commission. In line with its habitual cowardice, Congress this past September dispatched a few of its most pettifogging members to Andrews Air Force Base, where, behind closed doors, it was hoped that they might construct the facade of an agreement on the budget.

For the better part of 200 years it was the particular genius of the American democracy to compromise its differences within the context of an open debate. For the most part (i.e., with the tragic exception of the Civil War), the society managed to assimilate and smooth out the edges of its antagonisms and by so doing to hold in check the violence bent on its destruction. The success of the enterprise derived from the rancor of the nation's loudmouthed politics—on the willingness of its citizens and their elected representatives to defend their interests, argue their case, and say what they meant. But if the politicians keep silent, and if the citizenry no longer cares to engage in what it regards as the distasteful business of debate, then the American dialectic cannot attain a synthesis or resolution. The democratic initiative passes to the demagogues in the streets, and the society falls prey to the ravening minorities in league with the extremists of all denominations who claim alliance with the higher consciousness and the absolute truth. The eloquence of Dan-

iel Webster or Henry Clay degenerates into the muttering of Al Sharpton or David Duke.

The deliberate imprecision of the Constitution (sufficiently vague and spacious to allow the hope of a deal) gives way to rigid enumerations of privileges and rights. A democracy in sound working order presupposes a ground of tolerance, in Judge Learned Hand's phrase, "the spirit which is not too sure that it is right." I might think that the other fellow is wrong, but I do not think that he is therefore wicked. A democracy in decay acquires the pale and deadly cast of theocracy. Not only is the other fellow wrong (about abortion, obscenity, or the flag); he is also, by definition, an agent of the Antichrist.

4.

The Constitution presents the American people with as great a gift of civil liberties as ever has been granted by any government in the history of the world.

But liberty, like the habit of telling the truth, withers and decays unless it's put to use, and for the last ten years it seems as if the majority of Americans would rather not suffer the embarrassment of making a scene (in a public place) about so small a trifle as a civil right. With scarcely a murmur of objection, they fill out the official forms, answer the questions, submit to the compulsory urine or blood tests, and furnish information to the government, the insurance companies, and the police.

The Bush administration cries up a war on drugs, and the public responds with a zeal for coercion that would have gladdened the hearts of the Puritan judges presiding over the Salem witch trials. Of the respondents questioned by an ABC/*Washington Post* poll in September 1989, 55 percent supported mandatory drug testing for all Americans, 52 percent were willing to have their homes searched, and 83 percent favored reporting suspected drug users to the police, even if the suspects happened to be members of their own family. Politicians of both parties meet with sustained applause when they demand longer jail sentences and harsher laws as well as the right to invade almost everybody's privacy; to search, without a warrant, almost anybody's automobile or boat; to bend the rules of evidence, hire police spies, and attach, again without a warrant, the wires of electronic surveillance. Within the last five years the Supreme Court has granted increasingly autocratic powers to the police—permission (without probable cause) to stop, detain, and question a traveler passing through the nation's airports in whom the police can see a resemblance to a drug dealer; permission (again without probable cause) to search barns, stop motorists, inspect bank records, and tap phones.

The same Times Mirror survey that discovered a general indifference toward all things political also discovered that most of the respondents didn't care whether a fair percentage of the nation's politicians proved to be scoundrels and liars. Such was the nature of their task, and it was thought unfair to place on the political authorities the additional and excessive burden of too many harsh or pointed questions. "Let them," said one of the poor dupes of a respondent, "authoritate."

Democracy, of course, is never easy to define. The meaning of the word changes with the vagaries of time, place, and circumstances. The American democracy in 1990 is not what it was in 1890; democracy in France is not what it is in England or Norway or the United States. What remains more or less constant is a temperament or spirit of mind rather than a code of laws, a set of immutable virtues or a table of bureaucratic organization. The temperament is skeptical and contentious, and if democracy means anything at all (if it isn't what Gore Vidal called "the great American nonsense word" or what H. L. Mencken regarded as a synonym for the collective fear and prejudice of an ignorant mob) it means the freedom of thought and the perpetual expansion of the discovery that the world is not oneself. Freedom of thought brings the society the unwelcome news that it is in trouble. But because all societies, like all individuals, are always in trouble, the news doesn't cause them to perish. They die instead from the fear of thought—from the paralysis that accompanies the wish to make time stand still and punish the insolence of an Arab who makes a nuclear bomb or sells gasoline for more than twenty-five dollars a barrel.

Democracy allies itself with change and proceeds on the assumption that nobody knows enough, that nothing is final, that the old order (whether of men or institutions) will be carried offstage every twenty years. The multiplicity of its voices and forms assumes a ceaseless making and remaking of laws and customs as well as equations and matinee idols. Democratic government is a purpose held in common, and if it can be understood as a field of temporary coalitions among people of different interests, skills, and generations, then everybody has need of everybody else. To the extent that democracy gives its citizens a chance to chase their own dreams, it gives itself the chance not only of discovering its multiple glories and triumphs but also of surviving its multiple follies and crimes.

CHAPTER **2**

The Constitution

The political heritage of American government is strongly rooted in constitutionalism and the rule of law. The United States Constitution is the oldest written charter among Western democracies. It has four basic components: (1) to express the principles of democracy; (2) to define the relationships between citizens and government; (3) to state what citizens and government can and cannot do; and (4) to establish institutions for self-government.

DEMOCRATIC FOUNDATIONS: LOCKE AND JEFFERSON

We noted in Chapter 1 that a fundamental premise of democratic theory is that government receives its authority from the consent of the governed. What are the legal and constitutional relationships between government and the people? The American colonists considered this basic question when they severed their ties to Britain in the eighteenth century. To fully appreciate the philosophic foundations of the colonists' rationale in the Declaration of Independence (see Appendix), we turn first to John Locke, whose writings had great influence on Thomas Jefferson, the principal author of the Declaration.

Locke, the noted British philosopher of the seventeenth century, was concerned with why men establish political societies (governments). In his *Second Treatise, Of Civil Government,* he focused on the legal obligations between people and government that are established in a "social contract." When forming government, individuals move from a state of nature where their security is uncertain and where justice is a personal matter, to an organized society that is required to arbitrate and decide disputes impartially. The role of government is to enforce the law fairly and without personal bias or prejudice. At the same time, the members of society retain certain basic natural rights (the Declaration's "inalienable rights") that government may not take away. These include the rights to life, liberty, and property. Government may not deprive the people of their natural rights, nor may it act contrary to the expectations of the citizenry. Thus, the rulers of society are limited—they derive their authority from the consent of the governed, and they may be deposed if their actions are no longer considered legitimate.

Locke's ideas on the social contract, the natural rights of the people, and the reserved authority to alter the people's contractual obligations with government were incorporated directly into the Declaration of Independence. The Declaration provided the moral and legal basis for American separation from Britain in 1776. This was (and still is) a truly revolutionary statement of principles. Not only does the Declaration assert such "self-evident truths" as political equality and the rights to "life, liberty, and the pursuit of happiness," but it also states that "whenever any form of government becomes destructive of these ends, it is the right of the people to alter or to abolish it." Moreover, since changes in government are serious matters, the statement is qualified by warning: "Prudence, indeed, will dictate, that governments long established should not be changed for light and transient causes."

The Declaration of Independence established the political goals of the colonists in breaking off from Britain. First, they rejected rule by royal prerogative and sought government based on the consent of the people. They believed that executive power should be limited by popular representation in the legislative branch. Second, the colonists wanted a written constitution that clearly specified the powers of government in order to ensure that government was limited in its authority. Third, protections of human liberty were sought. Several of the colonies argued for a bill of rights to protect citizens against unwarranted intrusions of governmental power. Finally, the colonists wanted to prevent excessive concentration of power in the central government. They believed that power should be divided between the national government and the states in a federal system.

WEAKNESSES OF THE ARTICLES OF CONFEDERATION

Following the Revolutionary War and preceding the Constitutional Convention of 1787, the United States was governed by the Articles of Confederation, a document that provided for a very weak central government that was dependent on the thirteen states for nearly all its powers. The national legislature lacked the power to tax and to regulate interstate commerce; it could not act in any matters relating to war, foreign relations, money, or requisitions without the approval of at least nine of the thirteen states; and Congress could not enforce sanctions against the states for any of the decisions it made. The executive and judicial branches were even weaker than the legislature. There were no provisions for a chief executive (a president) nor was there any system of federal courts, except those that settled disputes on the high seas. Finally, the Articles were nearly impossible to change or amend since unanimous consent of the states was required. This was an obstacle that permitted any one state to exercise veto power over changes that the others might desire.

THE CONSTITUTIONAL CONVENTION

The Constitution is a remarkable document. Since it was drafted in 1787 it has withstood the test of time with relatively few changes. What were the intents and purposes of the Founding Fathers? What political strategies did they employ to achieve their objectives? The fifty-five men who went to Philadelphia in 1787 were determined to overcome the political and institutional defects of the Articles of Confederation. They were particularly concerned with developing a sense of national unity to overcome the commercial and trading disputes between the states that could not be resolved by the weak central government under the Articles. Foremost among the issues facing the Framers were those dealing with legislative representation, the conflicting interests of the larger and smaller states, and North-South disputes over slavery. In resolving these conflicts, the Framers were effective practical politicians who engaged in bargaining, negotiation, and compromise.

The political infighting at the Convention is especially interesting in analyzing the battles over legislative representation. Until a compromise plan could be worked out, the Framers were unable to proceed to other issues. Two very different proposals were debated: the big-state Virginia Plan and the small-state New Jersey Plan. The Virginia Plan—designed by James Madison—called for a strong national government with a dominant lower house elected directly by the people from districts proportional to state population. The upper chamber would be elected by the lower house from persons nominated by the state legislatures. Congress would have general legislative power to act in all matters where the states lacked authority. Congress would elect the chief executive for a fixed term and would also select members of the national judiciary.

The smaller states promoted the New Jersey Plan, which strengthened legislative powers in a unicameral Congress, consisting of state representation, with one vote per state delegation. Congress would elect a plural executive and a national judiciary to hear appeals from the state supreme courts.

The deadlock was resolved by the Connecticut Compromise, which established a bicameral Congress, with the House members elected from districts proportional to state population (the Virginia Plan); and the Senate chosen from persons elected by state legislatures (the New Jersey Plan). Each state was guaranteed two senators. Congress was given specified powers, while the states retained reserved powers (the New Jersey Plan). Following approval of the Connecticut Compromise, the Framers agreed on the three-fifths compromise dealing with slavery and taxation (which balanced the competing interests of the North and South) and the electoral college compromise (which combined an unusual arrangement of popular election and elite participation). Finally, members of the Supreme Court were to be nominated by the president and approved by the Senate.

JAMES WILSON AND THE CONSTITUTION

How did the constitutional framers make their decisions in 1787? What were their beliefs and values about organizing a new national government? In Article 4, Garry Wills, Professor of American culture at Northwestern University, offers an imaginary interview with James Wilson, one of the leading constitutional framers and a principal ally of James Madison in promoting the Virginia Plan. Wilson was also a signer of the Declaration of Independence and later served as one of the first justices on the Supreme Court.

While strolling through Philadelphia, Wilson makes several important points about drafting the Constitution in 1787 and how it has evolved over the past two hundred years.

First, Wilson emphasizes the secrecy and almost conspiratorial nature of the convention since the Articles of Confederation were scrapped without following procedures in that document. Second, Wilson advocates legislative supremacy and dismisses the traditional view that the Constitution establishes a government of checks and balances. Instead, Wilson argues that the three branches were set up to provide for efficiency. Third, he argues that the Framers were correct in establishing a new government because they adhered to public accountability. Ratifying state conventions had to approve the new Constitution. Fourth, Wilson states his preference for popular vote for all executive and legislative offices. (This, of course, was not contained in the original Constitution.) Finally, Wilson is concerned about the development of presidential prerogative in military issues, particularly when the president avoids requesting declarations of war from Congress. On this matter, Wilson anticipated the modern executive-legislative conflicts over warmaking authority, particularly during the Vietnam War.

THE MADISONIAN MODEL

What kind of national government was established under the Constitution? According to James Madison, the principal architect at the convention of the nation's government structure, the blueprint incorporated the principles of separation of powers and checks and balances. The Madisonian model is most effectively described in *The Federalist*, Number 51 (Article 5). *The Federalist*, written by Madison, Alexander Hamilton, and John Jay under the name of "Publius," was a series of eighty-five essays published in New York newspapers to convince the New York State Convention to ratify the

Constitution. The essays became the single most important source for understanding the political philosophy and meaning of the original Constitution.

Number 51 argues that government should be limited because uncontrolled political power can lead to tyranny. To prevent any of the three branches—executive, legislative, and judicial—from dominating the other two, each must be relatively independent. This is achieved by separation of powers. Also, the three branches would have checks and balances over each other to counteract power concentration and domination of any one branch over the other two. The limited government of the Madisonian model may prevent excessive power dominance, but it has the liability of ineffective governance. Many have criticized the Madisonian model as a deadlock of democracy where policy initiatives and innovation are difficult to achieve without extraordinary presidential leadership and congressional cooperation on major issues facing the country.

CHANGING THE CONSTITUTION

What are the strengths and limits of the Constitution? What does the Constitution mean today? Constitutional democracy has been increased in at least four ways since 1787.

First, voting rights and popular participation have expanded by several constitutional amendments. The right to vote without racial barriers was guaranteed in the Fifteenth Amendment (1870). The Seventeenth Amendment instituted direct popular election of U.S. senators (1913). Women's suffrage was provided in the Nineteenth Amendment (1920). Voting rights in presidential elections were extended to residents of the District of Columbia in the Twenty-third Amendment (1961). Poll taxes for all federal elections were prohibited in the Twenty-fourth Amendment (1964). The Twenty-sixth Amendment (1971) lowered the voting age to eighteen.

Second, slavery was abolished by the Thirteenth Amendment (1865). Third, the Bill of Rights was applied to the states in a series of Supreme Court decisions. Finally, the federal government assumed many domestic and international responsibilities beginning with the New Deal of the 1930s and continuing during and after World War II.

Contemporary constitutional obstacles to democratic government include conflicts between national government and state powers in the federal system; the difficulties of achieving policy agreement between the president and Congress (resulting from the cumbersome procedures of separation of powers and checks and balances); the disharmony between the executive and legislative branches over policy (caused by weak political parties); and the politicization of social issues by ideological conservatives who want their views of social policy to be placed in the Constitution (these views include prohibition of abortion, mandatory school prayer, and elimination of court-ordered busing to achieve racial balance in public schools).

Amending the Constitution is a very difficult and complex process. Aside from the Bill of Rights (the first ten amendments), which was part of the original Constitution, only sixteen other amendments have been approved from more than five thousand proposals. Amendments can be initiated in two ways: either by a two-thirds vote of both houses of Congress or by a two-thirds vote of state legislatures calling for a special constitutional convention. The latter method has never been used, although by 1984 thirty-two state legislatures (two less than required) had approved a special convention for a balanced budget amendment.

Constitutional amendments are approved in two ways. The most frequent method is by affirmative vote of three-fourths of the state legislatures. This has been used for all amendments except the Twenty-first Amendment (repealing the prohibition of liquor in the Eighteenth Amendment), when three-fourths of the states held special ratifying conventions.

The Enduring Constitution: Is Reform Needed?

In Articles 6 and 7, historian Richard Morris and various government officials and experts examine the strengths and problems of constitutional government after two hundred years. During the 1987 bicentennial of the Constitution, many people made observations on the Constitution. Most applauded the stability, longevity, and effectiveness of the U.S. Constitution as the oldest written charter among contemporary governments. Richard Morris emphasized the adaptability of the Constitution to various developments over time.

As shown in Article 7, the Committee on Constitutional Development, a private organization of government officials and citizens, did advocate some specific amendments to improve the electoral system and executive-legislative relationships. This group was particularly concerned with overcoming the problems of the Madisonian model and checking excessive executive power.

But other observers argued that institutional tinkering would not solve the inability of the president and Congress to work more cooperatively. Instead, they emphasized the need for revitalizing the party system and having more effective leadership. With the difficulties of amending the Constitution, it is probably more realistic to expect that change will take place by legislation, Supreme Court decisions, and the actions of government leaders. Constitutional interpretation will decide how government officials and citizens will be affected in various cases and public policy issues.

Upholding the Special Prosecutor Law:
A Case of Separation of Powers v. Checks and Balances

One example of how constitutional change can be achieved through executive, legislative, and judicial interaction is found in the political battle over the special prosecutor law. In 1988, the Supreme Court in the case of *Morrison v. Olson* upheld the right of Congress to establish procedures for appointing independent counsels under the Ethics in Government Act of 1978. This was an important constitutional issue involving a debate over whether or not separation of powers or checks and balances should prevail as the foundation of public policy. The Reagan administration challenged the independent counsel procedure as a violation of separation of powers. Congress argued that the 1978 law was a proper exercise of legislative checks and balances over the executive branch.

The issue before the Supreme Court was whether or not Congress could delegate power to the attorney general, after conducting investigations of alleged crimes by high executive branch officials, to ask a special three-judge federal appellate court to appoint a special prosecutor.

The Reagan administration argued that only the executive branch has the authority to appoint prosecutors. In its view, judicial involvement in the selection process violated executive powers in Article II of the Constitution.

The Supreme Court disagreed with this view. Instead, by upholding the powers of Congress, the Court established an important check and balance precedent. The executive branch could no longer claim constitutional authority to investigate its own officials accused of violating the law in such issues as Watergate and the Iran-Contra Affair.

The Special Prosecutor case demonstrates that constitutional change can occur as a result of political battles between the president and Congress. When the two branches disagreed over such a fundamental issue as prosecuting alleged abuse by high executive officials, the Supreme Court settled the matter through interpreting the laws and applying the Constitution.

James Wilson and the Constitution

4

Interview with a Founding Father
Garry Wills

How would one of the constitutional framers respond to the contemporary practices in America's basic governmental charter? In 1987, the United States celebrated the bicentennial of the Constitution. Garry Wills, author of several books on the Constitution, imagined he interviewed James Wilson in Philadelphia, the site of the Constitutional Convention of 1787. Wilson tells Wills that the convention was a conspiracy since the members were "plotting an overthrow of the government." Why does he argue this? Wilson cites several basic goals of the constitutional framers: accountability to the people, legislative supremacy, popular voting for all elective offices, and limits on presidential warmaking authority. How have these goals been achieved or changed in the two hundred years since the framing of the Constitution?

JAMES WILSON, IN BRIEF

He was born in Scotland in 1742 near St. Andrews, where he attended the university and divinity school. After four years of tutoring in Scotland and America, he read law with John Dickinson, the leading pamphleteer of the early Revolutionary cause. Wilson wrote his own pamphlet, one of the earliest statements of American independence from Parliament, which Thomas Jefferson greatly admired.

A signer of the Declaration of Independence, Wilson was cast as a conservative in his opposition to Pennsylvania's state constitution of 1776 and his defense of Robert Morris's bank. But he advanced the most radi-

cally "popular" theories at the convention that drafted the United States Constitution in 1787, where he was James Madison's principal ally in promoting the Virginia Plan. Wilson's speeches for the draft were the ones most cited in the ratifying period, during which he guided Pennsylvania's early endorsement of the Constitution by the two-thirds majority.

He also led the convention that rewrote the state constitution of 1776. In 1789, President Washington appointed him to the new Supreme Court, and in 1790 he began the first public law lectures devoted to expounding the Constitution. His decision against "states' rights" in the *Chisholm* v. *Georgia* case (1793) was countered by rapid passage of the

From *American Heritage*, May/June 1987, pp. 83–86, 88. Reprinted with permission from *American Heritage*, Volume 38, Number 4. Copyright © 1987 by American Heritage, a division of Forbes, Inc.

Eleventh Amendment, which John Marshall did not find ways to circumvent until 1821.

Born desperately poor, Wilson had admired Scottish "lairds" of the Enlightenment like Lord Kames of Edinburgh. In America he speculated heavily in land schemes, embarrassing the Adams administration when he was jailed for debt while trying to ride circuit as a Justice of the Supreme Court. He died, to many people's relief, in a tavern at Edenton, North Carolina, in 1798.

His red judge's robe looked faded and theatrical by daylight. People at the bus stop stared at him, and his face flushed near the color of the robe. But he busily ignored them.

"There were market sheds here, where we assembled." Judge Wilson is trying to re-create the route of the Grand Procession that marched through Philadelphia on July 4, 1788, to celebrate the ratification of the Constitution by ten states. We have started, where the parade did, at South and Third streets. "At ten piers along the way we had ships representing each new state; they saluted us with their cannon." He glanced absentmindedly back and forth across the street, trying to find a familiar building. "There's St. Peter's. It has not changed."

I tell him there is a house farther on, on the left, that he must have visited: the Powel House. "Is that it? It looks smaller now that it does not stand alone."

"And your house was just beyond, at Walnut?"

"Yes."

But he tries to hurry me by the site, which now holds an apartment building done in the bunker-colonial style of Society Hill's modern structures. I have to clutch his robe, to his obvious distress, and *make* him read the plaque. "This is one of the few places where your name is publicly displayed in Philadelphia. You are a signer of the Declaration of Independence, and you are buried in Christ Church yard; but the placard in front of the cemetery mentions only the other five signers there, not you."

"You know very well why." He eyes me with asperity. "I was buried first in North Carolina. It was not till—1906, was it?—that my body was brought back to Christ Church."

"You should remember the date. It is your body."

"I cannot keep track of what you do with things in this terrible century. Look what you have done to the Republic we left you. If you knew what it cost, you would take better care of it."

"What do you mean?"

"Presidents resigning in disgrace. . . . "

"Well, you died in disgrace, a Supreme Court Justice."

"A matter of private debt. Nothing I could not have settled in time, if they had only *given* me time."

"And you were an expert on finance, hired by the Bank of North America to explain the mystery of credit."

"I explained very well. But that was theory. I had a hard time making theory fit with facts in my life. Don't most people?"

"Then why be surprised that the Republic does not reflect your theory any more?"

"What disturbs me about the Republic is not the discrepancy between fact and theory but the lapse of theory altogether. Where is the ideal of the citizens in action?"

"That is why I wanted you to look at the plaque on this apartment building. It says that 'Fort Wilson'—the place where citizens attacked your house for harboring loyalists in the Revolution—stood here."

"That was a rabble—"

"It was a state militia—"

"—Out of the control of its own officers. That was the intimidation that went on under the Pennsylvania Constitution of 1776—the one I changed by the state convention of 1790."

"Did you think of this bloody battle at your house, of the six men killed there, when you marched past it nine years later in the Grand Procession?"

"No, there was no time for that. That procession was a miracle of timing and coordination. Every artisan company had its float or marching group. The whole town was put on wheels or on foot. Yet only one man marched as the embodiment of Pennsylvania; only one man gave a speech that day. I was that man."

"Well, yes, Dr. Franklin was bedridden by then."

"I gave Franklin's speeches in the drafting convention. He had turned to me by then for his politics. He had completely forsworn the old state constitution."

He was getting testy again. I reminded him that he was on loan for an interview today because there was so little demand for him. James Madison was signed up for every day of 1987 and for months afterward. George Washington was not granting interviews. Franklin, talking all day long, was booked forever. "Even William Paterson was harder to talk with than you."

"Yes," he said bitterly, "though Madison and I—the two Jemmys, they called us—blocked Paterson and rammed the Constitution through. I was the one who gave Madison his defense against the charge that we were traitors."

"Who were traitors?"

"All of us at the drafting convention. We were plotting the overthrow of the government, mon!" His Scots accent comes out when he waxes revolutionary. "We had all sworn oaths to the various constitutions—state and federal—and we meant to break them. Why do you think we were meeting in secret? If our legislatures had known what we were up to, they would have recalled us for break-ing our instructions. We had sworn that the Confederation should be perpetual, that it could not be changed without unanimous assent of the states. Yet our plan called for a breakup of that Confederation if any nine states could be found to ratify the new one. We posted guards at the State House so no one could hear what we were up to."

"But the world would know when you published the document."

"That's when we scurried back to our lairs as private citizens. The convention went out of existence; no one could find it after it broke up. George Washington took the records home to Mount Vernon, where no one would have the nerve to ask for them."

"Why would Washington break his oath to the Confederation?"

"Oh, he had none, laddie. He was one of the few of us who held no civil office under the Confederation. But he was encouraging others to break their oaths, as calm as could be. There were many who wanted to skulk out of that chamber and never meddle more with this dangerous business. But they had not the nerve to skulk out under his eyes, I tell you."

"I have always heard that Washington did practically nothing at the convention."

"He sat there. That did everything. If he had gone, we all would have. Franklin was too weak to protect us by that time. We needed something to hide behind. He gave us that."

"Was that his only purpose?"

"That was his good to us. We did him good, too, especially we Jemmys. We gave him a four-month course in government he would never forget. We knew we were tutoring the ruler if our plan went through. He fatigued you just by the intensity of his listening. I was speaking to him the whole time, and I spoke more than anyone but Madison and that insufferable ladies' man Gouverneur Morris. I poured out my learning for the man, and I certainly expected a higher post than the one he gave me."

"You wanted to be Chief Justice."

"Yes. I could understand the politics of his giving the job to Jay in the first place. But to be passed over for Rutledge and Ellsworth! That was humiliating."

"What do you think you taught Washington most forcefully in the convention?"

"Accountability to the people. They are the sovereigns; he is just their servant."

"Is that what is meant by *limited government*?"

"Republicanism is not necessarily more limited in what it does than any other form of government. It just differs in the *justification* for its energy."

"But what about the checks and balances we all learn about as central to the Constitution?"

"Do you have a text of the Constitution there? Find me the term *checks* in there. Find *balances* there."

"Well, but it pits one power against another."

"Show me where," Wilson says triumphantly, grabbing my little copy of the Constitution and waving it in my face. He always considered the document peculiarly his own. "It is an *empowering* document, not a limiting one. Just look at the Preamble. Each of the first three articles says that the powers of legislation, execution, and judging all shall be in the particular department."

"Yes, but those powers are meant to check each other."

"It's not in the text."

"It's just common sense. Three equal powers are bound to contend with and control each other."

"Equal?" His face reddened. "Where is *equal*? You cannot execute laws, or give judgement on the laws, until you *have* laws. There is no *equal* in the text or in the very

idea of a republic, a government in which people govern themselves by *laws*. As Madison put it in *The Federalist* (which, by the way, did not get near the circulation in 1787 of my two speeches on the Constitution), 'In republican government the legislative authority, necessarily, predominates.' "

"Then why have separate powers at all, if two are to be subordinated to the one?"

"Well, division of labor makes for efficiency. The Congress found that out under the Articles of Confederation when it had to deliberate on all the matters that should have gone to a separate executive or judiciary department. That Congress had to stretch the Articles, to create a kind of executive not provided for. But the real reason for separation is to prevent the same people from making general law and applying it to particular cases; that would corrupt the legislator by making private concerns his legislative duty."

"You talk like Rousseau."

Wilson looks over his shoulder with an impulse of caution. A bag lady on the corner of Chestnut Street, appraising his red dress, seems to think it a little too worn. "You noticed that about Rousseau, eh? I thought I kept it pretty hidden. Rousseau's name was not popular in my circles. I never used it."

"Sure you did. You cited *The Social Contract* three times in your law lectures of 1790."

"Oh, but I never published those; my son did after my death. I don't know what I would have done with the citations. They were just sketched in for the lectures. I meant to rewrite the lectures as the great treatise on American law." His speech dwindles off in reverie. "They would have made my name." He is gazing at what looks like the drawing of a house's frame lifted above actual houses along Third Street. "What is that?"

"It marks the site and the scale of Franklin's house."

"You mean that is Market Street ahead? Where are the stalls? This is where the guns from the harbor saluted me during the procession. I turned and bowed toward the docks."

"You later became familiar with another kind of dock."

He hesitated, about to turn away and leave me. But the expounding fever was upon him. He could never resist lecturing a pupil. "Rousseau, now, understood the real point of republican government: that the people never surrender their sovereignty to the government. They retained the power to change government anytime they want, any way they want."

"Why was that so important to you?"

"Don't you see? The opponents of the Constitution said we were breaking the Articles' rules for amendment—as if the people can make any authority higher than themselves. The people are not bound, Rousseau says, even by the social contract. They made it; they can unmake it at will."

"But how are the people as a whole to know when they want to overthrow a government?"

"They have to *find* a way. We *made up* the devices of the drafting convention and ratifying conventions. We broke all the rules—articles and state constitutions too—by an appeal back to the people."

"But the people did not vote directly on the Constitution, only for delegates to the ratifying conventions."

"That was the most directly democratic procedure that could be used at the time. Even most state constitutions had not been ratified except by state legislatures sitting on ordinary business—the same bodies that ratified the Articles."

"Well, Rousseau would not call that an expression of the general will. He wanted an assembly of all the citizens at one meeting."

"Yes, but he violated one of his own rules. His assembly, formulating the general will, had to resolve itself into a committee of the whole in order to make the particular government. That legal fiction did not separate his legislators from his governors in a real way. Our popular vote, followed by the delegates' action did—so long as the popular vote was a universal one."

"Which, of course, it was not in your day. Not even women voted then."

"They were not fully citizens yet. But those who were citizens voted. Besides, I was the only one at the drafting convention who wanted a popular vote for the President and senators as well as for representatives. You have caught up with me on senators but not yet on the President."

"Yet you helped invent the Electoral College, which still elects our President indirectly."

"Just as a second-best. I was for direct vote everywhere, in the Pennsylvania Constitution as well as the federal one. In fact, I was for mandatory voting. If one does not vote, one cannot be a citizen."

"Force them to be free?"

"Ah, you do have Rousseau on your mind, don't you? But how can you say a people is self-governing if it does nothing to formulate the general will? Don't you still force people to serve on juries?"

"Yes."

"Making laws is even more important than enforcing them. In time of war do you make citizens serve in the military?"

"Depends on the war."

"Well, governing a country well is more important than defending it. How many citizens vote now?"

"More than half."

"Do you still call your country a republic?"

"Of course. Don't you?"

He hands me back the Constitution with an air of defeat. "Don't you do anything to make people act like citizens?"

"Naturally. We have a public school system meant to form citizens."

"Do people attend?"

"They have to. It's required."

"You force them to go to school so they can vote intelligently, but you do not force them to vote? I knew you were absentminded about politics; I did not know you were simpletons. Who governs you instead of the people?"

"Well, we normally think of the government as headed by the President. We speak of the Carter government, for instance, or the Nixon government."

"And only half the people voted for these Presidents?"

"Well, normally about a half of the half that turned out."

"And what does this man of government do?"

"Makes policy, sets the agenda for Congress, defends the country."

"How does he defend the country?"

"As Commander in Chief."

"Are you at war?"

"Not at the moment."

"Then what power has he as Commander in Chief? He is that with regard only to the armed forces, not to the citizens."

"Well, we live in a different world from yours."

"So I notice." He is looking up at a jet's contrails.

"In an age of nuclear war," I continue, "the President has to be able to respond to the threat of attack with our own nuclear response."

"Of course—after Congress has declared war."

"I'm afraid there would not be time for that in these days. He would have a matter of minutes to decide on activating the codes that release our missiles."

"And there is no intervention between his deciding that and the action taking place?"

"No constitutional one."

The judge abruptly sits down on the dirty street curb, holding his wig. "So there is no Constitution left. This is worse than I thought."

"Well"—I try to cheer him up—"that is just for nuclear war. We hope that won't happen. It is a once-in-a-lifetime matter."

Wilson rises, still wary. "Are your other wars declared by Congress, before this super-President of yours wages them?"

"Some are. Most recent ones have not been."

He sits down again, this time with a deliberately forlorn air. "How does war get declared then?"

"The President sends troops off to Vietnam, or Beirut, or Grenada—or somewhere."

"And Congress does not question this kind of act?"

"It tries to, but the President opposes it with executive privilege."

Wilson jumps up and grabs the Constitution back. "Privilege? Where is that? What have you done to this Constitution? *Privilege* is not a republican term. It is like *prerogative*—something meant to protect government from the people. Government is legitimate only if it is an *expression* of the people. A people's own expression has to be transparent to it. The people have to know what they are doing through all their intermediaries."

"But *you* convened in secrecy at Philadelphia."

"We were conspirators, mon. We were overthrowing a government. But the government we *set up* was not a secret one. It was one the people ordained and established to rule themselves. Those who keep secrets from them are not their representatives, cannot be speaking for them.''

"Well, what should we do? Call a convention to amend the Constitution? The Constitution itself allows for that.''

"That's the difference between anything you call now and the one we held in 1787. Our form of government did not allow us to create a republic. We went ahead and did it anyway.''

We turned off Third Street, heading west toward where the Grand Procession had ended. Wilson's memory is caught up now in the excitements of that day. "The warship float began to labor up this incline, though it was drawn by ten horses. It had a 'crew' of twenty-five seamen on its decks.''

"Was that your favorite float?''

"No, my favorite was the New Roof at the Grand Federal Edifice, with its thirteen pillars upholding a dome. At the end of the march, at Bush Hill, I mounted that float and gave the one speech of the day.''

The judge is panting now as he climbs an incline between shops boarded up. "The whole city went out from its confines and gathered in the field, forming all the other floats in a circle around the Federal Edifice. I spoke from the center of the circle, praising what the people had wrought. No other government was formed with such popular participation and debate at every level. I can tell you what I said, from heart: The Constitution 'was discussed and scrutinized in the fullest, freest, and severest manner—by speaking, by writing, and by printing—by individuals

and by public bodies—by its friends and by its enemies. What was the issue? Most favourable. . . .' '' He was in full oration now, breathless but unstoppable—till the site of Bush Hill stopped him. We were on Sixteenth Street, crossing Spring Garden. The entire area was cluttered with dust from demolition and high-rise construction. Bulldozers were at work on the site where the entire city had gathered, once, to pledge itself to a new political creation. There was not a marker anywhere to recall that event.

"You have not fared well, Judge Wilson, in the hearts of your citizens.''

"My lodging there was always precarious, I am afraid. But I have never doubted their right to govern themselves, so long as they showed they were willing to govern.''

"Well, we do mean to remember your Grand Procession on its bicentenary.''

"On July 4, 1988?''

"No, we thought we would fold it together with the end of the drafting convention in September 1787. I suppose we have the date wrong.''

"That, among other things. What is it, precisely, you are celebrating in 1987?''

"The Constitution.''

"It is a funeral ceremony then?''

"Of course not. We are celebrating all the things that have happened to the Constitution, up to now. Come and see.''

"Oh,'' he said, with a stricken look. "I think not''—and his robe dimmed abruptly in the bulldozers' dust as he fled.

Separation of Powers: Checks and Balances

5

The Federalist, Number 51
James Madison

Factions and uncontrolled political power are the major problems addressed in The Federalist, Number 51. *Too much governmental power causes abuses that endanger personal liberty and security. This is a problem in relationships within the national government and between government and the people. For example, if the president gains excessive power at the expense of Congress, our constitutional system may be threatened by abusive exercises of authority. Such excessive power was evident in the Vietnam War, the Watergate scandal, and the Iran-Contra Affair. The federal system is a second check on possible excesses of concentrated political power. Since the national government and the states operate in the same geographic territory, individuals are protected because the two levels of government can counterbalance each other. This issue is discussed further in Chapter 4. A major question from this* Federalist *essay concerns the exercise of negative, as opposed to positive, political power: If separation of powers and checks and balances prevent abuses of authority, how can the government deal effectively with policy controversies and serious crises? Clearly, our governmental structure is not organized to facilitate hasty decisions. At the same time, we may be frustrated by the lack of governmental response to pressing social and economic problems.*

TO THE PEOPLE OF THE STATE OF NEW YORK

To what expedient, then, shall we finally, resort, for maintaining in practice the necessary partition of power among the several departments, as laid down in the Constitution? The only answer that can be given is, that as all these exterior provisions are found to be inadequate, the defect must be supplied, by so contriving the interior structure of the government as that its several constituent parts may, by their mutual relations, be the means of keeping each other in their proper places. Without presuming to undertake a full development of this important idea, I will hazard a few general observations, which may perhaps place it in a clearer light, and enable us to form a more correct judgment of the principles and structure of the government planned by the convention.

From the *New York Packet*, Friday, February 8, 1788.

In order to lay a due foundation for that separate and distinct exercise of the different powers of government, which to a certain extent is admitted on all hands to be essential to the preservation of liberty, it is evident that each department should have a will of its own; and consequently should be so constituted that the members of each should have as little agency as possible in the appointment of the members of the others. Were this principle rigorously adhered to, it would require that all the appointments for the supreme executive, legislative, and judiciary magistrates should be drawn from the same fountain of authority, the people, through channels having no communication whatever with one another. Perhaps such a plan of constructing the several departments would be less difficult in practice than it may in contemplation appear. Some difficulties, however, and some additional expense would attend the execution of it. Some deviations, therefore, from the principle must be admitted. In the constitution of the judiciary department in particular, it might be inexpedient to insist rigorously on the principle: first, because peculiar qualifications being essential in the members, the primary consideration ought to be to select that mode of choice which best secures these qualifications; secondly, because the permanent tenure by which the appointments are held in that department, must soon destroy all sense of dependence on the authority conferring them.

It is equally evident, that the members of each department should be as little dependent as possible on those of the others, for the emoluments annexed to their offices. Were the executive magistrate, or the judges, not independent of the legislature in this particular, their independence in every other would be merely nominal.

But the great security against a gradual concentration of the several powers in the same department, consists in giving to those who administer each department the necessary constitutional means and personal motives to resist encroachments of the others. The provision for defense must in this, as in all other cases, be made commensurate to the danger of attack. Ambition must be made to counteract ambition. The interest of the man must be connected with the constitutional rights of the place. It may be a reflection on human nature, that such devices should be necessary to control the abuses of government. But what is government itself, but the greatest of all reflections on human nature? If men were angels, no government would be necessary. If angels were to govern men, neither external nor internal controls on government would be necessary. In framing a government which is to be administered by men over men, the great difficulty lies in this: you must first enable the government to control the governed; and in the next place oblige it to control itself. A dependence on the people is, no doubt, the primary control on the government; but experience has taught mankind the necessity of auxiliary precautions.

This policy of supplying by opposite and rival interests, the defect of better motives, might be traced through the whole system of human affairs, private as well as public. We see it particularly displayed in all the subordinate distributions of power, where the constant aim is to divide and arrange the several offices in such a manner as that each may be a check on the other—that the private interest of every individual may be a sentinel over the public rights. These inventions of prudence cannot be less requisite in the distribution of the supreme powers of the State.

But it is not possible to give to each department an equal power of self-defense. In republican government the legislative authority necessarily predominates. The remedy for this inconveniency is to divide the legislature into different branches; and to render them, by different modes of election and different principles of action, as little connected with each other as the nature of their common functions and their common dependence on the society will admit. It may even be necessary to guard against dangerous encroachments by still further precautions. As the weight of the legislative authority requires that it should be thus divided, the weakness of the executive may require, on the other hand, that it should be fortified. An absolute negative on the legislature appears, at first view, to be the natural defense with which the executive magistrate should be armed. But perhaps it would be neither altogether safe nor alone sufficient. On ordinary occasions it might not be exerted with the requisite firmness, and on extraordinary occasions it might be perfidiously abused. May not this defect of an absolute negative be supplied by some qualified connection between this weaker department and the weaker branch of the stronger department, by which the latter may be led to support the constitutional rights of the former, without being too much detached from the rights of his own department?

If the principles on which these observations are founded be just, as I persuade myself they are, and they be applied as a criterion to the several State constitutions, and to the federal Constitution, it will be found that if the latter does not perfectly correspond with them, the former are infinitely less able to bear such a test.

There are, moreover, two considerations particularly applicable to the federal system of America, which place that system in a very interesting point of view.

First.   In a single republic, all the power surrendered by the people is submitted to the administration of a single government; and the usurpations are guarded against by a division of the government into distinct and separate departments. In the compound republic of America, the power surrendered by the people is first divided between two distinct governments, and then the portion allotted to each subdivided among distinct and separate departments. Hence a double security arises to the rights of the people. The different governments will control each other, at the same time that each will be controlled by itself.

Second.   It is of great importance in a republic not only to guard the society against the oppression of its rulers, but to guard one part of the society against the injustice of the other part. Different interests necessarily exist in different classes of citizens. If a majority be united by a common interest, the rights of the minority will be insecure. There are but two methods of providing against this evil: the one by creating a will in the community independent of the majority—that is, of the society itself; the other, by comprehending in the society so many separate descriptions of citizens as will render an unjust combination of a majority of the whole very improbable, if not impracticable. The first method prevails in all governments possessing an hereditary or self-appointed authority. This, at best, is but a precarious security; because a power independent of the society may as well espouse the unjust views of the major, as the rightful interests of the minor party, and may possibly be turned against both parties. The second method will be exemplified in the federal republic of the United States. Whilst all authority in it will be derived from and dependent on the society, the society itself will be broken into so many parts, interests and classes of citizens, that the rights of individuals, or of the minority, will be in little danger from interested combinations of the majority. In a free government the security for civil rights must be the same as that for religious rights. It consists in the one case in the multiplicity of interests, and in the other in the multiplicity of sects. The degree of security in both cases will depend on the number of interests and sects; and this may be presumed to depend on the extent of country and number of people comprehended under the same government. This view of the subject must particularly recommend a proper federal system to all the sincere and considerate friends of republican government, since it shows that in exact proportion as the territory of the Union may be formed into more circumscribed Confederacies, or States, oppressive combinations of a majority will be facilitated; the best security, under the republican forms, for the rights of every class of citizens, will be diminished; and consequently the stability and independence of some member of the government, the only other security, must be proportionately increased. Justice is the end of the government. It is the end of civil society. It ever has been and ever will be pursued until it be obtained, or until liberty be lost in the pursuit. In a society under the forms of which the stronger faction can readily unite and oppress the weaker, anarchy may as truly be said to reign as in a state of nature, where the weaker individual is not secured against the violence of the stronger; and as, in the latter state, even the stronger individuals are prompted, by the uncertainty of their condition, to submit to a government which may protect the weak as well as themselves; so, in the former state, will the more powerful factions or parties be gradually induced, by a like motive, to wish for a government which will protect all parties, the weaker as well as the more powerful. It can be little doubted that if the State of Rhode Island was separated from the Confederacy and left to itself, the insecurity of rights under the popular form of government within such narrow limits would be displayed by such reiterated oppressions of factious majorities that some power altogether independent of the people would soon be called for by the voice of the very factions whose misrule had proved the necessity of it. In the extended republic of the United States, and among the great variety of interests, parties, and sects which it embraces, a coalition of a majority of the whole society could seldom take place on any other principles than those of justice and the general good; whilst there being thus less danger to a minor from the will of a major party, there must be less pretext, also, to provide for the security of the former, by introducing into the government a will not dependent on the latter, or, in other words, a will independent of the society itself. It is no less certain than it is important, notwithstanding the contrary opinions which have been entertained, that the larger the society, provided it lie within a practical sphere, the more duly capable it will be of self-government. And happily for the *republican cause,* the practicable sphere may be carried to a very great extent, by a judicious modification and mixture of the *federal principle.*

Publius

The Enduring Constitution

6

A Few Parchment Pages
Two Hundred Years Later
Richard B. Morris

Richard Morris provides strong evidence for the endurance and adaptability of the Constitution. He begins with a sketch of the various regional compromises agreed to at the constitutional convention. Why were these compromises and concessions so important to the drafting of the Constitution? Professor Morris then considers how the Constitution should be interpreted. Does the original intent of the framers provide the best guide to constitutional interpretation? What were James Madison's views on this matter? Morris concludes his thoughtful essay with a discussion of constitutional adaptability. He refers to amendments, actions by the three branches of government, and public opinion. How have these activities redefined, expanded, or checked various powers in the Constitution?

The American Constitution has functioned and endured longer than any other written constitution of the modern era. It imbues the nation with energy to act while restraining its agents from acting improperly. It safeguards our liberties and establishes a government of laws, not of men and women. Above all, the Constitution is the mortar that binds the fifty-state edifice under the concept of federalism; it is the symbol that unifies nearly 250 million people of different origins, races, and religions into a single nation.

Over two centuries dozens of constitutions adopted in other countries have gone into the scrap heap. The United States Constitution has outlived almost all its successors. The longevity of the Constitution makes us wonder whether its thirty-nine signers planned it that way, and if they did, why doesn't the Constitution declare itself to be perpetual, unlike the weak "perpetual" union—the Articles of Confederation—that it succeeded? Somehow the adjective was overlooked in the federal convention, while the word *compact* was deliberately avoided in a vain attempt to forestall the issue of whether the Constitution was a compact between the states, which any party could disavow, or between the government and the people, which States' Righters might have found unacceptable.

However, the Constitution does start with a hint that it was aiming for longevity. The Preamble, in Gouverneur Morris's incomparable language, says that its purpose is "to

From *American Heritage*, Vol. 38, No. 4 (May/June), 1987, pp. 46-51. Reprinted by permission of the estate of Richard B. Morris.

form a more perfect Union" and "secure the Blessings of Liberty to ourselves and our Posterity. . . ." President Washington in his Farewell Address speaks of the "efficacy and permanency of your union." Nevertheless, both the supremacy and the permanence of the Constitution were to be challenged within a decade. To oppose the Alien and Sedition Acts of 1798, which curbed the actions of hostile aliens and held the press criminally accountable for "false" and "malicious" writings about the government, James Madison and Thomas Jefferson joined forces to write the Kentucky and Virginia Resolutions. These asserted that a state had the power to "interpose" when the government exceeded its powers as enumerated in the Constitution.

By 1828 the challenge of "interposition" had become the threat of "nullification" when John C. Calhoun endorsed South Carolina's refusal to obey a new tariff measure. In spite of vigorous support by Daniel Webster and President Andrew Jackson, the life-span of the Constitution seemed jeopardized on the eve of the Civil War as "nullification" gave way to "secession," and the Southern states claimed that the Constitution was dissoluble at the pleasure of any state that might wish to secede.

Confronted by a burgeoning secessionist movement, President Lincoln declared, "I hold that, in contemplation of universal law and of the Constitution, the Union of these States is perpetual." The word was out at last. The Union forged by the Constitution could not be dismantled. To put the issue beyond controversy required four years of war and a Supreme Court decision to settle the question of whether the Constitution was a compact of *sovereign states* or a compact of the *people of the states,* as was originally intended. The Supreme Court confirmed the military decision, denying the right of states to secede. In *Texas v. White* in 1869 it declared, "The Constitution, in all its provisions, looks to an inde-

structible Union, composed of indestructible States."

One of the clues to the mystery of the Constitution's durability is the plastic quality that makes it applicable to a rapidly changing society. At the convention it was the Committee of Detail's deliberate intention, in the words of its draftsman, Edmund Randolph, "to insert essential principles only" in order to accommodate the Constitution "to times and events" and "to use simple and precise language, and general propositions. . . ." Randolph's notion of confining a constitution to broad principles was a masterstroke that contributed immensely to that document's enduring suitability and relevance, and James Wilson of Pennsylvania contributed further by putting Randolph's draft into smoother prose. Finally, the Committee of Style and Arrangement, under the swift and sure guidance of Gouverneur Morris and his talented colleagues, gave us the final draft, a masterpiece of conciseness.

How different, indeed, from most modern state constitutions, which are often hugely long with their general principles buried under a heap of minute local and transitory details. The great charter, a few parchment pages adopted in eighty-four working days, is a broad blueprint of governance, timeless in character.

Another aspect of the working methods of the framers helps explain the relative speedy adoption and ratification of the Constitution. In 1839, on the fiftieth anniversary of the establishment of the national government, John Quincy Adams spoke of the federal Constitution as having been "extorted" from the "grinding necessity of a reluctant nation." He was attesting to the fact that only a combination of bold innovation, compromise, and concession made it possible to frame and ratify the Constitution. Adams may well have been overstating the case, for in fact, the overwhelming majority of the delegates to the Philadelphia convention were nationalists of one sort or another, convinced of the need to confer a taxing power on a central government, to invest it with jurisdiction over foreign and interstate commerce, and to establish a framework that would be the supreme law of the land.

Within this extraordinary company of statesmen there developed sharp differences about how such a constitution could be made to conform to truly republican principles, how vestiges of sovereignty could be left to the states, just what powers should be enumerated to the national (or federal) government, and how far the states could be restrained. The result was a series of compromises and concessions, some minor and easily settled, some major and involving prolonged debate.

School texts invariably refer to the Great Compromise by which the small states gained equality in the Senate while the House of Representatives was made proportional to population. But even within that compromise, credited to the Connecticut delegates, there were additional compromises. Once it was settled that the House was to be elected by the people, the issue arose as to how the Senate was to be elected—also by the people, as the democratic nationalist James Wilson proposed; or by the House, as Edmund Randolph recommended; or by the state legislatures, an idea set forth by John Dickinson. The last suggestion was the one adopted, and it was a tribute to the delegates' concern about setting up a federal rather than a national constitution, thereby recognizing that certain powers inhered to the states. The Senate represented the states, and Article V of the Constitution guaranteed that no state could be deprived of equal suffrage in the Senate. This equality of the fifty states is a cardinal element of our federal system, reinforced by the Tenth Amendment, according to which "the powers not delegated to the United States by the Constitution, nor prohibited by it to the States, are reserved to the States respectively, or to the people."

On the issue of choosing senators, James Wilson's vision proved the sharpest, for the Senate came in later years to be perceived as a tool of the big business interests that tended to dominate the state legislatures. The Seventeenth Amendment, which was ratified in 1913, provided for direct election of senators by the people, vindicating Wilson's original judgment.

While the large states won proportional representation in the House, the Northern states could hardly be expected to permit the South to count blacks, who were not eligible to vote, for purposes of that representation. Nor did the South care to include its slave population in the head count that would determine the amount of taxes it would have to pay in direct taxation. The result: Another compromise by which representation and direct taxes in the lower house would be based on "free persons," including servants bound for a term of years (a favored labor source of white labor in the tobacco states of Maryland and Virginia), and three-fifths of all other persons, "excluding Indians not taxed. . . ." As a result, in counting population a black was included as three-fifths of a white person. The compromise gave something to each side: for the South, more Southerners to be represented in Congress; for the North, more heads to tax.

If the Great Compromise resolved differences between the states about representation, the second major compromise resulted from a confrontation between North and South about commerce. Everyone had agreed that conferring power over commerce upon the national government, along with the power to tax, was a prime motive for calling the convention. But the South now had second thoughts. States that shipped farm staples to a world market believed that this would work to the advantage of the North—which was heavily engaged in trade and shipping—while adding disproportionate costs to Southern exporters. To protect themselves against possible discrimination, some in the South sought to require a two-thirds vote in each house for passage of commercial legislation. The scholarly and creative James Madison, rising above sectional prejudices, prevailed upon the convention to reject this proposal and to give Congress the power to regulate commerce by a simple majority vote.

Nonetheless, every regional concession brought its price and begot its compromise. Thus, the great slavery issue came to the fore when the delegates took up the matter of import and export duties. The South proposed that Congress be forbidden from levying a tax on the importation of slaves or from prohibiting their importation altogether. Virginians, who were finding slavery less profitable than did their more southerly neighbors, did not join the Southern bloc. Nevertheless, over the objections of Virginia's great libertarian George Mason and of a divided North, the delegates worked out a compromise whereby no prohibition on the importation of "such persons as any of the states now existing shall think proper to admit" could be permitted before the year 1808. Even the North was split on this crucial and emotional vote. Nor was there a solid South.

In this way was slavery acknowledged, though not by name in the Constitution, and confirmed in two other compromises: the three-fifths rule for representation to the House of Representatives and for direct taxes and the provision for the return to their owners of fugitive persons "held to Service or Labor. . . ."

And the Philadelphia delegates continued to compromise. First, it was decided that the chief executive was to be a single person, not a committee or plural executive, as previously

had been proposed. He would serve for four years (other proposals had ranged from a life term to a single seven-year term), and he was to be eligible for reelection. He would have a qualified veto (one that could be overridden by the legislative branch), not the absolute veto that some had urged. He would not be chosen by Congress, as the Virginia Plan had proposed, or selected directly by the people, as James Wilson would have preferred. Instead, the final decision, after countless proposals, was to have the President elected by electors who would be chosen in each state "in such Manner" as its legislators might "direct." This plan, perhaps conceived to propitiate the states, proved instead a victory for both nationalism and democracy, for very shortly after 1789 nearly all the state legislators provided for the election of their states' presidential electors by popular vote. If no candidate had a majority of the electoral vote, the ultimate choice would be made from the five highest candidates by the House of Representatives. However, in choosing the President, the House would vote by states, each state having one vote. Thus, the electoral college proved to be a compromise whereby the people, at least indirectly, would make the choice rather than the state legislatures.

Perhaps the ablest defense of all these compromises and concessions was made in *The Federalist*, in which Madison, while conceding that the Constitution was not a "faultless" document, admitted that the convention's delegates "were either satisfactorily accommodated by the final act; or were induced to accede to it out of a deep conviction of the *necessity of sacrificing private opinions* and *partial interests* to the *public good*, and by a despair of seeing this necessity diminished by the delays or by new experiments."

Finally, and certainly most important in terms of the safeguards for the people, the chief criticism leveled against the Constitution when it was finally submitted for ratification was the failure to incorporate a bill of rights. In ratifying the Constitution, a number of states included bills of rights among their recommendations. To ensure such compliance, New York even urged that a second convention be called. The prospect of another convention, which might very well undo the great work already accomplished, appalled James Madison. Once elected to the House of Representatives, the Virginian reduced more than two hundred proposed amendments to twelve, of which ten were ratified. The Bill of Rights, as those first ten amendments are called, proved to be the great concession that quieted public fears about the new government's guarantees of civil liberties. This concession was Madison's noblest heritage to the nation.

If there was controversy from the very start about the scope and intent of the Constitution, that controversy has continued down to the present day. In fact, it has heated up over the current insistence of the attorney general, Edwin Meese, that the Supreme Court in interpreting the Constitution is bound by the intent of the framers. This question, now being debated in many quarters, addresses the public's conception of the Constitution: Is it a charter carved in stone or a malleable document that can be interpreted in response to rapidly changing moral and social values and economic and technological demands? When Hamilton described the Constitution as looking "forward to remote futurity," how flexible did he consider it to be?

Are courts bound by the debates at the convention and the state ratifying conventions, or are they bound by the "express words" of the Constitution, and are we talking about the meaning of those words in 1787 or in the 1980s? Certainly the meaning that the drafters wished to communicate may differ from the meaning the reader is warranted to derive from the text.

What we do know, in studying the notes of debates on the framing of the Constitution, is that the framers expected the Constitution to be interpreted in accord with its *express language*. "Vague" or "indefinite" language was criticized, and there were debates then and to this day as to how much of the war-making power was given to the President and how much to Congress.

Since the proceedings of the convention were secret and mostly not published until after James Madison's death some fifty years later, there is no possibility that the framers wished future interpreters to extract intention from their private debates. Nevertheless, in the debates over ratification, the Antifederalists expressed worries that the Congress and the federal judiciary would construe broadly the enumerated powers. At the New York ratification convention John Jay sought to allay these fears by insisting that the document involved "no sophistry, no construction, no false glosses, but simple inference from the previous operation of things." And Madison took pains to point out that improper construction of the Constitution could be remedied through amendment or by election "of more faithful representatives to annul the acts of the acts of the usurpers."

One of the most revealing examples of determining the intent of the framers occurred in their own later arguments about the "necessary and proper" clause. Article I, Section 8 lists among the powers granted Congress: "To make all Laws which shall be necessary and proper for carrying into Execution the foregoing Powers, and all other Powers vested by this Constitution in the Government of the United States, or in any Department or Officer thereof." Now it so happens that both James Madison and Alexander Hamilton served on the Committee of Style that was responsible for the final wording of the Constitution. In *The Federalist*, No. 44 Madison argued for a liberal interpretation of the "necessary and proper" clause in a way that must have delighted Hamilton, who was later to take the same position in defending the creation of the First Bank of the United States. The convention had in fact rejected a proposal to give Congress explicit power to charter corporations. Only after Madison had become involved with Jefferson in what amounted to the opposition party's assault on Hamilton's financial policies did Madison in effect repudiate his *Federalist* position and adopt the theory of "strict construction."

Yet it was to be Hamilton's interpretation of the scope of the "necessary and proper" clause that President Washington accepted and that Chief Justice John Marshall later embraced. Indeed, Hamilton anticipated the later assumption by the Supreme Court of powers for the federal government on the basis of three clauses of the Constitution, which, in addition to the "necessary and proper" clause, included the general welfare clause—granting Congress power "to provide for the . . . general Welfare of the United States"—and the commerce clause, giving Congress the power to "regulate Commerce with foreign Nations, and among the several States, and with the Indian Tribes. . . ." There is no question that we today owe to the vision of the framers a Constitution that· can accommodate the modern welfare state under the general welfare clause and manufacturing within the commerce clause.

In *The Federalist*, No. 37 Madison, then sharing Hamilton's views, argued that the "intent" of any legal document is the product of the interpretive process, not of some fixed meaning that the author locks into the document's text at the outset. He ventured so far as to declare that even the meaning of God's Word "is rendered dim and doubtful by the cloudy medium through which it is communicated" when He "condescends to address mankind in their own language. . . ." It was

up to the courts, Hamilton argued in a later *Federalist* letter, to fix the meaning and operation of laws, including the Constitution, and the courts could be expected to use the "rules of *common sense"* to determine the "natural and obvious sense" of the Constitution's provisions.

The question of the intention of the Philadelphia framers came up in one of the first great and controversial decisions handed down by the Supreme Court presided over by John Jay. *Chisholm v. Georgia* (1793) raised the question, Could a state be sued by a private citizen of another state? The language of the Constitution was, to say the least, ambiguous; according to Article III, federal judicial power could extend to controversies "between a State and Citizens of another State. . . ." In the debates on ratification the framers went to great pains to deny that the Constitution would affect the state's sovereign immunity. Even Hamilton gave such assurances in *The Federalist*, No. 81. Yet a majority of the Court, construing the wording of Article III, held that the text was intended to *allow* suits against a state. But Georgia did not think so, and few amendments overruling a Supreme Court decision were adopted more speedily than the Eleventh Amendment, which in 1798 upheld the states' immunity to such actions.

How much weight did James Madison, often called the "father of the Constitution," give to the original intent of the framers? Very little, it seems, if we can judge from his insistence in his later years that "as a guide to expounding and applying the provisions of the Constitution, the debates and incidental decisions of the Convention can have no authoritative character." What counted in Madison's eyes were precedents derived from "authoritative, deliberate and continued decisions." Madison, who had originally phrased the Bill of Rights, sought to bind the states as well as Congress—a phrasing that mysteriously disappeared from the final product, which speaks only of Congress. He would have rejoiced at the modern Supreme Court's interpretation of the truly revolutionary Fourteenth Amendment, ratified in 1868 during the Reconstruction Era and holding that the states as well as the federal government are bound by the Bill of Rights.

Indeed, what has contributed to the durability of the Constitution is its capacity to adapt to a society so different from that of the Founding Fathers. Shortly before the Constitutional Convention assembled, a mob put an alleged witch to death in Pennsylvania, and just a few weeks later most of the delegates went down to the banks of the Delaware to see a demonstration of John Fitch's steamboat—so incongruous were the boundaries of knowledge at that time. A First Amendment setting up a wall of separation between church and state and guaranteeing freedom of religion was adopted by a people who were already facing one of the great fundamentalist religious revivals of our history.

The Constitution made provision for such adjustments. Even though the word *equality* is missing in that seminal charter, in time amendments were adopted that, among other things, ended slavery (ratified in 1865), provided for "the equal protection of the laws" and "due process of law" for all persons (ratified 1868); conferred voting rights regardless of "race, color, or previous condition of servitude" (ratified 1870); required the direct election of senators (ratified 1913); gave women the suffrage (ratified 1920); ended the poll tax as a bar to voting in federal elections (ratified 1964); and extended the suffrage to eighteen-year-olds (ratified 1971).

But not by amendments alone has the Constitution been reshaped. Actions of the three branches of government have broadened its text and applied its principles to specific situations only dimly perceived by the framers.

As early as George Washington's administration the principle of executive privilege was upheld, the rights of the President to dismiss appointees accepted, the cabinet—not mentioned in the Constitution—created, the right of the President to declare neutrality without consulting the Senate established, and the House of Representatives' power to withhold appropriations for treaties it did not approve of overruled. Finally, there emerged a party system—a system that none of the Founding Fathers anticipated—that Washington deplored in his Farewell Address, and that was considered a cause of faction and divisiveness. Yet today political parties are accepted as the touchstone of a democratic society, and the repression of opposition parties as one of the most visible symptoms of a totalitarian state.

Despite these enlargements and glosses upon the original Constitution made by both the President and Congress over the past two centuries, it is the High Court that bears the brunt of criticism for straying from the intent of the framers. Critics charge the Supreme Court with practicing what amounts to judicial legislation to effect due process, achieve equal justice, assure voting equality, and maintain the right of privacy even in cases in which it is dubious that a majority of the nation's citizens support some of its advanced positions.

In 1787 and 1788 and again today critics contend that judges, who are insulated from the electoral process, should not be entrusted with final interpretation of the laws. But no federal judge has even been impeached and removed from the bench because his decisions have run counter to public opinion. Only on grounds of "high crimes or misdemeanors"—not deviation from prevailing political norms—is a federal judge liable to impeachment and removal. To Alexander Hamilton the independence of the judicial branch was essential if the courts were to maintain their role as guardian of the Constitution's limits on power.

That independence is the central issue concerning the federal judiciary's role today. The Supreme Court is increasingly preoccupied with cases that deal with social and moral issues—the death penalty, desegregation, school busing, prayer in schools, abortion, privacy—and litigants insist that the justices fill the vacuum created by the lack of direction on these subjects from the two other branches of government that, unlike the Court, are subject to the electoral process.

No single branch of government can long evade the issue of accountability for interpreting the Constitution. The President fills vacancies on the Court, usually picking persons who reflect his constitutional views. In requiring the President to swear to "preserve, protect and defend the Constitution," the public expects him to determine if and when it is being threatened. Some Presidents, like Lincoln, looked neither to Congress nor to the courts in times of crisis. Deciding that the Union was indissoluble, Lincoln explicitly assumed the authority and took on the full burden of maintaining the Union.

Nor can Congress escape responsibility, since it is charged by the Constitution with enacting regulations concerning the Supreme Court's jurisdiction except when spelled out in Article III. Beginning with the Judiciary Act of 1789, Congress has set the parameters of the federal courts' jurisdiction and within those constitutional limitations can enlarge or diminish the scope of litigation that may be brought to trial in the federal courts.

Finally, we the people have the power of defining the Constitution through the ballot box, albeit that power has seldom been used directly to affect judicial decisions. The most startling exception was in 1936, when, not long after the election, the Supreme Court in obvious response to public opinion began to yield to the President's and Congress's constitutional views. But that example was dramatic and virtually without parallel. Indeed, few citizens consciously or systematically utilize their ballots to register constitutional interpretations. This omission leaves officials to resolve most conflicts themselves, but senators, representatives, and Presidents do so subject to the disapproval of voters, whereas the Court is politically unaccountable.

True, the Constitution contains a provision for amendment by calling a convention, but the framers, having themselves violated their instructions by overthrowing rather than revising the Articles of Confederation, were loath to expose their great work to a second convention. And despite the number of states that in recent years have gone on record to call for such a second convention, the wording of the calls are varied and imprecise and the dangers to the durable structure of the nation seem too great to bear the risk.

In the landmark case of *Cohens v. Virginia* (1821), Chief Justice John Marshall spoke of a constitution as having been "framed for ages to come" and as being "designed to approach immortality as nearly as human institutions can approach it." These are appropriate words for the Constitution's bicentennial celebration. An issue-laden document, always a storm center of dissent, the Constitution is, paradoxically, still held in affection, even veneration, by the people of America.

In the century ahead it should continue to function so long as it can meet the objectives that were set forth in the Preamble in the name of "We the People": to "insure domestic Tranquility, provide for the common defense, promote the general Welfare, and secure the Blessings of Liberty to ourselves and our Posterity. . . ." For two hundred complex years it has remained steadfast to these goals. No worthier aims can be set for the great charter as it moves into its third century.

Is Constitutional Reform Needed?

7

The World's Most Stable Democracy
Charlotte Saikowski

The next selection deals with the question of whether or not fundamental constitutional changes are needed. One side argues that the federal government is so divided and fragmented that it cannot make key decisions. Chronic deadlock or stagnation benefits special interests, not the public interest. Consequently, the Committee on the Constitutional System advocates specific structural changes for Congress, the cabinet, and the treaty-making process. Others argue that constitutional tinkering is unnecessary. They argue for political change, reforming campaign finance laws, and improving the quality of leadership. With which side do you agree? Does the Constitution need to be changed? Or, are other components of American government, politics, and leadership in need of improvement?

America is young as nations go. But it boasts at least one record of longevity: The United States has the oldest working written Constitution on Earth. The Constitution is not just a piece of parchment that is consulted only when convenient or expedient, but a living document that has helped produce the most stable government in the world.

Under it, the United States has survived a history of severe challenges, including the War of 1812, the Civil War, two world wars, waves of immigration, the Great Depression, and sweeping economic, social, and technological change.

No constitutional system today has endured so long. And no system has evoked so much admiration and bafflement. Many nations have sought, in varying degrees, to emulate American representative democracy.

Others are perplexed, even annoyed, by its disorderliness.

What George Washington, James Madison, and Alexander Hamilton—the three leading figures behind the Constitutional Convention of 1787—would think of their handiwork today and of how separation of powers has worked out in practice is a matter of speculation. Certainly the system has undergone extraordinary change since 1787:

- The national government has grown to a point of overpowering the role of the states, which were dominant when the nation was born.
- The presidency, which the framers expected to be relatively weak and sought to strengthen, has expanded into the nation's most powerful institution. With the widening role of

government and a steadily growing executive branch, the president has accumulated more and more authority. Power now is seen to reside largely at the White House.

- Congress, which the framers envisaged as the dominant force in government (and feared as a result), similarly has grown in size and remains powerful. But, with today's proliferation of committees and subcommittees, fragmentation of political power, and bloated staffs, Congress is less inclined to initiate policy than to let the president set the legislative agenda.
- The federal judiciary was expected to be the weakest branch of government. But down through the decades the Supreme Court has become a powerful vehicle for making public policy as it interprets the law.
- Political parties, which are not mentioned in the Constitution and which the framers thought would not be needed, were soon established as an integral part of the American political system. Though weakened today, they remain the means through which the national leaders and representatives are nominated and elected.

Despite the evolutionary changes in government, however, it is the stability and continuity of the American system that is most striking in 1987.

"The big story is the absence of change [in the system], given the amount of economic and social change," says Everett Carll Ladd, author of "The American Polity." "We still have separation of powers in all its glory—what the Founding Fathers had in mind has worked."

While most observers of American constitutional democracy agree that the present system of divided powers and checks and balances has served the nation extremely well, concern grows among some political leaders and scholars that it is not able to deal with the deluge of issues raised by an increasingly complex technological world and injected into the political arena.

GOVERNMENT IN GRIDLOCK

Proponents of reform say that, partly because of divided government (that is, when one party controls the White House and the other holds a majority in one or both houses of Congress—which has been the case 60 percent of the time since 1956), efforts to make decisions or strike compromises on such issues as the federal deficit and nuclear arms control have failed. Coherence and consistency are lacking in foreign and national-security policies. Painstakingly negotiated treaties are submitted to the Senate for ratification, only to be rejected. The result, these critics say, is chronic indecision, gridlock, or stagnation in government, which tends to benefit special interests at the expense of the general good.

"The separation of powers between the legislative and executive branches, whatever its merits in 1793, has become a structure that almost guarantees stalemate today," writes Lloyd N. Cutler, a former counsel to the president and a co-chairman of the bipartisan Committee on the Constitutional System. "As we wonder why we are having such a difficult time making decisions we all know must be made and projecting our power and leadership, we should reflect on whether this is one big reason."

Historian James MacGregor Burns echoes this theme in his book "The Power to Lead": "The American political system faces a pervasive crisis of self-confidence that only the rarest kind of leadership can overcome. The symptoms of the crisis take the long-observed form of political disarray, institutional stalemate, and governmental ineptitude and impotence."

Some reform advocates go so far as to favor moving closer to a parliamentary system of government. Under that system the executive officers of government are selected from the ranks of the legislative majority, thereby facilitating the ability of the majority party to carry out an overall program and be held accountable for its success or failure.

But the reformists appear to be a minority, even within the academic community. Interviews with scores of lawmakers, governors, and other public officials, as well as academics and everyday citizens, disclose an overwhelming predisposition to leave the Constitution alone.

"The genius of the framers was to set the broad principles and structure of a government that worked in their time but would be flexible enough for the indefinite future," says Clark Clifford, a lawyer and former high aide to Democratic presidents. "We have a document that works today and works well."

"Madison would be astounded, not by the great empire America became—which he expected—but by the pluralism of society made possible by the Constitution," comments Charles McC. Mathias Jr., a former US senator from Maryland.

"The Constitution has served us beyond the wildest expectations of the people who wrote it," remarks Sen. Bob Graham of Florida. "We don't need a constitutional convention to rewrite it."

Even the investigations of the ongoing Iran-contra affair are viewed as demonstrating the capacity of government to withstand shocks and adjust to a failure within one of its branches. "It shows the great virtues of the American system, based as it is on a separation of powers," says historian Arthur M. Schlesinger Jr. "The issue is whether the president is above the Constitution and the laws. The system guarantees that when a president abuses power, corrective forces exist to redress the constitutional balance."

While some observers worry about another "broken presidency," others maintain that the system of separation of powers will effectively respond to the situation. As the White House struggles to regain its standing, Congress will assert its authority, and the Supreme Court, in turn, will be carefully watching the legislature.

Most public officials and scholars acknowledge the existence of gridlock and the slowness of policymaking. But they contend that the problems and the solutions do not lie in the governmental structure.

"The answers are political not structural," says Thomas E. Cronin, author of "The State of the Presidency." "Democracy is not self-executing. We need gifted political leaders who can see the longer run and weave coalitions together. No structural gimmicks are the answer."

Americans sometimes fail to recognize that Britian's admired parliamentary government also runs into stalemates, because these tend to be hidden from view. The British prime minister is often blocked from acting because of confrontation with his or her Cabinet ministers.

REFORMS PROPOSED

"The parliamentary system is an illusion," comments Richard Neustadt, a Harvard scholar. "What you would get in the United States is the French Fourth Republic [which had a frequent turnover of governments]. You could not get party disciplines, so there would be constantly shifting coalitions."

There is no quarrel among experts that the American political system periodically needs adjusting to make for smoother governance.

Current ideas center on further reforming campaign-finance laws to strengthen the dam of control on the money flowing to candidates; revamping the swollen system of committees and subcommittees in Congress; revising the cumbersome budget process; making the president's national-security adviser subject to Senate confirmation; and setting up regional primaries and strengthening party rules.

Going further, the Committee on the Constitutional System, a private group that seeks to stimulate public debate, proposes changes that would require additional amendments to the Constitution. These include extending the terms of members of the House of Representatives from two to four years and of senators from six to eight years; permitting members of Congress to serve in the Cabinet; and relaxing the requirement that treaties be approved by a two-thirds vote of the Senate, either by lowering the requirement to 60 percent or by requiring only a majority vote of both houses.

Professor Burns, a member of the committee, says he believes that much of the misbehavior in the White House over the years, including the Iran affair, reflects a general institutional problem. "Because there's so much deadlock in the system and because the public demands action from the government, there is enormous pressure on the White House to short-circuit the system, and not always for malign reasons," he comments.

If there were more collaboration between president and Congress from day to day, Burns says, "we would avoid some of these abuses."

But few practitioners of politics seem to want to change the structure fundamentally. "The Constitution is a remarkable document that has endured for 200 years, and I don't want to mess with it on my watch," says Speaker of the House Jim Wright with a tinge of righteous indignation.

Many politicians and scholars observe that the framers of the Constitution did not intend representative democracy to be efficient. Their purpose was to create a system that would control men's greed for power and prevent the emergence of a monarchy or an oligarchy, thereby safeguarding individual liberty. Recognizing that men are capable of wicked as well as noble behavior, they sought to curb the former and encourage the latter.

"They feared both plebiscitary democracy and central tyrannical power," comments Princeton scholar Fred Greenstein. So the framers established a federal system of checks and balances to prevent the concentration of power.

Authority was divided between the federal and state governments and power was further divided among the three branches of the national government, each of which was expected to represent the public's interests. And Congress was further divided into two chambers, the House of Representatives and the Senate.

Professor Neustadt argues that the 55 men who met in Philadelphia in 1787 did not establish a system of separated powers of government but of "separated institutions sharing powers."

"It was not a separation of powers so much as the creation of redundancy, with each branch doing everything," says Martin Shapiro, a constitutional scholar at the University of California at Berkeley. "The system works well because of the redundancy—when one branch cannot do something, another does."

Thus, during the Great Depression, while Congress was reluctant to act, President Franklin Roosevelt had no compunctions about seizing the initiative. And when in the 1960s Congress and President John Kennedy failed to deal with the difficult issue of racial discrimination, the Supreme Court stepped in.

Democracy, moreover, requires consensus on, or at least strong majority support for, policies before they can be enacted. This often requires time. People do not always know what they think, especially given the complexity of today's issues. When opinion has not crystallized, this translates into inaction by government.

"The problem today is not at all that our leaders know what to do and are prevented from doing it by structural gridlock in the system," writes Professor Schlesinger in "The Cycles of American History." "The problem is that they know not what to do."

"You have to let water back up behind the dam," comments Rep. Morris Udall of Arizona.

"It's not an efficient decisionmaking process," agrees Rep. Dick Cheney of Wyoming. "The American people have an ambivalent attitude that is reflected in Congress. But the system is very efficient at giving everyone a shot."

This makes for stability in an extremely diverse and individualistic society, where the losers are willing to accept government decisions if they have taken part in the process.

"The democratic system keeps the debating going," says John P. Sears III, a lawyer and longtime GOP consultant. "It's good to take time because you can hear from everyone and, after they've had their say, they can live with [the eventual decision]."

Because the public was long indifferent to the widening federal deficit, for instance, neither the president nor Congress tackled the problem. But with opinion now shifting, the legislators are beginning to pull back on defense spending, and more talk is heard about the need to raise taxes.

'SOMETHING IS GOING ON'

"The problem is not the system, the problem is the people who are running the system," says Sen. Bill Bradley of New Jersey, one of the architects of last year's tax reform law. "There is no process fix that will give people the courage to confront problems or to take risks. Tax reform is important because it demonstrates that something can get done."

To some, the mere fact of government inaction does not mean that nothing has happened. Despite the groping for progress on nuclear arms control, for instance, no nuclear device has been exploded in anger since the detonations over Hiroshima and Nagasaki, and the unratified SALT II agreement remains largely observed by the US and the Soviet Union.

"Something is going on," says political scientist Nelson Polsby. "The people who complain and want to reform things believe their view is sovereign. The constitutional writers sympathized with the right [to voice] opposing views. The people who complain and want to reform things want their view to prevail."

Perhaps the most powerful argument against structural change is that the system has proved so resilient, allowing for self-correcting forces to assert themselves to counter potentially dangerous trends.

John Shannon, executive director of the Advisory Commission on Intergovernmental Relations, notes the current swing of the pendulum toward the states after decades of expansion of power in the national government. He, too, observes that Congress is beginning to deal with the deficit issue by denying President Reagan huge increases in defense spending.

"We always are looking at the problem," Dr. Shannon says. "We're so concerned with pathology that we don't recognize a healthy person."

UNDERLYING VALUES NOTED

The Constitution is not the sole reason that Americans govern themselves as they do, of course. Many nations have democratic constitutions; some follow, to a degree, the American model. Yet some are not robust, vital democratic republics.

Underpinning American democracy are also historical traditions, mores, and spiritual values that make it possible for the Constitution to operate.

It is perhaps in this intangible area that many thoughtful observers are seeing danger signs and a need for change.

John Gardner, a civic reformer and former Cabinet officer, points to the difficulty of holding a pluralistic society together when there is such preoccupation with individualism rather than the collective good. "It's hard to govern with a disintegration of shared values," he says.

"Democracy is not a law of nature," comments Richard Lamm, former governor of Colorado, pointing to the moral decay that destroyed many other civilizations. Uncontrolled greed, excessive self-interest, insufficient attention to education, apathy to work—these are signs of "creeping crisis," he warns.

But as Americans reflect on the state of their republic and the daunting challenges ahead, they take heart that the framers established a governmental system strong enough to withstand the tremors of crisis and flexible enough to permit change and evolution.

In Mr. Gardner's words, "The genius of our Constitution is that it makes renewal possible."

CHAPTER 3

Civil Liberties and Civil Rights

Constitutional government requires a balance between majority rule and the protection of minority rights. Throughout American political development, civil liberties and civil rights have been an arena of intense conflict. This chapter provides several examples of controversial issues under the Bill of Rights and the Fourteenth Amendment. In all these issues, decisions by the Supreme Court and actions by the president and Congress resulted in choices that dissatisfied certain groups while providing benefits to others:

1. How do the Bill of Rights and Supreme Court decisions protect minorities and dissenters?
2. Is governmental suppression of free speech by unpopular political minorities a justifiable way of protecting the community against potential or actual harm? Should the American flag be protected or do protesters have the right to burn the flag?
3. How does the Fourteenth Amendment provide constitutional equality for racial and other minority groups?
4. How far should the courts extend procedural rights to persons accused of serious crimes? Do such protections prevent the community from having effective law enforcement?

The original Constitution contained a number of provisions regarding individual rights such as protections against the writ of habeas corpus, which prohibits government officials from jailing a person without specific charges, or the passage of any bills of attainder, a statute which declares a person or a group guilty of a crime and establishes punishment without a fair trial. Many anti-Federalists considered these protections to be inadequate. They demanded a Bill of Rights and were prepared to use this as an issue in the original fight for ratification of the Constitution. The first session of the First Congress agreed, responding to the prompting of President George Washington and the prodding of James Madison.

The ten amendments to the Constitution were finally ratified in 1791. Such explicit protections as the First Amendment freedom of speech, press, assembly, and religious belief were included as well as rights against unreasonable searches and seizure (the Fourth Amendment); the protection against double jeopardy and forceful testimony against oneself (the Fifth Amendment); the right of due process of law that protects citizens against arbitrary procedures (the Fifth Amendment); the right to a speedy and public trial (the Sixth Amendment); and the protection against excessive bail and cruel and unusual punishment (the Eighth Amendment). This basic core of rights provides the foundation for the idea of limited government as it deals with the individual citizen.

Additional amendments have been added to the Constitution since 1791 that have applied these basic rights to the various states. Important examples are the Fourteenth Amendment, due process of law, and equal protection of the laws clauses that have greatly enhanced procedural protections for those accused of a crime and the provision of equality of opportunity for blacks and other minorities.

GOVERNMENT ACTORS IN CIVIL
LIBERTIES AND CIVIL RIGHTS POLICY

Civil liberties and civil rights policy making involves the three branches of the federal government, the states, and various interest groups. Using statutory and constitutional interpretation (judicial review), the Supreme Court began to apply the Bill of Rights to the states in 1898, although all but one of the cases where provisions of the Bill of Rights were read into the Fourteenth Amendment took place in 1925 and continued until 1969. During the 1950s and 1960s, the Supreme Court, under Chief Justice Earl Warren, greatly expanded protections of the First and Fourteenth Amendments for minorities.

In the executive branch, the president, the Justice Department, the Civil Rights Commission, and the Equal Employment Opportunity Commission are influential. The president determines initiatives and policy direction in selecting the attorney general and other Justice Department officials who are responsible for civil rights enforcement. President Johnson made the Civil Rights Act of 1964 and the Voting Rights Act of 1965 top priorities for congressional action. President Reagan and his attorney general, Edwin Meese, established a rigorous screening policy for federal court judgeships to ensure adherence to a conservative view on civil rights and civil liberties cases. President Bush has taken a strong position against quotas in affirmative action for women and minority employment.

The attorney general is the chief law-enforcement officer of the federal government and advises the president on civil rights and civil liberties issues. Within the Justice Department, the Civil Rights Division is responsible for enforcing the Civil Rights Act of 1964 and other laws that prohibit racial discrimination, protect voting rights, and provide equal access to education, jobs, housing, credit, and public facilities.

The Civil Rights Commission was established in 1957 to monitor, review, and report on federal civil rights activities. The Commission publicizes its findings through written reports but has no enforcement power. Until 1983, the Commission was considered an independent agency, free from executive control after presidential nominees had been approved by Congress. However, in 1983 President Reagan wanted to remove three members who opposed his conservative views on civil rights policy, particularly court-ordered busing and affirmative action. After a period of congressional resistance, a compromise was achieved to change the structure of the Commission. Instead of a six-member body, the Commission is now comprised of eight persons, four selected by the president and four by congressional leaders. The eight persons serve for a fixed term.

The Equal Employment Opportunity Commission was established by the 1964 Civil Rights Act. Its responsibilities include investigations and orders to public and private employers charged with violating racial, religious, sex, and age discrimination laws in hiring, firing, promotions, and other employment conditions. The EEOC is also responsible for enforcing nondiscrimination in employment under the 1963 Equal Pay Act and the 1967 Age Discrimination in Employment Act.

Congress is involved with civil liberties and civil rights policies through various standing committees of the House and Senate that review presidential initiatives, investigate and monitor executive branch actions, and review presidential nominees for the federal courts and the Supreme Court. One of the most important is the Senate Judiciary Committee, which recommends presidential nominees to the full Senate under the constitutional "advice and consent" function.

Various interest groups are also involved with civil liberties and civil rights policy. Some of the most active and influential are the American Civil Liberties Union, the National Association for the Advancement of Colored People, the Leadership Conference on Civil Rights, and the National Organization for Women. These organizations frequently take cases into the federal courts, lobby the executive branch and Congress, raise funds, and publicize important civil liberties and civil rights issues. For example, the Southern Christian Leadership Conference, led by Martin Luther King, Jr., was highly influential in pressuring the federal government to enact the 1964 Civil Rights Act and the 1965 Voting Rights Act.

The Bill of Rights as Protector of Minorities and Dissenters

In Article 8, Norman Dorsen of the American Civil Liberties Union explains how the Bill of Rights and Supreme Court interpretations protect minorities, dissenters, and protesters in America. Four constitutional areas are of particular interest: free expression, religious freedom, controlling state action against official misconduct, and preventing governmental discrimination. Dorsen argues that civil liberties are never secure. Each generation needs to defend them. There are strong opponents who appeal to necessity and patriotism to override constitutional protections for the weak, the unorthodox, and the despised.

FREEDOM OF POLITICAL EXPRESSION

The cornerstone of free expression rests on the right of freedom of speech. A vital debate on public issues was considered to be of particular importance to the architects of the Bill of Rights. Although the First Amendment spells out in clear terms that Congress may make "no law . . . abridging freedom of speech," the Supreme Court has never claimed that this right to free speech is guaranteed in all circumstances and situations. Do unpopular political groups have the right to free expression when the nation is at war? Can radical political parties advocate the forceful overthrow of the government when their chances for success are minimal? Can a member of the Ku Klux Klan publicly urge violent attacks against blacks and Jews? Over the years, the Supreme Court has developed "balancing" tests to determine permissible speech by controversial radical groups. The Court sought to weigh the right of free expression under the First Amendment against potential or actual dangers to the community.

In the case of *Schenck v. United States* (1919), the Supreme Court announced the "clear and present danger" test. Charles Schenck, General Secretary of the American Socialist Party, was convicted under the Espionage Act (intended to prevent disruptions against U.S. participation in World War I) for mailing circulars urging young men to resist the military draft. Justice Oliver Wendell Holmes upheld Schenck's conviction on the basis that his actions created a clear and present danger of bringing about evils that Congress had a right to prevent. According to Holmes, the First Amendment does not give a person the right to cause panic by shouting fire in a crowded theater.

The Court extended free speech restrictions with the "clear and probable danger" test in *Dennis v. United States* (1951). The case involved convictions of eleven top Communist party leaders under the 1940 Smith Act, which prohibited advocating the forceful overthrow of government. Chief Justice Fred Vinson upheld the convictions because Congress had the right to protect against potential armed rebellion. The Communist party clearly advocated violent action against the government. Its actions might occur at any time, thereby causing a clear and probable danger which Congress had a right to prevent.

In recent years, the Supreme Court has removed most restrictions on free expression by radical political minorities. This resulted from the Court's incitement standard announced in *Brandenburg v. Ohio,* decided in 1969. The case dealt with the conviction of Clarence Brandenburg, a Ku Klux Klan leader, who was arrested and convicted under Ohio's criminal syndicalism law, following his advocacy of mob action against blacks and Jews. The Supreme Court declared the state law unconstitutional because it censored Brandenburg. The state had to prove that Brandenburg's speech was likely to incite or produce "imminent lawless action." Under this approach, the state could not prevent the advocacy of force as an abstract doctrine. Brandenburg could only be restrained if his words were shown to cause actual incitement to violence. This case is considered a landmark Supreme Court decision because it requires the government to prove that a danger is *real* rather than imaginary. In doing so, the Supreme Court extended the First Amendment to speech that was not previously protected.

The Flag Burning Controversy

Should the Bill of Rights be amended to prohibit one kind of political expression deeply offensive to most Americans? This question caused considerable debate in Washington from 1989 to 1990. The controversy was sparked by the Supreme Court's 1989 ruling in *Texas v. Johnson* declaring that state's anti-flag burning law unconstitutional. In a 5–4 decision, the Court upheld the political expression rights of flag burners under the First Amendment.

President Bush strongly supported a flag protection constitutional amendment. He had considerable support from conservatives, war veterans in Congress, and public opinion. A *New York Times*/CBS poll disclosed 59 percent favored such an amendment, while 83 percent supported an anti-flag burning law.

Congress decided to pursue the legislative rather than the amending process to overturn the Supreme Court's decision. The House and Senate passed the 1989 Flag Protection Act, which made mutilating, defaming, burning, or trampling of the flag a federal crime punishable by up to one year in prison.

A few days after President Bush signed the bill into law, two groups burned American flags, one in Washington on the Capitol steps and another in Seattle. They were prosecuted under the federal law, but their cases were dismissed under the Supreme Court's earlier ruling in *Texas v. Johnson.*

The Bush administration appealed the constitutional rulings of the lower federal courts directly before the Supreme Court. In May 1990, the U.S. solicitor general argued that flag burning did not include any political ideas protected by the First Amendment. The defendants claimed that flag burning was expressive speech protected by the First Amendment. In their view, the federal government law was simply trying to circumvent the 1989 ruling in the Texas case.

As shown in Article 9, the Supreme Court affirmed its ruling in the Texas case by declaring the federal law unconstitutional in June 1990. The Court's decision in *U.S. v. Elchman* and *Haggerty v. U.S.* included a debate between Justices Brennan and Stevens over the clashing values of protecting political expression versus maintaining the integrity of the American flag.

Following the court's decision, President Bush called for a constitutional amendment. But neither the House nor the Senate could attain the required two-thirds votes. The flag protection amendment fell short by thirty-four votes in the House and nine votes in the Senate. Lack of constituent pressure was cited as a major reason for failure to obtain the required two-thirds vote.

The American flag is certainly a basic symbol of the country's freedom and liberty. Most believe that flag burning is deeply offensive. But only a tiny number of protesters engaged in such activity. Instead of amending the Bill of Rights for the first time in two hundred years, Congress accepted the Court's interpretation of the First Amendment.

Constitutional Equality

In Article 10, Stanley Katz demonstrates that constitutional equality for all Americans was never intended by the original Constitution nor by the Bill of Rights. American society was originally based on systematic inequality toward women and slaves. Women could not vote until 1920 and blacks were considered white men's property until the Civil War.

The Fourteenth Amendment, ratified in 1868, provided for legal equality by declaring that the states must afford "equal protection of the laws." But the framers of this amendment did not intend it to provide political, social, or individual equality. Neither did the Supreme Court.

In 1896, the Supreme Court delivered a decisive blow to advocates of racial equality. In the case *Plessy v. Ferguson,* the Court upheld the conviction of Homer Plessy, a man of "one-eighth African blood," for violation of the segregation rules of the Louisiana Railroad Accommodation Law. This resulted in the infamous "separate but equal" doctrine to prevent racial mixing in public places, including the public schools. Consequently, the Supreme Court upheld the so-called Jim Crow laws adopted by the Southern states following the Civil War for segregating schools, trains, restaurants, restrooms, and water fountains. Systematic legal segregation of the races was permitted under the "separate but equal" doctrine.

Katz observes that the real beginning of constitutional equality began with President Eisenhower's nomination of Earl Warren as Chief Justice of the Supreme Court. For the next decade, beginning in 1954, the Court became the nation's preeminent defender and expander of civil rights for minorities.

One of the most dramatic decisions of the Supreme Court took place in May 1954 when Chief Justice Earl Warren, speaking for a unanimous court, declared that racial segregation of the public schools was unconstitutional. *Brown v. Board of Education* arose from challenges by the National Association for the Advancement of Colored People (NAACP) against racially "separate but equal" schools in Kansas, South Carolina, Virginia, Delaware, and the District of Columbia. Southern school segregation, also known as *de jure* segregation, was a bulwark of white supremacy over blacks, since most white schools were far superior in buildings, curriculum, and teachers. In overruling *Plessy v. Ferguson,* the Court responded to the NAACP's claim that segregated schools resulted in a "sense of inferiority" affecting the motivation of black children to learn. The constitutional ruling was that "separate but equal" facilities produced unequal education for blacks and therefore violated the "equal protection of the laws" for blacks provided for in the Fourteenth Amendment.

To implement its decision in the *Brown* case, the Court specified that desegregation must be achieved "with all deliberate speed." It took nearly two decades to end Southern resistance to federal desegregation orders.

Outside of the South, *de facto* segregation was a serious problem because of segregated residential patterns and increasingly concentrated minority populations living in the central cities. City schools were predominantly black and Hispanic, while suburban schools tended to be all white. Achieving racial balance was very difficult in the larger city school systems. Cross-district busing of students outside their neighborhoods seemed to be the logical alternative for desegregating the city schools. Court-ordered busing was used as a desegregation remedy for the first time in 1971 when the Supreme Court ruled on a case involving the metropolitan school district of Charlotte, North Carolina. The *Swann v. Charlotte-Mecklenburg Board of Education* decision focused on whether the school board had complied with the removal of *de jure* segregation even though the resulting neighborhood school system perpetuated *de facto* segregation in student enrollments due to existing residential patterns. The Supreme Court found that the federal district court could order the school board to develop a busing plan to remove *de facto* segregation. Chief Justice Warren Burger upheld busing as a tool of school desegregation as long as the time or distance travelled did not significantly harm the students.

Katz concludes his review of constitutional equality by observing that we are now in an era of containment and potential conflict. The Supreme Court is no longer expanding minority rights, but limiting them by narrowly reinterpreting earlier court rulings.

AFFIRMATIVE ACTION, REVERSE DISCRIMINATION, AND QUOTAS

The notion that all people are created equal has never meant that all people possess the same talents or interests. When we try to put the principle of equality into practice in American society, we face the problem of determining which differences between people are relevant to differential treatment and which are not. Should the government establish public policies that in some significant way discriminate on the basis of race, religion, sex, or national origin? More specifically, should the government establish programs to aid minority groups in competition for jobs and higher education?

The federal government became involved in promoting equal employment opportunities as a result of Title VII of the 1964 Civil Rights Act, which established the Equal Employment Opportunity Commission. EEOC had authority to promote affirmative action by bringing suits against private employers and unions for engaging in job discrimination. Title VII also applied to state and local governments, public education institutions, and private employers.

Two important Supreme Court decisions in 1978 and 1979 dealt with fundamental challenges to affirmative action programs: Do preferential quota systems for minorities in medical schools and private firms result in "reverse discrimination" against whites who are denied access to the program?

In *Regents of the University of California v. Bakke* (1978), the California-Davis Medical School had a policy to set aside 16 percent of its entering class for minority students. Allan Bakke was a white applicant denied admission even though his test scores were higher than some of the minority applicants. Bakke charged that the admissions program discriminated against him and violated his rights under Title VI of the 1964 Civil Rights Act, which barred discrimination in any program receiving federal financial assistance. The Supreme Court agreed with Bakke. By a 5-4 vote, the Court invalidated the special admissions program as an inflexible and unjustifiably biased quota system that favored minorities over whites. At the same time, the Court agreed that race could be used as a factor in admissions when particular programs revealed a historic pattern of discrimination.

In the *Weber* case (*United Steelworkers of America v. Weber*) decided by the Supreme Court in 1979, the key issue focused on whether Title VII of the 1964 Civil Rights Act prevented a private company from establishing a voluntary affirmative action program that favored blacks over whites. By a 5-2 majority, the Court found that the Kaiser Aluminum Company was not prohibited from doing this. Voluntary racial quotas could be established where private firms attempted to prevent future charges of discrimination by the federal government. Consequently, Brian Weber, a white applicant for the special job-training programs, was denied admission and could not claim reverse discrimination under the law.

The Supreme Court in 1979 also dealt with a challenge to the constitutionality of a provision in the 1977 Public Works Employment Act. One part of this law set aside 10 percent of a $4 billion public works program for Minority Business Enterprises, companies in which black, Hispanics, and other specified minorities controlled at least a 50 percent interest. By a 6–3 vote, the Supreme Court upheld this affirmative action remedial plan. In the decision of *Fullilove v. Klutznick,* the Court found that Congress may use narrowly defined racial quotas to remove the effects of past discrimination in government contracts.

How did the Supreme Court apply the decisions of *Bakke, Weber,* and *Fullilove* to employment discrimination and affirmative action programs by local governments and school boards? In 1984, the Supreme Court rejected a claim that blacks were discriminated against under a seniority plan in the Memphis, Tennessee, Fire Department. In the case of *Firefighters Local Union 1784 v. Stotts,* the Court, by a 6–3 vote, ruled against an affirmative action plan that required someone with more seniority to be fired to preserve a minority-occupied job. According to Justice Byron White, preference for minorities in race-conscious affirmative action programs can apply only to actual "victims of discriminatory practice." Seniority rights can be violated only to aid specifically identified victims of discrimination.

Using the *Stotts* decision, William Bradford Reynolds, Assistant Attorney General for Civil Rights, claimed that all affirmative action plans are "morally wrong." The only available relief was to actual victims of past discrimination. This doctrine made it very difficult to win anti-discrimination suits against employers or unions because general affirmative action plans would be invalid. The victims would have to prove discrimination on a case-by-case basis. With the approval of Attorney General Edwin Meese, Reynolds attacked consent decrees issued by federal judges under which state and local governments agreed to use minority hiring goals to eliminate past employment discrimination against blacks, Hispanics, and women. The Justice Department sought to overturn affirmative action plans in fifty cities.

In 1986, the Supreme Court issued three decisions that appeared to support narrowly defined affirmative action remedies for minorities. These decisions refuted the Justice Department's opposition to affirmative action and particularly the argument that race-conscious remedies in employment can only assist specifically identified victims of past discrimination.

Hiring goals for minorities were upheld in the case of *Wygant v. Jackson Board of Education.* The case involved a challenge by white teachers to a layoff plan that called for removal of white teachers with more seniority before black teachers with less seniority. The Supreme Court agreed by a 5–4 vote that the white teachers were denied equal protection of the laws by this plan. This upheld the earlier Court decision in *Stotts.* However, at the same time, eight justices agreed that "adoption of hiring goals" favoring minorities might be an acceptable way for government employers to end past discrimination. Also, Justice Sandra Day O'Connor, who joined the majority, issued a separate concurring opinion that rejected the Reagan administration's argument that affirmative action hiring plans must be tied to remedying specific instances of discrimination.

Another aspect of racial preference was also nullified by the Court in 1989. In the *Richmond, Virginia v. Croson Co.* case, the Supreme Court overturned a local law setting aside 30 percent of the value of city construction projects. The Court stated that set-asides for minority contractors violated equal protection of the laws for non-minority contractors under the Fourteenth Amendment.

In two other 1986 cases, the Supreme Court upheld court-ordered affirmative action remedies for minority firefighters in Cleveland and for prospective minority employees in a New York City sheet metal workers' union.

In the *Cleveland Firefighters* case, the Supreme Court decided 6–3 that under Title VII of the 1964 Civil Rights Act, the lower federal courts may approve consent decrees to remove the effects of past employment discrimination. Court-ordered settlements of discrimination suits are permissible for municipal employers who agree to preferential hiring or promotion plans for minorities. The Vanguards, an organization of black and Hispanic firefighters, had sued the city for alleged discrimination in hiring and promotions. The Supreme Court upheld the federal court consent decree under which Cleveland agreed to a new affirmative action promotion plan. This plan promoted black and Hispanic firefighters ahead of whites with more seniority and higher test scores.

In the *Sheet Metal Workers* case, the Supreme Court approved a lower federal court order requiring the New York City union to implement a 29 percent minority membership goal by 1987. Such a preferential remedy was required to eliminate especially "egregious" discrimination against minority applicants that had persisted for over twenty years. As early as 1964, the New York State Human Rights Commission had found that the union deliberately excluded minorities from its apprenticeship program in violation of state law. Several court actions required the union to change this situation, but by 1975 only 3.19 percent of its membership was nonwhite. In 1982, the union was found in contempt of court for not meeting a deadline to implement the plan to increase nonwhite membership to 29 percent, based on the pool of nonwhite workers in the New York City area. Justice Brennan upheld this plan as a valid remedy for persistent discrimination and rejected the claim that affirmative action hiring plans can only be used to aid actual victims of unlawful discrimination.

In 1987 the Supreme Court extended affirmative action protection for women in the case of *Johnson v. Transportation Agency* by ruling for the first time that employers may sometimes favor women over better qualified men in hiring and promotion. In a 6–3 decision, the Court upheld an affirmative action plan by Santa Clara, California, giving job preferences to women over men. The Court rejected a suit by Paul Johnson who claimed he was denied promotion as a transportation dispatcher in favor of Diane Joyce, who received a lower test score. The Court's decision was considered the most comprehensive ruling on affirmative action.

Congress and the Bush administration engaged in a bitter dispute over whether or not women and minorities should be protected against discrimination in the workplace. President Bush vetoed the 1990 Civil Rights Act, claiming that employment quotas put too much of a financial burden on employers. Congressional Democrats disagreed, but could not get two-thirds majorities to override the veto. Bush's veto of civil rights legislation was the first one ever sustained by Congress. Only two other presidents, Andrew Johnson and Ronald Reagan, vetoed civil rights bills, but both were overridden by Congress.

The battle between President Bush and Congress over the 1990 and 1991 civil rights bills was triggered by a series of restrictive affirmative action decisions by the Supreme Court in 1989.

Two of the most important decisions (*Wards Cove v. Atonio* and *Martin v. Wilks*) eased the burden of proof for alleged discrimination by employers and restricted court awards of damages to victims of employment discrimination. Congress tried to reverse the Court decisions by reinstating compensatory damages, but President Bush vetoed the bill. He argued it would force employers to establish hiring quotas to avoid claims of discrimination by employees.

The employment discrimination issue was finally resolved in the fall of 1991 when Republican senators John Danforth (Missouri) and Robert Dole (Kansas), the minority leader, developed a compromise acceptable to the White House. To alleviate the Bush administration's concern over hiring quotas, the negotiators agreed that employment requirements must be "job related for the positions in question and consistent with business necessity." Without defining these terms, they instructed the courts to interpret the law as they had before the 1989 *Wards Cove* decision by the Supreme Court.

The Senate negotiators also convinced President Bush to permit jury trials and damages for all kinds of employment discrimination against women. Cash damages were permitted for the first time in cases of job discrimination based on sex. With these agreements, Congress approved the 1991 Civil Rights Act and President Bush signed it into law.

Many observers argued that the 1991 law was almost the same as the one President Bush had previously vetoed. The difference was a change in political climate, precipitated by David Duke, a candidate for governor in Louisiana. Duke, a former Nazi and Ku Klux Klan leader, bitterly attacked quotas and affirmative action. He claimed he was a Republican protecting white people's rights against blacks and other minorities. President Bush urged Louisiana voters to reject Duke, which they did by electing Edwin Edwards governor. Bush also modified his opposition to affirmative action, fearing that Duke's racist appeals might split Republican voters in the 1992 presidential campaign.

CRIME AND DUE PROCESS

The Anglo-American legal tradition has been concerned with the fair treatment of those accused of a crime. One of the great controversies of American politics in the last decade or so has been to determine how much "fairness" is due to the criminally accused. For some, fairness means procedural justice, that is, investigative and judicial proceedings conducted according to clearly established and predictable rules. For others, this scrupulous attention to established rules only "coddles" criminals. They believe that the law should provide for quick retribution against criminals so security can be established. Still others in our society contend that "due process of law" principles found in the Fifth and Fourteenth Amendments must mean a great equalizing of legal resources in the criminal justice system, giving every person, rich or poor, the same opportunity to establish an effective defense when accused of a crime.

The Warren Court was particularly concerned with broadening the protections afforded to persons accused of serious crimes. Throughout the 1960s, procedural rights were extended to the right of counsel, police powers to search and seize evidence without a court order were restricted, rights of prisoners were increased, coerced and involuntary confessions to the police were limited, and the scope of state death-penalty laws was narrowed. These reforms caused considerable controversy because many believed that the police and the courts were severely restricted in battling crime. Procedural guarantees to the accused limited society in protecting itself against lawless conduct.

Others argued that the police and the courts should follow the procedural guarantees contained in the Fourth, Fifth, Sixth, and Eighth Amendments of the Bill of Rights. A landmark decision in *Miranda v. Arizona*, decided by the Court in 1966, set strict guidelines for the police in obtaining confessions. (It is interesting to note that Miranda was eventually retried and convicted after the Supreme Court overturned his earlier case.)

The so-called Miranda rules require the police to provide the following warnings to any person arrested for an alleged criminal violation:

1. You have the right to remain silent and do not have to say anything at all.
2. Anything you say can and will be used against you in a court of law.
3. You have the right to talk to a lawyer of your choice and have the lawyer present while you are questioned.
4. If you cannot afford a lawyer, one will be appointed to represent you before any questioning.
5. If you wish to provide a statement, you have the right to stop any time you wish.

In Article 11, Paul Savoy argues that too much protection of alleged lawbreakers undermines citizen concern about public safety. Many people want more authority given to the police to fight violent crime and drug abuse. Savoy is particularly forceful in calling for modifications of search and seizure, the exclusionary rule, and restrictions on coerced confessions of those suspected of violent crime. He argues that the Fourth, Fifth, and Sixth Amendments were never intended to assist people in deliberately hiding incriminating evidence or lying to law enforcement officials.

Savoy's arguments were implemented by the Supreme Court in a series of decisions in 1990 and 1991. The Court had a very strong law-and-order majority, particularly with the arrival of Justice David Souter (appointed by President Bush in 1990).

The Court sided with accused persons only in one case, where it upheld the long-standing exclusionary rule. In a 5–4 decision in *James v. Illinois,* the Court held that illegally obtained evidence cannot be used at a trial to impeach the credibility of a defense witness.

Otherwise, the Court agreed with Paul Savoy that police powers can be expanded to fight violent crime and drunken driving. In 1990, the Court decided in *Michigan v. Sitz* that the police may conduct sobriety checks to prevent driving while intoxicated. Search warrants are not needed by the police. The same principle applies to suspected concealment of drugs or other illegal items that the police suspect to be in an automobile. The Court ruled in *Lehnert v. Ferris Faculty Association* that the police do not need a search warrant to examine bags, suitcases, and other containers in a car if they have reasonable cause to believe there are illegal items in the vehicle.

The Court also modified the Miranda warnings required to prevent involuntary or coerced confessions by the police. In *Pennsylvania v. Muniz,* the Court allowed videotaped bookings of drunken drivers at police stations to be presented at trials even if suspects were not told of their Miranda rights.

In *Arizona v. Fulmuinante,* the Court ruled 5–4 that coerced confessions do not always invalidate a conviction as long as other evidence used at the trial is sufficient to achieve a guilty verdict.

Finally, in a California case, *Riverside v. McLaughlin,* the Court ruled that a person may be imprisoned for as long as forty-eight hours before it is determined whether or not the arrest was proper. The Court overturned a lower court decision that upheld a thirty-six hour time limit.

THE CURRENT STATUS OF CIVIL LIBERTIES AND CIVIL RIGHTS

The Bill of Rights is the focus of resolving controversial issues. It is a cornerstone of our legal and political system, particularly when the elected branches are unable or unwilling to settle conflicts over basic rights and freedoms. In the twentieth century, government has sometimes been more flexible in protecting individual and minority rights while at other times it has imposed various restrictions. During the 1960s, the Supreme Court was very responsive in expanding political, social, and procedural rights under the Bill of Rights and the Fourteenth Amendment. By the 1980s and 1990s, political and religious conservatives attacked the Supreme Court's expansion of constitutional rights and liberties for minorities and persons accused of serious crimes. These conservatives also wanted prayer in the public schools, and restrictions against court-ordered school busing, affirmative action, and procedural rights for the accused. President Reagan symbolized opposition to Supreme Court decisions in these areas. He favored school prayer, opposed busing and abortion rights for women, was against affirmative action, and wanted substantial modification of the exclusionary rule for the police. The exclusionary rule prevented the police from using evidence obtained under improper search and seizure procedures against persons accused of crimes.

President Bush maintained Reagan's conservative views toward civil liberties and civil rights. Bush, like Reagan, wanted to appoint conservative federal judges who are tough on crime, drug abuse, and abortion rights, and support business interests over advocates of fair employment practices and affirmative action claims.

We will have more to say about the conservative direction of the Supreme Court in Chapter 11. It is clear that civil liberties and civil rights remain highly controversial and divisive issues. Groups and individuals who benefitted from earlier constitutional, judicial, and statutory protections are reluctant to yield them without a political fight. Electoral politics is rapidly replacing the courts as the arena for resolving these battles.

Evolution of Constitutional Protections

8

The Bill of Rights: Protector of Minorities and Dissenters

Norman Dorsen

Norman Dorsen, law professor at New York University and president of the American Civil Liberties Union, states that the basic principle of the Bill of Rights is to ensure individual liberty. His article explains how the first ten amendments have protected minorities and unpopular political dissenters, particularly in the First, Sixth, and Fourteenth Amendments. In the area of free expression, what was the evolution of constitutional protections for World War I protesters? In the 1960s and 1970s, which unpopular political groups had free speech protections? Why is the Supreme Court less favorable to protecting symbolic speech? Why did the Framers oppose government censorship? Which liberties have been identified by the Courts that are not found expressly stated in the Bill of Rights? Dorsen concludes by identifying some recent threats to individual rights and liberties. Is he correct in observing that anti-civil libertarians want to dominate the weak, the unorthodox, and the despised? Why does this occur in American society?

The American political system is built upon two fundamental principles. The first is majority rule through electoral democracy. This precept is firmly established in our culture. The second fundamental tenet is less established, less understood, and much more fragile. This is the principle that even in a democracy the majority must be limited in order to assure individual liberty.

The Bill of Rights—the first ten amendments to the Constitution—is the primary source of the legal limits on what the majority, acting through the government, can do. Such limits guarantee rights to all but in practice they often serve to protect dissenters and unpopular minorities from official wrongdoing. This process is indispensable to a free society, which in turn is the highest purpose of organized government. As John Locke wrote, "However it may be mistaken, the end of law is not to abolish or restrain, but to preserve and enlarge freedom."

How the Bill of Rights came to be appended to the original Constitution is a fascinating tale. How over two centuries it came to mean what it does today is a complex story

Reprinted from *this Constitution: A Bicentennial Chronicle,* No. 18, Spring/Summer 1988, pp. 20-24, published by Project '87 of the American Historical Association and the American Political Science Association.

which is not over yet. In the words of Chief Justice John Marshall, the Constitution is a document "intended to endure for ages to come, and, consequently, to be adapted to the various crises of human affairs."

The original Constitution protected civil liberty but it did so incompletely. The principal means it employed was structural—the ingenious carving up of governmental power both vertically and horizontally, through the creation of a federal system and the separation of powers within the national government.

It is well known that the Constitution created a national government possessing only limited powers, leaving to the states all other powers over its inhabitants. Although state authority could not be exercised inconsistently with the Constitution or acts of Congress, this formula nevertheless left the states with dominant authority over the people's welfare.

The Constitution also created a tri-partite division of national authority by reposing separate spheres of power in the Executive, Legislative and Judicial branches. While the chambers are not airtight, they serve to fulfill the theory of our government, which (as the Supreme Court said in 1874) "is opposed to the deposit of unlimited power anywhere."

The original Constitution did not merely seek to enhance civil liberty by dividing the authority to rule. It also contained some explicit safeguards. It provided that the privilege of habeas corpus, which requires a judge to release an imprisoned person unless he is being lawfully detained, may not be suspended except in cases of rebellion or invasion. The ex post facto and bill of attainder clauses seek to guarantee legislative fairness by prohibiting laws that make new crimes out of conduct that has already occurred and by requiring laws to operate generally and not against particular people. Article III guarantees a jury trial in all federal criminal cases, defines treason narrowly, and imposes evidentiary requirements to assure that this most political of crimes will not be lightly charged. Article VI prohibits religious tests as a qualification for public office.

But these safeguards were not enough. In 1787, many people were displeased by the absence of an explicit Bill of Rights in the newly-drafted Constitution, and some state conventions refused to ratify without a commitment, or at least a strong indication, that one would soon be introduced. The Framers promptly made good on this commitment, and the Bill of Rights was ratified in 1791. Thus the new nation's novel and creative structure that simultaneously provided for majority rule and limitations on that rule was in place.

Two further ingredients were needed to make the system work. The first occurred in 1803, when the Supreme Court unanimously ruled in *Marbury v. Madison* that the federal courts could enforce the Constitution by invalidating statutes passed by Congress that were inconsistent with it. In the twentieth century, the Supreme Court put the final component in place by holding that almost all provisions of the Bill of Rights restrict unlawful actions by state and local officials as well as the national government.

The Bill of Rights protects all Americans, but it is of particular value to minorities and dissenters. Supreme Court Justice Hugo Black expressed this thought eloquently in 1940:

Under our constitutional system, courts stand against any winds that blow as havens of refuge for those who might otherwise suffer because they are helpless, weak, outnumbered, or because they are non-conforming victims of prejudice and public excitement.

While the Supreme Court has not always been faithful to that trust, it has often used the Constitution to shield the powerless.

FREE EXPRESSION

The First Amendment guarantees of free speech and free press serve an especially important function in this respect by prohibiting the government from forcing everyone to espouse officially sanctioned opinions. Early Supreme Court cases on free speech were not promising. During World War I, appellants had been prosecuted for opposing enlistment in the armed services and protesting American involvement in the war, extremely unpopular positions at that time. The convictions were all affirmed in 1919, and the defendants jailed, some for many years. However, by 1931 an enthusiastic displayer of a red flag and the publisher of a "scandalous and defamatory" newspaper won their free speech and free press cases, although they were equally unpopular to most Americans. Fittingly, public debate and private reflection had begun to lead informed opinion to appreciate the value of free expression in a free society. Justice Oliver Wendell Holmes, who wrote the opinion sustaining the first convictions for speech relying on a "clear and present danger" standard, voted to reverse the later convictions.

From the 1930s through the 1950s, free speech claims were pressed by Communist activists and radical labor union leaders, and in the 1960s and 1970s by civil rights protestors, the Ku Klux Klan and the American Nazi Party. Although the results were mixed, in 1969 the Supreme Court enunciated the principle—broadly protective of free expression— that political expression cannot be punished unless it is directed to inciting or producing imminent lawless action and is likely to incite or produce such action.

The Court has not been as hospitable to claims under the First Amendment when "speech" and "non-speech" elements are combined in the same course of conduct. The Court has protected the right of children to wear an armband to class to protest the Vietnam War and the right to burn or disfigure the American flag for the same purpose. But it sustained the conviction of a man for burning his draft card as a protest against the war. More recently, it rejected protests against the government's policies towards poor people that were expressed through the form of sleeping outdoors in a public park.

The framers of the First Amendment expected it to promote democratic self-government and facilitate orderly social change through the medium of new and unfamiliar ideas; to check possible government corruption and excess; and to advance knowledge and reveal truth, especially in the arts and sciences. The framers recognized that some speech would be controversial, some even repugnant. But their belief in free speech rested upon the premise that censorship brought worse consequences. As Justice Brandeis wrote in 1927, "If there be time to expose through discussion the falsehood and fallacies, to avert the evil by the process of education, the remedy to be applied is more speech, not enforced silence."

A free society has confidence in its people to separate the wheat from the chaff. A wise and principled conservative, Justice John Marshall Harlan, recognized that "the constitutional right of free expression is powerful medicine in a society as diverse as ours." "It is designed," he said,

> . . . to remove governmental restraints from public discussion, putting the decision as to what views shall be voiced largely into the hands of each of us, in the hope that use of such freedom will ultimately produce a more capable citizenry . . . and in the belief that no other approach would comport with the premise of individual dignity and choice upon which our political system rests.

The desirability of protecting unpopular expression also rests on hard practical considerations. The government apparatus required to impose limitations on speech, by its very nature, tends toward administrative extremes. History has shown that the techniques of enforcement—chilling investigations, surveillance of lawful activity, secret informers, unauthorized searches of homes and offices—are often carried out by police or zealous officials without adequate concern for the consequences of their actions.

RELIGIOUS FREEDOM

The First Amendment also contains two clauses providing for religious liberty: one guarantees the "free exercise of religion" and the other bars laws that put state power behind religion or entangle the state with religious activities. These clauses also have served to safeguard minorities. This protection seems particularly appropriate because many of our early settlers—Puritans, Roman Catholics, Huguenots, and others—fled religious persecution in Europe, where the dominant national churches were often intolerant and cruel to those who professed dissenting beliefs. At different times in American history, Christian sects, Jews, Mormons, and atheists all have relied on the First Amendment guarantee of religious liberty to protect their rights against official and private discrimination; more recently Moslems, Buddhists, and the Unification Church have also done so. Few constitutional provisions have proved more decisively that guarantees of liberty must be accorded to all or they will erode.

CONTROLLING STATE ACTION

Additional provisions of the Bill of Rights protect unpopular individuals and groups from other kinds of state action. The Fourth Amendment guarantee that the people will be "secure in their persons, houses, papers, and effects, against unreasonable searches and seizures" can be traced to English history. In 1763, repeated abuses led William Pitt the Elder to defend in Parliament the sanctity of one's home:

The poorest man may in his cottage bid defiance to all the force of the Crown. It may be frail—its roof may shake—the wind may blow through it—the storm may enter, the rain may enter—but the King of England cannot enter—all his force dares not cross the threshold of the ruined tenement!

In response to such protests, Parliament enacted new legal protections in England. But high-handed treatment by British governors was, in the words of the Supreme Court, "fresh in the memories of those who achieved our independence and established our form of government." The right of a person to privacy in his or her home became one of the essentials of our constitutional system.

The lessening of restraints on official misconduct would undermine the rights of all. Although private property is not always a refuge, police and other officials must secure a judicial warrant based on probable cause or they must justify a search on other grounds. The alternative to these safeguards is a regime where no citizen is safe from a dreaded knock on the door by officers who, unaccountable to law, may violate privacy at their discretion, the very evil the Fourth Amendment was designed to prevent.

Similarly, the right to counsel contained in the Sixth Amendment prevents the government from misusing its power by providing that citizens are entitled to legal advice when accused of crime. In the famous Scottsboro case (*Powell v. Alabama*, decided in 1932), the Supreme Court reversed the death sentence of black teenagers who were convicted of raping two white women in a trial in which they were denied lawyers. A generation later, the Court held that the public must pay for lawyers if an accused lacks funds, recognizing that without the assistance of counsel it is virtually impossible for a defendant, guilty or innocent, to mount a creditable defense against a government charge.

EQUAL TREATMENT

Despite its broad reach, the Bill of Rights (like the Constitution itself) was incomplete because it did not address outright the issue of inequality or prohibit government discrimination. The original Constitution in several clauses countenanced slavery, and in most states the right to vote at the time of ratification was limited to property-holding white males. Although the Fourteenth Amendment attempted to erase disabilities against former slaves by prohibiting states from denying the "equal protection of the laws," the end of Reconstruction in the South after 1876 and unsympathetic Supreme Court decisions undercut the promise of equality for generations.

After a long campaign by civil rights groups, the Supreme Court in 1954 invalidated state-supported segregation in *Brown v. Board of Education,* and the movement towards equal treatment gathered momentum. Much public and private discrimination persists in the United States, but there have been enormous gains in recent decades as Congress, the Executive Branch, and the states, reinforced by judicial decisions, have provided increased protection for racial minorities, women, nonmarital children and other vulnerable groups.

JUDICIAL GUARDIANS

The courts have also identified certain liberties not expressly enumerated in the Bill of Rights but well grounded in the constitutional structure, such as freedom of association and the rights to travel and sexual privacy. These rights tend to come under attack when individuals wish to exercise them in a way that offends the majority. Thus, Alabama sought to interfere with the associational rights of the NAACP, the federal government sought to deny Communists the right to travel abroad, and many states imposed restraints on abortion. The protection of these individual rights not only comports with the premises of a free society but is supported by the language of the Ninth Amendment, which provides that "The enumeration in the Constitution, of certain rights, shall not be construed to deny or disparage others retained by people."

The Bill of Rights was not designed as an abstraction. If it were, the rights it contains would have no more value than the barren promises entombed in many totalitarian constitutions. To be real, rights must be exercised and respected. The political branches of government—legislators and executive officials—can be instrumental in protecting rights, but majoritarian pressures on elected representatives are great during times of crisis, when the stress on liberty is most acute. A nation threatened from without is rarely the best guardian of civil liberties within. As already noted, President Wilson presided over massive invasions of free speech during World War I. In addition, President Roosevelt approved the internment of Japanese Americans during World War II, and McCarthyism, the virulent repression of dissent, was a product of the Cold War of the late 1940s and early 1950s.

The vulnerability of politically accountable officials to popular pressure teaches that freedom is most secure when protected by life-tenured judges insulated from electoral retribution. The doctrine of judicial review, which gives the courts final authority to define constitutional rights, is the most important original contribution of the American political system to civil liberty. James Madison summed it up when he said in proposing a bill of rights, "Independent tribunals of justice will consider themselves in a peculiar manner the guardians of those rights; they will be an impenetrable bulwark against every assumption of power in the Legislative or Executive." Thus, judicial review reinforces the central premise of the Bill of Rights that even in a democracy the majority must be subject to limits.

While the principles of the Bill of Rights are timeless, experience teaches that civil liberties are never secure, but must be defended again and again in each generation. Examples of frequently repetitive violations of the Bill of Rights include police misconduct, school book censorship, and interference with free speech and assembly. Thus, the American Civil Liberties Union found it necessary to assert the right of peaceful demonstration when that right was threatened by Mayor Frank Hague's ban of labor organizers in New Jersey in the 1930s, by Sheriff Bull Connor's violence to civil rights demonstrators in Alabama in the 1960s, by the government's efforts to stop antiwar demonstrators in Washington in the 1970s, and by the legal barriers erected by the city of Skokie, Illinois, in 1977–78 to prevent American Nazis from parading.

The defense of the rights of Americans is often thankless. Strong opponents have invoked both necessity and patriotism while subverting liberty and dominating the weak, the unorthodox, and the despised. Government efficiency, international influence, domestic order, and economic needs are all important in a complex world. But none is more important than the principles of civil liberty and human dignity embodied in the Constitution and Bill of Rights, our proudest heritage.

Protecting Unpopular Political Expression

9

The Flag Burning Controversy
U.S. Supreme Court

In June of 1990, the U.S. Supreme Court, in a 5–4 decision, declared that a 1989 federal law protecting the American flag was an unconstitutional violation of the First Amendment. Congress passed the law in 1989 after the Supreme Court had invalidated a Texas law prohibiting flag desecration. Justices William J. Brennan and John Paul Stevens both agreed that flag burning is deeply offensive to most Americans. But they disagreed on whether government could prohibit such activity. For Brennan, the law sought to suppress free political expression. But Stevens argued that government has a legitimate interest to protect the flag because it is the symbol of fundamental American values. This case obviously represented two basic values of democracy in conflict: free expression under the First Amendment versus respect for the American flag. The conflict causes dilemmas. Which is more important, the flag or free speech? And, how should flag burners be treated?

THE MAJORITY OPINION

By Justice Brennan

In these consolidated appeals, we consider whether appellees' prosecution for burning a United States flag in violation of the Flag Protection Act of 1989 is consistent with the First Amendment. Applying our recent decision in *Texas v. Johnson* (1989), the District Courts held that the Act cannot constitutionally be applied to appellees. We affirm.

In No. 89-1433, [*U.S. v. Eichman*] the United States prosecuted certain appellees for violating the Flag Protection Act of 1989 by knowingly setting fire to several United States

Source: 110 L. Ed., 2d 287 (1990).

flags on the steps of the United States Capitol while protesting various aspects of the Government's domestic and foreign policy. In No. 89-1434, [*U.S. v. Haggerty*] the United States prosecuted other appellees for violating the Act by knowingly setting fire to a United States flag while protesting the Act's passage.

In each case, the respective appellees moved to dismiss the flag-burning charge on the ground that the Act, both on its face and as applied, violates the First Amendment. Both the United States District Court for the Western District of Washington and the United States District Court for the District of Columbia, following *Johnson*, held the Act unconstitutional as applied to appellees and dismissed the charges. The United States appealed both decisions directly to this Court pursuant to 18 U.S.C.A. Sec. 700(d) (Supp. 1990). We noted probable jurisdiction and consolidated the two cases. . . .

II

Last Term in *Johnson,* we held that a Texas statute criminalizing the desecration of venerated objects, including the United States flag, was unconstitutional as applied to an individual who had set such a flag on fire during a political demonstration. The Texas statute provided that "(a) person commits an offense if he intentionally or knowingly desecrates . . . [a] national flag," where "desecrate" meant to "deface, damage, or otherwise physically mistreat in a way that the actor knows will seriously offend one or more persons likely to observe or discover his action."

We first held that Johnson's flag-burning was "conduct 'sufficiently imbued with elements of communication' to implicate the First Amendment." We next considered and rejected the state's contention that, under *United States v. O'Brien,* we ought to apply the deferential standard with which we have reviewed Government regulations of conduct containing both speech and nonspeech elements where "the governmental interest is unrelated to the suppression of free expression."

We reasoned that the state's asserted interest "in preserving the flag as a symbol of nationhood and national unity," was an interest "related 'to the suppression of free expression' within the meaning of O'Brien" because the state's concern with protecting the flag's symbolic meaning is implicated "only when a person's treatment of the flag communicates some message." We therefore subjected the statute to " 'the most exacting scrutiny,' " quoting *Boos v. Barry,* (1988), and we concluded that the state's asserted interests could

not justify the infringement on the demonstrator's First Amendment rights.

After our decision in *Johnson,* Congress passed the Flag Protection Act of 1989. The Act provides in relevant part:

"(a)(1) Whoever knowingly mutilates, defaces, physically defiles, burns, maintains on the floor or ground, or tramples upon any flag of the United States shall be fined under this title or imprisoned for not more than one year, or both.

"(2) This subsection does not prohibit any conduct consisting of the disposal of a flag when it has come worn or soiled.

"(b) As used in this section, the term 'flag of the United States' means any flag of the United States, or any part thereof, made of any substance, of any size, in a form that is commonly displayed."

The Government concedes in this case, as it must, that appellees' flag-burning constituted expressive conduct, but invites us to reconsider our rejection in *Johnson* of the claim that flag-burning as a mode of expression, like obscenity or "fighting words," does not enjoy the full protection of the First Amendment. Cf. *Chaplinsky v. New Hampshire,* (1942). This we decline to do. The only remaining question is whether the Flag Protection Act is sufficiently distinct from the Texas statute that it may constitutionally be applied to proscribe appellees' expressive conduct.

The Government contends that the Flag Protection Act is constitutional because, unlike the state addressed in *Johnson,* the Act does not target expressive conduct on the basis of the content of its message. The Government asserts an interest in "protect[ing] the physical integrity of the flag under all circumstances" in order to safeguard the flag's identity " 'as the unique and unalloyed symbol of the Nation.' "

The Act proscribes conduct (other than disposal) that damages or mistreats a flag, without regard to the actor's motive, his intended message, or the likely effects of his conduct on onlookers. By contrast, the Texas statute expressly prohibited only those acts of physical flag desecration "that the actor knows will seriously offend" onlookers, and the former Federal statute prohibited only those acts of desecration that "cas[t] contempt upon" the flag.

Although the Flag Protection Act contains no explicit content-based limitation on the scope of prohibited conduct, it is nevertheless clear that the Government's asserted interest is "related 'to the suppression of free expression,'" and concerned with the content of such expression. The Government's interest in protecting the "physical integrity" of a privately owned flag rests upon a perceived need to preserve the flag's status as a symbol of our nation and certain national ideals.

But the mere destruction or disfigurement of a particular physical manifestation of the symbol, without more, does not diminish or otherwise affect the symbol itself in any way. For example, the secret destruction of a flag in one's own basement would not threaten the flag's recognized meaning. Rather, the Government's desire to preserve the flag as a symbol for certain national ideals is implicated "only when a person's treatment of the flag communicates [a] message" to others that is inconsistent with those ideals.

Impact of Flag Destruction

Moreover, the precise language of the Act's prohibitions confirms Congress's interest in the communicative impact of flag destruction. The Act criminalizes the conduct of anyone who "knowingly mutilates, defaces, physically defiles, burns, maintains on the floor or ground, or tramples upon any flag." Each of the specified terms—with the possible exception of "burns"—unmistakably connotes disrespectful treatment of the flag and suggests a focus on those acts likely to damage the flag's symbolic value. And the explicit exemption in Sec. 700(a)(2) for disposal of "worn or soiled" flags protects certain acts traditionally associated with patriotic respect for the flag.

As we explained in *Johnson:* "[I]f we were to hold that a state may forbid flag-burning wherever it is likely to endanger the flag's symbolic role, but allow it wherever burning a flag promotes that role—as where, for example, a person ceremoniously burns a dirty flag—we would be . . . permitting a state to 'prescribe what shall be orthodox' by saying that one may burn the flag to convey one's attitude toward it and its referents only if one does not endanger the flag's representation of nationhood and national unity."

Although Congress cast the Flag Protection Act in somewhat broader terms than the Texas statute at issue in *Johnson,* the Act still suffers from the same fundamental flaw: it suppresses expression out of concern for its likely communicative impact. Despite the Act's wider scope, its restriction on expression cannot be "'justified without reference to the content of the regulated speech.'" *Boos,:* see *Spence v. Washington,* (1974) (State's interest in protecting flag's symbolic value is directly related to suppression of expression and thus *O'Brien* test is inapplicable even where statute declared "simply . . . that nothing may be affixed to or superimposed on a United States flag"). The Act therefore must be subjected to "the most exacting scrutiny," *Boos,* and for the reasons stated in *Johnson,* the Government's interest cannot justify its infringement on first Amendment rights. We decline the Government's invitation to reassess this conclusion in light of Congress's recent recognition of a purported "national consensus" favoring a prohibition on flag-burning. Even assuming such a consensus exists, any suggestion that the Government's interest in suppressing speech becomes more weighty as popular opposition to that speech grows is foreign to the First Amendment.

III

" 'National unity as an end which officials may foster by persuasion and example is not in question.' " Johnson, quoting *West Virginia Board of Education v. Barnette,* (1943). Government may create national symbols, promote them, and encourage their respectful treatment. But the Flag Protection Act goes well beyond this by criminally proscribing expressive conduct because of its likely communicative impact.

We are aware that desecration of the flag is deeply offensive to many. But the same might be said, for example, of virulent ethnic and religious epithets, see *Terminiello v. Chicago,* (1949), vulgar repudiations of the draft, see *Cohen v. California,* (1971), and scurrilous caricatures, see *Hustler Magazine, Inc. v. Falwell,* (1988). "If there is a bedrock principle underlying the First Amendment, it is that the Government may not prohibit the expression of an idea simply because society finds the idea itself offensive or disagreeable." Johnson. Punishing desecration of the flag dilutes the very freedom that makes this emblem so revered, and worth revering. The judgments are affirmed.

THE DISSENT

By Justice Stevens

The Court's opinion ends where proper analysis of the issue should begin. Of course "the Government may not prohibit the expression of an idea simply because society finds the idea itself offensive or disagreeable." None of us disagrees with that proposition. But it is equally well settled that certain methods of expression may be prohibited if (a) the prohibition is supported by a legitimate societal interest that is unrelated to suppression of the ideas the speaker desires to express; (b) the prohibition does not entail any interference with the speaker's freedom to express those ideas by other means; and (c) the interest in allowing the speaker complete freedom of choice among alternative methods of expression is less important than the societal interest supporting the prohibition.

Contrary to the position taken by counsel for the flag-burners in *Texas v. Johnson,* it is now conceded that the Federal Government has a legitimate interest in protecting the symbolic value of the American flag. Obviously that value cannot be measured, or even described, with any precision. It has at least these two components; in times of national crisis, it inspires and motivates the average citizen to make personal sacrifices in order to achieve societal goals of overriding importance; at all times, it serves as a reminder of the paramount importance of pursuing the ideals that characterize our society.

The first question the Court should consider is whether the interest in preserving the value of that symbol is unrelated to suppression of the ideas that flag-burners are trying to express. In my judgment the answer depends, at least in part, on what those ideas are. A flag-burner might intend various messages. The flag-burner may wish simply to convey hatred, contempt, or sheer opposition directed at the United States. This might be the case if the flag were burned by an enemy during time of war.

Motivations of Flag-Burners

A flag-burner may also, or instead, seek to convey the depth of his personal conviction about some issue, by willingly provoking the use of force against himself. In so doing, he says that "my disagreement with certain policies is so strong that I am prepared to risk physical harm (and perhaps imprisonment) in order to call attention to my views." This second possibility apparently describes the expressive conduct of the flag-burners in these cases. Like the protesters who dramatized their opposition to our engagement in Vietnam by publicly burning their draft cards—and who were punished for doing so—their expressive conduct is consistent with affection for this country and respect for the ideals that the flag symbolizes.

There is at least one further possibility; a flag-burner may intend to make an accusation against the integrity of the American people who disagree with him. By burning the embodiment of America's collective commitment to freedom and equality, the flag-burner charges that the majority has forsaken that commitment that continued respect for the flag is nothing more than hypocrisy. Such a charge may be made even if the flag-burner loves the country and zealously pursues the ideals that the country claims to honor.

The idea expressed by a particular act of flag-burning is necessarily dependent on the temporal and political context in which it occurs. In the 1960's it may have expressed opposition to the country's Vietnam policies, or at least to the compulsory draft. In *Texas v. Johnson*, it apparently expressed opposition to the platform of the Republican Party. In these cases, the respondents have explained that it expressed opposition to racial discrimination, to the failure to care for the homeless, and of course, to statutory prohibitions of flag-burning. In any of these examples, the protesters may wish both to say that their own position is the only one faithful to liberty and equality and to accuse their fellow citizens of hypocritical indifference to—or even of a selfish departure from—the ideals which the flag is supposed to symbolize. The ideas expressed by flag-burners are thus various and often ambiguous.

Legitimate Government Interests

The Government's legitimate interest in preserving the symbolic value of the flag is, however, essentially the same regardless of which of many different ideas may have motivated a particular act of flag-burning. As I explained in my dissent in *Johnson,* the flag uniquely symbolizes the ideas of liberty, equality, and tolerance—ideas that Americans have passionately defended and debated throughout our history.

The flag embodies the spirit of our national commitment to those ideals. The message thereby transmitted does not take a stand upon our disagreements, except to say that those disagreements are best regarded as competing interpretations of shared ideals. It does not judge particular policies, except to say that they command respect when they are enlightened by the spirit of liberty and equality. To the world, the flag is our promise that we will continue to strive for these ideals. To us, the flag is a reminder both that the struggle for liberty and equality is unceasing, and that our obligation of tolerance and respect for all of our fellow citizens encompasses those who disagree with us—indeed, even those whose ideas are disagreeable or offensive.

Thus, the Government may—indeed, it should—protect the symbolic value of the flag without regard to the specific content of the flag-burners' speech. The prosecution in this case does not depend upon the object of the defendants' protest. It is, moreover, equally clear that the prohibition does not entail any interference with the speaker's freedom to express his or her ideas by other means. It may well be true that other means of expression may be less effective in drawing attention to those ideas, but that is not itself a sufficient reason for immunizing flag-burning. Presumably a gigantic fireworks display or a parade of nude models in a public park might draw even more attention to a controversial message, but such methods of expression are nevertheless subject to regulation.

A Question of Judgment

This case therefore comes down to a question of judgment. Does the admittedly important interest in allowing every speaker to choose the method of expressing his or her ideas that he or she deems most effective and appropriate outweigh the societal interests in preserving the symbolic value of the flag? (1) The importance of the individual interest in selecting the preferred means of communication; (2) the importance of the national symbol; and (3) the question whether tolerance of flag-burning will enhance or tarnish that value. The opinions in *Texas v. Johnson* demonstrate that reasonable judges may differ with respect to each of these judgments.

The individual interest is unquestionably a matter of great importance. Indeed, it is one of the critical components of the idea of liberty that the flag itself is intended to symbolize. Moreover, it is buttressed by the societal interest in being alerted to the need for thoughtful response to voices that might otherwise go unheard. The freedom of expression protected by the First Amendment embraces not only the freedom to communicate particular ideas, but also the right to communicate them effectively. That right, however, is not absolute—the communication value of a well-placed bomb in the Capitol does not entitle it to the protection of the First Amendment.

Burning a flag is not, of course, equivalent to burning a public building. Assuming that the protestor is burning his own flag, it causes no physical harm to other persons or to their property. The impact is purely symbolic, and it is apparent that some thoughtful persons believe that impact, far from depreciating the value of the symbol, will actually enhance its meaning. I most respectfully disagree.

Indeed, what makes this case particularly difficult for me is what I regard as the damage to the symbol that has already occurred as a result of this Court's decision to place its stamp of approval on the act of flag-burning. A formerly dramatic expression of protest is now rather commonplace. In today's marketplace of ideas, the public burning of a Vietnam draft card is probably less provocative than lighting a cigarette. Tomorrow flag-burning may produce a similar reaction. There is surely a direct relationship between the communicative value of the act of flag-burning and the symbolic value of the object being burned.

The symbolic value of the American flag is not the same today as it was yesterday. Events during the last three decades have altered the country's image in the eyes of numerous Americans, and some now have difficulty understanding the message that the flag conveyed to their parents and grandparents—whether born abroad and naturalized or native born. Moreover, the integrity of the symbol has been compromised by those leaders who seem to advocate compulsory worship of the flag even by individuals whom it offends, or who seem to manipulate the symbol of national purpose into a pretext for partisan disputes about meaner ends. And, as I have suggested, the residual value of the symbol after this Court's decision in *Texas v. Johnson* is surely not the same as it was a year ago.

Given all these considerations, plus the fact that the Court today is really doing nothing more than reconfirming what it has already decided, it might be appropriate to defer to the judgment of the majority and merely apply the doctrine of *stare decisis* to the case at hand. That action, however, would not honestly reflect my considered judgment concerning the relative importance of the conflicting interests that are at stake. I remain persuaded that the considerations identified in my opinion in *Texas v. Johnson* are of controlling importance in this case as well.

Accordingly, I respectfully dissent.

Protecting Minorities

10
Constitutional Equality
Stanley N. Katz

American constitutional government has been very slow and hesitant in providing everyone with equal treatment in all aspects of life. According to Stanley Katz of Princeton University, the original Constitution and the Bill of Rights contain only one reference to equality. And that dealt with equal representation of the states in the Senate, not with equality of people. Katz claims that American society from the late 1700s to the mid-1800s was based on systematic inequality. Why? Even with approval of the Fourteenth Amendment, only equal protection of the laws rather than equality was guaranteed. What was the high point of the Supreme Court's actions against equality? Katz observes that the Warren Court began the modern era of protecting substantive equality. How did this occur? What was the constitutional revolution promoted by the Warren Court? Do you agree with Katz that we are now in an era of containment conceiving further extensions of equality? Will future battles for equality provoke political conflict in the United States?

Most Americans remember Jefferson's dictum that "all men are created equal." Many of us believe that it is part of the United States Constitution. The hard fact is, of course that the word "equality" appears only once in the 1787 document, and it does not apply to citizens.

Not many lawyers, much less law students or concerned citizens, can find the single reference to "equality" in the text of the original Constitution. Surprisingly, it is in Article V, the amendment article, which defines the two unamendable clauses of the Constitution: the slave trade clause and that governing the representation of states in the Senate. Constitutional equality, as expressed literally in the text fashioned by the Framers, was no more than equal representation for all states in the upper house of the national legislature: "[N]o state, without its Consent, shall be deprived of its equal Suffrage in the Senate."

Why is there no reference to equality for individuals in the body of the Constitution? Perhaps the harder question is why the Bill of Rights did not guarantee equality, since the first ten amendments specified other individual rights which are at best only implied in the original Constitution. Yet neither the word nor the concept of "equality" appears in the Bill of Rights, unless by implication in the rights reserved "to the people" in the Ninth

Reprinted from *this Constitution: A Bicentennial Chronicle*, No. 18, Spring/Summer 1988, pp. 31–35, published by Project '87 of the American Historical Association and the American Political Science Association.

Amendment, or, for some people and under certain circumstances, in the First Amendment or in the Due Process Clause of the Fifth Amendment.

THE SPIRIT OF '87

The fact of the matter is that it would be very surprising if equality were mentioned, much less guaranteed, in the 1787 document. The Declaration of Independence, from which Jefferson's statement comes, differed from the 1787 constitution in two important ways: (1) the Declaration was the product of a revolutionary tradition, promulgated at the very peak of American ideological fervor, and (2) it was a political manifesto, designed to rally domestic and foreign support of the revolutionary cause rather than to serve as a framework document for governmental organization.

Progressive historians, following Carl Becker and Merrill Jensen, have long argued that the political thrust of the revolutionary movement was democratic. The Revolution was thus properly institutionalized in the Articles of Confederation format, which severely limited the power of the central government and tended to favor the social distribution of political power. From this perspective, the movement for the Philadelphia Constitution was reactionary, since the more highly centralized 1787 governmental structure could be used by a merchant minority for its own purposes, contrary to the will of the majority. For the Progressives, then, the exclusion of equality as a formal constitutional value in 1787 seems historically predictable. But even those historians who do not consider the Constitution to be a counterrevolutionary document must acknowledge that the ideological thrust of 1787 was different from and certainly less egalitarian than that of 1776.

The spirit of '76 was republican. It held up for emulation the Jeffersonian conception of a community of independent, self-reliant, property owning farmers tied together by their commitment to place the good of the community before their individual self-interest. Republicanism thus implied the ultimate goal of equality among those productive workers in the political community (a definition which by no means included a demographic majority). Most historians now argue that important elements of this republican ideology persisted well into the nineteenth century.

LIBERALISM

But, as Joyce Appleby has reminded us, liberal ideology began to play a role in American political thought in the late eighteenth century. Liberalism contended that social good was achieved through the cumulation of the pursuit of individual self-interest. Liberalism thus implies a different sort of equality, one measured at the "front end" as individual opportunity and perceived as a starting point rather than a social goal. The tension between republicanism and liberalism was apparent in 1787-1788, but the fact is that neither ideology required a commitment to general social equality or egalitarianism. Both, for different reasons, required guarantees of participation for those entitled to membership in the political community. And both accommodated themselves to the reality that not all Americans were entitled to be political actors.

Slavery, the "peculiar institution" was only the most obvious reason why the framers could not (or would not) write equality into the United States Constitution. How could the Constitution advert to equality as a general value when nearly one in every five "Americans" was enslaved? The subject of slavery was so politically sensitive that the Framers omitted any overt reference to it. To state the obvious, if some people were to count as three-fifths of a person for the purpose of calculating representation in the lower house, how could equality be a constitutional norm?

But the case against equality does not need to rest on the tragedy of slavery. Americans in 1787 never proclaimed themselves in favor of the sweeping egalitarianism announced six years later in France. Our society was based upon systematic inequality, about which there was not much dissent. Women did not hold a legal or political status equal to that of men, nor did Indians or free blacks claim equality with whites. The society (differentiated from state to state and region to region) was based on the recognition of a hierarchy of statuses rather than a conception of universality of rights, the Declaration of Independence notwithstanding. Some Americans aspired to more in 1776, but the Federalist triumph in 1787–88 constituted a victory for social realism and the acceptance of federal constitutional inequality, or at best equality only for that minority of Americans defined as being within the political community.

An 1806 law suit in Virginia, *Hudgins v. Wrights,* will perhaps make the point. A few years earlier, Chancellor George Wythe had freed a young woman claiming to be an Indian from the ownership of a slaveholder who alleged that she was black. The law of Virginia then presumed Indians to be free unless proven otherwise, and blacks to be slaves unless proven free. Wythe went further, however, and announced that Virginia's 1776 Declaration of Rights, which declared all men to be free and equal, was in itself a constitutional guarantee of the presumption of freedom and equality. When the case was appealed to Virginia's Supreme Court, however, Justice St. George Tucker, scathingly rejected Wythe's argument for egalitarianism. Virginia Declaration, said Tucker, was

> notoriously framed with a cautious eye to this subject [slavery], and was meant to embrace the case of free citizens, or aliens

only; and not by a side wind to overturn the rights of property, and give freedom to those very people whom we have been compelled from imperious circumstances to retain, generally, in the same state of bondage that they were in at the revolution, in which they had no concern, agency or interest.

In Virginia, as in the United States generally, few people thought that revolutionary prescription of equality had general constitutional implications.

Locke had spoken of life, liberty, and property (which Jefferson translated as "life, liberty and the pursuit of happiness"), and property, rather than equality, was explicitly protected in the Constitution of 1787–91 through, for example, the clauses prohibiting states from issuing paper money or impairing the obligation of contracts. The protection of private property was essential to nationalists interested in economic development through private enterprise. But the notion that some measure of equality of economic opportunity was necessary to civil liberty, did not imply, for most Americans, that equality was similarly requisite to political liberty. Voting qualifications set by the states for the first federal election in 1788 testified to the prevailing view that only men of property had the kind of stake in government that entitled them to participate in it.

The federal constitutional solution at the founding held sway for nearly three quarters of a century, although some states moved in a more egalitarian constitutional direction. Meanwhile, the nation grew in dramatic and unexpected ways, and both its growth and practices, such as the creation of political parties and the emergence of judicial review, altered the constitutional system significantly. A number of systemic failures also began to emerge, but none so terrifying and nearly mortal as the inability to cope with the intertwined problems of slavery and regionalism.

The solution to these problems was forged in the cataclysm of the Civil War and Reconstruction. We must nevertheless acknowledge the failure of constitutional change as a response to the antebellum crisis. Constitutionalism could do little better than Chief Justice Roger Taney's dictum in the Dred Scott case (1857) that "the negro has no rights which a white man is bound to respect." The point is not so much that the Supreme Court could not manage a statesmanlike response to the conflict (although that is true) as that the entire constitutional system could not produce a politically acceptable consensus upon which a democratic solution could be based.

Ironically, this devastating constitutional failure came at precisely the moment that political equality for white men had succeeded as the decisive political value. The franchise had been expanded, legal protections were extended to some new groups, and general legislation began to replace special interest statutes. The Jacksonian attack on monopoly also moved governments in a more egalitarian direction. Some of this movement occurred in national politics, but it would be left to the new Republican party, with its program of "free soil, free labor and free men," to work out a liberal (though certainly not republican) federal constitutional regime for the postbellum United States.

THE FOURTEENTH AMENDMENT

It was only with the ratification of the Fourteenth Amendment in July 1868 that egalitarian values explicitly entered the Constitution. Section 1 of the amendment, in its final clause, forbade the several states to "deny to any person within [their] jurisdiction the equal protection of the laws." Notice two things in the language: (1) "equal protection of the laws" rather than "equality" is guaranteed by the clause, and (2) this protection is afforded only against nonegalitarian activities of the states. To this day there is no explicit constitutional guarantee against comparable incursions of the federal government, although in *Bolling v. Sharpe* (1954), the decision that desegregated the District of Columbia public schools, the Supreme Court found that the due process clause of the Fifth Amendment included a requirement of equal protection.

Perhaps more important, most of the Framers (and ratifiers) of the Fourteenth Amendment pretty clearly intended the Equal Protection clause to cover what they called "civil" (rather than political or social) rights. These were the rather narrow legal rights specified by the 1866 Civil Rights Act: the right to own property, the right of contract, the right to testify in court, and the like. Civil rights were specifically designed to confer upon the freed slaves the capacity to participate in the liberal society into which they had so suddenly been thrust. Neither Abraham Lincoln nor any but the most radical abolitionists imagined full social integration as a plausible political goal. Lincoln himself opposed both black suffrage, and "everything looking to placing negroes upon a footing of political and social equality with whites" although he defended for them "a perfect equality of civil and personal rights under the Constitution." The road from constitutional "equal protection" to full individual equality has not yet been completed, though there is no doubt that the first stones were put in place from 1866 to 1868.

While Congress attempted to provide a somewhat broader conception of civil rights (and therefore, to some extent, of equality) in the 1875 Civil Rights Act, for nearly a century the history of constitutional equality was written by the Supreme Court. The story is a mean-spirited one, for the court contracted the scope of the equal protection clause in several ways. First, it developed a constitutional doctrine of "state action" that required a showing of overt and official activity on the part of public officials as a trigger mechanism for equal protection complaints. The amendment had, to be sure, forbidden any "State" to "deny to any person within its jurisdiction the equal protection of the laws," but its sparse language did not specify that the denial had to be overt rather than passive, direct rather than indirect. Second, the Court determined that the protection of "persons" in the clause comprised all conceivable legal persons, including those fictive legal persons known as business corporations. The cumulative result of this jurisprudence was a narrowing of the scope of protection for human beings and an expansion of scope for the protection of business activity. The enunciation of these doctrines in the *Slaughterhouse Cases* (1873) and the *Civil Rights Cases* (1883) dramatically limited the potential constitutional equality for individuals, even the freedmen who were the intended beneficiaries of the Fourteenth Amendment.

Plessy & Brown

This counter-egalitarian judicial trend reached its fulfillment with the Court's 1896 decision in *Plessy v. Ferguson*, holding that Louisiana's legislative policy of racial segregation in public transportation did not violate the equal protection clause. Here was an instance of self-evident "state" action appearing to deny equality of treatment to blacks, which the Court justified by accepting the argument that comparable accommodations, however separate, were constitutionally "equal." For the Supreme Court at the century's end, "equal" had become synonymous with "equivalent." The *Plessy* reasoning was subsequently invoked to constitutionalize racial segregation (Asian as well as black) in public education, politics, and practically everywhere else in southern public life (*Gong Lum v. Rice,* 1927).

Although some cases hinted at the potential egalitarian scope of the equal protection clause, constitutional guarantees of equality remained limited throughout the first four decades of the twentieth century. Equal protection, scoffed Oliver Wendell Holmes, was the "usual last resort of constitutional arguments" (Buck v. Bell, 1927). The low point of equal protection came, in fact, when the Supreme Court, deferring to an alleged national security claim, refused constitutional protection to the Japanese American citizens interned in 1942.

From 1868 until 1954, constitutional equality meant at most nominally fair legislative classification and statutory application. Statutes necessarily sort individuals into groups; the equal protection doctrine served at least to limit the potential arbitrariness of such state classifications. But the force of the principle was weakened by judicial deference to state justification of apparently inequitable classifications, and, in matters of race, by the Supreme Court's reluctance to re-examine the *Plessy* doctrine (that is, its substitution of equivalence for equality). Individual equality was at best a weak constitutional value in postbellum America.

Substantive equality (the notion that everyone is entitled to equal treatment in all aspects of life) began to enter the Constitution in 1954. The decision of the Court in *Brown v. Board of Education of Topeka,* proclaiming that state-decreed racial segregation of public schools violated the Fourteenth Amendment principle of equal protection of the laws, began a constitutional as well as a social revolution. *Brown* carefully avoided reversing *Plessy* by confining the reasoning only to public education. But it is obvious that the Warren Court must have found a stronger reading of equality in the Fourteenth Amendment than had the Brewer Court in 1896. "Separate" can only be "equal" if the concept of equality is narrow. After 1954, in cases dealing with many activities other than education, the Supreme Court began to define the content of the new equality.

Race was of course the major substantive component in the Warren Court's reinterpretation of constitutional equality. The Court declared that race was meaningfully a "suspect" legislative category (following up the abortive hint in *Korematsu*), subject to judicial "strict scrutiny." What this meant in practice was that state schemes employing race or other suspect classifications would not enjoy the presumption of constitutionally traditionally accorded state actions. Rather, such schemes would have to be justified by showing that they were necessary to achieve fundamental state purposes, that they did not violate "fundamental rights and interests," and that they could be accomplished in no less onerous a manner. The tables were thus turned, for previously state programs were given the benefit of the constitutional doubt and were upheld unless blatantly unrelated to legitimate public ends.

This infusion of political and social substance into constitutional equality was probably the most important aspect of the "revolution" in constitutional law begun by the Warren Court. The process continued, for the most part, under the Burger Court, with the result that for almost thirty years after the *Brown* decision new categories of equality gained constitutional protection, in whole or in part. Alienage, ethnic origin, and illegitimacy perhaps gained the most, but progress was also made against gender and wealth discrimination. Equality emerged as a normative standard in the constitutional evaluation of political representation ("one person, one vote"), the rights of defendants in criminal proceedings, and the right of interstate travel. This trend was given enormous velocity by Congress, with the passage of the Civil Rights

Acts of 1957, 1960, 1964, 1965, and 1968. Civil rights now took on a richer range of meaning, extending to employment, public accommodation, education, and many other significant realms of public activity. Age, gender and other previously discriminated categories of the American population were specifically "included in" by the new legislation. For Americans coming of age since the Warren Revolution, equality had become an operative, meaningful public value.

CONTAINMENT

By the time of Warren Burger's retirement from the chief justiceship in 1986, the Supreme Court had gone far toward the fulfillment of the promise of constitutional equality, but the Court had also stopped short in a number of important areas. Above all, the number of "suspect" categories did not expand. Many had hoped (or feared) that gender would be included, but the Court drew back from this step in *Frontiero v. Richardson* (1973). There were some early indications that wealth discrimination might also enter the charmed circle, but that too was not to be. Welfare benefits, exclusionary zoning, municipal services, and school finance failed to receive even the "heightened scrutiny" applied to gender discrimination which would have made them subject to more stringent tests of equality.

Archibald Cox has remarked that "Once loosed, the idea of Equality is not easily cabined." That conclusion seemed persuasive during the years of the Warren Court, but it now appears that federal constitutional equality has been contained, if not diminished. Once the Court moved beyond the fulfillment of the promise of racial equality, it had no clear sense of where and how far to take the concept. The belief that further development ought to rest with the legislature is doubtless prudent, but it also shows how incomplete the American constitutional notion of equality is as we approach the twenty-first century.

At the moment, equality seems most likely to reemerge as the framework for political conflict in the United States. As Rousseau once noted: "This equality, they say, is a chimerical speculation which cannot exist in practice. But . . . [it] is precisely because the force of things always tends to destroy equality that the force of legislation must tend to maintain it." We will see how important equality is to Americans in the next century. They cannot assume that it has been guaranteed them by their constitutional heritage.

Protections for the Accused: Should They be Changed?

11
When Criminal Rights Go Wrong
Paul Savoy

One of the most controversial and divisive issues under the Bill of Rights is whether or not the procedural guarantees found in the Fourth, Fifth, and Sixth Amendments are intended to protect the innocent and the guilty. Paul Savoy, a former prosecutor and law professor, argues that only the innocent should have such protections. In his view, liberal judges have applied these protections too expansively to accused lawbreakers. Violent crime and drug abuse have frightened so many people that they favor tougher prosecution. Savoy supports modification of restraints against search warrants, the exclusionary rule, and self-incrimination. Do you agree or disagree? When the police make serious procedural errors in collecting evidence or in questioning suspects, should the accused waive their constitutional rights and confess willingly to their crimes? Savoy's arguments also suggest that defenders of procedural rights are soft on crime. Is this accurate? Are modifications of procedural guarantees the best way to achieve justice for both the accused and the victims of crime?

It has become one of those commonplaces of bicentennial speeches and Fourth of July orations to cite reports by pollsters that if the Bill of Rights were put to a vote today, a surprisingly large number of citizens would fail to ratify some of our most fundamental freedoms. A 1989 survey conducted by *The National Law Journal* showed that Americans are so fearful about the drug-driven crime epidemic that more than half of those polled who expressed an opinion favored cutting back the constitutional rights of criminal defendants and overruling Supreme Court decisions that limit police conduct in gathering evidence.

When Americans reject the ideals of one of our founding documents, we are urged to believe, as Garry Wills observed on the occasion of the 200th anniversary of the Declaration of Independence, that something has gone wrong with America; that somehow, in failing to subscribe to the Supreme Court's interpretation of certain 18th-century ideals, America "has ceased in part to be itself." What we have failed to consider is the possibility that what may be misguided are the orthodox teachings of the American legal establishment, not the majority opinions of the American people.

The approach of the 200th anniversary of the ratification of the Bill of Rights provides a timely opportunity for the legal profession to consider an unsettling idea: There may be considerable validity to the profound, though poorly articulated, intuition of the public at large that the procedural guarantees of the Constitution are not to be used to undermine a defendant's responsibility for his criminal acts. Because readers will be (and should be) extremely skeptical of the claim that much of what law schools have been teaching and courts have been espousing since the advent of the Warren Court era may be fundamentally flawed, a heavy burden rests with those who would challenge the prevailing orthodoxy.

TAKING RIGHTS TOO SERIOUSLY?

Having provided the framework for what was surely the most ambitious and idealistic effort in the history of the Supreme Court to bring the Constitution to bear upon flagrant abuses in the administration of criminal justice, liberals have become willing to accept the assumptions and principles of that 1960s revolution as dogma beyond accountability to serious moral or intellectual inquiry. Deeper and more mature reflection on the history and purpose of the procedural guarantees of the Constitution—including most prominently the Fourth Amendment prohibition of unreasonable searches and seizures and the Fifth Amendment privilege against compulsory self-incrimination—will show that these fundamental rights were not intended, and should not be construed, to protect the guilty.

In 1957, Edgar Smith was convicted of murdering a 15-year-old girl and sentenced to die in the electric chair. High school sopho-more Vickie Zielinski had disappeared on her way home from visiting a friend, and her battered body was found the next day in a sand pit on the outskirts of the small New Jersey town where she lived. Her skull had been crushed with a 44-pound boulder, leaving a gaping hole in her head and her brains scattered along the bank.

In 1969, the Supreme Court ordered a hearing to determine if incriminating statements Smith made to police had been obtained in violation of his constitutional rights. Although Smith acknowledged that he had not been mistreated by the police officer who conducted the interrogation, and three psychiatrists testified that the statements were "the result of his free will and rational choice," a federal court in New Jersey ruled the statements were inadmissible because they were obtained under "coercive" circumstances: Smith had not been advised of his rights to remain silent or his right to counsel, and his interrogation had extended over a period of more than 10 hours. After 14 years on Death Row, Smith, who continued to assert his innocence, was released from prison because, without his statements, there was insufficient evidence to retry him for first-degree murder.

Five years after his release, in 1976, Smith finally did confess to killing Vickie Zielinski—at a trial in San Diego in which he was convicted of kidnapping and attempted murder after abducting another woman and stabbing her with a six-inch butcher knife as she struggled to escape. "Don't ask me why I did it," Smith later wrote from San Quentin Prison regarding the San Diego attack. "Ask those self-righteous public servants why they gave me the opportunity to do it."

No constitutional controversy has generated as much public furor, nor elicited a more unsatisfying response from the legal profession, than the debate over the rights of people accused of crimes. The notion that criminals have constitutional rights may offend the average citizen concerned about the increase in drug-related crime and gang violence, but every law student soon learns that the common sense of the common man is wrong. The basic premise of our constitutional system of criminal justice is that a defense attorney has the duty to raise every available legal defense without regard to the actual guilt or innocence of his client. If cross-examination can be used to discredit a nervous and easily confused witness, use it, even though you know he is telling the truth. If the evidence has been illegally seized, move to suppress it, even though it establishes incontrovertible proof of your client's guilt. If the eyewitness's identification is tainted by an improperly conducted lineup, challenge it, even if the witness has correctly identified your client as her assailant. If the police interrogated your client without advising him of his right to remain silent, move to exclude his confession, without regard to whether it is truthful or whether your client is actually guilty of the kidnapping and murder with which he is charged.

"Defense counsel has no obligation to ascertain or present the truth," explains Justice Byron White in a classic statement of the criminal lawyer's role. "Our system assigns him a different mission. . . . [and] permits counsel to put the State's case in the worst possible light, regardless of what he thinks or knows to be the truth." If an injustice results, in the sense that a guilty person escapes a punishment he deserves, it results because the Constitution, according to the received view, not only permits it, but requires it. "The constitutional rights of criminal defendants are granted to the innocent and the guilty alike," Justice William Brennan reminds us in a recent affirmation of this fundamental principle of constitutional jurisprudence. Beginning in the early sixties, the constitutional rights of crimi-

nal defendants came to be defended in such eloquent and eminently reasonable terms that no one with a modicum of civic virtue could disagree. That all people, without regard to guilt or innocence, are entitled to claim the procedural decencies of the Constitution in resisting the power of government to invade their freedom and privacy—who would dispute such a ringing affirmation of human dignity and the rule of law? Few statements about the Bill of Rights seem so obvious from the text or sound so seductive. And yet few are so deeply and grievously flawed.

In the 1980s, the perception that there is something radically wrong with the prevailing liberal view of the rights of people accused of crimes became widespread. Outrage about the extent to which victims are satisfied to the rights of criminals is evident in the wave of films in the last several years that depart from the Perry Mason school of criminal law, in which all clients are innocent. The outrage is there in *The Jagged Edge,* the story of a defense lawyer portrayed by Glenn Close, who skillfully wins an acquittal for her client in a murder trial, only to discover that she is about to become his next victim. It is there in *Star Chamber,* in which a group of trial judges, fed up with having to dismiss cases against guilty defendants on technicalities, deputize themselves to try the culprits in *absentia* and order their execution by hired hit men. And in *True Believer,* James Woods portrays San Francisco attorney Tony Serra, a sixties defender of political activists turned eighties drug lawyer, who is berated by a disenchanted young associate for "using exalted principles to get off scumbags," until he gets a chance to redeem himself by defending an innocent man.

By the end of the 1988 presidential campaign, drugs and violent crime had vaulted to the top of the American political agenda. The defeat of Michael Dukakis became the most visible symbol of the deep fissures and contradictions in "liberal" that have made it synonymous with "soft-on-crime."

There is considerable irony in the extent to which liberalism has taken the heat for coddling criminals. Despite its rhetoric of liberty and human dignity, the due process school of criminal procedure is not a legitimate child of classical liberal thought. John Stuart Mill, the founding father of liberal legal theory, actually denounced as "sophistry" and as "palpably untenable and absurd" those arguments invoked by barristers in early 19th-century England to rationalize the use of procedural rules to defeat the prosecution of clients they knew were guilty of the crimes with which they were charged. "The benefit which would arise from the abolition of the exclusionary rule," Mill wrote in a postscript to Jeremy Bentham's classic treatise on the law of evidence, "would consist rather in the higher tone of morality that would be introduced into the profession itself." The exclusionary rule to which Mill was referring was the attorney-client privilege, which, in the context of criminal defense practice, "gives an express license to that willful concealment of the criminal's guilt, which would have constituted any person [besides the criminal's lawyer] an accessory to the crime." With Bentham, Mill called for a reform of legal ethics:

"We should not then hear an advocate boasting of the artifices by which he had [manipulated] . . . a deluded jury into a verdict in direct opposition to the strongest evidence; or of the effrontery with which he had, by repeated insults, thrown the faculties of a bona fide witness into a state of confusion, which had caused him to be taken for a perjurer, and as such, disbelieved. Nor would an Old Bailey counsel any longer plume himself upon the number of pickpockets whom, in the course of a long career, he had succeeded in rescuing from the arms of the law. The professional lawyer would be a minister of justice, not an abettor of crime; a guardian of truth, not a suborner of mendacity."

The so-called "liberal" model of criminal procedure that prevails in the United States today is actually an odd coupling of free-market theory with a particularly interventionist form of governmental regulation—not regulation of the private sector, but regulation of government by government: regulation of the police by the courts. It is governmental regulation in the name of individualism, not the traditional individualism of Jefferson or John Stuart Mill, but the free-enterprise individualism of modern libertarianism decked out in the pious rhetoric of the founding fathers.

STAPLES OF INJUSTICE

In the early morning hours of May 5, 1979, the badly burned body of Sandra Boulware was discovered in a vacant lot in the Roxbury section of Boston. An autopsy revealed that she had died of multiple compound skull fractures caused by repeated blows to the head. After an investigation, police linked the homicide to one of the victim's boyfriends, Osborne Sheppard, and obtained a warrant authorizing a search of Sheppard's house. Police officers found several pieces of incriminating evidence there, including a pair of bloodstained boots, a hairpiece belonging to the murdered woman, and strands of wire similar to wire fragments found on the victim's body.

Sheppard was found guilty of first-degree murder after a trial in which these items were received in evidence. Two years later, the Massachusetts Supreme Judicial Court overturned the conviction on the ground that the evidence had been illegally seized. Because Detective Peter O'Malley had applied for a search warrant on a Sunday, the local courthouse was closed, and he could not find an application form for the warrant. O'Malley finally obtained a warrant form designed for narcotics cases, but he failed to delete the reference to "controlled substances" in the part describing the evidence to be seized. O'Malley had included a detailed description of the evidence in an affidavit that accompanied the warrant application, and the warrant would have been valid if the judge had written "see attached affidavit" on the form and stapled the affidavit to the warrant. But the judge issued the warrant without making the necessary changes. The mistake proved fatal, insofar as the Fourth Amendment requires that a warrant "particularly describe" the evidence to be seized. Because of a failure to staple two pieces of paper together, the state's highest court reversed Sheppard's murder conviction.

In 1984, the U.S. Supreme Court agreed to hear the case. By then, the Burger Court had already begun whittling away at the 1961 Warren Court decision in *Mapp v. Ohio,* which established the principle that evidence seized in violation of the Fourth Amendment is inadmissible in state as well as federal prosecutions. In an opinion written by Justice White and joined by five other members of the Court, Sheppard's conviction was reinstated and the exclusionary rule was modified to incorporate a "good faith" exception. This exception permits illegally seized evidence to be used against a defendant if the police officer who conducted the search reasonably believed that it was authorized by a valid warrant. Affirming earlier indications of the Burger court that the exclusionary rule is not to be regarded as a "personal constitutional right of the person aggrieved," the conservative majority in *Sheppard* concluded that illegally seized evidence should not be excluded when the benefits of the rule in deterring police misconduct are outweighed by its costs in freeing guilty defendants.

Civil libertarians denounced the Court's decision as tantamount to repealing the Fourth Amendment. Liberal defenders of the exclusionary rule, including Justices William Brennan and Thurgood Marshall, who both dissented from the Court's ruling in the Sheppard case, maintained that the exclusionary rule is not a discretionary remedy that the Court is free to balance against the costs of letting guilty defendants off, but rather, "a direct constitutional command." In a widely quoted speech delivered the following year, Justice Brennan, one of the two remaining members of the Warren Court majority, lamented the Court's failure in the post-Warren years to fulfill its historic mission "as a protector of the individual's constitutional rights."

The debate between liberals and conservatives over the good-faith exception to the exclusionary rule has manifested itself in the form of a question that captures the constitutional crisis in a more compelling way than might at first appear—as a kind of Zen koan for our times: *Does a police officer's reasonable belief in the reasonableness of an unreasonable search make the search reasonable?* The cabalistic nature of such constitutional conundrums is not so much a function of some profound legal mystery as it is a symptom of the breakdown of the ruling doctrines that have shaped the Court's thinking about them. Behind the smoke and mirrors of the constitutional arguments is one simple and fundamental disagreement between liberals and conservatives that everyone could understand if candid explanations were not ruled out by the legal profession's allegiance to the cult of complexity: Liberals believe that everyone is entitled to claim the protection of the Fourth Amendment, without regard to their guilt or innocence; conservatives, while they pay lip service to this constitutional canon, do not actually believe it—and with good reason. That a person driving a car with a corpse in the trunk and a five-year-old kidnap victim on the floor has some legitimate expectation of privacy is about as ludicrous a proposition as one could imagine. But back on the record, Everyman's car is his castle.

More than 30 years ago, before *Mapp* was decided and the ideological silos had hardened, Edward Barrett, former dean and professor emeritus of the University of California at Davis, posed the commonsense question in an article in the *California Law Review:* "If one were to look only to the rights of the defendants, why would it not be reasonable to take the position that by engaging in [criminal activity] within their houses, they have waived their constitutional right to privacy and could in no event complain of the police entries?" A closer reading of certain celebrated 18th-century cases, frequently cited by liberal jurists and commentators as "landmarks of English liberty," supports Professor Barrett's suggestion that criminals should not have any right to use their privacy to conceal criminal activity. It appears that the original purpose of the Fourth Amendment was not to create a personal sanctuary where even the criminal might claim a legitimate expectation of privacy, as modern authorities assert, but rather to protect law-abiding citizens from invasions of privacy by overzealous law enforcement officers.

COMMON LAW, COMMON SENSE

In 1763, the Chief Justice of the English Court of Common Pleas, later elevated to the peerage as Lord Camden, authored an opinion which would immoralize him, in the words of Samuel Johnson, as the "zealous support of English liberty by law." John Wilkes, a member of Parliament, and 49 other individuals had been arrested the preceding year and charged with seditious libel in connection with their publication of one of a series of political pamphlets that contained an unusu-

ally bitter attack both on Charles II and on the use of general warrants to search for evidence of violations of an unpopular tax on cider. A general warrant was issued by the secretary of state, pursuant to which Wilkes' house was ransacked and all his private papers seized. Wilkes brought a civil suit against the governmental official responsible for the execution of the warrant and won a judgment of 1,000 pounds.

Although Lord Camden roundly condemned the use of general warrants as "totally subversive of the liberty of the subject," a careful reading of his opinion makes it clear that the guilt or innocence of the householder was far more relevant to the validity of the search than the standard liberal accounts suggest. The chief justice declared that although the warrant was unsupported by probable cause, "If upon the whole, they [the jury] should esteem Mr. Wilkes to be the author and publisher [of the pamphlet], the justification [for the search] would be fully proved."

A long line of distinguished authorities, from Sir Matthew Hale's classic 18th-century work on the English common law of liberty to the American Law Institute's modern *Restatement of Torts,* confirm the conclusion that under common law, an arrest, even though made without a warrant or probable cause, violated no right of the accused *if he was actually guilty of the crime for which he was arrested.* It was the common sense of the common law that the criminal had no standing to complain of being caught.

This is not to say that in acting without probable cause or in failing to obtain a valid warrant, the police have not violated the Fourth Amendment, but only that in so acting, *they have violated no personal right of a felon.* On this revisionist view of the Fourth Amendment, the function of the exclusionary rule, when invoked by a factually guilty defendant to object to illegally seized evidence, is not to vindicate any personal right of the accused but actually enables him as a representative of the public interest to enlist the judiciary in protecting the collective security of the rest of us. The defendant, in effect, is "asserting that he must be recognized as a private attorney general, protecting the Fourth Amendment rights of the public at large," explains Columbia University Professor of Constitutional Law Henry Monaghan.

The public debate over the exclusionary rule has proceeded as if the issue were "the rights of the suspect" versus "the rights of society." Formulating the problem in such terms misapprehends the true nature of the rights asserted by the criminal defendant. When a defense attorney moves to suppress the 400 pounds of cocaine with which his client was caught red-handed, what is actually being defended is not a personal right of the defendant, but the right of drug traffickers to defend the rights of the rest of us without our consent—a prerogative that leading constitutional scholars are beginning to recognize has no basis in the Bill of Rights.

The Court has no power per se to reverse a conviction because the police have violated the Constitution. The rights guaranteed by the Constitution normally may be enforced only by someone whose own personal protection was infringed by the violation. In the rare instance when individuals are permitted to assert the rights of third parties or of the public at large, the Court has held that some relationship must exist that makes the individual asserting the right an adequate representative of the members of the public in whose behalf the right is claimed.

We have done something strange and almost incomprehensible in our constitutional system of criminal justice. On the one hand, the justices have closed the federal courthouse door to law-abiding citizens seeking to protect their own rights with public interest lawsuits and have refused to issue injunctions against police misconduct even when individuals have been seriously injured as a result of those abuses. (In a lawsuit challenging the use of choke-holds by the Los Angeles Police Department, the plaintiff, who had been strangled into unconsciousness by a police officer during the course of a stop for a traffic infraction, was denied injunctive relief against the use of the holds, even though by the time the Court heard the case in 1983, 16 deaths had occurred as a result of the departmental practice.) On the other hand, the Supreme Court has deputized criminals to protect the constitutional rights of law-abiding citizens. The factually guilty defendant, however, insofar as he seeks to enforce the public interest by obtaining exemption from punishment, is a most improbable and inadequate representative of the public interest.

The real objection to using illegally seized evidence against a factually guilty defendant is not that such use is contrary to the Constitution, but that a court is normally unable to determine whether a defendant is guilty of using his privacy for criminal purposes without considering the very evidence that has been unlawfully seized. The Supreme Court has declared that "an arrest is not justified by what the subsequent search discloses." Perhaps it is time for the Court to reconsider this doctrine and permit the fruits of the search to be used, not to justify the search, but to determine whether the defendant was using his privacy for criminal purposes, thereby reserving the exclusionary rule for people who maintain a legitimate expectation of privacy.

A DUBIOUS PRIVILEGE

After being arrested at his home in Phoenix, Arizona, Ernesto Miranda was picked out of a lineup by an 18-year-old victim as the man who had kidnapped and brutally raped her.

Two officers then took Miranda into a separate room to question him. At first he denied his guilt, but after two hours of interrogation, he gave a detailed oral confession and then wrote out and signed a brief statement in which he admitted and described the crime. Although unmarked by any of the traditional indicia of coercion, Miranda's oral and written confessions were held inadmissible because the police had failed to advise him of his right to remain silent and his right to a lawyer. As Justice John Harlan suggested, in dissenting with three other members of the Warren Court from the majority's ruling almost 25 years ago in *Miranda v. Arizona* "one is entitled to feel astonished" that the Constitution can be read to create such a dubious privilege: *a right of criminals to conceal their crimes.*

To be sure, the law has long regarded torture and other blatant forms of coercion as unlawful means of obtaining a confession, for the reasons that a coerced confession is likely to be untrustworthy and that the use of physical brutality offends civilized standards of fair play and decency. But when a confession is indisputably true, and the police have not used the blackjack or the third-degree, the reason for the privilege is more difficult to fathom. This is not to dispute the wisdom of the Court's decision in *Miranda* requiring that, before questioning, people in police custody be advised of their rights under the Fifth and Sixth Amendments. A decision about whether to invoke a constitutional right should be the product of an informed and independent choice, and advising a person that he has such a right contributes to his freedom to choose.

The more obvious question, but one that is rarely asked about *Miranda,* is why a criminal suspect should have a right to remain silent in the first place. Even as conservative a critic of *Miranda* as former Attorney General Edwin Meese conceded that "if a person doesn't want to answer, that's [his] right."

However, as Judge Henry Friendly once observed, "no parent would teach such a doctrine to his children." The guilty, according to the moral standards that prevail outside the courtroom, should own up to their guilt, while the innocent, one would think, have nothing to fear by telling the truth.

CARVIN' MIRANDA

Describing the complex of values embodied in the Fifth Amendment privilege against compulsory self-incrimination, Chief Justice Warren, in his opinion for the Court in *Miranda,* explained that the privilege has come to be recognized in part as an individual's "right to a private enclave where he may lead a private life." Elsewhere, the Court has said of the privilege that it is "intended to shield the guilty and imprudent as well as the innocent."

Despite the Court's confident pronouncements, however, the conclusion that a person who has committed rape or any other crime has a privacy interest in not answering a police officer's questions is supported neither by the historical record nor by evolving standards of fair play and decency. The story of the historic struggle for the privilege as a protest in behalf of the guilty and the innocent alike against the abuses of inquisitorial methods of interrogation is largely a fairy tale.

The privilege traces its roots in Anglo-American history to early 17th-century England, when the infamous Star Chamber and the ecclesiastical courts prosecuted various religious and political offenses by requiring Puritan dissenters to take an oath and answer questions regarding deviations from the established faith. The resistance of dissident preachers and pamphleteers to these proceedings took the form of the defense that "no man is bound to accuse himself," and received its most articulate exposition from the Levellers, whose ideas furnished the intellectual bulwark of the Puritan Revolution. This much about the history of the Fifth Amendment is generally known and agreed upon by constitutional scholars and jurists.

What is not generally known is that the Levellers articulated the privilege not as a right of the guilty and the innocent alike, but as a protection for those who sincerely believed they were innocent—either in the sense that they had not committed the acts with which they were charged, or more commonly, that they had a conscientious belief that the crimes of which they were accused were beyond the power of government to punish (heresy, seditious libel, and treason were the usual offenses). According to John Lilburne, the most prominent and prolific of the Levellers leaders, the right to remain silent was a right "that no man be questioned, or molested, or put to answer for anything, *but wherein he materially violates the person, goods, or good name of another.*" [Emphasis added.]

The opposition in England to compulsory self-incrimination, although related to resistance to torture and other physically abusive forms of interrogation, went far beyond those concerns. The privilege proceeded primarily from the objection to the moral compulsion associated with the oath and the dilemma it created for *people of conscience* either to lie under oath or to tell the truth and thereby risk conviction for offenses they believed the state was without power to punish. A petition circulated in 1648 by the Levellers contained what was perhaps the first formal declaration of the privilege in language clarifying its relation to the oath and leaving no doubt that its roots were planted in the soil of conscience: "That all Statutes for all kinds of Oaths, whether in Corporations, Cities, or other, which ensnare conscientious people . . . be forthwith repealed and nulled, *and that nothing be imposed upon the consciences of any*

to compel them to sin against their own consciences." [Emphasis added.]

The privilege against self-incrimination was thus originally conceived as an essentially spiritual principle that permitted a person who had a conscientious belief in his innocence to assert what was tantamount to be right of passive resistance against an unjust law or a false accusation. The modern use of the privilege that best exemplifies its original purpose was the exercise of the Fifth Amendment during the McCarthy era. Given the Cold War climate of the fifties, a Supreme Court that could not quite bring itself to declare that active membership in the Communist Party was protected by the First Amendment could nevertheless find in the procedural guarantee of the Fifth Amendment a politically safe way of permitting people of conscience to resist legislative inquisitions into left-wing departures from the established democratic faith.

Even when freedom of conscience is not at stake, the privilege operates to protect the innocent. Contrary to popular belief, an innocent person may have a great deal to lose by telling the truth. For example, an innocent person, by admitting certain elements missing from the prosecution's cases, such as his presence at the scene of the crime, or that he owned the murder weapon, or even that it was he who fatally stabbed the victim (though in self-defense), has a legitimate concern that by telling the truth he may contribute to his being convicted of a crime he did not in fact commit or for which he had sufficient justification. The right to remain silent thus reflects our unwillingness as a society to permit an *innocent* person to become the instrument of his own conviction.

Give the purpose of the privilege to protect the innocent and those who hold a conscientious belief in their innocence, a revised set of *Miranda* warnings that would be more consistent with the history of the privilege, as well as contemporary standards of fairness and justice, should include, in addition to the existing admonitions regarding the right to consult with an attorney, the following: 1) If you believe you are innocent, you are not required to make a statement, or to answer any questions; 2) If you are guilty, you have a legal duty to answer questions and to state truthfully the circumstances concerning your commission of the offense with which you are charged.

The implications of this revisionist interpretation of the Fifth Amendment may have applications beyond the administration of *Miranda* warnings. Two years before *Miranda*

was decided, in *Murphy vs. Waterfront Commission,* the Supreme Court made it clear that "by requiring the government in its contest with the individual to shoulder the entire load," the privilege against self-incrimination provides the constitutional core of the presumption of innocence. Rethinking the Fifth Amendment may thus ultimately require rethinking the presumption of innocence as well as Justice White's classic statement of the criminal lawyer's role—"to put the State's case in the worst possible light, regardless of what he thinks or knows to be the truth." In a subsequent article, I will explore this most troubling and difficult aspect of the defense of criminal cases.

CHAPTER 4

Federalism and Intergovernmental Relations

American government combines centralization and decentralization of political power in a system of federalism. The federal system has a division and sharing of powers between the national government and the states. The Constitution shows how this is accomplished with guaranteed state representation in Congress, enumerated legislative powers in Article I, Section 8, and powers reserved to the states in the Tenth Amendment. Our political party system is decentralized.

Federalism differs from highly centralized unitary and very decentralized confederal systems. Under a unitary system, the people grant broad powers and authority to a central government, which then controls any other territorial units within the nation-state. Most Western European democracies are unitary systems, including Britain, France, the Netherlands, Belgium, Sweden, Norway, Denmark, and Finland. The American state governments are unitary authorities, having direct control over counties and local govements. Under the Articles of Confederation, the states had the most important authority and granted limited powers to the weak central government. Two examples of contemporary confederation are Switzerland, with language-based cantons exercising broad governmental powers, and the General Assembly of the United Nations, which lacks power to enforce its decisions without the agreement of member nation-states.

According to Daniel Elazar (see Article 13), more than seventy percent of the world's population lives under some kind of federal arrangement. There are more than three hundred federal-type states including the United States and the European Community. Some examples are Canada, Australia, India, and Germany.

The pro-democracy movement in the Soviet Union included demands by several of the republics for more autonomy and even independence from the central government. Considerable conflict took place before the

Baltic republics—Estonia, Latvia, and Lithuania—gained independence from the U.S.S.R. in 1991.

CONSTITUTIONAL FOUNDATIONS

What were some of the basic reasons for establishing our federal system? When the Founding Fathers debated the new Constitution in 1787, they were concerned with the weakness of the national government. Not only did the states predominate under the Articles of Confederation, but the new nation lacked a mechanism to raise revenue (the power to tax). The national government relied on voluntary contributions from the states. It did not have unified military capability to protect itself from foreign attacks. General George Washington had encountered this problem during the Revolutionary War when many of the colonies were reluctant to supply him with arms and troops. The United States was weak militarily and diplomatically in 1787. Consequently, there were two essential foundations of the federal bargain: an *expansion* condition and a *military* condition. The Framers created centralized federalism by expanding territorial control to meet an external threat. Such expansion could not be achieved by conquest, so concessions were made to the constituent units. In addition, the federal bargain was accepted by the constituent units because of external military-diplomatic threats or opportunities. The federal arrangement provided more protection to member states than if they acted alone.

The Constitution reflects the federal bargain by defining the basic *legal* boundaries of national and state authority. The principal constitutional provisions are Article I, Section 8 (delegated national powers), the Tenth Amendment (state-reserved powers), and several constitutional amendments which restrict state powers in matters of racial discrimination and voting rights.

Delegated, or enumerated, national government powers found in Article I, Section 8, include responsibilities over taxation, interstate commerce, coining money, declaring war, the military, and federal courts. The constitutional Framers agreed in 1787 that these were the powers needed to have an effective national government. Congress was given power "to make all laws which shall be necessary and proper for carrying into execution the foregoing powers. . . ." This section is frequently referred to as the "elastic clause," or the implied powers of Congress, following the Supreme Court decision in *McCulloch v. Maryland* discussed on the next page.

The states are granted reserved powers in the Tenth Amendment. In the 1800s and early 1900s, the Supreme Court interpreted "reserved powers" strictly, that is, the states retained all powers not delegated to the national government. More recent Supreme Court decisions have favored national power when it conflicts with the states. For example, in 1985 the Supreme Court ruled that federal minimum wage and hour standards should cover all employees of publicly owned mass transit systems. The decision changed a "new federalism" view of the Tenth Amendment which held in 1976 that the Tenth Amendment gave the states special protections and set affirmative limits on the federal government's power to interfere in state affairs.

Daniel Elazar (Article 13) argues that Supreme Court decisions in the 1980s resulted in "prefectorial federalism," by which congressional mandates were approved as a condition for aid to the states. This type of federal-state relationship gives Congress control over how the states may use federal aid and what kinds of federal standards and regulations apply to federal grants.

The federal government also restricts state authority in the three famous post-Civil War constitution amendments: the Thirteenth Amendment which prohibits slavery; the Fourteenth Amendment which prevents states from depriving persons of life, liberty, or property without due process of law or equal protection of the laws; and the Fifteenth Amendment which prohibits the states from denying voting rights on the basis of race. Three other prohibitions on state powers are the Nineteenth Amendment, which guarantees women's voting rights, and the Twenty-sixth Amendment, which sets the legal voting age at eighteen. States are prohibited from levying poll taxes in the Twenty-fourth Amendment.

McCULLOCH V. MARYLAND: THE DOCTRINE OF IMPLIED POWERS

What is the relationship between the formal constitutional provisions dealing with national and state powers and the realities of intergovernmental cooperation and conflict? Obviously, the Founding Fathers could not anticipate future nation-state problems and the political processes by which these controversies would be resolved. The Supreme Court assumed the role of umpire in the federal system. Under the leadership of Chief Justice John Marshall, the Supreme Court became involved in deciding nation-state disputes. When the State of Maryland challenged the authority of Congress to charter a national bank, Marshall wrote a landmark decision which greatly expanded the powers of Congress. In the case of *McCulloch v. Maryland* (1819), the chief justice declared that the so-called elastic clause of Article I, Section 8, of the Constitution, which refers to congressional authority "to make all laws which shall be necessary and proper," requires a very broad interpretation and implementation because: ". . . This provision is made in a constitution intended to endure for ages to come, and, consequently, to be adapted to the various crises of human affairs. . . ." Thus, even though the delegated powers of Congress include no provisions to charter a national bank, such power is implied from the "necessary and proper" clause.

Such implied powers are quite broad and subject only to the following conditions:

> . . . Let the end be legitimate, let it be within the scope of the Constitution, and all means which are appropriate, which are plainly adapted to that end, which are not prohibited, but consist with the letter and spirit of the Constitution. . . .

Chief Justice Marshall's decision in *McCulloch v. Maryland* not only expanded the powers of Congress by broadening the interpretation of the elastic clause, but it also established the principle of national supremacy in disputes with the states. When national and state authority clashed over controversial issues, the Supreme Court decided in favor of Congress, particularly when such legislative authority was constitutionally permissible. Throughout his tenure as chief justice, Marshall consistently strengthened national power. As the United States expanded its territory during the early decades of the nineteenth century, many of his decisions affirmed national authority.

PHASES OF FEDERALISM

Marshall's "nation-centered" interpretation is not the only view of American federalism. As Richard Leach indicates in Article 12, other theories have dealt with states' rights, dual federalism, intergovernmental cooperation, creative federalism, and new federalism. More recent examples of federalism in action are President Carter's targeted aid to assist distressed cities and President Reagan's extremely decentralized New Federalism, which proposed to return more than forty federal programs to the states. However, Leach is less concerned with examining theories about the federal system than he is with understanding the practical nature of nation-state relations. He argues that intergovernmental cooperation is the key to analyzing how the national, state, and local governments work with each other. Thus, federalism is a "*process . . . a way of doing things,* rather than . . . a set of abstract principles." If there is no set pattern of intergovernmental relations, then theorizing about federalism may be irrelevant. Most importantly, Leach observes, our federal system should be viewed pragmatically. "Workable federalism is marked by diversity, trial and error, and experimentation on the one hand, and it is problem-oriented on the other."

INTERGOVERNMENTAL FISCAL COOPERATION

Cooperation is the keynote of modern federal-state relations. Our federal system is characterized by a sharing of government functions and responsibilities. Rather than a "layer cake" of legal separation, the nation works together to overcome the formal fragmentation of many units of government.

Centralization and decentralization are not competing concepts. Rather, "government close to the people" depends on the nature of cooperative policies which best serves national, state, and local needs. In fact, our governmental and political structure in Congress, the bureaucracy, pressure groups, and political parties illustrate the accommodation required to achieve common policy objectives. Morton Grodzins, a political scientist, called federal-state cooperation "marble-cake" federalism.

Marble-cake federalism underwent further changes in intergovernmental fiscal relations in the 1970s and 1980s. As federal grants increased and became more specialized, a "picket-fence" arrangement between federal, state, and local bureaucracies administering federal grants emerged during the Nixon and Carter administrations in the 1970s. The picket-fence analogy referred to administrative specialization in functional grant areas such as education, environmental regulation, and transportation.

Other observers found that increased federal fiscal domination, through the proliferation of grants, resulted in a "fruit-cake" analogy in the 1970s. Federal incentives to the states and local governments resulted in their excessive dependency on available grants.

Federal aid cutbacks during the Reagan and Bush administrations produced a "do-it-yourself" federalism by states and localities. The subnational governments had to find ways to cope with less federal financial assistance by experimenting and solving problems on their own initiative.

By the 1970s, cooperative federalism involved three principal types of federal aid to state and local government: categorical grants, block grants, and general revenue sharing.

Categorical grants are federal payments for specific programs, subject to a variety of federal matching requirements and administrative regulations which recipients must follow. Categorical grants are attractive to states and localities, but the federal granting agencies leave relatively little room for state and local discretion. For example, they must comply with civil rights regulations and personnel guidelines, equip buildings and transportation for the handicapped, follow water pollution controls in building water and sewer systems, and protect historical landmarks.

In the 1980s, the Reagan administration reduced federal spending for categorical programs to $70 billion. This was part of the effort to control domestic spending and reduce federal budget deficits. Reductions resulted in program elimination, spending cuts, and conversion of categorical grants to block grants by consolidating programs with reduced funding.

Even with these cuts, federal aid to states and localities increased to $134 billion by 1990 for such categorical programs as mass transportation, public works (highways, public housing, hospitals, airports) and education. But the greatest proportion of federal grants was for entitlement programs rather than construction or public works. Entitlement programs involved distribution of federal aid by specific criteria or formula rather than by state or local project applications to federal administrative agencies. Federal entitlements include such antipoverty programs as Medicaid, food stamps, and public assistance. By 1990, $75 billion of federal aid was allocated to these entitlement programs while project grants had been reduced from $70 billion to $59 billion.

Block grants consolidate related categorical programs into broad functional areas. They became popular in the late 1960s and 1970s as a way of reducing federal administrative controls and providing the states with more program discretion than they had under categorical grants. Block grants are defended as a way of promoting decentralization, as being more efficient than categorical grants, and as better serving the needs of the recipients. The first block grant was the Partnership for Health Act of 1966, followed by the Omnibus Crime Control and Safe Streets Act of 1968, and the Comprehensive Employment and Training Act of 1973. The Housing and Community Development Act of 1974 demonstrated the block grant concept most effectively. Under this act was the Community Development Block Grant (CDBG), which included ten previous categorical programs that were folded into a single block grant. By 1982, there was a total of eleven different federal block grant programs, nine of which were enacted in 1981.

General revenue sharing (GRS) was approved in 1972 as a guaranteed form of federal aid to the states and local governments with few administrative requirements. States and localities received GRS on a quarterly basis according to congressional allocation formulas. They were only required to file reports revealing how money was spent rather than follow complex federal regulations. States were originally included in 1972 and received GRS until 1980. GRS was very popular with state and local officials because money could be spent with virtually no restrictions. However, the Reagan administration and Congress eliminated GRS in the 1987 federal budget as a cost-cutting measure. Many mayors and county officials were dismayed that local taxes were increased and many programs curtailed with the elimination of GRS.

REAGAN'S NEW FEDERALISM

President Reagan's New Federalism represented a dramatic reversal in the federal commitment to assist state and local governments. Reagan favored a plan of extreme decentralization under which most federal categorical programs would end and the states would become responsible for aiding cities, suburbs, and metropolitan areas. Reagan believed that the federal government should minimize both the financial and administrative direction of national grants programs. In 1981, the New Federalism was part of a larger economic recovery program designed to reduce federal domestic spending, to lower federal income taxes, to increase defense spending, and to balance the federal budget. The first phase of the New Federalism included major cuts for a variety of social services, including nutritional, housing, and transportation programs. More than fifty categorical aids were folded into nine block grants with a 25 percent reduction in federal funding. The second phase called for a restructuring of federal-state functional responsibilities, including the return of $47 billion in federal programs to the states. Strong objections by governors and mayors thwarted action by Congress to follow through on this second phase. However, congressional enactment in 1985 of the Gramm-Rudman-Hollings budget deficit reduction plan continued the elimination, if not the return, of many federal programs traditionally supported for states and localities.

Bush's New Federalism Plan

In 1991, President Bush proposed a single consolidated grant of $15 to $21 billion a year to the states. The goal was to give the states complete control over federal categorical and block grants in five broad program areas: education, environmental protection, health and human services, housing and urban development, and crime and antidrug programs.

Unlike President Reagan's 1982 decentralization plan, the Bush administration said it would guarantee the $15 to $21 billion a year for five years in federal payments to the states. The most costly federal program to be returned to the states included financing administrative costs of welfare programs like Medicaid, Aid to Families with Dependent Children, and food stamps. The costs of these programs are expected to grow by 62 percent, to $8.3 billion, in 1996. The Bush administration assumed that the states would absorb these costs and reduce grants for construction of sewage treatment plants by 56 percent and grants for low-income energy assistance by 83 percent.

A major criticism of the Bush plan was that governors or mayors were not consulted in developing the proposal. Many mayors were concerned that state control over a consolidated grant would further reduce federal aid to cities.

After considering the proposal, the National Conference of State Legislatures and the National Governors' Association came up with their own plan modeled after President Bush's initiative. State officials proposed consolidating child care, job training, clean water management and agricultural extension-service programs. The governors proposed a ten-city pilot program to test the feasibility of pooling administrative costs of Medicaid, AFDC, and food stamps into a singly consolidated grant.

The Bush plan did not take into account the severe budget deficits faced by state and local governments. Decentralization can be a desirable goal in intergovernmental fiscal relations, but states and localities needed new revenue in the early 1990s to overcome the effects of a prolonged economic recession.

Federal-State Relations: Centralization, Decentralization and Innovation

Efforts by recent presidents to reduce, eliminate, and consolidate program assistance to state and local governments suggest that long-term decentralization is occurring in the federal system.

Articles 13 and 14 discuss two different aspects of these decentralizing trends. Daniel Elazar is relatively optimistic that state governments can play a positive role in developing new domestic policy initiatives. States can become laboratories in experimenting with new ideas. But Elazar does not tell us where the revenues will come from to finance them. However, he is persuasive that reduced federal domination over the states can produce beneficial results.

Jonathan Walters points out that the national organizations representing mayors, cities, counties, and governors have not yet decided how to cope with the continuing cuts in federal assistance. Some want to fight for budget restorations and challenge federal mandates as a condition for receiving aid. Others seek to create a national clearinghouse which would provide information on how states and localities are experimenting with innovative approaches in an era of federal reductions.

The 1990s represents a time for state and local governments to meet the challenge of changing relationships with the national government. Do-it-yourself federalism is the reality. Innovation may be the strategy for providing the programs and services for people. The Ford Foundation is providing awards to state, local, and individual innovators. Innovation is a way of "doing more with less." Creative ideas dealing with targeting available funds, eliminating bureaucratic interference, and developing public-private partnerships may be the future direction of fiscally-strapped state and local governments.

Federalism and the Political Process

12
Federalism and Theory*
Richard H. Leach

How has American federalism developed over time? Richard Leach shows that federal-state relations reflect a variety of approaches, each of which represents an adjustment to different political circumstances. Denying that federalism is a fixed "theory," Leach argues there have been a variety of pragmatic responses to nation-state relations. For example, Chief Justice John Marshall was a leading advocate of "nation-centered" federalism. He tried to strengthen the authority of the national government against challenges made by the states (McCulloch v. Maryland, 1819). Other competitive and cooperative varieties of federalism have characterized American political experiences. Since Leach's views were written in 1970, how has federalism developed? What is the most effective balance between the goals of centralization and decentralization?

Federalism has been a subject of controversy in American government and politics since the beginning of the Republic. It continues so today. For it is at the center of American governmental action. It is, as the late Morton Grodzins wrote, "a device for dividing decisions and functions of government . . . It is a means, not an end."[1] It ordinarily involves two major levels of government, each, at least in democratic societies, assumed to derive its powers directly from the people and therefore to be supreme in the areas of power assigned to it. Each level of government in a federal system insists upon its right to act directly upon the people. Each is protected constitutionally from undue encroachment or destruction by the other. To this end, federalism

entails a point of final reference, usually a judiciary. The people in federal systems are held to possess what amounts to dual citizenship. Sovereignty, in the classic sense, has no meaning; divided as power is, the element of absoluteness which is essential to the concept of sovereignty is not present. Federalism is concerned with process and by its very nature is a dynamic, not a static, concept. In operation, it requires a willingness both to cooperate across governmental lines and to exercise restraint and forebearance in the interests of the entire nations. . . .

But precisely what "federalism" means is not now and never has been clear. We can only be sure that the framers of the Constitution regarded it as one of several ways to limit

Reprinted from *American Federalism* by Richard H. Leach, by permission of W.W. Norton & Company, Inc. Copyright © 1970 by W. W. Norton & Company, Inc.

the power of government in the United States. Thus any attempt to argue for a particular relation between the national government and the states—in particular for a precise division of powers between them—must fall flat for lack of constitutional corroboration. Nor are clear directions given with regard to other aspects of federalism. Instead of a rigid set of principles, what the framers gave us was a flexible instrument concerned with function and the practice of government. Federalism is thus something which is able to respond to changing needs and circumstances and is not bound by the tenets of a particular political theory.

But that there is in effect no basic theory of American federalism has not prevented both plain and eminent men from arguing vehemently that such a theory exists. So many and so vociferous have proponents of various conceptions of federalism been over the years that the literature is voluminous. The leading theoretical contentions are summarized under two main categories in the paragraphs that follow.

COMPETITIVE THEORIES
Nation-Centered Federalism

The concept of nation-centered federalism was the first to be advanced. Alexander Hamilton laid the basis for nation-centered federalism in his numbers of *The Federalist,* in his state papers, and by his actions as Secretary of the Treasury under George Washington. Later, John Marshall, as Chief Justice of the United States, constantly emphasized national power and indeed visualized judicial review "as a means of keeping the states within bounds."[2] The nation-centered theory of federalism posits the idea that the Constitution is a document emanating from and ratified by the American people as a whole. It follows that the government which the whole people created is the focal point of political power in the United States and that it has the principal responsibility for meeting the needs of the American people. Between them, Hamilton and Marshall expounded the idea that, in Marshall's words in *McCulloch v. Maryland,* the national government "is the government of all; its powers are delegated by all; it represents all, and acts for all . . . The nation, on those subjects on which it can act, must necessarily bind its component parts. But this question is not left to mere reason; the people have, in express terms, decided it by saying, 'this constitution, and the laws of the United States, which shall be made in pursuance thereof, . . . shall be the supreme law of the land' . . . " Nor is it merely its popular base which gives the nation primacy. As Abraham Lincoln pointed out in his first Inaugural Address, "The Union is much older than the Constitution. It was formed, in fact, by the Articles of Association in 1774. It was matured and continued by the Declaration of Independence in 1776. It was further matured, and the faith of all the then thirteen States expressly plighted and engaged that it be perpetual, by the Articles of Confederation. . . . " And finally, in 1787, one of the declared objects for ordaining and establishing the Constitution was "to form a more perfect Union." What else needs to be pointed out to demonstrate the centrality of the Union at the outset? And the intervening years did nothing to alter the original emphasis on the national government.

Nor is there anything incompatible in emphasizing the national government and at the same time defending the existence and utility of states and state governments. As Chief Justice Roger Taney put it in 1869 in *Texas v. White*[3] (the case which tested whether the government of Texas was responsible for the bonds issued by the state's Confederate government during the Civil War),

. . . The perpetuity and indissolubility of the Union, by no means implies the loss of distinct and individual existence, or of the right of self-government by the States. Under the Articles of Confederation each State retained its sovereignty, freedom, and independence, and every power, jurisdiction, and right not expressly delegated to the United States. Under the Constitution, though the powers of the States were much restricted, still, all powers not delegated to the United States, nor prohibited to the States, are reserved to the States respectively, or to the people. And we have already had occasion to remark at this term, that "the people of each State compose a State, having its own government, and endowed with all the functions essential to separate and independent existence," and that "without the States in union, there could be no such political body as the United States." Not only, therefore, can there be no loss of separate and independent autonomy to the States, through their union under the Constitution, but it may be not unreasonably said that the preservation of the States, and the maintenance of their governments, are as much within the design and care of the Constitution as the preservation of the Union and the maintenance of the National government. The Constitution, in all its provisions, looks to an indestructible Union, composed of indestructible States.

Thus the national government has a dual responsibility to the people under the Constitution, a responsibility for the preservation and defense of both the Union as a whole and each and every individual state, which adds but a further reason for its primacy.

State-Centered Federalism

State-centered federalism developed in resistance to the nationalism of Hamilton and Marshall and was first articulated in the Virginia and Kentucky Resolutions in 1798. Later on, the full-blown theory of state-centered federalism was polished and perfected, particularly by southerners, as its usefulness in rationalizing the differences between that section of the country and the rest of the nation became more apparent. Thomas Jefferson and John C. Calhoun were the chief (but far from the only) developers of this variation on the theme.[4] The theory of state-centered federalism holds that the Constitution resulted from state action. It was, after all, the states which sent delegates to Philadelphia, and state ratifying conventions which confirmed the completed document. Moreover, to protect the states, the framers set absolute limits to the power of the national government in Article I, section 8, and specifically guaranteed state power in the Tenth Amendment. James Madison spoke to the point in *Federalist 45*:

. . . It is not preposterous, to urge as an objection to a government, without which the objects of the Union cannot be attained, that such a government may derogate from the importance of the governments of the individual states? . . . The powers delegated by the proposed Constitution to the federal government are few and defined. Those which are to remain in the State governments are numerous and indefinite. The former will be exercised principally on external objects. . . . The powers reserved to the several States will extend to all the objects which, in the ordinary course of affairs, concern the lives, liberties, and properties of the people, and the internal order, improvement, and prosperity of the States.

The chief focus of citizen and governmental attention, believers in this theory are convinced, should be to guard against any enlargement of national power. For basic to the theory of state-centered federalism is the conviction that there is only a limited amount of power available to government in the United States and that the constitutional delegation of power, as narrowly construed as possible, is all that safely can be exercised by the national government. Any extension beyond those narrow limits amounts to usurpation of power which rightfully belongs to the states.

Dual Federalism

In one sense, the Civil War was fought between proponents of nation-centered and state-centered federalism. With the victory of the North, it might be assumed that the nationalist concept became the dominant and unchallenged interpretation of federalism in the United States. In fact, this was not the case. Even before the war, the Taney Court had begun to develop the concept of dual federalism, which the Supreme Court after the war embellished and utilized well into the twentieth century; and it gained adherents outside the bar and the judiciary as the corporation, which sought freedom from the restraints of both national and state government, came fully into its own. Proponents of dual federalism profess to believe that the Constitution created a governmental system with "collateral political spheres," to use John Taylor of Carolina's phrase. The national and state governments form two separate centers of power, from each of which the other is barred and between which is something like a jurisdictional no-man's land in which both are barred from entering. Each government in its own sphere is sovereign, and there is an essential equality between them. As Taylor put it in his *Construction Construed and Constitutions Vindicated,* published in 1820, "the federal constitution, so far from intending to make its political spheres morally unequal in powers, or to invest the greatest with any species of sovereignty over the least, intended the very reverse"—the distribution of equal power between the states and the national government. "The reason," Taylor continued, "why great spheres derived no authority from magnitude to transgress upon small spheres, is, that both are donations from the same source [i.e., the people]; and that the donor did not intend that one donation should pilfer another, because it was smaller." The donation is inviolable, and it is the clear duty of the several branches of the national government, as well as of state governments, to maintain it so, not so much to protect the governments involved, but to assure the freedom of the people. For "the strength of the government lies in the people," Taylor concluded.

> *They are the protectors and supervisors of the collateral political spheres, which they have created. If one of these spheres should acquire sufficient power to control the others, it would, like an officer of a monarch, who can control all the other officers of the government, obtain a supremacy over the monarch himself. . . .*

COOPERATIVE THEORIES

Cooperative Federalism

Despite the triumph of dual federalism in the years following the Civil War, neither the nation-centered nor the state-centered varieties were abandoned, in part probably because the heat of the Civil War was so long in dying down, both sides continuing to fight the battle long after the war was over. Perhaps because the arena of argument seemed to be full, the concept of cooperative federalism was slow in jelling and was not given explicit expression much before Morton Grodzins described it in the 1950s. The flavor of the cooperative theory is best caught in the title of a book by Grodzin's student, Daniel Elazar, *The American Partnership.*[5] Elazar illustrates how from the very beginning all levels of government in the United States have collaborated in performing governmental functions. Far from comprising separate and independent layers of government as suggested by proponents of the competitive theories, the American form of government is cooperative, a blending of governments, resembling a "rainbow or marble cake, characterized by an inseparable mingling of differently colored ingredients, the colors appearing in vertical and diagonal strands and unexpected swirls. As colors are mixed in a marble cake, so functions are mixed in the American federal system."[6] In this view, the Constitution visualized a single mechanism of government in the United States, with many centers of power, which among them were to perform all the functions required of government by the American people. Even before the Constitution, intergovernmental cooperation was utilized to establish primary and secondary education; and the framers of the Constitution were so conscious of "the essential unity of state and federal financial systems"[7] that they provided for the federal government's assumption of the states' Revolutionary War debts. It is a fundamental principle of American federalism that the national government will use its resources in harmony with state and local programs and policies. During the nineteenth century that principle was manifest in steadily increasing intergovernmental cooperation in all the important functional areas of American government, and the twentieth century confirmed the practice. Shared functions, without regard to neat allocations of responsibility, is thus the core of American governmental operation and of the theory of federalism as well. Intergovernmental collaboration rather than the priority of particular governmental levels is the working principle of the federal system.

Creative Federalism

Creative federalism is that theory of federalism first used and described by Governor Nelson Rockefeller in his Godkin Lectures at Harvard in 1962.[8] The idea was picked up and made central to this program by President Lyndon B. Johnson after his election in 1964. Creative federalism is an extension of cooperative federalism in that it emphasizes cooperation. It differs in its recognition of local and private centers of power as well as national and state centers, and in its concern for the development of cooperation not only between the national and state governments but between them and local governments and private organizations as well. All are regarded as a working team, dedicated to positive action in solving the problems facing the nation, with perhaps a different combination of forces at work in each different problem area, and with the national government not always the senior partner. In both its stress on the responsibility of the private sector of American life in the problem-solving process and its concern that action and innovation take place before problems become critical, it is unique among the theories of federalism so far espoused in America.

New Federalism

President Richard Nixon described his concept of "new federalism" in a nationwide television speech on August 8, 1969, and again before the National Governors Conference on September 1. It was later given more explicit form in testimony before Congress by the assistant director of the Bureau of the Budget.[9] Its major theme is to rechannel "power, funds and authority . . . increasingly to those governments closest to the people . . . to help regain control of our national destiny by returning a greater share of control to state and local authorities."[10] It stresses *responsible decentralization:* "Washington will no longer try to go it alone," President Nixon said. Washington will "refrain from telling states and localities how to conduct their affairs and [will] seek to transfer ever-greater responsibilities to the state level."[11] To make the transfer possible, a system of revenue sharing must be established. It also emphasizes *a strong concern with basic systems.* Instead of piecemeal action on parts of problems, intergovernmental strategies for attacking broad problem areas must be worked out. Welfare and manpower programs were the first two such areas to be singled out for attack. Finally, the "new-federalism" places *greater emphasis on the effective implementation of government policies,* particularly at the state and local level, where acceptance of the concept "would impose . . . new obligations and new challenges" on government in terms of improved quality of performance. The thrust of the "new federalism" is to deemphasize the national government's role in the partnership of governments and to strengthen that of state and local governments. "Washington will no longer dictate," President Nixon promised. "We can only toss the ball; the states and localities will have to carry it."[12] The new federalism has not yet developed the specifics as to how to make this possible, particularly in financial terms, and until it does, *The New York Times* remarked editorially, it will likely be little "more than a rhetorical phrase."[13]

A recital in chronological order of the several theories of federalism which have been developed in the United States should not be misinterpreted; the subsequent development of one theory by no means served to crowd its predecessors off the stage. Not only did the first two claimants of attention continue to make themselves heard, but as each new concept was developed, proponents of the earlier theories hardened their positions. Thus the stage became more crowded, more confused, and certainly more noisy.

To a large extent the "debate" over the theories of federalism has not been a debate at all. For the most part, it has been conducted at presidential press conferences and in political addresses, in legislative committee chambers and court rooms, in the pages of the daily press and in scholarly journals and reports, but not in the streets and by the people as a whole. Indeed, it would be difficult to demonstrate that there is now or ever has been a widespread public understanding of federalism. If some southerners seem to have consistently supported one theory as opposed to any of the others, their advocacy is based not so much on participation in the debate and understanding derived therefrom as on habit and stereotype. It has always been difficult to find out what the popular conception of federalism is, and this is because the people are very likely confused as to what federalism means, as much by the several interpretations of the "truth" offered them through the years as by the vacuum left by the framers.

An example of that confusion is found in a survey of federalism as viewed by governmental officials concerned with the administration of federal grant-in-aid programs, recently conducted by the Senate Subcommittee on Intergovernmental Relations.[14] The survey showed that, while none of those interviewed had consciously articulated a theory of federalism or even given much thought to the need to do so, "the respondents [did] have a general idea of what intergovernmental relations are and how they should operate. In short, the survey made it clear . . . ,"[15] that state and local officials involved in federal grant-in-aid programs hold views of federalism quite different from those of federal officials. Moreover, the study revealed that neither the state and local officials nor the federal officials were in agreement among themselves as to the several elements of the theories they espoused. As the report itself put it, "These contrasting [theories] . . . are based on contrasting emphases and principles." The federal officials were chiefly concerned with doing a professional job of administering aid programs and generally held an anti-state and anti-local official bias, which understandably made their views "completely unacceptable" to the state and local officials, who generally insisted on a more formal statement of principles and were concerned with such concepts as "balance" and "parity."[16] The views of neither group of officials, however, conformed in every respect to one of the theories described earlier in this chapter. Indeed, the subcommittee concluded, governmental officials probably held atypical views of the federal system.

One is left at the end of even so careful an analysis of concepts of federalism more confused than ever as to just what the theoretical bases of American federalism are—or one's confusion is finally dispelled as he is led to understand once and for all that considerations of theory are irrelevant to an understanding of federalism. For the most important conclusion to be drawn from the Senate study is that most respondents agreed their commitment was to a *process,* to *a way of doing things,* rather than to a set of abstract principles. The most frequently occurring words in the views of both sets of officials are *function, program, activity, administration,* in considering all of which *collaboration* and intergovernmental *relations* are fundamental. Federalism from both points of view—more from the federal than from the state and local, to be sure—is seen as a complex working arrangement to permit the accomplishment of commonly held objectives. It is an arrangement whose virtue lies in what it permits to be accomplished rather than in the degree to which it adheres to a set of binding tenets. And accomplishment can only be secured by a large amount of interrelation. Above all, the conclusion is inevitable that intergovernmental cooperation is the key to modern federalism. Meeting the problems of modern America with the right programs and policies involves *all* levels of government, working together in a variety of ways. The older competitive theories of federalism took into account only the actions of and relations between the government of the United States and those of the states, and even the more recently developed theories of cooperative and creative federalism are focused chiefly on them. Yet federalism is much more than that. It involves as a matter of inheritance and practical necessity at least three levels of action—national, state, and local—and five sets of relations—national-state, interstate, state-local, interlocal, and national-local. To the extent that theories of federalism overlook this elemental truth, they are inapplicable and invalid from the outset. Only the theory of creative federalism seems to take interaction between all levels of government into account. . . .

Implicit in all the theorizing about federalism is the belief that men plan and act rationally in devising their governmental systems. There is no clear evidence that they do. Even the revered framers of the American Constitution were men affected by many forces, only some of them within the control of their reason, as they worked to create the federal system. It is all well and good to speak, as Paul Ylvisaker does in *Area and Power,*[17] of "the proper areal division of powers." Proper according to what logic? what criteria? what reasoning? Persons working in practical intergovernmentalism are more likely fettered than aided by such notions of "propriety."

American federalism is based on the theory of limited government. Beyond that, it answers not to theoretical dictates. Nor is it likely that it will be adjusted to meet theoretical demands in the future. Theory, in other words, has not been causative in American federalism. The framers of the Constitution bequeathed us an open-ended system. We can only be the losers if we try to close it off by adopting any set of theoretical principles, any model, any construct. As in so many other areas, the framers in building federalism built better than they knew—and we are the beneficiaries.

NOTES

1. Morton Grodzins, "The Federal System," Ch. 12 in *Goals for Americans. The Report of the President's Commission on National Goals* (Englewood Cliffs, N.J., Prentice-Hall, 1965), p. 265.

2. The phrase of Benjamin F. Wright, *The Growth of American Constitutional Law* (Boston: Houghton Mifflin, 1942), p. 38.

3. 7 Wallace 700 (1869).

4. See Alpheus T. Mason, *The States' Rights Debate.* A Spectrum Paperback (New York, 1964).

5. Daniel Elazar, *The American Partnership* (Chicago: Univ. of Chicago Press, 1962).

6. Grodzins, "The Federal System," Ch. 12 in *Goals for Americans, op. cit.,* p. 265.

7. *Ibid.,* p. 268.

8. Nelson A. Rockefeller, *The Future of Federalism* (Cambridge: Harvard Univ. Press, 1962).

9. See the statement of Richard P. Nathan, September 25, 1969, reprinted in *Congressional Record* 115: S11429 (September 26, 1969). The italicized phrases are from his testimony.

10. President Nixon before the National Governors Conference, reprinted in *Congressional Record* 115: H7533 (September 4, 1969).

11. Quoted in *The New York Times,* September 3, 1969, p. 1.

12. *Ibid.*

13. *Ibid.,* p. 46.

14. *The Federal System as Seen by Federal Aid Officials* Committee Print. December 15, 1965. 89th Congress, 1st Session.

15. *Ibid.,* p. 95.

16. *Ibid.,* pp. 96, 97, 99.

17. Arthur Maass, ed., *Area and Power. A Theory of Local Government* (Glencoe, Ill.: Free Press, 1959).

Federal-State Relations: Centralization and Decentralization

13

Opening the Third Century of American Federalism: Issues and Prospects

Daniel J. Elazar

In this informative article, Daniel Elazar, director of the Center for the Study of Federalism at Temple University, continues the discussion of the New Federalism mentioned by Leach in the previous article. He updates recent developments by showing contradictory trends in the federal system. The courts have upheld congressional mandates against the states, while the Reagan and Bush administrations promoted decentralization and more state responsibility for domestic programs. Elazar argues that Reagan's dual federalism view did not work. Why not? Elazar also discusses a new direction by the states. What does he mean by this? What are the characteristics of the new noncentralization? According to Elazar, what are the four main functions of the national government in the federal system? Do you agree with this list, or are there other federal responsibilities? What are the strengths and limitations of the states in facing future challenges?

At the beginning of its third century, the condition of American federalism is best characterized as ambiguous but promising. This, in itself, represents a great advance for noncentralized government over the situation that prevailed between 1965 and 1980, during which the trend was rather unambiguously centralizing.

In an earlier *Annals* article, I set out the shifting patterns of American intergovernmental relations in the twentieth century.[1] Table 1

summarizes that analysis and brings it up to date. In the intervening 25 years, federal intervention into state and local affairs reached its apogee and then began to collapse of its own weight, assisted by the electoral triumph of Ronald Reagan and his dual-federalism, states' rights ideology. At the most, the various New Federalisms that preceded the Reagan administration sought to replace noncentralization— the constitutional diffusion of power among federal, state, and local centers that makes the

From *The Annals*, Vol. 509 (May 1990), pp. 12-21. © 1990 by The Academy of Political and Social Science. Reprinted by permission of Sage Publications, Inc.

1. Daniel J. Elazar, "The Shaping of Intergovernmental Relations in the Twentieth Century," *The Annals* of the American Academy of Political and Social Science, 359:10-22 (May 1965).

TABLE 1 Twentieth-Century Patterns of American Federalism

Year	Period	Economic Era	Political Condition	State of Intergovernmental Relations
1900 1910	Transition (1895–1911)	Concentrated enterprise capitalism (1877–1913)	GOP majority party	Passing of nineteenth-century cooperative programs. New experiments in collaboration under T. Roosevelt. Widespread state experimentation has important influence on public.
 1920	Progressive agrarianism (1911-21)	Transition era (1913–33)	(Democratic administration, 1913–21)	Wilson's New Freedom lays foundation for twentieth-century cooperative federalism.
    1930	Normalized entrenchment (1921–31)		1928 Critical elections 1932	GOP restoration starts second period. Existing cooperative programs continued and improved but no significant new federal starts. State experimentation again significant.
     1940	Crisis-oriented centralism (1931–45)		Democrats forge majority coalition, become majority party.	New Deal explosion in federal-state cooperation, heading off centralization through temporary concentration of power in Washington. Expansion of federal-local and unilateral federal programs along with cooperative ones.

TABLE 1 —*Continued*

Year	Period	Economic Era	Political Condition	State of Intergovernmental Relations
1950 1960	Noncentralist restoration (1946–61)	Regulated capitalism (1946–)	(GOP administration, 1953–61) 1956 Critical elections 1960	Fourth period brings great expansion of small cooperative programs, great expansion of state government expenditures, and increased concern with states' role.
1970	Concentrated cooperation (1961–68)		Democratic majority coalition reforged	Fifth period brings new emphasis on stimulatory action and new threat of centralization from outside of the cooperative system.
1980	Coercive cooperation (1969–81)		Divided federal government	Under guise of cooperative federalism, federal government tries to coerce the states into following and implementing mutual policies set in Washington. Breakdowns in Washington begin reversal of this trend.
1990	Neodualism (1981–)	Deregulation and neomarket capitalism	1980 Critical elections 1984	Reagan administration reintroduces ideology of dual federalism and states' rights. Fiscal realities shift governmental initiative to the states. Strong reduction in federal aid.

relationships between those centers ones of true partnership—with decentralization—namely, a federal center deciding what the states and localities should or should not do.[2]

The most striking aspect of American federalism in the 1980s was the existence of very strong contradictory trends within the federal system. On one hand, in its *Garcia* and *South Carolina* decisions, the U.S. Supreme Court compounded all of its previous errors with regard to the proper constitutional relationship between the federal government and the states.[3] The Court stood the Constitution on its head so as to give the Congress of the United States the last word in determining the federal-state relationship in matters deemed to be within the purview of the federal government under the commerce clause of the federal Constitution. In doing so, the Court threw over 200 years of constitutional understanding and nearly that many years of precedent. The Court did exactly what the Constitution pledged not to do, that is to say, make one of the parties to any inter-governmental controversy the arbiter of the results.

If the states and localities, through their political influence in Congress, have been able to hold the line on a number of the issues directly confronted in U.S. Supreme Court decisions, they have lost the battle with regard to congressional mandates, whereby the Congress, in Court-justified actions, orders the states to do this and that without any pretense of winning them over through federal aid or making those orders contingent upon accepting federal grants.[4] This is prefectorial federalism. A decade ago, prefectorial federalism seemed to be emanating from the executive branch of the federal government.[5] In the intervening years, the executive branch, headed by President Reagan, turned out to be generally a friend of federalism while Congress, increasingly detached as it is from state and local ties, turned out to be unfriendly, in a manner that once seemed characteristic only of the U.S. Supreme Court.

The transformation of American politics from a state and local party-based system to a free-for-all among individuals supported by various national economic, cultural, social, and political interests through political action committees has meant that fewer members of Congress have had direct experience in state and local government.[6] Increasingly, candidates for Congress are new to the political arena and depend on projecting their personalities by raising enough funds from political action committees and individuals to meet today's outrageous campaign costs. Hence they come

2. Cf. Jeffrey L. Mayer, ed., *Dialogues on Decentralization,* vol. 6, *Publius: The Journal of Federalism* (Fall 1976); Robert B. Hawkins, Jr., and George Packard, eds., *Government Reorganization and the Federal System,* vol. 8, *Publius: The Journal of Federalism* (Spring 1978).

3. *Garcia v. San Antonio Metropolitan Transit Authority,* 469 U.S. 528 (1985); *South Carolina v. Baker,* 56 U.S.L.W. 4311 (1988). Cf. U.S. Advisory Commission of Intergovernmental Relations, *Federalism and the Constitution: A Symposium on Garcia* (Washington, DC: Advisory Commission on Intergovernmental Relations, 1988).

4. U.S. Advisory Commission on Intergovernmental Relations, *Regulatory Federalism* (Washington, DC: Advisory Commission on Intergovernmental Relations, 1984).

5. Daniel J. Elazar, "Is Federalism Compatible with Perfectorial Administration?" *Publius: The Journal of Federalism,* 11:3–22 (Spring 1981).

6. U.S. Advisory Commission on Intergovernmental Relations, *The Transformation in American Politics* (Washington, DC: Advisory Commission on Intergovernmental Relations, 1986); Hedrick Smith, *The Power Game* (New York: Random House, 1988).

to Washington without state and local political roots. They settle their families within the Beltway year round, and, although they continue to work their districts, they do so as visitors more than as residents. Thus they have no strong personal commitments to state and local government interests, much less to the constitutional rights of the states.

THE STATES REASSERT THEMSELVES AS POLITIES

Nevertheless, within this deteriorating constitutional and political framework, the states have become stronger and more vigorous than ever. They have reasserted themselves as polities and have become the principal source of governmental innovation in the United States as well as the principal custodians of most domestic programs. In this extraordinary turnaround, they have been helped by the catastrophes that have befallen previous presidents and by the positive efforts of the Reagan administration to have the federal government turn over certain functions to the states, free certain revenue sources to accompany them, and reduce federal regulatory interventions in state affairs and the processes of state governance.[7]

Fifteen years ago, the crisis of the Nixon administration—Watergate, the Arab oil embargo, the national truckers' strike, and the collapse of South Vietnam—paralyzed the federal government. The states, particularly the governors, acted to fill the vacuum in the true spirit of federalism, and in a manner that demonstrated the virtues of federalism as providing useful redundancy and fail-safe mechanisms, so that when one part of the political system cannot function, other parts can take over. The states organized the distribution of limited oil and gas resources, governors settled the truckers' strike, and state and local agencies came to the fore in resettling Southeast Asian refugees. State officials discovered that they had powers of their own derived from the very existence of their states as states and did not need to wait for federal initiatives or permission, in other words, that the states are indeed polities. Moreover, they enjoyed exercising those powers and did so well.

By 1975, as the United States was about to enter a new political generation, the states were off and running. The states' innovative role continued to expand through the late 1970s, in part because of the relative paralysis of the Carter administration, which was sympathetic to fostering a greater state role in the federal system and whose relations with the states were generally good and constructive.

At the same time, in the years following the Warren Court, the formerly unambiguously activist U.S. Supreme Court entered a period of rather diffuse retrenchment. Many state supreme courts began to pick up the slack through the development of a new, vibrant state constitutional law, building state constitutional foundations for public policy in everything from individual rights to relations between religion, state, and society, and to fairer distributions of public services. The constitutional legitimacy of these grounds was increasingly recognized by liberals and conservatives alike on the U.S. Supreme Court, each for his own reasons. State constitutional law became a field of academic and legal interest

7. U.S. Advisory Commission on Intergovernmental Relations, *The Question of State Government Capability* (Washington, DC: Advisory Commission on Intergovernmental Relations, 1985); Robert B. Hawkins, Jr., ed., *American Federalism: A New Partnership for the Republic* (San Francisco: Institute for Contemporary Studies, 1982).

beyond the courts, a sure sign of its new importance.[8]

In the mid-1970s, the Court began to look more favorably upon state actions in a number of fields previously subjected to preemptive decisions by their predecessors. For a while, until *Garcia,* it even seemed as if the Tenth Amendment would be reinvigorated through such decisions as *Usery.*[9] Even today, the Court's decisions on federalism are distinctly mixed, with state prerogatives being preserved at least half of the time.

THE REAGAN BALANCE SHEET

President Reagan, from the moment of his election, began to reshape American attitudes toward the federal government and the states in particular. The president enunciated a traditional dual federalist view of the American system, but by enunciating it forcefully, he compelled even committed centralists to respond in federalist terms and to justify their extraordinary reliance on federal intervention in those terms. With his flare for communication, Reagan brought federalism into the headlines in a way unexcelled by any president in this century.

By its decisive actions in so many fields, the Reagan administration demonstrated that it was still possible to take hold of the reins of government and begin to reverse seemingly irreversible trends, including the at least seventy-year-long thrust toward greater government permeation of society. Yet fulfilling Reagan's promise to strengthen the states within that system, and thereby strengthen the system as a whole, has not been easy. There are several reasons why this is so.

First, even when there was general agreement in principle, there was great disagreement around the country and even in the administration as to what should be turned over to the states. The Reagan administration was no more immune to this problem than was any other. Indeed, its people suggested new federal interventions almost as frequently as they suggested federal withdrawals. Second, the states were not necessarily willing to accept added responsibilities as solely theirs if the costs—fiscal or political—were high. Third, there was a tendency in the administration to rely on simple notions of separating federal and state functions as a basis for making policy rather than on gaining an understanding of the possibilities of strengthening the states by restoring classic patterns of intergovernmental cooperation. Much of the problem relates to a misunderstanding of the principles of federalism and how they informed the American political system in better days.

The Reagan administration failed to secure the adoption of the most visible portions of its New Federalism program, but by shifting federal government priorities, reorganizing existing grant programs, and reducing federal domestic expenditures as a proportion of the total federal budget, it did succeed in introducing new attitudes among state and local officials and their constituents. The latter learned that it was no longer possible to turn to Washington for solutions to most of their problems and that, therefore, it was necessary to rely on their own efforts. All this was

8. U.S. Advisory Commission on Intergovernmental Relations, *State Constitutions in the Federal System* (Washington, DC: Advisory Commission on Intergovernmental Relations, 1989); John Kincaid, ed., *State Constitutions in a Federal System,* vol. 496, *The Annals* of the American Academy of Political and Social Science (Mar. 1988).

9. *National League of Cities v. Usery,* 426 U.S. 833 (1976).

accompanied by a shift in the orientation of the federal departments and regulatory agencies in favor of loosening or reducing federal regulation of state and local activities and oversight of intergovernmental programs.[10]

On the other hand, the Reagan administration did not succeed in restoring anything approximating dual federalism, even in the limited areas in which it made proposals. Quite to the contrary, the general sense that cooperative federalism was the only kind of federalism possible was much strengthened from both directions, that is to say, among those who would have hoped for more federal activity and those who hoped for less.

Moreover, whenever an issue came forward in which an increased federal role was perceived by the administration to be beneficial to its interests, it acted in what has by now become the usual way of opting for the expansion of federal powers. Three examples of this will suffice: the federal act allowing tandem trailer-trucks on most federally aided highways, thereby preempting state standards; the enactment of a requirement that states raise the minimum drinking age to 21 or lose a percentage of their federal highway funds; and further federal preemption of state banking laws, thereby initiating a process of nationalization of the banking system. Still, all told, the Reagan administration pointed the United States in a new direction. In doing so, it galvanized and focused the shift that had begun to be evident even earlier.

A NEW DIRECTION

The twentieth century has been a time in which objective conditions have fostered centralization. Whether the states and localities acted responsibly or not in meeting the century's challenges, they found the federal government stepping in. Especially during the first postwar generation (1946–76), there was an environment basis for centralization. The nation's economic system became increasingly centralized as locally owned firms were purchased by national—and multinational—corporations. The civil rights revolution led to substantial federal intervention in the legal and educational systems. Even organized religion underwent centralization as the various denominations developed strong national offices with extensive bureaucracies. The country's mass communications system, which so influences the public, led the pack toward an almost exclusive focus on Washington as the single center of political power.[11]

There are many signs that objective conditions in the twenty-first century will require different responses. Conditions of size and scale will reduce the utility of the federal government as a problem solver and increase that of the states. The idea that new models of intergovernmental, interorganizational, and public-private activity are needed has attracted increasing attention across the entire political spectrum, from Robert Reich's *Next American Frontier* to John Naisbit's *Megatrends*[12] and from conservative advocates of old-fashioned

---

10. Richard S. Williamson, *Reagan's Federalism: Reagan's Efforts to Decentralize Government* (Lanham, MD: University Press of America and Center for the Study of Federalism, 1990); Richard P. Nathan and Fred C. Doolittle, *Reagan and the States* (Princeton, NJ: Princeton University Press, 1987); David A. Caputo, Richard L. Cole, and Delbert A. Taebel, eds., *Assessing New Federalism*, vol. 16, *Publius: The Journal of Federalism* (Winter 1986).

11. Daniel J. Elazar. "Cursed by Bigness or Toward a Post-Technocratic Federalism," *Publius: The Journal of Federalism*, 3:239 (Fall 1973).

12. Robert Reich, *The Next American Frontier* (New York: Penguin, 1983): John Naisbit, *Megatrends: Ten New Directions Transforming Our Lives,* 6th ed. (New York: Warner, 1983).

states' rights to environmentalists interested in the greening of America. Even ten years ago, similar ideas, whatever their intellectual value, ran against the realities of American civil society.

By the late 1980s, concrete changes in the thrust toward centralization had become evident. While the trend toward further integration of the national economy has not abated—witness the movement toward nationwide interstate banking—America's new economic concerns focus on industrial redevelopment and improving foreign markets. Both are spheres in which the states have played and are likely to continue to play a prominent role over-lapping into international relations, constitutionally a federal preserve.[13]

The federal role in the nation's education system—in everything but civil rights matters—had begun to decline by the mid-1970s. During the Reagan administration, federal intervention in state and local affairs on civil rights matters also diminished, first in the actions of the executive branch and most recently in U.S. Supreme Court decisions. Moreover, recent criticism of the results of the American education system has led to greater state involvement in funding and setting minimum educational requirements and achievement standards. What seems to be emerging is a combination of an increased variety of educational options locally, both public and private, often on a nonterritorial basis, coupled with state standard setting to establish certain basic requirements for all who pass through the schools.

Noncentralization has come back even more strongly to the religious sphere. The transfer of power to the national offices of the mainstream denominations had stopped by the early 1970s as church members voted with

their feet against the policies of those bodies. Since then, the national offices have retreated, and the great national seminaries have lost much of their influence. The revival of fundamentalism, which tends to be highly localistic or, failing that, based upon individual evangelists with their own regional or national followings, has increased noncentralization in the religious sphere. As fundamentalists became involved in politics, they brought some of that noncentralization with them. Even when they seek national solutions, by and large their national political activity has been devoted to repealing federal policies that interfere with what earlier had been considered issues in the domain of the states, such as abortion and school prayer.

Communications is the sphere in which there has been the least amount of change. Political news, especially in the electronic media, still seems to be heavily national in orientation, flowing from Washington and concentrating on the White House. In this respect, the media, following the line of least resistance, have lagged behind the overall trends in American society. In doing so, they have lost the confidence of the American people. Cable television offers the promise of more public affairs programs that do not originate in Washington or New York, even if that promise has not yet been fulfilled.

What is characteristic of this new noncentralization is that it does not represent a retreat from nationalization to an older style of territorial democracy but a movement to a new stage that combines territorially based and nonterritorially based actors in a mulidimensional matrix. Technological change has made much of the old centralization obsolete, or is rapidly doing so, but the new technology

13. Ivo D. Duchacek, ed., *Federated States and International Relations*, vol. 14, *Publius: The Journal of Federalism* (Fall 1984); John Kincaid, "State Offices in Europe," *Comparative State Politics Newsletter*, 6:22 (Aug. 1985).

is certainly not restoring the simpler territorial democracy of a more rural age. American civil society is becoming more multidimensional than ever, having to accommodate great diversity in an urbanized environment, people with different life-styles rubbing shoulders with one another as well as different stages of economic growth, educational aspiration, religious commitment, and social group expression.

If the system has become too complex simply to turn things back to the states, it has also become too complex simply to rely upon the federal government. There are too many forces in a country of 250 million people spread over 3.5 million square miles. States, localities, and sections offer points of identification and expression that have vitality in their own right and offer real opportunities to deal with the challenges of a multidimensional society.

Changes in the patterns of urban settlement will continue to reinforce that trend. At the beginning of the century, urbanization had encouraged centralization; at mid-century, metropolitanization helped to shift government in the direction of decentralization. Now the spread of low-density urban settlement in the countryside is restoring the impulse for noncentralization.[14] Finally, the closer integration of an international community whose members will increasingly rely on federal principles in their own organization will increase the international role of the states, including a closer relationship with their counterparts in other federal systems. Today over 70 percent of the world's population lives under federal arrangements of one kind or another, from the United States of America to the European Community. The 160-plus politically sovereign states are interacting with the 300-plus federal states in ways that are diminishing the differences between them.[15]

NEW DIMENSIONS AND FIRST PRINCIPLES

In order to cope with these new dimensions, it is necessary to go back to first principles—not for formulas, but to reexamine them and to discover how they can help us deal with the new environment that must be served by the American federal system.

First and foremost, we must recall that the nation and each of the 50 states is a polity in its own right, in the fullest sense. While the federal and state governments may serve each other in some administrative capacity by mutual agreement, neither is designed to be the administrative arm of the other per se.[16] Together they form a governmental matrix established by the American people, not a power pyramid with the federal government on top, the states in the middle, local governments on the bottom, and—by implication—the pyramid as a whole resting on the backs of the people. The general government—that nineteenth-century term has great merit for its precision and the clarity it brings to the subject—sets the framework for the matrix as a whole by defining and delineating the largest arena. The states, whose boundaries are constitutionally fixed, provide the basic decision-making arenas within the matrix. Both together provide the constitutional basis for the diffusion of powers necessary to prevent hierarchical

14. Cf. John Herbers, *The New American Heartland* (New York: New York Times Books, 1986).

15. Daniel J. Elazar, *Exploring Federalism* (Tuscaloosa: University of Alabama Press, 1987).

16. Daniel J. Elazar, "The Rebirth of Federalism: The Future Role of the States as Polities in the Federal System," *Commonsense,* 4:1–8 (1981).

domination, given the human penchant for hierarchies.[17]

Since the beginning of the Republic, the elements in the matrix have worked together to develop common policies and programs, with most important actors being involved, through the political process, in most important details of most steps in problem definition, planning, programming, budgeting, implementation, and evaluation of most policies of mutual interest to them. Empirically, students of federalism pointed this out more than two decades ago, through detailed case studies of federalism, the party political process, and the role of Congress, particularly in the quadrangle that links state—and/or local—administrators, their federal counterparts, their congressional representatives, and their common professional associations or interest groups.[18] Congressional-administrative preclearance of proposed legislation and administrative regulations is a regular feature of American government and has been since 1790. Plans for programs are developed, more often than not, in consultation with representatives of the interested parties. Unfortunately, the inroads of the new hierarchies into the manner in which all this is done has put the traditional system in jeopardy.

The problem for federalism, then, is not that the federal and state governments must cooperate in the governance of the country, but that, in the 1960s, the federal government, under the guise of cooperative federalism, changed its role from being supportive—from playing a backstopping role—to being coercive and even preemptive.

Recognizing the interlocking character of the federal system, a proper theory of federalism suggests that the federal government should only deal with (1) the application of the framing principles of the United States Constitution; (2) extraterritorial issues, such as foreign affairs and defense; (3) boundary questions between the constituent entities of the federal system; and (4) backstopping the states and their localities in matters of national concern. It need not—indeed, should not—deal with any of these on an exclusive or preemptive basis. It is clear that this coercive federalism has failed. Coercion of the states and localities not only leads to a strong negative reaction on the part of the principals involved and the public in general but also is tied closely with the failure of managerialism, the ideology of those who sought to replace traditional federalism with a power pyramid.

REFOCUSING ON THE STATES

There was a time when the American public—reformers and conservatives, interested parties of all kinds—looked to their states as the arenas in which to fight great battles and do great things. Indeed, that was the case even though American society was in many respects a national society from the first and certainly became more intertwined nationwide in the wake of the Industrial Revolution. Now that is happening again. The New Deal quite properly represented a recognition that the states could not go it alone, at least not after the U.S. Supreme Court had so limited their powers that reform was stymied unless Congress acted. But—to carry the principles of the New Deal to absurd extremes—to assume that, because the states cannot go it alone in some things, they cannot go it alone in any or that

17. Daniel J. Elazar, *American Federalism: A View from the States,* 3d ed. (New York: Harper & Row, 1984).

18. Daniel J. Elazar, *The American Partnership* (Chicago: University of Chicago Press, 1962); Morton Grodzins, *The American System,* ed. Daniel J. Elazar (Chicago: Rand McNally, 1966).

they cannot lead in those things that are done cooperatively is simply to misread American reality and American aspirations.

On the other hand, because powers really are diffused throughout the matrix, usually in a rather untidy way, it is very difficult to decide to transfer power from Washington. In the past, presidents who tried to do so discovered that in order to decentralize, they first had to centralize. Today, in an age of hierarchy assumers, a president can be a successful centralizer to a great degree, but there is no guarantee that an administration strong enough to overcome the noncentralization inherent in the system will so willingly part with hard-won powers. For those who believe in the utility and virtues of federalism, the substitution of decentralization for noncentralization is not an advance. The Reagan administration grasped the idea apparently lost in the previous generation that while, under normal circumstances, the elements in the matrix do work together to develop common policies and programs, the secret of a successful federal system lies precisely in the right of the elements not to act under certain conditions.

FEDERALISM AND THE CURSES OF BIGNESS

Through bitter experience, it has been discovered that, in very large bureaucracies, coordination is well-nigh impossible at the top because the people on the top can barely control and are frequently at the mercy of their own organizations. Moreover, in a system of interlocking arenas—which is what exists in the United States despite all the talk about levels—there is no real top to do the coordinating. Similarly, students of public administration have begun to note the failure of

managerial techniques widely touted as means to come to grips with contemporary problems. Certainly, the idea that such techniques would automatically result in efficiency and economy has long since gone by the boards. We now know how bureaucracies create their own inefficiencies and diseconomies. Beyond that, there has been a discovery that the new management techniques—the planning-programming-budgeting system and zero-based budgeting are prime examples—often are inappropriate to the political arena with its lack of precise, agreed-upon goals and its basic purposes of conciliating the irreconcilable and managing conflict.

On a different but closely related plane, Americans are beginning to sense the failure of consumerism, namely, the redefinition of people primarily as consumers and their institutions primarily as vehicles for the satisfaction of consumer wants. At the very least, the redefinition of government as a service-delivery mechanism and citizens as consumers leads to an unmanageable acceleration of public demands.[19] It also leads to the evaluation of all institutions by a set of standards that, being human institutions, they are bound not to meet. Not the least of the problems of the consumer model is the abandonment of the principle that people have responsibilities as well as rights, and that they have obligations to each other, if not to the polity in the abstract, which, when neglected, imperil democracy by undermining its very foundations.

Simultaneously, the actions of the U.S. Supreme Court and, to some extent, the Congress offer vigorous testimony to the danger faced by the states and the federal system, demonstrating once again the need for strong constitutional protections for federalism even where there is the best will in the world on

19. Cf. Norton E. Long, "The Three Citizenships," *The Journal of Federalism,* 6:13–32 (Spring 1976).

the part of those actively engaged in the political arena to be good federalists.[20] The founding fathers understood this need, which is why they wrote such protections into the Constitution.

The possibilities of an increased role for the states are better for yet another reason. Until the mid-1970s, states' rights were inevitably associated with arguments on behalf of slavery, racial segregation, and discrimination against nonwhites. However erroneous such arguments may have been in principle, in practice states' rights were used effectively as a shield for racism and discrimination. That problem has been overcome as a constitutional issue. It is clear that the federal Constitution and, for that matter, the vast majority of state constitutions are color-blind. This is the constitutionally correct position in a civil society dedicated to the proposition that "all men are created equal and endowed by their Creator with certain inalienable rights." For the first time in American history, believers in federalism can argue that protecting the rights of the states is important for the sake of liberty and is not entangled with racism and discrimination. Hence, as the United States moves into the third century of American federalism, within the limits of a reality that will never conform as closely to our models as we would like and that might not pass certain aesthetic tests, there is a serious opportunity to strengthen the basic noncentralization of the American system in new ways.

20. John Kincaid, "A Proposal to Strengthen Federalism," *Journal of State Government,* 62: 36–45 (Jan.–Feb. 1989).

Federal Aid to States and Local Governments

14
Lobbying for the Good Old Days
Jonathan Walters

With substantial federal aid cutbacks to state and local governments, Washington-based lobbies representing governors, mayors, counties, and local governments are reconsidering their goals and objectives. Federal cuts have reduced their influence. Jonathan Walters interviewed past and present leaders of the National League of Cities, the U.S. Conference of Mayors, the National Association of Counties, and the National Governors' Association. City and county interest groups are trying to restore funding, delay new federal regulatory mandates, and maintain traditional programs from the federal government. The governors' group has a different agenda. What is it? Walters also talked to a former mayor, John Mercer, who is promoting a new Office of Federalism. How would this clearinghouse assist states and localities? Why is it opposed by state and local interest groups?

At 1313 E. 60th St. on Chicago's South Side, at the edge of the University of Chicago campus, stands a chunky, gray stone building that has been there since the turn of the century. Its mass reflects the stolid, unpretentious work that once went on inside. It was the headquarters of the Public Administration Clearinghouse, established in the early 1920s to help mayors, city councils, governors and state legislatures do a better job.

"1313" was a heartland headquarters for a grass-roots cause. It was the birthplace of the National League of Cities and housed the organizations from which the National Governors' Association and the National Conference of State Legislatures eventually sprang.

Today the work of such groups, and the setting of some of them, has changed dramatically. The National Governors' Association sits at the foot of Capitol Hill in Washington, in the Hall of the States, a marble and glass monument to the NGA's shift in focus from simple membership service to monitoring and lobbying the federal government. Just a few blocks away is the new glass-enclosed headquarters of the National League of Cities, equidistant between the Capitol and the White House and likewise well-positioned to wield influence. Visitors enter a two-story main lobby dominated by the group's name spelled out in gigantic block letters sweeping along a central staircase. The effect is impressive, bespeaking power and importance.

Among members of those organizations, however, a debate is going on about just how powerful and important they really are, and whether it is time for some institutional soul-searching. In the past decade, as federal grant programs have been slashed and more governmental work—and cost—has been dumped back onto states and localities, the influence of their government interest groups over Washington has waned considerably. Many of their past leaders—and some who are active now—argue that this is the time to embark on a major shift and return to their roots, to the role they once played at 1313 E. 60th St., providing the information and the ideas that helped members do their jobs.

George Latimer, former mayor of St. Paul, Minnesota, completed his term as president of the National League of Cities in 1984. He was convinced by then that the group was facing in the wrong direction. "It struck me," he says, "that the shift away from Washington was occurring, and that it had been since about 1978. We never really responded to that curve. We continued to act as though all the action was in Washington.

One hears similar complaints from the rank and file. Tom Jones, information officer for Shelby County, Tennessee (Memphis), insists that what counties need most is information about how other counties are solving their problems. He wants his organization, the National Association of Counties, to provide it. But it doesn't. He worries that its staff has been mesmerized by the federal government: "They see Washington as the center of the universe."

The leaders of these groups have heard all those arguments. "We are an urban advocacy organization." says Tom Cochran, executive director of the United States Conference of Mayors, one of the most ardently Washington-focused government interest groups in the city. In Cochran's view, it is the primary job

of the conference to keep Washington's feet to the fire and alert members to federal action.

The debate over this issue is more intense among the local interest groups than among the ones speaking for states. The governors' association has always been shaped as much by the personalities of its 50 members as by its Washington presence. The National Conference of State Legislatures has never had more than a mild case of Potomac Fever; its national headquarters is in Denver. But as the era of federal disengagement enters its second decade, the question of purpose is one that all these groups, state as well as local, are having to confront. Should Washington remain the center of their universe when the federal government is all but ordering them to solve their own problems with their own money?

To those who argue for a shift in focus, there is no better symbol of the problem than the past decade of effort by cities and counties to resurrect federal revenue sharing. The critics consider it a long and futile run at the federal treasury that has done little more than drain the groups' resources while sticking them with a "tin-cup" reputation. The National League of Cities still lists revenue sharing as a category of domestic spending in some current documents. Former Phoenix Mayor Terry Goddard, who was president of the league in 1989, argues that the organization has lost precious years clamoring for the return of revenue sharing, for example, when it probably should have been teaching cities how to cope with the loss.

Meanwhile, as a string of other programs, such as Urban Development Action Grants and Comprehensive Employment Training Act public jobs, were eliminated, the interest groups merely turned up the decibel level and poured new resources into trying to get the programs back. The programs have not come back. League of Cities figures show that federal grants to local government have declined from about $50 billion to about $19 billion in the past 10 years. Meanwhile, the interest groups have been unable to make any progress on some important Washington issues that do not involve any cost to the federal government, such as re-regulation of cable TV (which holds out the prospect of higher licensing fees to cities) and taxation of interstate mail order sales, which is money waiting to be put in the bank for states and localities.

A glance through the pages of *Nation's Cities Weekly, County News* or *U.S. Mayor* provides some unmistakable clues to what the interest groups are interested in. There are articles about federal defense spending, about the details of the Gramm-Rudman law, about the effort to reduce capital gains taxes. *County News* recently ran a front-page story showing President Bush signing a declaration of "National County Government Week," to celebrate the job counties do in governing. Inside the paper, story after story discussed ways in which the administration is actually forcing counties to do their governing with less and less federal support.

A recent front-page story in *Nation's Cities Weekly* relates league president Sidney Barthelemy's trip to Washington "to meet with President George Bush" on the president's "America 2000" education plan. In fact, there was no private meeting. Barthelemy was just one of the crowd assembled to hear the president lay out a tentative plan for abstract educational goals that mean little to those running schools right now. There is little in any of these papers about how localities are coping with their current problems, or much on new solutions they might want to try.

The Mayor's Conference, true to its current and unrelenting assault-on-Washington approach, has always been based in the nation's capital. It was founded there in 1932 with the encouragement of Franklin D. Roosevelt, who wanted to cement his relationship with the big-city political machines that helped elect him.

But the other interest groups have a different history. They did not start out obsessed with the federal government. They were drawn in gradually as the federal role in state and local political life kept expanding. In 1954, the National League of Cities (originally the American Municipal Association) moved to Washington from Chicago, to be followed soon after by the National Association of Counties. The states held off longer. It was not until 1967 that the National Governors' Association arrived, splitting off from the Council of State Governments, which remains as an apolitical, technical assistance and research group based in Lexington, Kentucky.

There is still a great deal going on in Washington for these groups to be concerned with. The federal government will funnel more than $130 billion to states and localities this year, and continues to impose new and burdensome mandates, often without the funds to implement them. None of the major government interest groups could afford not to have a Washington presence. But increasingly, their influence is at the margins: pushing to avoid decimation of existing programs and fighting for delays in the implementation of environmental and health-related mandates. "It's been a rear-guard action," Terry Goddard concedes.

Goddard, Latimer and other critics say the governmental entity that localities ought to be most concerned about these days—and lobbying hardest—is states. Total state aid to localities increased more than 60 percent between 1982 and 1988, from $88 billion to nearly $143 billion, according to the National Association of State Budget Officers. The number of people on state staffs increased from 3.5 million in 1978 to more than 4.2 million in 1988. Annual state expenditures, meanwhile, rose from nearly $204 billion in 1978 to almost $585 billion in 1988. In the process, states have taken on an ever-expanding menu of responsibilities.

John Thomas, who recently resigned as executive director of the National Association of Counties and now heads the American Society for Public Administration, thinks this is the crucial issue. "County governments live and die at the state legislature," he says. "What Congress does to us is irrelevant in many ways."

Latimer, likewise, believes national organizations should offer localities more advice and technical assistance in dealing with state legislatures and state bureaucracies. "Even with all the complexity of Washington," he says, "it's still simpler working there than trying to take on 50 states. So I think the tendency of national staff is to leave the states alone. I think that is altogether a mistake, that we could have more influence if they focused on state and local activities."

There are clear reasons why the league, the mayors' conference and the counties' association have a hard time seeing it that way. They were the groups that arrived in Washington first; they were the big winners when federal programs for urban redevelopment started up in earnest in the 1960s. After decades as political creatures of the states, dependent on legislatures for their livelihood and their very existence, localities suddenly found themselves participants in the world of domestic policy, treated as seriously by Washington as the states in whose shadow they had always lived.

President Nixon delivered an added bonus to the local organizations in the 1970s when he turned to them for help in implementing the grant programs. Millions of dollars were funneled to the league, the mayors' conference and the counties' association for research and technical assistance. The money was used by the groups to help localities come up with ideas and programs for using the federal money, and to help them stay true to the strings that were attached to it.

The era of urban programs had less effect on the state organizations. Both the governors' association and the National Conference of State Legislatures spent most of the Johnson and Nixon years going about their regular business of helping their membership succeed at state government. These groups did score heavily with the passage of federal revenue sharing to states in 1972. They expanded their Washington operations and began devoting more of their resources to mining the federal government for funds.

Proportionately, though, it was the local organizations that were changed the most by federal assistance. So it was that when the cuts came in the 1980s, it was not only the localities that were hurt—it was the groups representing them. In the early 1980s, the Washington staff of the National Association of Counties went from 140 to 60. The National League of Cities cut back from about 120 to 65; the mayors' conference from 120 to about 75.

All three groups insulated their lobbying operations from the cutback. Lobbyists would be needed, after all, to recoup the losses. The mayors' conference has the same number of lobbyists today that it did when federal funding was at its peak. "It was technical services that got cut," says Tom Cochran, the executive director.

To the extent that the National Governors' Association developed a Washington focus in the '80s, it was not built around the quest for federal help. It was built around the effort to create a personal showcase in national politics and policy debate for its 50 members, and especially for its chairmen, who became the object of increasing media attention during their single-year terms. Lamar Alexander, chairman of the governors' association in 1986, inaugurated the practice of having the association specialize in research on a single topic each year; his topic was education. The effort helped give Alexander publicity and prestige he has carried with him ever since and also helped make him Secretary of Education earlier this year.

By the mid-1980s, the states, like the cities and counties, were comfortably ensconced in Washington headquarters buildings that bespoke the importance of the federal connection. But the connection was not quite the same for the states as it was for the localities. When it came to federal aid, the balance was tilting further toward the states every year. Even programs aimed ultimately at benefiting the localities were increasingly funneled through the states. In 1980, 25 percent of total federal grants went to localities, 75 percent to states. By 1988 it was 15 and 85.

That may or may not be one reason why the Washington organizations of the states have been considerably more muted during recent years in their denunciations of the federal aid cutbacks. Both Bill Pound, executive director of the state legislators' conference, and Ray Scheppach, executive director of the governors' association, like to point out that their groups were favoring a reduced federal deficit while the local organizations were clamoring for more federal aid. This is not an easy attitude for many of the locals to accept, as it was the localities that were most directly affected by the cuts and had to deal most directly with the consequences.

The whole situation has clearly left the organizations that represent the localities in a tough position: Should they accept the assumption that their members need to be more self-sufficient, and return to the role they once played in Chicago, when the first priority was providing services to their members; or should they continue to be the "urban advocacy" organizations Tom Cochran is determined to maintain at all costs?

The staying power of that latter view was demonstrated in March at the winter meeting of the National League of Cities in Washington. Mayor Barthelemy of New Orleans, the league president, called on the federal government to declare an operation "Urban Storm" to save the nation's cities. Many of the mayors present, big-city and smaller-city alike, approved of the strategy. "I don't call us 'whiners,'" said Mayor Steve Hettinger of Huntsville, Alabama. "I say we're the dreamers; we try to reflect a vision of what should be." From the anti-Washington faction, however, the reaction was one of sarcasm. "It's always the national agenda," said George Latimer, "even when there is no agenda."

Donald J. Borut, executive director of the league, has said since the start of his tenure last year that he wants his organization to become a showcase for "ideas that work," and to celebrate entrepreneurial local government. He sends at least 20 letters a week to members soliciting examples for such celebration. There has been no organized effort, however, to become a force for generating new ideas, or to be the place where they are given a hard look for real value or transferability. Borut says developing such an analytical capability would be too expensive. Rather, he says, the group is going to concentrate on acting as a conduit for all ideas.

Meanwhile, the traditional Washington focus is symbolized by Frank Shafroth, the league's indefatigable top lobbyist, who since the days of the big federal budget cuts has taken to calling himself "Dr. Doom." Shafroth has never given up his conviction that the federal government has the resources to help troubled cities, if only it had the desire. "We are on course now to spend more than $500 billion to bail out the S&L industry," Shafroth says. "It is clear in this country that where we have the will, dollars are irrelevant."

At the mayors' conference, it is full speed ahead for the traditional priorities—Community Development Block Grants, federally assisted public housing and federal aid for transportation. Cochran says his organization has no real choice but to lobby for those programs. "The governors can go to Hilton Head," he says. "and come up with five-year education plans. But I'm sitting here and the phone is ringing every day and someone has to deal with what is going on with AIDS and drugs. That's the difference in being a mayor and a governor."

Expressed that way, the debate over strategy sounds like an either-or affair. It does not have to be. Tucson Mayor Thomas Volgy, who is active within both the league and the mayors' conference, is looking for ways in which those groups can pursue both missions. He cites, for example, the local economic crises set off by military base closings. "That's a classic situation," Volgy argues, "where the league and the conference need to attack the issue at the federal level, but also provide technical services, to assess the nature of the problem, find local solutions."

In Volgy's view, the local groups have done a good job on this one issue. But he concedes that the resources may not be there to do it on more than a few subjects at the same time. "You need to provide that in 35 different categories, beg, borrow or steal," he says. "We're doing it well on about two. We still have 33 to go."

There are those who think that localities cannot afford to wait, however, and that the groups need to shift their resources accordingly. Among them is John Mercer, former mayor of Sunnyvale, California, now minority counsel to the U.S. Senate's Committee on Governmental Affairs. As a mayor, he says, he was routinely frustrated by the lack of good information available at the local level through the national organizations, and by the lack of

evaluation and analysis of those ideas that were passed along. Typical, he says, was a conference session put on several years ago by the National League of Cities entitled "14 Ways to Raise Revenues." The session drew a standing-room-only crowd. Then the summary of the session was handed out: a list of 14 taxes that localities could increase. "That's not exactly what we had in mind," says Mercer. What Mercer and his colleagues wanted was to learn, for example, how some cities use ground leases of underutilized public property to attract business, "not how to raise taxes," he says.

Terry Goddard, whose term as president of the league ended two years ago, concedes Mercer's point. Even under his own tenure, Goddard says, "the league put out pamphlets that I thought were pretty worthless: everything everyone's ever said about a particular issue," without evaluation or analysis. "What works in Phoenix might fall flat on its face in Des Moines."

Mercer's experience as a mayor has prompted him to push for legislation in Congress creating an Office of Federalism, to act as a clearinghouse for good state and local government ideas. The point, he says, is to create a center that does more than simply pass ideas along for what they are worth. Those that did not hold up under scrutiny would be jettisoned; those that proved out would be packaged in such a way that they could be easily applied. At the other end, the legislation would give states and localities an opportunity to comment to the office on the effects of federal mandates.

Much stands in the way of such an idea, however, including lukewarm support on the part of some of the state and local government interest groups. Don Borut, speaking for the league, formally opposed the Mercer proposal in a letter to the Senate. "I laud and promote any effort that will bring more information to local officials," Borut says, "but it's an issue of credibility. . . . One of the things that is really important is a sense of trust in the source of information. [City officials] look to their peers and colleagues. They will tend to put greater faith in information from another mayor."

There is also, however, a question of pride and political turf. Agreeing to such a clearinghouse represents tacit agreement that the government interest groups are not doing an adequate job of providing services, and perhaps agreement as well that states and localities ought to start counting on the federal government more for ideas than for money.

The idea of a federal information clearinghouse may or may not be the answer. But the opposition to it reflects the difficulty that is likely to confront any organized effort to change the focus of the state and local interest groups. All these groups are staffed at top levels by people who have spent their profes-sional lives learning to understand and operate in Washington. It is not going to be easy to persuade them to face in a different direction. "When these groups are interviewing people for jobs," says John Mercer, "they're not say-ing: 'Do you have expertise in municipal man-agement?' No, it's: 'What do you know about the Hill?' "

But it is not just the staffs in Washington that are resistant to change: It is, in many cases, the membership as well. They, too, have learned to view the American political system as dominated by the federal govern-ment. John Thomas learned that lesson as di-rector of the National Association of Counties. "People in county governments know that the states are where the action is," he says, "but they don't like to admit that. They see their national organization as the way to play in the Washington ball game."

Political Participation: Influencing Government

CHAPTER 5

Interest Groups

Interest groups are essential to democracies for providing the people with effective channels to pressure government for the achievement of specific goals. In our modern, postindustrial, technological age, governments have become so large and complex that individuals, acting alone, often find executives, legislators, and administrators inaccessible and unresponsive. By joining interest groups, citizens are able to pool their concerns and are better able to get their views across to government.

An interest group may be defined as any group of people who organize to advance their political interests and to influence public policy. Interest groups develop around economic issues, in response to government policy, when advocates generate followings around particular issues, and when counterorganizations form in opposition to other groups. The United States has many politically active organizations and associations because of the nation's social diversity, governmental fragmentation, and the weakness of political parties. Interest groups represent nearly every conceivable issue and constituency. The system of separation of powers and checks and balances produces for interest groups many different points of access to government policy makers. The decline of political parties has created a power vacuum that is filled by the increased influence of interest groups at all levels of government. As discussed in Chapter 7, the media has also filled the power vacuum caused by political party decline.

THE DANGER OF FACTIONS

Biased policy objectives can threaten the foundations of a democratic political system. James Madison recognized this problem in *The Federalist,* Number 10 (Article 15) when he warned against the danger of *factions.* These consist of "a number of citizens, whether amounting to a majority or minority of the whole, who are united and actuated by some common impulse of passion, or of interest, adverse to the rights of other citizens, or to the permanent and aggregate interests of the community." Madison claimed that the unequal distribution of property was the major cause of factions. However, government cannot deal with the causes of factions because to do so would interfere with human liberty. Attention must be directed to the effects, which in Madison's view can be controlled by the system of separation of powers and checks and balances.

A modern version of Madison's concern for factions is found in Theodore Lowi's discussion of "interest group liberalism."[1] Lowi analyzes the excessive influence of pressure groups on pubic policy. Lowi's definition of the term "liberal" differs from the designation usually associated with party politics. He considers liberalism comparable to the unrestricted marketplace economics of the early nineteenth century. The policy "liberal" believes that the public interest is best served by the free competition of private interests. Lowi points out that the consequence of group liberalism is the *status quo,* conservative policy.

This occurs because certain interest groups capture and control government agencies without having to compete for policy rewards. By gaining influence through appointments and lobbying, interest groups do not have to compete for policy rewards. For example, retired military officers go to work for defense contractors and have an inside track to their former colleagues in the Pentagon. Public policy thus serves only the corporate or other entrenched elites. Administrative agencies tied to these elites are subject to the pressures of the powerful interests. This creates serious obstacles to policy change.

According to Lowi's concept, interest group liberalism results in strong pressure groups but a fragmented and weak government. This is a condition of hyperpluralism. The proliferation of interest groups causes paralysis in national policy making. Government officials attempt to respond favorably to various group demands with the result that conflicting pressures cancel out incompatible policy goals. Government policy becomes confusing, and contradictory.

GROUP THEORY OF POLITICS: ELITIST BIAS

Interest groups can be understood by a group theory of politics. According to E. E. Schattschneider (Article 16), group theory assumes that the struggle between contending groups produces public policy. Individuals with common interests and goals join together to bring their demands to the attention of government. Public policy represents the outcome of bargaining, negotiation, and compromise between different groups, each of which seeks to maximize its power and influence. Coalitions are formed between policy makers and interest groups in order to achieve agreement on the content of public policy. However, Schattschneider argues that any organization is a "mobilization of bias." Special interest groups represent only a narrow range of political bias. In fact, the pressure system has an upper-class bias which excludes most citizens. It is unbalanced in favor of a small minority. Consequently, while the people may belong to many different organizations, they rarely participate in developing policy proposals. This is particularly a problem with the representatives of interest group leaders acting on behalf of the membership and lobbying tactics employed in government.

Competing Interpretations of Interest Group Power

Schattschneider argues that interest groups are dominated by an elite bias. In addition to elitism, there are three other explanations of how they develop and exercise influence. These include pluralism, democratic elitism, and hyperpluralism.

Elitism is said to exist when small and unrepresentative groups exercise a disproportionate share of power. Several writers have argued that American politics is dominated by an "establishment" or "power structure" of relatively few actors who make the key decisions. Wealth, political influence, or bureaucratic expertise are sources of elite power. Many years ago, C. Wright Mills argued in *The Power Elite* (1956) that the United States is ruled by an interlocking power elite comprised of the military, big corporations, and political-governmental experts in the executive branch. Karl Marx argued that capitalists controlled national economies by exploiting the working classes. Max Weber found bureaucratic power dominant in Western nations. Elite dominance is found in certain policy-making arenas, such as national defense, national security, and foreign affairs.

Elitism is evident in American economic and political institutions. According to Thomas R. Dye, power is concentrated in 100 corporations which control more than half of the nation's industrial assets; fifty foundations which control 40 percent of all foundation assets; twenty-five universities which control two-thirds of all private endowment funds; and the three major television and cable news networks that account for 90 percent of national news reaching the public. Elite theorists argue that the most powerful citizens control and make public policy. Dye identified 7,314 elites in corporations, the media, law, foundations, the military, and cultural areas. About 40 percent of the top elite held government positions at some time during their careers.[2]

Pluralism exists when power is shared among representative sectors of the population, when public policy is shaped by a wide range of competing groups, when no single group dominates others, and when benefits from public policy are widely shared in society. Pluralism is generally associated with the American system of separation of powers and checks and balances. Pluralists argue that American government is fragmented and decentralized, thereby providing many different points of access to government decision makers. The federal system is a good example of the decentralization of power in a pluralistic nation (see Chapter 4). Political office seekers need to form coalitions of diverse groups in order to get elected. Government officials need to bargain, negotiate, and compromise in achieving their public-policy goals.

Are interest groups dominated by elites or is pluralism more evident? According to Thomas R. Dye and L. Harmon Zeigler, democratic elitism best explains how interest groups operate. In contrast to Mills's notion of a conspiratorial or selfish elite, Dye and Zeigler take the position that the top leadership groups act on behalf of the people. The irony of democracy, they observe, is that "elites must govern wisely if government 'by the people' is to survive."[3] Elites are not opposed to popular sovereignty; in fact, they may act in the public interest and actively seek to improve the welfare of the masses. But elites clearly differ from the masses in the amount of power and resources at their disposal. Elites maintain stability. They have the power to act when the masses are poorly informed, passive, and apathetic; and elites generally agree on the "rules of the game" of their organizations and government.

Other theorists argue that American politics can best be explained by hyperpluralism, an exaggerated form of power decentralization and fragmentation characterized by an excessive number of interest groups that refuse to bargain, compromise, and negotiate to resolve disputes. Single-issue groups demand support for their stand on issues and condemn opponents who refuse to agree with them. In recent years, these have included pro- and anti-abortion groups, pro- and anti-gun-control groups, and pro- and anti-nuclear groups. Such groups make government subordinate to their demands by moving from one arena to the next until they win. Many times, they end up in the state and federal courts, using litigation to pressure executives, legislatures, and administrators. Hyperpluralism can result in relatively weak and ineffective government because of the intensity and political determination of single-minded groups.

LOBBYING STRATEGIES AND TACTICS

When interest groups influence public policy, they employ pressure strategies and lobbying tactics. Strategies may be positive, for example, seeking benefits on behalf of members, or negative—trying to prevent government from acting on matters deemed harmful to the group. For example, big business (such as the U.S. Chamber of Commerce or any large corporation) and organized labor (the AFL-CIO or the United Automobile Workers) frequently pressure government on such specific matters as tax benefits, subsidies, investment incentives, collective bargaining, and minimum wages. As a government responds to these demands, the special interest groups achieve results for their constituencies that would not be possible otherwise. The effectiveness of interest group demands depends on their focus on a specific policy area, communication with public officials, and the strength of organizational skills. Additionally, such groups are enhanced by the size of membership, access to monetary and other resources, cohesiveness, leadership skills, and the receptivity of public officials to their demands.

Publicity, lobbying and pressure are tactics used by interest groups to achieve their objectives. Organized interests seek to mold public opinion to a point of view that creates a favorable image or which assists the groups in attaining particular legislative goals. In this sense, interest groups employ campaigning methods to protect or obtain a public-policy objective. For example, the American Medical Association was highly successful for many years in preventing the enactment of medical care for the elderly by organizing a skillful propaganda campaign which attacked Medicare as "socialized medicine." The AMA provided literature to physicians for display in their waiting rooms, took out paid advertisements in newspapers and magazines, and engaged in massive letter-writing campaigns to congressional representatives. Additionally, the AMA took sides in electoral contests by offering campaign funds to legislators who opposed the various Medicare bills.

Interest groups also engage in direct lobbying with legislators. Almost every important interest group maintains headquarters in Washington from which lobbyists are sent to Congress to discuss legislative proposals. When the lobbyist testifies before a congressional committee, offers advice on a bill, or provides dinners, cocktail parties, and other amenities, he or she is attempting to influence legislators to a point of view favored by the lobbyist's group. Lobbying is most effective on issues of a technical or specialized nature. On such matters, the lobbyist can provide expertise, information, and advice to legislators and the bureaucracy. At the national level, the president, Congress, and the voters (or public opinion) are more influential in initiating policy proposals, particularly on those matters of nationwide concern.

There is a very close relationship between interest groups and government policy makers. When they collaborate with each other iron triangles, or policy subgovernments, result. These are political alliances uniting members of a government agency, a congressional committee or subcommittee, and an interest group with similar views and preferences in the same area of public policy. Iron triangles or subgovernments develop around legal, economic, political, and social considerations. Various congressional enactments and executive orders guarantee interest group representation on governmental advisory committees. Politically, the president identifies leading group personnel to serve as cabinet-level secretaries or assistant secretaries. The interest group can have close economic and social contacts with governmental agencies which deal directly with their needs. The military-industrial complex is a good example, particularly in the areas of defense contracts and weapons systems. The Pentagon is accustomed to dealing with small groups of aerospace and other corporate firms in awarding huge contracts to the private sector.

A crucial problem developing from these relationships is "cooptation," which occurs when the governmental agency becomes a captive of the organized private groups. Public policy becomes a product of very narrow interest group demands. The governmental agency may have to yield control over some of its programs to retain support for other policy goals.

Lobbyists at Work: Old Breed Versus New Breed

Congress, the president, and the federal bureaucracy are pressured by many interest groups. Lobbying activity increased dramatically in the 1980s. In 1987, the number of officially registered Washington lobbyists was more than 23,000, up from 5,600 in 1981. More importantly, there are another fifty or sixty thousand lobbyists and workers in non-government law firms and trade association offices.

According to Hedrick Smith (Article 17), Washington lobbyists can be classified into two broad categories: old and new breed. Old-breed lobbyists are members of top law firms and former government officials who have set up private consulting firms in the nation's capital. These people play retail politics. They establish social contacts with federal officials and seek access to news on various policies, decisions, and pending legislation. They sell their influence to clients who want to get inside information on these matters.

In the 1980s, the new-breed form of lobbying began to replace the traditional approach. While seeking the same kinds of access as the old-breed lobbyists, the new-breed uses more organized, direct pressure campaigns, usually directed at legislators. This "wholesale politics" includes grassroots coalitions, public relations campaigns, television advertisements, and mass mailings. In effect, the new-breed lobbyists are selling their clients promotional marketing, through which legislators and the executive branch are convinced to act or not act on certain policies and pending legislation. The goal is to inundate federal officials with a mass of pro- or anti-campaign material, aimed at achieving the client's goals.

When new-breed lobbying is combined with interest group political action committee (PAC) contributions to federal officials, the combined effect can be very powerful. PAC influence will be discussed in Chapter 7.

Interest Group Pressure Campaigns

Some policy issues mobilize enormous interest group pressure campaigns in Washington. For many years, proposed gun control legislation brought out the membership of the National Rifle Association to oppose it. The NRA has long been recognized as one of the most powerful single-issue lobbies in national politics. Founded in 1871 by National Guard officers to improve citizen marksmanship, the NRA has 2.6 million members, a $60 million annual budget, and vigorous support from its members. Both Presidents Reagan and Bush are lifetime members of the NRA.

Before 1990, the only meaningful gun control legislation was approved in 1968, following the assassinations of Senator Robert Kennedy and the Reverend Dr. Martin Luther King, Jr. It restricted the sale of handguns and sawed-off shotguns and required gun dealers to keep detailed records of firearm buyers. Importation of handgun components was prohibited.

Otherwise, the NRA succeeded in protecting its claim that the Second Amendment protects the right of every citizen "to keep and bear arms." The NRA conveniently ignored the introductory words of this amendment, "A well-regulated militia, being necessary to the security of a free State. . . ."

Two developments challenged the NRA's monopoly lobbying position against gun control. First, a wave of drug-related crime against the police included the use of rapid-fire semiautomatic weapons, against which the police were at a serious disadvantage. Also, assault weapons were increasingly killing large numbers of people. Law enforcement officials began to lobby for federal and state prohibitions against assault weapons. In 1990, President Bush and Congress agreed to prohibit the manufacture and sale of several types of these weapons.

A second development that threatened the NRA is explained in Article 18. The NRA's near-monopoly voice against gun control was challenged by Sarah and James Brady. Unlike other proponents of gun control, the Bradys had considerable prestige and sympathy from President Bush and Congress. Why? Jim Brady, President Reagan's press secretary, was nearly killed in 1981 when John Hinckley tried to assassinate the chief executive. Brady suffered severe brain damage and was confined to a wheelchair.

Sarah Brady became active in Handgun Control, a lobby group opposing the NRA. Sarah and Jim Brady organized a personal interest group campaign effort to achieve enactment of the Brady bill, a required seven-day waiting period to purchase handguns. When President Reagan endorsed the Brady bill in March 1991, it gained momentum in Congress. Subsequently, Congress approved the Brady bill, but President Bush threatened to veto it because it was part of an omnibus crime bill which contained provisions the President did not want.

Wayne King's portrait of the Bradys' efforts in Article 18 tell us that personal lobbying requires enormous commitment, travel, and persuasive skills. The Bradys needed to combine both the old- and new-breed types of lobbying efforts discussed by Hedrick Smith in Article 17.

CONCLUSION: INTEREST GROUP PROS AND CONS

Interest group power has generated considerable debate in recent years. Their formidable resources—membership size, financial clout, organization, and intensity on issues—have led many people to conclude that interest groups have disproportionate influence on public policy. Interest groups are attacked as elitist, single-minded, intrusive, and power hungry. PACs may be corrupting U.S. elections through excessive campaign contributions. Defenders argue that individuals, acting alone, cannot effectively influence public policy without collective action. Nearly everyone belongs to some kind of interest group. Interest groups are politically active because political parties have declined in influence, prestige, and public attractiveness. Interest groups fill a power vacuum in American government. They supply information to public officials, gain support for issues, endorse or oppose candidates, and demonstrate on behalf of their goals through lobbying, marches, picketing, and letter-writing campaigns.

NOTES

1. Theodore Lowi, *The End of Liberalism,* 2d ed. (New York: W. W. Norton & Co., 1979), Chapter 3.
2. Thomas R. Dye, *Who's Running America? The Bush Era,* 5th ed. (Englewood Cliffs, N.J.: Prentice-Hall, 1990), 275–76.
3. Thomas R. Dye and L. Harmon Zeigler, *The Irony of Democracy,* 7th ed. (Monterey, Calif.: Brooks/Cole, 1987), 3.

The Danger of Factions

15
The Federalist, Number 10
James Madison

The Federalist, Number 10, by Madison deals with a central problem of all governmental systems: how to balance majority will with minority rights to prevent tyranny or oppression. Madison warned against the danger of "factions" that might hinder popular control of government. Factions may be "adverse to the rights of other citizens, or to the permanent and aggregate interests of the community." Madison was apprehensive that such factions would influence government out of proportion to their numbers, which would result in a tyranny of the minority; or, conversely, that majority factions would overwhelm the rights and interests of other groups in society causing a tyranny of the majority. See The Federalist, Number 51, Article 5, for an analysis of separation of powers and checks and balances as a structural solution to the problem of factions.

TO THE PEOPLE OF THE STATE OF NEW YORK:

Among the numerous advantages promised by a well-constructed Union, none deserves to be more accurately developed than its tendency to break and control the violence of faction. The friend of popular governments never finds himself so much alarmed for their character and fate, as when he contemplates their propensity to this dangerous vice. He will not fail, therefore, to set a due value on any plan which, without violating the principles to which he is attached, provides a proper cure for it. The instability, injustice, and confusion introduced into the public councils, have, in truth, been the mortal diseases under which popular governments have everywhere perished; as they continue to be the favorite and fruitful topics from which the adversaries to liberty derive their most specious declamations. The valuable improvements made by the American constitutions on the popular models, both ancient and modern, cannot certainly be too much admired; but it would be an unwarrantable partiality, to contend that they have as effectually obviated the danger on this side, as was wished and expected. Complaints are everywhere heard from our most considerate and virtuous citizens, equally the friends of public and private faith, and of public and personal liberty, that our governments are too unstable; that public good is disregarded in the conflicts of rival parties; and that measures are too often decided, not according to the rules of justice and the rights of the minor party, but by the superior force of an interested and overbearing majority. However anxiously we

From *The Daily Advertiser*, November 22, 1787. This essay appeared in *The New York Packet* on November 23 and *The Independent Journal* on November 24.

may wish that these complaints had no foundation, the evidence of known facts will not permit us to deny that they are in some degree true. It will be found, indeed, on a candid review of our situation, that some of the distresses under which we labor have been erroneously charged on the operation of our governments; but it will be found, at the same time, that other causes will not alone account for many of our heaviest misfortunes; and particularly, for that prevailing and increasing distrust of public engagements, and alarm for private rights, which are echoed from one end of the continent to the other. These must be chiefly, if not wholly, effects of the unsteadiness and injustice with which a factious spirit has tainted our public administrations.

By a faction, I understand a number of citizens, whether amounting to a majority or minority of the whole, who are united and actuated by some common impulse of passion, or of intent, adverse to the rights of other citizens, or to the permanent and aggregate interests of the community.

There are two methods of curing the mischiefs of faction: the one, by removing its causes; the other, by controlling its effects.

There are again two methods of removing the causes of faction: the one, by destroying the liberty which is essential to its existence; the other, by giving to every citizen the same opinions, the same passions, and the same interests.

It could never be more truly said than of the first remedy, that it is worse than the disease. Liberty is to faction what air is to fire, an ailment without which it instantly expires. But it could not be less folly to abolish liberty, which is essential to political life, because it nourishes faction, than it would be to wish the annihilation of air, which is essential to animal life, because it imparts to fire its destructive agency.

The second expedient is as impracticable as the first would be unwise. As long as the reason of man continues fallible, and he is at liberty to exercise it, different opinions will be formed. As long as the connection subsists between his reason and his self-love, his opinions and his passions will have a reciprocal influence on each other, and the former will be objects to which the latter will attach themselves. The diversity in the faculties of men, from which the rights of property originate, is not less an insuperable obstacle to a uniformity of interests. The protection of these faculties is the first object of government. From the protection of different and unequal faculties of acquiring property, the possession of different degrees and kinds of property immediately results; and from the influence of these on the sentiments and views of the respective proprietors, ensues a division of the society into different interests and parties.

The latent causes of faction are thus sown in the nature of man; and we see them everywhere brought into different degrees of activity, according to the different circumstances of civil society. A zeal for different opinions concerning religion, concerning government, and many other points, as well of speculation as of practice; an attachment to different leaders ambitiously contending for preeminence and power; or to persons of other descriptions whose fortunes have been interesting to the human passions, have, in turn, divided mankind into parties, inflamed them with mutual animosity, and rendered them much more disposed to vex and oppress each other than to cooperate for their common good. So strong is this propensity of mankind to fall into mutual animosities, that where no substantial occasion presents itself, the most frivolous and fanciful distinctions have been sufficient to kindle their unfriendly passions and excite their most violent conflicts. But the most common and durable source of factions has been the various and unequal distributions of property. Those who hold and those who are without property have ever formed distinct interests in society. Those who are creditors, and those who are debtors, fall under a like discrimination. A landed interest, a manufacturing interest, a mercantile interest, a moneyed interest, with many lesser interests grow up of necessity in civilized nations, and divide them into different classes, actuated by different sentiments and views. The regulation of these various and interfering interests forms the principal task of modern legislation, and involves the spirit of party and faction in the necessary and ordinary operations of the government.

No man is allowed to be a judge in his own cause, because his interest would certainly bias his judgment, and, not improbably, corrupt his integrity. With equal, nay with greater reason, a body of men are unfit to be both judges and parties at the same time; yet what are many of the most important acts of legislation, but so many judicial determinations, not indeed concerning the rights of single persons, but concerning the rights of large bodies of citizens? And what are the different classes of legislators but advocates and parties to the causes which they determine? Is a law proposed concerning private debts? It is a question to which the creditors are parties on one side and the debtors on the other. Justice ought to hold the balance between them. Yet the parties are, and must be, themselves the judges; and the most powerful faction must be expected to prevail. Shall domestic manufacturers be encouraged, and in what degree, by restrictions on foreign manufactures? Are questions which would be differently decided by the landed and the manufacturing classes, and probably by neither with a sole regard to justice and the public good. The apportionment of taxes on the various descriptions of property is an act which greater opportunity and temptation are given to a predominant party to trample on the rules of justice. Every shilling with which they overburden the inferior number is a shilling saved to their own pockets.

It is in vain to say that enlightened statesmen will be able to adjust these clashing interests and render them all subservient to the public good. Enlightened statesmen will not always be at the helm. Nor, in many cases, can such an adjustment be made at all without taking into view indirect and remote considerations, which will rarely prevail over the immediate interest which one party may find in disregarding the rights of another or the good of the whole.

The inference to which we are brought is, that the *causes* of faction cannot be removed, and that relief is only to be sought in the means of controlling its *effects*.

If a faction consists of less than a majority, relief is supplied by the republican principle, which enables the majority to defeat its sinister views by regular vote. It may clog the administration, it may convulse the society; but it will be unable to execute and mask its violence under the forms of the Constitution. When a majority is included in a faction, the form of popular government, on the other hand, enables it to sacrifice to its ruling passion or interest both the public good and the rights of other citizens. To secure the public good and private rights against the danger of such a faction, and at the same time to preserve the spirit and the form of popular government, is then the great object to which our inquiries are directed. Let me add that it is the great desideratum by which this form of government can be rescued from the opprobrium under which it has so long labored, and be recommended to the esteem and adoption of mankind.

By what means is this object attainable? Evidently by one of two only. Either the existence of the same passion or interest in a majority at the same time must be prevented, or the majority, having such coexistent passion or interest, must be rendered by their number and local situation unable to concert and carry into effect schemes of oppression. If the impulse and the opportunity be suffered to coincide, we well know that neither moral nor religious motives can be relied on as an adequate control. They are not found to be such on the injustice and violence of individuals, and lose their efficacy in proportion to the number combined together, that is, in proportion as their efficacy becomes needful.

From this view of the subject it may be concluded that a pure democracy, by which I mean a society consisting of a small number of citizens, who assemble and administer the government in person, can admit of no cure for the mischiefs of faction. A common passion or interest will, in almost every case, be felt by a majority of the whole; a communication and concert result from the form of government itself; and there is nothing to check the inducements to sacrifice the weaker party or an obnoxious individual. Hence it is that such democracies have ever been spectacles of turbulence and contention; have ever been found incompatible with personal security or the rights of property; and have in general been as short in their lives as they have been violent in their deaths. Theoretic politicians, who have patronized this species of government, have erroneously supposed that by reducing mankind to a perfect equality in their political rights, they would, at the same time, be perfectly equalized and assimilated in their possessions, their opinions, and their passions.

A republic, by which I mean a government in which the scheme of representation takes place, opens a different prospect, and promises the cure for which we are seeking. Let us examine the points in which it varies from pure democracy, and we shall comprehend both the nature of the cure and the efficacy which it must derive from the Union.

The two great points of difference between a democracy and a republic are: first, the delegation of the government in the latter to a small number of citizens elected by the rest; secondly, the greater number of citizens and greater sphere of country over which the latter may be extended.

The effect of the first difference is, on the one hand, to refine and enlarge the public views, by passing them through the medium of a chosen body of citizens, whose wisdom may best discern the true interest of their country, and whose patriotism and love of justice will be least likely to sacrifice it to temporary or partial considerations. Under such a regulation, it may well happen that the public voice, pronounced by the representatives of the people, will be more consonant to the public good than if pronounced by the people themselves, convened for the purpose. On the other hand, the effect may be inverted. Men of factious tempers, of local prejudices, or of sinister designs, may by intrigue, by corruption, or by other means, first obtain the suffrages, and then betray the interests of the people. The question resulting is, whether small or extensive republics are more favorable to the election of proper guardians of the public weal; and it is clearly decided in favor of the latter by two obvious considerations.

In the first place, it is to be remarked that, however small the republic may be, the representatives must be raised to a certain number in order to guard against the cabals of a few; and that, however large it may be, they must be limited to a certain number in order to guard against the confusion of a multitude. Hence, the number of representatives in the two cases not being in proportion to that of the two constituents, and being proportionally greater in the small republic, it follows that, if the proportion of fit characters be not less in the large than in the small republic, the former will present a greater option and consequently a greater probability of a fit choice.

In the next place, as each representative will be chosen by a greater number of citizens in the large than in the small republic, it will be more difficult for unworthy candidates to practise with success the vicious arts by which elections are too often carried; and the suffrages of the people being more free, will be more likely to centre in men who possess the most attractive merit and the most diffusive and established characters.

It must be confessed that in this, as in most other cases, there is a mean, on both sides of which inconveniences will be found to lie. By enlarging too much the number of electors, you render the representative too little acquainted with all their local circumstances and lesser interests: as by reducing it too much, you render him unduly attached to these, and too little fit to comprehend and pursue great and national objects. The federal Constitution forms a happy combination in this respect; the great and aggregate interests being referred to the national, the local and particular to the State legislatures.

The other point of difference is, the greater number of citizens and extent of territory which may be brought within the compass of republican than of democratic government; and it is this circumstance principally which renders factious combinations less to be dreaded in the former than in the latter. The smaller the society, the fewer probably will be the distinct parties and interests composing it; the fewer the distinct parties and interests, the more frequently will a majority be found of the same party; and the smaller the number of individuals composing a majority, and the smaller the compass within which they are placed, the more easily will they con-

cert and execute their plans of oppression. Extend the sphere, and you take in a greater variety of parties and interests; you make it less probable that a majority of the whole will have a common motive to invade the rights of other citizens; or if such a common motive exists, it will be more difficult for all who feel it to discover their own strength and to act in unison with each other. Besides other impediments, it may be remarked that, where there is a consciousness of unjust or dishonorable purposes, communication is always checked by distrust in proportion to the number whose concurrence is necessary.

Hence, it clearly appears that the same advantage which a republic has over a democracy in controlling the effects of faction is enjoyed by a large over a small republic,—is enjoyed by the Union over the States composing it. Does the advantage consist in the substitution of representatives who enlightened views and virtuous sentiments render them superior to local prejudices and to schemes of injustice? It will not be denied that the representation of the Union will be most likely to possess these requisite endowments. Does it consist in the greater security afforded by a greater variety of parties, against the event of any one party being able to outnumber and oppress the rest? In an equal degree does the increased variety of parties comprised within the Union, increase this security? Does it, in fine, consist in the greater obstacles opposed to the concert and accomplishment of the secret wishes of an unjust and interested majority? Here, again, the extent of the Union gives it the most palpable advantage.

The influence of factious leaders may kindle a flame within their particular States, but will be unable to spread a general conflagration through the other States. A religious sect may degenerate into a political faction in a part of the Confederacy; buy the variety of sects dispersed over the entire face of it must secure the national councils against any danger from that source. A rage for paper money, for an abolition of debts, for an equal division of property, or for any other improper or wicked project, will be less apt to pervade the whole body of the Union than a particular member of it; in the same proportion as such a malady is more likely to taint a particular county or district, than an entire State.

In the extent and proper structure of the Union, therefore, we behold a republican remedy for the diseases most incident to republican government. And according to the degree of pleasure and pride we feel in being republicans, ought to be our zeal in cherishing the spirit and supporting the character of Federalists.

Publius

The Mobilization of Bias

16
The Scope and Bias of the Pressure System
E. E. Schattschneider

What is the role of interest groups in the American political system? How do such groups develop and what are their goals and objectives? This essay by E. E. Schattschneider provides analysis of the "pressure system," indicating the distinguishing features of group theory, the bias of special interest groups, and the relationships between interest groups and government. He shows that group theory is related to the types of interests involved—special or public—and the differences between organized and unorganized interests. These criteria indicate that organization is a "mobilization of bias," a theme discussed by James Madison in The Federalist, Number 10. Also, the pressure system has a strong upper-class bias which excludes most people. Why is this so? What are the major flaws of the pressure system? What does Schattschneider mean by the "socialization of conflict"? What are the relationships between business and the Republican party?

The scope of conflict is an aspect of the scale of political organization and the extent of political competition. The size of the constituencies being mobilized, the inclusiveness or exclusiveness of the conflicts people expect to develop have a bearing on all theories about how politics is or should be organized. In other words, nearly all theories about politics have something to do with the question of who can get into the fight and who is to be excluded.

Every regime is a testing ground for theories of this sort. More than any other system American politics provides the raw materials for testing the organizational assumptions of two contrasting kinds of politics, *pressure politics* and *party politics*. The concepts that underlie these forms of politics constitute the raw stuff of a general theory of political action. The basic issue between the two patterns of organization is one of size and scope of conflict; pressure groups are small-scale organizations while political parties are very large-scale organizations. One need not be surprised, therefore, that the partisans of large-scale and small-scale organizations differ passionately, because the outcome of the political game depends on the scale on which it is played.

To understand the controversy about the scale of political organization it is necessary first to take a look at some theories about interest-group politics. Pressure groups have played a remarkable role in American politics,

Scattered excerpts from *The Semi-Sovereign People*, copyright © 1960 by E. E. Schattschneider and renewed 1988 by Holt, Rinehart and Winston, Inc., reprinted by permission of the publisher.

but they have played an even more remarkable role in American political theory. Considering the political condition of the country in the first third of the twentieth century, it was probably inevitable that the discussion of special-interest pressure groups should lead to development of "group" theories of politics in which an attempt is made to explain everything in terms of group activity, i.e., an attempt to formulate a universal group theory. Since one of the best ways to test an idea is to ride it into the ground, political theory has unquestionably been improved by the heroic attempt to create a political universe revolving about the group. Now that we have a number of drastic statements of the group theory of politics pushed to a great extreme, we ought to be able to see what the limitations of the idea are.

Political conditions in the first third of the present century were extremely hospitable to the idea. The role of business in the strongly sectional Republican system from 1896 to 1932 made the dictatorship of business seem to be part of the eternal order of things. Moreover the regime as a whole seemed to be so stable that questions about the survival of the American community did not arise. The general interests of the community were easily overlooked under these circumstances.

Nevertheless, in spite of the excellent and provocative scholarly work done by Beard, Latham, Truman, Leiserson, Dahl, Lindblom, Laski, and others, the group theory of politics is beset with difficulties. The difficulties are theoretical, growing in part out of sheer overstatements of the idea and in part out of some confusion about the nature of modern government.

One difficulty running through the literature of the subject results from the attempt to explain *everything* in terms of the group theory. On general grounds it would be remarkable indeed if a single hypothesis explained everything about so complex a subject as American politics. Other difficulties have grown out of the fact that group concepts have been stated in terms so universal that the subject seems to have no shape or form.

The question is: Are pressure groups the universal basic ingredient of all political situations, and do they explain everything? To answer this question it is necessary to review a bit of rudimentary political theory.

Two modest reservations might be made merely to test the group dogma. We might clarify our ideas if (1) we explore more fully the possibility of making a distinction between public-interest groups and special-interest groups and (2) if we distinguish between organized and unorganized groups. These reservations do not disturb the main body of group theory, but they may be useful when we attempt to define general propositions more precisely. If both of these distinctions can be validated, we may get hold of something that has scope and limits and is capable of being defined. The awkwardness of a discussion of political phenomena in terms of universals is that the subject has no beginning or end; it is impossible to distinguish one subject from another or to detect the bias of the forces involved because scope and bias are aspects of limitations of the subject. It cannot really be said that we have seen a subject until we have seen its outer limits and thus are able to draw a line between one subject and another.

We might begin to break the problem into its component parts by exploring the distinction between public and private interests. If we can validate this distinction, we shall have established one of the boundaries of the subject.

As a matter of fact, the distinction between *public* and *private* interests is a thoroughly respectable one; it is one of the oldest known to political theory. In the literature of the subject, the public interest refers to general or common interests shared by all or by substantially all members of the community. Presumably no community exists unless there is some kind of community of interests, just as there is no nation without some notion of national interests. If it is really impossible to distinguish between private and public interests, the group theorists have produced a revolution in political thought so great that it is impossible to foresee its consequences. For this reason the distinction ought to be explored with great care. . . .

In contrast with the common interests are the special interests. The implication of this term is that these are interests shared by only a few people or a fraction of the community; they *exclude* others and may be *adverse* to them. A special interest is exclusive in about the same way as private property is exclusive. In a complex society it is not surprising that there are some interests that are shared by all or substantially all members of the community and some interests that are not shared so widely. The distinction is useful precisely because conflicting claims are made by people about the nature of their interests in controversial matters. . . .

The distinction between public and special interests is an indispensable tool for the study of politics. To abolish the distinction is to make a shambles of political science by treating things that are different as if they were alike. The kind of distinction made here is a commonplace of all literature dealing with human society, but *if we accept it, we have established one of the outer limits of the subject;* we have split the world of interests in half and have taken one step toward defining the scope of this kind of political conflict.

We can now examine the second distinction, the distinction between organized and unorganized groups. The question here is not whether the distinction can be made but whether or not it is worth making. Organiza-

tion has been described as "merely a stage or degree of interaction" in the development of a group.

The proposition is a good one, but what conclusions do we draw from it? We do not dispose of the matter by calling the distinction between organized and unorganized groups a "mere" difference of degree because some of the greatest differences in the world are differences of degree. As far as special-interest politics is concerned the implication to be avoided is that a few workmen who habitually stop at a corner saloon for a glass of beer are essentially the same as the United States Army because the difference between them is merely one of degree. At this point we have a distinction that makes a difference. The distinction between organized and unorganized groups is worth making because it ought to alert us against an analysis which begins as a general group theory of politics but ends with a defense of pressure politics as inherent, universal, permanent, and inevitable. This kind of confusion comes from the loosening of categories involved in the universalization of group concepts.

Since the beginning of intellectual history, scholars have sought to make progress in their work by distinguishing between things that are unlike and by dividing their subject matter into categories to examine them more intelligently. It is something of a novelty, therefore, when group theorists reverse this process by discussing their subject in terms so universal that they wipe out all categories, because this is the dimension in which it is least possible to understand anything.

If we are able, therefore, to distinguish between public and private interests and between organized and unorganized groups we have marked out the major boundaries of the subject; *we have given the subject shape and scope.* We are now in a position to attempt to define the area we want to explore. Having cut the pie into four pieces, we can now appropriate the piece we want and leave the rest to someone else. For a multitude of reasons *the most likely field of study is that of the organized, special-interest groups.* The advantage of concentrating on organized groups is that they are known, identifiable, and recognizable. The advantage of concentrating on special-interest groups is that they have one important characteristic in common; they are all exclusive. This piece of the pie (the organized special-interest groups) we shall call the *pressure system.* The pressure system has boundaries we can define; we can fix its scope and make an attempt to estimate its bias. . . .

By the time a group has developed the kind of interest that leads it to organize, it may be assumed that it has also developed some kind of political bias because *organization is itself a mobilization of bias in preparation for action.* Since these groups can be identified and since they have memberships (i.e., they include and exclude people), it is possible to think of the *scope* of the system. . . .

The business or upper-class bias of the pressure system shows up everywhere. Businessmen are four or five times as likely to write to their congressmen as manual laborers are. College graduates are far more apt to write to their congressmen than people in the lowest educational category are. . . .

The obverse side of the coin is that large areas of the population appear to be wholly outside the system of private organization. A study made by Ira Reid of a Philadelphia area showed that in a sample of 963 persons, 85 percent belonged to no civic or charitable organization and 74 percent belonged to no occupational, business, or professional associations, while another Philadelphia study of 1,154 women showed that 55 percent belonged to no associations of any kind. . . .

The class bias of associational activity gives meaning to the limited scope of the pressure system, because *scope and bias are aspects of the same tendency.* The data raise a serious question about the validity of the proposition that special-interest groups are a universal form of political organization reflecting *all* interests. As a matter of fact, to suppose that everyone participates in pressure-group activity and that all interests get themselves organized in the pressure system is to destroy the meaning of this form of politics. The pressure system makes sense only as the political instrument of a segment of the community. It gets results by being selective and biased; *if everybody got into the act, the unique advantages of this form of organization would be destroyed, for it is possible that if all interests could be mobilized the result would be a stalemate.*

Special-interest organizations are most easily formed when they deal with small numbers of individuals who are acutely aware of their exclusive interests. To describe the conditions of pressure-group organization in this way is, however, to say that it is primarily a business phenomenon. Aside from a few very large organizations (the churches, organized labor, farm organizations, and veterans' organizations) the residue is a small segment of the population. *Pressure politics is essentially the politics of small groups.*

The vice of the groupist theory is that it conceals the most significant aspects of the system. The flaw in the pluralist heaven is that the heavenly chorus sings with a strong upper-class accent. Probably about 90 percent of the people cannot get into the pressure system.

The notion that the pressure system is automatically representative of the whole community is a myth fostered by the universalizing tendency of modern group theories. *Pressure politics is a selective process* ill designed to serve diffuse interests. The system is skewed, loaded, and unbalanced in favor of a fraction of a minority.

On the other hand, pressure tactics are not remarkably successful in mobilizing general interests. When pressure-group organizations attempt to represent the interests of large numbers of people, they are usually able to reach only a small segment of their constituencies. Only a chemical trace of the fifteen million Negroes in the United States belong to the National Association for the Advancement of Colored People. Only one five hundredths of 1 percent of American women belong to the League of Women Voters, only one sixteenth hundredths of 1 percent of the consumers belong to the National Consumers' League, and only 6 percent of American automobile drivers belong to the American Automobile Association, while about 15 percent of the veterans belong to the American Legion.

The competing claims of pressure groups and political parties for the loyalty of the American public revolve about the difference between the results likely to be achieved by small-scale and large-scale political organization. Inevitably, the outcome of pressure politics and party politics will be vastly different.

A CRITIQUE OF GROUP THEORIES OF POLITICS

It is extremely unlikely that the vogue of group theories of politics would have attained its present status if its basic assumptions had not been first established by some concept of economic determinism. The economic interpretation of politics has always appealed to those political philosophers who have sought a single prime mover, a sort of philosopher's stone of political science around which to organize their ideas. The search for a single, ultimate cause has something to do with the

attempt to explain *everything* about politics in terms of group concepts. The logic of economic determinism is to *identify the origins of conflict and to assume the conclusion.* This kind of thought has some of the earmarks of an illusion. The somnambulatory quality of thinking in this field appears also in the tendency of research to deal only with successful pressure campaigns or the willingness of scholars to be satisfied with having placed pressure groups on the scene of the crime without following through to see if the effect can really be attributed to the cause. What makes this kind of thinking remarkable is the fact that in political contests there are as many failures as there are successes. Where in the literature of pressure politics are the failures?

Students of special-interest politics need a more sophisticated set of intellectual tools than they have developed thus far. The theoretical problem involved in the search for a single cause is that all power relations in a democracy are reciprocal. Trying to find the original cause is like trying to find the first wave of the ocean. . . .

The very expression "pressure politics" invites us to misconceive the role of special-interest groups in politics. The word "pressure" implies the use of some kind of force, a form of intimidation, something other than reason and information, to induce public authorities to act against their own best judgment. In Latham's famous statement already quoted the legislature is described as a "referee" who "ratifies" and "records" the "balance of power" among the contending groups.

It is hard to imagine a more effective way of saying that Congress has no mind or force of its own or that Congress is unable to invoke new forces that might alter the equation.

Actually the outcome of political conflict is not like the "resultant" of opposing forces in physics. To assume that the forces in a

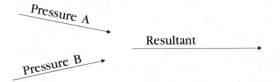

political situation could be diagramed as a physicist might diagram the resultant of opposing physical forces is to wipe the slate clean of all remote, general, and public considerations for the protection of which civil societies have been instituted.

Moreover, the notion of "pressure" distorts the image of the power relations involved. *Private conflicts are taken into the public arena precisely because someone wants to make certain that the power ratio among the private interests most immediately involved shall not prevail.* To treat a conflict as a mere test of the strength of the private interests is to leave out the most significant factors. This is so true that it might indeed be said that the only way to preserve private power ratios is to keep conflicts out of the public arena.

The assumption that it is only the "interested" who count ought to be re-examined in view of the foregoing discussion. The tendency of the literature of pressure politics has been to neglect the low-tension force of large numbers because it *assumes that the equation of forces is fixed at the outset.*

Given the assumptions made by the group theorists, the attack on the idea of the majority is completely logical. The assumption is that conflict is monopolized narrowly by the parties immediately concerned. There is no room for a majority when conflict is defined so narrowly. It is a great deficiency of the group theory that it has found no place in the political system for the majority. The force of the majority is of an entirely different order of magnitude, something not to be measured by pressure-group standards.

Instead of attempting to exterminate all political forms, organizations, and alignments that do not qualify as pressure groups, would it not be better to attempt to make a synthesis, covering the whole political system and finding a place for all kinds of political life?

One possible synthesis of pressure politics and party politics might be produced by *describing politics as the socialization of conflict.* That is to say, the political process is a sequence: conflicts are initiated by highly motivated, high-tension groups so directly and immediately involved that it is difficult for them to see the justice of competing claims. As long as the conflicts of these groups remain *private* (carried on in terms of economic competition, reciprocal denial of goods and services, private negotiations and bargaining, struggles for corporate control or competition for membership), no political process is initiated. Conflicts become political only when an attempt is made to involve the wider public. Pressure politics might be described as a stage in the socialization of conflict. This analysis makes pressure politics an integral part of all politics, including party politics.

One of the characteristic points of origin of pressure politics is a breakdown of the discipline of the business community. The flight to government is perpetual. Something like this is likely to happen wherever there is a point of contact between competing power systems. It is the *losers in intrabusiness conflict who seek redress from public authority. The dominant business interests resist appeals to the government.* The role of the government as the patron of the defeated private interest sheds light on its function as the critic of private power relations.

Since the contestants in private conflicts are apt to be unequal in strength, it follows that *the most powerful special interests want private settlements* because they are able to dictate the outcome as long as the conflict remains private. If A is a hundred times as strong as B he does not welcome the intervention of a third party because he expects to impose his own terms on B; he wants to isolate B. He is especially opposed to the intervention of public authority, because public authority represents the most overwhelming form of outside intervention. Thus, if

$$\frac{A}{B} = \frac{100}{1},$$

it is obviously not to A's advantage to involve a third party a million times as strong as A and B combined. Therefore, it is the weak, not the strong, who appeal to public authority for relief. It is the weak who want to socialize conflict, i.e., to involve more and more people in the conflict until the balance of forces is changed. In the schoolyard it is not the bully but the defenseless smaller boys who "tell the teacher." When the teacher intervenes, the balance of power in the schoolyard is apt to change drastically. It is the function of public authority to *modify private power relations by enlarging the scope of conflict.* Nothing could be more mistaken than to suppose that public authority merely registers the dominance of the strong over the weak. The mere existence of public order has already ruled out a great variety of forms of private pressure. Nothing could be more confusing than to suppose that the refugees from the business community who come to Congress for relief and protection *force* Congress to do their bidding.

Evidence of the truth of this analysis may be seen in the fact that the big private interests do not necessarily win if they are involved in public conflicts with petty interests. The image of the lobbyists as primarily the agents of big business is not easy to support on the face of the record of congressional hearings, for example. The biggest corporations in the country tend to avoid the arena in which pressure groups and lobbyists fight it out before congressional committees. To describe this process exclusively in terms of an effort of business to intimidate congressmen is to misconceive what is actually going on.

It is probably a mistake to assume that pressure politics is the typical or even the most important relation between government and business. The pressure group is by no means the perfect instrument of the business community. What does big business want? The *winners* in intrabusiness strife want (1) to be let alone (they want autonomy) and (2) to preserve the solidarity of the business community. For these purposes pressure politics is not a wholly satisfactory device. The most elementary considerations of strategy call for the business community to develop some kind of common policy more broadly based than any special-interest group is likely to be.

The political influence of business depends on the kind of solidarity that, on the one hand, leads all business to rally to the support of *any* businessman in trouble with the government and, on the other hand, keeps internal business disputes out of the public arena. In this system businessmen resist the impulse to attack each other in public and discourage the efforts of individual members of the business community to take intrabusiness conflicts into politics.

The attempt to mobilize a united front of the whole business community does not resemble the classical concept of pressure politics. The logic of business politics is to keep peace within the business community by supporting as far as possible all claims that business groups make for themselves. The tendency is to support all businessmen who have conflicts with the government and support all businessmen in conflict with labor. In this way *special-interest politics can be converted into party policy.* The search is for a broad base of political mobilization grounded on the strategic need for political organization on a wider scale than is possible in the case of the historical pressure group. Once the business community begins to think in terms of a larger scale of political organization the Republican party looms large in business politics.

It is a great achievement of American democracy that business has been forced to form a political organization designed to win elections, i.e., has been forced to compete for power in the widest arena in the political system. On the other hand, *the power of the Republican party to make terms with business rests on the fact that business cannot afford to be isolated.*

The Republican party has played a major role in *the political organization of the business community,* a far greater role than many students of politics seem to have realized. The influence of business in the Republican party is great, but it is never absolute because business is remarkably dependent on the party. The business community is too small, it arouses too much antagonism, and its aims are too narrow to win the support of a popular majority. The political education of business is a function of the Republican party that can never be done so well by anyone else.

In the management of the political relations of the business community, the Republican party is much more important than any combination of pressure groups ever could be. The success of special interests in Congress is due less to the "pressure" exerted by these groups than it is due to the fact that Republican members of Congress are committed in advance to a general probusiness attitude. The notion that business groups coerce Republican congressmen into voting for their bills underestimates the whole Republican posture in American politics.

It is not easy to manage the political interests of the business community because there is a perpetual stream of losers in intrabusiness conflicts who go to the government for relief and protection. It has not been possible therefore to maintain perfect solidarity, and when solidarity is breached the government is involved almost automatically. The fact that business has not become hopelessly divided and that it has retained great influence in American politics has been due chiefly to the overall mediating role played by the Republican party. There has never been a pressure group or a combination of pressure groups capable of performing this function.

Lobbying: Strategies and Tactics

17
Old-Breed and New-Breed Lobbying
Hedrick Smith

Hedrick Smith, a journalist, wrote The Power Game: How Washington Really
Works *in 1988. The strategies and tactics of old- and new-style lobbyists
are a key to understanding the Washington power arena. Old-breed lobbying is an insider influence game of powerful lawyers and former government officials seeking to bring benefits to their clients and to elected
officials. How do these insiders get access? Smith characterizes their activities as "retail lobbying." What is this? The new-breed of lobbyists use public relations, television, mass-mailings, and grass-roots coalitions. How did
this type of lobbying expand in the 1980s? What are some examples of
new-breed lobbying cited by Smith?*

In the abstract, lobbying kindles an image of
wickedness only barely less disreputable than
the skullduggery of the Mafia. It conjures up
Upton Sinclair's exposés of the beef and sugar
trusts or Thomas Nast's oils of robber barons
closeted in back rooms, their corpulent figures
framed in thick black strokes against a backdrop in red.* It has the illicit aroma of cigar
smoke, booze, and money delivered in brown
envelopes. Or it smacks of big labor muscling
congressional minions. But that is a caricature,
for lobbying has changed immensely with the
rise of mass citizen protests in the 1960s over
civil rights and the Vietnam War. It changed
further with the breakup of the old power

baronies, the arrival of new-breed politicians,
and the intrusion of campaign techniques.

Of course, plenty of lobbyists still practice
old-fashioned lobbying. At heart, the old-breed
game is inside politics. That is why so many
lobbyists are former members of Congress,
former White House officials, former legislative staff aides, former cabinet officers. Their
game thrives on the clubbiness of the old-boy
network. It turns on the camaraderie of personal friendships, on expertise born of experience. It taps old loyalties and well-practiced
access. It draws on the common bond of old
battles and the certain knowledge that you
may lose on this year's tax bill, but you'll be

  * Upton Sinclair was an American socialist and writer whose most famous work, *The Jun-
gle* (1906), helped arouse public opinion over unsanitary conditions in the meat-packing industry, which led to the creation of the Food and Drug Administration (FDA). Thomas Nast was a
political cartoonist for *Harper's Weekly* during and after the Civil War. He is probably most
famous for popularizing the symbols of the Democratic and Republican parties, the donkey and
the elephant.

back to revise it next year, and that yesterday's foe may be tomorrow's ally. It depends on relationships for the long haul.

The superlobbyists of the old-breed game are people such as Clark Clifford, a courtly, genteel former White House counsel to Harry Truman and secretary of defense to Lyndon Johnson; Robert Strauss, the wisecracking former Democratic party chairman and Mr. Everything for Jimmy Carter; and Howard Baker, between stints as Senate majority leader and White House chief of staff. Close behind are Tommy Boggs, the able, likable, paunchy son of Representative Lindy Boggs and the late House Democratic Majority Leader Hale Boggs; Charls Walker, an astute, drawling Texas-born tax attorney with high Treasury experience in the Nixon years; and Robert Gray, secretary to the Eisenhower cabinet, who got to know the Reagans in California. These inside fixers cannot do what was possible a generation ago. Yet in a game where access and reputation are the coin of the marketplace, king rainmakers still have influence.

For the essence of the old-breed game is *retail* lobbying: the one-on-one pitch. It is Bob Strauss's note to Treasury Secretary Jim Baker to help a friend seek appointment to the World Bank. It is Howard Baker's contact with an old Senate colleague to see that some client gets a break on the "transition rules" of a tax bill. It is Bob Gray's phone call to the White House to ask the president to address some convention or to wangle an invitation to a state dinner for an industrial big shot. It is breakfast with a committee staff director who is drafting intricate legislation. It is little favors such as tickets to a Washington Redskins football game or helping Ed Meese's wife get a job. It is knowing which buttons to push.

"The best lobbyists' work is basically just socializing," former Speaker O'Neill's spokesman, Chris Matthews, advised me. "They know members of Congress are here three nights a week, alone, without their families. So they say, 'Let's have dinner. Let's go see a ball game.' Shmooze with them. Make friends. And they don't lean on it all the time. Every once in a while, they call up—maybe once or twice a year—ask a few questions. Call you up and say, 'Say, what's Danny going to do on this tax-reform bill?' Anne Wexler [a former Carter White House official, now a lobbyist] will call up and spend half an hour talking about left-wing politics, and suddenly she'll pop a question, pick up something. They want that little bit of access. That's what does it. You can hear it. It clicks home. They'll call their chief executive officer, and they've delivered. That's how it works. It's not illegal. They work on a personal basis."

An inside tip can be gold. Right after Reagan's inauguration in 1981, John Gunther, executive director of the U.S. Conference of Mayors, got a tip from a cabinet staff aide that the Reagan administration was planning to kill the revenue-sharing program which funneled billions to states, counties, and cities. The timing was serendipitous. The next day a mayors' delegation was scheduled to lunch with the president. Over lunch, the mayors of Peoria, Indianapolis, Denver, and Columbus lobbied Reagan and top aides. The program escaped the guillotine for several years, though it was ultimately reduced.

In another case, a former Reagan White House official turned lobbyist told me that a Washington lawyer telephoned him on behalf of a businessman who had a $497,000 cost overrun on a contract with the Department of Housing and Urban Development. In one telephone call, my lobbyist source learned that HUD had already decided to pay the contractor $350,000 and would tell him in about two weeks. My friend phoned the lawyer back, but before he could speak, the lawyer said his client was willing to pay the lobbyist ten percent of whatever he got. My source stopped in mid-sentence and replied, "Well, let me see what I can do." With some misgivings, but rationalizing that the contractor or the lawyer could have made the same phone call, my source waited a couple a days and then called back to report that the contractor would get $350,000. He never claimed to have fixed the deal, but he got a check for $35,000—for simply knowing whom to ask.

"A lot of it is direct contact," Christopher Matthews commented. "You see Tip, he'll be out at a country club playing golf [usually Burning Tree Country Club], and some lobbyist will walk up to him just as he's about ready to tee up his ball and say, 'Tip, you know, I got to tell you one thing. Do me one favor. Just don't push that state-and-local tax thing through on the tax bill.' You don't think that has an impression? Of course it does. They know what they're doing. Tip's mood can be affected by who the heck he's seen over the weekend. And these guys do their homework. They know right where these members socialize. You think it's an accident some guy walks up and talks to Tip on the golf tee? No. It's smart. It's natural. It's easy."

That is classic old-breed lobbying, and as an old-breed politician, Tip O'Neill was particularly susceptible. Indeed, practically no politician is immune to the flattery and personal attention that are the essence of old-breed lobbying. I remember an article in 1978 about Tongsun Park, a Korean lobbyist who had been close to O'Neill and who wound up getting several other congressmen indicted for taking illegal campaign contributions from a foreigner. But the article, by William Greider in the *Washington Post,* was emphasizing something else: Park's simple but shrewd understanding that politicians need to feel loved.

"Park exploited this weakness with his Georgetown parties and gifts, but that hardly makes him unique," Greider wrote.

The most effective lobbies on Capitol Hill, whether it is the Pentagon or the Farm Bureau, have always been the ones that played most skillfully to the Congressmen's egos. The military treats them like generals, flies them around in big airplanes and fires off rocket shows to entertain them. The Farm Bureau awards them plaques and holds banquets in their honor. Politicians are not different in this respect from the rest of us, except that many of them have a stronger personal need for ego gratification. It's what drew them into politics in the first place, the roar of the crowd and all that.

Now, picture a scrambling politician who works his way up the local ladder, who finally wins a coveted seat in Congress and comes to Washington to collect his glory. The first thing he discovers is that glory gets spread pretty thin in this town. . . . He hardly ever sees his name in the daily newspaper unless he gets into trouble or creates an outrageous media stunt which the press can't resist. When he opens the mail from home, it is a hot blast of complaints, demands, threats. In the last decade, his status has declined considerably, displaced by the new celebrities who dominate Washington's glitter: movie stars, cause advocates, rock musicians, even members of the news media. In this environment, politicians, some of them anyway, will behave like the rest of us—they will devote their attention to people who appreciate them. Lobbyists appreciate Congressmen. They thank them constantly for their hard work. They provide them with the trappings, however phony, of exalted status. They protect a Congressman, with small favors, while the rest of the world beats up on him.[1]

Old-breed lobbying also thrives on an aura of influence, a promise of the inside track, the hint of priceless contacts. A certain amount of this promise of influence is hokum. There is no year-in, year-out box-score, but even the big-name lobbyists "rainmakers" lose major battles or settle for much less than they had hoped for. "One of the great myths around is that wheelers and dealers can come in there and write policy and have their way in whatever they want—it's simply not the case,'' asserts Norm Ornstein, one of the best-known scholars on Congress, who is at the American Enterprise Institute for Public Policy Research. "You pick any big shot, and you're dealing with *some* wins and losses. Any sophisticated person is going to know that you hire a Tommy Boggs, and that doesn't mean you buy victory. What you buy with a Tommy Boggs is access. Very few people are gonna say they won't see him. You buy acumen. This is somebody who understands how the process works.''

Ornstein's skepticism is well taken, for lobbyists are prone to oversell their influence; but his assertion that lobbyists do not write policy is too sweeping. Their effectiveness, suggested David Cohen, codirector of the Advocacy Institute, depends largely on the public visibility of issues. Large issues like the MX missile, environmental legislation, the Voting Rights Act, or broad provisions of tax law are ''less susceptible to the superlobbyists because they are highly visible,'' Cohen argues—correctly, I think. "But when you're dealing with invisible issues and the narrower details of legislation, you can still use the superlawyers and the superlobbyists.''

Access is the first arrow in any lobbyist's quiver, especially lobbyists of the old breed. Scores of times I have been told that votes are won simply by gaining an audience with a time-harassed congressman, so he could hear your case. In this access game, the lobbyist's first rule is to make his own services so reliable and indispensable that officeholders become dependent on him—for his information, his contacts, his policy advice, not to mention his money. "A good lobbyist is simply an extension of a congressional member's staff,'' I was told by Terry Lierman, an energetic health lobbyist and former staff aide for the Senate

Appropriations Committee. "If you're a good lobbyist and you're working something, all the members know where you're coming from,'' Lierman said. "So if they want information and they trust you, they'll call *you* for that information.''

That takes expertise. For instance, Representative Tony Coelho, a California Democrat, pointed out how lobbyists work hand in glove with the members and staffs of the highly specialized subcommittees of the House Agriculture Committee. They help craft legislation that covers their own sector. "There are lobbyists who are extremely influential in the subcommittees,'' Coelho asserted. "They know more about the subject than the staff or the committee members. The Cotton Council will be writing legislation for the cotton industry in the cotton subcommittee.''

A top real estate lobbyist explained the premium value of expertise in the final stages of writing a tax bill and why lobbyists gather by the score outside the committee room. "There are very arcane, very turgid, complicated sections of the tax code, and members and their staffs often are not as familiar with how they apply to the industry as we are,'' explained Wayne Thevnot, president of the National Realty Committee. "So if you've got entrée there and you understand the process and you're present, you can influence the specific drafting of these proposals. Staff and others will come out and seek you out in the halls and say, 'We're on the passive-loss provision, and this is the material-participation test that the staff is proposing. Does that work? Does that solve your problem? And, if not, how can we correct it?

AIPAC has institutionalized its influence through this technique.* Tom Dine and other staffers draft speeches and legislation for many members of both House and Senate, offering detailed rundowns on the Arab-Israeli military balance, or doing spot checks on Middle Eastern visitors, "We'll get a call from a congressional staffer, say at nine in the morning, and they want a speech on an issue," one midlevel AIPAC legislative assistant disclosed. "By ten-thirty, they'll have a speech." AIPAC has a research staff of fifteen people, well-stocked with papers on many topical issues. Practically every senator or House member known as a spokesman on Israeli issues and scores of lesser lights have leaned on this service or gotten AIPAC's staff to ghostwrite or edit op-ed articles on Middle East issues.

Charles Peters, in his slim and knowing handbook on Washington, *How Washington Really Works,* argues that the name of the game for politicians and administration officials is survival, and lobbyists work to become an integral part of the survival networks of people in power. "The smart lobbyists knows he must build networks not only for himself, but for those officials he tries to influence," Peters wrote. "Each time the lobbyist meets an official whose help he needs, he tries to let that official know—in the most subtle ways possible—that he can be an important part of that official's survival network.

Ultimately, that urge to prove a vital part of an officeholder's network gets into campaign money and demonstrating clout with the voters. And that begins to bridge from the old inside game of lobbying to the new outside game.

The new-breed game reflects the organic changes in American politics and the institutional changes in Congress. Its medium is mass marketing; its style is packaging issues; its hallmark is wholesale lobbying. New-breed lobbying borrows heavily from the techniques of political campaigns, with their slick P.R., television advertising, orchestrated coalitions, targeted mass mailings, and their crowds of activists. It is the National Rifle Association generating three million telegrams in seventy-two hours and blanketing Capitol Hill with so many phone calls that members cannot make outgoing calls. It is the "gray lobby" dumping up to fifteen million postcards and letters on Jim Wright in one day to warn Congress not to tamper with Social Security cost-of-living adjustments.* It is legions of insurance and real estate lobby agents swarming Capitol Hill as a tax markup nears a climax. It is political consultants and campaign strategists elbowing superlawyers aside, to generate grass-roots support for their lobbying clients or to do public-relations campaigns.

For example, when Jonas Savimbi, the Angolan rebel leader, wanted to push his cause in Washington in late 1985 and to bring pressure on Congress and the administration to supply him with missiles to combat Soviet tanks and jets, he paid a fancy $600,000 fee to Black, Manafort, Stone, and Kelly, a hot-shot lobbying firm set up by a group of young political campaign managers and consultants. The firm, whose campaign work gave it ties to the Reagan White House and influential Republican senators, not only arranged entrée at the highest levels of the administration and Congress, but it orchestrated a massive public-relations blitz for Savimbi. In his two-week visit, the jaunty, bearded anti-Communist rebel had scores of press interviews and television appearances. Suddenly Savimbi became a

---

* AIPAC, or the American Israeli Public Affairs Committee, is a foreign policy lobby that seeks to provide U.S. financial aid to Israel and to deny aid to Arab nations that are at war with Israel. It is also active in coordinating the activities of a large number of pro-Israeli PACs, channeling money to candidates who support pro-Israeli positions, and coordinating efforts against opponents.

* Representative Jim Wright, a Democrat from Texas, was elected Speaker of the U.S. House of Representatives for the session beginning in January 1987.

cause célèbre, which helped him get the weapons.

There are literally hundreds of deals like these, tapping the ranks of political campaign specialists for lobbying. That is an important shift away from reliance on lawyers and former government officials for lobbying—a shift symptomatic of how the new politics have altered the Washington power game.

The essence of the new-breed game is grass-roots lobbying. It developed in the 1960s with the advent of citizen protest. The civil rights movement, mass marches against the Vietnam War, and then Ralph Nader and public-interest groups such as Common Cause opened up mass lobbying. Those movements spawned a new generation, a new cadre of players trained in grass-roots activism, many of whom settled into the Washington power game. Business was initially slow to react, but it arrived with a vengeance to play on the new terrain in the late 1970s and gained the upper hand in the 1980s. Now old-breed and new-breed lobbyists jostle, borrowing techniques from each other.

The new game has made lobbying a boom industry. It takes a lot more money and manpower than it did in the old days to touch all the power bases in Congress, and the campaign techniques of working the grass roots shoot costs up exponentially. The swarm of lobbyists in Washington seems to reach new highs every year: from 5,662 registered with the secretary of the Senate in 1981 to 23,011 in mid-1987 (registration is required to work the halls of Congress legally), plus another fifty or sixty thousand more lobbyists and workers in law firms and trade association offices. In the new Washington, practically no big client will settle these days for a single lobbying firm. The style now is "team lobbying" to make all the necessary contacts and to handle all aspects of the influence game: a law firm, a public-relations outfit, a lobbying firm, plus grass-roots political specialists.

One hallmark of new-breed lobbying is its strange political bedfellows. With Congress split for six of the past eight years between a Democratic-controlled House and a Republican-dominated Senate, bipartisan lobbying coalitions became a necessity. Even in 1978, when the Chrysler Corporation was looking for a government bailout loan, it pulled together a big Democratic law firm (Patton, Boggs and Blow) and a big Republican lobbying firm (Timmons and Company). The latest pattern is for each firm to have its own in-house bipartisan coalition. For example, Bill Timmons—who regularly runs Republican national conventions—hired Democratic lobbyists such as Bill Cable from the Carter White House staff and Howard Paster, formerly with the United Auto Workers union.

It is not unusual for lobbying partners to wind up on opposite sides of political campaigns. One striking example is the highly respected firm of Wexler, Reynolds, Harrison & Schule, which principally pairs Anne Wexler, a liberal Democrat from the Carter White House, and Nancy Reynolds, a close confidante and White House aide to Nancy Reagan. In the hot 1986 Senate campaign, their rivalries stretched across the country; Wexler and Reynolds ran fund-raisers for rival candidates in Senate races from Florida and Maryland to Idaho and Nevada. "We don't think anything of it," Anne Wexler told me. "Our having contacts on both sides benefits our clients."

The swarm of lobbyists is so great that members of Congress have grown jaded—quick to challenge Washington lobbyists for evidence that their case has real pull among the voters. Danny Rostenkowski, chairman of the House Ways and Means Committee, told me that while his committee was drafting the 1986 tax bill, he refused to see Washington lobbyists—though he would grant time to constituents from home. And Tom Korologos, an old-breed lobbyists who learned the power game in the 1960s under Utah Senator Wallace Bennett and as congressional liaison in the Nixon White House, concedes: "We have a different breed of congressman who is more active, more publicity prone, more responsive to his district. . . .

"On the Senate side in the old days you could go talk to two or three committee chairmen," Korologos recalled, "you could talk to John Stennis and Russell Long and Allen Ellender and Warren Magnuson, and you had a policy. You had a defense bill. You had an oil policy. Now, you've got to talk to fifty-one guys. So you fly in the Utah plant manager to see Orrin Hatch and Jake Garn [Utah's two senators], and the Utah plant manager gets in to see 'em. If he doesn't get in, he goes back home and goes to church on Sunday and bowling on Monday and to coffee on Tuesday and says, 'I was in Washington, and the son of a bitch wouldn't see me.' And let that spread around for a while. Political graveyards are filled with statesmen who forgot the folks back home."

"The logistics of trying to persuade Congress have changed enormously," agreed Jim Mooney, for years a top House Democratic staff aide and now chief lobbyist for the cable-television industry. "What's changed is there are so many more groups now and simultaneously a diminution of power in the power centers of Congress. You've got to persuade members one by one."

In the new game, another maxim is that lobbyists must demonstrate that the home folks are with them to prove their political legitimacy. "There's a suspicion on the part of elected officials toward paid lobbyists," acknowledged David Cohen, the public-interest lobbyist. "They often sense a gap between leaders and the rank and file, whether labor unions or other organizations like church groups. I don't think you're a player unless you have a constituency to mobilize."

In an earlier era, labor unions had a near monopoly on lobbying with a mass base. Disgruntled farmers also rolled their tractors onto the Capitol Mall to demonstrate mass anger. Business has now entered that game. Mass-marketing techniques are being used even by people like Charls Walker, a traditional Washington insider whose normal style is lobbying at intimate dinners for selected members of Congress. After serving as an inside tax adviser to the 1980 Reagan campaign, Walker got important tax write-offs for business written into the 1981 tax bill. But more recently he has enlisted help from new-breed lobbyists.

"When a member says to you, 'Go convince my constituents,' then you are thrown into those arenas," Walker explained to me. "You get into targeted mail and all that sort of stuff. The lobbying business is moving toward a full service which will include not just your legislative experts and administration experts, but your public-relations experts, experts in grass-roots communications, targeted communications, cluster-group approaches, grass-roots coalition building." Charls Walker was talking the lingo of the modern political campaign, and in fact, the old-breed lobbyists are turning increasingly to campaign consultants.

Note

1. William Greider, *The Washington Post*, November 5, 1978.

Interest Group Campaigning

18
Sarah and James Brady, Target: The Gun Lobby
Wayne King

In March 1981, John Hinckley attempted to kill President Reagan. The President survived a shot in the chest, but James Brady, his press secretary, suffered severe brain damage which confined him to a wheelchair. Several years later Jim and Sarah Brady became active in lobbying for a seven-day waiting period before purchasing a handgun. Wayne King, a New York Times reporter, explains how the Bradys' personal lobbying efforts in Congress and the states are at odds with the pro-gun position of the National Rifle Association. What are the strategies and tactics of the Bradys in seeking gun control? How is the NRA trying to defeat the Brady bill? How does this article relate to Smith's discussion of old-breed and new-breed lobbying in Article 17?

It was not John Hinckley's murderous assault on President Reagan and her husband, Jim, in March 1981 that turned Sarah Brady into America's most implacable foe of easy access to handguns. It was her son, Scott. It happened in 1985, in her husband's peaceful hometown of Centralia, Ill. Scott, then 5 years old, crawled into a family friend's pickup truck, spied a plaything on the seat, picked it up and pointed it in fun at his mother, who was climbing in behind him.

"Don't do that, Scott," she said. "Don't ever point a gun at anyone, even a toy." She looked closer and paled. It was not a toy. "It was a loaded .22 pistol," the same kind of $29 gun Hinckley used to shoot her husband.

Sarah Brady calmly, carefully took the gun from her son. She found out later that the fam-

ily friend had been carrying the pistol because he had been involved in a bitter labor dispute and figured he might need it. But the potential disaster brought everything crashing in on her. "I stormed about it for days and weeks," she says. "And then back in Washington I picked up the paper and saw that the Senate was getting ready to vote on the McClure-Volkmer bill."

McClure-Volkmer—introduced by Republican James A. McClure of Idaho and Democrat Harold L. Volkmer of Missouri—was strongly backed by the National Rifle Association, which had long pushed to neutralize the Gun Control Act of 1968. The 1968 act wasn't an especially tough piece of legislation to begin with. It built on the National Firearms Act of 1934 and the Federal Firearms Act of 1938, and, among other restrictions, prohibited gun dealers from selling to minors and the importing of nonsporting weapons. Even so, it in effect allowed any adult who wanted a hunting rifle to go down to the local gun store and buy one. You could buy a pistol with nothing more than proof of residence and your oath that you were not crazy or a convicted felon. Few people checked to see if you were telling the truth. You could buy a machine gun if you paid $200 for a Federal tax stamp, underwent a background check by the Bureau of Alcohol, Tobacco and Firearms and your local police chief didn't object.

But the Gun Control Act did require gun dealers to keep records of who bought firearms, in case the weapon they sold ended up being used to kill somebody. And it banned interstate and mail-order sales, like the one in which Lee Harvey Oswald bought, for $21.45, the 6.5-millimeter Mannlicher-Carcano he used to kill John F. Kennedy in 1963. But the 1968 act had long grated on the N.R.A. and other proponents of easy access to firearms.

"McClure-Volkmer would have annihilated the '68 Act," says Sarah Brady. She was not then, nor is she now, hysterical about guns. Her father, an agent for the Federal Bureau of Investigation, wore a .38 to work. He and her brother and uncles all hunted for sport, and Sarah Brady sees no evil in it. Her husband's boss, Ronald Reagan, was a member of the N.R.A.; so is George Bush.

But her son had pointed a loaded pistol at her and the emotionally disturbed man who had shot her husband had no difficulty buying guns or the kind of exploding bullets called Devastators. The bullets that hit the President, a policeman and a Secret Service agent did not explode; the one that entered Jim Brady's brain did.

They got Brady to George Washington University Hospital within 10 minutes and managed to save his life, sawing open his skull all the way across his forehead and getting out the fragments and doing other things like lancing his left eyelid to keep the pressure from blinding him in case he did survive, which few thought likely. But he did, and although he walked out, literally, on Nov. 23, 1981, both he and his wife knew he was badly, and permanently, hurt.

He really could not walk (he could only manage a few steps at a time) and the pain was horrible. He cried and screamed and sometimes he would blank out and howl like an animal. After a year or so, he tried to write his name and it would come out JIMMMMMMMMMMMMMMMMM, or he would count and it would go, 1,2,3,3,3333333333333.

"But it was the summer that Scott got hold of the gun that really finished me," says Sarah Brady. "And then the McClure-Volkmer bill. I thought, 'This is ridiculous.' and I called Handgun Control Inc. and I said, 'Can I do anything to help?'

"Charles said: 'Can you do anything to help? Yes, I think so.' "

Charles J. Orasin, president of Handgun Control—a citizens group based in Washington that lobbies, in its words, "to keep handguns out of the wrong hands"—signed up Sarah Brady to write letters to members of the Senate, in which she urged them to turn back the worst excesses of McClure-Volkmer. She also spoke to a number of the Senators in person. And she wrote op-ed pieces about the issue for national newspapers.

But in May 1986 the McClure-Volkmer bill became law. For the N.R.A., though, it was a Pyrrhic victory. The organization had spent millions in its efforts to roll back the 1968 act, and the concessions it won were less than they had worked to get. Gun dealers could sell, over the counter, certain guns to out-of-staters, as long as the sale was legal in the state of the buyer and seller. Dealers could now sell ammunition by mail, but not firearms.

And a last-minute addition to the bill banned the further manufacture of machine guns for private sale and made conversions of semiautomatic weapons to machine guns more difficult.

The day after the bill was approved by Congress, the entire 17-member public relations staff of the N.R.A. was summarily dismissed. The gun lobby denies that the dismissals and passage of the watered-down bill were connected.

Although the image of James Brady, face down on the sidewalk outside the Washington Hilton, haunted the debate that his wife carried to Congress in the mid-1980s, he himself stayed out of it.

For one thing, he was still technically the White House press secretary and would be until Reagan left office in early 1989. It was Brady's duty to keep his mouth shut. "Me and my boss really didn't see eye to eye on it," he says today. For another, it was Sarah Brady's cause, not his. On behalf of Handgun Control, she lobbied vigorously for legislation circumscribing the buying of firearms; he was concerned with the rights of the disabled. As he puts it: "If the Raccoon wouldn't go out and heal the disabled, the Bear wouldn't go out and confiscate anybody's guns."

Jim Brady, who has a nickname for everybody, calls his wife the Raccoon because she has large dark circles around her eyes, especially when she's tired. Most days, she is trim and vivacious, but sometimes she looks gaunt and relentless. He is a bulky and tenacious man, and so he is the Bear.

Brady is unsure as to when he decided to break his silence on the issue of gun control. "I fell down on the road to Tarsus one day and was blinded," he says, in mock allusion to the epiphany of St. Paul. But decide he did. Certainly having his name taken off the White House masthead in January 1989 had much to do with it.

Once the decision was made, Brady pursued the task of fighting for gun control with characteristic zeal. Despite his severe physical handicaps, he traveled with his wife on about a dozen trips around the country pressing for gun control. On Nov. 21, 1989, he testified before a Senate judiciary subcommittee on behalf of Senate Bill 1236. The bill, which has been around since 1987 in various forms and was named after Jim and Sarah Brady, basically asks for a gun-purchase waiting period of seven days, during which time a background check of the purchaser can be made.

"Are you going to continue to pander to the special-interest groups that whine about a little inconvenience and other such lamebrain foolishness?" Jim Brady asked the subcommittee.

The first Handgun Control print advertisement featuring Jim Brady appeared early this year. "Ever since I was shot," it said, "I have watched from my wheelchair as the gun lobby blocked one sane handgun control bill after another. But I'm not just watching anymore. I'm calling on Congress to pass a commonsense law—the Brady bill requiring a seven-day 'cooling off' period before the purchase of a handgun. So police have time to check if the buyer has a criminal record.

In the ad, Brady cited polls showing that 91 percent of Americans—and 87 percent of American handgun owners—support the bill, as does every major law-enforcement organization in the country. In fact, he continued, "it seems the only people against the Brady bill are psychopaths, criminals, drug dealers and the gun lobby."

"Can we beat the gun lobby?" Brady then asked. His answer: "Yes."

He was wrong.

In late October, the Brady bill was bottled up in the House and never reached the floor. Undeterred, the Bradys say they will try again when the new Congress convenes on Jan. 3. Their overriding goal is passage of the Federal bill. Even with its passage, the Bradys and other gun control advocates say there is much else to be done: educating people about handgun violence and safety, implementing efficient and thorough background checks, finding ways to curb traffic in handguns among private owners and making sure that gun laws, once in place, stay in place.

"The gun lobby never gives up," Sarah Brady says. "You get a good law and they do everything they can to undo it."

The Bradys lobby, speak, write letters, take part in radio and television commercials, monitor politicians' positions on gun issues, keep a close eye on the National Rifle Association and its allies in Congress. In recent months, Sarah Brady stole a march on the N.R.A. with her effective involvement in political campaigns. All of this, of course, is standard operating procedure for active members of public-interest pressure groups, but with a difference: the Bradys are living symbols of what can happen to lives if lawmakers refuse to listen.

"This is what Jim likes to call our traveling dog and pony show," says Sarah Brady, opening a joint appearance before the American Bankers Association in Orlando, Fla., in October.

"Pony," interjects Jim, stationed alongside her in a wheelchair, stage-gesturing at his chest. "I'm the pony."

"Well," she sighs, "I guess I know what that makes *me*."

It's corny, but it gets a chorus of guffaws from the bankers, who seemed a bit too quiet as they filed into the conference room at the Orange County convention center, near Sea World, to hear the Bradys talk about their lives and guns and a crippling assault by a would-be Presidential assassin. Not normally the stuff of comedy.

Although she is married to a man who will remain largely paralyzed and in constant pain for the rest of his life, there is nothing about Sarah Brady that spells martyr. Driven by a consuming mission, she is not someone who attracts or accepts the slightest hint of pity. She does not lecture, she does not plead, she does not seem angry. She is rail thin, green-eyed and blond. Her smile is a tad horsy, but it will light up a room. She is very funny. A bit of Imogene Coca, if you go back that far; Candice Bergen, if you don't.

Despite the paralysis that affects much of his body, and the fatigue and the terrible pain (and the phenobarbital that he takes to control seizures), Jim Brady is still the irrepressible fellow who was nearly dismissed from his job as Reagan's campaign press secretary. That was in 1980, when he was in a plane full of reporters shortly after President Reagan made his curious observation in Ohio that trees cause more pollution than cars and factories. Brady peered out of the window, pointed out a forest fire and shouted: "Killer trees! Killer tress!"

He looks better in person than in still photos, probably because of the relentless good humor and vitality. But his right eye droops, there is that angry scar across his forehead and most days he cannot walk more than a few steps at a time. To watch him, *hear* him, get into or out of a car or in and out of his wheelchair is to comprehend only slightly what this man goes through. He moans and curses and stifles outright screams. "Oh, oh God, oh, goddamn, oh, ohhh, ohhhHHHHHH. . . . " He calls his physical therapists "physical terrorists."

Sarah Brady is relentlessly cheerful. When she is with her husband, she seems neither to lead nor to follow, although she is something of the senior partner by virtue of health and mobility. Rather, she is *there*. "Gradually things shifted to where Sarah was basically in control," says Mollie Dickenson, who wrote a book about the Bradys called "Thumbs Up," which is being turned into an HBO movie starring Beau Bridges as Jim and Joan Allen as Sarah. "Jim has adjusted to his limits."

The Bradys, in fact, have one of those rare partnerships in which each is finely tuned to the other. They are independent—neither finishes the other's sentences—but they function like two people sawing wood. They do not always travel or appear together. He travels as vice chairman of the National Organization on Disability; as chairman of Handgun Control, she is often somewhere else supporting gun control legislation. But sometimes they play dog and pony.

Sarah Brady recounts their meeting and courtship: he a small-town boy from Centralia, she only slightly less a small-town girl, born in Missouri and raised in Alexandria, Va. They met in the late 60's when he trekked to Washington to plead for money for a Congressional campaign he was managing in Illinois, and she was the finance liaison for the Republican Party.

"It took me a while to discover he was not just interested in the money," she says.

"The money," he interjects. "It was the money."

The bankers like that.

She tells of their long-distance courtship and their marriage in 1973, when she was 31 and he 32. She recounts his campaigning first for John Connally and then for Ronald Reagan, and his wild hope that he might be named White House press secretary after Reagan was inaugurated as the 40th President of the United States on Jan. 20, 1981. He was, and they drank Dom Perignon well into the night.

Those were heady times. An elegant woman invited them to a dinner party, and Sarah recalls going home to tell Jim: "Somebody named Kay Graham has invited us to a dinner party." She had never heard the chairman and chief executive officer of the Washington Post Company called anything but

Katharine Graham. "And I had never been to a dinner party where they didn't put the coats on the bed. It was a whole new experience—valet parking and coat checks in the hall."

Meanwhile, relatives from Centralia were sleeping on the floor at home, "and Scott, who was 2, thought his dad worked for Ronald McDonald." And then: "Jody Powell, who was Jimmy Carter's press secretary, left Jim a bulletproof vest on his desk, and a note: 'Jim, it's not the bullets that will get you, it's the gnats and the ants.'

"But for Jim, it was a bullet that got him. . . . "

The Ingram Mac-10 is the very essence of deadly. Originally designed by the Military Arms Corporation as a weapon for close combat, the Mac, as it is called, is not much bigger than the old Army Colt .45. In full automatic mode, the machine gun will spit out 15 rounds a second. For covert operations, the easily concealable weapon could be fitted with a silencer.

In the early 1980's, the semiautomatic Mac was not only the gun of choice among drug dealers, it was also one that a neo-Nazi terrorist group called the Order had been acquiring and converting to machine guns. One of the converted weapons was used to kill the Denver talk-show host Alan Berg, who was Jewish and an acid-tongued critic of racism.

In May 1985, I walked into a gun show in the convention center in Jackson, Miss., to find out as a Times reporter just how easy it was to buy a semiautomatic Mac. I bought one—now made under different names by various manufacturers—in less than 45 minutes, no questions asked. The gun itself, offered by a private individual at one of the more than 100 tables and booths set up by gun traders and collectors, cost $600, cash.

Because the transaction was ostensibly between two private gun collectors—not a commercial operation that would have mandated a seller's license, buyer identification, proof of residence and a permanent record—no formalities applied. And because the gun was, by itself, a semiautomatic version of the Mac and not a machine gun, no Federal tax stamp, or license, was required.

Ten feet away, at another booth, I bought, for $29.95, a conversion kit that, with little more than a drill press and a bit of skill, would turn the pistol into a fully automatic machine gun. At still another booth, I bought, for $90, the guts of a silencer to fit the weapon. On sale for $39.95 at another counter was the metal sleeve to contain the guts. With the guts and sleeve I could straightaway create a foot-long silencer for my aspiring machine gun.

I didn't buy the sleeve. Possession of a silencer without a Federal tax stamp is punishable by up to 10 years in prison. Possession of an unregistered converted gun could mean another 10 years.

It was a nice, sunny Sunday.

The next day, the whole deadly apparatus snuggled into a soft case not much bigger than a desk dictionary (the gun seller threw it in at no cost), I walked into the Federal Building in downtown Jackson and turned it over to Gary Peach, an agent at the Bureau of Alcohol, Tobacco and Firearms. I had no need for a would-be machine gun with silencer. Peach was not happy with my purchase of the weapon, but he conceded it had been legal (with the possible exception of its having been made to an out-of-state resident, which nobody bothered to check) so long as I hadn't made the conversion.

Today, the "open bolt" semiautomatic versions of the Mac, along with the kits to convert them, are classified as machine guns, no matter how they are sold. But the unconverted gun had been legally for sale for about two decades, and an estimated 33,000 were purchased by individuals. Nobody knows how many conversion kits were sold, but in the gun's early days they were widely available, the idea being to provide "an affordable machine gun"—some at a little over $200.

But even in semiautomatic mode, modern military assault weapons (like the AK-47, the M-16 and the Uzi), along with their civilian counterparts (the AKM, the AR-15 and the Uzi-Carbine), will lay down a devastating stream of rapid fire. Indeed, when Patrick Purdy walked into a schoolyard in Stockton, Calif., two years ago and began blazing away at children with an AK-47, many people thought it was a machine gun, so rapid was the fire.

Handgun Control's advertisements point out that people in the United States seem to murder each other with stunning regularity. In 1988, the last year for which such statistics are available, 7 people were murdered with handguns in Britain; 19 in Sweden; 53 in Switzerland; 8 in Canada, and 8,915 in the United States.

Other troubling statistics: there are some 200 million firearms in the United States, virtually one for every man, woman and child in the nation; an estimated 60 to 70 million are handguns. On the average, a child under 14 is killed every day with a handgun. Every day, according to the Justice Department, 25 people are murdered with handguns, 33 women are raped by a man with a gun, 575 people are robbed at gunpoint and 1,116 are assaulted with a gun. Every day.

Given the staggering number of guns out there, Handgun Control concedes the odds of some of them falling into the hands of criminals are astronomical. "But we do know that most guns used in crimes are new guns," Sarah Brady says, "and we can do something about that."

America's fascination with firearms is steeped in both its history and its mythology. It is entwined with liberty, the flag gallantly streaming in the rockets' red glare, bombs bursting in air. Americans wrested their free-dom from King George at gunpoint, and the guns they brought to the battlefield were often their own. When Americans went West, they carried their rifles with them. Guns in hand, the pioneers battled the Indians and fed themselves and won the West.

Davy Crockett, the Alamo, Hopalong Cassidy, Wyatt Earp, the O.K. Corral, Gary Cooper at high noon—all that merges with the six-shooter justice in a thousand Saturday westerns in which the good guy only got hit in the shoulder and the bad guys got blown away. An aging John Wayne, reins in his teeth, a Colt .45 in either hand, tells the baddies: *Fill your hands.* The good guys always win. Because they are better with a gun.

Ask Jim Brady.

"I'm not here to sell wheelchairs," he told a television reporter in Orlando who wanted to know what his motives were. "If anything, I'm here to stop the growth of wheelchairs. I know how easy it is to blow somebody away with a piece. John Hinckley knows how easy it was for him to get his handguns. Could we have stopped him? I don't know. But I know we can stop many others. I don't want to go through this again."

The battle waged by the Bradys and Hand-gun Control against the N.R.A. for the hearts and minds of America's gun-owning public, and the public in general, is a classic David and Goliath struggle.

The National Rifle Association was founded in 1871 and has about three million members and an operating budget of $86 million. Pete Shields, a native of Delaware, helped found Handgun Control Inc. in 1974 after his 23-year-old son was murdered with a handgun in California. His organization has 250,000 active members (although it has the names of a million supporters—signers of petitions, contributors and others—in its computers) and an operating budget of $6.5 million.

Given its war chest and membership, the N.R.A. has long vied with the American Medical Association as Washington's most powerful lobby. Its tactics are blunt and direct: reward friends and punish enemies. For years it perpetuated the misconception that the Founding Fathers decreed in the Constitution that the ordinary American has a "right to keep and bear arms." Thus, emblazoned across the face of the National Rifle Association's headquarters in Washington are the words, "The right of the people to keep and bear Arms shall not be infringed."

Those are, of course, the words of the Second Amendment to the Constitution. But they are artfully truncated. The Amendment says: "A well-regulated Militia, being necessary to the security of a free State, the right of the people to keep and bear Arms shall not be infringed." The key words are "a well-regulated Militia."

If the words of the Amendment are not clear enough, the United States Supreme Court has, over the past 114 years, ruled at least three times that the Second Amendment has not the slightest thing to do with an individual's right to bear arms ("or to arm bears, either," Jim Brady likes to say) but rather to the right of the states to raise an armed militia.

In *U.S. v. Miller,* perhaps the most trenchant of the decisions, the Court ruled in 1939 that a man named Jack Miller was not protected from prosecution by the Second Amendment for carrying a sawed-off shotgun across state lines. In that case, the court specified that the shotgun had "no reasonable relationship to the preservation or efficiency of a well-regulated militia."

Resolutely blind to these rulings, pro-gun forces also argue that gun controls don't really do any good. "It is the very places that have the strictest gun laws that have the most crime," says James Jay Baker, chief lobbyist for the National Rifle Association's Institute for Legislative Action.

Baker cites places like New York and Washington, which have very strict gun laws and very high rates of violence. To bolster that claim, he points to the nation's capital as having the highest number of murders. This argument, however, ignores the fact that cities like Washington and New York are awash in illegal guns because it is a simple matter to go elsewhere to get them.

In one analysis, the Federal Bureau of Alcohol, Tobacco and Firearms found that 96 percent of the guns used in crimes in New York City were purchased *outside the city* and almost exclusively outside the state. The same is true in Washington, where one can buy a gun just over the line in Virginia. Virginia, Florida and Georgia form the biggest source of illegal handguns in the East.

Increasingly, the public and legislators are confronted with the problem of easy access to guns in some states. In Georgia, in 1987, an Atlanta woman named Mozella Dansby, distraught at being passed over for a promotion at work, bought a gun and used it the next day to shoot two of her supervisors and then to kill herself. Atlanta has a gun-purchase waiting period, so the woman went to nearby Smyrna, which has no such law, to buy the gun.

There are other examples, and they occur frequently enough to cause more and more state legislatures to defy the once indomitable gun lobby to adopt waiting periods. In fact, there is clear evidence that the power of the N.R.A. may be waning.

Ronald Reagan, in 1988, signed a bill outlawing plastic handguns, which are difficult or impossible to detect in airport screening machines. Reagan, who bought and taught his wife, Nancy, to shoot "a tiny little gun" that she kept by her bedside, also caused some consternation among pro-gun partisans in June 1988 when he said there were "certain things I would go for" in the area of gun control,

such as a waiting period for handgun purchases by individuals—the heart of the Brady bill.

Not only is there increased public awareness of the handgun problem, there has also been the defection of most major police groups, once staunch allies of the N.R.A. The role played by Sarah Brady and Handgun Control, and more recently by Jim Brady, has also clearly been a factor.

"She has been very effective," concedes James Baker, the N.R.A. lobbyist, "but in large part because of her personal situation." John M. Snyder, chief lobbyist for the Citizens Committee for the Right to Keep and Bear Arms, conceding Sarah Brady's effectiveness, also maintains it is "based on emotion."

Over the past year, Sarah Brady has made two dozen trips around the country on behalf of gun control. She campaigned for handgun control laws in Florida, Virginia, Maryland, Rhode Island and Connecticut. She directed the lobbying and education efforts by Handgun Control in New Jersey and California. Handgun Control lent support to, but had little active involvement in, the handgun reform efforts in Oregon, Massachusetts and Iowa.

A lifelong Republican activist, Sarah Brady campaigned this year for Senators Tom Harkin and Paul Simon, both Democrats, because of their strong stands on gun control. She endorsed Senator John Kerry in Massachusetts, for the same reason, and Representative George E. Brown Jr. in California, who beat an N.R.A.-backed Republican candidate.

Although she did not play a role in Richard Swett's campaign, she noted that "It's significant that one of the most ardent N.R.A. supporters on the House Judiciary Subcommittee on Crime, Representative Chuck Douglas, lost to a backer of the Brady bill, Dick Swett," also a Democrat. The gun issue might have played a part in a Maine House race in which Democrat Thomas H. Andrews, a supporter of a waiting period for handgun sales, defeated Republican David F. Emery, allied with the pro-gun forces.

With her husband often at her side, Sarah Brady is increasingly successful at selling gun control at the state level. In Florida, state and law-enforcement organizations joined them in backing a three-day waiting period to buy a handgun, and a constitutional amendment to do that was approved by 84 percent of the state's voters last month. In 1988, a similar measure was soundly defeated in the Legislature.

In the last two years, California, Virginia, Maryland, Oregon, Delaware, New Jersey, Connecticut, Iowa and Rhode Island have passed some form of gun control legislation, mandating either a waiting period or a system of background checks for buyers of handguns and assault weapons, or both. Some banned the sale of assault weapons.

Nearly half the states now have restrictions on gun sales. At the Federal level, however, after a promising beginning, there was considerable frustration this fall as House Speaker Thomas S. Foley bottled up the Brady bill despite clear evidence of strong support. A bill to ban assault weapons did not come to a House vote after its surprise passage in the Senate.

Foley's publicly stated reason for not allowing the Brady bill to be considered as part of a pending crime bill was that time was critical and he did not want to bog the crime bill down with attachments and amendments, particularly when he felt the Brady bill was not likely to be acted on in the Senate. Nonetheless, he allowed an amendment, strongly supported by the N.R.A., from Jolene Unsoeld, his colleague from Washington State, also a Democrat.

While the crime bill banned the assembly of assault weapons of foreign design from imported or domestic parts, Unsoeld's amendment allowed assembly from *domestic parts.* The bill sailed through. The day after she introduced the amendment, Unsoeld got a campaign donation of $4,950 from the N.R.A.'s political action committee.

Unsoeld denied any deal with the N.R.A., as did Foley. But the public-interest group Common Cause found that of 49 representatives who received more than $10,000 each from the N.R.A. over the past five years, 48 voted for the Unsoeld amendment, with Foley, who got $14,850, not voting. Common Cause also found that the 257 House members who voted for the Unsoeld amendment received an average of $5,432 from the N.R.A.'s political action committee. That adds up to $1.4 million.

At the Brady's appearance before the American Bankers Association in Orlando, it is Jim's turn on the podium. Seated in his wheelchair, he begins by saying: "I'm glad to be here. All things considered, I'm glad to be anywhere."

His speech unfolds in a laconic monotone. His manner of speaking has been severely impaired, slowed by the damage to his brain and by the sedation, and it sometimes slurs and stumbles. It takes the audience a little while to adjust to the curiously flat See-Dick-Run recitation. But it is funny, with asides about banning the Beach Boys from the Bicentennial celebration and calling Reagan's Bitburg appearance "a class piece of advance work if ever I saw one."

The audience warms, but things—at first imperceptibly, then noticeably—begin to fall apart. Brady stumbles over a word or two, says "abruptry" for "abruptly" and then clearly leaves out part of a sentence. He goes back and corrects it.

"Read correctly," quips Sarah.

"You read it." he says.

He stumbles again and the audience is very, very still.

"I have a new set of challenges . . ." he begins and trails off. Then he hiccups. " . . . a new, a new . . . beginning. . . ."

Another hiccup. Someone coughs.

Sarah Brady, who has been listening and watching and smiling, continues to smile.

"Say, excuse me, Jim," she says.

"Excuse me, Jim," he says.

There is a roar of relieved laughter.

Then he does it again. Hiccup.

"Excuse me, Jim," he continues, and he is back on track.

"I have spent eight years in rehabilitation, lots of P.T. pain and torture—the physical terrorists learn their black arts from the Marquis de Sade. But because of my terrorists, I walk better, I talk better . . . and I hiccup better." Sarah laughs. Everybody laughs, but a few blink hard while they do it.

And when Jim Brady stops speaking, there is a silence. Then applause—waves and waves of it.

CHAPTER 6

Public Opinion, Political Parties, and Campaigns

PUBLIC OPINION

Public opinion polls have become an important influence in American politics. Candidates use them to determine voter trends before an election. Incumbents use their results to determine levels of public approval and attitudes on policy issues. The media makes extensive use of polls in news stories and in describing voter preferences during campaigns.

Public opinion can be defined as the aggregate of citizens' personal views on public questions. Three aspects of public opinion are political opinions, political attitudes, and values. Political opinions are general judgments on current policies, leaders, and events. Political attitudes are more deeply held views on enduring social issues such as race relations, abortion, crime, and the environment. Political values disclose people's ideas and commitments involving their fundamental beliefs about the proper direction of government.

Charles Kenney in Article 19 presents an interesting overview of the evolution of public opinion polls in American society. The discredited predictions of 1936 and 1948 have been replaced by a large industry of accepted and reliable polling firms, including Gallup, Harris, and media conglomerates such as CBS and the *New York Times*. Kenney tells us about the construction of random samples, the components of a survey, and their use by candidates and elected officials. He also provides several guidelines for effective citizen interpretation of poll findings.

What are some findings of recent public opinion polls? Before the Persian Gulf War, the Times Mirror Center for the People found increasing alienation from government and "a growing socioeconomic schism within the country." In a survey of 3,000 respondents, the *Times Mirror* poll found that even with the personal popularity of President Bush, "cynicism toward the political system in general is growing as the public in unprecedented numbers associate Republicans with wealth and greed, Democrats with fecklessness and incompetence."[1]

American cynicism and alienation toward government and policy issues seem to get worse the farther away these issues are from the public's home base. Recent polls suggest that almost 70 percent of the public has a negative view of Congress, but 51 percent approve of their own individual legislators.[2] An April 1990 poll found that 84 percent believed that pollution was getting worse, but 56 percent said the problem was not serious where they lived.[3]

POLITICAL PARTIES

Political parties are instruments for organizing power and providing opportunities for popular participation and control of government in a democratic society. The major objective of a political party is to win elections by mobilizing the voters. As an important link between government and society, political parties offer various groups access to government and a means to participate in the political system.

Political party systems can be organized in three different ways: one-party, two-party, and multiparty systems. One-party systems are found in authoritarian or military regimes. The dominant party usually prohibits any opposition in campaigns and elections. The goal of elections is to legitimize and ratify the policies of the party in power. Multiparty systems are found in most Western parliamentary democracies. Consisting of three or more parties, this system aims for legislative majorities and the formation of executive cabinets, with the Prime Minister as both the legislative party leader and the dominant figure in the cabinet. Some parliamentary multiparty systems, such as Israel, need to form party coalitions before a cabinet can be established.

The United States has a two-party system (with a variety of temporary and weak third and minor parties). The Democratic and Republican parties comprise the oldest continuous two-party competition of any Western democracy. They are dominant at the national level because of their success in capturing a majority of votes in presidential elections and in winning a majority of seats in either the House or the Senate to organize and control Congress. At the state level, the two parties have dominated elections for governors and state legislators. As long as third or minor parties are unable to govern by electing chief executives or legislators, it is certain that the Democratic and Republican party labels will remain important. The two-party system provides the majority party with the power to govern and a loyal opposition that criticizes the party in power and offers alternatives to the voters with the prospect that it can replace the party in power.

PARTY DEVELOPMENT

Political parties are not mentioned in the Constitution. In fact, James Madison warned against the dangers of factions in *The Federalist*, Number 10. However, party factions developed as soon as the new government went into effect in 1789. Differences revolved around the extent of national authority in relation to the states. This Federalist–anti-Federalist competition entered the 1800 presidential election when Thomas Jefferson opposed the incumbent, President John Adams. From that time to the present, political parties have dominated our governmental system.

According to James L. Sundquist in Article 20, Americans have always had an ambiguous attitude toward political parties. He attributes this to the original Madisonian model of American government, which was an effort to prevent the evils of faction from becoming dominant (See *The Federalist*, Number 10, in Chapter 5). The constitutional framers devised a government structure that fragmented and dispersed power among the three branches and between the national government and the states. The goal was to prevent any faction or political party from dominating the system.

Throughout American political history, one of the two major parties has been dominant over the other for a considerable period of time. Following an important or *critical* election, the voters shift loyalties to a new party coalition, which maintains control over the executive and legislative branches and defines how policy issues will be resolved. Several party eras are evident in American politics. Following Thomas Jefferson's victory over John Adams in 1800, the Democratic-Republican party dominated national politics for the next twenty-four years with virtually no opposition. Jefferson won a second term in 1804; James Madison followed with two terms as did James Monroe. The Federalist party disappeared and was absorbed into the grand ruling coalition.

The second major party era lasted from about 1824 until the Civil War. It was characterized by the election of Andrew Jackson in 1828, the formation of the Democratic party (based on Western, Southern, and new immigrant voters), and the development of a national party convention to determine presidential candidates and party platforms. The first Democratic party convention was held in 1832. Opposition during this era came from the Whig party, which was most influential in Congress through notables such as Daniel Webster and Henry Clay. The Whigs occasionally elected aging and popular generals to the White House.

The Civil War signaled the disintegration of the Democrats as the party defending Southern slavery, the disappearance of the Whigs, and the emergence of the Republican party. With the election of Abraham Lincoln in 1860, the Republicans became the dominant presidential and congressional party for the next sixty-two years. Following Lincoln, the Republicans won thirteen of the next seventeen presidential elections, with only Grover

Cleveland (1884 and 1892) and Woodrow Wilson (1912 and 1916) elected on the Democratic label. During this time, the Republicans also controlled Congress and filled nearly all the seats on the Supreme Court.

The most dramatic change in party fortunes since 1860 occurred in 1932, with the election of Franklin Roosevelt as president, the return of Democratic party dominance in Congress, and the New Deal setting the domestic policy agenda. Following Roosevelt's four elections to the White House (1932, 1936, 1940, and 1944), presidential contests have been dominated by the Republican party, with seven victories in the eleven contests from 1948 to 1988. The Democrats have consistently won control of the House since 1952. The Republicans gained control of the Senate in 1980 for only the third time in the past fifty-two years. In 1986, the Democrats recaptured control of the Senate by a margin of 55–45. The Democrats retained control of both houses of Congress in the 1988 and 1990 elections.

PARTY FUNCTIONS: DECLINE OF TRADITIONAL ROLES

The Democratic and Republican parties can be characterized as loosely organized coalitions of diverse interests. The principal types of party roles include party leaders, activists, supporters, and voters. In examining these roles, what are the major functions of political parties?

First, the chief objective of the Republicans and Democrats is to win public offices in national, state, and local elections. To do so, the parties provide the voters with candidates who articulate their views on relevant issues. The linkage between parties and the electorate is crucial in understanding how and why the voters behave the way they do. In this sense, parties provide channels of expression for public opinion and serve as organizing agents for different groups who wish to participate in elections. This is one of the primary functions of a party: to control and direct the struggle for power.

Second, parties provide opportunities to become actively involved in practical politics. Before the electorate can be organized, the party itself must have an effective scheme of operations. This requires teams of workers who engage in such activities as voter registration, canvassing, and assisting voters to the polls on election day. The party activists may also hold party offices and become involved in fund raising and designating candidates to run in primary elections. They may also seek to attend national or state party conventions that nominate candidates for such high offices as president or governor.

Third, political parties are a means of gaining control over government. After winning elections, the office holders are in a position to form majority coalitions in government to control the agenda and the outcome of decisions on important issues. Thus the party in government has the power to make policy decisions based on the mandate it receives from the voters.

Parties often have difficulty keeping their promises and translating voter expectations into public policies.

Political parties are no longer promoting coherent policy development and government. They are failing to perform three major roles: maintaining coalitions of voter loyalty, managing elections through nominating candidates and simplifying voting choices, and effectively governing after elections take place.

There are some hopeful signs for party revival. There may be a slight increase in party identification for both the Democrats and Republicans, and party loyalty is more closely tied to policy concerns than in the past. The two major parties are becoming better organized with strong national committees, lengthy direct mailing lists, large budgets, professional staffs, and polling and advertising services for candidates.

PARTY DECENTRALIZATION

Decentralization is another major feature of American political parties. Nominations, campaigns, and electoral contests are predominantly a product of state and local rather than national issues. Loose collections of state and local officials also dominate national party committees; this makeup results in a decentralized structure that is difficult to coordinate except when under the control of a strong national party chairperson. The federal system, the separation of powers, nominating procedures, and the financing of campaigns all cause a power flow from the decentralized organizations to the top.

Public policy is affected by party decentralization. First, there are many access points in government through which elected officials, interest groups, and individuals can take action. Second, there is considerable participation by states and local communities in the development and administration of national programs. Third, representatives and senators seek to serve their constituents by reflecting local and state perspectives. Finally, the president attempts to represent the diverse wings of both parties in making cabinet, administrative, and judicial appointments.

PARTY FRAGMENTATION AND PROSPECTS FOR REFORM

In recent years party loyalty has declined drastically. The independent voter, who disavows party labels, regularly splits the ticket in electoral contests. Furthermore, many people are increasingly skeptical about the goals and objectives of the parties. Fewer people are voting today than ten years ago—reflecting a growing dissatisfaction toward party politics. Parties no longer provide incentives for people to vote. Most big-city political machines have disappeared. The machines formerly offered material benefits to urban voters, which significantly expanded voter participation. Reforms of the Progressive Era (1900–1917) attacked graft and corruption of the city political machines, thereby weakening the most centralized form of party organization. The New Deal of the 1930s introduced the modern welfare state. This further weakened the parties by removing the material incentives they could offer to voters. More recently, parties have become quite fragmented with the increasing importance of television and highly personalistic presidential campaigns. Presidential candidates need to run decentralized campaigns during the primaries in order to get sufficient delegate support for the nomination. Television news emphasizes personalities rather than issues. The result has been diminished voter participation and heightened distrust of political institutions.

NATIONAL PARTIES AND THE PRESIDENCY

Presidential nominations and campaigns attract the most public attention and media coverage since the presidency is the nation's highest elective office. The quest for the presidency offers the supreme challenge to contenders. It takes enormous time, effort, stamina, funding, and media appeal to make a serious bid for the presidency. Some have characterized it as an endurance contest where only the fittest survive.

The presidential campaign consists of two stages: nomination politics and electoral politics. In the nomination stage, the potential candidate needs to start very early—perhaps as soon as the last presidential election has ended, although most contenders wait until the midterm congressional elections are over. During these early days, or "invisible primary" stage, the candidate needs to develop name recognition, raise money, assemble a campaign staff, identify salient issues, work well with the media, and develop self-confidence. Once a decision is made to run, the contender needs to plan and organize for the primary elections.

The initial contests for presidential contenders include attracting delegate support for the party conventions in Democratic and Republican party caucuses and primary elections. Party caucuses and primaries usually take place between February and June of the presidential election year. Presidential nomination systems have evolved over the years from congressional caucuses (until 1828), to national party conventions during the era of Jacksonian democracy (1840), to presidential primaries, the first of which was held in Wisconsin in 1905. Today, three-quarters of convention delegates are selected in the primaries. Some have argued that the primary season has become a time-consuming media spectacle where front-runners gain momentum while others fall by the wayside.

The emphasis on primary contests by prospective presidential candidates has greatly reduced the importance of national party conventions. Instead of selecting the presidential candidate, most national party conventions since 1960 have ratified the nominee who won a majority of delegates during the primary season. Today, party conventions are media spectacles for those nominees and presidential incumbents seeking reelection. Party conventions are most important for television coverage, adopting the party platform, and, most importantly, selecting the vice presidential candidate.

According to D. Grier Stephenson, Jr. in Article 21, the 1988 presidential primary introduced a new regional primary in ten southern states called Super Tuesday. The goal was to have strong southern influence on the selection of the Democratic party's nominee. However, that did not occur since no prominent southern conservative competed. While Tennessee Senator Albert Gore did well, the results of Super Tuesday boosted the prospects of liberal Michael Dukakis and civil rights proponent Jesse Jackson, neither of whom was a southerner. Also, Super Tuesday did not guarantee any Democrat the nomination.

On the Republican side, Super Tuesday provided the boost George Bush needed to clinch the nomination. Bush swept nearly all Republican delegates in the regional primary.

Stephenson provides convincing evidence that nomination reforms adopted by the Democrats for 1992 almost guarantee the reelection of President Bush. The Democrats have been so concerned about fairness and proportionality in delegate selection that they have been unable to select a nominee who appeals to the general electorate. Republicans unite more easily behind their presidential nominee. Democrats are more concerned with competing for the delegates who will nominate them rather than developing an overall message that appeals to the general electorate.

The party convention, held in the summer months of July or August, provides a bridge between nomination and electoral politics. The party convention normally supports the candidate who won the most delegates in the primaries and builds unified support for the candidate in the forthcoming campaign.

The post-convention presidential election campaign is quite brief, lasting only two to three months, and places extraordinary pressure on nominees to maintain party unity while appealing to the general voter. The media and public-opinion polls play a large role in predicting who is ahead and why.

POLITICAL PARTIES AND THE MEDIA

Television today is an influential aspect of presidential campaigns. While more expensive than other communications media—the press, news magazines, radio—television reaches more potential voters and brings the candidates directly into the voters' homes. Candidates are buying TV time for advertisements that create a favorable image. Campaign strategists seek to reassure the voters that a candidate's views are safe, reliable, and comforting.

Consequently, a candidate's TV message is brief rather than one that stimulates serious thought or detailed discussion of issues.

According to Gary Orren and William Mayer in Article 22, the media, particularly television, have replaced political parties as the principal intermediary between candidates and voters. Particularly in national elections, candidates have disavowed party labels and run highly personalistic campaigns. Their fund-raising efforts are directed at purchasing advertisements and getting positive television coverage.

Political parties lose influence when the media assume the principal role of informing the voters on elections and campaigns. The parties formerly had a monopoly in this crucial communications function. But today, individual candidates and the media dominate the electoral process.

Orren and Mayer are concerned that the democratic process is suffering as a result of personalized campaigns and the dominant role of the media. The biggest problem is that the media are not accountable in the way in which they report on campaigns.

Campaigns have become massive advertising and promotional efforts. The media are obsessed with instant polls and reporting on non-issues. Many voters were disgusted with the excessive negative campaigning in the 1988 presidential election.

It is not surprising that voter turnout is at an all-time low in national elections. This topic will be discussed further in the next chapter.

NOTES

1. Michael Oreskes, "Alienation From Government Grows, Poll Finds," *New York Times*, 19 Sept. 1990, p. A26, col. 1–6.
2. Steven A. Holmes, "When Grass Looks Greener on This Side of the Fence," *New York Times*, 21 April 1991, p. E6, col. 1–2.
3. *Ibid.*

Public Opinion: Polls and Political Survey Research

19
They've Got Your Number
Charles Kenney

Candidates for elective office have made increasing use of public opinion polls ever since John F. Kennedy hired pollster Louis Harris in the 1960 presidential campaign. Charles Kenney, a staff writer for Boston Globe Magazine, *provides a useful introduction to the use and abuse of polling information. He traces the evolution of the accuracy of polls and problems that need to be overcome to give the polling industry credibility with both the public and candidates. Why were the* Literary Digest *and Gallup Polls discredited in the 1936 and 1948 presidential campaigns? In discussing how polls work, Kenney identifies three types of errors that pollsters should avoid. What are these? What are the five key steps in constructing a survey of public opinion? Why is development of a random sample so important? How do candidates use survey findings? Kenney concludes by showing how citizens can read polls intelligently. What should we look for to test the accuracy of polling results reported on television and by the print media?*

America's first great polling fiasco came not during the 1948 presidential campaign, when so many pollsters predicted that Thomas E. Dewey would beat Harry S Truman, but during Franklin Delano Roosevelt's 1936 campaign for reelection. In those days, a New York magazine called *Literary Digest* ran the oldest and most highly publicized survey on presidential campaigns. It had picked the winner of presidential races from 1920 through 1932. In 1936, the *Digest* wanted to conduct the broadest possible survey, so its editors, in a rather spectacular blunder, settled upon two lists: a compilation of names from telephone directories and a list of people who had registered automobiles.

Months before the election, the *Digest* mailed out 10 million mock ballots to people whose names appeared on the two lists. By late October the *Digest* received 2,376,523 completed ballots. On the basis of that information, the *Digest* predicted that Alfred M. Landon would defeat Roosevelt in a landslide, that the president would receive a mere 41 percent of the vote. (Naturally, Democrats challenged the *Digest's* findings, none more vigorously than a group of Massachusetts Roosevelt supporters who offered to bet the

From "They've Got Your Number," by Charles Kenney, August 12, 1987, *Boston Globe Magazine.* Reprinted by courtesy of the *Boston Globe.*

Digest's editors $100,000 that FDR would win. The editors declined the wager.)

As it turned out, of course, Roosevelt won in a landslide, taking 63 percent of the popular vote and winning every state except Maine and Vermont. So spectacularly wrong was the *Literary Digest* poll that it brought down upon itself the swift and fierce wrath of polling skeptics (and partisan Democrats). Only days after the election, Sen. Kenneth D. McKellar, a Tennessee Democrat, proposed a congressional investigation into the *Digest* poll and suggested that the federal government strictly regulate all straw polls. Nonbelievers in the infant quasi-science of polling wondered, along with believers: How could the *Digest* poll have been *so* wrong?

Henry E. Brady, an associate professor of political science at the University of Chicago and an expert on polling, says the *Digest's* flaw was as obvious as it was fatal. "In the midst of the Depression," says Brady, "only the rich had telephones and automobiles." As a result, he says, the *Digest* wound up with a sample in which there were too many wealthy people and Republicans and not enough poor people and Democrats.

Thus did *Literary Digest* commit polling's mortal sin: It did not base its survey on a random sample of the electorate. Random sampling is the *only* way to conduct an accurate poll because only a purely random sample guarantees that every voter in the population has an equal chance of being questioned.

Since the *Digest* catastrophe delighted polling skeptics 51 years ago, the survey-research business has changed radically. What was then a fledgling business has grown into a massive industry. Where once only a few national pollsters struggled to find buyers for their numbers, today hundreds of polling companies provide tens of thousands of surveys to a seemingly insatiable clientele that includes national, regional, and even local newspapers,

and radio and television stations as well as politicians running for every imaginable office. For numbers and analyses that are sometimes insightful, sometimes meaningless, the purchasers of polls pay anywhere from $5,000 to more than $50,000. An average telephone survey—a good one—costs about $20,000.

By far, the greatest number of surveys conducted in the United States these days are not political but market research—on every conceivable type of product from liquid laundry detergents to teen-age movie idols. Our focus here, however, is on political-survey research, where, as the business has grown—particularly during the past 10 to 15 years—the quality of polls has improved. Pre-1970s methods could be maddeningly slow, clumsy, and imprecise. Results published weeks or more after a survey was conducted were as stale as last month's news. Today, largely through the use of computers and telephones, polls are strikingly fast and often as fresh as today's bread. And because today's survey methods are more sophisticated, polls are more reliable than ever before.

Polling is not a science, but it is constructed on a foundation of sound, widely accepted scientific principles. Some of the best pollsters, well grounded in mathematics and probability theory, are also artful analyzers of raw data (the worst pollsters are ignorant of methods *and* politics). The work of the best people can be precisely executed methods that lead to brilliantly inspired insight. Other pollsters, entrepreneurs who have gotten in on the boom times to make a buck, produce polls that are quick and dirty, overnight wonders by schlock operators with shaky methodology.

Polls from the fascinating to the ridiculous, the perplexing to the unfathomable, will be on display during the next 14 months, leading up to the 1988 presidential election, a campaign during which Americans will be inundated with polls as never before. But as you face all those numbers, graphs, and charts, there's no need to throw up your hands and give in to the avalanche. Understanding polls is easier when you know where they come from; why they work (or don't work); how they are conducted; who uses them (and for what); who conducts them; and what distinguishes a good poll from a bad one.

And if you think it odd that this relatively young industry has so captured the American imagination, consider that our hunger for information about ourselves—and even more so for glimpses of what lies ahead—is as old as civilization.

"There is a constant need in society for prediction, forecasting; for what academics call the 'reduction of uncertainty.' People want to know what's going to be around the corner in life," says Gary Orren, an associate professor at Harvard's John F. Kennedy School of Government.

"Almost every society has an important place for oracles, soothsayers, prophets. You'd be hard-pressed to find any group that doesn't have someone who serves that role of prediction and forecasting. Pollsters are the 20th century's version of soothsayers."

POLLS AND POSSUMS

Early pollsters were a favorite target for tart-tongued commentators who saw the new business as a fraud. In 1939, a Louisiana newspaper called *The American Progress* reported on a trip by some of George Gallup's interviewers to New Orleans: "Three months ago a half-dozen post-graduate 'Social Science Workers' from Princeton University, augmented by seven or eight East Side New Yorkers who had never in their lives seen a possum, tasted a sweet potato, or chewed a

plug of tobacco, arrived in New Orleans to conduct a so-called survey of public opinion.

"After taking a few sightseeing trips, getting some fancy grub at the famous restaurants in New Orleans, looking at some swamps, and sending picture postcards back home, they then wrote some mystic figures in their little black books and hurried back to their boss, a low-ceiling guy with bifocal glasses who sits enthroned way up there in Princeton, New Jersey, like the Wizard of Oz and peers owlishly at figures all day long until he looks like a left-handed figure 4.

"And out of this hocus-pocus of numbers and dope sheets and form charts, lo and behold, if up didn't jump the Gallup Poll!"

A popular target for mockery, Dr. George Gallup Sr. was also probably the most important figure in polling history. The University of Chicago's Brady says Gallup did no less than "institutionalize political polling."

Gallup, who grew up in Iowa, began his survey work during the 1920s, while he was teaching journalism at the University of Iowa. For years he experimented with dozens of different methodologies, finally settling upon a random probability method of interviewing voters—an approach that was the subject of his PhD dissertation in 1928. Using his then-revolutionary methods, Gallup received some national exposure in 1934 when he polled, rather accurately, as it turned out, some of that year's congressional races. The following year Gallup founded his company and began by selling the results of his surveys—in the form of a column that he wrote—to 35 newspapers.

Respect for Gallup soon increased, when, as the *Digest* poll was found to be worthless, Gallup and two other fledgling polling companies—Crossley and Roper—all predicted a landslide for Roosevelt. That inspired some confidence in the new business, but it wasn't long before pollsters suffered a hugely discouraging setback. In the 1948 presidential election, the major survey-research organizations—with Gallup very much in the lead—stopped polling several weeks before the election, in the belief that few voters change their minds late in a campaign. Gallup and the others predicted that Dewey would win. But as Truman triumphantly showed the next morning, in the famous photo with the now-notorious headline announcing a Dewey victory, the pollsters stopped too soon to detect a massive late shift in support for Truman. Dark days followed: Gallup was widely ridiculed, and his client list shrank. A book was mailed to his company entitled *What Dr. Gallup Knows about Polls*. Its pages were blank.

Since that embarrassment of 1948, two devices have improved the speed and quality of polls: computers and telephones. Until the late 1960s, most surveys were conducted by hired interviewers, men and women who visited voters in their homes, clipboards in hand, a process that usually took at least an hour per interview. While long interviews provided pollsters with more information than they could get on the phone, in-person interviewers couldn't be supervised as closely as phone callers, and the possibility of bias—as slight as a knowing glance or rolled eyes during an interview—was always there. The answers from those interviews—mounds of paper—were hand-tabulated, which could take days or even weeks. Today, interviews can be conducted in minutes over the phone, and results can be produced by computer within hours.

"The telephone is a leap forward for public opinion polls," says Geoffrey D. Garin, president of Garin-Hart Strategic Research in Washington. "Because such a large percentage of the American population lives in households equipped with phones—it's up in the 90s—you can contact people very quickly and much less expensively and with relatively little bias. Now we can do things virtually over-

night. Between having telephones and computers there are campaigns where we will do the interviewing from 6 in the evening until 9:30 and complete 400 interviews. It will be key punched and processed at my office and by 12 o'clock that night, sitting in front of the results on my computer at home, I can be on the phone with the campaign manager, talking about the results and the implications for the campaign."

HOW POLLS WORK: A LAYMAN'S GUIDE

On the face of it, the notion that by talking with 1,500 Americans one can accurately reflect the views of 120 million voters seems preposterous. The idea, however, is rooted in time-honored principles of probability theory. The notion is simply this: If a random sampling of a universe is taken, that sampling will accurately represent the entire universe.

Edward H. Lazarus, a partner in the Washington polling firm of Information Associates, taught political science and survey methodology at Yale before going into the polling business full time. Lazarus says that "a randomly selected sample would be in every way representative of the population at large because every individual in the universe has an equal probability of being picked. If that holds true, your attitudes, demographics, geography will be represented proportionally in the sample."

Garin, of Garin-Hart Strategic Research, explains that the "reliability of a sample is almost never perfect. You can't interview a sample and be absolutely sure the results are identical to what you'd get if you interviewed everybody in the universe. There is a margin of error. If you do everything perfectly right there is still a margin of error, and the most important part of determining the margin of error is the sample size."

A mathematical formula based on probability and statistical theories places the margin of error for a sample size of 400 at plus or minus 5 percent. Garin says that means that "in 95 out of 100 cases, the difference between the results of the survey and the results of interviewing everybody in the universe would not differ by more than 5 percent in either direction."

Perhaps the most mind-boggling aspect of polling is that the size of the universe being polled is irrelevant to the accuracy of the survey. Neil Beck, a political science professor at the University of California at San Diego, takes this point a little further, into what might seem like the ionosphere of mathematics. A random sampling of 1,000 voters, says Beck, would just as accurately reflect the views of 10,000 voters as it would 20 trillion voters. In fact, he says, the theory of probability assumes the population being studied is an infinite number. Laymen don't understand it, Garin says, "but it's the truth."

Most pollsters, says Garin, don't interview fewer than 400 people because the margin of error rises exponentially as the sample size goes down. When a sample drops to 200, for example, the margin of error rises to 7 percent, a sample of 800 yields a margin of error of about 3.5 percent, while a sample of 1,500—the standard size used in polls of the United States—has a margin of error of about 2.5 percent.

Most pollsters select their sample of people to be interviewed from lists of voters or randomly selected phone numbers (random-digit dialing). The advantage to using voter lists is that the pollster is sure the people surveyed are eligible to vote, while the advantage of random dialing is that even voters with unlisted numbers may be reached. Both methods are considered reliable.

Modern polling is far from trouble-free, however. Orren says there are three kinds of errors pollsters make. The first, which is the least frequently made, according to Orren, is a sampling error. These aren't as egregious as the *Literary Digest* mistake in '36, but the absence of randomness still renders a survey worthless.

The second type is known as a "measurement error," which usually involves poorly worded questions. For example, some pollsters ask voters whether they rate a politician's performance as excellent, good, fair, or poor. What does a voter who says "fair" mean? asks Orren. " 'Fair' for some people means pretty good." For others it means not so good. Because of the ambiguity, "fair" shouldn't be offered as a category, says Orren.

The third type of mistake, says Orren, is a "specification error," meaning "you've got a bad theory looming behind your questions. It means you might get the right answers to the wrong questions." For example, he says, he once did a survey on busing in a Boston suburb and found that most residents favored busing as a means to achieve school integration. However, he found that many of the people polled didn't much care about the issue. Among those who did care about it—enough to vote for or against a politician based on his position on busing—opposition to busing was overwhelming. Pollsters often make the mistake, says Orren, of conducting polls based on the belief that "everyone cares about everything and that it has the same political consequences for everyone."

THE MAKING OF A POLL

Most of the best and most reputable pollsters follow similar methods in conducting their surveys for clients who are running for public office, using five essential steps:

1. ***Draft a questionnaire.*** All pollsters ask voters interviewed for standard demographic

data such as age, income, race, party identification, and so on. And most also ask about a politician's performance and whether voters like the politician. Once the questionnaire is drafted, the pollster submits it to the politician for approval. Each question adds time on the phone during the interview process—and so to the cost—so Washington pollster Ed Lazarus says that in formulating a question, he asks himself: "What would we or could we do differently if we knew the answer to this question?" If the answer is that very little or nothing would be done differently, he doesn't ask the question.

2. ***Generate a sample.*** Samples can be drawn in dozens, if not hundreds or thousands, of ways. Some pollsters select their samples from voting lists, others use telephone books. Like many pollsters, Lazarus buys his samples. He pays for a computer-generated list of randomly selected phone numbers—minus most business phones—in the state he's polling. This method is more likely than some others to produce a random sample because it reaches people with unlisted phone numbers. In a statewide race, particularly in a large state, most pollsters do at least 800 interviews. This size sample—which is not dramatically more accurate than one with 400 interviews—permits a pollster to break out subgroups—women, blacks, or residents of a particular media market, for example. If the sample is much smaller than 800, it will probably include too few members of subgroups for a reliable analysis. If Lazarus wants 800 completed interviews, he begins with a list of about 5,000 numbers. Many numbers aren't attached to working phones, some business numbers slip through, some people refuse to talk, others (in the case of random dialing) aren't registered to vote, and still others aren't at home to answer the phone. That makes call-backs crucial. One of the most important features of any good survey is that

interviewers always try to call back a voter who is not home on the first try. Says Harrison Hickman, "We want to make sure every person has an equal opportunity to be selected, and you're not doing that if you're only calling each person one time."

3. ***Conduct the interviews.*** Rare is the pollster these days who has interviews conducted in person. Hiring someone to visit a voter costs about twice as much as a phone interview. Some survey companies have phone banks in their offices and hire and train a cadre of callers. Others, like Lazarus, contract their calls out to a telephone-interviewing service. Lazarus uses a company in suburban Philadelphia to which he ships the phone numbers and the questionnaires. Does it make a difference who makes the calls? A big difference, says Lazarus. "It's important that it be someone who is not going to irritate or annoy you by their voice or diction or language, someone who can establish a rapport quickly so the respondent has an investment in this process." Lazarus says it is important that the callers not know about or care about the candidates. Callers in Philadelphia aren't concerned with the outcome of a U.S. Senate race in Nevada or California and therefore won't be biased in their interviewing. The longest phone interviews pollsters will conduct run 35 or 40 minutes, and some, like Lazarus, are uncomfortable trying to keep voters on the phone for more than 25 minutes. Surveys conducted early in a campaign take three, four, or even five nights to complete. Near the end of a heated campaign, most pollsters complete a new survey every night, between the hours of 6 and 9:30.

4. ***Process the results.*** After the interviews are completed, the questionnaires are key punched so the data can be processed by a computer. The computer provides hundreds, sometimes thousands, of pages of data, mostly

in the form of cross-tabulations such as the popularity of a candidate among women, the major issue among Hispanics, or the character trait most appealing to undecided voters.

5. *Analyze the results.* The pollster studies the data, searching for particularly salient information. The pollster will then provide the client with answers to major questions, such as job rating and the horse race. Over the course of a few days, or sometimes weeks—particularly if it is *very* early in the campaign—the pollster then prepares a detailed, written report. The report is generally delivered when the pollster makes an oral presentation to the client, which usually lasts for several hours and consists mainly of advice—based on the survey findings—about what direction the campaign should take.

The *real* last step, of course, is getting paid. A statewide telephone survey of 800 interviews with a lengthy questionnaire runs between $20,000 and $30,000. In general, phone surveys cost in the neighborhood of $30 to $35 per interview—about $12,000 to $15,000 for a 400-sample survey; about $45,000 to $55,000 for a 1,500-sample survey.

HOW POLLS ARE USED

Newspapers, magazines, and television and radio stations use polls as news items. Candidates use them to formulate strategy. The oft-repeated cynic's cliché about polls holds that candidates read them so they can pander to the populace. But candidates who shift directions with every political zephyr don't often go far in politics—Americans generally see to it that their elected leaders have a bit more heft than that. Do unscrupulous candidates use polls for manipulative purposes? Of course, but probably far less often than doubters suggest.

The cynical notion that politicians use surveys to tailor their positions to the majority of voters has grown rather tired through the years. A politician shifting views on major topics purely to remain in tune with the polls would quickly become transparent. That is not to say that politicians don't use polls to help them get elected—that's precisely what they do. How can a poll help? Let's say, for example, that a candidate for president finds that because of his position on oil-import quotas he has no chance at all of winning Louisiana. But he has a remote shot at taking New Jersey. That small bit of information is valuable because it tells a campaign that it should not waste its major resources—advertising dollars and the candidate's time—in Louisiana but might profitably concentrate on New Jersey.

Or let's say that a state representative is running for mayor of Boston and finds through a poll that he is quite popular throughout the city with one exception—elderly voters don't much like him. Let's say this candidate, as a state rep, had a strong record of supporting causes popular among senior citizens, but, for some reason, the poll reveals that many seniors don't see this candidate as a friend (perception and reality are often at odds in politics). That poll data is of immense value because the problem that has been detected through the survey can be corrected. The candidate can step up activity among the elderly, visiting more senior centers. And the campaign can target direct-mail and radio advertising to the elderly, focusing on the candidate's record on senior-citizens' issues.

Predictably, pollsters get rather grumpy when asked about the use of polls for what some see as manipulation. Harrison Hickman, of Hickman-Maslin Research in Washington, D.C., says polls provide information that allows his clients to be shown in the best possible light. A trace of indignation creeps into Hickman's voice when he poses what he clearly considers an absurd question: "We should be obligated to tell the *worst* side of our client's story?"

Polls are a way for candidates to listen to the voters, says Hickman. And once a candidate has begun executing the strategy—that is, attempting to communicate as specific message about himself or his views through news stories and advertising—a poll is a way to measure whether the message is getting through to voters.

Oddly enough, even though polling had been around for at least 30 years, the first candidate to have a pollster working within his campaign was John F. Kennedy in 1960. His pollster was Louis Harris, leader of one of the oldest and most established polling companies in the nation.

THE BIG-NAME POLLSTERS

While polling companies have sprouted up around the country to fill the demand of local and regional media outlets and to service candidates for lesser offices, the pollsters who handle the major campaigns could easily fit in a small jet. Most pollsters—Democrat and Republican alike—seem to agree that the best in the business are two well-established, very successful Republicans: Richard Wirthlin of Decision Making Information in Washington, whose best-known client currently occupies the White House, and Robert Teeter, president of Market Opinion Research in Detroit. Both men are considered very smart and thoughtful, and both understand not only the science of polling but political strategy.

Among the Democrats, the well-respected pollsters include Peter Hart of Garin-Hart, William Hamilton, Edward Lazarus, Harrison Hickman, and Edward Maslin, all based in Washington. Perhaps the most controversial of all American pollsters is Patrick Caddell, who gained fame as a wunderkind barely out of his

teens in the 1972 McGovern presidential campaign. Some colleagues consider Caddell a brilliant strategist; others regard him as a has-been.

A number of the major pollsters come from academia, where they studied and taught political science, statistics, and survey methodology. But many other pollsters operating throughout the country have little if any formal training. Polling is an unregulated business. There is no licensing authority or professional association. Anyone with a basic knowledge of polling and a personal computer can open up shop.

READING POLLS INTELLIGENTLY

At times during the next year or so it may seem that you hear or read about two or three different polls a day. The key to becoming a smart consumer of polling information is to look for a few indications that often reveal the differences between polls you can trust and polls you can't.

Perhaps the most important aspect of any poll is its author. As a general rule, you can feel safe in trusting polls conducted by the likes of Wirthlin, Teeter, or the major national newspapers or television networks.

Next, make sure the precise question asked is printed in full. Read the question carefully. Does it strike you as fair? Or does it seem, through loaded wording, to have an inherent bias that tilts the respondent toward a particular response?

Not all polls provide information about methodology, but look for how the sample was selected. If the people interviewed were selected either from voter lists or through random-digit dialing, you can feel comfortable about it.

Next, look for a sample of at least 600 interviews. If fewer than 400 people were polled, you can skip the survey. If it consists of at least 400 randomly selected people, the overall results may be fine. But if the sample is only 400, or even 600, don't trust results from subgroups. A poll with a sample of 400 would have a subsample of, say, undecided voters, that was simply too small to analyze intelligently.

Also look for a sample where voters are screened so that the results reflect the attitudes of voters who are likely to vote, particularly in primaries. Some pollsters force respondents to pass tough screens. They ask not only whether the voter plans to vote but whether he or she voted in the past few elections, if the voter can name the candidates running for certain offices, and if the voter knows the date of the election.

Finally, see when the poll was conducted. If all the interviews were done over the Labor Day weekend, when people with the opportunity are likely to be away on vacation, chances are very good that the survey overrepresents poor and working people and underrepresents the wealthy. If the interviews were done only during the day, the survey probably oversampled women and older people.

Ours is a healthy if not voracious appetite for polling information, yet there seems little doubt that our collective hunger will be sated by the heaps of polling offered for our consumption during the coming election season. Many of us will even become statistics as we are interviewed by pollsters for whom we, as randomly selected individuals, represent the attitudes, hopes, and frustrations of, say, 80,000 other Americans. That is a heavy responsibility, indeed, and if the soothsayers and oracles of our times are to operate with any intelligence, we ought to cooperate and provide honest responses to their queries.

So even if you are approached by "Social Science Workers" from Princeton University, augmented by seven or eight East Side New Yorkers who had never in their lives seen a possum . . . ," you might set skepticism aside momentarily, if not in honor of probability theory, then at least for civility's sake.

Political Parties: Prospects for Reform

20
Strengthening the National Parties
James L. Sundquist

In this article, James Sundquist of the Brookings Institute tells us that political parties are viewed as having two different roles. The Madisonian model (discussed in The Federalist, Number 10) *views American government as a system without parties. Parties are viewed with suspicion. Many candidates seek political office by running against or ignoring party labels. In contrast, the responsible party model calls for accountability of the governing party in elections. Why has the responsible party model never been popular in the United States? Sundquist identifies two principal obstacles to strengthening parties. What are these? He also identifies several recent steps taken to strengthen national parties. Sundquist is skeptical of increasing party discipline. Why? Also, campaign contributions to candidates by the congressional parties do not seem to hold much promise. When will parties become more cohesive?*

Political parties have always occupied an ambiguous position in American public life. They are profoundly mistrusted—yet accepted. Their constant maneuvering for petty advantage is reviled and ridiculed, but millions of people call themselves either Democrats or Republicans and cherish the ideals of their party with a religious fervor. Parties have been credited with such supreme achievements as saving the Union and rescuing the country from the Great Depression. But they have also been accused of placing partisan advantage ahead of the national good, of failing to conceive farsighted programs, of running away from problems and responsibilities, and sometimes of deep and pervasive corruption.

It was the last of these that led, during the Progressive era, to a passionate reformist crusade to destroy the strength and influence of the party organizations that, at the end of the nineteenth century, had reached their zenith of power and plunder. Throughout this century the Progressive reforms have been serving that purpose, until by now the objective has been largely accomplished. Governmental administration has been cleansed of the grosser forms of corruption—in most places, anyway—but in the process the party organizations have been shorn of much of the patronage that had given them their armies of loyal workers. The direct primary gradually reduced, and by today has virtually eliminated,

Reprinted by permission of the Brookings Institution From A. James Reichley, editor, *Elections American Style*, (Washington, D.C.: The Brookings Institution, 1987), pp. 195-201; 213-221.

the organizations' control of, or even influence on, nominations for office, including the presidency itself. By law some states prohibit party organizations from making endorsements in primaries or from participating at all in nonpartisan general elections for mayors and city council members. With their organizations thus stripped of both nominating functions and active workers, political parties have in most places lost the motivation and the competence to organize, finance, and manage general election campaigns as well, and these responsibilities in contests for major offices have gravitated to a new and growing professional elite of private campaign management and consulting firms.

But as the traditional political party organizations die—whether victims of reformist zeal or of simple obsolescence—what becomes of the functions that political parties have performed well, at least at times, and that only the parties can perform? Are there, indeed, such functions? A new school of reformers is now answering that question emphatically in the affirmative. "Our political party system," proclaims the Committee for Party Renewal (CPR), ". . . is in serious danger of destruction. Without parties there can be no organized and coherent politics. When politics lacks coherence, there can be no accountable democracy. Parties are indispensable to the realization of democracy. The stakes are no less than that."[1] And the Committee on the Constitutional System (CCS), in its 1987 report, declares that "the weakening of parties in the electoral arena has contributed to the disintegration of party cohesion among the officials we elect to public office," and that "the decline of party loyalty and cohesion at all levels of the political system" is a principal cause of "the failures and weaknesses in governmental performance."[2]

Anyone who would renew or remold an institution must have a model. The ambiguity in the popular attitude toward political parties and the confusion as to the role they should play arise from a conflict between two models of the American governmental system that has been left unsettled throughout the whole two centuries of national life. The first model was embodied in the Constitution, with James Madison its principal designer. It contemplated a national government without national political parties. But when the founding generation assumed responsibility for operating the new government, it discarded that model almost at once and embraced an alternative conception in which national parties occupied a central place. The nation's political leaders have ever since used parties as the means for gaining control of government and then for mobilizing the resources of the legislative and executive branches to enact and carry out programs. Yet the notion that organized parties, rather than unaffiliated and disconnected individuals, should take responsibility for the affairs of government—and be held accountable by the voters—has never been fully embraced in the country at large, and the Constitution has not been altered to accommodate it. Elements of both models are therefore reflected in America's institutional structures, political practices, and fundamental beliefs. And over the decades, the struggle to reconcile the models and achieve a workable blending of the two has come up against the hard fact that, in essential respects, the models are irreconcilable.

THE MADISONIAN MODEL: A SYSTEM WITHOUT PARTIES

The Constitution that emerged from the Convention of 1787 made no place for parties. At that time, only the faint forerunners of modern political parties had appeared anywhere in the world. Factions had taken shape within legislative bodies in both the American states and in England, but they were not formally organized, and political organizations formed by citizens of the new states for purposes of particular elections were still local and rudimentary. Insofar as the Constitution's framers at Philadelphia referred to these groupings at all, they condemned them. They were usually termed factions or cabals rather than parties, and they were denounced as responsible for the "corruption" and "intrigue" of legislative bodies.

Accordingly, in designing the institutions of the new government, the men of 1787 deliberately sought to erect barriers against the development and influence of parties. Indeed, the basic tripartite structure of the government, as well as the division of the legislative branch into two houses, can be seen as having that essential purpose. The framers scattered power in order to forestall the evils of concentration in any individual or group, that is, in any one faction or party. They feared that a transient popular majority might be able to seize the House of Representatives and try to impose its will on the country, but they designed the Senate as a body of elder statesmen with long, overlapping terms who would rise above factionalism, and conceived the presidency, possessed of a veto in the legislative process, as the very embodiment of the nonpartisan ideal.

It was to ensure that kind of presidency that the framers, after extensive debate over the merits of the two obvious means of selecting a president—first, by the legislature, or second, by the people through direct election—ultimately rejected both. Either, they concluded, would encourage factionalism. "If the Legislature elect, it will be the work of intrigue, of cabal, and of faction," contended Gouverneur Morris of Pennsylvania at the midpoint of the Convention; ". . . real merit will rarely be the title to the appointment."[3] But others feared that factionalism and intrigue could come to dominate a direct national election. "The people are uninformed," argued Elbridge Gerry of Massachusetts. Their "ignorance . . . would put it in the power of some one set of men dispersed through the Union and acting in Concert to delude them into any appointment."[4] To render the presidential election free of factions, the framers invented their alternative, the electoral college. The electors chosen in each state would be public-spirited and eminent citizens who would have no other duty, and officeholders would be ineligible to serve. They would not meet as a body but would cast their votes separately, in their own states. "As the electors would be chosen for the occasion, would meet at once, and proceed immediately to an appointment, there would be very little opportunity for cabal, or corruption," reasoned Madison.[5] The electoral college, then, would function as a more elaborate version of a civic club's nominating committee or an institution's search committee. Merit, achievement, and competence alone would be the touchstones. Parties or cabals would be excluded.

In *The Federalist*, Number 10, Madison advanced as one of the Constitution's central merits that it would tend "to break and control the violence of faction," which he equated with party. No more powerful diatribe against the evils of parties has been penned in the United States or perhaps in any country than his famous essay. In it he denounces "the violence of faction" as "this dangerous vice" that introduces "the instability, injustice, and confusion" that have "been the mortal diseases under which popular governments have everywhere perished." In the new American states, public measures were "too often decided, not according to the rules of justice, and the rights of the minor party, but by the superior force of an interested and overbearing majority." All this was due "chiefly, if not wholly" to "the unsteadiness and injustice, with which a factious spirit has tainted our public administrations."

Creating the new union would help in "curing the mischiefs of faction" by raising decisions to the national level. There they would be more likely to be in the hands of representatives "whose enlightened views and virtuous sentiments render them superior to local prejudices and to schemes of injustice." A "greater variety of parties" would lessen the chance that any one party could "outnumber and oppress the rest." "Factious leaders" in individual states could not "spread a general conflagration through the other states." In later papers, particularly numbers 47, 48, and 62, Madison extols the separation of powers as the means to forestall the "tyranny" and "sinister combinations" that would follow if all elements of the government were to be controlled by any one individual or political faction.[6]

THE RESPONSIBLE-PARTY MODEL

The opposing model for organizing a government recognizes not only the inevitability but the necessity of parties and assigns them the role that they everywhere seek and come naturally to assume. This is the model that has been adopted in various forms by most of the other advanced democracies of the world, and it is the one that inspires the recommendations of such contemporary American reformist groups as the CPR and the CCS.

In this model, political parties are formed because groups of people, each sharing a philosophy and a set of goals, desire governmental power in order to carry out their programs. In competition with one another, they present their programs to the people in an open and free election. The party or coalition that wins the support of a majority of the people gains control of the government and enacts its program. The minority party or parties form an

opposition, with power to criticize, debate, and delay but not to block. After a few years the voters in another election render a verdict on the majority's stewardship. If they approve what has been done, they return the ruling party or coalition to office. If they disapprove, they turn the incumbents out and entrust power to an opposition party or combination of parties. At all times, one of the parties, or a combination, is responsible for the government, possesses authority commensurate with its responsibility (subject to check by the judiciary if it exceeds its constitutional powers), and is fully accountable for whatever the government (except for the judiciary) does. In the metaphors of political science textbook writers, the political party is the tie that binds, the glue that fastens, the bridge or the web that unites the disparate institutions that make up the government. Without parties, democracy on a national scale simply could not work.

Yet one can readily perceive why Madison and his colleagues saw such a model as dangerous. If a majority party can win the whole of governmental power, what is to prevent it from oppressing the minority? As Madison saw it in *Federalist,* Number 10, the natural party division would be between "those who hold, and those who are without property," between "those who are creditors, and those who are debtors." He feared that a majority party made up of the propertyless would exhibit "a rage for paper money, for an abolition of debts, for an equal division of property." He put his faith in the geographical scale of the country and in the division of powers among the branches of government. Others, however, demanded more ironclad guarantees against the tyranny of the majority, and those guarantees emerged from the First Congress, under Madison's own leadership, as the Constitution's Bill of Rights.

In the European countries, as monarchs either surrendered their power or were deposed, institutions evolved according to the responsible-party model. The executive authority was assumed by the legislative body in the fusion of power known as the parliamentary system. The larger, always popularly elected, legislative house achieved a dominant position. If a party won a majority of that house, it attained a virtual monopoly of governmental power—limited only by such restraints as might be embodied in a written constitution, and by whatever residual powers that were assigned to a smaller, and often indirectly elected, second chamber. Most continental European countries also adopted proportional representation, which fostered a multiplicity of parties and hence reduced the likelihood that any one party might obtain undivided control of the government. Yet, with these modifications the responsible-party model has prevailed throughout the democratic world save in America.[7]

THE OBSTACLES TO STRENGTHENING PARTIES

The fundamental barrier to strengthening political parties is the survival in popular culture of the Madisonian model. Rejected almost unanimously by the country's political elite for two centuries, the Madisonian ideal of a factionless government has never lost its hold on the public. Factionalism is derided, and wherever possible averted, in the multitude of private organizations with which individual citizens are familiar. Why then, they ask, must politicians divide into factions that spend their energies in recrimination and petty squabbling rather than getting together to do what is best for the country?

The machines that were the target of antiparty legislation nearly a century ago have by now virtually disappeared, and the strongest political organizations in the country are those held together not by public jobs and other forms of patronage but by ideology and philosophy. Yet the antiparty rhetoric of the Progressive era still rings loudly in political campaigns. Both Jimmy Carter and Ronald Reagan trumpeted their antiestablishment sentiments, and candidates at every level still find their road to victory by running against a party organization wherever one exists—the "man against the machine." So advocates of stronger parties must struggle against the widespread and often prevailing view that powerful party organizations are more a menace than a boon.

A second obstacle, related to the first, is the self-interest of individual politicians. A stronger party is by definition one with a stronger center, possessing some institutional means of fostering unity and cohesion. But for reasons stated early in this chapter, the individual politician who does not aspire to national leadership usually finds more to lose than to gain by strengthening the center. With a loose, decentralized structure the state or local leader can follow the national party and its leaders when their policies are popular at home or defy them when they are not. The self-interest of thousands of politicians is a centrifugal force within the party structure that is operative constantly; centripetal political forces develop now and then, but most of the time they are overbalanced.

RECENT PROGRESS TOWARD STRONGER PARTIES

Yet advocates of stronger parties are the beneficiaries of one profound trend in American politics and one series of deliberate actions, and both of these give hope.

The promising trend is that the two major parties have both become, and are still becoming, more homogeneous ideologically. This trend is the simple consequence of the party realignment that began in the 1930s and has been working its way, gradually but inexorably, through the political system. Simply put, the minority wings, once strong enough to disrupt the internal unity of the two parties, have been dying out. The "four-party system" James MacGregor Burns condemned a generation ago for producing "the deadlock of democracy" is now much more nearly a genuine two-party system.[8]

First to fade were the progressive Republicans. The progressive wing of the GOP, which spanned the generations from Theodore Roosevelt through the La Follettes and George Norris to Nelson Rockefeller and George Romney, was powerful enough as recently as twenty years ago to contest seriously for the presidential nomination. But the progressive Republicans are now an ineffectual remnant. Their counterparts, the conservative Democrats, have been vanishing as well, although more slowly. Virtually confined to the South since the New Deal era, they have from the 1960s been gradually losing their base there to the burgeoning Republican party. As conservative Democrats have ended their careers one by one—usually through retirement rather than defeat—their successors have typically been either conservative Republicans or Democrats cut in the mold of their national party. Thus Republicans occupy the seats once held by such archconservative senators as Harry F. Byrd and A. Willis Robertson of Virginia and James O. Eastland of Mississippi, while new Democratic senators arriving from the South tend to be moderates, such as Terry Sanford of North Carolina and Bob Graham of Florida, or even bear the liberal label, like Wyche Fowler of Georgia. A corresponding transformation has taken place in both parties in the House.[9]

The deliberate actions are those taken by congressional Democrats over the past two decades to impose discipline on party dissenters. Any article on strengthening political parties written earlier than twenty years ago

would have opened and closed with a call for destruction of the seniority system in the Congress. That has now been accomplished on the Democratic side. As long as seniority was automatically honored, any Democrat, no matter how out of step with the majority of the party in Congress, could acquire all the plenary power of a committee chairmanship through mere longevity. Through that device some of the Senate and House committees most crucial to the enactment of the Democratic party's program were turned over to conservative Democrats who voted regularly with the Republicans against the majority of their own party. Sooner or later the situation was bound to prove intolerable. Finally the revolution occurred: liberals in the House forced through the party caucus a series of rules changes that not only scrapped seniority but reduced the arbitrary power of committee chairmen. The revolt was solidified in 1975 when the caucus deposed three chairmen. And it has continued to exercise disciplinary power. In 1987 the caucus voted to remove Les Aspin of Wisconsin from the chairmanship of the House Armed Services Committee, reversing itself only after Aspin humbly promised to accept its guidance on major questions of military policy.[10] The caucus has also assumed, and exercised, the power to instruct the Democratic committee majorities to bring specific measures to the House floor.

With this power of discipline, the caucus has been revived as an instrument for building policy consensus. In their drive to assert control over party policy, the liberals won a demand for regular monthly party caucuses plus additional meetings on petition of fifty members—a dramatic departure from the once-every-two-years tradition that had prevailed for a quarter of a century. The caucus has proved to be an effective consensus-building mechanism, particularly in the long and acrimonious debate over the Vietnam War when the passion of the antiwar Democratic majority eventually persuaded some reluctant senior party figures to abandon their support. Since then it has expressed itself on a wide range of measures, including the issues of defense policy that led to Aspin's pledge of conformity. In early February 1987 the caucus denounced the Reagan administration's resumption of underground nuclear testing and urged the administration instead to begin negotiations with the Soviet Union for an agreement banning such tests.

Institutional change has occurred less formally in the clublike Senate, but the arbitrary power of Democratic committee chairmen has been effectively curtailed there as well. Within the committee structures in both houses, democratic norms now prevail.

Finally, the new Democratic party rule that guarantees seats in the quadrennial presidential nominating convention to 80 percent of the party's members of Congress may prove to be an important move in the direction of greater party cohesion. While most members will no doubt be guided by the sentiment of their states' voters as expressed in primaries and caucuses, and while they are unlikely to vote as a bloc in any case, their influence will be enhanced. In a close convention contest a determined network of House and Senate leaders could conceivably be decisive in selecting a nominee experienced in dealing with Congress, as opposed to an outsider like Jimmy Carter whose misfortunes in his relationships with the legislators and the rest of the party establishment spurred the rules revision.

So, whenever the next Democratic president is elected, advocates of responsible-party government may yet expect to see a close approximation to their model. Given reasonable luck in the presidential nominating lottery, today's more homogeneous Democratic party should be able to attain a degree of cohesion under presidential leadership that observers of the party system have not seen—except for the honeymoon years of Lyndon Johnson—in half a century.

Perhaps that cohesion will provide a satisfactory enough version of responsible-party government. But if additional measures to strengthen parties could be taken, the possibilities are worth considering. Any such measures, however, are sure to be difficult. If they were easy, they would already have been adopted, for those who lead the two national parties would assuredly prefer to lead stronger organizations.

THE LIMITED OPPORTUNITIES FOR FURTHER ACTION

The first obvious possibility for further action is for the majorities in Congress to impose party discipline not merely to get measures out of committee but to get them passed. The means to that end is the binding caucus, which both houses last used with full effectiveness in the first Congress of the Wilson administration, in 1913–14. Through that device two-thirds of the Democratic caucus could bind the entire membership to vote with the majority.[11] When the rule was invoked, however, the Democrats laid themselves open to attack by the Republican opposition and its supporters in the media and elsewhere, as well as by independents revolted by the spectacle of coercion. Rule by "King Caucus" developed into a major political issue. Chastened by the public reaction and by intraparty opposition as well, Senate Democrats abandoned the device after the Wilson era. The House party discarded it, too, after a brief revival in the early New Deal period. Any proposal for its reintroduction would undoubtedly arouse an even more adverse response in today's climate of political individualism, which makes the suggestion futile at the outset.

Another instrument employed by strong parties in other countries also appears beyond consideration in the United States. That is control by the national party, in one or another degree, over the selection of candidates for the national legislature. On reflection, it has to appear anomalous that anyone, no matter how ideologically opposed to the program and philosophy of the Democratic or Republican party, may run for Congress as the party's candidate, take his or her seat with the party upon election, and receive choice committee assignments as a matter of right from the party caucus. Yet neither party has ever developed mechanisms at any level for screening candidacies. Even to design such a mechanism would be difficult. Some have suggested that the copyright laws be made the vehicle, with only persons authorized by the national party allowed to use the party label. But the idea of national control of nominations has too antidemocratic a ring—smacking, like the binding caucus, of thought control—ever to acquire noticeable support. In emergencies, like the one that developed in Illinois in 1986 when two unacceptable candidates won Democratic nominations for state office, the party can devise extraordinary remedies, as the Democrats did in that case by organizing a temporary new party. Moreover, the principal reason for advocating control of candidacies disappeared on the Democratic side when the seniority system was scrapped, for while a dissenter can win committee assignments, he or she can now be denied on ideological grounds the power of a chairmanship. This, if the issue arises, would be the easier solution for the GOP as well.

In its 1950 report the American Political Science Association Committee on Political Parties proposed creation of a national council in each party to set party policy as a means for moving toward a more responsible two-party system. The council, to consist of about fifty members from both inside and outside government, would draft the preliminary party platform and, after its adoption by the convention, interpret it. The council would also make recommendations "in respect to congressional candidates," and perhaps presidential candidates as well. But any such proposal also founders on the rock of self-interest. Why would a president and leading legislators who had won governmental office through arduous election campaigns voluntarily share their policymaking power with outsiders and submit to their restraints? That was the experience when the Democratic National Committee, influenced by the APSA committee report, established its Democratic Advisory Council after the 1956 election. The party's congressional leaders simply declined to join.[12] The council issued well-considered policy pronouncements, but it spoke for only a segment of the party and could not serve its purpose as an institution to unify the party.

There remains one other instrument of discipline: money. Dependent as legislators are on campaign contributions, the power to grant or deny financial assistance can in theory by a powerful disciplinary tool. The national Republican party in recent years has demonstrated the capacity to raise and distribute an enormous treasury. The Democrats' capability is by no means comparable, but it has been improving. Is money a potential means, then, for tightening party discipline within Congress to achieve responsible-party government?

In theory, yes. In practice, probably not to a significant degree. Because discretionary power over congressional campaign funds would be a powerful device to achieve central control, the resistance that arises against central control of any aspect of party organization would in this case be commensurately potent. But even if discretion were granted to the national party committees, their self-interest would steer them away from exercising it as an instrument of party discipline. The overriding objective of the national party in congressional campaigns is to win a majority of seats. To this end, the party's self-interest is to support any candidate with a chance of victory, and to support most generously the candidates in the closest races, where additional spending is most likely to pay off in victories. In the heat of a campaign the national party officials making money decisions do not ask about the voting regularity of a party's incumbents or extract voting promises from nonincumbents. They ask only about election prospects. They take polls and are guided by the numbers.[13]

So it is that in these days of Republican opulence no complaints have been heard that the national party has been using its funds in a discriminatory fashion to penalize legislators who have deviated from the Reagan party line. After the 1986 election the party was proud to announce that it had "maxed out" on every candidate, that is, given the maximum amount permissible by law to its nominee in every race. No one was disciplined. Indeed, one true believer in party discipline, Patrick J. Buchanan, the White House director of communications, could complain after the election that President Reagan had been "travelling the nation as no other president before him, fighting to save the Senate for . . . Republicans, throwing his arm around men—some of whom had cut-and-run on him in every major engagement he has fought since he came to the White House."[14]

In any case, cash contributions to congressional campaigns by national party committees are now so tightly limited by law that the potential for monetary discipline is not great. In House campaigns a party committee is treated as just another political action committee limited to contributing the same $5,000 a race (in Senate contests the ceiling is $17,500). Compared with what the array of PACs can put

into closely contested races, these sums are a pittance, particularly in the case of the senior members of key committees who—if any member needed discipline—might need it the most. Any major influence by party committees has to be exerted indirectly, through advice given by party officials to friendly PACs, rather than directly through the party's own funds.

The limits on party contributions could, of course, be raised by new legislation, but the Democrats are hardly likely to use their Senate and House majorities to enhance the advantage that the richer Republican party would get from freer spending. And if a large share of congressional campaign funds were to come from the public treasury, that would not change matters either. In the bill introduced in January 1987 as S. 2 by Democratic Senators David L. Boren of Oklahoma and Robert C. Byrd of West Virginia, the majority leader, the public funds would be distributed among candidates by formula, with the party not even serving as a channel.

Money, then, is not likely to become the powerful centralizing force within the parties that at first sight might appear possible. The handling of money has yielded to, and been conformed to, the prevailing pattern of decentralization in the party structure. And it is likely to remain that way, no matter how the sums at the disposal of the parties might be increased. The members of Congress who would write any public financing law and who already have the decisive voice in determining the national parties' policies for distributing congressional campaign funds will see to that.

Deliberate attempts, then, to strengthen political parties run counter to deep-seated public attitudes, to the self-interest of the politicians who would have to initiate change, and to the structure of governmental and political institutions, including the electoral system. The feasible actions have already been taken—notably the crucial decisions in the 1970s to assert majority rule within the congressional parties. There is a solid basis for hope, however, in political trends beyond the influence of even the political elite itself—the continuing realignment of the party system that is producing the homogeneity on which party cohesion and strength at the governmental level must rest.

If, when one party again wins single-party control of the presidency and Congress, it succeeds in coping effectively with the problems of the country, the value of the responsible-party concept will have been demonstrated and the model will win a wider public acceptance. More people will then see the role of parties as those who believe in the responsible-party model see it—as institutions crucially necessary to formulate governmental programs, to enact and execute those programs, and to account for them to the electorate afterward.

Only such a period of success can provide the necessary popular support for institutional changes that will further the same ends. In the meantime, such changes of any consequence will simply have to wait.

NOTES

1. Statement read by James MacGregor Burns, then chairman of the committee, at the Jefferson Memorial, Washington, D.C., September 2, 1977. The committee, formed in 1976, is composed of political scientists and Democratic and Republican party activists.

2. Committee on the Constitutional System, *A Bicentennial Analysis of the American Political Structure* (January 1987), pp. 3, 5. The committee, organized in 1981, is made up of present and former members of Congress, former executive branch officials, academics, and others concerned with structural weaknesses in the govern-ment. Its cochairs are Lloyd N. Cutler, former White House counsel; C. Douglas Dillon, former cabinet member; and Senator Nancy Landon Kassebaum, Republican of Kansas.

3. Max Farrand, ed., *The Records of the Federal Convention of 1787*, rev. ed., 4 vols. (Yale University Press, 1966), vol. 2, p. 29, proceedings of July 17, notes of James Madison.

4. Ibid., p. 57, July 19, and p. 114, July 25, Madison notes. He even identified one existing national organization that was "respectable, United, and influential" enough to have the power to elect the president—the Order of the Cincinnati.

5. Ibid., pp. 110–11, July 25, Madison notes.

6. The authorship of number 62 has been disputed, but the weight of scholarly opinion now appears to ascribe it to Madison rather than Hamilton.

7. And, some would add, except in France under its current constitution. Executive powers are divided uneasily between the president and the premier, who may be of different parties.

8. James MacGregor Burns, *The Deadlock of Democracy* (Prentice-Hall, 1963).

9. The homogeneity of the congressional Republicans has, of course, been demonstrated throughout the Reagan years. But Democratic unity has also improved; see A. James Reichley, "The Rise of National Parties," in Chubb and Peterson, eds., *New Direction*, p. 197.

10. House and Senate Republicans also permit departures from seniority in selecting chairmen or ranking minority members of committees, but no member has yet been penalized. In a contested case in 1987, Senate Republicans upheld seniority in assigning Jesse Helms of North Carolina to the ranking minority post on the Foreign Relations Committee.

11. Except for those who formally communicated their intention not to be bound, citing one or more of several permissible

grounds. That privilege was, however, not often invoked.

12. However, two members of the party's liberal wing in the Senate—Hubert Humphrey and Estes Kefauver—did join the Advisory Council at the outset. Senators John F. Kennedy and Stuart Symington joined late in 1959.

13. A national party committee under presidential control might on occasion be tempted to intervene in a party primary against a recalcitrant member (despite the unhappy experience of President Franklin Roosevelt in his attempted "purge" of anti-New Deal Democrats in 1938). Early in 1986 President Reagan's political operatives were reportedly encouraging Governor Richard L. Thornburgh of Pennsylvania to challenge Senator Arlen Specter in that state's 1986 Republican primary. While the White House ultimately turned away from that course, it may have achieved a measure of discipline for a limited time through the threat to support Thornburgh. Significantly, the Senate Campaign Committee did not participate in threatening an incumbent senator.

14. *Washington Post,* December 8, 1986.

National Parties and the Presidency

21

Choosing Presidential Candidates: Why the Best Man Doesn't Necessarily Win

D. Grier Stephenson, Jr.

The most important task for the national Democratic and Republican parties is to nominate a presidential candidate every four years. D. Grier Stephenson, professor of government at Franklin and Marshall College, discusses the evolution of the party nominating process from congressional caucuses to nominating conventions to presidential primaries. Selection of party convention delegates has become increasingly democratized. No longer do party bosses determine who will be the presidential nominee. Stephenson identifies three candidate strategies for succeeding in the primaries. What are these? He also discusses the regional primaries of 1988, particularly Super Tuesday. What were the intended goals and unintended results of Super Tuesday? How have the Democrats changed delegate selection rules for 1992? Do you agree with Stephenson that the Democrats nominating procedures put them at a disadvantage with the Republicans? How might the Democratic party improve its competitive opportunities with the Republicans in 1992?

Nov. 8, 1988, witnessed the nation's 51st presidential election. Rare two centuries ago, election of heads of government is a common feature of many political systems today. What is not common is the American way of selecting presidential candidates. For 1988, this process actually had begun at least two years before, as candidates made plans, raised money, and built organizations. The goal was a majority of the delegates at the national parties' nominating conventions.

An appreciation of the politics of nomination in 1988 and the outlook for 1992 requires a brief examination of the earliest devices for selecting candidates, the development of the presidential primary, and the impact of changes after 1968. This will demonstrate that a party's nomination machinery and its chances for victory at the polls are linked directly.

By 1800, party caucuses in Congress were recommending nominees to the state legislatures, who, in turn, selected members of the Electoral College. After the Federalists declined as a political force, this meant that the

From *USA Today Magazine*, March 1989, pp. 20–25, by the Society for the Advancement of Education.

members of the majority party in Congress, in effect, were selecting the next president.

In 1824, nomination by Congressional caucus began to break down. Candidate William Crawford, the choice of the Democratic caucus, found himself with anything but full party support in the nation. Alongside Crawford appeared others designated by state legislatures and state party conventions. The failure of the Congressional caucus to unite Democratic factions explains why no candidate received a majority of the electoral vote that year. The decision fell to the House of Representatives, and John Quincy Adams became the next president.

Anti-Masonics tried an alternative device— the nominating convention. In this case, necessity was truly the mother of invention. Having no Congressional representatives, they resorted to a meeting outside that body, assembling in a Baltimore saloon. Some 116 delegates from 13 states filled the room.

Dissidents who soon would be labeled Whigs did the same thing—even meeting in the same saloon. A convention, composed of delegates of the state parties, seemed an ideal way of choosing a candidate who could rally widespread support. The Democrats were convinced. In 1836, their national convention picked Martin Van Buren (until 1988, this was the last time a sitting vice president who was nominated as president won).

The convention persisted. By contemporary standards, however, party rank-and-file had little to do directly with selection of presidential nominees. Party leaders still narrowed November's choices for the electorate, rather than the other way around. This was the era of the proverbial smoke-filled room, when state party chieftains shuffled, cut, and dealt the deck. Conventions often required multiple ballots before a nominee emerged. Yet, the time-consuming process could unite the state parties for the campaign that lay ahead. To no

one's surprise, this system made presidential candidates acutely sensitive to the needs and wishes of state party organizations.

A surge of reform made its impact early in the 20th century. Leaders such as Robert La Follette of Wisconsin and Hiram Johnson of California demanded a larger role for the people in the nomination process. Voters would elect delegates to the national conventions and express a preference for the party's presidential nominees.

As early as 1912, nearly one-third of the states provided for some kind of popular election of convention delegates. By 1916, half the states had a Democratic or Republican presidential primary, and a few had both. Among Democrats, 54 percent of the convention delegates were chosen by primaries in 1916, a figure that would not be surpassed until 1972. For Republicans, 59 percent of the delegates were the products of primaries, a number not exceeded until 1976.

Still, popular participation went only so far. Most primaries did not generate binding results—*i.e.,* delegates were not required to vote for a particular candidate. Party leaders influenced how delegates actually voted. Theodore Roosevelt learned this the hard way. In 1912, 42 percent of the Republican delegates were chosen in primaries. Even though Roosevelt won nine of the 10 primaries he entered, including William Howard Taft's home state of Ohio, Taft got the nomination.

Partly because influence by party leaders continued to overshadow preferences of the rank-and-file in presidential primaries, voter turnout in primaries declined. States began to abandon the primary as a delegate selection device. By 1936, only 40 percent of the delegates of the two major parties were chosen in primaries.

During the first two-thirds of the twentieth century, primaries were *a* route to the nomination, but by no means *the* route. They were no substitute for careful cultivation of state party leaders. In 1952, Tennessee Senator Estes Kefauver entered 13 of the 17 Democratic primaries, a large number for that day. He won 12 of the 13, but the party nominated Adlai Stevenson.

The strategy became one of picking and choosing primaries carefully. John Kennedy, for example, entered and won the West Virginia primary in 1960 as a way of debunking the wisdom that a Catholic could not be elected president. Until the 1970s, primaries mainly were seen as devices to reflect an existing consensus within a party. Few viewed the primary as a tool to forge such a consensus—that had to be done before primary season. Except for Republican Thomas E. Dewey in 1940 and Kefauver in 1952, the front-runner *before* the first primary was the convention choice between 1936 and 1968.

CHANGES AFTER 1968

A different world of presidential campaign politics emerged after 1968. Then-Vice President Hubert Humphrey was the last candidate of either major party who did not enter a single presidential primary in the year he was nominated. The old La Follette-Johnson notion of popular control of the candidate-selection process took on a new life.

The searing experience of the Vietnam War, Humphrey's nomination, and his subsequent defeat at the polls pushed the Democratic Party toward significant change. For the first time, the national party began to have a say in how delegates were chosen. Beginning with the Democratic nomination in 1972, state delegations had to reflect more closely the complexion of the party in terms of race, gender, and age, as well as the preferences of those who voted in primaries and attended caucuses. Party professionals no longer had the control they once had over how delegates

would vote. The presidential primary and caucus became the setting for guerrilla warfare within the parties.

First for the Democrats and then for the Republicans, the primary provided the opportunity to build popularity and support, not merely a way to reflect the backing one already had acquired. The new era also offered candidates ample opportunity to lose support they already had. Being the front-runner meant that a candidate occupied the seat of vulnerability. Democrat Edmund Muskie's campaign in 1972 declined after George McGovern's stronger-than-expected showing in the New Hampshire primary. Ronald Reagan's challenge to President Gerald Ford in 1976 almost cost the latter the nomination. George Bush gave the Reagan campaign a jolt in Iowa in 1980, treatment Reverend Pat Robertson accorded Bush in the Iowa caucus in 1988.

DIFFERENT TACTICS

New tactics followed the new rules. First, *do better than expected.* It became possible to win in defeat and to lose in victory. Gary Hart's very distant second-place finish in Iowa in 1984 helped to make him the man Walter Mondale had to beat. In 1976, Carter went from "Jimmy Who" to the cover of *Time* because he got 28% of the vote in the New Hampshire primary. In 1988, Michael Dukakis got 36% in the same state, and the media yawned.

Second, *"get there firstest with the mostest."* General Nathan Bedford Forrest's cavalry battle tactics in the Civil War worked in presidential politics, too. Doing well, especially in a crowded field, required a candidate to launch a campaign early; target states like Iowa and New Hampshire, which traditionally had some of the first caucus and primary battles; build a local organization; and pour in time and money. By-passing these contests was out of the question for serious contenders, while coming in first or second generated the invaluable three M's—media, momentum, and money.

Third, and above all, *enter as many primaries and caucuses as possible.* Contests produced delegates, who, in turn, represented votes at the convention. Accordingly, one could not expect to win a party's nomination by entering no primaries or just a few.

The unique feature of nomination politics in 1988 was "Super Tuesday," an event which shook some of this conventional wisdom, but reaffirmed the rest. On March 8, 20 states, 10 of them in the old Confederacy, spread over a territory as large as Europe, selected delegates to the Democratic and/or Republican national conventions. This was almost a complete regional event, with 16 primaries and four caucuses, most for both parties. No previous day in a presidential election year had seen such a concentration, much less a regional one. Some 88,000 Democrats took part in the Iowa caucus on Feb. 8, and there were 123,360 Democratic votes cast in the New Hampshire Primary on Feb. 16. On Super Tuesday, Democratic votes totaled 9,568,290.

What was Super Tuesday supposed to accomplish? The Democratic Leadership Council and Democratic-dominated legislatures in the South devised the day as a way of diminishing the magnified echoes of Iowa and New Hampshire, traditionally the sites of the first delegate selection contests in the nation. Liberal candidates within the party had stood a better chance of obtaining the nomination because of the boosts they received in the earliest contests. Then, except for 1976, they went on to lose the election to the Republicans. Selection of so many delegates early would force candidates to "come south and talk southern." Moreover, no candidate in Iowa or New Hampshire could fail to keep one eye focused ahead on Super Tuesday. In short, Super Tuesday was supposed to infuse new meaning into the words "southern strategy."

Yet, no conservative southern Democrat ran for president in 1988, even though Senator Albert Gore of Tennessee tried to wear the mantle. Rev. Jesse Jackson, South Carolina born, but Illinois nurtured, and Richard Gephardt of Missouri were also in the race, but the more conservative Senator Sam Nunn of Georgia and former Governor (now Senator) Charles Robb of Virginia were not. Some thought Super Tuesday was a party without a guest of honor, the right idea in the wrong year. Nevertheless, the dampened hopes of some did not stop Gephardt, Gore, and Jackson from trying to fill the void.

What were Super Tuesday's most immediate consequences? The first was unintended. It sharply boosted the campaigns of a conventional liberal from Massachusetts (Michael Dukakis) and a black neopopulist and civil rights activist from Illinois (Jesse Jackson). Dukakis and Jackson ran just behind the more conservative Gore in the southern states on March 8 and ahead of him when non-southern Super Tuesday states were counted.

Still, Super Tuesday made Gore—who had not exerted a serious effort in either the Iowa caucus or the New Hampshire primary—a credible candidate. In place of getting there "the firstest with the mostest," he adhered to the rule of "better late than never." He clearly was not playing percentage politics. Gore knew that no one had lost the New Hampshire primary and won the White House in decades. Instead, he worked hard to secure endorsements from state and local officials in southern states. If Gephardt boasted the longest list of Congressional endorsements, Gore did best at statehouse and courthouse levels.

Ultimately, Super Tuesday bestowed insufficient delegates for any Democrat to "clinch" the nomination. For the Democrats, Super Tuesday was "Slim-down Tuesday," eliminating Gephardt, Hart, and Paul Simon from serious consideration and sending Dukakis, Gore, and Jackson into later contests closely matched. Especially valuable for Dukakis was the fact that he was able to demonstrate broad regional appeal among Democratic voters in the South.

As a second, also unintended, consequence, Super Tuesday was a "Knock-out Tuesday" for the Republicans. Bush's near sweep of delegates effectively halted the campaigns of Jack Kemp and Pat Robertson and left Bob Dole counting on little more than a stumble by Bush later in the campaign.

Super Tuesday clearly made these results possible. The day's effects were greater in the Republican Party because half its primaries included a winner-take-all possibility. A candidate who did well at the polls did even better in the delegate count. For example, Bush received 54 percent of the Republican vote in Georgia, but captured all 48 delegates. Democrats may not have designed Super Tuesday to allow the Republicans to settle their nomination early, but it did.

Super Tuesday left the Democratic competition unsettled because, in contrast to the Republican primaries, most of the Democratic contests awarded delegates on a proportional basis, provided a candidate reached a threshold of 15 percent in a district. With the vote largely divided among three candidates, no one came out a clear winner. In Georgia, for example, Jackson received 40 percent of the popular vote and 36 delegates; Gore won 32 percent of the vote and 31 delegates; and Dukakis gathered 16 percent of the vote and 10 delegates.

Within six weeks, Gore was effectively out of the race for the nomination because he failed to make a credible showing in any of the primaries outside the South, especially in the industrial states of the Northeast. The race for the Democratic nomination soon was condensed to one between Dukakis and Jackson. By the time of the last primaries in June, Dukakis greatly had outpaced Jackson in votes and delegates.

Third, Super Tuesday proved the value of large campaign war chests, effective organizations, and a large array of loyal volunteers. If Iowa and New Hampshire made "retail" politics possible, Super Tuesday was almost entirely "wholesale." With so many contests, gone were the opportunities to focus on a single state with a person-to-person campaign built on slim resources.

Fourth, as a result of economics and technology, Super Tuesday and the rest of the 1988 presidential primaries and caucuses witnessed the elimination of the near monopoly on campaign news enjoyed by the three major television networks. To provide extensive coverage of a dozen presidential candidates from the serious launchings of campaigns in 1987 through the dozens of primaries and caucuses in 1988 was not only a logistical burden, but a financial drain. Today's technology allows local television stations and other news services to produce their own reports and to receive other stations' coverage in a way not financially or technically possible a short time ago. It was cable network C-SPAN's coverage of New Hampshire, after all, that led to Delaware Sen. Joseph Biden's undoing in 1987, months before the primary. Local television news thrives on "Tarmac politics," a fact Gary Hart discovered in 1984. At the rate of a half-dozen airport appearances a day, candidates see few voters, but many voters later see the candidates via electronic wizardry. In the primary season, as in the fall campaign, candidates now often shy away from the massive rallies that were the hallmark of American presidential politics only a few years ago. In the "old days," campaign directors tried to obtain the largest crowd estimate possible from the local sheriff or police chief. Big turnouts were a way of conveying growing support for a candidate nationally. Now, for the most part, the emphasis is on staging "events" for the cameras.

TOWARD 1992

Super Tuesday's effects will be felt in 1992 and beyond. American political history gives no indication that this campaign innovation will be the last. Each innovation begets another.

Other states may band together to create regional primaries of their own. One alliance of states may cause others to unite in self-defense. Congress even may require regional primaries. (In 1988, it considered legislation which would direct the Federal Election Commission to fix dates for a series of six regional primaries.) If this happens, there will have to be a reevaluation of the early and isolated Iowa and New Hampshire events. However, their elimination would reduce the ability of relatively unknown candidates to use the early contests as a basis for building a national following. This strategy greatly helped Carter in 1976, Hart in 1984, and Gephardt in 1988. Regional primaries at the outset would work against such people because too many delegates would be at stake too soon. The result might be domination by "celebrity" candidates—those already enjoying high name recognition, in or out of politics.

Even without Congressional direction, a series of regional primaries in 1992 probably will encompass fewer states than Super Tuesday's 20. Five or six regional primaries, each with eight to 10 states, might be a better way of balancing "retail" against "wholesale" campaigning. Newcomers would not confront an obstacle so massive as Super Tuesday; neither would they enjoy a state-by-state path of stepping stones to the nomination.

If Congress does not require regional primaries, but if the regional idea catches on, it may accelerate the movement toward "front-loading"—the shifting of primaries and caucuses to an earlier date in the delegate selection season during presidential election years. By the first Tuesday in April, seven percent of the delegates had been chosen in 1968, 17 percent in 1972, 33 percent in 1976, 42 percent in 1980, 52 percent in 1984, and 57 percent in 1988. Super Tuesday occurred relatively early in 1988. In 1992, other groupings of states may try to move to the front of the line to magnify their influence. If so, the national parties or Congress may have to restore order and dictate that different regions take turns going first. Front-loading was supposed to reduce the length of the campaign season, but has had the opposite result. The immense amount of money needed to compete simultaneously in 20 states early in 1988 required candidates to start running even sooner than before. This reality means that the presidential campaign of 1992 began on Nov. 9, 1988—the day after the election.

There already have been significant changes in the Democratic Party's rules for 1992. All primaries and caucuses now must allocate delegates proportionally to the number of votes a candidate receives. While most states in 1988 selected delegates in this way, some large ones did not. Some allowed direct election primaries, wherein voters balloted directly for delegates by district and a winner-take-all result was possible. (Candidate A wins the most votes in each of five districts; candidate B places second to candidate A in five districts; candidate A receives the delegates from all five districts.) Other states used a bonus primary, whereby the winner in each district won one extra delegate, with the rest divided proportionally. Direct election primaries, for example, gave Dukakis 46 percent of the primary vote and 56 percent of the delegates; in the same states, Jackson received 29 percent of the primary vote, buy only 12 percent of the delegates. In states using proportional representation primaries, Dukakis received 40 percent of the vote and 43 percent of the delegates, while Jackson received 30 percent of the vote and 34 percent of the delegates.

A second rule change affects superdelegates, who are unelected and officially unpledged, but are chosen for the convention because of the political and party offices they hold. First introduced for the 1984 Democratic convention in an effort to reestablish the role of the national party and elected officials in the choice of a presidential candidate, superdelegates totaled 644 at the 1988 convention. In 1992, the number will be reduced to about 250, consisting of all Democratic governors, many of the Democratic members of Congress, party "elders" such as former presidential candidates, the chairs of the state party organizations, and the chair and other principal officers of the Democratic National Committee. Assuming that no candidate arrives at the convention in 1992 with a majority of the delegates, this change shifts influence from the national party toward grass-roots participation. In 1988, however, even with the large number of superdelegates, Michael Dukakis had obtained more than enough delegates by June for the nomination in the primaries and the caucuses.

Neither change necessarily will improve the Democrats' chances for nominating an electable candidate in 1992. George Bush's election in 1988 marked the fifth Democratic defeat in the past six presidential elections.

The combination of current Democratic nominating procedures and those who choose to participate in the primaries and caucuses nearly assures the nomination of a candidate who will be less than acceptable to the voting population in the general election.

In 1988, for example, Dukakis received 9,727,000 votes in the states which held presidential primaries. This represented 42.5 percent of the total, but nearly 90,000,000 people voted in the November election. To win the nomination, one must appeal to the few; to win the election, one must appeal to the many. A poignant reminder is Texas Sen. Lloyd Bentsen, who consistently had the lowest "negatives" of any of the four national candidates in 1988. Yet, the politics of the present Democratic candidate selection process makes it almost impossible for a Bentsen to be nominated as president. Even in 1976, when Bentsen made a try at the nomination, he won only six delegates from his home state.

Granted, Republican victory in 1988 was immeasurably aided by Reagan's popularity and the widely heralded peace and prosperity of his eight years in office. It is always harder to run against relative satisfaction—to convince voters that they are neither as secure nor as well off as they think. Moreover, Bush and the Republicans deserve credit for effectively characterizing Dukakis as outside the "mainstream" and seizing the political center themselves, tasks made easier by Democratic nomination politics. It was little wonder, therefore, that Bush attracted 54 percent of the voters and won 40 states.

Political Parties and the Media

22

The Press, Political Parties, and the Public-Private Balance in Elections

Gary R. Orren and William G. Mayer

In this article, Orren and Mayer of Harvard University make two key points. First, political parties have lost the important role of informing and communicating with the voters, especially in presidential campaigns. Instead, candidates at all levels of government run personalized campaigns. The second point is that much of campaign politics has become a private industry, with many of the functions formerly provided by political parties now performed by hired consultants, pollsters, and especially by the mass media, particularly television news shows. The electronic media are now the principal brokers between candidates and voters. How does this broker role affect candidates and voters? Orren and Mayer argue that the media have "both a public and a private face." What do they mean by this? What are the prospects of holding the media more accountable in campaign reporting?

COMMUNICATING WITH VOTERS

Political parties and the mass media have fought a long battle for dominance in *communicating with and educating the electorate.* The key issue has been this: Who will control the stream of messages that bombards the voters during an election campaign? In other words, who will determine the inputs upon which the citizenry will base its voting decisions?

For most of the nineteenth century, political parties were the dominant instrument of campaign communications and probably of political education generally. From the 1830s on, grassroots party organizations sprang up in every city, county, and rural hamlet in the na-

tion. One of their main functions was to carry the parties' message to the electorate. Party precinct workers went from door to door, selling the merits of the party slate. As Ralph Whitehead once noted, the party organization served as a "labor-intensive communications medium."

Adding to their effectiveness, such party machines in many locations enjoyed a virtual monopoly on political communications. In city neighborhoods with large immigrant populations that did not speak English, the precinct captain or ward boss became a kind of ambassador to the outside world, interpreting political developments for the new Americans. Needless to say, the information provided this way was far from neutral or objective. Farms

Reprinted from pp. 205-210; 218-224 in *The Parties Respond: Changes in the American Party System*, edited by L. Sandy Maisel, 1990, by permission of Westview Press, Boulder, Colorado.

and small towns, too, were a lot more isolated in the age before television, radio, and modern highways. So although rural politics in the strong-party era has been less well studied than urban politics, it is safe to say that party organizations served as an important source of political news for many rural residents.

Even where other sources of political news were available, most of them worked with—or for—the party organizations, rather than against them. In 1850 census listed only 5 percent of newspapers as "neutral" or "independent." The other 95 percent were propaganda organs for political parties, nurturing the growth of party organizations and cultivating devoted mass followings. They served as the principal weapons in the intense partisan battles of the age. Scores of campaign newspapers, published strictly for electioneering, sprang up throughout the nation. One of the most successful was Horace Greeley's *Log Cabin*, devoted to perfecting the image of William Henry Harrison.

In fact, the most important editors of this period were essentially politicians who wielded newspapers, fortifying and arousing the party faithful with catchwords and slogans. Many of these editors became leaders of state and local party organizations. Thurlow Weed, for example, used the newspaper he published, the *Albany Evening Journal,* to organize the Whig party in New York. The distinction between the press and the party nearly vanished.

Toward the end of the nineteenth century, however, the partisan press began to wane, and with it the centrality of political parties in communicating with the electorate. Newspapermen started writing about the emergence of a press free from party domination. By 1880, one-fourth of the country's newspapers were independent of party control, and by 1890 about one-third. By 1940 nearly half the papers were independent, and

only a quarter had outright partisan ties. And, of course, it was the press itself that led the reform assault against local party machines around the turn of the century. Political leaders like Theodore Roosevelt and Woodrow Wilson used newspapers as a counterforce against party organizations to establish their own direct links with the public.

Today journalism has become a far more professional occupation, bound by an ethic of objectivity. Network television has perfected the nonpartisan approach to news. This has happened partly because of economic pressure to attract the largest possible audience and partly because of regulations requiring balanced reporting and equal time to opposing candidates and parties.

Starting in the Progressive Era, from the mid-1880s to the early 1920s, the strong local party organizations also began to crumble. In this case, the media were not the immediate cause of death. The chief executioners were civil service laws, though in many cases the newly independent press helped lead the fight to enact such laws. Going door to door is not especially interesting work, and the only people who would do it regularly, election after election, were those whose livelihood depended on it. As patronage gave way to civil service, then, local party organizations gradually fell apart.

The last hurrahs of the old party machines occurred at different times in different parts of the country, depending on the local political culture and the resourcefulness of reform leaders. But by 1960 at the latest, party organizations were no longer an important force in large sections of the country. A study carried out in Detroit in 1956, for example, found "a viable Democratic organization in less than half of the precincts, and a working Republican organization in about one-third of the precincts." The state of party organization in Minneapolis in the late 1940s led to a similar verdict: "Roughly 100 of the 634 possible precinct captaincies will be unfilled and not over half the remainder are filled by active precinct workers who can be depended upon at all times." In the national election surveys that the University of Michigan has conducted regularly since 1952, the percentage of American adults who report having been contacted by a party worker has never risen above 25 percent.

But even where the party precinct organizations endured, their monopoly was a thing of the past. The immigrants were gradually assimilated, and rural areas were transformed by revolutions in communications and transportation. Today, a party precinct worker who knocks on a typical American door has to counter the messages that voters have been receiving from television and newspapers. It is not a fair fight, to say the least. In 1980, for example, 86 percent of the Michigan survey sample said they had watched the campaign on television, 71 percent had read campaign stories in the newspaper, 47 percent had heard programs or discussions on radio, and 35 percent had used magazines—buy only 24 percent had been contacted by a party worker.

Thus, even if the old precinct organizations were more active, it is questionable how effective they would be. When the typical American adult has watched television for six hours a day for much of his life and thus learned to accept a televised view of reality, how likely is it that he will believe an alternative vision presented by a party precinct worker who visits once or twice before an election? Studies have invariably found that precinct work has little effect on voter choice in major, high-media elections. Using survey data from 1952–1964, Gerald Kramer found that the effect of precinct canvassing in presidential and congressional elections was very small and frequently counterproductive. In

one especially good study, Cutright and Rossi conducted extensive surveys of party precinct workers in the city of Gary, Indiana. After controlling for socioeconomic characteristics, the team tried to relate variations in precinct activity to variations in the two-party share of the vote. In the 1956 presidential election, they found that for both Democrats and Republicans, an active committeeman increased his party's share of the vote by only about 4 percent.

Further evidence comes from a survey William Mayer conducted in 1980 in Chicago, then one of the few places in the United States that still had a strong party organization. When asked which of seven sources they relied upon most for information about politics and elections, 73 percent mentioned television, 63 percent named newspapers, and only 7 percent cited their party organization precinct captain. When asked which source they trusted more, the results were: television 43 percent, newspapers 38 percent, precinct captains 3 percent. Asked which they distrusted, 46 percent said precinct captains versus 15 percent for television. Simply put, when faced with a conflict between Walter Cronkite and a local party minion, the average voter sided with Cronkite.

One qualification does need to be added to this picture: Party organization may still be an important force in lower-level elections such as for state legislature or city council and perhaps in some congressional elections as well. Precinct captains can't compete with television anchors, but in these elections they don't need to. The typical state legislative race receives little or no television coverage and may not get much attention in the newspapers, either. With such a dearth of information, the voter may listen to party workers simply because they are the only source available. For example, in the same city where Cutright and Rossi showed that party activity had only a minimal impact on the presidential vote, they found that precinct work accounted for 80 percent of the variation in the Democratic primary vote for offices such as county commissioner and county surveyor.

Of course, communication is not just a one-way process. The voters have grievances, demands, and ideas that they want to communicate to political leaders. But here as well, the last thirty years have seen parties supplanted by media. When Franklin Roosevelt wanted to find out what was on the public mind, he often called on party leaders like Ed Kelly in Chicago and Ed Flynn in New York, whose positions and precinct organizations supposedly put them in closer touch with the electorate. Today, the public pulse is monitored largely by opinion polls—some conducted by parties, most by media organizations—or polling firms like Gallup and Harris that sell their results to media clients.

Some readers might interject here that we have ignored an important part of the loop: Parties, it might be argued, also benefit from the mass media. They can use television and newspapers to send their message more effectively to the electorate. But this argument ignores an important distinction: In general, it is not the *parties* but the *candidates* who try to communicate with the voters. And candidates, not surprisingly, are generally uninterested in selling the electorate on the merits of their party as a whole. Modern campaigns, as Robert Agranoff has noted, are "candidate-centered." Their task is to stress the strengths of their own candidate or to attack the weaknesses of the opponent. In either case, they rarely put much emphasis on partisan ties. Indeed, many modern campaigns—like Jimmy Carter's and Gary Hart's bids for the Democratic presidential nomination—actually ran against the party apparatus, portraying it as out of touch, unresponsive, and illegitimate. If precinct organizations were still the main link

to the voters, such candidates would have to make their peace with the party.

One reason precinct organizations are no longer the main link is that they have lost their monopoly on communicating with voters. A new cadre of campaign consultants, independent of political parties, has risen to prominence—if not preeminence—in election campaigns. More and more, campaigns rely on hired guns for advice and services such as advertising, polling, direct mail, and fund raising. The ascendancy of this elite corps of campaign professionals has accompanied, and at the same time hastened, the retreat of party organizations.

Recently the parties, led by the Republicans, have been jumping on the communications bandwagon. They have tried to become major service organizations for campaigns, paying for or supplying polling, advertising, fund raising, and the like. They have even sponsored advertising that promotes the record and virtues of the party. Some observers believe that this new sophistication will resuscitate political parties, as they become repositories of technical expertise and services. But candidates will not readily relinquish their independence and return control to the parties. In the jockeying for campaign supremacy among the media, the consultants, the candidates, and the parties, it is the parties who will come up short.

The substantial literature that has grown up in recent years around modern congressional elections makes much the same point. Members of Congress get reelected by making very personalistic appeals to their local districts. They emphasize the services they have delivered to the voters, the interests and constituencies they stand up for, their effectiveness in guaranteeing the district its fair share of the federal pork barrel—but not their party affiliation. Indeed, the whole purpose of such campaigning is to insulate the representatives

TABLE 1 Key Intermediary Functions in Elections

Function	Formerly Performed by	Currently Performed by
Communicating with voters	Political parties	News media Candidate campaigns (and their consultants)
Evaluating candidates	Political parties	News media
Selecting party nominees	Political parties	Voters
Recruiting candidates	Political parties	No group or institution (individuals decide on their own)
Mobilizing voters	Political parties	Political parties } Interest groups } very weakly
Clarifying electoral choices	Political parties	Candidate campaigns) Political parties (weakly)

from larger national trends, and thus to make sure they will get reelected even if their party's record is unpopular.

The media, of course, are not the principal movers behind candidate-centered campaigns. The decisions to downplay partisan themes are taken, in the first instance, by the candidates and their managers. But the media make such campaigns possible. They offer candidates a channel to the electorate that bypasses the party organization. They also focus the public's attention on candidates rather than political parties.

> For instance, television made it possible for the first time for millions of Americans to see and hear a live speech by a president, without being in the physical presence of the president. This in itself has bred a new sense of familiarity of citizens with the president, a familiarity that [the presidents] can exploit in their election campaigns and tenure in office. After all, you cannot televise an entire political party but you can televise an individual candidate. What works best on television is the candidate-centered campaigns, with all the attention to personality, individual character, appearance, poise, and de-

meanor that mark the television campaign. An older campaign strategy, which centered on party label, and endorsement of party bosses, has not translated nearly as well into the television era.

Print journalism, too, has increasingly focused on candidates. One study that monitored presidential election coverage in five major newspapers and magazines found that candidates were mentioned about twice as often as parties in the 1950s and roughly five times as often in 1980. The press, once the prime reinforcer of partisanship, now highlights candidates instead.

The function of educating the electorate, then, is one that has been usurped almost entirely from political parties. The role has passed to the media and to the individual candidates and campaigns.

Table 1 summarizes our discussion of who is now performing which traditional party functions. The mass media have largely supplanted political parties as the conduit through which candidates communicate with voters and through which voters become educated on election issues. Individual campaigns have taken over much of this function as well. They now control such activities as fund raising, field operations, polling, press relations, getting out the vote, and especially advertising.

The media have also become the principal institution that evaluates the candidates and their standing in the races, judging whether they are strong or weak, worthy or unworthy, doing well or doing poorly.

Nevertheless, there are ways in which the media cannot fill the parties' shoes. As direct primaries have increasingly drawn the public into the nomination process, the function of selecting candidates has passed to the voters themselves. Moreover, two of the functions once reserved for parties are no longer performed by any institution, at least not vigorously. Candidate recruitment is virtually a thing of the past. And while psychological attachment to a party still has some power to get people to the polls, voter mobilization is not a hallmark of contemporary American politics.

To a greater extent, the parties continue to clarify and structure electoral choices for voters. They do this less effectively than they once did. Yet even in a country where distinctions between parties are relatively weak, the party label still serves as a symbol for a cluster of policies and principles that yields helpful cues to the voters.

THE PUBLIC-PRIVATE BALANCING ACT

As the preceding discussion should suggest, political parties and the media, as intermediary agencies, are inevitably two-sided institutions. They have both a public and a private face; they are, one might say, *semipublic institutions*. In order to link the public to political leaders and government, these institutions must be privately organized and operated. (Otherwise, they would simply be creatures of the very leaders or government they were try-

ing to influence.) But they also play a vital role in the political and governing process and serve important public functions.

In the case of political parties, this public-private duality has taken shape gradually since the nineteenth century. Originally, parties were little more than aggregations of like-minded individuals who came together to promote various interests and policies and to gain the benefits of political power. Parties were never mentioned in the Constitution and not in state law until the late 1800s. Eventually, however, many Americans came to feel that, since the parties exercised such important political power, they should be regulated by the government. The first step in this direction came with the adoption of the partisan version of the Australian ballot (a ballot marked in secret and printed, distributed, and counted by public authorities) in the 1880s, in which state governments officially recognized party-nominated slates of candidates. Having bestowed legal status on the parties, the states next found it necessary to determine who was entitled to the party label, which led to the adoption of the party primary in the early 1900s. "By 1920," wrote Austin Ranney, "most states had adopted a succession of mandatory statutes regulating every major aspect of the parties' structures and operations." This trend probably reached its zenith in 1944, when the U.S. Supreme Court, in outlawing the whites-only primary, declared that a party whose nomination system was prescribed in state law became, in effect, "an agency of the state."

The courts thereby announced that political parties were institutions that performed important public functions. But if parties become too closely regulated by government, if they really are nothing more than creatures of the state, then they lose the flexibility and self-governing capacity that are necessary to represent public demands and grievances. And so, more recently, the pendulum has started to swing back in the opposite direction as the Supreme Court has affirmed the private status of political parties. In a series of decisions handed down over the last two decades, the Supreme Court has consistently upheld the superiority of national party rules over state laws, declaring that "a political party's choice among the various ways of determining the makeup of a state's delegation to the party's national convention is protected by the Constitution."

Within the Democratic party, controversial battles and debates over presidential nomination rules have also reflected this public vs. private duality. Party reformers who criticized the "smoke-filled room" traditions of the party tried to make the presidential selection process more public and more accountable. They sought to broaden participation and make room for divergent points of view. Party regulars, on the other hand, defended rules and procedures that enhanced the influence of party professionals and strengthened peer review. They hoped to keep the selection of nominees essentially an internal affair.

The mass media also exhibit both a public and a private face. As with political parties, Supreme Court rulings support both faces of the media. For example, the Court has recognized that the press plays a unique and critical role in a self-governing democracy by providing the information necessary for the public to make intelligent political choices. Moreover, as the Court has noted, the press provides a "powerful antidote to any abuses of power by government officials" and helps keep them "responsible to the people whom they were elected to serve." However, the Court has also made clear that the government cannot *require* the press to perform these public functions. Newspapers, for instance, are private entities, not "common carriers" obligated to accept the messages of anyone who wants

space in the news columns or on the editorial page. In short, the First Amendment does not permit government to meddle in the process by which newspaper editors decide what and what not to publish. By and large, the same is true of broadcasters, although the Court has upheld statutes and regulations by the Federal Communications Commission (FCC) that require licensees to provide air time to others under certain narrow circumstances.

Media professionals disagree whether the press is more public or more private. For example, a raging debate over the proper role of television news recently broke out at NBC. On one side stood those who saw network news as a public service that should be shielded from the financial imperatives of other businesses. The news division, in their view, ought to be subsidized by the profits of the network's entertainment division. On the other side were those who claimed that the news media are private businesses subject to the demands of the marketplace. The news department must carry its own financial weight.

In a democracy, intermediaries like political parties and the press are neither wholly public nor wholly private. Indeed, the appropriate question is not whether they are more public or more private but where they should fall on the public-private continuum to best perform their mediating functions. One's assessment of how well political parties and the media are doing their jobs depends largely on how satisfied or dissatisfied one is with their positions on this continuum.

Elections are among the most public activities in a democracy. However, we conduct them these days in the most private of ways. Much of our discomfort with recent campaigns can be traced to this privatized style of electioneering. It pervades almost every aspect of contemporary electoral politics, resulting in an "electronic plebiscitary democracy."

The most striking feature of the system of electronic plebiscitary democracy is direct, continuous, highly intense communication between Presidents (and would-be Presidents) at one end, and scores of millions of people at the other. The politicians reach the people via polls. In this relationship, the politicians act almost solely in their capacity as popular leaders and scarcely at all in their capacity as party officials or government managers. The people act almost solely in their capacity as atomized individual television-watchers, and scarcely at all in their capacity as citizens of states and communities or members of political parties or other voluntary associations.

The privatization of modern campaigns is especially evident in the role of television. Public rallies and speeches have given way to televised appearances in which candidates speak directly to individual voters in the privacy of their homes. The viewers' attention is focused squarely on the personal qualities of the candidates. The spotlight shines brightly on day-to-day squabbles among the candidates and even brighter on their gaffes. The bulk of the coverage is about who's in the lead, and more recently, about the inside strategy and tactics of the candidates. The main casualty of this preoccupation with personality and process is serious public discourse. Little effort is made to connect the campaign to the central issues of the day—the issues that will shape the way people are governed after election day.

Unlike other Western democracies, the United States leaves the ownership and control of television largely in private hands. For the most part, broadcast media are privately owned and commercially financed. In these advertiser-driven media, pressure for audience ratings is intense. Indeed, commercial television today can no longer afford the luxury of insulating the news from the ratings. Inevitably, entertainment values intrude in all programming, including the news, which more and more is produced to hook and please the audience.

Campaigns exploit this to the hilt. According to Michael Deaver, Ronald Reagan's former aide and image maker: "The media, while they won't admit it, are not in the news business; they're in entertainment. We tried to create the most entertaining, visually attractive scene to fill that box, so that the networks would have to use it." The campaigns ration the media's access to the candidates, providing instead alluring photo opportunities and dramatic visuals.

Succumbing to the need for tight structure and fast pacing to beat the competition, networks and local stations chop the candidates' words into shorter and shorter sound bites. In the twenty years since 1968, the typical sound bite in presidential campaigns has shrunk from forty-three seconds to a mere nine.

Privatized democracy also finds expression in the candidates' and the media's reliance on public opinion polls. More and more, citizens' involvement is reduced to the passive and private act of registering their opinions in a poll, a shallow form of participation at best. Even more troubling is the hold that polls have over news coverage. Not only does poll-based information command a substantial and growing portion of the news, but the amount and content of coverage that candidates receive is to a large extent determined by their standing in the polls.

Our system defends the right of private entrepreneurs to sell consulting services to campaigns. Today every would-be prince wants a gang of these Machiavellis on the campaign payroll. These technical experts, who set the strategy, message, and tone of so many campaigns, are not attached to more permanent, public, and hence more accountable, organizations like political parties. Reinforcing privatized democracy, they sell services like polling, direct mail, and paid advertising that establish direct pipelines between campaigns and voters. In most democracies, candidates cannot purchase advertising time. In the United States, they can, and the results have been less than encouraging. Increasingly, the airwaves are filled with highly personal, crudely manipulative attack ads designed to sully an opponent's reputation. By and large, the press has permitted the admen to set the campaign agenda and dialogue with these ads. And although the ads are sometimes misleading or false, and of dubious relevance to the office at stake, the press has not vigorously dissected them or held their authors accountable.

The chorus of lamentations about deficiencies in the selection of leaders grows louder with each passing election. Everyone has their favorite complaints. Yet the problem lies deeper than any particular shortcoming. It can be traced to the process of intermediation itself.

Political columnist David Broder and network executive Timothy Russert have recently been crusading to get the U.S. media to assume greater public responsibility in covering election campaigns. They have issued a plea for a more vigilant press corps. As they envision it, the press would help keep the news agenda focused on relevant and nontrivial issues; scrutinize nonelected consultants; carefully monitor, dissect, and criticize campaign advertising; insist on more substantive candidate debates; and demand regular and routine access to the candidates in press conferences. Other journalists have urged that the networks provide free air time in the evening to candidates or parties during campaigns, a common practice in other democratic countries. With this more public posture, the press would hardly be a neutral messenger that simply reports the news as it occurs.

If adopted, these ideas might go some way toward reducing the excessive privatization that has marked recent campaigns. But two ca-veats are worth bearing in mind. First, one ought to ask how realistic many of these proposals are. In the heat of the 1992 campaign, will the media actually live up to such high standards? In the end, the news media are private, profit-making businesses that hope to attract large audiences. Their behavior is governed by news and entertainment values, not political values. As Thomas Patterson has put it, "The issue for the press is not which candidates would be good for a majority of the country but which are material for good news stories." Although many observers criticized the media's obsession with polling in 1988, there are few signs that any major media organizations are planning to stem this tide in 1992.

The other caveat is that even if they do police election campaigns more aggressively, the media will somehow have to be held accountable. If the press becomes more assertive, more prescriptive, and more judgmental, then how can we redress the possible errors and abuses of a powerful and unelected elite? Expecting news organizations to monitor each other seems a vain hope. According to some, the media already are the Fourth Estate, yet they are not subject to the kinds of checks and balances that restrain the other three. Calls for an accountable press, however, understandably make journalists and defenders of the press nervous. While it seems natural enough to hold candidates or intermediaries like political parties accountable, the idea of applying such restraints to the news media is not easily reconciled with the cherished ideal of a free press.

The decline of parties has made the media the most powerful intermediary in American politics. The press must now face head-on a question it has too often tried to avoid: What public purposes should it serve while preserving its status as a private, nongovernmental institution?

CHAPTER **7**

Voting, Elections, and the Media

VOTING AND NON-VOTING

Voting is one of the basic means for active citizen participation. Elections determine who controls executive and legislative offices and the shaping of public policy. Accordingly, democratic theory holds that voting should be a rational choice made by informed citizens. Thomas Jefferson believed that grassroots democracy was ensured when citizens participated equally in governing community affairs. Voting in town meetings was meaningful because all citizens shared power, control, and responsibility over local policies—a model of participation rooted in the ancient Greek city-state.

In the early nineteenth century, only adult white males who owned property could vote. Since then, most legal exclusions against voting have been eliminated. The Fifteenth Amendment, ratified in 1870 but not effectively implemented until the 1965 Voting Rights Act, removed racial barriers against black votes. The Nineteenth Amendment provided voting rights to women in 1920. The Twenty-sixth Amendment, approved in 1971, lowered the voting age to eighteen years.

Why do people vote? FIve reasons frequently cited include citizen duty, information about politics, concern for elections, attention to politics, and political efficacy. Regular voters have a strong sense of citizen obligation, and voting demonstrates good citizenship. Consistent voters have more information about and pay attention to politics. They feel that their votes do make a difference in elections. Such voters have a high sense of political effectiveness.

Voting turnout is directly related to the issue of American voting behavior. There are two contrasting views of American voters: dependent or responsive. The dependent voter, a product of the 1950s, is considered poorly informed and relatively uninvolved with public affairs. The dependent voter is a straight party-ticket voter. He or she responds to socioeconomic factors, including family background, ethnic identification, or occupation. Dependent voters are party loyalists unconcerned with issues.

In contrast, responsive voters, who emerged during the 1960s and 1970s, are issue-oriented, carefully considering their votes in relation to the major problems facing the nation. Responsive voters reject party labels and split their tickets in elections. Their actions can result in shifting election results from Democrats to Republicans, depending on the major issues being contested.

Over the last thirty years, participation by American voters has steadily decreased to the point where a minority of eligible voters is electing the president and members of Congress. According to Curtis Gans in Article 23, the high point of voting turnout was 62.8 percent in the 1960 presidential election. Since then, the decline in voting continued through the 1988 presidential election when slightly less than half of the eligible voters participated.

In 1984, about 174 million Americans could have voted for either Ronald Reagan or Walter Mondale for the presidency. Mr. Reagan won a landslide re-election victory with 59 percent of the votes cast, but 47 percent of potential voters—about 82 million people—did not vote.

Voting turnout hit rock bottom in 1988. George Bush won a relatively easy victory over Michael Dukakis, but Bush's election was based on receiving only about 27 percent of the eligible vote, the lowest percentage to elect a president in the twentieth century. Various estimates disclosed that only half of the voting age population went to the polls in 1988. This was the lowest voter turnout since 1924.

Voting participation in the off-year congressional elections is even worse. In 1986 and 1990, slightly more than one-third of potential voters participated. The turnout of 37.3 percent in 1986 was the lowest since 1942, and a reduction of almost 4 percent from 1982. In 1990, the 67.7 million Americans who voted represented only 36 percent of the 186 million eligible voters.

Gans observes that the United States is among the three least-participating democracies in the world along with Switzerland and India. In contrast, voter turnout is exceptionally high in many western democracies. Germany, Italy, and Australia usually exceed 90 percent or more; in France, Holland, and Denmark, voter turnout is 80 percent or better; and in Japan, Britain, and Canada, it is 70 percent.

Why don't people vote? In Article 23, Gans identifies five groups of nonvoters, including those who never voted (poor, young, less educated, unemployed, homeless); alienated dropouts; the disenfranchised; and the apathetic or lazy person who always finds excuses not to vote.

A 1988 *New York Times* CBS News poll revealed a profile of the typical non-voter in the presidential election. In comparison with the voter, the non-voter was more likely to be under 30 years of age to have an annual income under $25,000 to have less than a college education and to have changed residence in the last two years.[1]

Gans recommends two ways to improve voter turnout: remove procedural barriers and improve the quality of American politics, institutions, leadership, and discourse.

Both Gans and others have recommended changes in voter registration procedures. Raymond Wolfinger, professor of political science at the University of California, supported a proposal for a National Voter Registration Act in 1990.[2] This would have required state and local election officials to communicate with each other and with the Postal Service on all applications for drivers' licenses and renewals, and to automatically reflect reported address changes in voter registration rolls. The previous address would be purged. States would also be required to provide voter registration by mail.

According to Wolfinger, universal registration would increase voter participation. He observes that 85 percent of registrants voted in the three presidential elections before 1988. The figures dropped to 69 percent in 1988 because few efforts were made to increase voter registration.

But Gans concludes that American discontent with the quality of political life is the more powerful explanation for why people don't vote. These issues are discussed in the articles by Sabato, Fischer, and Woodruff.

CAMPAIGN FINANCE: POLITICAL ACTION COMMITTEES

Presidential and congressional campaigns cost an enormous amount of money. In 1988, spending on the presidential campaigns was an estimated $125 million, a $25 million increase over 1984. The average spending for a senator elected in 1988 was $3.7 million, a 22 percent increase over 1986. Winning candidates for the House spent an average of $393,000, an increase of 10 percent over 1986.

Federal financing for presidential races began in the 1970. The 1974 Federal Election Campaign Act (FECA), a post-Watergate reform, provided public funding for presidential campaigns. At the nomination stage in 1984, the Federal Election Commission (FEC) provided up to 50 percent of $20 million to candidates who raised $5,000 in each of twenty states, with no more than $250 from any one individual contributor. During the electoral politics stage, the FEC will finance the total cost of the presidential campaign if the candidates agree not to accept any private donations or spend more than $50,000 personally. In 1988, the Bush and Dukakis campaigns each received $46.1 million in public funds for the general election and another $8.3 million from their National parties.

Congressional campaigns are not publicly funded. Instead, political action committees (PACs) have replaced political parties as the major source of funding for congressional races. According to Larry Sabato (Article 24), a PAC is a segregated nonparty campaign fund established by a labor union, business corporation, trade association, congressperson or senator, or prospective presidential candidate solely for political purposes. PACs have expanded enormously, because in 1974 FECA limited individual contributions to $1,000 but allowed PACs to contribute $5,000 to primary and general election campaigns. PAC recipients were required to file reports with FEC. In 1989–90, some 4,950 PACs contributed about $100 million to congressional candidates and campaigns, including $79 million to incumbents and $6.5 million to challengers.

What are the problems with PAC contributions? First, the PACs seem to contribute the most funds to key incumbents serving on committees that deal directly with the interest group's concerns. Are the PACs using "legalized bribery" to get legislation by rewarding favored congressmen and senators? Or do such contributions simply provide access to key legislators? Another criticism is that PAC contributions have raised the cost of campaigns. Since PAC funds represented a large proportion of these increased costs, it appears that congressional candidates will need to raise huge sums to remain in office or to replace incumbents. Some would argue that candidates are trying to buy elective offices rather than represent constituencies.

Sabato argues that the PAC system represents the modern version of James Madison's argument about the expansion of factions in a democracy (see *The Federalist*, Number 10, in Chapter 4). The more factions or PACs, the more likely democracy will be strong because no one group will dominate the political system. The recent proliferation of PACs results in a balancing of liberal and conservative, labor and business, Democratic- and Republican-oriented groups.

Sabato observes that PACs have been a negative influence in deceptive fund-raising practices, in contributions favoring incumbents over challengers, and in the dominance of narrow policy issues of great concern to interest groups. He recommends a variety of reform to reduce PAC influence, including raising the cap on individual and corporate contributions to candidates, increasing the financial flexibility of political parties, restoring the income tax credit option for political contributions, and public financing of congressional campaigns. His principal suggestion is to increase disclosure of PAC sources of funding so that contributors to PACs will know how their money is being used.

In 1991, the Senate debated legislative proposals to reduce PAC influence. The Democratic party's proposal was sponsored by Senate Majority Leader George Mitchell and David Boren of Oklahoma. The Republican proposal was promoted by Minority Leader Robert Dole.

Both reforms would have abolished PAC contributions to federal campaigns. However, they differed substantially on alternative sources of campaign funding. Republicans opposed any ceilings on candidate spending limits. Democrats wanted voluntary spending limits, ranging from $950,000 to $5.5 million, based on a state's voting-age population.

ELECTING THE PRESIDENT

One of the most complex procedures in American politics is electing the president. The electoral college, a product of the Constitutional Convention of 1787, represented a compromise for selecting chief executives following George Washington. The Framers debated direct popular election and indirect election by the state legislatures, finally agreeing to combine both methods in the electoral college. State legislatures would choose "wise men" to nominate and select the president. The large states were rewarded with the most electoral votes while the small states were guaranteed a minimum of three votes. The state legislatures had the option of giving the people a vote in selecting electors. If no candidate received a majority of electoral votes, the House of Representatives would select the winner. Most of the Framers believed this would happen after George Washington because the electoral college would fail to produce a majority for one candidate.

How does the electoral college operate? When people vote for president, they are actually voting for slates of electors chosen by state political parties pledged to a particular candidate. Most states do not print the names of electors on the ballot. Each state is allotted as many electoral votes as it has senators and representatives in Congress. The District of Columbia has had three electors since passage of the Twenty-third Amendment. There are 538 electoral votes with 270 needed for a majority. The candidate who receives the most popular votes in a state receives all of the electoral votes in a "winner-take-all" system. About six weeks after the election, the electors meet in their state capitals to cast their ballots. The state electoral ballots are counted before a joint session of Congress during the first week in January. If no candidate receives a majority, the president is chosen by the House from among the three leading candidates, with each state casting one vote.

The constitutional Framers probably never expected the electoral college to continue in its original form. However, as political parties emerged, they found the electoral college an effective means for capturing the presidency. Instead of independent electors, they became party functionaries acting on behalf of their party's candidate by voting automatically for the winner of the state's popular votes.

Some reformers have advocated changing the electoral college system to avoid and prevent several problems. For example, Thomas Cronin has proposed a "national bonus plan" that would combine the existing system with 102 bonus electoral votes awarded to the candidate who wins the most popular votes nationwide. Cronin's goal is to prevent the election of a president who fails to receive a majority of the nationwide popular votes. Over the years, several other reforms have been suggested to replace the electoral college. The simplest proposal is to eliminate the electoral college and choose the president by a majority of the national popular vote. Another suggestion is proportional voting by which each candidate who receives a fraction of the state's popular votes would win the same fraction of electoral votes. This would eliminate the "winner-take-all" effect of the present system. Others have recommended retaining the electoral college but eliminating the office of elector. This reform aims to remove the problem of the so-called "faithless" elector, who may vote for a candidate other than the one the political party supports. Public-opinion polls show that the public favors direct popular election of the president. However, Congress is not likely to change the existing system until a serious problem occurs.

NEGATIVE TELEVISION ADS

One of the reasons why many people have a negative attitude toward elections and are not voting might be the proliferation of negative attack ads on television. While political campaigns have always included mudslinging, many believe that the 1988 election represented an all-time low in negative, non-issue campaigning.

Instead of focusing on substantive matters, the Bush campaign decided to portray Michael Dukakis as a dangerous liberal who was soft on crime, lacked patriotism, and favored pollution. The Bush campaign spent millions on television ads referring to Willie Horton, the Pledge of Allegiance, and the pollution of Boston Harbor. Willie Horton, a black man, was a convicted murderer who raped a woman after his release under a Massachusetts furlough program. The Pledge of Allegiance involved Dukakis' veto, in conformity with court decisions, of state legislation requiring schoolchildren to state the Pledge. And Dukakis was blamed for Boston Harbor's pollution since the state had received federal aid to clean it up.

The nature of these attacks on Dukakis by the Bush organization were so personal that they avoided many of the issues facing the country in 1988. The goal was to denigrate the opponent to the point where Dukakis lost all credibility with the voters, Dukakis' failure to respond to the negative ads proved to be a severe liability in the campaign.

Raymond Fischer in Article 25 goes beyond the immediate creators of negative campaign ads and correctly places blame on the press and the public. He argues that reporters never questioned the negative ads of 1988. The press played no watchdog role as it had in 1980 and 1984 in challenging the substance of ad attacks. Similarly, most citizens, in Fischer's view, passively view these negative ads and never complain about their validity. The unfortunate conclusion is that such attacks work. In 1990, Jesse Helms used a vicious, racist attack ad against civil rights in his Senate reelection campaign in North Carolina. The ad likely provided Helms with the margin of victory over his black opponent.

Fischer suggests several reforms to reduce the impact of negative television ads. These are worth considering. Otherwise, the quality of campaigns will most likely continue to deteriorate.

THE MEDIA, POLITICS, AND ELECTIONS

This chapter has shown the crucial role of television in modern electoral politics. In Chapter 6, we discovered that the media has replaced political parties as the key intermediary between voters and candidates. Television and the press tell American citizens who the candidates are, the progress of their campaigns, their standings in the polls, and who will win on election day. The media has become a modern version of ancient fortune-telling and prophecy.

Judy Woodruff, a reporter for the "MacNeill-Lehrer News Hour" on public television, is deeply concerned about the failure of the media to be responsible and accountable in political reporting. In Article 26, Woodruff tells us that news shows are increasing, but the quality of reporting has diminished.

The major television networks treat electoral reporting almost the same way as commercial advertisements. The more the candidate can say in the least amount of time is preferred. So-called sound bites of presidential candidates in 1988 were as short as seven seconds, down from thirteen seconds in 1984. The media is not interested in detailed reports on issues, candidates' histories, inconsistencies, or the substance of their attacks on opponents. Television, in particular, is catering to a simplistic, trivialized presentation of American politics. It is no wonder that so many potential voters are turned off and do not vote.

One suggestion to improve the quality of reporting in presidential campaigns is for the media to change in 1992. Timothy J. Russert, Washington Bureau Chief of NBC news, provides some useful guidelines.[3]

First, he recommends that the networks report the content and accuracy of candidates' basic "stump speeches" early in the campaign. This type of speech offers an overview of where the candidate stands on issues, values and philosophy.

Second, Russert warns against televising so-called photo opportunities arranged by the candidates' campaign managers. These are staged events intended to place the candidate in a highly favorable setting for a television sound bite. Instead, Russert argues for a discussion or report on the record of the candidate's stand on the policy for which he is seeking promotional media coverage.

Third, Russert wants analysis of television ads presented in the campaign. Campaign ads should be dissected and analyzed for substance, content, and verification. In his view, there should be truth in advertising.

Finally, Russert favors at least four televised debates, involving the two candidates and a single anchor reporter from ABC, CBS, CNN, and NBC. The debates would focus on economic policy, social policy, foreign policy, and general campaign issues. There would be no panels, no props, no rigid rules. The candidates would face each other, defending and explaining their views. This would bring presidential debates back to the way they were conducted in 1960 and 1976.

While Russert's recommendations may not be the only way to improve the quality of media reporting in presidential campaigns, they provide a good start. Something needs to be done to get the potential voter interested in electoral politics. Otherwise, we can expect Gans' negative predictions of diminished citizen interest in voting to continue to come true.

The articles in this chapter show why there is so much cynicism toward electoral politics in America. Fundamental reforms are indeed needed to improve the quality of electoral politics in the United States, particularly at the national level. Otherwise, weakened political parties, increased political money, deceptive advertising, and trivialized non-issue campaigns will continue in 1992.

NOTES

1. E. J. Dionne, Jr., "If Nonvoters Had Voted: Same Winner, But Bigger," *New York Times*, 21 Nov. 1988, p. B16, col. 3–6.
2. Raymond E. Wolfinger, "How to Raise Voter Turnout," *New York Times*, 6 June 1990, p. A27, col. 1–4.
3. Timothy J. Russert, "For '92, The Networks Have to Do Better," *New York Times*, 4 March 1990, p. E23, col. 2–3.

Voting and Non-Voting

23
Remobilizing the American Electorate
Curtis B. Gans

In this provocative discussion, Curtis Gans, Executive Director of the Committee for the Study of the American Electorate, argues that voting is both the "lowest common denominator act" of citizen participation and that "it is a highly complex act." Gans is troubled that voting participation has declined significantly in the last thirty years. He identifies five different types of non-voters. Who are they? He also argues for removing procedural barriers to voting, but concludes that this is insufficient. Which procedural barriers to voting still need to be reformed? Gans believes there are basic flaws in American government, political parties, policy, and the media which contribute to American nonparticipation in elections. Unless these problems are corrected, American faith in the democratic process will continue to erode. Do you agree with Gans? Who benefits from low levels of voter participation? Who loses?

REMOBILIZING THE
AMERICAN ELECTORATE

Curtis B. Gans

Consider, if you will, two slices of recent American political history:

—In 1963 President John F. Kennedy—for reasons of principle (he believed that the rate of political participation in the United States was unconscionably low) and for reasons of politics (he knew that the majority of non-participants had a demographic profile that was likely to benefit the Democratic Party)—established a commission to recommend ways in which voter participation in America might be enhanced.

Shortly after his death that commission reported its recommendations that included: the abolition of poll taxes and literacy tests; the enfranchisement of minorities and youth between the ages of 18–20; shortening the time between the close of registration and voting; voter outreach programs; mail registration; bilingual ballots; liberalization of state and local residency requirements, among other items. With one minor exception—a recommendation of an election day holiday—every one of the recommendations have been implemented in whole or in part (only 20 states have mail registration).

Yet, in every election (save 1982 and aberrationally 1984) since that time voter turnout had been declining. From a high point of 62.8% of the eligible voters who cast their ballot in the election in which President Kennedy was elected in 1960, we have fallen to levels

From *Policy Studies Review*, Vol. 9, No. 3 (Spring 1990), pp. 527–537. Reprinted by permission of the author and the Policy Studies Organization.

of only 53% in the 1980s. In both presidential and congressional elections, we have fallen approximately ten percent in our rate of participation. Fully 20 million Americans who formerly regularly or sporadically voted, no longer do so. We are the lowest participating democracy in the world with the occasional and possible exceptions of Switzerland and India.

Similarly consider more recent events. In the 1984 presidential election, in part due to the polarization of the electorate generated by the policies of the Reagan administration, voluntary organizations across the American political spectrum engaged in an unprecedented level of voter registration activity. More than 25 million dollars was spent in soft foundation money, hard political money, and in-kind contributions of housing, personpower and material to enroll various groups of voters thought likely to enhance the voting strength of one interest or party.

At the same time, state governments spent more than $250 million to enroll voters. Many of them conducted vastly expanded programs of voter outreach more extensive than they had ever done before.

In this year of registration, many barriers to citizen participation fell. Mississippi eliminated dual registration for the first time. The homeless were enfranchised in the District of Columbia, Pennsylvania, and New York. Volunteer registrars were permitted for the first time to solicit registration in public agencies and in some states, agencies were empowered to distribute welfare, provide licenses and the like and were for the first time also empowered to enroll prospective voters. In addition, the media spent literally millions of dollars of free air time, exhorting citizens to register and vote.

All this activity did produce a significant increase in registration (10.8 million new registrants and 3.2 percentage point increase in the percentage of eligibles who were registered), but it did not produce a significant increase in turnout. The turnout of eligible Americans increased by 0.7 percentage points. The turnout of registered Americans decreased by 2.1 percentage points and the turnout of those mobilized to register by voluntary organizations was lower than that of those who registered to vote on their own.

Consider finally one piece of academic literature on this topic. In a landmark study of the 1972 and 1974 Current Population surveys, Raymond Wolfinger and Steven Rosenstone (1980) identified the categories of the most likely voter. That voter is likely to be older, more educated, more stable, married, and rooted in his or her community. Since 1971 the average age of Americans has been increasing. Since 1960 the percentage of Americans attending and graduating from college has nearly doubled, and since the mid-1960s society has become less mobile. Yet voter participation, by and large, has declined. (Only in the area of marriage, does theory correlate with fact. We are less married and more divorced society than we were in the 1960s and 70s, but I would hesitate to recommend marriage as a cure to non-voting.)

It is not at all irrelevant (and perhaps central to the theme of this paper) to speculate the turnout trends might have been different had the Kennedy reforms been enacted and the demographic changes taken place without: mid-sixties strife, the war in Vietnam and Watergate, inadequate images of public leadership provided by Presidents Johnson, Nixon, and Carter; without growing complexity in our society and growing confusion about how to deal with it; without the growth of governmental and nongovernmental institutions and a feeling of public helplessness in the face of them; without the speeding up of our perceptions and attention span by television and the decay of our integrating institutions.

Nor is it irrelevant to speculate what might have happened to the massive efforts to mobilize Americans to vote in 1984 or 1988 had there not been economic prosperity, a personally popular President in office, a laughable campaign run by the Democrats and a huge gap between the two principals on election day.

For it seems clear that the principal causes of continued low and declining voter participation—in which only half of our electorate votes in presidential elections and only a third in congressional elections—lies not in voting laws and procedures, not in mobilization and demography, but in the quality and content of our politics. By and large a smaller percentage of the electorate is voting because a smaller percentage of the electorate believes in the efficacy of their ballots, in their ability to affect events and to, through the democratic process, better the quality of their lives.

I would like to suggest that a continued low turnout and a continuing decline in voter turnout poses a series of specific threats to the health and welfare of American democracy:

- Voting has been shown in a number of surveys to be a lowest common denominator act—that people who do not vote are not likely to participate in any other form of social, civic, or political activity. Thus to the extent that fewer and fewer Americans vote, the more likely it is that our politics will be increasingly dominated by those who are intensely interested and that our politics will be increasingly subject to the centripetal forces of narrow specialized interest.
- To the extent that fewer and fewer people vote the course of public policy can be affected. If public employees constitute, as they do, one sixth of the American electorate and if they vote heavily, as they do, then in a presidential election in which half of the rest of the electorate votes, their voting strength becomes one-third. In a congressional election in which only a third vote, their force becomes nearly one-half. Then try to abolish an agency, reform civil service or privatize some public services.
- If voting is, as has been shown a lowest common denominator act, then the potential for the necessary voluntarism that is so intrinsic to the health of the American society also diminishes.
- And if non-participation is, as has been shown, a symptom of both disinterest and disengagement, then the potential for demagoguery and even authoritarianism is enhanced.

There may be no optimal level of participation for this democracy or any democracy, but a continued low and declining rate of participation threatens the health and welfare of this democracy and it must be reversed.

Democracy is not only the most humane form of government, it is also the most fragile. It depends not only for its legitimacy but also for its health and well-being on the involvement of the governed.

Government may not be, as many people now seem to feel, the answer to all of society's ills, but unless the American people wish to abdicate to oligarchic or authoritarian rule, the resolution of societal problems must come through the democratic political process. The continuing withdrawal of American people from voting and political participation threatens not only wise governance, but the underlying vitality of the political process and the democratic ideal. We are simply and bluntly in danger of becoming a nation governed of, for and by the interested few.

Having said all of this, it might be well to look at who these non-voters are. For if we are to begin to address both the generic problem of non-participation or the more particular problem of participation of certain important sub-groups, it would be well to know the lay of the land.

In 1976, my organization, the Committee for the Study of the American Electorate, undertook a survey of a scientifically selected sample of nonvoters to attempt to ascertain who they were and why they were not participating. And while I found that survey less than fully satisfying as a total answer to the problem (although surely more satisfying than anything that has been done before or since), it does provide some clues.

For the purpose of this discussion, I would like to categorize non-voters in four broad groups. Any such categorizing is, of course, imperfect, but the categories may serve to show at least something of the nature of the problem that confronts us.

By far the largest group are chronic non-voters, people who have never, or in Gilbert and Sullivan's phrase "hardly ever," voted. They tend to come from families who have never voted. They tend to be poorer, younger, less educated, more unorganized working class, more unemployed, more minority, more Southern, more rural, and more urban underclass than the rest of the population. They are also likely to be participants in nothing else. With the exception of a few chronic non-voters in the South who participate in fundamentalist religion (and who are likely to have been the source of the Reverend Jerry Falwell's additions to the voter rolls of the 1980s), the chronic non-voter tends to participate in no organized political, social, religious, or civic activities. They are a nation larger than France within our own midst, who, if one were to describe them in terms applied by the Bureau of Labor Statistics to elements of the labor force, would be out of voting force.

The second group are those who have dropped out of the political process in the past two decades, some 20 million Americans. They are still more heavily weighted to the poorer and more minority segments of our population. But they also include a 40 percent component who are educated, middle-class, professional, and white collar workers in the suburbs in the middle-Atlantic, northeastern, and western states. These people were in our survey the most alienated and the most motivated by events and by a belief that their vote no longer had any efficacy, either in the improvement of their individual lives or the conduct of public policy.

The third group is the young. For the lowest participating group in America is the nation's youth. Bluntly, fewer young people are voting than ever before. They are becoming socialized to participate at a slower rate than previous generations and their interest in politics as a group is substantially lower than the rest of the nation.

The fourth major group, smaller than the others, is the approximately one-tenth of the non-voters who still perceive themselves to be, or who actually are blocked by impediments in the political process, ranging from feeling intimidation at the polls or from the polling procedures, to insufficient places of registration and/or voting, too short registration and/or voting hours, inadequate outreach and the like.

Finally, there are those who are truly apathetic or lazy. They cannot be quantified by our survey data because all respondents tend to give rational answers to what they perceive to be deviant behavior. But behind some of these rational answers lurks a person who does not give a damn. But for the overwhelming majority of non-voters, their non-participation is on one basis or other a rational act.

Reversing the trend toward non-participation is as important as it will be difficult to achieve. There are not magic formulas. Voting is a very complex act. Participation is a product of our upbringing and schooling, of the laws and rules governing the political process, the issues of the day, the forces within our society, the influences of the media and the quality of our lives. Any attempt to reinvigorate the electorate will involve addressing all of these aspects of the problem if any solution is to be achieved.

I have suggested that the laws and procedures governing elections are not the principal reason why the United States continues to have low and declining participation rates. I would like now to suggest that these laws and procedures are not totally irrelevant.

Rosenstone and Wolfinger (1980), using complex statistical modeling argue that if we remove all barriers to participation, the rate of voting would increase by 9.1 percentage points. (One has to marvel at such precision.) The evidence in the four states that adopted election day registration suggests that if all barriers to participation were removed the base level of voter turnout would increase by 2–4 percentage points. But whether you accept the statistical estimate of the academicians or the real evidence of actual experiments, we are talking about from 4 to 13 million voters who might participate if all barriers were removed.

America need not continue to be the only democracy in the world that puts the burden for qualifying to vote on the citizen. Is it necessary to continue to have both registration and voting when every other nation in the world makes voting, by and large, a one step act in which the state conducts the registration and all the citizen need to do is vote. We could and should adopt election day registration, a voter identification card or best of all a system such as in Canada in which the state conducts a bipartisan canvass of eligible voters, insures that fraud at the ballot box is minimized and requires of the citizen no more than he appear to vote (Crotty, 1980, 1977).

In the absence of such sweeping changes, it would be useful to explore ways to bring the United States closer to this ideal by further shortening the time between the close of registration and election, eliminating any disparities between states and local registration practices and practices in federal elections and adopting those means of making it easier to register and vote such as liberalized and uniform deputy registration laws and drivers license registration to name but two.

One of the principal objections to adopting a registration system such as the Canadian system of universal enrollment is the problem of cost. It would be possible, however, to recover that cost by holding fewer elections. There is no earthly reason why I, when a citizen of the District of Columbia, should have been called upon to vote in an election in which the only office in contention was the powerless advisory neighborhood council. Nor as a resident of Virginia should I be called upon to vote four times in one year—for sheriff and county commissioner in one election; in a primary for Congress in a second; in a caucus for presidential nominee in a third; and for all constitutional federal offices in a fourth. It should be possible to consolidate our elections and by doing so focus greater interest and eliminate the protected state of certain local offices.

It should also be possible to constructively reduce the length of our ballots. There are no good reasons why stepping stone offices such as secretaries of state and attorneys general, which are implementing rather than policy-making offices, should be elected. Similarly we could reduce the number of other elected offices and the number of ballot propositions. With ballots a mile long and information about them scarce, it is no wonder that the public says in opinion polls that it is confused and that there are discouragingly long lines at the polling places.

To eliminate some of those lines we might have more polling places and slightly longer hours (although not a 24 hour voting day or an election day holiday for which there is no evidence turnout might be enhanced).

It would also be desirable to eliminate those last vestiges of discrimination and obstacles to voting that exist in law and practice. There is no reason why voters should be purged for failure to vote in a particular election. Our studies have shown that states with permanent registration tend to have both higher registration and turnout compared to states that purge their rolls on the basis of non-participation at any interval. The system needs to be protected from fraud and abuse by purging those who have moved or died and this should be done on a regular basis, but those who have exercised their right to eschew the franchise in a particular election should not be penalized in future elections. For those who move, it should be possible to expedite both their purging and their re-registration in their new localities by the simple expedient now being proposed in law of providing change of address forms, not simply to potential mailers and post offices, but to registrars in both new and old places of registration.

Systems of dual registration, in which a voter must register in one place in federal elections and at another for local elections should be eliminated, as they were in 1984 in Mississippi. There is no reason why registration places should be opened for two unadvertised hours every two years as they currently are in the Upper Marlboro, Maryland. And deputy registrars should be deputized easily and uniformly. In the immediate past election, it was next to impossible for anyone who

wanted to register not to get registered in Fairfax County, Virginia so seriously did local registrars take their outreach responsibilities. But one hundred miles to the south and west, operating under the same laws, it was impossible for new registrants to get registered because no one was allowed to be deputized. A liberal uniformity should be the order of the day.

It should also be possible to provide adequate information to voters so that they can make rational voting decisions at the ballot box. In a 1984 survey my committee commissioned of new registrants, the overwhelming majority reported their lack of understanding of what was at stake. In any given election, the mass media, notably television, gives adequate coverage (although it, too, could be improved) of presidential elections and perhaps senatorial, gubernatorial, and mayoral elections, the latter largely limited to cities of substantial size. But it is next to impossible in both print media or television or radio to know what is at stake in other elections. In some areas, the League of Women Voters attempts to fill the gap and in some locales local newspapers cooperate with the League in publishing ballot guides for voters. But there is no reason why such guides should not be available to everyone in which the qualifications and positions of each candidate are listed and each ballot proposition discussed.

There are a number of larger issues that need to be assessed. If young people are, as they are, the lowest cohort in the electorate, we need to examine whether the quality of civic education in our schools is adequate, whether there are co-curricular outlets to give opportunities for and foster political participation, and whether parents use television as a child pacifier at the expense of such things as reading and discussion.

We need to look at whether we have adequate leadership training institutions that teach civic responsibilities. The relatively high levels of participation that existed in the late 1950s and early 1960s did not occur in a vacuum. They occurred because there were training institutions such as the California Democratic Clubs, the New York reform movement, the Newman Clubs and Wesley Foundations, the U.S. National Student Association, to name a few that saw as their mission the development of meaningful political involvement.

We need, in addition, to examine the structure of the modern campaign; the degree to which sophisticated survey techniques have campaigns focus on likely voters, leaving non-voters alone and creating an ever-diminishing pool of voters; of the tendency to rely almost exclusively on paid political advertising as the sole means of campaigning and thus denigrating active involvement in creating a "Silent Spring" for American politics; of ever-spiraling costs that make access to and participation in politics available only to those who are wealthy or who have access to collective wealth. We need to both establish a floor in public financing of campaigns that might limit the deleterious potential of overweening interest of those with money and provide the wherewithal that more could participate in politics. A ceiling at the point of campaign costs' greatest hemorrhage—the media—should be enacted.

But if we were to accomplish all of these reforms we would barely be able to scratch the surface of the problem. For unless the public believes it is voting for something meaningful and that its vote will make a difference, low voter participation will continue to be the order of the day.

The simple answer to reversing the trend toward non-participation is, of course, to have candidates who speak relevantly to the issues of public concern and who can deliver upon their political promises once in office.

Life and reality are rarely so simple. For this relatively simple formulation of an answer runs smack against six central political problems afflicting our political life—the problems of policy, parties, institutions, media, governance, and involvement.

A.   Policy—We may lament the quality of our candidates. Such laments have been common for the past twenty years. Yet, leadership does not spring full blown upon the political scene. The business of a politician is, in its best sense, to move the center of America in creative directions and to preserve the option to move in other directions. It involves very fine antennae about how far one can move to the center without making one's self irrelevant. The problem within America today is that there is no such center of ideas to which the politicians can repair. If all our politicians sound like throw-backs to the New Deal (or, as in the case of a president, to the 1920s), it is because they are repairing to the only safe ground they know. The problem lies not with our leaders but with the state of the art.

For three decades, we had such a consensual center. Out of the two great crises of the 1930s and 1940s, the Great Depression and World War II, there emerged a national consensus. On the domestic side we had Keynesian economics and the New Deal, a programmatic federal response to each perceived problem taken ad seriatim. On the foreign side, we had an increasing American global role in the containment first of fascism and later of communism. We argued about issues but only in degree. Was this domestic program necessary? How much aid should we be sending abroad and should it be military or economic?

That consensus broke down in the 1960s. The war in Vietnam revealed the limits of American power and resources in the world and questioned the nation's ability to assume a truly global role. The blight of our cities and the pollution of our environment were but two ways that showed that treating our problems ad seriatim might bring by-products as bad as the disease the original programs were designed to cure. Burgeoning and unresponsive bureaucracies showed the limits to the maxim "let the federal government do it."

But if that consensus that existed fell apart, it has not been replaced. We are living in a time of ideological interregnum, a time which, if the logicians had their way, would be called "not p." In the syllogism, "if not p, then q." We have made it clear that "p"—the policies of the past—have not worked. We have not replaced them effectively with new consensual policies.

In retrospect, Roosevelt had an easier time, because he could accomplish those changes in outlook in an atmosphere of perceived crisis. In many ways the problems confronting us are nearly as great, but the perceived sense of crisis is not there. Thus, it becomes an exercise in leadership, an exercise no less necessary because it is difficult.

B.   Political Parties—If the candidate has difficulty in knowing what to say because of a lack of central American consensus, then he also has difficulty as an office-holder in delivering upon his promises because there is no organizational force to discipline the individual office-holder and make him part of a collective.

That is the traditional role of the political party, which should serve as the training ground for leadership, the mobilizer of voters, the mediator of contending factions, the sorter of public programs for contending interests, the disciplinarian of individual self interest, the enactor of policies and the implementor of legislation. But political parties are now in disarray. Their patronage functions have been supplanted by government, their informational

functions by television, their role in the conduct of campaigns by money, media, and political consultants.

They are in disarray also for other reasons—in that they either stand for something irrelevant or they stand for nothing at all. In the ideal world, we would have a two party system that would resemble two of Britain's parties—Liberal and Labor. We would be debating between those whose primary concern is the quality of life and those whose primary concern is the wherewithal to live. Instead, we have that particular combination of right-wing reactionary populism and big business greed that is the underpinning of the Republican Party, and the mush that is the cacophony of interests unbridled by some central thread of national interest that is the Democratic Party.

The cohesion and coalition that kept the Democratic Party together for three decades broke down for natural and sometimes salubrious causes. The Democrats had been welded together by the policies of the New Deal into a coalition of ethnic, racial and religious minorities, the poor, liberals, big city organizations, and Southern conservatives. It broke down, in part, because those policies were successful for some. The nation was no longer two-thirds poor and thus the economic appeals of New Deal liberalism were not enough for those who had escaped poverty. It broke down because of the advent of the civil rights movement and the clear indication that the party could no longer avoid the issue of race in pursuing a theory of trickle-down economics. It broke down because big city organizations no longer were as powerful, being robbed of their strength by federal employment and televised communications. It broke down because after the Voting Rights Act, there was no longer One South but many. It broke down because the war in Vietnam revealed more than one strain of liberalism. It broke down because certain more conservative ethnic groups freed from the fears of poverty could vote their fears of social change. But for whatever reasons it broke down, it cannot be put back together in the same format.

Similarly, the Republican Party became a shell of its former self through natural causes. The Goldwater revolution of 1964 was not countered by any organizing efforts by liberal and moderate Republicans. Resistance by business, always at the core of the Republican Party, to regulation in the quality of life drove out many good-government Republicans. The excesses of Richard Nixon and Spiro Agnew and the Vietnam War drove out still more. Those who did not go to the political sidelines went into the Democratic Party, helping to create the mess that currently exists.

We will not have a healthy democracy or a strong two party system until their alignment, not simply the method by which we conduct our presidential nominating campaigns, is sorted out. Unless the Republican Party is broader or is supplanted by a new party; unless the Democratic Party becomes narrower and more focused, it is unlikely that we can call upon our leaders to deliver upon their promises.

C.   Institutions—Related to the problem of political parties is the problem of institutions. Parties are the political support groups necessary for the outreach and mobilization that make the enactment of programs possible. Part of the problem of institutions is simply that the institutional base of American society has atrophied as the public has been atomized by television, cable and video-cassette recorders. Institutions are weaker because people participate less. Part of the problem is that some of our institutions have grown so large as to make them unresponsive, a trend accelerated by the Reagan Administration's policies on such things as mergers, family farms, and the media. Part of the problem of institutions is that some, notably issue groups, have grown narrower and narrower in the nature of their concerns and more intransigent in their modes of operation.

But perhaps a more critical problem is the degree to which traditional institutions no longer stand for what they once did. Rather than being adversaries, business and labor are in an entente for jobs and production to the detriment of other elements of society. Unions, once the place where the common man could repair, have too often (and not without significant exceptions) become the protector of the long-term employed at the expense of the unemployed and marginally employed. The middle class liberals, once a reliable source of support for redistributive policies, are increasingly both figuratively and literally concerned in cultivating their own interests. Because of this and because the nature of the issues and political terrain has vastly changed since the 1930s, it is unlikely that there will ever be the type of permanent coalition that, for a time, the policies of the New Deal forged.

But we can and should have interest groups that accurately reflect the interests of their issue or class, and have beyond that a broader perspective aimed at the total welfare of society.

We can and should have different coalitions for different societal problems, groups capable of working temporary concert to achieve shared societal aims. Too often now the interest of one group tends to resist cooperation with another for the public good. We need, in short, to return civility and perspective to the conduct of our politics and rekindle an outlook that seeks ways to cooperate with others in temporary coalition for the common good.

D.   Media—There is also the problem of media. For if the politician had the consensus through which to lead, the parties through which to implement programs, the institutions through which to back programs, there would still be the problem of communications.

If there has been one technological development over the last two decades that has acted for the betterment of American politics, it has been invention of the pill and the intrauterine contraceptive devices that have liberated women to take their rightful role in American politics. If there is one such development that has acted to society's detriment, it has been television.

It has served to atomize our society; weaken our institutions; reduce participation by making people spectators and consumers rather than involved participants; decreased reading, comprehension and conversation; and increased public confusion. It gives information in undifferentiated blips and by highlights of the most visually exciting. It has, in addition, established unreal expectations for our political system by creating heroes and as quickly destroying them and by offering in its advertising panaceas that give the society a belief it can have equally rapid social panaceas.

There is also the problem that media poses in covering campaigns: their inability to focus on more than two candidates at a time; their propensity for emphasizing the sporting aspects of politics; their disinterest in the substance of the issues at stake and the character of the office seeker; their arrogance in declaring, from their polls and their seat of the pants judgments, winners before the political process itself has had the ability to choose winners; their insensitivity to the needs for public debate; and their control over the conduct of the campaigns.

But perhaps the most pertinent concern of all is the degree to which there is, in the television message, no sense of history, no sense of the slow pace of political progress, no sorting through the important from the unimportant but visually exciting. We expect relief from societal ills as quickly as one allegedly gets relief of hemorrhoids from "Preparation H." In a political campaign, it is easier to focus on a politician's gaffes than on his record; it is easier to talk about a James Watt's remarks relating to the membership of a commission than his record in despoiling the environment.

I do not believe the problem of television will be solved unless there is a sixty minute national news program that might make possible greater news in depth; some control and self-control in the viewing habits of Americans; and some regulation in the conduct of campaigns through television. The networks were not licensed, in one pundit's phrase, to coin money. They have a responsibility to the public for the grant of dominance of the airwaves. They must be brought to some sense of responsibility in their conduct and historicity in their coverage.

E.   Governance—Underlying all of the problems associated with non-voting is the problem of governance. For at the root of public cynicism is a disillusionment with the quality of government. The problem quite simply is that the experience of each and every citizen is a constant reminder that government is not the problem-solver many expect it to be. Those riding our freeways find that a trip that once took a half hour now takes an hour. Those who are sandwiched in subway cars during rush hour; those who as in Boston have watched an experiment in busing to achieve integration produce neither integration nor enhance education; those who fly find increasingly delayed flights, all must reflect that there has to be a better way.

We have been a great society in our ability to respond to great crises. We have a terrible record in anticipating crises or the by-product of technological progress. As a result, the legitimate public perception is that government does not work very well; that we now pay more for less in quality, service and humane life styles. In such a situation, non-voting can be seen as an increasingly rational response to the world they perceive.

The Reagan revolution has run its course. Now we need defense of constructive governance. More, we need constructive governance, anticipatory governance, a task as necessary as it will be hard to achieve.

F. Involvement—Willie Velasquez preached the gospel that mobilizing voters is ineffective unless the newly franchised voter can see concrete results from their involvement. Yet, our society has, in general, been reducing the possibilities for involvement of its citizenry during the last decade, and especially during the years of the Reagan Administration. Legal services, citizen action, class action are among the words that are being dropped from our vocabulary as we move to consolidate ever larger institutions and more elitist power. In cities like Boston where little city halls were stated with bright hopes of involving citizens in the search of better communities and better government have deteriorated into patronage machines. Many have folded into non-existence.

Unless we find sources for involvement, not simply in elections, and unless those sources for involvement yield better condi-tions for those who are involved, we can expect an increase in public cynicism about the political enterprise.

Finally, a few words about voting. I have suggested that voting is a lowest common denominator act and that it is a highly complex act. It is also a religious act. It rests upon the premise that no matter how clear it is that the individual's vote in many elections does not count because very few elections are decided by one vote, citizens want to contribute to a general will that will either give or withhold assent to a particular candidate or set of policies. It is this religious faith in the democratic process that is presently being eroded.

The essence is that such faith will not be easily rekindled. It involves looking at the whole of our polity and addressing the root causes of the problem. The problem we face is large and to deal with it we should not think small.

NOTES

Crotty, W. (1977). *Political reform and the American experiment.* New York: Thomas Y. Crowell.

Crotty, W. (1980). The franchise: Registration changes and voter representation. In W. Crotty (Ed.), Paths to political reform (pp. 67–114). Lexington, MA: Lexington Books/D.C. Heath.

Wolfinger, R. E., & Rosenstone, S. J. (1980). *Who votes?* New Haven: Yale University Press.

Campaign Finance:
Political Action Committees

24
Real and Imagined Corruption in
Campaign Financing
Larry Sabato

Campaign finance is a crucial matter in determining the success of candidates seeking the presidency, legislative office, and state and local elected positions. Since political parties have declined in their fund-raising functions, political action committees of various interest groups have become an important source of financing congressional campaigns. Larry Sabato of the University of Virginia weighs the arguments for and against PAC influence on elected legislators. Does PAC money buy congressional votes? What other factors influence how a Senator or House member votes? Sabato suggests several reforms to reduce the influence of PACs. Which of these proposals might be most effective? Will more comprehensive campaign expense disclosure reduce the deceptive and fraudulent practices of PACs?

THE AGE OF PACS

While many PACs of all political persuasions existed before the 1970s, it was during the 1970s—the decade of campaign reform—that the modern PAC era began. Spawned by the Watergate-inspired revisions of the campaign finance laws, PACs grew in number from 113 in 1972 to 4,157 by the end of 1986, and their contributions to congressional candidates multiplied from $8.5 million in 1972 to $130.3 million by 1986. This rapid rise of PACs inevitably proved controversial, yet many of the charges made against them are exaggerated and dubious. It is said that PACs are disturbingly novel and have flooded the political system with money, mainly from business. While the widespread use of the PAC structure is new, special-interest money of all types has always found its way into politics, and before the 1970s it did so in less traceable and far more disturbing and unsavory ways.

In absolute terms PACs contribute a massive sum to candidates, but it is not clear that there is proportionately more interest group money in the system than before. As Michael Malbin has argued, the truth will never be known because the earlier record is so incomplete.[1] The proportion of House and Senate campaign funds provided by PACs has certainly increased since the early 1970s, but individuals, most of whom are unaffiliated with PACS, still supply over three-fifths of all the money raised by House candidates and

From A. James Reichley, editor, *Elections American Style*, (Washington, D.C.: The Brookings Institution, 1987), pp. 157-162; 167-174.

three-quarters of the campaign budgets of Senate contenders. Although the importance of PAC spending has grown, PACs clearly remain secondary to individuals as a source of election funding.

Apart from the argument over the relative weight of PAC funds, critics claim that PACs are making it more expensive to run for office. There is some validity to this assertion. Money provided to one side funds the purchase of campaign tools that the other side must then match in order to stay competitive. In the aggregate, American campaign expenditures seem huge. Congressional candidates in the 1986 election spent a total of about $450 million, for instance. Will Rogers's remark has never been more true: "Politics has got so expensive that it takes lots of money to even get beat with."

Yet these days it is enormously expensive to communicate, whether the message is political or commercial. Television time, polling costs, consultants' fees, direct-mail investment, and other standard campaign expenditures have been soaring in price, over and above inflation.[2] PACs have been fueling the use of new campaign techniques, but a reasonable case can be made that such expenses are necessary and that more and better communication is required between candidates and an electorate that often appears woefully uninformed about politics. PACs therefore may be making a positive contribution by providing the means to increase the flow of information during elections (though one can legitimately question whether thirty-second TV spots can enlighten anyone).

PACs are also accused of favoring incumbents, and except for the ideological ones, PACs do display a clear preference for incumbents. But the same bias is apparent in contributions from individuals. Facing all contributors is a rational, perhaps decisive, economic question: why waste money on non-

incumbents if incumbents almost always win? On the other hand, the best challengers—those perceived as having fair to good chances of winning—are generously funded by PACs. Well-targeted PAC challenger money clearly helped the Republicans win a majority in the U.S. Senate in 1980, for instance, and in turn aided the Democrats in their 1986 Senate takeover. It is true that PACs limit the number of strong challengers by giving so much early money to incumbents and thus helping to deter potential opponents. But the money that PACs channel to competitive challengers late in the election season may then increase the turnover of officeholders on election day. PAC money also certainly increases the level of competitiveness in congressional races without an incumbent candidate.

Another line of attack on PACs is more justified. The undemocratic character of the process by which some PACs choose which candidates to support completely severs the connecting link between contributor and candidate. As political scientist David Adamany has noted, this unhealthy condition is most apparent in many of the ideological nonconnected PACs, whose free-style organization and lack of a parent body make them accountable to no one and responsive mainly to their own whims.[3]

Leaders of ideological PACs insist that their committees are democratic in the sense that their contributors will stop giving if dissatisfied with the PACs' candidate choices. But these PACs, like most independent committees, raise money by direct mail. Except for perhaps an occasional news article, the average donor's only source of information about the PAC's activities is its own direct mail, which, not surprisingly, tends to be upbeat and selective in reporting the committee's work. Moreover, as political scientist Frank Sorauf has stressed, since direct mail can succeed with a response rate of only 2–5 percent and prospecting for new donors is continuous, decisions by even a large number of givers to drop out will have little effect on PAC fund-raising.[4]

Ideological PACs are not alone in following undemocratic practices. When the AFL-CIO overwhelmingly endorsed Democrat Walter Mondale for president in 1983, making available to him the invaluable resources of most labor PACs, a CBS/*New York Times* poll showed that among the union members they interviewed, less than a quarter reported having had their presidential preferences solicited in any fashion. If a democratic sampling had been taken, the AFL-CIO might not have been so pro-Mondale. The CBS/*Times* poll indicated that not only was Mondale not favored by a majority of the union respondents, he was in a dead heat with Senator John Glenn for a plurality edge. Nor can many corporate PACs be considered showcases of democracy. In a few the chief executive officers completely rule the roost, and in many the CEOs have inordinate influence.

Does PAC Money Buy Congressional Votes?

The most serious charge leveled at PACs is that they succeed in buying the votes of legislators on issues important to each committee's constituency. That many PACs are shopping for congressional votes seems hardly worth arguing. That PAC money buys access to congressmen is similarly disputed by few. But the "vote-buying" allegation is generally not supported by a careful examination of the facts. PAC contributions do make a difference, at least on some occasions, in securing access and influencing the course of events on the House and Senate floors. But those occasions are not nearly as frequent as anti-PAC spokesmen often suggest.

PACs affect legislative proceedings to a decisive degree only when certain conditions prevail. First, the less visible the issue, the more likely that PAC funds can influence congressional votes. A corollary of this rule might be that PAC money has more effect on the early stages of the legislative process, such as agenda setting and votes in subcommittee meetings, than on later and more public floor deliberations. Press, public, and even "watchdog" groups are not nearly as attentive to initial legislative proceedings.

Second, PAC contributions are more likely to influence the legislature when the matter at hand is specialized and narrow or unopposed by other organized interests. PAC gifts are less likely to be decisive on broad national issues such as American policy in El Salvador or the adoption of an MX missile system. Additionally, PAC influence in Congress is greater when large PACs or groups of them are allied. In recent years business and labor, despite their natural enmity, have lobbied together on a number of issues including defense spending, trade policy, environmental regulation, maritime legislation, trucking legislation, and nuclear power. The combination is a weighty one, checked in many instances only by a tendency for business and labor in one industry (say, the railroads) to combine and oppose their cooperating counterparts in another industry (perhaps the truckers and Teamsters).

It is worth stressing, however, that most congressmen are not unduly influenced by PAC money on most votes. The special conditions I have outlined simply do not apply to most legislative issues. Other considerations—foremost among them a congressman's party affiliation, ideology, and constituents' needs and desires—are the overriding factors in determining a legislator's votes. Much has been made of the passage of large tax cuts for oil and business interests in the 1981 omnibus tax package. Journalist Elizabeth Drew said there was a "bidding war" to trade campaign contributions for tax breaks benefiting the independent oil producers.[5] Ralph Nader's Public Citizen Group charged that the $280,000 in corporate PAC money accepted by members of the House Ways and Means Committee had helped to produce a bill that "contained everything business ever dared to ask for, and more." Yet, as Robert Samuelson has convincingly argued, the "bidding war" between Democrats and Republicans was waged not for PAC money but for control of a House of Representatives sharply divided between Reaganite Republicans and liberal Democrats, with conservative "boll weevil" Democrats from the southern oil states as the crucial swing votes.[6] The Ways and Means Committee actions cited by Nader were also more correctly explained in partisan terms. After all, if these special interests were so influential in the writing of the 1981 omnibus tax package, how could they fail so completely to derail the much more important (and, for them, threatening) tax reform legislation of 1986?

The answer goes beyond the tug of party ties, of course. If party loyalty can have a stronger pull than PAC contributions, then surely the views of a congressman's constituents usually take precedence over those of PACs. PAC gifts are merely a means to an end: reelection. If accepting money will cause a candidate embarrassment, then even a maximum donation is likely to be rejected. If an incumbent is faced with a choice of either voting for a PAC-backed bill that is very unpopular in this district or forgoing donations from the PAC or even a whole industry, the odds are that he will side with his constituency and vote against the PAC's interest. The flip side of this proposition makes sense as well: if a PAC's parent organization has many members or a major financial stake in the congressman's home district, he is much more likely to vote the PAC's way—not so much because he receives PAC money but because the group accounts for an important part of his electorate. Does Senator David Durenberger of Minnesota vote for dairy price supports because he received 11 percent of his PAC contributions from agriculture, or because the farm population of his state is relatively large and politically active? Do congressmen generally vote the National Rifle Association's preferences because of the money the NRA's PAC distributes or because the NRA, unlike gun-control advocates, has repeatedly demonstrated the ability to produce a sizable number of votes in many legislative districts?

If PACs have appeared more influential than they actually are, perhaps it is partly because many people's views of congressmen have been tainted by scandals such as Abscam. The spectacle of a congressman exclaiming on candid camera, "I've got larceny in my blood!" leaves a powerful impression. It is both disturbing and amusing that the National Republican Congressional Committee felt obliged to warn PAC-soliciting Republican candidates: "Don't *ever* suggest to the PAC that it is 'buying' your vote should you get elected." Yet all knowledgeable Capitol Hill observers agree that there are few truly corrupt congressmen. Simple correlations notwithstanding, when legislators vote for a PAC-supported bill, it is usually because they have been convinced of the merits of the case by arguments or pressure from their party leaders, peers, or constituents rather than by money from the PAC.

When the PAC phenomenon is viewed in the broad perspective, and when the complex nature of the congressional and electoral process is fully considered, what matters most to congressmen as they vote is merit, as defined by the specifics of each case, general ideological beliefs, party loyalty, and the interests of district constituents. It is ludicrously naive to contend that PAC money never influences congressmen's decisions. But it is irredeemably cynical to believe that PACs always, or even usually, push the voting buttons in Congress.

REFORMS THAT MAKE SENSE

As I have discussed, one sure way to lessen the importance of PACs is to shore up competing institutions and to increase the pool of alternative money. To begin with, the $1,000 limit on an individual's contribution to each candidate per election should be raised to recover its loss to inflation since 1974. Both the $1,000 cap and the companion limit of $25,000 on what an individual is permitted to donate to all candidates in a calendar year should be permanently indexed to the inflation rate. Restoring the value of individual contributions will offset somewhat the financial clout of the PACs.

Much more vital is the need to enhance the financial flexibility of the political parties. While individuals and PACs represent particular interests and further the atomization of public policy, the parties encompass more general concerns and push the system toward consensus. Their role is absolutely central to American democracy's future health and success; thus the parties should be accorded special, preferential treatment by the campaign finance laws. The original Federal Election Campaign Act of 1971 (FECA) was not especially generous to the parties, though neither was it particularly injurious, considering that it allowed coordinated expenditures by the party on behalf of a slate of candidates, and established relatively liberal limits on contributions and expenditures for parties. The 1979 amendments to FECA helped by allowing state and local parties to spend unlimited amounts on materials for volunteer activities and get-out-the-vote drives. The most useful party advantage of all under current law may be the greatly reduced postage rates allowed party mailings, funded by a congressional subsidy.

But parties can be aided still further. The current limits on contributions to party committees ($20,000 a year for an individual and $15,000 for a multicandidate PAC) should be substantially increased. Additionally, contributors should be permitted to underwrite without limit the administrative, legal, and accounting costs parties incur. A modest level of public funding from general tax revenues or some of the surplus existing in the Federal Election Campaign Fund (derived from the income tax check-off) should be provided each year to the national party committees for party-building activities, or, alternatively, taxpayers should be permitted to take a tax credit for their gifts to parties (see below).

It would be wise, too, for Congress to reclaim a portion of the public's airwaves and require that television and radio stations turn over a dozen five-minute blocks of prime time each year to both the state parties and another dozen blocks to both national parties (rather than to individual candidates) so that more generic, institutional advertising can be aired even by the relatively underfinanced Democrats. (Politicians should still be free to make unlimited additional purchases to promote their individual candidacies.) The parties should have wide discretion in determining the uses to which the time is put. They may wish to conserve it all for the general election, or they may allocate some of it to help the party's endorsed slate in the primary.

The relative failure of the Democratic party at fund raising, so far at least, stands in the way of more substantial reforms. Republican National Committee chairman Frank Fahrenkopf is surely correct in wondering "why the United Auto Workers or NCPAC can spend an unlimited amount of money supporting or opposing candidates for federal office [by means of independent expenditures] and not the Republican or Democrat parties." At some point the amounts party committees can give or spend on behalf of their nominees should be considerably increased, but this will probably not be acceptable until the Democratic party becomes better funded. The long-term objective is clear; beef up the parties so that PACs will be limited indirectly. Candidates and the political system will then benefit from the infusion of more party funds and power, and the influence of PACs will decrease without their being shackled by unfair and unworkable restrictions.

Public Finance Proposals

President Theodore Roosevelt first proposed in 1907 that the cost of campaigns be borne by the federal treasury, and since 1976, as a result of the Watergate scandals, presidential campaigns have been publicly financed. But three major attempts in the late 1970s to extend the presidential system to congressional races fell short. More recently Senators Boren and Byrd have seriously proposed partial public financing of Senate campaigns, but it is questionable whether such a bill can be enacted in the foreseeable future.

If and when public financing of congressional elections is passed, it should be designed in ways that benefit the political system. Public funds should be given to candidates as *floors* rather than as *ceilings*. Under this system, every congressional candidate at the primary election level who can raise a qualifying amount (say $50,000) in small contributions (perhaps $250 and under) should be eligible for matching funds from the federal treasury for all similar small gifts, up to a maximum per candidate of something between $50,000 and $75,000. Then in the general election, congressional nominees of the major parties would receive a flat amount (a floor) in public funds (perhaps $150,000) to ensure that they had the minimum financial base needed to conduct a modern campaign. Beyond that, in both the primary and general election, they should be permitted to raise as much as they can in unrestricted fashion from PACs and individuals. This approach guaran-

tees at least basic competition in each district and augments the ability of candidates to communicate with voters while preserving for individuals, PACs, and interest groups a rightful and legitimate role in elections. A ceiling on expenditures, by contrast, almost certainly benefits incumbents since challengers must usually spend a great deal more than average to defeat an incumbent. Moreover, a ceiling restricts the flow of communications between candidates and voters and unfairly minimizes the direct participation of PACs in the political process. And as is true of other limitations on PAC contributions, a public-funds ceiling would squeeze PAC money into less accountable and less desirable channels, such as independent spending. A public-funding scheme should also transmit treasury money through the national or state political parties, permitting them to keep a certain percentage for their own administration and partybuilding activities and perhaps also allowing them some degree of flexibility in allocating funds to their nominees.

Realistically, these reform measures do not now have a good chance of enactment. Congressmen are probably not going to subject themselves to additional leverage by their parties, nor are they going to do any favors for their opponents by enacting public-funding floors that favor challengers rather then ceilings that favor themselves. Representative Richard Cheney, Republican of Wyoming, said it best: "If you think this Congress, or any other, is going to set up a system where someone can run against them on equal terms at government expense, you're smoking something you can't buy at the corner drugstore."[7]

Probably the best form of public financing with a reasonable chance of passage is the tax credit option. The 1986 tax reform bill eliminated the 50 percent tax credit for all contributions to candidates, PACs, and political committees of up to $50 for an individual and

$100 on a joint return. A useful and feasible reform would restore the old credit and increase it to 100 percent, but only for contributions to political parties, or to House and Senate candidates from the contributor's own state, not for gifts to PACs. Special-interest groups should not be restricted as they go about fulfilling their legitimate purposes, but their political activities should not be subsidized by the taxpayers.

Reforming the tax credit incentive in this way would remove the inducement for giving to PACs and augment the motivation for party giving. It would also encourage candidates to expand their base of small, in-state contributors rather than simply concentrating on national PACs and large individual donors. And while challengers would benefit from a form of public financing that increases the electoral money supply without capping expenditures, incumbents would perhaps be in a better position to take advantage of the small-donor tax credit because of their superior resources and higher name recognition. Not incidentally, recent elections have underlined the need to stimulate more small individual contributions. Gifts of under $100 to House general election candidates declined from 36 percent of all campaign money in 1978 to 18 percent in 1982 and 15 percent in 1984. Increasing the tax credit for small gifts would encourage participation from more citizens while providing another indirect check on PACs.

This reform might also help to stem another unhealthy development, the aggregation of large personal debts accumulated by candidates (especially nonincumbents) during their campaigns. By 1984, 12 percent of all money raised by Senate candidates and 8 percent of all funds secured by House candidates were in the form of loans, either borrowed from banks or given from their own personal fortunes. These loans can place elected representatives under great pressure once in office, as they raise money to repay the banks or themselves.

The Importance of Disclosure

Probably the most universally supported and certainly the most successful provision of the campaign finance law is the disclosure requirement, under which PACs and candidates are required at various intervals to reveal their contributors and their expenditures. Disclosure provisions not only expose the motives and decisions of PACs and politicians, but also alert competing interests to the need for mobilization.

Disclosure is no cure-all, however. As David Adamany has pointed out, the disclosure laws generate more information than can be mastered by the media or the voters.[8] The volume of financial disclosure reports filed with the Federal Election Commission is crushing. Despite inadequate funding, the FEC does an admirable job in making the information available to press and public, but it is usually well after election day before any thorough analysis of the data can begin, which is too late to affect the election results. Still, disclosure serves many useful purposes, from permitting post-election enforcement of the laws to allowing connections to be made between campaign contributions and votes cast on the floor of Congress. Disclosure itself generates pressure for more reform. When campaign finance was out of sight, it was out of most people's minds; now that the trail of money can be more easily followed, indignation is only a press release away. Disclosure is the single greatest check on the excesses of campaign finance, for it encourages corrective action, whether judicial or political. It is such an essential and welcome device in American democracy that it should be broadened to bring to light a number of abuses or perceived abuses in the PAC community.

No PAC practice is so distasteful as the distortion and deception found in many direct-mail solicitations, especially from the ideological committees. PACs using any form of direct-mail fund-raising should be required to enclose a copy of all letters with their periodic FEC reports. Direct-mail fund-raising is notoriously prone to exaggeration and deceptive promise. Robert Timberg documented a number of such cases in a newspaper series on PACs. The Life Amendment PAC, an antiabortion organization, sent out a letter begging for money to save the seat of antiabortionist Representative Henry Hyde, Republican of Illinois, who was described as being in mortal danger of defeat. In fact Hyde, who had no prior knowledge of the letter and repudiated it, was in a safe Republican district. Another antiabortion group calling itself "Stop the Baby Killers" promised in 1979 to give maximum contributions to candidates opposing a number of "Political Baby Killers" (liberal Democratic congressmen), and to pay for polls, in-kind campaign consultants, and campaign training seminars for volunteers. In truth, the group made not a single contribution of any size to a candidate in 1979 or 1980, conducted no polls, and held no campaign seminars. What happened to the $189,000 the group raised? About $146,000 was used to pay three for-profit direct-mail firms with ties to the organization itself.

The political right wing has no monopoly on such travesties. Other disturbing examples came from the ideological left. Of the nearly $1.7 million raised by Congressman Edward Markey's two PACs (the U.S. Committee Against Nuclear War and the National Committee for Peace in Central America) from 1982 to 1986, less than 3 percent was contributed to candidates sympathetic to the Massachusetts Democrat's causes. Markey's PACs broke repeated promises to 50,000 contributors that their money would be used to train and elect liberal contenders, lobby legislators, and conduct polling, canvassing, and phone banks.

The FEC has received many complaints about fraudulent political fund-raising, and this may be only the tip of the iceberg. Unless a reporter happens to receive a copy of a questionable solicitation or a contributor takes it upon himself to trace his money through the FEC, little is heard about most direct-mail pieces.

Just as private charities are required to do in many states, PACs using direct mail should be forced to disclose in each letter and on each contributor card how much of all money raised is devoted to fund-raising and administrative costs. Granted, prospecting for direct-mail donors is a necessary and expensive first step in the process, but it takes only a couple of paragraphs to explain this to letter recipients. They may not like what they read and consequently may refuse to give, but they are entitled to know how their money will be spent if any degree of accountability is to exist. Furthermore, all PACs, not just those using direct mail, should be required to report their list of candidate selections to their contributors. Most PACs already do this, but the ideological PACs are usually exceptions.

Beyond PACs, broadened disclosure is needed in other areas. Both national parties have a "building fund" to pay the costs of the headquarters facilities. Corporations, unions, and individuals contribute millions of dollars to these funds, which, for the most part, remain hidden from public view. Tens of millions have been similarly given in "soft money"—donations channeled through the national and state parties that normally would be illegal under federal election law because the money comes directly from corporate or union treasuries or exceeds maximum contribution limits. This "soft money" remains barely legal because it is spent primarily by the *state* parties in states where direct corporate or labor union treasury contributions are permitted, ostensibly to affect only non-federal races. The distinction, of course, is artificial since voter registration and turnout programs inevitably influence all contests on the ballot.

Finally, some presidential candidates, as well as some large PACs, have established tax-exempt foundations that exist primarily to prepare the groundwork for their sponsor's White House bids. Yet these foundations can accept unlimited donations from groups and individuals and do not have to disclose the identities of any donors. Some potential candidates have voluntarily revealed their foundations' benefactors, but they should not have the choice. This subterfuge should be exposed and disclosed.

Particularly if these reforms are adopted, the perpetually starved Federal Election Commission must be funded at a much more generous level to accommodate the increased crush of paper that comes with broad disclosure.

NOTES

1. Michael J. Malbin, "The Problem of PAC-Journalism," *Public Opinion,* vol. 5 (December-January 1983), pp. 15–16, 59.

2. See Larry Sabato, *The Rise of Political Consultants* (Basic Books, 1981); see also "Campaign Spending Report: Where the Money Goes," *National Journal,,* vol. 15 (April 16, 1983), pp. 780–81

3. David Adamany, "The New Faces of American Politics," *Annals of the American Academy of Political and Social Sciences,* vol. 486 (July 1986), pp. 31–32.

4. Frank J. Sorauf, "Accountability in Political Action Committees: Who's in Charge?" paper prepared for the 1982 annual meeting of the American Political Science Association, pp. 21–22.

5. Elizabeth Drew, "Politics and Money, Part I," *New Yorker* (December 6, 1982), pp. 38–45.

6. Robert Samuelson, "The Campaign Reform Failure," *New Republic* (September 5, 1983), pp. 32–33.

7. Quoted in Richard A. Armstrong, "Election Finance and Free Speech," *Newsweek,* July 18, 1983, p. 11.

8. David Adamany, "PAC's and the Democratic Financing of Politics," *Arizona Law Review,* vol. 22, no. 2 (1980), pp. 597–98.

Negative Election Ads

25
The Negative 1988 Presidential Campaign
Raymond L. Fischer

Campaign funds are used principally to purchase television advertisements. The 1988 presidential contest was one of the most issueless and negative campaigns in recent memory. George Bush's campaign advisers convinced him to use negative attack ads against Bob Dole in the primaries and against Michael Dukakis in the general campaign. Unfortunately, they worked effectively for Bush. The campaign for president became a mud-slinging contest. Raymond Fischer of the University of North Dakota tries to affix blame for the unusual degree of negativism in 1988. Why didn't the press do its job? Why is the public willing to accept negative TV ads? Fischer concludes by suggesting several reforms to improve the quality of presidential campaigns. Which of these are most effective? What are the prospects of achieving these reforms?

Reacting to the 1988 presidential campaign, Walter Mondale assessed, "I feel sick. There is no substance. The candidates are hidden. The negatives have taken over and it's mud every night." The election is over, but the distaste of the campaign lingers on. Following 18 months of headlines proclaiming how low and empty the campaign was; stories about mud-slinging, attack ads, sound bites, and one-liners; and cartoons portraying the candidates covered with mud or hurling invectives, the American public determined the election without purging the sour taste. As they neglected the issues and used misleading TV ads, rumor-mongering, and deceptive practices, the candidates stand accused of carrying on one of the most trivial and excoriating campaigns in history. Social and political scientists now can begin to sift through the facts and put the campaign in its proper perspective. Why was it so bad? More importantly, can anything be done to make future campaigns more palatable?

George Bush has been accused of taking the low road to the White House, of slinging several tons of mud—much more than Michael Dukakis—and flooding the airwaves with a barrage of attack ads. Bush claims that he became negative because the Democratic convention was negative and attacked him. However, Bush was that way long before either convention—in fact, during the primaries. Why?—because it works.

Following the caucuses, Bush left Iowa knowing he had placed third behind Sen. Robert Dole and Pat Robertson—an embarrassing showing in a state that he had won eight years earlier. Winning in New Hampshire was

Reprinted from *USA Today Magazine*, March, 1989, pp. 20-22. Copyright 1989 by the Society for the Advancement of Education.

imperative; yet, shortly before the primary, polls showed Bush merely even. Roger Ailes, his media advisor, implored Bush to "go negative," and Ailes had just the vehicle—the so-called "Senator Straddle" ad that portrayed Dole as "waffling" on several issues. Although Bush was hesitant at first, he ultimately agreed to try it. This 30-second ad, scheduled for every available time slot until the primary, dominated the final days of the New Hampshire campaign. As a result, Bush won New Hampshire by 10 points and was on his way. He never looked back.

During the long Memorial Day weekend, Bush and his trusted aides and friends met to map out the campaign against Dukakis. The most important information shared by the group was a marketing company's research showing that the general public knew very little about the candidates, their stands on issues, and their earlier accomplishments. The study revealed that Dukakis' veto of the bill requiring schoolchildren to say the Pledge of Allegiance, stand against the death penalty, and sanction of weekend furloughs to first-degree murderers were sufficient to brand him a liberal. Consequently, they labeled Dukakis accordingly and pounded home the so-called issues repeatedly. They looked upon Dukakis as a blank canvas in the mind of voters; they would fill the canvas and began by painting it black—with mud.

Dukakis, as had Dole, planned to stay above the mudslinging and base the campaign on issues and accomplishments. However, when he found himself on the defensive early in the campaign and ultimately behind in the polls, he felt compelled to fight the battle with the "proper" or "necessary" weapons. So, Dukakis became entangled in the negative ads, sound bites, and one-liners. However, it was too little and too late.

Every campaign in U. S. history has included vilification of the other candidate. In the first contested election, Republican supporters of Thomas Jefferson circulated handbills that accused John Adams of being a monarchist and an aristocrat, while the Federalists were calling Jefferson an atheist, a freethinker, and an enemy of the Constitution. Years later, Andrew Jackson was charged with ordering several executions of his own soldiers, massacring Indians, stabbing a man in the back, personally shooting a soldier who disobeyed him, and hanging three Indians. William Henry Harrison was branded a pitiable, superannuated dotard and accused of military incompetence. In 1948, Democratic ads included fast-moving, humorous programs filled with one-liners aimed at the opposition. One asked the audience to identify a person from a clue, then came dead silence, followed by the announcer's explanation, "Governor Dewey, who says nothing on any issue." In 1952, Adlai Stevenson observed that "the people might be better served if a party purchased 30 minutes of radio and TV silence during which the audience would be asked to think quietly for themselves."

With the emergence of firms specializing in political media in the early 1960s and the founding of the American Association of Political Consultants in 1969, political advertising became an art—often one of negative attack ads. The American public has a tendency to forget how negative some of the more modern election campaigns have been. During the 1976 campaign, columnist George Will commented that, "until Dole took wing in his debate with Walter Mondale, it was unclear when this campaign would hit bottom." Almost all of the ads for Jimmy Carter and Gerald Ford were concerned with the personal elements of the opponent—not with issues. One ad cartooned a mirror in which a smiling Carter looked at a frowning image as Actor Cliff Robertson listed Carter's inconsistencies. Both candidates ended the campaign with numerous attack ads. In fact, Ford's ads were credited for his narrowing the gap in the polls. One Carter ad accused the Ford Administration of following outdated, insensitive, unjust, and wasteful economic policies and criticized Ford for voting against Medicare, food stamps for the elderly, and adequate housing. This campaign also introduced the now popular threat of the vice president being a "heartbeat away" from the presidency.

In 1980, attack ads were plentiful. During the primaries, Carter's ads attacked Sen. Edward Kennedy, and Kennedy and the Republicans returned fire. Following the Democratic convention, Republican ads included statements made by Kennedy about Carter. Although Ronald Reagan rarely attacked Carter personally, a loophole in the election laws permitted independent political action committees to air a plethora of ads denouncing Carter. In response, Reagan was depicted as dangerous and lacking in compassion in Carter's ads. Reagan later stated that his views had been "distorted in an effort to scare people through innuendos and misstatements of [his] position." Ultimately, Carter suffered from voter backlash, which accused him of creating a "dirty campaign." The "meanness issue" accelerated.

In 1984, the attack ads aired by the Republican Party devastated Mondale. Like Dukakis, Mondale learned too late that, in a presidential campaign, one must fight fire with fire. The epitome of negative campaign ads occurred in the 1986 campaign, when irrelevant and inflammatory attack ads played a major role in helping the Democrats regain control of the Senate. How soon the American public forgets!

WHO IS TO BLAME?

Are the candidates to blame for using a technique that works? Indeed, they are. Negative, non-issue campaigns have become an art. However, politicians and their parties are not the only ones at fault. The press and the public must be called to account as well.

In 1980 and 1984, the press intensely scrutinized nationally telecast advertising. When either candidate made questionable claims or cast unfounded aspersions, the media made the facts public. Several major newspapers and TV newscasters probed Reagan's "sins of omission and commission" complaint. Press vigilance exposed many half-truths and innuendos and printed the facts and the truth.

However, in 1988, the media just did not do their job. *Time* referred to the campaign coverage as "a burnt-out genre . . . with none of the [old] magic." One reporter suggested that the "watch dog" media turned into lap dogs. A few programs such as public TV's "MacNeil-Lehrer Report," CNN's "Inside Politics '88," and ABC's "Nightline" did provide in-depth coverage. Yet, most reporting merely repeated charges and distortions when analysis was in order. The media relinquished control of campaign coverage to the candidates, especially Bush, who had learned from Reagan's mastery use of the media during the 1984 election. Staged-for-TV events frequently provided the "visual" needed for news programs, and carefully programmed one-liners provided the "sound bites." From the beginning, Bush, and later Dukakis, remained as inaccessible as possible; neither traveled nor lodged with the press. There is no question that the candidates and their advisors controlled the media in this campaign. Not only that, the media actually praised the experts for their work.

Reporters seemed to bend over backwards to be "fair." Although it was obvious that Bush began "slinging mud" earlier and more often than Dukakis, reporters appeared to blame or vindicate both men equally. For example, Bush was more adept than Dukakis at using misleading TV spots, but reporters seldom set the record straight. Only in the "whispering campaign" did reporters outdo themselves in disclosing such rumors as Dukakis' mental health, Kitty Dukakis burning an American flag, and Bush's affairs—all unfounded, but blown out of proportion.

Although one network president promised to improve coverage of the next election by concentrating on long-range issues, all of the networks should reevaluate their campaign coverage and resolve to provide the public with more than "pretty pictures" and sound bites. Reporters deliberately must point out that events have been staged and sound bites planned; they must correct the half-truths, point out the inconsistencies, and ask questions concerning the issues. The media must be held accountable.

The American public should share in the blame. Jaded and more concerned with personalities than issues, people are more apt to listen to the negative ads than to ask what a candidate stands for. The environment, the trade deficit, the budget—issues that should have been discussed in this election—are of public concern. However, as long as some form of "peace and prosperity" exists, public apathy will rear its ugly head.

Nevertheless, something can be done about apathy. The U. S. has a notoriously low voter turn out, which plummeted even below the previous average in 1988. Some countries require voting and fine citizens who do not. The carrot-and-stick method has potential—a fine for not voting and a tax reduction for voting. At the polling places, each voter might receive a receipt with a number and authorization signed by the voter in the presence of election officials. The number would ensure that the person who voted was registered to vote and the receipt could be enclosed in tax returns for a dollar or percentage reduction in Federal and/or state income taxes.

Another reason for apathy is related to the length of the campaign. Although some candidates begin the next campaign as soon as an election is over, a reasonable time line might restrict active campaigning and curtail the use of media. Canada limits campaigning in national elections to 55 days and precludes advertising on "any electronic media or in any periodical publications until the 29th day before [the election]."

Something also can be done about the paucity of qualified candidates. Further limiting national campaign costs might encourage additional candidates to seek nomination. Signed into law on Feb. 7, 1972, the Federal Election Campaign Act (FECA) limited the amounts candidates for Federal office could spend on communication media and broadcast advertising. The act limited Richard Nixon's and George McGovern's spending to no more than $8,400,000 on broadcasting after the nomination, but the 1974 amendment repealed the media spending ceilings. The act also limited personal expenditures by presidential candidates to $50,000 during their campaign.

The election of 1976 was the first presidential campaign to utilize Federal funds made available by the FECA amendment. Any candidate who raised at least $5,000 in contributions of $250 or less in each of 20 states qualified for matching funds. In return, candidates agreed to a spending ceiling, which was $13,100,000 in 1976. Matching funds ceased 30 days after a candidate failed to receive at least 10% of the vote in two consecutive primaries. In the general election, Carter and Ford each received $21,800,000, and the amendment allowed national parties to raise and spend an additional $3,200,000. The imposed ceiling resulted in a decrease in total campaign spending. Subsequent FECA amendments might reduce the ceiling further.

On Jan. 30, 1976, the Supreme Court ruled that the $1,000 limit on individual contributions and the $5,000 ceiling on contributions of political action committees (PAC's) were constitutional. However, they also ruled that the limit of PAC's *independent* of a candidate's campaign were unconstitutional, which opened the door to much of the financial trouble now incurred in elections. PAC advertising in the 1980 presidential race took on giant proportions—growing from less than $2,000,000 for both candidates in 1976 to almost $12,000,000 for Reagan, but only $50,000 for Carter, four years later.

The independent PAC loophole must be closed. The imposed ceilings should be lowered, and the media spending ceilings should be reimposed. Canada assures its citizens that anyone over 18 may become a candidate for an election "without fear of being overwhelmed by a more wealthy opponent." It severely limits not only the amount of expenditures and time, but also imposes fines and/or imprisonment, and disqualifies a candidate for five years for conviction of illegal practices and seven years for corrupt practices.

Legislatures concerned about escalating costs of advertising have drafted bills that would require the public and/or mass media to assume some or all of the expense. Such a measure would be difficult to administer, though legislation might set limits for total time and expenditures and insist that radio and TV ads appear exclusively on public radio and TV. Yet another proposal would limit the types of ads—for example, "talking head" ads only.

CHANGING THE CAMPAIGNS

The debates should be mandatory and actual debating should occur. In 1988, Canada again led the way with wide-open, no-holds-barred parliamentary debates during the campaign. Given a topic to discuss, the candidates questioned and interrupted each other. Many of the innuendos and half-truths concerning free trade with the U. S. were brought out into the open, discussed freely, and laid to rest. The participants proved that they were knowledgeable on issues.

Ideally, presidential candidates should participate in at least three debates spaced equidistant throughout the campaign; the vice-presidential candidates should debate only once. Because panelists complicate these confrontations with their own politics and prejudices, one highly respected moderator should state the issue for each debate and allow the candidates to make opening statements. Then, the candidates should question and respond until they have exhausted the issue—not until time runs out. The moderator should interrupt only if things get out of hand. When debates have become something to dread and the candidates' goal is avoiding mistakes, rather than revealing how they think and feel about relative issues, it is time for a change.

Rep. Lee Hamilton (D.-Ind.) would like to add another element to the presidential campaigns. In addition to TV debates, TV ads, and routine news coverage, he would require the candidates to address a single major issue in each of the final six-eight weeks. One at a time, each candidate would make a statement on a single issue and then submit to in-depth questioning by a panel of experts. The videotaped sessions would appear throughout the week. In this way, the public could gain meaningful comparison of the candidates' policies and have a better idea of the positions and ability to express themselves. New York

Gov. Mario Cuomo has suggested that each candidate hold several press conferences during the campaign and submit to unlimited questioning until their positions on major issues of the day are made absolutely clear.

An editorial in the *Washington Post* called the 1988 presidential campaign a "terrible campaign, a national disappointment." Indeed, it was the epitome of a no-issues campaign based on attack ads and little substance—one that *used* the media. Will anything be done to change future campaigns? Unfortunately, the answer is probably not. After each of the last four elections, network officials promised that the next would be different and the coverage issue-oriented. However, the coverage has been different only in the degree of deterioration.

Will the candidates change? They probably won't, because experience from past campaigns has made managing the media an art. Hopefully, some future candidate will realize that the public is fed up with no-issue, "dirty" campaigning and instead take the high road to the White House. This will occur only if the public and the press make it happen. There is no law to require debates, and only one elected incumbent, Reagan, has chosen to face his opponent. Most incumbents have used the "Rose Garden" technique—avoiding debates and staying as far as possible from the media.

Will the procedure change? They might, because legislation has been suggested after all recent campaigns—some even drafted—and the Federal Election Campaign Act did pass in 1972. However, the public must insist that Congress draft and amend laws.

It is time for voters to show an interest in presidential campaigns and demand some changes. They must know where the candidates stand on major issues, have the opportunity to observe them under pressure, and demand coverage that provides essential information. Presidential election campaigns could become even more heavily managed and innocuous. The public could see and know even less about future candidates unless something is done now. American voters must know enough about the issues and candidates to elect a president who will lead the U. S. competently. After all, the fate of the nation very well may depend upon the ability of voters to make the right choice.

The Media, Politics, and Elections

26

Can Democracy Survive the Media in the 1990s?

Judy Woodruff

Judy Woodruff is a reporter on public television's "MacNeill-Lehrer News Hour." She argues that democracy works well where a free press exists. However, the American media is not doing its job very well. In elections, candidate sound bites are now about seven seconds. Television ads for candidates have become increasingly negative. The problem is that the quantity of news has not kept pace with quality. What evidence does Woodruff offer to support this observation? How are the networks distorting the news? What is needed to make television news reporting more accountable and responsible? Why is Woodruff concerned about the future of media reporting?

Let's examine the media from two perspectives—international and domestic—the latter being more complicated, naturally. If we step back and look at the rest of the world, I think we would agree that democracy generally has flourished where a free press has existed. Examples readily come to mind, including England, France, West Germany, and Japan. When the press has been restricted, for whatever reason, it has come hand in hand with a move away from democracy, whether in Panama, South Africa, China, or wherever.

Most of the movement recently has been in the other direction. Thanks in part to Mikhail Gorbachev, communism is on its deathbed and *glasnost* is changing the way the press operates in the Soviet Union and gradually in the rest of the Eastern Bloc. Who would have dreamed even a year ago that we would see this? It is truly an exciting time to be a journalist watching and reporting these ongoing changes.

The argument used to be that, with a free press, democratic nations engaged in too much harmful self-criticism and generally were less tidy than totalitarian regimes that were not saddled with an inquisitive media. When Libya's Muammar al-Qaddafi wants something done, he doesn't have to answer questions from a bunch of nosy reporters. You can bet that China's Deng Xiaoping and his cronies were not bothered by a pushy press after their bloody crackdown at Tiananmen Square. South Africa has similar muzzles on the press.

Nevertheless, the notion that a controlled press brings stability has been all but disproven

Reprinted from *USA Today Magazine*, May 1990, pp. 24–26. Copyright © 1990 by the Society for the Advancement of Education.

by what has transpired in Eastern Europe and Nicaragua. What a controlled press does is suppress temporarily a population's opinions and people's hopes and aspirations. All that is stifled does not disappear, however, and what is forced into hiding is almost sure to bubble up later in clandestine ways that hardly produce stability. So, on an international level, a free press goes hand in hand with a democratic form of government.

Focusing on the U. S., the question is: Can the world's best democracy survive, given the way our free press sometimes functions? I will take the liberty of mostly discussing television, since that is where my experience has been. When I think back to the time when I entered journalism and began covering government and political campaigns, it is as if everything back then moved in slow motion. Politicians gave speeches, made statements, and/or answered questions and they usually could expect a reasonable facsimile of what they said to be reported in the newspaper and on television. Entire thoughts were transmitted in a condensed form, to be sure, but it felt as if there were substantive airings of views that took place. When I covered the Democratic primary in the Georgia gubernatorial race in 1970, Carl Sanders and Jimmy Carter had a real disagreement over how to improve the state's education system. There was some criticism of the other candidate by each side—Carter said Sanders was too wealthy to understand the problems of the little guy, while Sanders claimed Carter was inexperienced—but it did not seem to dominate the campaign the way it does today.

In the early 1970s, when I covered the Georgia legislature and there was a big debate under way about the budget, or taxes, or even whether wide-load trucks should be able to travel state roads, my news director gave me three, four, or sometimes five minutes to tell the story on the six o'clock news. I used 45-second or one-minute-long excerpts of various state senators and representatives engaging in floor debate or speaking in an interview or at a news conference. The politicians were not all handsome, well-coiffed fellows, articulate to a fault, and many of them spoke in a kind of shorthand that I and everyone else had to decipher.

Nowadays, a campaign run the way those were in 1970 or a politician who does not know how to speak in sound bites would not last 10 minutes in a competitive situation. In the 1988 presidential campaign, the average network news sound bite lasted seven seconds, down from 13 seconds in 1984. Television advertising in the late 1980s became so mean-spirited and personal in its attacks on other candidates that, as long-time Republican consultant Doug Bailey put it, "If you don't go negative—even heavy negative—you are considered a wimp!" George Bush's campaign commercials helped erase any lingering "wimpy" impressions of him; indeed, they had the effect of making Michael Dukakis seem weak. Just recall the prison furlough and Boston harbor pollution ads and the unforgettable scene of Dukakis riding in an army tank, wearing that wonderful helmet!

NEGATIVE ADVERTISING

In 1989, the predictions that negative advertising is here to stay came true. During the gubernatorial race in Virginia, the Republican ran ads accusing the Democrat of being soft on rapists. In the New York mayoral campaign, there was an unrelented barrage of negative ads from both sides. Meanwhile, in the New Jersey governor's race, the Democrat accused his Republican opponent of having toxic dumps in his back yard. All of these things are misleading or at least exaggerated and, in some cases, right on the edge of what is factual.

What also has changed about the negative ads is that they are assumed to be true! Unless the other side runs a denial right away, the ads are taken at face value. How does most of television news cover these campaigns and commercials? We usually play it as it lays. We don't bother with much perspective or analysis—we don't have time.

As for covering government, there is not a chance in the world that I would be given three, four, or five minutes on a legislative debate if I were working today for a commercial station. It would be more like a minute and a half to two minutes, with average 10-second sound bites. The legislators or members of Congress who get interviewed nowadays, are the most articulate ones, the ones who have learned how to look good and talk short for television. Issues that used to be explored in depth now are dealt with in abbreviated form with lots of helpful visuals and as little detail as possible to save time.

If I were to ask you if TV news—local, network, weekend, or weekday—is contributing to a more informed electorate, what would your answer be? Certainly, more people are hearing and seeing more about government and political developments than ever before. There are more television channels reaching into more communities: weekend network news shows; early morning, late night, and middle of the night news; and public affairs talk shows on over-the-air and cable television channels. There are more shows with groups of pundits sitting around telling us what to think. When "The MacNeil/Lehrer Report" went on the air in 1975, it was an unusual format. Now, everywhere you look, there is another interview or talk show or, more recently, a quasi-information-entertainment show, trying to win an even bigger audience.

Second, the local and network news broadcasts are far better illustrated (with eye-catching graphics), sometimes better written,

and often reported by a more experienced professional, who even may be a specialist in his or her area. When we watch Bob Bazell reporting on science or medicine news for NBC, or Carl Stern on the Supreme Court, we know we are hearing from someone who makes it his business to know the issues and the people involved in the story.

So, much is improved, and nowhere is it clearer than when there's a breaking story such as a hostage crisis in Lebanon, an earthquake, or an election night. The big networks cover these exhaustively. The technological advances are mind-boggling, including satellites that produce a picture in an instant wherever a microwave truck can get a signal out. The world has shrunk dramatically and we can witness starvation in sub-Saharan Africa, terrorism in the Middle East or by Columbia's drug cartels, or the brutal repression of college student in Tiananmen Square. The sounds, even without the picture, are powerful. Who can forget CBS reporter Richard Ross describing the approach of the Chinese soldiers and their assault on him and his camera crew as transmitted by Ross' portable telephone in contact with his office in New York?

THE TRADE-OFF

So, we are bombarded by events, newsmakers, and fast-breaking developments. However, there has been a trade-off in exchange for all this technology and fast-paced, eye-catching delivery of the news. The trade-off has been an explanation of what it all means for the rest of the world, the nation, our community, our culture, and our families.

It seems to me that, as the quantity of news has increased, the quality has diminished. Political campaigns play themselves out in the willingness of too many news organizations to take candidates and their campaign statements and commercials at face value.

There is too little questioning of facts, challenging of assertions, and offering of background information that might put today's attack on an opponent into perspective. Political consultant Doug Bailey claims there is too little, "truth-telling" going on. Lies sit out there unchallenged till they become political lore. When a candidate airs a new commercial, Bailey says, the media immediately should dissect it to discern if it is truth or fiction, exaggeration or innuendo, or just plain misleading.

When candidates, as they did skillfully in the presidential campaigns of 1980, 1984, and 1988, stand day after day carrying American flags in front of cheering high school students, but don't say anything new of any substance—other than more attacks on the opponent and a recitation of familiar positions—that ought to be reported exactly as it happened. If there is no news, as on most nights of the 1988 presidential campaign, then Tom Brokaw, Dan Rather, and Peter Jennings ought to do what the former president of CBS News, Richard Salant, said several years ago. When the candidates aren't addressing the issues, he advised, the networks should go on the air and say, "George Bush or Michael Dukakis didn't say a damn thing today. So, instead, we are going to report on his record in public office or his past statements on the budget deficit." The news media are far too timid about looking into the past records of candidates and searching out the contradictions, the inconsistencies, as well as the accomplishments. We are just plain lazy sometimes. It's easier to cover the mudslinging.

There's little doubt that one factor that exacerbates all this is the increasing emphasis on profits at the network news headquarters. When the Loews Corporation bought CBS, General Electric bought NBC, and Capital Cities Broadcasting bought ABC, a much greater concern about the bottom line was introduced. I think we have to ask if the corporate chieftains calling the shots at the networks care more about their quarterly profit and loss statements than they do about journalism. Not that there is anything wrong with the good old American free market system—that is what made us great, after all. I just think that the question has to be raised simultaneously.

The networks have faced the double whammy of competition from cable, independent stations, video tapes, and all the other visual offerings that the public can choose instead of ABC, CBS, or NBC. The networks' share of the audience has dropped and, as that has taken place, the commitment to long-form news gradually has eroded. How often do you see documentaries on the networks anymore? What we see instead are the new prime-time "news and entertainment" shows, which are cheaper to produce than pure entertainment. In some instances, they have raised questions among critics and journalists about the validity of what they present. In a lengthy front-page report, *The Wall Street Journal* took the networks to task for their policy of using dramatic re-enactments, rather than real news footage, to tell a story. Maybe I am an old fuddy-duddy, but I agree with the *Journal* when it says that these re-enactments, which have been used on all three networks, are further blurring the distinction between fiction and reality in television news. *The New York Times* made the same point in an editorial, stating that journalists have a duty to the truth and to their audiences. How will the public know what is real and what is not after watching these shows?

Closely akin to the re-enactments, which are coming out of network news divisions, are programs like the docudrama aired on ABC based on the book *The Final Days* by Watergate reporters Bob Woodward and Carl Bernstein. ABC admitted the program was not wholly factual, and attorney Leonard Garment, who was counsel to former Pres. Nixon, said it was a lot worse than that. In an op-ed piece in *The New York Times,* he condemned it as "littered with false pictures, false sequences, and words that were not spoken by the people who spoke them." Garment asserted that the last scene of the program, which shows Nixon collapsing in front of Henry Kissinger, is pure fiction. Garment predicted that the show will be defended as a piece of journalism and protected by the First Amendment. He also forecast that, if the courts diminish First Amendment protection over the next decade, it will come in the area of docudramas. He obviously had an axe to grind in a show about the Nixon Administration, but I think he had a point when he said it will be difficult to invoke the First Amendment—one of the cornerstones of our Constitution—as a protection for shows like "Cops," "Most Wanted," and "A Current Affair," all of which employ docudrama techniques, which, he claimed, are far removed from any respectable definition of journalism. If someone sues a network, what jury will believe a dramatic re-enactment over the testimony of people who actually participated in the event? He raised a point for all of us in television journalism to think about. Once the erosion of the press' freedoms begins, how easy will it be to stop?

As we look to the future, will we find more robust news media in this country, ever more vigilant in their watchdog role, overseeing how elected and appointed officials are handling the public trust, raising tough questions, demanding answers, looking after the public interest, and holding politicians accountable? Or will we find, in the year 2000, in the words of ethicist Michael Josephson, that "the operative definition of newsworthiness will favor virtually unrestricted use of personal, sensitive, and intimate facts." In other words, will we find the worst of today's journalistic ethics and practices magnified a dozen times over? I would like to say that it will not happen, but the trend over the past few years has not augured well for a turnaround in the 1990s.

Some of us in the media, especially television, have gotten caught up in the size of our audience, the profits to be made, catering to short attention spans, and seeking the sensational. Consequently, we seem to have forgotten something basic—that we are here to serve the public, to bring them the information they need to make informed judgments about their community, the nation, and the planet. What could be more important at a time when the world has grown smaller and the problems seem more complicated, if not more difficult, than ever before? If the media don't feel that responsibility, if television news, which reaches more people than any other medium, does not feel some responsibility, then who will? Will Americans read more? The trend does not seem to be moving in that direction.

When my colleagues argue, as I have in the past, that television is only one of the sources of information to which Americans have access, I repeat a statistic that I have heard recently—the average number of books people in Great Britain read last year was eight. The is not very impressive, until you hear that the average in the U. S. is one-quarter of a book!

We are in for some pretty exciting, uncertain times. If communism is not dead, it is dying, and democracy is one the ascendancy. Will journalism, especially television journalism, operate in these other countries as it has in the U. S.? Or is there something uniquely flawed and simultaneously strong about our system that will let democracy succeed in spite of the new journalism we practice? It is something to think about. I am usually an optimist, but I still am undecided about this question.

Political Action: The Machinery of Government

CHAPTER **8**

The Presidency

The presidency occupies a central role in American government. The chief executive is the focus of leadership, authority, and policy direction. Presidential power expands in response to demands for decisive action that neither Congress nor the courts can fulfill. The dispersal and decentralization of Congress delays and limits swift, unified decisions in critical situations. Congress is more likely to follow presidential initiatives, particularly in defense policy and international relations. The president has access to secret and complex information from advisers and the executive bureaucracy that Congress cannot effectively challenge. The Supreme Court cannot initiate new policy in redefining constitutional powers or interpreting legislation, but must wait for appeals and cases and controversies brought by contending parties, which can often be a very slow and time-consuming process. Furthermore, the courts must depend on Congress for appropriations and the president to enforce their decisions.

Only the president, with control of the executive branch and an overview of public-policy priorities, can respond to the extraordinary chaotic events of the twentieth century—two world wars, the cold war with the Soviet Union, the threat of nuclear holocaust, the Korean and Vietnam wars, conflict in the Middle East between Israel and the Arab states, economic depression and recovery, and various energy, poverty, and urban crises. These and many other problems have required presidential leadership to protect, defend, and define the national interest.

CONSTITUTIONAL FOUNDATIONS

When the Founding Fathers wrote the Constitution, they were reacting, in part, to the excesses and abuses of executive power imposed by the British Crown during the colonial and Revolutionary War experiences. Consequently, the Framers focused major attention on the details of legislative representation and authority as a check on executive power. They designed a tripartite system of separation of powers and checks and balances to achieve an equilibrium between the executive and legislative branches (see *The Federalist*, Number 51).

Alan Shank in Article 27 observes that the Madisonian model of separated government is intended to limit executive authority. In contrast, Alexander Hamilton argued in *The Federalist*, Number 70, that "energy" in the executive is "a leading character in the definition of good government." The Hamiltonian view supports positive executive leadership to protect the country against foreign attacks and to provide for effective administration of the laws.

Shank compares and contrasts effective presidential achievements in domestic and foreign policy. Congress, state and local governments, and interest groups are identified as obstacles to presidential domestic initiatives. In contrast, chief executives have much more flexibility in foreign affairs, particularly in international crises and military interventions. The Vietnam War and the Iran-Contra Affair are cited as abuses of executive power in the international arena.

PRESIDENTIAL LEADERSHIP

The president's leadership skills are much more than the product of formal constitutional powers. Today, presidential power is defined in active and positive terms rather than in negative or passive ways. Most modern presidents have positive leadership approaches that include promoting executive policy initiatives in Congress, extolling the president's ceremonial role as the leader of the entire nation, rising above party politics, displaying heroic qualities, and establishing plebiscitary leadership by directly communicating with the masses. Most presidents no longer accept the Madisonian view of limited presidential authority. An example of such an approach was adopted by William Howard Taft, who considered the roles of Congress and the courts as considerably more important than that of the president, and who, as *chief magistrate,* would not undertake any new initiatives unless specifically authorized by the Constitution, acts of Congress, or judicial rulings.

Abraham Lincoln was the most important nineteenth-century president to provide precedents for extraordinary presidential authority in confronting wartime crisis. At the outbreak of the Civil War, Lincoln found it necessary and expedient to suspend various constitutional provisions. In attempting to restore national unity, he assumed legislative and judicial powers and suspended the civil liberties of certain Southern agitators. Such constitutional usurpation was temporary. When the crisis subsided, the president restored the full provisions of the "peacetime" constitution.

Theodore Roosevelt was the first modern president to define the activist role of the chief executive in shaping public policy. He argued that the president is the "steward" of the national interest, a leader who may undertake new authority unless specifically restricted by the Constitution, Congress, or Supreme Court decisions. Thus, presidents have a general constitutional prerogative to expand their powers in response to particular situations that require their involvement.

World wars required Woodrow Wilson and Franklin D. Roosevelt to assume new powers in controlling the national economy and in conducting diplomatic negotiations with foreign nations. The 1917 Lever Act represented a significant legislative delegation of power to the president in preparing the national economy for entry into World War I. In 1936, the Supreme Court decided that the president has exclusive authority to represent the nation in foreign affairs. The president's preeminent role provides discretion and freedom from statutory restrictions "which would not be admissible were domestic affairs alone involved." Subsequently, President Roosevelt entered into secret arrangements with Prime Minister Winston Churchill to trade American warships for British bases in the West Indies before the United States formally entered World War II. Roosevelt then presented his *fait accompli* policies to Congress, which were approved in the Lend Lease Act of 1941.

A countervailing criticism of strong presidential leadership emerged in the 1970s, when Arthur Schlesinger, Jr., characterized the Johnson and Nixon administrations as "imperial presidencies." Unchecked executive authority led to concerns about reasserting a Madisonian balance between the executive and Congress. This view gained widespread public support during the 1973–1974 congressional investigations of the Watergate scandals. During the summer months of 1973, the Senate Select Committee on Presidential Campaign Activities heard more than thirty witnesses testify about the break-in of the Democratic national party headquarters in June 1972. The national TV audience, the seven senators, and their legal staff expressed disbelief that President Nixon's most trusted advisers never informed him about either the Watergate burglary or the subsequent coverup. John Dean, the counsel to the president, revealed many sensational details about Watergate and directly implicated the president after revealing Nixon's efforts to keep the defendants silent. Presidential advisers Ehrlichman and Haldeman strongly defended Nixon. More than a year after Dean's disclosures, President Nixon, under pressure from Judge John Sirica, Special Prosecutor Leon Jaworski, and the House Judiciary Committee, disclosed that he indeed had obstructed the administration of justice by directing the Central Intelligence Agency to stop an investigation of Watergate by the FBI just a few days after the break-in had occurred.

Watergate is one example of executive abuse of authority. The failure of the Johnson administration to keep Congress fully informed about escalating the Vietnam War is another. A third example was the controversy with Congress over aiding the Nicaraguan Contras during the Reagan administration. Critics such as George Reedy in *Twilight of the Presidency* (1970) argued that presidents tend to be treated as "kings" because they are frequently isolated from criticism by approving staff members. Also, the longer they are in office, presidents tend to become divorced from reality. Presidents begin to consider themselves omnipotent, without the necessity of checks by Congress or public opinion.

Looking now at specifics, what does it take to be a good president? What kinds of characteristics are needed to bring the best qualified persons to the presidency? Character, temperament, intelligence, and communication skills are important. The public wants presidents to look like presidents—such as Roosevelt, Kennedy, and Reagan. Presidents need tremendous stamina and resiliency. As for character, they need integrity, magnanimity, and compassion. They need presence, dignity, moral and physical courage, and self-confidence. Presidents require superior intelligence and common sense. Contenders must offer the country a vision of where it is going. They need to communicate effectively with the public, using television as a major resource.[1]

Personal character is an important component in assessing presidential leadership. In a well-known book, *The Presidential Character,* James David Barber argues that a president's personality, as shaped by character, world view, and political style, will affect performance as chief executive. These characteristics are developed during childhood, adolescence, and early adulthood. Presidential personalities fall into a typology of two variables: activism or passivity toward the duties of the office and positive or negative attitudes toward the political environment. Barber establishes four categories of presidential character: active-positive, active-negative, passive-positive, and passive-negative. In his opinion, active-positives are best for the country while active-negatives are potentially the most dangerous. Active-positives include Franklin Roosevelt, Harry Truman, and John F. Kennedy. These men had confidence and flexibility and enjoyed working to achieve their policy objectives. They had well-defined goals and sought to implement them even though they were not always successful. Active-positives are strong chief executives. In contrast, active-negatives are power seekers who show tendencies of ambitious striving, aggression, and struggling for power in a hostile environment. They can become compulsive, withdrawn, and increasingly isolated if their policy views do not succeed. Active-negatives do not like to admit mistakes.

Lyndon Johnson and Richard M. Nixon are two recent examples of active-negative presidents. Johnson was obsessed with the Vietnam War, escalating it to a point where he lost the support of the press, draft-age youth, and middle-class families whose sons were being killed. Nixon was forced to resign from office, following the coverup fiasco of Watergate, when the president was heard plotting to obstruct justice on the infamous White House tapes.

When all these leadership attributes are put together, presidents will be faced with many public expectations, some of which may conflict with each other. In Article 28, Thomas Cronin points out that public expectations and demands on presidents are so complex that chief executives frequently face contradictory situations. These expectations have consequences for the public support a president receives as well as for the kinds of actions taken to maintain that support. The paradoxes of the presidency may result in a no-win or Catch-22 condition. Can any one person be effective as a gentle and decent but forceful and decisive leader at the same time? Can the chief executive be apolitical in representing all the people and political with Congress in promoting and defending legislative programs?

PERSUASION AND INFLUENCE: ACHIEVING POLICY GOALS

After a president is elected, the first tasks are to establish an administration (see Chapter 9) and to set policy initiatives. The president needs an agenda that will guide Congress and the public toward domestic and foreign policy goals. This is leadership in government.

Many years ago, Richard E. Neustadt argued in *Presidential Power* (1960) that effective policy leadership requires persuasion and influence rather than commands or coercion. Neustadt views the president's role within the context of a Washington establishment, consisting of influential members of the bureaucracy, Congress, pressure groups, advisers, and the press. All of these actors have their own sources of power. Effective presidential leadership requires skillful management of this influence structure. Presidential commands diminish power and reputation because the president uses the leadership resources which might be employed in other policy areas.

In Article 29, Marcia Lynn Whicker and Todd Areson provide useful guidelines for newly elected presidents to be effective policy persuaders. In surveying recent presidents, the authors provide six suggestions for specific policy initiatives, including simplicity, clear priorities, optimism, unifying themes, appeals to sacrifice, and innovation.

As messengers or agenda-setters, presidents can develop the art of persuasion by being orderly, being good media performers, demonstrating understanding of issues, creating a vision of the future, and motivating followers.

Interestingly, the authors consider President Bush a persuader without a message. In other words, Bush has an effective mastery of the persuasive arts. He has been less successful in conveying coherent policy goals to Congress and the public other than the unifying theme of forcing Saddam Hussein's Iraqi forces out of Kuwait in 1991.

Domestic and Foreign Policy Leadership

In 1966, Aaron Wildavsky, a political scientist at the University of California, wrote a landmark essay. In his view, there are "two presidencies." He argued that presidents are more effective in achieving defense and foreign policy goals than in attaining their domestic initiatives. Chief executives had a bipartisan consensus that lasted from the end of World War II until the Vietnam War. Postwar presidents had nearly unqualified support in containing Soviet communism and its expansionist goals.

The Supreme Court provided the president with a preeminent constitutional role in international affairs. In the case of *United States v. Curtiss Wright* (1936), the Court ruled that the president has exclusive authority to represent the nation in foreign affairs. The chief executive has discretion and freedom from statutory restrictions "which would not be admissible were domestic affairs alone involved."

In 1989, Wildavsky and his colleague, Duane Oldfield, reassessed the two presidencies concept. In Article 30, they discover increased conflict and tension between the executive and Congress over a variety of military and international issues. In their view, the Vietnam War ended consensus and bipartisanship over foreign policy. The president is now constrained by legislators and interest groups which seek accountability for presidential initiatives. This was particularly evident in the 1973 War Powers Resolution and the Iran-Contra Affair during the Reagan presidency.

While the War Powers Resolution has not prevented any chief executive from sending troops into combat, it has resulted in considerable congressional debates, disputes, and demands for presidential justifications. In fact, Congress debated giving President Bush authority to conduct the Persian Gulf War in 1991 even after Bush had sent 400,000 troops into Saudi Arabia.

The Iran-Contra Affair caused considerable disagreement between congressional Democrats and the Reagan administration. Congress refused to appropriate funds to aid the rebels in Nicaragua. But the Reagan administration decided to defy Congress through secret private fund-raising and by establishing a covert non-government operation to channel the profits from arms sales to Iran to aid the Nicaraguan Contras. President Reagan's administration suffered severe criticism as a result of these disclosures. In 1987, Congress engaged in heated debates and conducted a full-scale investigation.

Oldfield and Wildavsky conclude by saying that presidents still have considerable flexibility and support for independence in foreign policy. President Bush has based much of his presidency on these three points. First, the president selects foreign arenas where no side feels it has a viable solution. The Middle East is one of the best examples. This is where President Bush conducted the Persian Gulf War in 1990–91.

Second, the president can appeal directly for public support in the media and thereby bypass Congress. President Bush did this in gaining strong endorsement for his Middle East actions against Iraq.

Finally, the president is commander-in-chief and chief diplomat. Despite the War Powers Resolution, President Bush did not officially notify Congress until after he dispatched 400,000 troops to Saudi Arabia. Some congressional critics were displeased about Bush's notification procedures. And Bush independently made many arrangements with foreign leaders and the United Nations in preparing for the Persian Gulf conflict to force Iraq out of Kuwait.

NOTE

1.   "Job Specs for the Oval Office," *Time*, 13 Dec., 1982.

Constitutional Foundations

27

The Presidency and
Constitutional Development
Alan Shank

What are the constitutional sources of executive authority? In this article, the original views of James Madison and Alexander Hamilton are compared and contrasted. The Madisonian model has already been referred to several times. Madison, particularly in The Federalist, *Number 51, favored balanced and limited government. Consequently, executive power was checked to prevent abuses. In contrast, Alexander Hamilton, in* The Federalist, *Number 70, supported vigorous executive leadership and an expansive view of Article II in the Constitution. Article 27 goes on to compare these two interpretations in the exercise of executive power in domestic and foreign policy. The Madisonian view is applicable to the former, while Hamilton's views apply to the latter. What are the three limits to presidential power in domestic policy? How can they be overcome? How have strong presidents dominated foreign policy? What are some examples of executive abuse in foreign policy? In which areas does the president share power with Congress?*

The presidency occupies a central constitutional role in American government. The chief executive is the focus of leadership, authority, and policy direction. Presidential power expands in response to demands that neither Congress nor the courts can fulfill. The modern presidents, beginning with Franklin Roosevelt, have been the principal leaders in responding to world war, economic crisis, budget deficits, and various international tensions. These foreign and domestic challenges require presidential leadership to protect, defend, and define the national interest.

When the Founding Fathers wrote the Constitution, they were reacting, in part, to the excesses and abuses of executive power imposed by the British Crown during the colonial and revolutionary war experiences. They were also trying to develop an independent executive branch that was not included in the Articles of Confederation. The Framers focused major attention on the specifics of legislative power and authority as a check on executive power. They designed a tripartite system of separation of powers and checks

Reprinted and adapted from *The Constitution and the American Presidency,* Edited by Martin Fausold and Alan Shank, pp. xvii–xxiv, by permission of the State University of New York Press. Copyright © 1991 State University of New York.

and balances to achieve an equilibrium between the executive and legislative branches.

According to James Madison, the principal architect of the federal government's structure at the Constitutional Convention, the system of separated powers and checks and balances was necessary to control political power.[1] In *The Federalist*, Number 51, Madison argued that too much governmental power causes abuses that endanger personal liberty and security. Uncontrolled power can lead to tyranny. If the executive gains power at the expense of the legislature, the constitutional system could be threatened. To prevent any of the three branches—executive, legislative, judicial—from dominating the other two, each must be relatively independent. This is achieved by separation of powers. Also, the three branches would have checks and balances over each other to counteract power concentration and domination of any one branch over the other two.

The Madisonian model is one of limited government. Neither the executive nor the legislative branch is dominant. However, the Madisonian emphasis on balance and equilibrium between the executive and legislative has two principal liabilities: It is an inherently adversarial structure and it frequently produces stalemate or inaction. Forrest McDonald[2] argues that the Founding Fathers distrusted executive power so much that they created a constitutional design which made it difficult for the two branches to cooperate. Separation of powers was favored over the British choice of a ministerial system which merged the executive and legislative branches and reduced the Crown to a ceremonial role in the 1720s. The constitutional conflicts between the two branches make policy initiatives and innovations difficult to achieve without extraordinary presidential or legislative leadership and executive-legislative cooperation. McDonald argues that his has been infre-

quent except for wartime and economic crises.

In contrast to the Madisonian model of checking potential executive abuses, Alexander Hamilton, in *The Federalist*, Number 70, struck a particularly modern note by arguing for "energy" in the executive, "as a leading character in the definition of good government." Hamilton believed that vigorous executive leadership was "essential to the protection of the community against foreign attacks; it is not less essential to the administration of the laws."

Hamilton's essay identified several important characteristics of a strong presidency. First, the president should be vigorous in carrying out constitutional roles and responsibilities by demonstrating "energy." If he does this, then "good" or "effective" government will result. Second, the president's authority in international and domestic policy is equally important. He is responsible for protecting the nation and administering the laws. Third, the constitution provides the president with four sources of authority to meet his responsibilities. These are unity (a single executive), duration in office (a four-year term with unlimited reeligibility until enactment of the Twenty-second Amendment), adequate compensation, and competent powers (found in Article II of the Constitution).

The formal constitutional powers of the president enable the chief executive to be both independent and interdependent in policy-making responsibilities. Congress cannot control the president. The chief executive is protected by the Madisonian concept of separation of powers. The president also shares power with Congress. This makes the executive both an independent and coterminous branch of the national government. Second, the executive participates in the policy-making process as an equal partner with Congress.

Through "competent powers," the executive checks and balances the legislative branch.

The Hamiltonian chief executive is a strong leader who protects the nation against foreign attacks, administers the laws, and secures liberty against the dangers of ambition, faction, and anarchy. Nearly all of the strong presidents of the nineteenth and twentieth centuries defended their constitutional authority in Hamiltonian terms. When abuses of presidential power occurred, Congress usually asserted the Madisonian model of equilibrium and checks and balances.

Most presidents prefer the Hamiltonian view of executive power. They exercise active and positive leadership rather than defer to Congress in negative or passive ways. Thomas Jefferson, Andrew Jackson, Abraham Lincoln, Theodore Roosevelt, Franklin Roosevelt, and Harry Truman were all vigorous leaders. Together with the presidents serving from 1952 to the present, they promoted executive policy initiatives in Congress, exercised a ceremonial role as leader of the entire nation, rose above party politics and became national leaders, and, since John Kennedy, established a plebiscitary relationship with the public through direct communication in televised speeches and messages from the Oval Office.

The Hamiltonian model of vigorous executive leadership is more applicable to presidential foreign policy leadership and crisis management than it is to the domestic policy arena.

Presidents have had much more flexibility in foreign policy initiatives than in domestic policy proposals. Unless some kind of economic catastrophe (e.g., the Great Depression of the 1930s) occurs requiring the exercise of extraordinary executive powers, presidents must acknowledge a sharing of domestic policy initiatives with an active and involved Congress.

Constitutional checks and balances, fortified by Madison's warning in *The Federalist,* Number 51, that "ambition must be made to counteract ambition" usually have modified or delayed executive domestic policy initiatives. We can see this in the proposals by Truman for civil rights; in Eisenhower's initiatives to return various federal programs to the states; in the delays to enact Kennedy's New Frontier initiatives in civil rights, aid to education, and health insurance for the elderly; in the resistance to Nixon's decentralization efforts and welfare reform proposals under New Federalism initiatives; in Carter's energy and urban policy proposals; and in the inability of Reagan to go as far as he wanted in cutting federal spending for the poor and the needy and to return programs to the states and the private sector. Exceptions to this usual pattern include FDR's First New Deal, Johnson's Civil Rights and War on Poverty initiatives, and Reagan's early budget and tax cuts and increases in military spending.

The reasons for executive inability to act quickly on domestic policy initiatives are not difficult to identify. After the president announces proposals in the State of the Union address, his initiatives must gain support from interest groups, state and local governments, and Congress. Each of these competitors can counteract the "ambition" of a "vigorous executive" (to use the notions of Hamilton and Madison).

Interest groups, which are not mentioned in the Constitution, are referred to by Madison as "factions" in *The Federalist,* Number 10. These are the non-governmental associations which influence domestic policy by promoting benefits for their members and preventing government action harmful to their members. Interest groups provide campaign funds to members of Congress and get support for their views. The president must convince interest groups to support his initiatives or find ways to counteract them. Frequently, he is unsuccessful or stalemated.

The federal system of fifty state and thousands of local governments presents a situation of considerable complexity and fragmentation of power for an ambitious domestic policy president. The president is required to build coalitions and gain support from many governors and mayors. There is a sharing of responsibility between national policy goals and the actual provision of services by state and local governments.

Congress sees itself as a partner with the president on domestic policy, both from the standpoint of its seventeen clauses of power in Article I, Section 8, of the Constitution and from the constituency-based nature of Congress in serving the people back home. Congress expects the president to lead the House and Senate in domestic initiatives, but Congress also expects to deal with the president in the final determination of policy results. Consequently, Congress expects the president to persuade, bargain, negotiate, and compromise. It expects the president to give and take. This takes time and effort from an ambitious president. The president needs to expend enormous political resources and capital to achieve major domestic policy initiatives.

The three principal limits to domestic policy—interest groups, the intergovernmental system, and Congress—can be overcome by a vigorous Hamiltonian-type president. This has occurred on at least two occasions since 1945: Johnson's initiatives on civil rights, voting rights, and the Great Society antipoverty and aid to education program in 1964–65; and Reagan's $35 billion budget cuts, $225 billion tax cuts, and huge increases in defense spending in 1981. The ingredients for their achievements were clear: enormous landslide election victories, partisan support in Congress, quick response by Congress in the early months of the new administration, public support for the new president resulting from assassination—in the case of Johnson, sympathy for Kennedy. For Reagan, an unsuccessful assassination attempt resulted in favorable media publicity and enough interest group support to overcome strong opposition. Both presidents benefited from a combination of effective leadership and a perceived need for change which mobilized huge voting support in Congress early in their presidencies. Without these ingredients, most presidents faced the normal obstacle course on domestic policy. James MacGregor Burns has characterized this obstacle course as a "deadlock of democracy,"[3] which means protracted battles with Congress and interest groups on major domestic policy initiatives of any president.

According to Forrest McDonald,[4] contemporary examples of executive-legislative policy deadlock or stalemate include electoral politics and the Twenty-second Amendment. The Republican party has an electoral advantage over the Democrats in presidential contests, while the Democrats dominate the House of Representatives. Control of the Senate has become more competitive. Consequently, the presidency and at least one house of Congress are usually in partisan disagreement over domestic policy. The Twenty-second Amendment, limiting the president to two terms, produces a lame-duck syndrome in the president's second term. The president and Congress do not need each other, and an adversarial relationship occurs. By the third year of the second term, the president usually shifts attention away from domestic initiatives to foreign policy.

The president is much less interdependent with Congress in foreign policy initiatives. In *The Federalist*, Number 69, Hamilton carefully distinguished between the sharing of powers and independence of the American executive in foreign policy, particularly in acting as commander in chief and in making treaties. The sharing of presidential authority contrasted sharply with the British King who had nearly absolute powers in these two areas. The King had "the entire command of all the militia" while "the president will only have command of such part of the militia of the nation as by legislative provision may be called into the actual service of the Union . . . The President is to have power, with the advice and consent of the Senate, to make treaties . . . The King of Great Britain is the sole and absolute representative of the nation in all foreign transactions."

The strong presidents of the past two centuries dominated U.S. foreign policy. They shared power with Congress in treaty-making and appointments and needed appropriations for military and other foreign actions. At the same time, the presidency, beginning with FDR, became nearly autonomous in two important areas: the national security state and warmaking powers. The absence of effective constitutional constraints created a potential for enormous abuses of executive power. Arthur Schlesinger, Jr., characterized this problem as the danger of an "imperial presidency."[5]

World War II, Cold War, Soviet aggression, the nuclear age, the worldwide responsibilities of the United States, international crises and emergencies—all of these factors have resulted in a demand for strong presidential leadership in the last fifty years. Presidents have sufficient constitutional and legislative authority to meet these challenges. The president is the commander in chief of the armed forces, the principal negotiator of treaties and executive agreements, and the chief diplomatic representative of the nation, and he has congressional authority to appoint certain officials, such as the NSC adviser, without senatorial approval. The principal legislative enactment which guarantees strong foreign policy leadership is the 1947 National Security Act. This law established the Central Intelligence Agency,

the National Security Council, the Defense Department, and the Joint Chiefs of Staff. The president was provided an enormous institutional apparatus and bureaucracy to conduct intelligence-gathering, to coordinate information from the State and Defense Departments, to unify the armed services and their military commanders, and to engage in covert activities. This institutional structure is essential to a strong foreign policy presidency.

The problem of the foreign policy presidency, as stated earlier, is unchecked authority and the potential for abuse. This has occurred on at least three occasions since 1945: the Vietnam War, Watergate, and the Iran-Contra Affair.

The Vietnam War showed that the president can initiate and conduct war which has no resolution, which has misguided objectives, and which lacks the necessary support from Congress and the American people. President Nixon's extension of the Vietnam War into Cambodia was as questionable as Lyndon Johnson's earlier escalation. The abuse of power was obvious: The conduct of a full-scale war in a distant part of the world requires the support of more than a group of executive "cold warriors" making policy in the White House. An isolated executive became unaccountable to Congress and the public and caused great damage to the country.

The same holds true for Watergate and the Iran-Contra Affair. When President Nixon used the CIA to prevent the FBI from investigating Watergate and established "plumbers" and enemies lists, he showed contempt for constitutional procedures and the rights of individuals. The "third-rate" burglary of the Democratic Party Headquarters became a political fiasco for Nixon, leading to calls for his impeachment and resulting in his eventual resignation from office. The point is that Nixon used the national security apparatus to develop the coverups in Watergate.

The Iran-Contra Affair of the Reagan presidency also shows the dangers of isolation when the executive develops a foreign policy without consulting with Congress or informing the American public. Here the issue was gaining the release of American hostages in Lebanon by trading arms to Iran and then using the profits from these arms sales to aid the rebel forces in Nicaragua. Reagan's problem was that Iran was a State Department-designated "terrorist" country which had held American hostages since 1979 during the Carter presidency. The Ayatollah Khomeini was one of the most hostile anti-American demagogues in the world. Further, Congress had specifically prohibited arms shipments to the Nicaraguan Contras at the very time that Lt. Col. Oliver North, General Richard Secord, and Albert Hakim were involved in establishing secret Swiss bank accounts and overseas offshore companies to channel funds to the Contras. The point is that the national security apparatus was used for these covert and illegal activities. The National Security Council staff assumed operational functions, when in fact the 1947 law confined them to staff functions. Further, according to the Tower Board report, President Reagan was unaware of the Contra diversion and mismanaged this entire affair.

The last point to be made about the unilateral nature of presidential actions concerns the war power. Since 1945, the United States has been involved in two full-scale wars in Korea and Vietnam, along with military engagements in Lebanon, Grenada, Libya, Panama, and elsewhere without having a single declaration of war by Congress. The constitutional requirement of having Congress initiate war by declaring it, has been superseded by presidents who are both the initiators of war and its conductors.

Congress enacted the War Powers Resolution in 1973 over President Nixon's veto in an effort to regain constitutional participation in the war power. The resolution requires that the president inform Congress within forty-eight hours after U.S. troops are committed to combat, and that the president must consult with Congress. Combat must end within sixty days unless Congress extends the deadline for return of U.S. troops. Four observations can be made about the War Powers Resolution. First, every president from Nixon to Bush has claimed that the law is an unconstitutional limitation on the executive's powers as commander in chief. Second, no president has consulted with Congress prior to committing U.S. troops. Third, the power of Congress to force the withdrawal of troops within sixty or ninety days may constitute a legislative veto. Such legislative vetoes were declared unconstitutional by the Supreme Court in 1983.[6] Finally, the Supreme Court has refused to rule on the enforcement provisions of the War Powers Resolution.

CONSTITUTIONAL AUTHORITY AND THE PRESIDENT

Three kinds of presidential powers are found in the Constitution—in Article II and in the lawmaking process section of Article I: powers exercised by the president alone, powers that are shared with the Senate or both houses of Congress, and negative powers to prevent action by Congress. Exclusive presidential authority found in Article II includes serving as commander in chief of the armed forces, granting pardons and reprieves for federal crimes, receiving ambassadors, faithfully executing the laws, and appointing officials to lesser offices. Presidential powers shared with the Senate include the treaty-making process (requiring two-thirds approval) and the appointment of ambassadors, judges, and other high cabinet and executive officials.

The president also shares powers with both houses of Congress in the legislative process. A bill becomes a law either with the president's approval or by a two-thirds vote overriding a veto. Negative powers include presidential vetoes of legislation, executive privilege or the power to withhold information from Congress, and impoundment of appropriated funds. Neither executive privilege nor impoundment are mentioned in the Constitution. These powers are the result of Supreme Court decisions (executive privilege) or legislative authorization (impoundment). Another type of negative executive power is the president's authority to order sequestration (across-the-board budget cuts) under the Gramm-Rudman-Hollings law when the president and Congress cannot agree on a budget deficit-reduction plan.

NOTES

1. The following discussion on the competing interpretations of executive power in the Constitution and *The Federalist* is based upon the editor's introduction and collection of essays compiled in *The Federalist Papers,* edited by Isaac Kramnick (New York: Viking Penguin, 1987).

2. Comments of Forrest McDonald at "The Constitution and The Presidency Conference," held at SUNY-Geneseo, April 16, 1988.

3. James MacGregor Burns, *The Deadlock of Democracy* (Englewood Cliffs, N.J.: Prentice-Hall, 1963).

4. Comments of Forrest McDonald at "The Constitution and The Presidency Conference," held at SUNY-Geneseo, April 16, 1988.

5. Arthur M. Schlesinger, Jr., *The Imperial Presidency* (Boston: Houghton Mifflin, 1973).

6. *Immigration and Naturalization Service v. Chadha,* 77 L. Ed. 2d, (1983), 317. For a further discussion on the implications of the *Chadha* decision as it affects the War Powers Resolution, see James L. Sundquist, "The Implications of *Chadha,*" in *Reforming American Government,* edited by Donald L. Robinson (Boulder, Col.: Westview Press, 1985), 248–53.

Presidential Leadership

28
The Presidency and Its Paradoxes
Thomas E. Cronin

Presidents are confronted with a variety of public expectations, many of which may conflict with each other. As the most visible national leader, the president has heavy demands on time, energy, and resources. As Clinton Rossiter once argued, the president's list of required leadership talents includes everything from a to z, such as serving as head of the political party, of Congress, of the bureaucracy, of foreign policy, and so on.

Thomas Cronin focuses on a crucial set of problems: What happens to presidents when contradictory demands are made in particular political, personal, or policy-making situations? Can we continue to have a "paradoxed" presidency? Cronin's article deserves close attention, particularly its discussion of effective leadership and the assessment of candidates who seek the presidency.

Why is the presidency such a bewildering office? Why do presidents so often look like losers? Why is the general public so disapproving of recent presidential performances, and so predictably less supportive the longer a president stays in office?

The search for explanations leads in several directions. Vietnam and the Watergate scandals must be considered. Then too, the personalities of Lyndon Johnson and Richard Nixon doubtless are factors that soured many people on the office. Observers also claim that the institution is structurally defective; that it enourages isolation, palace guards, "groupthink" and arrogance.

Yet something else seems at work. Our expectations and demands on the office are frequently so paradoxical as to invite two-faced behavior by our presidents. We seem to want so much so fast that a president, whose powers are often simply not as great as many of us believe, gets condemned as ineffectual. Or a president often will overreach or resort to unfair play while trying to live up to our demands. Either way, presidents seem to become locked into a rather high number of no-win situations.

The Constitution is of little help in explaining any of this. Our founding fathers purposely were vague and left the presidency defined imprecisely. They knew well that the presidency would have to provide the capability for swift and competent executive action, yet they went to considerable lengths to avoid

Presented at the American Political Science Association Meetings, Chicago, Illinois, September 1-6, 1976. An earlier version of this essay appears in *Skeptic Magazine* (Sept./Oct. 1976). Reprinted by permission of the author. Copyright held by Thomas E. Cronin.

enumerating specific powers and duties so as to calm the then persuasive popular fear of monarchy.

In any event, the informal and symbolic powers of the presidency today account for as much as the formal ones. Further, presidential powers expand and contract in response to varying situational and technological changes. Thus, the powers of the presidency are interpreted in ways so markedly different as to seem to describe different offices. In some ways the modern presidency has virtually unlimited authority for nearly anything its occupant chooses to do with it. In other ways, however, our beliefs and hopes about the presidency very much shape the character and quality of the presidential performances we get.

The modern (post-Roosevelt II) presidency is bounded and constrained by various expectations that are decidedly paradoxical. Presidents and presidential candidates must constantly balance themselves between conflicting demands. It has been suggested by more than one observer that it is a characteristic of the American mind to hold contradictory ideas simultaneously without bothering to resolve the potential conflicts between them. Perhaps some paradoxes are best left unresolved. But we should at least better appreciate what it is we expect of our presidents and would-be presidents. For it could well be that our paradoxical expectations and the imperatives of the job make for schizophrenic presidential performances.

We may not be able to resolve the inherent contradictions and dilemmas these paradoxes point up. Still, a more rigorous understanding of these conflicts and no-win or near no-win situations should encourage a more refined sensitivity to the limits of what a president can achieve. Exaggerated or hopelessly contradictory public expectations tend to encourage presidents to attempt more than

they can accomplish and to overpromise and overextend themselves.

Perhaps, too, an assessment of *the paradoxed presidency* may impel us anew to revise some of our unrealistic expectations concerning presidential performance and the institution of the presidency and encourage in turn the nurturing of alternative sources or centers for national leadership.

A more realistic appreciation of presidential paradoxes might help presidents concentrate on the practicable among their priorities. A more sophisticated and tolerant consideration of the modern presidency and its paradoxes might relieve the load so that a president can better lead and administer in those critical realms in which the nation has little choice but to turn to him. Like it or not, the vitality of our democracy still depends in large measure on the sensitive interaction of presidential leadership with an understanding public willing to listen and willing to provide support when a president can persuade. Carefully planned innovation is nearly impossible without the kind of leadership a competent and fair-minded president can provide.

Each of the paradoxes is based on apparent logical contradictions. Each has important implications for presidential performance and public evaluation of presidential behavior. A better understanding may lead to the removal, reconciliation, or more enlightened tolerance of the initial contradictions to which they give rise.

1. ***The paradox of the gentle and decent but forceful and decisive president.*** Opinion polls time and again indicate that people want a just, decent, humane "man of good faith" in the White House. Honesty and trustworthiness repeatedly top the list of qualities the public values most highly in a president these days. However, the public just as

strongly demands the qualities of toughness, decisiveness, even a touch of ruthlessness.

Adlai Stevenson, George McGovern and Gerald Ford were all criticized for being "too nice," "too decent." (Ford's decisive action in the Mayaguez affair was an exception—and perhaps predictably his most significant gain in the Gallup Poll—11 points—came during and immediately after this episode.) Being a "Mr. Nice Guy" is too easily equated with being too soft. The public dislikes the idea of a weak, spineless or sentimental person in the White House.

Morris Udall, who was widely viewed as a decidedly decent candidate in the 1976 race for the Democratic nomination, had to advertise himself as a man of strength. He used a quote from House Majority Leader Thomas P. O'Neill in full-page newspaper ads which read: "We need a Democratic president who's tough enough to take on big business." "Mo Udall is tough." The image sought was unquestionably that of toughness of character.

Perhaps, too, this paradox may explain the unusual extraordinary public fondness for President Eisenhower. For he was at one and the same time blessed with a benign smile and reserved, calming disposition and yet he also was the disciplined, strong, no-nonsense five-star general with all the medals and victories to go along with it. His ultimate resource as president was this reconciliation of decency and decisiveness, likability alongside demonstrated valor.

During the 1976 presidential campaign, Jimmy Carter appeared to appreciate one of the significant by-products of this paradox. He noted that the American male is handicapped in his expressions of religious faith by those requisite "macho" qualities—overt strength, toughness and firmness.

Carter's personal reconciliation of this paradox is noteworthy: "But a truer demonstration of strength would be concern, compassion, love, devotion, sensitivity, humility—exactly the things Christ talked about—and I believe that if we can demonstrate this kind of personal awareness of our own faith we can provide that core of strength and commitment and underlying character that our nation searches for."

Thus this paradox highlights one of the distinctive frustrations for presidents and would-be presidents. Plainly, we demand a double-edged personality. We in effect demand the *sinister* as well as the *sincere*, President *Mean* and President *Nice;* tough and hard enough to stand up to a Khrushchev or to press the nuclear button, compassionate enough to care for the ill-fed, ill-clad, ill-housed. The public in this case seems to want a soft-hearted son of a bitch. It's a hard role to cast; a harder role to perform for eight years.

2. *The paradox of the programmatic but pragmatic leader.* We want both a *programmatic* (i.e., committed on the issues and with a detailed program) and a *pragmatic* (i.e., flexible and open, even changeable) person in the White House. We want a *moral* leader yet the job forces the president to become a *constant compromiser.*

On the one hand, Franklin Roosevelt proclaimed that the presidency is preeminently a place for moral leadership. On the other hand, Governor Jerry Brown aptly notes that "a little vagueness goes a long way in this business."

A president who becomes too committed risks being called rigid; a president who becomes too pragmatic risks becoming called wishy-washy. The secret, of course, is to stay the course by stressing character, competence, rectitude and experience, and by avoiding strong stands that offend important segments in the population.

Jimmy Carter was especially criticized by the press and others for avoiding commitments and stressing his "flexibility" on the issues. This prompted a major discussion of what became called the "fuzziness issue." Jokes spread the complaint. One went as follows: "When you eat peanut butter all your life, your tongue sticks to the roof of your mouth, and you have to talk out of both sides." Still, his "maybe I will and maybe I won't" strategy proved very effective in overcoming critics and opponents who early on claimed he didn't have a chance. Carter talked quietly about the issues and carried a big smile. In fact, of course, he took stands on almost all the issues, but being a centrist or a pragmatic moderate his stands were either not liked or dismissed as non-stands by liberals and conservatives.

What strikes one person as fuzziness or even duplicity appeals to another person as remarkable political skill, the very capacity for compromise and negotiation that is required if a president is to maneuver through the political minefields that come with the job.

Most candidates view a campaign as a fight to win office, not an opportunity for adult education. Barry Goldwater in 1964 may have run with the slogan "We offer a *choice* not an echo" referring to his unusually thematic strategy, but Republican party regulars, who, more pragmatically, aspired to win the election preferred "a *chance* not a *choice*." Once in office, presidents often operate the same way; the electoral connection looms large as an issue-avoiding, controversy-ducking political incentive. Most presidents also strive to *maximize their options,* and hence leave matters up in the air or delay choices. J. F. K. mastered this strategy, while on Vietnam L. B. J. permitted himself to be trapped into his tragically irreparable corner because his options had so swifty dissolved. Indeed this yearning to maximize their options may well be the core element of the pragmatism we so often see when we prefer moral leadership.

3. *The paradox of an innovative and inventive yet majoritarian and responsive presidency.* One of the most compelling paradoxes at the very heart of our democratic system arises from the fact that we expect our presidents to provide bold, innovative leadership and yet respond faithfully to public opinion majorities.

Walter Lippmann warned against letting public opinion become the chief guide to leadership in America, but he just as forcefully warned democratic leaders: Don't be right too soon, for public opinion will lacerate you! Hence, most presidents fear being in advance of their times. They must *lead us,* but also *listen to us.*

Put simply, we want our presidents to offer leadership, to be architects of the future, providers of visions, plans and goals, and at the same time we want them to stay in close touch with the sentiments of the people. To *talk* about high ideals, New Deals, Big Deals and the like is one thing. But the public resists being *led* too far in any one direction.

Most of our presidents have been conservatives or at best "pragmatic liberals." They have seldom ventured much beyond the crowd. John Kennedy, the author of the much acclaimed *Profiles in Courage,* was often criticized for presenting more profile than courage; if political risks could be avoided, he shrewdly avoided them. Kennedy was fond of pointing out that he had barely won election in 1960 and that great innovations should not be forced upon a leader with such a slender mandate. Ironically, Kennedy is credited with encouraging widespread public participation in politics. But he repeatedly reminded Americans that caution was needed, that the important issues are complicated and technical, and best left to the administrative and political experts. As Bruce Miroff writes in his *Pragmatic Illusions,* Kennedy seldom attempted to change the political context in which he operated:

> *More significantly, he resisted the new form of politics emerging with the civil rights movement: mass action, argument on social fundamentals, appeals to considerations of justice and morality. Moving the American political system in such a direction would necessarily have been long range, requiring arduous educational work and promising substantial political risk. The pragmatic Kennedy wanted no part of such an unpragmatic undertaking.*

Presidents can get caught whether they are coming or going. The public wants them to be both *leaders* of the country and *representatives* of the people. We want them to be decisive and rely mainly on their own judgment, yet we want them to be very responsive to public opinion, especially, to the "common sense" of our own opinions. It was perhaps with this in mind that an English essayist once defined the ideal democratic leader as "an uncommon man of common opinions."

4. *The paradox of the inspirational but don't-promise-more-than-you-can-deliver leader.* We ask our presidents to raise hopes, to educate us, to inspire. But too much inspiration will invariably lead to dashed hopes, disillusion and cynicism. The best of leaders often suffers from one of their chief virtues—an instinctive tendency to raise aspirations, to summon us to transcend personal needs and subordinate ourselves to dreaming dreams of a bolder, more majestic America.

We enjoy the upbeat rhetoric and promises of a brighter tomorrow. We genuinely want to hear about New Nationalism, New Deals, New Frontiers, Great Societies, and New American Revolutions; we want our fears to be assuaged during "fireside chats" or "a conversation with the president," to be told that "the torch has been passed to a new generation of Americans . . . and the glow from that fire can truly light the world."

We want our fearless leaders to tell us that "peace is at hand," that the "only fear we have to fear is fear itself," that "we are Number One," that a recession has "bottomed out" and that "we are a great people." So much do we want the "drive of a lifting dream," to use Mr. Nixon's trite phrase, that the American people are easily duped by presidential promises.

Do presidents overpromise because they are congenital optimists or because they are pushed into it by the demanding public? Surely it is an admixture of both. But whatever the source, few presidents in recent times were able to keep their promises and fulfill their intentions. Poverty was not ended, a Great Society was not realized. Vietnam dragged on and on. Watergate outraged a public that had been promised an open presidency. Energy independence remains an illusion just as crime in the streets continues to rise.

A president who does not raise hopes is criticized as letting events shape his presidency, rather than making things happen. A president who eschewed inspiration of any kind would be rejected as un-American. For as a poet once wrote, "America is promises." For people everywhere cherishing the dream of individual liberty and self-fulfillment, America has been the land of promises, of possibilities, of dreams. No president can stand in the way of this truth, no matter how much the current dissatisfaction about the size of big government in Washington, and its incapacity to deliver the services it promises.

William Allen White, the conservative columnist, went to the heart of this paradox when he wrote of Herbert Hoover. President Hoover, he noted, is a great executive, a splendid desk man. "But he cannot dramatize his leadership. A democracy cannot follow a leader unless he is dramatized."

5. *The paradox of the open and sharing but courageous and independent presidency.* We unquestionably cherish our three-branched system with its checks and balances and its theories of dispersed and separated powers. We want our presidents not only to be sincere but to share their powers with their cabinet, the Congress and other "responsible" national leaders. In theory, we oppose the concentration of power, we dislike secrecy and we resent depending on any one person to provide for all our leadership. In more recent years (the 1970's in particular) there have been repeated calls for a more open, accountable and deroyalized presidency.

The other side of the coin, however, rejects a too secularized presidency. It rejects as well the idea that complete openness is a solution; indeed it suggests instead that the great presidents have been the strong presidents, who stretched their legal authority, who occassionaly relied on the convenience of secrecy and who dominated the other branches of government. This point of view argues that the country in fact often yearns for a hero in the White House, that the human heart ceaselessly reinvents royalty, and that Roosevelts and Camelots, participatory democracy notwithstanding, are vital to the success of America.

If some people feel we are getting to the point where all of us would like to see a demythologized presidency, others claim we need myth, we need symbol. As a friend of mine put it: "I don't think we could live without the myth of a glorified presidency, even if we wanted to. We just aren't that rational. Happily, we're too human for that. We will either live by the myth that has served us fairly well for almost two hundred years, or we will probably find a much worse one."

The clamor for a truly open or collegial presidency was opposed on other grounds by the late Harold Laski when he concluded that Americans in practice want to rally round a president who can demonstrate his independence and vigor:

> *A president who is believed not to make up his own mind rapidly loses the power to maintain the hold. The need to dramatize his position by insistence upon his undoubted supremacy is inherent in the office as history has shaped it. A masterful man in the White House will, under all circumstances be more to the liking of the multitude than one who is thought to be swayed by his colleagues.*

Thus it is that we want our president not only to be both a lion and a fox, but more than a lion, more than a fox. We want simultaneously a secular leader and a civil religious mentor; we praise our three-branched system but we place capacious hopes upon and thus elevate the presidential branch. Only the president can give us heroic leadership, or so most people feel. Only a president can dramatize and symbolize our highest expectations of ourselves as an almost chosen people with a unique mission. Note too that only the president is regularly honored with a musical anthem of his own: "Hail to the Chief." If it seems a little hypocritical for a semi-sovereign people to delegate so much hierarchical deference and semi-autocratic power to their president, this is nonetheless precisely what we continually do.

We want an open presidency and we oppose the concentration of vast power in any one position. Still, we want forceful, courageous displays of leadership from our presidents. Anything less than that is condemned as aimlessness or loss of nerve. Further, we praise those who leave the presidency stronger than it was when they entered.

6. ***The taking-the-presidency-out-of-politics paradox.*** The public yearns for a statesman in the White House, for a George Washington or a second "era of good feelings": anything that might prevent partisanship of politics-as-usual in the White Hosue. In fact, however, the job of a president demands a president to be a gifted political broker, ever-attentive to changing political moods and coalitions.

Franklin Roosevelt illustrates well this paradox. Appearing so remarkably nonpartisan while addressing the nation, he was in practice one of the craftiest political coalition builders to occupy the White House. He mastered the art of politics—the art of making the difficult and desirable possible.

A president is expected to be above politics in some respects and highly political in others. A president is never supposed to act with his eye on the next election; he's not supposed to favor any particular group or party. Nor is he supposed to wheel and to deal or twist too many arms. That's politics and that's bad! No, a president, or so most people are inclined to believe, is supposed to be "president of all the people." On the other hand, he is asked to be the head of his party, to help friendly members of Congress get elected or reelected, to deal firmly with party barons and congressional political brokers. Too, he must build political coalitions around what he feels needs to be done.

To take the president out of politics is to assume, incorrectly, that a president will be so generally right and the general public so generally wrong that a president must be protected from the push and shove of political pressures. But what president has always been right? Over the years, public opinion has been usually as sober a guide as anyone else on the political waterfront. Anyway, having a president constrained and informed by public opinion is what a democracy is all about.

In his reelection campaign of 1972, Richard Nixon in vain sought to reveal himself outwardly as too busy to be a politician: he wanted the American people to believe he was too preoccupied with the Vietnam War to have any personal concern about his election. In one sense, Mr. Nixon may have destroyed this paradox for at least a while. Have not the American people learned that we *cannot* have a president *above* politics?

If past is prologue, presidents in the future will go to considerable lengths to portray themselves as unconcerned with their own political future. They will do so in large part because the public applauds the divorce between presidency and politics. People naively think that we can somehow turn the job of president into that of a managerial or strictly executive post. (The six-year single term proposal reflects this paradox.) Not so. The presidency is a highly political office, and it cannot be otherwise. Moreover, its political character is for the most part desirable. A president separated from or somehow above politics might easily become a president who doesn't listen to the people, doesn't respond to majority sentiment or pay attention to views that may be diverse, intense and at variance with his own. A president immunized from politics would be a president who would too easily become isolated from the processes of government and too removed from the thoughts and aspirations of his people.

In all probability, this paradox will be an enduring one. The standard diagnosis of what's gone wrong in an administration will be that the presidency has become too politicized. But it will be futile to try to take the president out of politics. A more helpful approach is to realize that certain presidents try too hard to hold themselves above politics—or at least to give that appearance—rather than engaging in it deeply, openly and creatively enough. A president in a democracy has to act politically in regard to controversial issues if we are to have any semblance of government by the consent of the governed.

7. *The paradox of the common man who gives an uncommon performance.* We like to think that America is the land where the common sense of the common man reigns. We prize the common touch, the "man of the people." Yet few of us settle for anything but an uncommon performance from our presidents.

This paradox is splendidly summed up by some findings of a survey conducted by Field Research Corp., the California public opinion organization. Field asked a cross section of Californians in 1975 to describe in their own words the qualities a presidential candidate should or should not have. Honesty and trustworthiness topped the list. But one of his more intriguing findings was that "while most (72%) prefer someone with plain and simple tastes, there is also a strong preference (66%) for someone who can give exciting speeches and inspire the public."

It has been said that the American people crave to be governed by men who are both Everyman and yet better than Everyman. The Lincoln and Kennedy presidencies are illustrative. We might cherish the myth that anyone can grow up to be president, that there are no barriers, no elite qualifications. But the nation doesn't want a person who is too ordinary. Would-be presidents have to prove their special qualifications—their excellence, their stamina, their capacity for uncommon leadership.

The Harry Truman reputation, at least as it flourished in the mid 1970s, demonstrates the apparent reconciliation of this paradox. Fellow-commoner Truman rose to the demands of the job and became an apparent gifted decision-maker, or so his admirers would have us believe.

Candidate Carter in 1976 nicely fit this paradox as well. Local, down-home, farm boy next door, makes good! The image of the peanut farmer turned gifted governor and talented campaigner contributed greatly to Carter's success as a national candidate, and he used it with consummate skill. Early on in his presidential bid Carter enjoyed introducing himself as a peanut farmer *and* a nuclear physicist— yet another way of suggesting he was down-to-earth and yet cerebral as well.

A president or would-be president must be bright, but not too bright; warm and accessible, but not too folksy; down to earth, but not pedestrian. Adlai Stevenson was witty and clever, but these are talents that seldom pay in politics. Voters prefer plainness and solemn platitudes, but these too can be overdone. Thus, Ford's talks, no matter what the occasion, dulled our senses with the banal. Both suffered because of this paradox. The "Catch 22" here, of course, is that the very fact of an uncommon performance puts distance between a president and the truly common man. We persist, however, in wanting both at the same time.

8. *The national unifier/national divider paradox.* One of the paradoxes most difficult to alleviate arises from our longing simultaneously for a president who will pull us together again and yet be a forceful priority setter, budget manager and executive leader. The two tasks are near opposites.

We remain one of the few nations in the world that calls upon our chief executive also to serve as our symbolic, ceremonial head of state. Elsewhere these tasks are spread around. In some nations there is a monarch *and* a prime minister; in other nations there are three visible national leaders—the head of state, a premier, and a powerful party head.

In the absence of an alternative, we demand that our presidents and our presidency act as a unifying force in our lives. Perhaps it all began with George Washington who so artfully performed this function. At least for a while he truly was above politics and a near unique symbol of our new nation. He was a healer, a unifier and an extraordinary man for all seasons. Today we ask no less of our presidents than that they should do as Washington did.

However, we have designed a presidential job description that impels our contemporary presidents to act as national dividers. They necessarily divide when they act as the leader of their political party; when they set priorities that advantage certain goals and groups at the expense of others; when they forge and lead political coalitions; when they move out ahead of public opinion and assume the role of national educator; when choosing one set of advisors over another. A president, as creative leader, cannot help but offend certain interests. When Franklin Roosevelt was running for a second term some garment workers unfolded a great sign that said, "We love him for the enemies he has made." Such is the fate of a president on an everyday basis; if he chooses to use power he usually will lose the good will of those who preferred inaction over action. The opposite is of course true if he chooses not to act.

Look at it from another angle. The nation is torn between the view that a president should primarily preside over the nation and merely serve as a referee among the various powerful interests that actually control who gets what, when and how and a second position which holds that a president should gain control of governmental processes and power so as to use them for the purpose of furthering public, as opposed to private interests. Obviously the position that one takes on this question is relevant to how you value the presidency and the kind of person you'd like to see in the job.

Harry Truman said it very simply. He noted there are fourteen or fifteen million Americans who have the resources to have representatives in Washington to protect their interests, and that the interests of the great mass of other people, the hundred and sixty million or so others, is the responsibility of the President of the United States.

Put another way, the presidency is sometimes seen as the great defender of the people, the ombudsman or advocate-general of "public interests." Yet is sometimes also (and sometimes at the same time) viewed as hostile to the people, isolated from them, wary of them, antagonistic, as inherently the enemy.

This debate notwithstanding, however, Americans prize the presidency as a grand American invention. As a nation we do not want to change it. Proposals to weaken it are dismissed. Proposals to reform or restructure it are paid little respect. If we sour on a president the conventional solution has been to find and elect someone else whom we hope will be better.

9. *The longer he is there the less we like him paradox.* Every four years we pick a president and for the next four years we pick on him, at him, and sometimes pick him entirely apart. There is no adequate pre-presidential job experience, so much of the first term is an on-the-job learning experience. But we resent this. It is too important a job for on-the-job learning, or at least that's how most of us feel.

Too, we expect presidents to grow in office and to become better acclimated to the office. But the longer they are in office, the more they find themselves with more crises and less public support. There is an apocryphal presidential lament which goes as follows: "Every time I seem to grow into the job, it gets bigger."

Simply stated, the more we know of a president, or the more we observe his presidency, the less we approve of him. Familiarity breeds discontent. Research on public support of presidents indicates that presidential approval peaks soon after a president takes office, and then slides downward at a declining rate over time until it reaches a point in the latter half of the four-year term, when it bottoms out. Thereafter it rises a bit, but never attains its original levels. Why this pattern of declining support afflicts presidents is a subject of debate among social scientists. Unrealistic early expectations are of course a major factor. These unrealistic expectations ensure a period of disenchantment.

Peace and prosperity, of course, can help stem the unpleasant tide of ingratitude, and the Eisenhower popularity remained reasonably high in large part because of his (or the nation's) achievements in these areas. For other presidents, however, their eventual downsliding popularity is due nearly as much to the public's inflated expectations as to a president's actions. It is often as if their downslide in popularity would occur no matter what the president did. If this seems unfair, even cruel, this is nonetheless what happens to those skilled and lucky enough to win election to the highest office in the land.

And all this occurs despite our conventional wisdom that the *office makes the man:* "that the presidency with its built-in educational processes, its spacious view of the world, its command of talent, and above all its self-conscious historic role, does work its way on the man in the Oval Office," as James MacGregor Burns put it. If we concede that the office in part does make the man, we must also admit that time in office often unmakes the man.

10. *The what it takes to become president may not be what is needed to govern the nation paradox.* To win a presidential election it takes ambition, ambiguity, luck, and masterful public relations strategies. To govern the nation plainly requires all of these, but far more as well. It may well be that too much ambition, too much ambiguity and too heavy a reliance on phony public relations tricks actually undermine the integrity and legitimacy of the presidency.

Columnist David Broder offers an apt example: "People who win primaries may become good Presidents—but 'it ain't necessarily so.' Organizing well is important in governing just as it is in winning primaries. But the Nixon years should teach us that good advance men do not necessarily make trustworthy White House aides. Establishing a government is a little more complicated than having the motorcade run on time."

Likewise, ambition (in very heavy doses) is essential for a presidential candidate, but too much hunger of the office or for "success-at-any-price" is a danger to be avoided. He must be bold and energetic, but carried too far this can make him cold and frenetic. To win the presidency obviously requires a single-mindedness of purpose, and yet we want our presidents to be well rounded, to have a sense of humor, to be able to take a joke, to have hobbies and interests outside the realm of politics—in short to have a sense of proportion.

Another aspect of this paradox can be seen in the way candidates take ambiguous positions on issues in order to increase their appeal to the large bulk of centrist and independent voters. Not only does such equivocation discourage rational choices by the voters, but it also may alienate people who later learn, after the candidate has won, that his views and policies are otherwise. LBJ's "We will not send American boys to fight the war that Asian boys should be fighting," and Richard Nixon's "open presidency" pledges come readily to mind. Their pre-presidential stands were later violated or ignored.

Political scientist Samual Huntington calls attention to yet another way this paradox works. To be a winning candidate, he notes, the would-be president must put together an *electoral coalition* involving a majority of votes appropriately distributed across the country. To do this he must appeal to all regions and interest groups and cultivate the appearance of honesty, sincerity and experience. But once elected, the electoral coalition has served its purpose and a *governing coalition* is the order of the day. This all may sound rather elitist, but Harvard Professor Huntington insists that this is what has to be:

> *The day after his election the size of his majority is almost—if not entirely—irrelevant to his ability to govern the country. What counts then is his ability to mobilize support from the leaders of the key institutions in society and government. He has to constitute a broad governing coalition of strategically located supporters who can furnish him with the information, talent, expertise, manpower, publicity, arguments, and political support which he needs to develop a program, to embody it in legislation, and to see it effectively implemented. This coalition must include key people in Congress, the executive branch, and the private-sector "Establishment." The governing coalition need have little relation to the electoral coalition. The fact that the President as a candidate put together a successful electoral coalition does not insure that he will have a viable governing coalition.*

Presidential candidate Adlai Stevenson had another way of saying it in 1956. He said he had "learned that the hardest thing about any political campaign is how to win without proving that you are unworthy of winning." The process of becoming president is an extraordinarily taxing one that defies description. It involves, among other things, an unending salesmanship job on television.

Candidates plainly depend upon television to transform candidacy into incumbency. Research findings point out that candidates spend well over half their funds on broadcasting. Moreover, this is how the people "learn" about the candidates. Approximately two-thirds of the public report that television is the best way for them to follow candidates and about half of the American public acknowledge they got their best understanding of the candidates and issues from television coverage.

Thus, television is obviously the key. But the candidate has to travel to every state and hundreds of cities for at least a four-year period to capture the exposure and the local headlines before earning the visibility and stature of a "serious candidate." For the most part, it becomes a grueling and gasping ordeal, as well as a major learning experience. In quest of the Democratic nomination for president, Walter F. Mondale of Minnesota spent most of 1974 traveling some 200,000 miles, delivering hundreds of speeches, appearing on countless radio and television talk shows, and sleeping in Holiday Inn after Holiday Inn all across the country. He admits that he enjoyed much of it, but says, too, that he seldom had time to read or to reflect, not to mention having time for a sane family life. Eventually he withdrew on the grounds that he simply had neither the overwhelming desire nor the time to do what was necessary in order to win the nomination.

Mondale's was not a sufficiently power-hungry ambition, witness his remarks:

> *I love to ponder ideas, to reflect on them and discuss them with experts and friends over a period of time, but this was no longer possible. It struck me as being unfortunate and even tragic that the process of seeking the Presidency too*

often prevents one from focusing on the issues and insights and one's ability to express them, which are crucially important. I believe this fact explains many of the second-rate statements and much of the irrational posturing that are frequently associated with Presidential campaigns. In any case, after eighteen months I decided this wasn't for me. It wasn't my style and I wasn't going to pretend that it was. Instead of controlling events in my life, I was more and more controlled by them. Others have had an easier time adapting to this process than I did, and I admire them for it. But one former candidate told me, three years after his campaign had ended, that he still hadn't fully recovered emotionally or physically from the ordeal.

What it takes *to become* president may differ from what it takes *to be* president. It takes a near-megalomaniac who is also glib, dynamic, charming on television and hazy on the issues. Yet we want our presidents to be well-rounded, not overly ambitious, careful in their reasoning and clear and specific in their communications. It may well be that our existing primary and convention system adds up to an effective testing or obstacle course for would-be presidents. Certainly they have to travel to all sections of the country, meet the people, deal with interest group elites and learn about the bracing issues of the day. But with the Johnson and Nixon experiences in our not-too-distant past, we have reason for asking whether our system of producing presidents is adequately reconciled with what is required to produce a president who is competent, fair-minded, and emotionally healthy.

CONCLUSIONS

Perhaps the ultimate paradox of the modern presidency is that it is always too powerful and yet it is always too inadequate. Always too powerful because it is contrary to our ideals of a government by the people and always too powerful as well because it must now possess the capacity to wage nuclear war (a capacity that unfortunately doesn't permit much in the way of checks and balances and deliberative, participatory government). Yet, always too inadequate because it seldom achieves our highest hopes for it, not to mention its own stated intentions.

The presidency is always too strong when we dislike the incumbent. On the other hand the limitations are bemoaned when we believe the incumbent is striving valiantly to serve the public interest as we define it. For many people the Johnson presidency captured this paradox vividly: many of the people who felt that he was too strong in Vietnam felt too that he was too weakly equipped to wage his war on poverty (and vice versa).

The dilemma for the attentive public is that curbing the powers of a president who abuses the public trust will usually undermine the capacity of a fair-minded president to serve the public interest. In the 187 years since Washington took office, we have multiplied the requirements for presidential leadership and we have made it increasingly more difficult to lead. Certainly this is not the time for a mindless retribution against the already fragile, precarious institution of the presidency.

Neither presidents nor the public should be relieved of their respective responsibilities of trying to fashion a more effective and fair-minded leadership system simply because these paradoxes are pointed out and even widely agreed upon. It is also not enough to throw up our hands and say: "Well, no one makes a person run for that crazy job in the first place."

The situation I have analyzed in this essay doubtless also characterizes governors, city managers, university presidents and even many corporate executives. Is it a new phenomenon or are we just becoming increasingly aware of it? Is it a permanent or a transitory condition? My own view is that it is neither new nor transitory, but more comparative and longitudinal analysis is needed before we can generalize more systematically. Meanwhile, we shall have to select as our presidents persons who understand these contrary demands and who have a gift for the improvisation that these paradoxes demand. It is important for us to ask our chief public servants to be willing occasionally to forego enhancing their own short term political fortunes for a greater good of simplifying, rather than exacerbating, the paradoxes of the presidency.

While the presidency will doubtless remain one of our nation's best vehicles for creative policy change it will also continue to be an embattled office, fraught with the cumulative weight of these paradoxes. We need urgently to probe the origins and to assess the consequences of these paradoxes and to learn how presidents and the public can better coexist with them. For it is apparent that these paradoxes serve to isolate and disconnect a president from the public. Like it or not, the growing importance of the presidency and our growing dependence on presidents seem to ensure that presidents will be less popular and increasingly the handy scapegoat when anything goes wrong.

Let us ask our presidents to give us their best, but let us not ask them to deliver more than the presidency—or any single institution—has to give.

BIBLIOGRAPHICAL NOTE

Because of the essay nature of this article I have not provided footnotes, nor have I cited the considerable number of articles and books that have assisted me in its writing. Let me acknowledge here my debt to many of the more important items cited and not. Especially helpful were Arthur Schlesinger's *The Imperial Presidency* and James MacGregor Burns' *Presidential Government.* I have profited too from numerous essays written by Fred Greenstein, Michael J. Robinson, James Stimson, Rexford G. Tugwell and Aaron Wildavsky. See also, Bruce Miroff, *Pragmatic Illusions* (McKay, 1976), Henry Fairlie, *The Kennedy Promise* (Doubleday, 1973), Walter F. Mondale, *The Accountability of Power* (McKay, 1975), Harold Laski, *The American Presidency* (Harper, 1940) and Michael Novak, *Choosing Our King* (Macmillan, 1974). The writings of David Broder, James David Barber and Alexander George always inform essays such as this. See finally, Harlan Cleveland's *The Future Executive* (Harper & Row, 1972) and *The American Commonwealth,* 1976 (Basic Books, 1976), especially the essays by Samuel Huntington and Aaron Wildavsky.

Persuasion and Influence: Achieving Policy Goals

29

The Art of Presidential Persuasion

Marcia Lynn Whicker and Todd W. Areson

In the following article, Whicker and Areson of Virginia Commonwealth University explain how presidents can achieve policy goals through persuasion and influence. After the elections are over, the chief executive assumes the tasks of governance. One of the most important is developing a coherent policy agenda. The power to persuade Congress and the public on executive priorities includes the content of the message and how it is presented. According to the authors, what are six message guidelines for presidents? How well has President Bush done in developing his domestic and foreign policy messages since this article was written in 1989? How does Bush compare and contrast with other presidents? Whicker and Areson also discuss the importance of the president as an effective messenger. What are the authors' six guidelines for the president as messenger? How does Bush compare and contrast with previous presidents as an effective messenger? Do you agree or disagree with the authors' conclusion that Bush is more persuasive as messenger than he is in the content of policy proposals?

Traditionally, presidents are given a "honeymoon" period by the press and public in the early days of their administrations, during which praise flows more liberally than criticism. Skillful leaders have used this time to establish their priorities, convey them to the nation, and persuade Congress, the press, and the American people to become team players in implementing this vision for the country.

John F. Kennedy used his honeymoon period to recruit "the best and the brightest" to government service and excite the nation with a vision of a New Frontier—in space, civil rights, and foreign relations. Lyndon Johnson enjoyed an unusually long honeymoon because of the tragic circumstances surrounding his ascension to the White House. In 1964, coupled with his massive electoral mandate, he used popular support to push through major civil rights and anti-poverty legislation.

Most recently, Ronald Reagan used his honeymoon to cut Federal income taxes drastically and implement other aspects of supply-side economics. In a short period, he shifted the nation's agenda from a liberal one, oriented toward social and redistributive programs, to a conservative one, intent on reestablishing a strong U.S. military role abroad.

George Bush may find his honeymoon period curtailed, compared to his predecessors. Several factors will undercut his ability to establish and implement policy goals. While Bush won the popular vote by 54–46% and by an even larger margin in the Electoral College, political pundits did not interpret this as a mandate. Furthermore, campaign coverage did not emphasize the major issues confronting the nation, but, rather, focused on trivial, personal aspects even more than usual.

Bush must work with an opposition Congress, since Democrats strengthened their majorities in both the Senate and House. After the election, Democrats were feeling belligerent, non-conciliatory, and put off by the effective hardball tactics and negative advertising used by the Bush campaign. What impact will these feelings have on deliberations between the Administration and Congress? How long can the "ruffled feathers" be expected to persist?

Even more ominous for the Bush Administration are the massive twin Federal and trade deficits—a legacy of the "Reagan Revolution." These deficits effectively would handcuff any president. In a fall, 1988, NBC News poll, the concerns most often cited by voters were the deficit, followed by drug abuse and "new programs for the middle class." Without a supportive Congress, Bush will be hard-pressed to simultaneously maintain the prosperity of the Reagan years, satisfy voters' concerns, and address nagging fiscal problems.

Finally, in contrast to his predecessor, Bush lacks the performance skills that Reagan used to extend his honeymoon period. While his image shifted during the campaign from being too soft and "wimpish" to tough and dirty, neither held the broad appeal of Reagan's avuncular, optimistic personality. Nor, after 30 years in the public eye, does Bush

have the advantage and excitement of being a fresh, new face on the political scene.

Under these less than salutary circumstance, what can Bush do to extend his honeymoon period and demonstrate his accumulated knowledge of governance? As the nation's chief executive, how can he enhance his ability to persuade Congress, the public, and the press to endorse his policy goals? An examination of honeymoon periods of modern presidents reveals several conditions that increase persuasiveness and the capacity to govern. Some deal with the message; others, the messenger.

The Message

It must be simple   The public has become accustomed to receiving information in "sound bites" on the evening news, and even they are shrinking in size. Two recent studies document that one-liners decreased from an average of 45 seconds in 1978 to 15 seconds in 1984 and nine seconds in 1988—an 80% reduction. The old "KISS" theory (keep it simple, stupid), long a dictum of managerial behavior, also applies to presidential persuasiveness. While this does not preclude complex solutions to complicated problems, it does imply that the communication of those efforts and answers must be simple and straightforward.

Bush's comments about being "the education president" during the campaign and wanting to make "kinder the face of the nation" in his inaugural address were tailored to sound-bite size—effectively conveying an image in few words. He also used the sound-bite technique to his advantage and the detriment of his opponent by hanging several images on Michael Dukakis. These included the Pledge of Allegiance ban; the Massachusetts "revolving door" furlough program, personified by Willie Horton; Boston Harbor pollution, symbolizing Dukakis' position on the environment; and the liberal image of Dukakis as a "card-carrying" member of the American Civil Liberties Union. Earlier, Bush had failed to use simple messages effectively to explain his role in the Iran-contra affair or his position on the Noriega drug scandal.

It must convey clear and limited priorities Presidents who overload the national agenda during their first few weeks in office fail to communicate a clear and manageable program behind which the public can unite. Carter failed to limit his to manageable proportions, while Reagan arrived in the Oval Office with a predetermined plan to cut taxes, reduce regulation and the role of government, and increase defense spending.

Bush did not use the campaign to create a mandate to address a limited number of key issues, talking instead about new programs in education, child care, and environmental cleanup; waging war on drugs; and new weapons systems. Only in his revision of the proposed fiscal year 1990 Reagan budget did he effectively establish limited priorities among the plethora of issues facing the U.S. Instead, he specified only his preferences for additional expenditures, leaving it up to Congressional Democrats to determine where compensating cuts in discretionary programs should be made to provide the additional funding.

It must be hopeful and optimistic As a motivator, optimism is easier to sustain for the long term than pessimism. Scapegoat techniques work better to demobilize opposition forces in the short run than motivate the public in the long run. Carter's now-famous "malaise in America" speech, while intended to motivate people to overcome social problems, had the opposite effect. Reagan, in contrast, constantly gave upbeat, optimistic speeches that discussed successes of individuals even in the face of massive societal problems. His emphasis on "pride in America" restored the public's faith in itself and the country. While engaging in a negative, "low-road" campaign, Bush immediately shifted to positive images (decency, fiscal restraint, and responsibility) and a spirit of bipartisanship once he was elected.

Unifying themes are more persuasive than divisive ones Effective presidents, like all persuasive chief executives, are team and coalition builders who unite their supporters, even across major cleavages. Reagan began the process of pulling "Reagan Democrats"—blue-collar and ethnic voters—into the Republican Party by appealing to patriotic and unifying themes. The Democrats, on the other hand, by stressing care of the poor, homeless, and minorities, emphasized differences among major subgroups and were less persuasive. Bush confronts the delicate problem of needing to unify the Republican base further to cope with broadening gaps between the rich and the underclass, the well-educated and illiterate, and light- and dark-skinned Americans. Yet, he must do so while appealing to common concerns, rather than to zero-sum politics and divisiveness.

Persuasive messages link appeals to sacrifice with promises of gain Americans have become accustomed to rising living standards and advertising's appeals to their self-interest. In an era of instant credit and short-term gratification, sacrifice is not commonly expected or called for. Not since Kennedy—admonishing Americans to ask not what their country could do for them, but what they could do for their country—has a president so blatantly appealed to the concept of personal sacrifice for national gain.

The U.S. capitalist system is predicated on notions of profit and individual gain. Juxtaposing a self-interested, profit-driven capitalist economy with political rhetoric calling for pain and loss seems both incongruous and distasteful in the minds of many citizens, even if necessary. In dealing with the twin deficits,

Bush and Richard Darman, his Budget Director, have avoided calling for tax increases so far, thus eschewing any mention of this type of political pain. Many experts predict this approach will lead to long-term economic decay, if not more immediate disaster. If and when Bush retracts his read-my-lips promise of no new taxes, he'd best link clearly in the public's mind any increases with the benefits to be gained from such actions.

Messages that contrast sharply with the policies of the previous chief executive are more persuasive than those that advocate continuity Kennedy's bold New Frontier advocated bearing any burden to bring freedom to the rest of the world and revamping society at home to address social inequities. This contrasted markedly with Eisenhower's mandate to pull back from international intervention, especially in Korea, and return the country to normalcy after two wars in as many decades. Reagan's optimistic and patriotic "Morning in America" message sharply differed from Carter's theme of "malaise." While Carter told the American people their government could not do everything, Reagan implied it could do almost anything.

Part of the appeal of a sharp contrast is that a media-reared public has become accustomed to constant bombardment by new images, messages, advertisements, films, and themes. Contrast is interesting; continuity is boring. Another factor is that social conditions change, and new messages are often more appropriate than old. However, Bush was elected to extend the Reagan Revolution, rather than break with the past.

The Messenger
Presidents perceived as strong and competent are more persuasive than those considered weak and ineffective Leadership skills are tied intimately to presidential persuasiveness. Presidents regarded as

strong, decisive, and confident are perceived as better leaders, more capable of achieving their stated objectives and policies, than those considered weak, indecisive, and hesitant. Richard Nixon, often unlikeable and by some standards devious, still was regarded as strong until the Watergate scandal undermined his public support. He used this strength to convince the public to reverse its official orientation toward Red China and to withdraw from Vietnam on a delayed schedule.

Carter, by contrast, was viewed as weak, plebian, obsessed with details, and ineffectual. He was not able to persuade Congress to pass his initiatives or gain wide public support for many of his policies. Reagan, however, enjoyed widespread public support, partially based on his presidential stage presence and friendly nature. He used this popularity to power his agenda through Congress.

In the early stages of his presidential campaign, Bush worked under the handicap of being perceived as weak, ineffectual, and wimpish, despite a record as a successful businessman, war hero, and high-level public manager. By the end of the campaign, he had turned this image around so the public considered him the stronger and more competent candidate. This turnaround, however, was brought about by negative, divisive tactics, a short-run approach. To extend his honeymoon, Bush will need to create an image of strength based on constructive accomplishments.

Presidents who present themselves as part of an orderly decision-making apparatus are more persuasive than those who are always personally in charge Reagan often was called the "Teflon president," because his public blunders and misstatements did not seem to stick to him and, consequently, cause him to suffer political repercussions. In part, this quality arose from Reagan's ability to project himself as the chief executive of an orderly, efficient corporate structure that would and did carry on even when he faltered. Recognizing that presidents are only human, the public believes that no one person can be omniscient, always making the best decision. Nor, given the American bias against strong authority, does it want such an infallible leader.

Good presidents are team builders and team players; persuasive presidents are also. Bush earns good marks on this score, having spent most of his public career as a team player and agency executive.

The persuasive president is a good media performer   Franklin D. Roosevelt, John F. Kennedy, and Ronald Reagan have been among our best presidents in using the media to accomplish their purposes. Jimmy Carter and Gerald Ford were less effective media performers and less persuasive presidents. Increasingly, presidents need to use the media not only to communicate their priorities to the public, but also to Congress, the press, and peer world leaders.

In many crucial ways, the media have replaced political parties as the gatekeepers of political success. Presidential scholars long have recognized that the relationship between press and president is one of mutual manipulation. Our most persuasive presidents have been more successful in this manipulation than the press. Bush has not been regarded as a good media performer, lacking the pizazz and polish of Reagan. During the campaign, however, he compensated by hiring good media consultants and ad men. As president-elect, he held more press conferences than Reagan during his last year in office.

The persuasive president demonstrates an understanding of the issues   Persuasiveness depends upon presenting a coherent, consistent message. To be persuasive, presidents must have a clear understanding of the issues to communicate

their essence to crucial audiences. Inundated with information, signals, and demands from many quarters, persuasive presidents are quick studies, able to ask the key questions, extract the major dimensions of a problem or proposal, frame reasonable solutions, and express these important points succinctly.

Presidents need a fundamental knowledge of public-sector problems, traditions, and institutions as well as the great intellectual capacity to be able to absorb them. Roosevelt, Truman, Kennedy, Johnson, and Nixon all demonstrated this ability. Bush's background and previous career experiences indicate he, too, can sort out the trivial from the important and convey the latter. Already, he has spoken of the multiple challenges facing the nation: strengthening the economy, broadening educational opportunities, improving the environment, reducing crime, and improving the operation of the intergovernmental system.

The persuasive president creates a vision of the future, which becomes the operating framework guiding his administration   As chief executives, presidents need to excite the populace with a vision and sense of direction for the country. Persuasive presidents not only must create a national agenda, but also provide the means for implementing their vision through programs and policies. The New Deal, Fair Deal, New Frontier, and Great Society were visions put forth by modern presidents. Reagan painted a view of a "Norman Rockwell America," where individualism triumphed and once again reigned supreme. Bush has not created his vision yet, although he has provided an outline—a "kinder, gentler America as part of a more peaceful, democratic world."

Persuasive presidents motivate their followers by demonstrating enthusiasm and manipulating emotion-laden symbols   Reagan was a master at using patriotic symbols to convey his vision of a stronger, revitalized nation. This mastery and his unabashed pride in the U.S. engendered a contagious public enthusiasm that helped him implement his agenda. Confronted with a public weary of presidential imperialism and regality, Carter adopted symbols of the common man, wearing sweaters when talking to the nation on television, walking to his own inauguration, and curtailing the use of limousines for top officials. Only belatedly did Carter realize that he had demythologized the presidency more than the public wanted or would allow.

Johnson used symbols from his Texas roots to convey a larger-than-life sense of the White House and its power. Kennedy used the arts and symbols of youth to convey a sense of vigor, vitality, and hope. Eisenhower is best remembered for his creation of the image of the looming military-industrial complex, to warn the nation of a questionable direction. Like Eisenhower, Bush has used the negative con-

cepts of environmental pollution and crime, and even converted a normally positive symbol—the Pledge of Allegiance—into a question of patriotism. He gained electoral victory, however, on the positive symbols of peace and prosperity.

Over all, Bush as a messenger is more persuasive than the message he is bearing. As a messenger, he ranks from moderate to high on significant attributes that enhance persuasiveness. His message, however, ranks from moderate to low in its persuasiveness. Generally, presidents more easily can alter their message than their attributes as messenger. This provides hope that Bush can and will increase the effectiveness of his message in his role as the nation's chief executive officer and, by doing so, will increase his persuasiveness—a crucial element of effective presidential governance.

Domestic and Foreign Policy Leadership

30
Reconsidering the Two Presidencies
Duane M. Oldfield and Aaron Wildavsky

This article is a reconsideration of Wildavsky's "two presidencies" essay of 1966. Wildavsky contended that the president has more initiative, flexibility, and power in achieving foreign policy success over domestic goals. In reviewing more recent developments, the authors identify conflict and partisan divisions between the presidents and Congress over foreign policy. How did this occur? What are the foreign policy perspectives of congressional Democrats and Republicans? How has consensus evolved into dissensus over foreign policy? The authors conclude by identifying three ways that presidents can remain dominant in foreign policy. What are these? Considering President Bush's overwhelming preference for a foreign policy presidency, how has he overcome the obstacles to success identified by the authors? Oldfield and Wildavsky's observations can be also applied to the case study on the Persian Gulf War found in Chapter 12.

More than twenty years ago, Aaron Wildavsky made a claim, in *Trans*-action, that has led to seemingly endless debate.

> The United States has one President, but it has two presidencies; one presidency is for domestic affairs, and the other is concerned with defense and foreign policy. Since World War II, Presidents have had much greater success in controlling the nation's defense and foreign policies than in dominating its domestic policies.

Did the "two presidencies" phenomenon ever exist? If so, why did it exist? Has it now departed from the political scene? In 1966 Wildavsky felt confident stating that "in the realm of foreign policy there has not been a single major issue on which Presidents, when they were serious and determined, have failed." Today such a claim would be hard to sustain. The Iran-Contra scandal, exacerbated by the Reagan administration's frustrating failure to win Congress over to its Central American policies, is a case in point. A reassessment of the two presidencies thesis is in order.

Too often. discussion of the two presidencies is limited to "success rates." Certainly, Wildavsky claimed that presidential success—however measured—was more likely in foreign policy but equally important were the reasons that lay behind this claim. "The Two Presidencies" argued that foreign and domestic policy are shaped in distinct political arenas, marked by quite different political configurations. First, given the international responsibilities assumed by the United States in the aftermath of World War II, foreign policy has come to dominate the president's agenda. The pace of international events is rapid, decisions are irreversible, and success or failure is quickly apparent. Events in obscure corners of the world come to be seen as integral aspects of global conflict. Therefore presidents devote more and more of their resources to foreign policy questions. Second, foreign policy is largely outside the field of partisan conflict. Unlike the case of domestic policy, the president does not inherit a detailed party program: "Presidents and their parties have no prior policies on Argentina and the Congo." Third, for a variety of reasons, the president's competitors in the foreign policy arena are weak. Relatively few interest groups are active; Congress is deferential; the public is uninformed and unable to provide policy direction. An expanded, expert staff allows the president to challenge the entrenched interests of the military and the State Department.

The overall picture is that of a foreign policymaking process insulated from the pluralistic pressures normally associated with American democracy. The battle of interest groups, parties, and bureaucracies fades into the background. What emerges is a rather apolitical, technical realm of presidential problem-solving: "In foreign affairs . . . he can almost always get support for policies that he believes will protect the nation—but his problem is to find a viable policy." This picture of the foreign policymaking process is evidently wrong today. What went wrong?

THE END OF CONSENSUS

Various studies cast serious doubt on the conclusions of "The Two Presidencies" outside of the period in which the thesis was proposed. Only Dwight Eisenhower was clearly more successful in foreign policy. Presidents cannot count upon bipartisan support when they find a workable policy. From Richard Nixon's Vietnam policies and Gerald Ford's attempts to intervene in Angola to Ronald Reagan's difficulties gaining support for the *contras* and the Strategic Defense Initiative (SDI), it has become clear that presidential control of foreign policy is not so complete as Wildavsky claimed.

The controversy over Reagan's SDI provides a useful perspective on these issues. One would expect this to be a technical issue. Will the proposed system be effective in combating incoming missiles? How much will it cost? How quickly can it be developed? If, as "The Two Presidencies" claims, foreign policy is a realm of technical problem-solving, the debate over the SDI could be expected to exemplify it.

This is not how the debate has unfolded. Presidential success has not been easy. If the questions involved are technical, we are left to account for the fact that the debate has split neatly along party lines. The SDI became a litmus test for candidates of both parties in the 1988 presidential campaign. When the debate did turn technical it became clear that the executive branch had no monopoly on expertise. The president's arguments for the SDI were subjected to expert criticism from a wide variety of sources.

The most important issue is that of ideological and partisan divisions. Wildavsky used McNamara as an example of a man who "thrives because he performs; he comes up with answers he defends." Yet the sort of "answers" a McNamara provided can be widely accepted only if participants in policy debates are asking the same questions, accepting a similar framework for interpreting the evidence. Shortly after the publication of "The Two Presidencies" it became clear that McNamara's techniques could not overcome ideological divisions over United States policy in Southeast Asia. Nor could the expertise of the Kissinger Commission resolve more recent controversy over Central American policy. Ideological and partisan differences are too intimately involved; different questions are being asked, different evidence cited.

If we look at key foreign policy votes from the Eisenhower through the Carter administrations, we find that a majority of the opposition party supported only Eisenhower more than half the time. After the Eisenhower administration, opposition members' level of support has run below, usually well below, 50 percent for each chamber of Congress in each administration. Party differences on foreign policy remain very large. Leon Halpert's study of House voting patterns under President Reagan comes to a similar conclusion:

> The recent characterization of foreign policy as a field engendering greater partisan based controversy and competition is empirically buttressed by our data . . . when partisanship developed on foreign policy matters during these years it evoked the most intense interparty conflict.

When basic agreements concerning the direction of foreign policy break down, bipartisan deference to the president is unlikely to survive. Let us look in more detail at the changes that have undermined the two presidencies thesis.

TWO FOREIGN POLICIES

"The Two Presidencies" is time and culture bound. It succeeds in showing that the Eisenhower administration had greater support in foreign and defense than in domestic policy, and in explaining why. It fails in that both the patterns of behavior and the reasons for their maintenance did not exist in the decades before or after the 1950s. In addition to being time bound, the thesis is also culturally limited. The shared values that sustained consensus on defense during the 1950s gave way in the late 1960s to different ones with far different results.

Bipartisanship was never complete. Partisan battles over "missile gaps" and the "loss" of China were intense. Wildavsky, in "The Two Presidencies," had little use for the concept of a "cold war consensus." Yet looking back from the perspective of the last twenty years, this consensus appears to have had a bit more reality to it. The breakdown of this consensus has profoundly altered the operation of the two presidencies.

Not only is the president more likely to face opposition, the nature of foreign policy conflicts has changed as well. In the 1950s and early 1960s, partisan battles tended to be about performance, or lack thereof, in pursuit of commonly shared objectives, as in the missile gap debate. Recent years have seen more fundamental disagreement concerning the objectives of American foreign policy.

A persuasive account of these changes is provided by Michael Mandelbaum and William Schneider, in *Eagle Entangled,* edited by Kenneth Oye et al. They argue that Vietnam and détente led to serious divisions within the then dominant internationalist public. Two groups emerged. Liberal internationalists support cooperative endeavors—arms control, giving economic aid to poorer nations, strengthening the United Nations—but put less emphasis on fighting communism. They show little support for the use of force. Conservative internationalists see a much more hostile world environment in which American interests and values must be actively defended. They support a strong military. Less educated and less interested in world affairs, noninternationalists remain suspicious of both cooperative and competitive international commitments. The crucial development is the rise of serious ideological divisions among the active, educated internationalists. For it is with their demands that foreign policymakers must deal.

Mandelbaum and Schneider's data fit into a larger pattern of cultural change affecting both foreign and domestic policy. Whereas, during Eisenhower's time in office, defense and domestic issues were on separate ideological dimensions, so that public officials who disagreed on one would frequently agree on the other, afterward the two spheres of policy became fused along a single ideological dimension. What has to be explained is how and why major issue areas that at one time were fairly separated became fused.

In the Eisenhower era, once the old isolationist forces had been defeated, there was widespread agreement on the desirability and efficacy of American national political institutions. There was the slave world with its captive nations; it was bad and dangerous. There was the free world with its liberty loving alliances. It was good. Protecting good against evil was the role of the United States as "the leader of the free world."

Compared to today, the range of national issues in the 1950s was woefully narrow. A liberal was a person who believed in a greater role for the federal government in providing social welfare. A conservative wanted less. Social issues, such as prayer in school and abortion, were unheard of. Civil rights for blacks were on the agenda but not prominent. Environmental issues were discrete entities, not a movement. Foreign policy mattered, but it was not debated on principles that divided the parties.

The presidency of John F. Kennedy proved to be the dividing line. Recall that Kennedy ran on the basis of a stronger defense in which, among other things, the alleged "missile gap" figured prominently. When he told the American people how much he regretted the Bay of Pigs fiasco, Kennedy said it was so awful that he would never speak of it again. Remarkably, from the perspective of the 1980s, he got away with it. Kennedy's relationships with the media were excellent, a phenomenon that used to be standard but has not recurred since. Kennedy may have reduced one barrier in being the first Catholic to become president, but he was not a champion of civil rights. His exhortations to the American people involved reaching the heights of technology (in the space program) or bearing international burdens, not redressing injustices or inequalities at home. America was good; it had only to extend that goodness outward and onward.

The hostile reaction to the war in Vietnam, which began in Kennedy's time and was extended by his successor, Lyndon Johnson, is usually credited with turning many Americans against military intervention abroad and institutions they suspected of deceiving them at home. No doubt the war was a factor. But if the cause was the war, and only or mainly the war, then we cannot explain what happened afterward. For one thing, there was no national consensus on the war, aside from its inefficacy, or on the American use of force in the international arena. At the same time, there was no new massive use of force. Yet that did not stop the mounting criticism of those in authority, a cascade so constant it has begun to seem like a natural condition, the opposite, say, to the "end of ideology" thesis in the 1950s.

The split on foreign policy was intensified by increasing division over domestic policy. Merely to list the major movements that began or became prominent from the late 1960s onward—not only civil rights but women's rights, gay rights, children's rights, animal rights, environmentalism, grey power, and more—is to trace the emerging differences.

Of special interest to us is the fact that these issues do not appear at random but are politically clustered. All of these issues belong to the Democrats in that their party has become the advocate while the Republicans have become the opponents of using government to protect these rights. Even more striking, foreign and domestic issues line up quite nicely, with the Republicans urging more for defense with less for social welfare and "rights" and Democrats willing to do less for defense and more for rights and welfare.

Here we have it: foreign as well as domestic issues now divide the parties; and there are many more issues—social, civil, rights, ecological, defense—to divide the parties. American parties are becoming more ideologically distinct. Conservative southern Democrats are moving toward the Republican party. Liberal Republicans are now an endangered species. While diversity still exists in each party, particularly at the mass level, the parties are slowly edging their way toward internal ideological unity. In Congress, despite earlier academics' fears of weakening party ties, partisan voting is on the rise. In 1987, *Congressional Quarterly's* measure of party unity voting in the House, reported by Janet Hook in 1988, hit its highest level since such measurements began in 1955. Warren Miller and Kent Jennings, in *Parties in Transition,* document growing ideological differences between the parties' convention delegates. Indeed, each party's activists are more united internally and more distant from each other than at any other period for which data exist.

Cleavages on international issues are coming to reinforce, rather than cut across, domestic cleavages. The Democrats and Republicans have become the parties of, respectively, liberal and conservative internationalism. In the 1950s, the division between internationalists and noninternationalists occurred within each party. Eisenhower had the more isolationist Taft wing of the party to deal with. Many Southern Democrats did not share their northern counterparts' enthusiasm for international commitments. In the mid-1960s and early 1970s a significant change of position took place. Northern Democratic support for defense spending and military foreign aid dropped dramatically. Support for economic foreign aid remained high in keeping with the principles of an emerging liberal internationalism. Republican and southern Democratic support for defense spending and military foreign aid rose dramatically as conservative internationalism emerged among them.

In order to draw implications for the two presidencies thesis from these developments, we must try to specify the dimensions along which contemporary cleavages occur, dimensions that serve to unify the parties against each other so as to wipe out the differences in treatment of foreign and domestic policy that took place during Eisenhower's presidency. If we inquire about which values unite the Democratic party of the 1980s, the answer is straightforward: greater equality of condition. The main purpose of the movements we have discussed is to reduce power differences between blacks and whites, women and men, gays and straights, on and on. It is precisely the influx of feminists and blacks, and the exit of southern Democrats who oppose their views, that has given the activist corps of the Democratic party its special stamp.

The Republican case is equally clear but a bit more complex because they are arrayed along two dimensions, corresponding roughly to economic and social conservatism. In the period from the 1930s through the mid-1960s, to provide a brief historical dimension, the United States could correctly be called a capitalist country, compared to most others, but there were few talented defenders of its legitimating values. Perhaps capitalism was too firmly ensconced to require constant overt justification. In any event, in the 1970s and 1980s there arose a considerable cadre of capitalist intellectuals who provided new designs for public policies from privatization to the flat tax. More animated and self confident than their predecessors, backed by the apparatus of modern economics, they constituted the free market or equal opportunity dimension of Republicanism.

In mentioning modern social movements, we deliberately left out one that informs the contemporary Republican party, Protestant fundamentalism. Believers in patriarchy, sharing hierarchical values, the fundamentalists sought to maintain social distinctions within family and society. Thus they gave the Republican party a second dimension. Social and economic conservatives disagree about governmental efforts to enforce social norms, but they are sufficiently close on a limited economic role for government, including opposition to such measures as affirmative action in hiring and promotion, as well as opposition to international communism, to constitute a viable coalition.

How, we still have to ask, were the domestic and foreign policy concerns joined through these dimensions? Our hypothesis is that the egalitarians who gravitated to the Democratic party viewed defense as taking away from welfare, therefore inegalitarian. In a corresponding manner, they saw the United States as a First World country beating down upon Third World countries, that is, as engaging in inegalitarian behavior abroad. Liberal internationalist policies were to help address these inequalities and to free up resources for use at home.

Republican social and economic conservatives viewed life in the United States much differently. American institutions, to them, were marvelous except that they were not pushed as deeply and as far as they would like. Freer markets and stronger adherence to moral norms would suit them. At home they wanted less government because the underlying institutions were benign. Abroad, they favored a conservative internationalist policy both to protect democratic capitalism and to project its institutions further where they would do even more good.

DISSENSUS UNDERMINES

How has the rise of ideological and partisan divisions affected the operation of the two presidencies? Let us take a quick look at the political configuration within which foreign policy was made in the 1950s and early 1960s. An internationalist consensus (a belief in the legitimacy of American institutions and the need to extend them) among northern Democrats and the Eisenhower wing of the Republican party led to a situation in which fundamental disagreement over objectives was rare. Internationalism was particularly strong among political elites. "Responsible" opinion among politicians, academics, and the press held that the United States must be willing to uphold its international obligations even if—as in the case of Korea—this was expensive and unpopular. Elites were held to have a duty to stick together so as to educate the public away from its dangerous tendencies toward isolationism. Internationalism was in the public interest.

In such an environment, Wildavsky's description of the two presidencies had some validity to it. Where fundamental disagreement was not present, Congress was often willing to give the president the benefit of the doubt. The president's advantages in terms of access to information, public stature, and ability to take rapid and decisive action all contributed to congressional deference. The executive branch was seen as the bastion of internationalism, while the Congress was viewed as more likely to support irresponsible parochialism. This led to elite support for presidential control of foreign policy. Given the high value upon presidential leadership, "responsible" opinion was reluctant to directly attack the president. Although presidents were likely to suffer the consequences if their policies did not succeed, they did have relatively broad discretion to initiate policies they believed necessary.

With the breakdown of consensus, the situation changes. If members of Congress disagree with the basic objectives of a president's foreign policy, deference is much less likely. Expert execution counts for little if the policy is deemed to be fundamentally flawed or immoral, inegalitarian or un-American. Instead if uniting in an attempt to educate the apathetic public (noninternationalists), elites now appeal to that group as a source of support in their wars against each other. As ideological and partisan divisions have come to reinforce each other, prospects for unity erode further. Foreign policy has become more like domestic policy—a realm marked by serious partisan divisions in which the president cannot count on a free ride.

The old system of foreign policymaking was further weakened by a number of additional changes in American political life. The press had grown less deferential in all areas. A more educated and active public is also a more ideological public. Thus ideologically ori-

ented interest groups have come to play a greater role in the process of presidential nomination. There are also more domestic groups with foreign policy agendas, not only Jews on Israel, but blacks on South Africa, Poles on Poland, and more. All these changes have added to the difficulty of keeping foreign policy isolated from public scrutiny and pressure.

From the viewpoint of the 1950s this looks unusual, but perhaps the 1950s are a poor benchmark. Conflict and shared control of foreign policy are normal in the American system. Divided power is, after all, a hallmark of the system the founding fathers devised. We agree with Bert Rockman who writes, in a 1987 issue of *Armed Forces and Society:*

> This relatively rare circumstance [the post-World War II "bipartisan national security consensus"] has since been shrouded in legend as a norm from which America's recent foreign policy-making process has deviated, moving from consensual premises and presidential leadership to conflicting premises and to frequent policy disagreement.
>
> The institutional supposition behind this traditional concept of a foreign policy based on consensual premises is one of a virtually exclusive presidentialist approach to American national security policy-making, and one thereby removed from the tugs and pulls and parochial pressures of domestic policy-making. . . . The "repluralization" of national security policy-making, of course, is intimately related to the growth of fundamental disagreement about policy course. But the American system of government also provides considerable opportunities for the opposition to influence policy that are unparalleled.

WHAT REMAINS?

Twenty years ago, "The Two Presidencies" exaggerated the degree of presidential control over American foreign policy. Given the changes we have discussed, is anything left of the two presidencies?

First, it is important to point out that partisan and ideological division do not affect all areas of foreign policy equally. Many positions do not fit neatly into opposing ideological frameworks (the Arab/Israel conflict, for example). Or, as in the case of the Persian Gulf, no side feels that it has a viable solution to the problem. In these situations, the president may be given more leeway to develop an approach of his own.

Second, the fact that foreign policy has become more like domestic policy does not mean that presidents cannot win; they simply must win differently. After all, presidents have been known to prevail on domestic issues. The new environment favors a plebiscitary presidency; public appeals replace establishment consensus. The president, symbol of the nation and center of media attention, is not without resources in such an environment.

Third, much of the president's power in foreign policy lies outside of the measures of success we have focused upon in this article. Easily measured, success in Congress has been the central concern of the two presidencies literature. Yet the obvious must be stated. The president is commander-in-chief, and this does matter. There is little Congress can do about a Grenada invasion or, for that matter, a decision to initiate nuclear war. Nor can Congress play the president's diplomatic role. It can express its preferences concerning arms control; it may frustrate the president's plans by refusing to further arm the Nicaraguan *Contras;* but without presidential action little that is positive can be done.

WHAT IS TO BE DONE?

In the era of blessed consensus now gone, things were better—or so it is claimed. We would all love consensus . . . around our own values. Reagan called for bipartisan support of his Central American policies; Democrats claim all would have been well had he not been so divisive. Consensus consists of the other side giving in. As the parties divide more neatly, over more issues, the temperature of national politics rises. According to the theory of cross-cuttings cleavages, when decision makers agree on some issues while disagreeing on others, they have an incentive to moderate their conflict in order to work together when necessary. When the same people take opposing sides over more and more issues, by contrast, each difference tends to deepen mutual hostility. Nowadays there is a lot more than a "dime's worth of difference" between the major political parties. Disagreement of this sort, combined with the separation of powers, can be a recipe for stalemate.

President Bush began his administration with a call for a return to the politics of consensus. "A new breeze is blowing, and the old bipartisanship must be made new again," he declared in his inaugural address. The honeymoon may last for a while; some of the Reagan era's more divisive foreign policy issues have receded in importance; but, in the long run, we believe that the politics of bipartisanship are unsustainable. The public is more educated and ideological than it used to be, the divisions we have discussed are deeply rooted in the party system. Neither side is likely to give in. Yet dissensus is not necessarily a bad thing. It is desirable that foreign policy be openly and frequently debated. Perhaps contacts with more minds from diverse perspectives would have avoided past blunders. Perhaps the inability to find a publicly acceptable rationale for the growing involvement in Vietnam or for giving arms to "moderates" in Iran should have sent up warning signals. Whatever short-run difficulties it causes, public debate is more likely to lead to a policy that can be supported in the long run. On some issues, such as the intermediate-range nuclear forces (INF) treaty, debate may lead to agreement across party lines. On others we may, for the moment, have to learn to live with disagreement. Attempting to suppress debate with pleas for consensus and presidential discretion cannot hide the reality of ideological division. Nor does it place much faith in our democratic process.

CHAPTER 9

The Executive Branch and the Bureaucracy

The president, Congress, and the courts receive the most public and media attention on important decisions. However, the federal bureaucracy does most of the work of government. Government agencies are major actors in public policy. The "politics-administration" dichotomy between legislative enactment and bureaucratic implementation of policy is no longer considered valid. Because Congress must approve the creation of new agencies and provide appropriations for programs, there is a close legislative-agency relationship. There are continuous struggles within and between departments, agencies, and commissions over the development, promotion, and implementation of policy. The president is the manager of the bureaucracy. The institutionalized presidency is designed to aid the chief executive in this task. The courts are frequently asked to rule on agency policies and regulations dealing with complex economic, environmental, energy, and civil rights matters. Interest groups find the bureaucracy a source of support in promoting their views.

EXECUTIVE MANAGEMENT

The president is generally considered to be the major initiator and formulator of important policy proposals. Over the last forty years, several institutions have developed to aid the president in carrying out the executive function. These are part of the contemporary institutionalized presidency—the White House staff and the Executive Office of the President (EXOP). The EXOP is not a single governmental agency, but a collection of individuals and organizations who assist the president in such bodies as the Office of Management and Budget, the Council of Economic Advisers, and the National Security Council. The EXOP differs from the cabinet-level departments in that the EXOP has advisers and institutions directly responsible to presidential initiative, coordination, and control. Members of the White House staff are not subject to senatorial approval.

The institutionalized presidency has several assets: the system provides important advice to the president; it helps in the implementation of policy; the system is flexible according to the White House occupant; the advisers provide a buffer to outside criticism; and there is a constant comprehensive overview of major policy issues. There are also certain risks and liabilities in the presidential advisory system: its value is directly dependent on the administrative skills of the president. The president must be able to utilize the staff advice. Institutionalization takes up much of the president's time and energy. Time tends to be channeled toward those areas that are most institutionalized. There is also the danger of isolating the president from outside criticism. Finally, the president needs the cabinet-level bureaucracy because it is responsible for most of the implementation of public policy.

Franklin Roosevelt initiated the modern presidential advisory system under the Executive Reorganization Act of 1939. FDR kept the White House staff small, did not give aides fixed assignments, and relied on nongovernmental sources for policy advice. He had a competitive and personalized style of executive management. Lyndon Johnson also employed a loosely structured staff system designed to maximize his personal influence over policy making. LBJ demanded a great deal of personal loyalty from his aides and exercised considerable domination over the White House staff.

Eisenhower and Nixon employed a formalistic style of management, combining broad delegation of authority with a hierarchical structure headed by a chief of staff to coordinate it. Sherman Adams and H. R. Haldeman were the principal domestic staff coordinators under Eisenhower and Nixon, while Henry Kissinger was the dominant foreign policy adviser during the Nixon years. Eisenhower also met regularly with the cabinet, while Nixon sought to combine EXOP centralization with a super-cabinet reorganization plan.

John F. Kennedy had a collegial or team approach, which dismantled much of Eisenhower's advisory machinery and replaced it with a more flexible system. Aides were not given fixed assignments and they were encouraged to participate in a variety of issues. For example, Attorney General Robert Kennedy played a key role in the Cuban Missile Crisis of 1962. President Kennedy generated a sense of teamwork among his aides to avoid the potential isolation of the president under the formalistic system and the chaos resulting from the highly personalized management style.

Due to the increasing complexity of policy issues, Presidents Ford, Carter, Reagan, and Bush have all used variations of the formalistic management approach. Carter's major contribution was to upgrade the vice president as a principal policy adviser. Walter Mondale was given an office in the White House and participated in several important issues. In his first term, President Reagan relied on four principal advisers—Edwin Meese, James Baker, Michael Deaver, and William Clark—in a hierarchical arrangement similar to that of Eisenhower and Nixon. He also promoted a new cabinet council concept, which was a flexible policy network intended to coordinate White House and cabinet officials in developing common policy goals. The Reagan approach reduced much of the traditional conflict between the White House staff and the cabinet.

President Reagan's executive management style was to delegate considerable authority to the White House staff. In contrast to Presidents Kennedy, Nixon, and Carter, Reagan did relatively little reading of staff papers before making a decision. In his second term, President Reagan changed the White House staff system by making former Treasury Secretary Donald Regan the White House chief of staff. Regan became the most powerful chief of staff under any recent president. Using a corporate, hierarchical approach, Regan gained personal control over all the administrative details and domestic and foreign policy initiatives of the Reagan presidency. He had daily management of all speeches, scheduling, paperwork, and policy priorities. Regan, a former Marine and head of the Wall Street brokerage firm of Merrill Lynch, had a tough approach to managing the White House, demanding total loyalty of subordinates. He seemed to be involved in all aspects of the Reagan presidency and characterized himself as a conservative pragmatist. Some criticized Regan's style as harsh and irritating, particularly in his relationship with Congress. Nonetheless, Regan became the most influential presidential adviser in recent times, maintaining the president's confidence so that Reagan could continue his own style of presidential leadership without becoming involved in the daily routine of managing the presidential office. Regan's autocratic leadership style reportedly isolated President Reagan in 1986 from all of the details of the transfer of arms to Iran for the release of American hostages. Mr. Regan became increasingly aloof from Congress and the press. Following the issuance of the Tower Commission Report in February 1987, President Reagan summarily dismissed Donald Regan and replaced him with Howard Baker, the former Senate majority leader. In contrast with Regan, Baker's management style was open, friendly, and accommodating with Congress and the media.

President Bush has developed a combination of Kennedy's collegiality with Reagan's reliance on a tough chief of staff. Unlike Reagan, Bush is much more involved with policy details, particularly in foreign affairs and military matters. In this arena, Bush is the leader of a tightly knit group of advisers, including Secretary of State James Baker, National Security Advisor Brent Scowcroft, Secretary of Defense Dick Cheney, and General Colin Powell, Chairman of the Joint Chiefs of Staff. Bush and his staff organized the capture of General Noriega in Panama in 1989 and Operation Desert Storm to remove Saddam Hussein's Iraqi troops from Kuwait in 1991.

In domestic policy, Bush worked very closely with Chief of Staff John Sununu, the former Governor of New Hampshire, before his dismissal in 1991. Sununu had strong influence over legislative proposals, congressional relations, and court appointments. He had a reputation for being tough and even arrogant with the press and Congress, both Democrats and Republicans. Unlike Donald Regan, Sununu was very close to President Bush and they appeared to agree on all domestic policy and political issues. In this respect, Sununu's role was more comparable to the staff role played by H. R. Haldeman under President Nixon.

Sununu's successor was Samuel Skinner, who previously served as transportation secretary. Skinner's main tasks were to coordinate policy initiatives on the economic recession and health care during President Bush's 1992 re-election campaign. Like Sununu, Skinner was considered a tough political operator, but without his predecessor's confrontational style. Skinner had a more moderating approach in dealing with the White House staff, Congress, the press, and interest groups.

In Article 31, Bradley Patterson, a former White House staff aide under Eisenhower, Nixon, and Ford discusses the growth and expansion of the presidential advisory system. He makes interesting observations about staff accountability, anonymity, and ethical standards. In his view, the future of the White House staff will remain consistent with the past. The best advisory system, in his view, is dependent upon what the president wants it to be. This is accurate, but Patterson needs to consider how abuses of the advisory system, such as Watergate and the Iran-Contra Affair, can be prevented.

TYPES OF GOVERNMENT AGENCIES

The constitutional Framers had very little to say about federal bureaucracy. The only reference is found in Article II where the president is given power to appoint with Senate approval "all other officers . . . whose appointments are not herein provided for, and which shall be established by law." The cabinet was not mentioned. Consequently, the federal bureaucracy emerged as a result of presidential requests to Congress to respond to various problems and needs.

By the 1990s, nearly three million civilians worked for the federal government in four principal types of agencies. Cabinet-level departments are headed by presidentially-appointed and Senate-approved secretaries. There are presently fourteen cabinet departments. The newest, established by Presidents Carter and Reagan, are the Energy, Education, and Veterans Affairs departments. President Bush and Congress considered elevating the Environmental Protection Agency to cabinet level status. Second, a variety of independent agencies and commissions have functions similar to the cabinet departments but are not located within them. These include the Environmental Protection Agency, Office of Personnel Management, and General Services Administration, the government's office of property and supply. Third, the independent regulatory commissions, including the Interstate Commerce Commission, Nuclear Regulatory Commission, and Federal

Trade Commission, oversee and regulate various parts of the private economic sector. The greatest increase in these boards and commissions occurred during the 1930s when Roosevelt's New Deal responded to the Great Depression. Finally, there are several government corporations that are organized like private-sector firms, with some designed to make a profit. They include the U.S. Postal Service; the National Rail and Passenger Corporation (Amtrak); the Federal Deposit Insurance Corporation, which protects bank depositors; and the Tennessee Valley Authority, which sells electricity to customers. In the 1980s, Congress created the Resolution Trust Corporation to manage the bailout and sell the assets of the failed savings and loan banks.

BUREAUCRATIC GROWTH AND EXPANSION

Bureaucracies are complex; they are organized in a hierarchical fashion with a superior-subordinate authority arrangement, assigning specific tasks to staff, who are career employees. All levels of government have bureaucracies; so do large-scale corporations and business firms. Many years ago, Max Weber, a German sociologist, claimed that bureaucracy was a form of complex social organization developed in response to the growth of technology and industry in developed nation-states. Technological complexity, political pressures, and economic growth account for the expansion of governmental bureaucracy. First, as U.S. society became more technologically developed in the 1800s, legislators and political generalists were unable to deal with the resulting issues. The government service was transferred from amateurs to professional specialists. Public administration became a vocation to train managerial specialists. Second, as relationships between government agencies and economic interest groups developed in the early twentieth century, new departments were established to reflect the agency-clientele ties. These include the Agriculture, Labor, and Commerce departments. A third explanation for agency expansion is that bureaucracy is a response to economic, social, and international crises. This was particularly evident in the 1930s and 1960s. President Roosevelt's New Deal included establishment of many temporary agencies to cope with the Great Depression. Lyndon Johnson's Great Society included a War on Poverty, which brought about the Office of Economic Opportunity and other agencies to administer new social programs. International crisis also results in increasing government bureaucracy. Many new agencies develop after the nation's involvement in major wars. Temporary programs become permanent after conflicts are resolved. This can be seen in the national defense bureaucracy. Following World War II, President Truman and Congress approved the National Security Act, which created the Defense Department, the Central Intelligence Agency, and the National Security Council.

Managing the Federal Bureaucracy

One of the president's most important tasks is to manage the bureaucracy effectively. The reason is that executive departments and agencies can be allies or obstacles to major policy goals. In Article 32, Alana Northrop considers that the bureaucracy can either be an enemy, a helpmate, or a noncontender with the president.

Northrop identifies bureaucratic maintenance of power and "iron triangles" as two principal obstacles to presidential policy objectives. The bureaucracy seeks to be independent in shaping policy and allies itself with powerful congressional committees and interest groups to achieve its goals.

However, these obstacles may be myths. Northrop argues that executive agencies and career civil servants are frequently willing to help the president, even to the point of abolishing their own programs. She cites three examples during the Reagan administration where this in fact occurred. Northrop believes career bureaucrats are helpful and adaptable. Those who are not leave the government.

To be an effective manager of the bureaucracy, the president, in Northrop's view, needs to be less of a critic. Instead, the chief executive needs to form a clear policy perspective, make effective appointments of experienced men and women, and use a supportive bureaucracy. Presidents should avoid making end runs around executive agencies since they may result in scandals such as Watergate and Iran-Contra. If encouraged to cooperate, the bureaucracy can assist the president in making policy changes and developing new proposals.

The Bureaucracy in Action: Implementation and Evaluation

In addition to assisting the president with policy initiatives, administrative agencies are also involved in the policy activities of implementation and evaluation.

Implementation involves activities specifically directed toward the application of a policy to solving a problem identified by government. It includes money spent, laws enforced, and employees hired. Administrative implementation is the action side of government. It usually occurs after the president and Congress agree on a legislative bill, after the president issues an executive order, or following a court ruling specifying that a certain action take place.

Bureaucracy is involved in implementing policies in at least three ways. First, an organizational structure is needed to establish resources, responsible units, and methods for putting a policy or program into effect. Second, administrators need to interpret and translate the approved law or policy into acceptable plans and directives. Third, the agency takes action by providing services, payments, or other direct activities to put the policy or program into effect.

After the policy or program is implemented, administrators, lawmakers, chief executives, interest groups, and the public want to know how well or how poorly the program is working. This is called policy evaluation. Administrative agencies may conduct in-house studies or hire outside consultants to do technical assessments of a program. Congress may become involved in oversight of the bureaucracy through hearings, investigations, and commissioning independent studies from the General Accounting Office. The president may ask the Office of Management and Budget to provide evaluations of administrative programs. Interest groups may conduct their own independent assessments of particular policies and programs.

Implementation and evaluation are both directly addressed in Article 33 by James Gleick concerning the 1990 census. The policy directive for the census is found in Article I, Section 2 of the Constitution. A decennial census must be conducted to determine the apportionment of representatives in the House "among the several states." The Constitution states that the "actual enumeration" is made "every ten years, in such a manner as [Congress] shall by law direct."

Legislative authority for conducting the census is assigned to the Census Bureau of the Commerce Department. Gleick contends that the implementation and evaluation of the 1990 census caused many problems. He is critical of how data was collected by census takers and the administrative assessment of the questionnaire mail form returned by respondents. A particularly severe problem was overcounting and undercounting. The 1990 census included more affluent people, due to dual residences, and fewer lower-income, minority, and homeless people because of the difficulties of locating them in large cities.

Aside from Gleick's valuable critique of the 1990 census, considerable political implications result from the census count. First, there is an impact on the distribution of power in the House of Representatives and state legislatures in allocating legislative seats and designing districts. Second, many federal aid formulas are based on state and local population figures. Areas which have a population undercount receive fewer funds than they are entitled.

As a result of these problems, the Census Bureau concluded in July 1991 that the total population was 249 million. Commerce Secretary Robert Mosbacher accepted the original count and rejected "adjusted" figures that resulted in an estimated count of 254 million. Why did the Census Bureau come up with an adjustment? The Commerce Department had settled a lawsuit brought by several large cities challenging the original count as an underenumeration of inner-city residents particularly blacks and Hispanics. The adjustment census would have benefited such large cities as New York, Chicago, and Detroit. But the new figures also reduced the relative share of population for New York State, Pennsylvania, Wisconsin, and Massachusetts.[1]

If Mr. Mosbacher had accepted the adjusted figures, California and Arizona would be the biggest winners in the House of Representatives. California would gain eight new seats, instead of seven, while Pennsylvania would lose one more seat than expected. The unadjusted census showed that California, Florida (four seats), and Texas (three seats) were the biggest winners for the reapportioned House in 1992.

All of this suggests that James Gleick is correct in recommending changes in how the Census Bureau conducts the enumeration of the American population. Perhaps the Census Bureau should combine random sampling procedures used by public opinion pollsters (see Chapter 5) with revised procedures for a headcount. This seems reasonable considering the great deal of resistance, non-compliance, and errors made by people in 1990 when they were contacted by the Census Bureau and individual enumerators.

NOTES

1. Felicity Barringer, "Adjustments to the Census Count Would Widen Gains by Winners," *New York Times,* 14 June 1991, p. A1, col. 1-2; and Peter Passell, "Can't Count on Numbers," *New York Times,* 6 August 1991, p. A1, col. 5-6.

The White House Staff

31
The Essence of White House Service
Bradley H. Patterson, Jr.

Bradley Patterson, who served for fourteen years on the White House staffs of Eisenhower, Nixon, and Ford, provides an effective description of how various aides and offices assist the chief executive. He raises interesting questions about the size of the White House staff and its accountability. Which is the key issue: size or control? Should White House aides speak for the president? Patterson also discusses anonymity and high ethical standards for presidential aides. Why are these important principles? In considering the future, Patterson mentions a few innovations. Should White House operations be reformed? Would a permanent secretariat improve the advisory system? What guidelines should be used by the president in organizing the advisory system? Do you agree or disagree with Patterson's guidelines?

I pray Heaven to bestow the best of blessings on this House and all that shall hereafter inhabit it. May none but honest and wise men ever rule under this roof. —John Adams

The time when Presidents and their aides were regarded as upright citizens devoted to the service of the nation had long since passed. Since Vietnam and Watergate much of the big-time media have tended to regard every public official, elected or appointed, as a suspect from the day he takes office, and public service as a crime waiting to happen. —Donald Regan

Why there is a White House staff, what it does, what its elements are—the previous chapters have given a photomontage of the ring of power that supports the modern president.

Questions now arise. How large is the staff, and what limits its size? What principles govern the staff's use of its influence?

THE WHITE HOUSE STAFF COMMUNITY

What is the size of the entire White House staff family? Its major elements are totaled as of the fall of 1987.

Such is the community which de facto is the White House environment and which serves the presidency of today.

It never stays still; any table of figures (including this one) is but a stroboscopic photograph of a buzzing, swiftly altering scene. Staffers, consultants and advisers, both high and low, continually join and leave the ranks; the numbers and totals change daily.

As the table makes clear, the security and military support staffs are the largest part of the White House establishment. These men and women are not on the White House

---

TABLE 1   Major Units of the White House Staff Community

The White House Office	
(Including the Office of Policy Development)	568
The National Security Council staff	190
The Office of the Vice President	98
The 45 percent of the Office of Administration that directly supports the	
White House	91
The Executive Residence	
(Including National Park Service staff regularly on the grounds)	129
The Military Office	1,300
U.S. Secret Service:	
Uniformed Division (White House Police)	500
Presidential Protection Detail	100
Vice Presidential Protective Detail	100
White House Technical Security	100
Engineering and Maintenance	
(From the General Services Administration, the Telephone Company)	190
Full-time Total	3,366
Part-time staff:	
Military personnel who support the White House on a less than full-	
time basis	2,500
Regular volunteers	500

---

payroll, nor are they "detailed" there in the sense of being borrowed away from their regular duties in other agencies; the White House is their duty station. They, the Residence staff, and many others are career professionals; while their presence in the White House is at the president's pleasure, they serve every succeeding president with equal and neutral competence. They are not policy officers, of course, but are an indispensable underpinning of the immediate presidential community.

The practice of borrowing personnel is decades old at the White House. Some 200 of the 947 employees in the first four of the elements listed are detailees; 85 of the 190 NSC staffers, for instance, are from outside the White House. Former President Ford disapproves of the practice of details:

Having somebody from a department in the White House—on the staff—tends to project a departmental view more than an independent White House view. . . . If you bring somebody in from a department, that department has a foot in the door and is undermining the independent judgment of the White House itself.

Ford's apprehensions are justified. In the first Reagan term, a staff officer on detail from one of the agencies told the author that his agency head made it clear to him: "Represent *my* interests over there at the White House or your promotions are in jeopardy." The staff officer in question refused to play the advocate role and the vindictive agency head aborted the promised raise.

Notwithstanding Mr. Ford's warning, presidents continue to use detailed employees, masking the true size of the staff. In July of 1987, the General Accounting Office issued a public reminder that many detailees at the White House were not being reported to the Congress, as a 1978 law requires.

In addition to detailees, White House staff offices in the Executive Office Building regularly use volunteers, and student interns, to pinch-hit in cases of illness but also to help relieve the inexorably increasing workloads. Considerations of security underlie the general rule that volunteers are not used in the West Wing, the East Wing, or the Residence, but the rule has been bent; volunteers, for instance, have assisted the first lady's staff in her Press and Advance Offices.

As the reader will now be observing, there is probably no ready answer for one who might ask: what is the total budget of the White House? The published figures for the White House Office, the vice president, the Office of Policy Development, the National Security Council, and the Executive Residence would have to be augmented by a substantial percentage of Treasury's uniformed and civilian Secret Service totals, by significant National Park Service and General Services Administration contributions, and by Defense's outlays for White House communications, facilities and aircraft, and the military personnel to support them. Even that cumulative total would have to be enlarged by gleaning, one by one, the costs of the many detailees, which are imbedded in the budgets of a dozen odd departments and agencies.

However large are the gross numbers of dollars or people, the ring of power itself is smaller. There are one hundred White House staff members with presidential commissions. Among them is the senior circle, the heads of the twenty major offices. Even within that ring, there are, in every White House, a very few who are the president's most intimate associates.

The size of the contemporary White House staff is not the result of mindless, willy-nilly empire-building; it is a direct consequence of the presidential demand for the tasks the staff performs. The threat of terrorism, for example, leaves the president no choice but to require security support in depth. The president's pastoral role, quantified in the volume of mail, telephone calls, tourists, hardship cases, messages, cards, and gifts, nearly overwhelms the place; the five hundred volunteers are used to keep the staff's heads above the flood.

Services added by earlier presidents as useful innovations—the Situation Room, the News Summary, the photographer, for example—have now proven their worth, and are standard White House elements. With more and more institutions reaching *in* to the presidency, and affording additional avenues of persuasion (interest groups, state and local officials, political coalitions), the White House has organized itself—and grown—to reach *out* to exploit those opportunities. As other authors have so well demonstrated, the president puts great store in "going public"; the "White House bubble machine" is a staff apparatus that no future president will forgo.[1]

Above all else, the centrality of the president's personal role in leading and coordinating the Executive Branch has occasioned the increase in his own staff resources. The thirty Cabinet departments and agencies are every chief executive's proud professional resource, but their disparate priorities must be marshaled and synchronized—a task the Constitution itself implies that presidents must do. As a Brookings scholar recently wrote:

> . . . over time the built-in advantage of the White House will prevail: presidents will incrementally enhance its competence, problems and issues will be increasingly drawn into it for centralized coordination and control, expectations surrounding previous patterns will slowly break down, new expectations will form around a White House-centered system, and the new

expectations will further accelerate the flow of problems and issues to the White House—thus enhancing the need for still greater White House competence.[2]

The more centrifugal the inevitable cacophony outside that White House gates, the more potent becomes the centripetal strength within.

Presidents have sworn to try to slice down the White House staff—but none have really done so. Can the staff be trimmed? One searches first for do-nothing hangers-on at the White House. There are few if any.

Are there superfluous offices? Only if a president is willing to deprive himself of functions already being performed. While in theory a new president has a clean slate, outside the White House there are expectations that condition his choices. Governors, legislators, state party chiefs, interest groups, and the news media would be the first to decry an "isolated" presidency if the intergovernmental, legislative, political, public liaison, or communications staffs were abolished.

Short of abolition, a president could ordain that the core functions continue but their staffs be smaller. He might pare his Public Liaison Office, cutting back its policy briefings, for instance, for the Business Roundtable or the Urban League. The president, however, needs the informed influence of just such groups in the halls of Congress. He could delegate sub-Cabinet patronage to his Cabinet members, shrinking his presidential personnel staff. President Carter tried that and recognized too late that he was giving up too much authority.

Reduce the Residence staff? Abandon Camp David? Instruct the first lady to be less active? Size per se is not the true issue in the management of the White House. As former Chief of Staff Richard Cheney urges,

> I don't think we should place artificial constraints on the President. If the President says he needs 500 people to do the job,

give him 500; if he thinks he needs 700, give him 700. It's a minor price to pay for having a president who is the leader of the free world. . . . A trillion dollar federal budget, 4.2 million federal civilian and military employees—we can afford to give the President of the United States however many persons he needs on his personal staff.

"The president is the best judge of what he needs to do his job," added a House appropriations staff officer. "We give him what he asks for and then, if he screws up, we can criticize him. We have made very, very few cuts in the White House Office requests."

To be a countervailing magnet to the atomizing particles in the polities of the nation and the world, the American president needs and deserves all the personal staff resources he can control. "Control" is the nub. The limit on White House staff size is the point at which the president senses that he can no longer govern what the least of his staff do or say. This limit is a dynamic arrangement, not an arbitrary figure. It should not be an imposed number, but will depend on the internal communications and disciplinary systems that the president and his chief of staff establish. If information flows readily from senior staff to mid-level officers, if the latter, for instance, are invited as experts or note-takers to presidential meetings, they can accurately relay the president's priorities, and a large staff is manageable. As the assistant Cabinet secretary attending Eisenhower Cabinet meetings, the author could and did convey to other White House colleagues or to inquiring departmental experts the precise thrust and emphasis of the presidential decisions rendered in those sessions. If there is constipation in communications, however, even a small staff would lack direction.

Is the staff now beyond control?

ACCOUNTABILITY

The Iran-contra escapade has indeed given the public the impression that the White House staff is a freewheeling bunch, pursuing not the president's agenda but their own. Some may seemingly have interposed themselves—the president allegedly unknowing—between the chief executive and his line subordinates.

That impression is understandable but wrong. No major enterprises take place in the White House environs without the president's knowledge and consent. The seniormost ring of White House staff are close to the president, and he to them, their confidences intimately shared, the mutual respect intense. The chances that they would keep secrets from one another—especially they from him—are close to zero.[3]

The senior staff will constantly be the transmitters of the chief executive's wishes; on occasion they will—or will be told to—mask the president's hidden hand behind a directive ostensibly their own. Some disgruntled recipients of such orders may mistakenly believe—or may choose to believe—that the instructions emanate not from the president's choice but from the staff's own arrogance. They, too, are wrong. "If Bob Haldeman tells you something, you are to consider it as a communication directly from me and to act on that basis," President Nixon once told J. Edgar Hoover. "If Ham or Stu or Jack calls on my behalf, take their word as coming directly from me," President Carter told his Cabinet. "You have been overly reluctant to respond when the White House staff calls you." For their part, rarely do senior staff need the kind of reminder President Johnson often gave: "You make sure you know what I think before you tell . . . [an outsider] what you think I think."

It is the use by lower-ranking aides of the presidential "we" that most quickly provokes challenges to the staff's reliability. "If you have hundreds of people doing that, there is no way you can keep them out of mischief," commented Kennedy assistant Ted Sorensen. Neustadt adds:

> Only those who see the President repeatedly can grasp what he is driving at and help him or dispute him. Everybody else there is a menace to him. Not understanding they spread wrong impressions. Keeping busy, they take their concerns for his.[4]

There is, however, a sharp, fast antidote to mischief-making by the more junior staff, a kind of pruning saw that rests in the hands of any on the receiving end of White House badgering. Should a query fired back to a White House superior produce the response that the original caller was not close to the presidential trunk, but out on a limb of his own, the saw cuts quickly, the limb is severed and with it collapses the aide's credibility if not his employment. Among Cabinet officers, governors, ambassadors, or legislators, the pruning saw is likely to be unsheathed whenever they hear "the White House calling." At the White House, every mid-level or junior assistant soon learns that he or she operates under that sharp-toothed discipline.

The disciplinary saw also cuts two ways. Johnson assistant Califano tells of the evening when he asked his associate, Lawrence Levinson, to pass on a presidential request to Secretary of Labor Willard Wirtz. The secretary doubted the younger aide's authenticity and paid the request no heed. Explaining his hesitation to an irritated president the next morning, Wirtz received the following admonition: "If you get a call from anyone over here, if you get a call from the cleaning woman who mops the floors at three A.M. and she tells you the President wants you to do something, you do it!"

Johnson, however, followed a very different principle where Secretary of Defense

McNamara was concerned. In a 1965 interview, he declared, "I've told Bob McNamara if anybody calls him and says he speaks for me, let me have the name of that man right away and I'll fire him."

NO ROOM FOR SPECIAL PLEADERS

President Carter's experience with Midge Costanza and Nelson Cruikshank, detailed earlier, illumines another principle at the heart of White House service: there is no place in the White House for narrow advocates; crusaders are ultimately forced out. What Costanza did in the Roosevelt Room and Cruikshank before a House committee, Reagan aide Pat Buchanan repeated in Lafayette Park: pushing a cause beyond the president's own priorities. There is only one route in the White House for the man or woman who climbs on a white horse: out the back door.

THE PASSION FOR ANONYMITY

There is a maxim of staff conduct that governs throughout the institution: the staff is to do its work behind the scenes. Part I catalogued the assignments that White House staff undertake—policy development, implementation enforcement, information-gathering, crisis management—missions that unavoidably breed polarities between them and Cabinet officers. Such tensions are inherent in the methods presidents now use in administering the Executive Branch.

While the polarities are unavoidable, they are exacerbated manyfold if the White House staff member is in the newspapers, implying that he or she is the centerpoint of the action. Louis Brownlow's advice, given over fifty years ago, is still valid today: White House staff should stay out of the limelight.

Occasional background briefings by senior White House officers may be appropriate; perhaps sufficient visibility could be permitted to offset a false mystique of "sinister forces" behind the presidency. If, however, White House men and women become featured speakers, TV personalities, and press-conference performers, the public will wonder and Cabinet officers will rightfully complain: "Who is running the place?" In the end, the president will ask the same question.

THE UNFORGIVING ETHICAL STANDARD

New recruits may chafe at the ethical requirements for government service—conflict-of-interest statutes and financial disclosure requirements. At the White House, those are merely the minima. The White House is a glass house, shot through with floodlights of scrutiny from a skeptical press and a hostile political opposition, watched by a changeable public. It is expected to be a model for public service and it cannot help but be a target for attack on even the least of peccadilloes. Its rules of conduct reflect its honored—and vulnerable—circumstance. The basic ethical standard in the White House is so old and clear that it still comes as a surprise to see any staff officers falling afoul of the rule. The *appearance* of impropriety is itself the impropriety. Will a staffer's acceptance of favors from outsiders, for instance, in fact compromise his or her judgment? No matter; it will look that way—enough to fail the test. The "appearance" rule is not in any law; it is tougher than law. It is the unrelenting standard for men and women who serve near the presidency.

White House staff can have no personal agendas other than helping the president. Political, professional, or financial ambitions in their years ahead have to be put aside, or one runs the risk of using the office for personal gain and of putting selfish priorities ahead of presidential objectives, instead of the other way around.

Even after leaving the staff, some officers have disregarded the proprieties of their relationship with the president. Many have rushed into print with one-sided, first-person accounts of their erstwhile internal feuds, even before their president has left office. In thus undermining the confidences of a sitting president, they weaken him before the world and, in turn, ever so little undermine the trust which future presidents and their staffs must try to reestablish. A few former aides have even been convicted of violating the conflict-of-interest laws, tainting their own White House service with the stain of avarice.

THE WHITE HOUSE OF THE FUTURE

As Hamilton would remind us, the raucous pluralism of American society will long continue to be the frustrating environment for those who govern. In a world balanced between peace and war, and in a nation buffeted by competing prescriptions for the division of its resources, parties, legislators, Cabinets, and presidents will forever be making their decisions in an environment of supercharged advocacies and pressures.

Can anything "bring us together"?

John Gardner looks at the White House:

Whatever may be said for the parties and for Congress, the best present hope of accomplishing the orchestration of conflicting interests, the building of coalitions and the forging of coherent national policy is the President. It is his natural role. He begins the process long before election as he seeks to put together the constituencies he needs. In this day of media-dominated campaigns, the coalition of constituencies may appear to be less needed to gain electoral victory; but it is as needed as ever if the President is to govern effectively after victory.

The President's capacity to balance conflicting forces and forge coherent pol-

icy and action should be substantially strengthened.[5]

It is the thesis of this book that the development of the modern White House staff has become a necessary part of that strengthening.

Presidents will continue to rely on such strength, yet they do so wrenched by two apparently contradictory imperatives: on the one hand, the presidential staff, both structure and people, must be kept loose and flexible, a president never encumbering himself with formal White House machinery incompatible with his style of governing; on the other hand, the core functions of the contemporary White House, which this book describes, are inescapably a part of the modern presidency—no chief executive can permit himself to be without them. The answer to the dilemma lies in choosing an incoming staff who can do the old work in new ways, who will be able to fulfill the conventional responsibilities with unconventional innovation.

The path through this contradiction is narrow. The innovations must be dramatic enough for a new president to boast that he has "reformed" White House operations, without actually diminishing the powers of governance which the existing systems afford him. A new president, for instance, will want changed diplomatic and military policies; he will have a new national security assistant and staff to help develop them. There is no alternative, however, to a coordination system *at* the White House for national security affairs; to disestablish the entire role is to guarantee chaos. . . .

Apropos of dramatic innovation, thoughtful observers have recently been asking a challenging question: must the top staff all be ejected when a new president arrives? Why should not the White House of the future preserve more than its professional administrative cadre—why not set up a permanent core of senior civil servants in its policy ranks?

Former domestic assistant Stuart Eizenstat recommends retaining perhaps ten career men and women, in the form of a permanent secretariat, directly responsible to the chief of staff. Such officers would be experienced in government, neutral in politics, have at hand copies of the policy papers of the recent presidents, and be linked to all the agencies' information systems. Half of this continuing secretariat, Eizenstat suggests, would concentrate on national security issues, half on domestic affairs. They would be expected to say to a new president—supplementing the policy memoranda to him from his incoming staff—"Here is the inner story of what the former president(s) did and why; here is the historical precedent; here are the risks involved in changing the past policies."

Is this a realistic suggestion? Amid the competitive tumult of a new president's first months, would careerists be welcome or their voices be heeded? In the modern White House, there have been very few cases from which to learn, and two of the highly regarded officers who personified such bridging between administrations of different parties come to differing conclusions. One distinguished career officer, General Andrew J. Goodpaster, overlapped for eight weeks from Eisenhower's into Kennedy's White House. From that experience he believes there is little in the past to give encouragement for the success of a senior "permanent secretariat" in the White House staff itself. A second careerist, Harold Saunders, served on the NSC staff from 1961 (Kennedy) to 1974 (Nixon) and advocates a repetition of that transition model in future NSC staffs.

Eizenstat's suggestion may be visionary; certainly it would be realizable only if the incoming president is convinced that it would be in *his* interest to insist on having a stanchion of continuity in such a swirl of impermanence. More likely, the White House of the future will continue to rely on the informal counsel of former presidents or senior staff alumni in person, rather than inject rigidities into what must always be a flexible policy environment.

Before launching any innovations, a future White House staff needs to know what it is they are reforming. Presidential public administration here enters virgin territory. With few exceptions, postelection communication between incoming and outgoing White House staff members has been at best perfunctory. Transition briefings are of course provided for newcomers within the Cabinet departments, but conversations among new and old White House office heads have often not gone beyond handing over the floor plans. Such communication gaps are harmful to good government. Between election and inauguration, therefore, private forums are needed where newly designated staff leaders can put their inherent superciliousness aside and give a hearing to the observations of those who have preceded them. Each White House of the future deserves the benefits of the experience each presidency has accumulated.

After a presidential change, the alumni of the years just gone begin to draw together to recall—and celebrate—the unforgettable intensities they shared. Eisenhower administration veterans gather in reunion luncheons and dinners; the Judson Welliver Society includes all the speechwriters present and past; the 1600 Club welcomes the White House Communications Agency insiders. Every few months the February Group of Nixon-Ford alumni convenes, its national directory of names and addresses kept current, its newsletter chatty with nuggets about new promotions, new marriages, old memories.

Within weeks of inauguration, a new White House staff comes to reflect, as did its predecessor, the president's own policies, priorities, and style. The older core functions continue, juggled perhaps into different hierarchies, adorned with new labels. Fresh adjustments are frequently made, practices fine-tuned, faces often changed. The White House staff then becomes no more than and no less than what the chief executive wants it to be; the instructions it gives are his orders and the procedures it specifies are the ones he desires.

If the Cabinet, the Congress, or the country are persistently offended by what a White House staff says and does, there is just one person in whose hands to heap their woe: the president of the United States. Ask not the White House staff to be what he is not. Should a president, fully informed, insist on unwise decisions, it is not they who will reverse him. Should he be malicious or dishonorable, it is only the more independent institutions of our nation—the Congress, the courts, the press—not the White House staff, who must guard the republic.

The essence of White House service, however, is not the notorious dishonor of a few, but the quiet honor of thousands. The newest staff intern remembers what the oldest White House veteran never forgets—John Adams' prayer inscribed over the fireplace in the State Dining Room and quoted at the beginning of this part. That invocation reaches staff members as well; few of them fail to be humbled by the sense of obligation that those words instill. Implied within them is a further admonition: whether high or low in the staff, even in the midst of partisanship, one's duty is not only to the ruler of the present, but to the White House of the future, to the president of today and to the presidency of tomorrow.

The true reward of White House service reaches, also, beyond the excitement of the moment, is deeper than the seductive allure of the trappings of office. The energetic and intellectually aggressive men and women who make up the White House staff are driven not so much by the thirst for fame in the present but by the prospect of nudging the future—of "hacking a few toeholds on history," in the words of one.

A president is elected to effect a coherent program of change, battling all the while the incoherencies of pluralism beyond the White House gates. The White House staff are his ring of power in this battle, tolerating the personal pressures and accepting anonymity as lesser sacrifices for a larger goal.

NOTES

1. See Samuel Kernell, *Going Public* (Washington, D.C.: *Congressional Quarterly Press*, 1986), and Grossman and Kumer, *Portraying the President*.

2. Terry M. Moe, "The Politicized Presidency," in John E. Chubb and Paul E. Peterson, eds., *The New Direction in American Politics* (Washington, D.C.: Brookings Institution, 1985), pp. 244-45.

3. While former Security Assistant Admiral John Poindexter testified to a congressional committee that he did not tell the president about the NSC staff's diversion of funds to aid the Nicaraguan contras, the author's own past experience at the White House makes him unable to put credence in that story. Even the committee itself commented, "Preempting a decision by the President to provide political deniability—which Poindexter testified that he did—was totally uncharacteristic for a naval officer schooled in the chain of command." (Iran-contra Report, p. 272).

4. Richard Neustadt, "Presidential Leadership: The Clerk Against the Preacher," James Sterling Young, ed., *Problems and Prospects of Presidential Leadership*, Vol. 1 (Lanham, Md: The University Press of America, 1982), p. 33.

5. John W. Gardner, *Toward a Pluralistic but Coherent Society* (Queenstown, Md.: Aspen Institute for Humanistic Studies, 1980), pp. 20-21.

Managing the Federal Bureaucracy

32
The President and the Bureaucracy: Enemies, Helpmates or Noncontenders?
Alana Northrop

The White House Staff and the Executive Office of the President have been used to manage the vast federal bureaucracy. Alana Northrop, political science professor at California State-Fullerton, considers whether or not the federal bureaucracy helps or hinders the chief executive in achieving policy goals. What are the two principal arguments that the bureaucracy is an obstacle to the president? What case examples are cited by the author to demonstrate that the bureaucracy can assist the president? Northrop also identifies four ways that the chief executive can be an effective manager. What are these? Do you agree or disagree with Northrop that the real problem with bureaucracy is its critics? How does the bureaucracy aid the president in developing policy changes and ideas?

The bureaucracy, the vast support staff in the executive branch which runs the wheels of government, has been under attack since the founding of the United States. But the attack has recently been gaining new steam. Public opinion polls over the last quarter century have charted an increase in the public's mistrust of the bureaucracy.[1] And starting with Nixon's presidency, the White House has purposely sought to end run the bureaucracy.[2] Carter and Reagan, in turn, even campaigned for the presidency by saying the problem with government was government.

Professional students of government have also contributed to this growing critique of the bureaucracy. A common argument in any textbook that deals with the bureaucracy is that bureaucracies seek to maintain themselves and that bureaucrats independently shape public policies. Both these characteristics of bureaucracies are said to work against the public will or the will expressed through elected officials. For example, in order to maintain or enhance their agencies, bureaucrats are said to seek larger budgets irrespective of broader social needs. Moreover, they can use their expertise to make a self interested case to Congress or the White House, neither of which have the parallel level of expertise to see through the self interested presentations.

The iron triangle argument, also found in government textbooks, complements the

From *The Presidency In Transition*, Vol. VI, No. 1, 1989, pp. 184–191. Reprinted with permission from the Center for the Study of the Presidency, publisher of *Presidential Studies Quarterly*.

above bureaucratic characteristic argument because it too sets the bureaucracy in opposition to the president and his political appointees. Essentially, this theory suggests that interest groups and their relevant administrative agency and congressional committee form an alliance that is so strong that the president cannot dictate or direct change. In fact, if this theory is valid, it provides a rationale for presidents or their staffs executing sweeping end runs around the bureaucracy.

In summary, we have an old but growing view of the bureaucracy as uncontrollable and in opposition to the public will. Moreover, this view is supported by a preponderance of professional scholarship on American government. No wonder a major concern of a newly elected president is how to wrest the reins of government from the bureaucracy.

While the preceding view of the bureaucracy may be overwhelmingly popular, it would be a mistake for presidents to act on its premise. A solid case can be made for the bureaucracy actually being a helpmate to the White House instead of an enemy. Moreover, most day to day operations of government do not involve disputes, discussions, or debates over what elected or appointed officials want to accomplish and what bureaucrats will let them accomplish. This chapter argues that if presidents continue to maintain negative views of the bureaucracy, the ability of presidents to direct the bureaucracy and thus to govern will decline.

THE BUREAUCRACY AS HELPMATE

Let us first consider the argument that bureaucracies seek to maintain themselves. This argument makes instinctive sense. Man has a need for self preservation and security. Not only is one's job and career clearly related to these needs, but also one forms an identity with his/her organization. Thus, we would expect career civil servants to seek to maintain their programs when they were threatened. Yet, civil servants do in fact help to end their own programs and even do so willingly. Take three recent cases under the Reagan Administration.[3]

Housing Secretary Samuel Pierce decided that housing vouchers for low income housing made more sense than federally subsidized new construction. Thus, in his 1982 budget request he asked for support for housing vouchers, not new construction. Congressional approval for the voucher program took two years. During those two years career civil servants designed the voucher program. Eventually they even ran it. Moreover, given the quick turnover of political executives in HUD, the careerists had to literally pick up the ball when the changing political leadership left a managerial void.[4] Thus, here is a case in which bureaucrats not only helped kill their own program but also directed the political executives in how to do so.

An example of bureaucrats actually ending federal involvement in an area versus supplanting one program for another comes from the Department of Transportation. Under Secretary Dole's leadership the careerists worked effectively with her staff to transfer authority to National and Dulles Airports from the federal government to a regional authority.[5]

Bureaucrats also helped end the Regional Health Planning Program. The demise of this program was an early agenda item of the Reagan administration and was strongly supported by some of the career staff who were affiliated with the program.[6] A career manager was even given the sole objective of managing the elimination of the program.

Bureaucrats can, consequently, end programs. In each of the above cases, the career civil servants did not oppose change.[7] Although bureaucracies may seek to maintain themselves, the maintenance is not necessarily static. Bureaucracies can and do willingly change. One conclusion is that the survival of organizations may take an evolutionary form as does that of humans.

The results of the 1982 survey of members of the Federal Executive Institute Alumni Association, who were typically senior level administrators, complement the preceding three cases. The executives ranked organizational stability, budget stability, and organizational growth at the bottom of eleven organizational goals.[8] As the authors of that study concluded, "Being able to count on certain levels of funding and/or expanding one's organization are either not highly desired or, more likely, not realistic in today's era of tight budgets and less government."[9] Thus, we have evidence that bureaucrats, both in their actions and values, do not always seek to maintain their agencies or programs.

The professional values of civil servants may help to explain the bureaucracy's "helpmate" role. James Pfiffner found that "most career executives will willingly support a new administration and not resist its legitimate policy initiatives."[10] In essence, he found that serving your boss is a professional value held by many civil servants. So when policy directives change, the career bureaucrat continues to do his or her job even though it may have a new content or direction. This aspect of administrative professionalism may help explain why bureaucrats work dedicatedly to end or alter their own agencies' programs.[11]

The changing character of career bureaucrats may also help explain their adaptability. For example, Aberbach, Rockman, and Copeland have found today's careerists and political appointees moving to the right in ideological values.[12] Hence, as the president with a new agenda reflects changes in social values, as Reagan did, so too will the personnel in the bureaucracy. These complementary shifts can therefore result in shared agendas between the administration and the career bureaucrats, not inherent conflicts in their policy positions.

Finally, it should be noted that dissemblers do choose to leave government service.[13] Thus, another explanation for the adaptability of careerists is continuing self selection to serve. Of course, this explanation can only explain the helpmate nature of the bureaucracy to a small degree, since we do not see massive retirements or self terminations with each change of administration.

THE BUREAUCRACY AS NONCONTENDER

Not only can bureaucrats be helpmates rather than enemies, they can also be in a noncontentious relationship with the president. For example, although the federal government performs thousands of tasks and services, the president and his cabinet can only concentrate on a few policies due to time and political limitations. In addition, the more energy and political know-how one exerts on even a smaller subset of policies, the more successful a president or cabinet secretary will be. Reagan's first term legislative successes demonstrate this phenomenon, as does Elizabeth Dole's successes as Transportation Secretary.[14] However, time and strategy limitations also mean that thousands of policies are not in question. In other words, the potential for bureaucratic opposition to the directives of political appointees is not present in a vast range of policy areas.

The noncontentious nature of the bureaucracy is also due to the fact that the need for change grows out of past administrative experiences. Changes in the housing program, the transfer of National and Dulles Airports, and the ending of the regional health planning program all had roots before Reagan took office. Moreover, public policy was generally ready for change and moving in that direction before

Reagan took office. "Jimmy Carter earned Arthur M. Schlesinger Jr.'s rebuke that he was the most conservative Democratic president since Grover Cleveland, because in important respects he represented that shift."[15] Thus, so-called political control of the bureaucracy evolves from the bureaucracy. A new president or cabinet secretary may "supposedly" initiate dramatic changes in policy, but many times the groundwork is already there. In fact, some scholars argue that almost all dramatic changes in policy come from policy succession rather than new ideas.[16]

THE ROLE OF THE PRESIDENT IN SUCCESSFUL ADMINISTRATION

So far we have evidence that the commonly held view of bureaucrats in opposition to the administration is supported more in theory than in practice. This being the case, it may be possible for the president to capture the bureaucracy and therefore implement his campaign promises. What type of presidency will have a greater chance of successfully holding the reins of government?

To begin, a potentially effective president must have a clear ideological mindset. This is important on two counts. First, a clear ideological mindset allows the president and his staff and perhaps even the bureaucracy to interpret his election as a mandate to accomplish policy change. Second, a clear ideological mindset allows his political appointees to think as he does or would. In essence, a president is extremely dependent on his political appointees to carry out his policy agenda and to control the bureaucracy on a daily basis. A president does not have the time to set or review all the policy agendas of the cabinet departments, nor is he interested in doing so. Thus, he must depend on his appointees.

For example, Treasury Secretary Donald Regan recalls that he never met alone nor discussed with President Reagan aspects of economic, fiscal, or monetary policy.[17] Regan, like other political appointees, had to discover on his own what the president would like to have done. The task is obviously easier as well as more likely to be accomplished if there is a clear presidential ideological framework to begin with and if the political appointee shares that perspective. For instance, the three cases earlier cited about policy change in the Reagan administration fit the Reagan framework of deregulation and transferring federal authority and were viewed as such.[18]

To be effective, a president must also take care to appoint politically experienced men and women. If the bureaucracy is amenable to changes in directives, then the keys to the bureaucracy-president linkage are the political appointees. The political appointees must be politically experienced for several reasons. First, they receive little or no training prior to starting their new duties. One day one is a congressperson, and the next day one is Director of the Office of Management and Budget. Secondly, their tenure in position is short, and so critical time is lost if they have to not only learn their new job but also about policies, bureaucracy, Congress, etc. And thirdly, external politics are as important as the internal politics for effective administration. Thus, an effective private sector manager is often ill prepared for running a government agency or department.

Finally, a president and his appointees who seek to redirect public policy need a supportive bureaucracy. As noted earlier, there is empirical evidence to suggest that active support exists.

In conclusion, a president can be an effective administrator but much depends on him. He must have a clear ideological mindset; he must pursue only a few issues; and he must carefully select compatible political appointees with political experience. Finally, presidential effectiveness also rests on the recognition of the helpmate role of the bureaucracy.

RECOGNIZING THE REAL PROBLEM WITH BUREAUCRACY: ITS CRITICS

We have argued that career bureaucrats are helpmates of the White House due to their professionalism, their values that parallel societal value changes, and because dissemblers leave government. But we have also noted the increasing criticisms of the bureaucracy, as well as the campaign denunciations and tendencies of the White House to circumvent the bureaucracy. These negative attitudes and actions do not bode well for the helpmate role of the bureaucracy.

First, the increasing attack on the bureaucracy over the last quarter century is paralleled by the decline in working conditions and morale.[19] In fact, only one quarter of a recent sample of senior level federal administrators advise "bright, competent young people" to seek careers in federal government (only 5% recommend careers in state or local government).[20] Paralleling this, "the percentage of students interested in public service has dropped over the last 20 years from 12% to 6%."[21] Second, organizational changes instituted by recent administrations to gain more firm control over the bureaucracy actually have had the opposite effect. For instance, an argument can be made that the capacity of the bureaucracy to change direction is impaired if the bureaucracy is decapitated with each change of administration. The net effect of such organizational changes is to reduce the sheer number of career bureaucrats in critical leadership positions, leaving managerial responsibilities to new, inexperienced political appointees.[22] Third, the view of the bureaucracy as standing in the president's way has

led to White House machinations resulting in scandals on the level of Watergate and Iranscam.

What these three trends suggest is a situation that threatens the effectiveness of the bureaucracy, the presidency, and therefore government. To the extent that the career civil service is populated by less skilled professionals, there may not be as many bureaucrats who want to (1) do their jobs well, (2) work *with* the political appointees, and (3) pass on the organizational and political memories and know-how necessary for implementing the president's agenda. And to the extend that energies are directed to reorganizing the bureaucracy, then energies are diverted from the real task of governing. Finally, end runs risk scandals. The net result is the president's agenda is sacrificed. Thus the real problem with bureaucracy is its critics. And if the criticisms are not countered, the chance of an effective presidency will be greatly reduced.

CONCLUSION

Presidents need bureaucrats. But on most day to day issues, bureaucrats are noncontenders with presidents and their political appointees. And on many other issues, bureaucrats are helpmates, not enemies standing in the president's and his appointees' ways. In fact, many policy changes and ideas come from the bureaucracy. And it is the bureaucracy's expertise, experience and professionalism that is critical to the effective administration of new as well as old policies.

Yet, what is more critical to effective administration is the president. In this chapter we have tried to dispel the myth that the bureaucracy stands in the way of a president's success. We have actually turned that myth on its head. For much depends on the president. What he represents in terms of world view, the kind of men and women he appoints to office, and how he chooses to administer (e.g., proactive versus reactive, overload versus underload) are all critical to a president's success. And how very nice for him, for *he* can control these critical ingredients to his success.

NOTES

1. M. P. Fiorina, "Flagellating the Federal Bureaucracy," Society, 20 (March/April 1983), p.67.

2. J. D. Aberbach and B. A. Rockman, "Mandates or Mandarins? Control and Discretion in the Modern Administrative State," *Public Administration Review,* 48, (March/April 1988), p. 607.

3. P. Ingraham, "Applying Models of Political-Career Relationships to Policy Implementation," a paper presented at the American Political Science Association's Annual Meeting, Chicago, IL, September 3, 1987.

4. *Ibid.*

5. *Ibid.*

6. *Ibid.*

7. *Ibid.*

8. W. H. Schmidt and B. Z. Posner, "Values and Expectations of Federal Service Executives," *Public Administration Review,* 46 (September/October 1986), p. 448.

9. *Ibid.*

10. James P. Pfiffner, *The Strategic Presidency: Hitting the Ground Running* (Chicago: The Dorsey Press, 1988), p. 104.

11. R. C. Kearney and C. Sinha, "Professionalism and Bureaucratic Responsiveness: Conflict or Compatibility," *Public Administration Review,* 48 (January/February 1988), p. 575.

12. J. D. Aberbach, B. A. Rockman, R. M. Copeland, "The Changing Federal Executive," a paper presented at the American Political Science Association's Annual Meeting, Chicago, IL, September 3, 1987.

13. S. Stehr, "Rethinking the Role of the Federal Career Executive," a paper presented at the American Political Science Association's Annual Meeting, Chicago, IL, September 3, 1987. FEIAA Newsletter, 1985.

14. Ingraham, *loc. cit.*

15. Henry Fairle, "After the Revolution," *The New Republic,* May 9, 1988. p. 15.

16. Brian Hogwood and B. Guy Peters, *Policy Dynamics* (London: Wheat Sheaf, 1983).

17. Donald Regan, *For the Record,* (New York: Harcourt Brace Jovanovich, 1988) excerpted in *Time* May 16, 1988, p.38

18. Ingraham, *loc. cit.*

19. Schmidt and Posner, *op. cit.,* 450. A. Northrop and J. L. Perry, "Change in Performance of the Federal Bureaucracy During the Carter-Reagan Transition: Evidence from Five Agencies," *Public Administration Quarterly,* (Winter, 1986), p. 463, B. Rosen, "Crises in the U.S. Civil Service," *Public Administration Review,* 46 (May/June 1986), p. 210.

20. Schmidt and Posner, *loc. cit.*

21. *Los Angeles Times,* June 19, 1988.

22. P. W. Ingraham, "Building Bridges or Burning Them? The President, the Appointees, and the Bureaucracy," *Public Administration Review,* 47 (September/October 1987), p. 425.

The Bureaucracy in Action

33
The Census: Why We Can't Count
James Gleick

Every ten years, the Census Bureau of the U.S. Department of Commerce is required to conduct a count of the population. The principal reason is to determine the allocation of seats in the House of Representatives. To determine this, each state's population must be counted. James Gleick explains that 350,000 people were hired to enumerate the 1990 population. He argues it is virtually impossible to count all the people in the country. What are the obstacles to one-by-one enumeration? Millions of people mailed in census forms. What happens with the forms that were improperly completed? What are the problems with underzealous census takers? How are some people undercounted and overcounted? Gleick contends that "coverage improvement" works best in counting the first 100 million of the estimated 250 million Americans. Why? What are the political impacts of more accurate counts of blacks, Hispanics, homeless, and illegal aliens? Should the Census Bureau use better sampling methods to enumerate the population? How can the census be made more accurate?

When the nation's greatest and most troubled exercise in counting finally comes to an end—when the last form flicks through the machines, when the last enumerator turns in the last Questionnaire Misdelivery Record Nonresponse Follow-Up, when the last lawsuit is filed—the 1990 census seems certain to stand as a bleak landmark in the annals of arithmetic. The United States Census has become an institution clinging to what many statisticians consider a myth: the idea that the Government can count the nation's population the way a child counts marbles—1, 2, 3 . . . 249,999,998, 249,999,999, 250,000,000. The population is too large, too mobile and too diverse to count that way.

We are a moving target, flowing in and out of what ecologists would consider an impressive variety of habitats, displaying an ever-greater reluctance to cooperate with our enumerators. There are too many doors to knock on, and too many people living without doors. Some demographers complain that the results are grossly out of date before the numbers can be released. "The decennial census was a great invention; so was the steam locomotive a great invention," says Leslie Kish, a statistician at the University of Michigan. "I think it will be phased out."

When Dale R. McCullough, a population biologist, used to take deer surveys, he would arrange scores of volunteers in a sort of skirmish line that swept across fields and marshes. He could get a close count, as long as he used about one census taker per deer. When it comes to people, though, he doesn't think much of the skirmish-line approach. "Accounting for animals that are secretive is always a problem," he says. By and large, scientists don't count that way anymore. John Bahcall, an astrophysicist at the Institute for Advanced Study, in Princeton, N.J., counts stars. Although his objects stand more or less still and don't slam doors in the faces of their enumerators, they have their own ways of telling lies and hiding from investigators. Stars cluster unpredictably. Clouds of interstellar gas obscure parts of the sky. So Bahcall's profession has developed a body of techniques for overcoming "selection effects"—that is, bias.

"There's a lot of bias associated with census questions," he says. "You don't know by what fraction homeless people are underrepresented, you don't know by what fraction yuppies are overrepresented. That's the main problem we face again and again in astronomy."

Supermarket chains taking inventory of their stocks have learned that the best approach—not just the cheapest, but often the most accurate—is to count small random samples of each product and then extrapolate from the part to the whole. Accounting firms making giant corporate audits rely on sampling, too. "They never nowadays check every transaction or even run through a large proportion of them—that's dumb," says Persi Diaconis, a Harvard statistician. "If you take a random sample, and every transaction is clean, then the laws of probability tell you that the whole thing is clean."

Diaconis warns that sampling for the census, however, can be dangerous. A sample never quite mirrors the whole. Still, experience has shown that worse errors arise when bored, tired clerks and accountants try to count each can of peas, each box of cereal, each receipt and invoice.

The hazards of one-by-one enumeration have never been so plain as in the 1990 census, now consuming the labor of a record 350,000 workers. Over the last four months, the census has been staggered by a rate of noncooperation that exceeded the estimates of the most severe critics. Nearly twice as many Americans as ever before either failed or refused to mail back census forms. In some large cities, response rates fell below 50 percent. The difficulties have broken both budget and schedule.

By the original June 6 deadline for the door-to-door phase, the bureau had begun closing shop at fewer than 30 or its 487 field offices nationwide. In some poor urban neighborhoods, which have long been systematically undercounted, the count dragged on into this month. A special follow-up survey, meant to help correct the undercount, has been delayed in many cities. Distortions in the census, of course, become distortions in the fabric of political power, through the apportionment of the nation's Congressional districts and the states' legislative districts.

Officially, the bureau is keeping a stiff upper lip. "I think the census is going quite well," says Charles D. Jones, associate director for the decennial census. "This is the first census that's ever had any extensive automation, and it's working excellently." June 6 was never a serious deadline, he says: "This was an idealized goal. We knew we couldn't make it."

"And if we fail we get beaten over the head with it," adds Barbara Everitt Bryant, President Bush's new Census Bureau director.

The ideal census, the one that exists in the popular imagination, is the one the Government described in March: "The enumeration is based on evidence that physical persons are in a particular location or block at a particular time," it said. "Each tally corresponds in principle to a particular person."

The final 1990 tally is expected to come to something like 250,128,752. A scientist would state the number differently, more like "250 million plus or minus 4 million"—using "error bars" or "confidence intervals" to express the range of error and avoid implying a false precision. Bureau statisticians, however, maintain contradictory views of their product: on the one hand they recognize the error, study the error, and struggle to minimize the error; on the other hand they report the results as though they were certain and pure. "The Census Bureau takes the position that somehow the total population counts are derived from an accounting process that isn't subject to error, and that therefore error bars have little meaning," says Kirk M. Wolter, who was chief of the bureau's Statistical Research Division until 1988. "Obviously that isn't true, or you and I wouldn't be having this conversation."

Many demographers, economic researchers and public-opinion pollers accept the idealization as a convenience. In calculating their own sampling error, they assume that the census data is itself error-free. They may know that the census enumeration does not correspond to the population of the United States. But they consider it a precise count of something. Of what? Says Charles E. Metcalf, head of Mathematica Policy Research, a New Jersey research group: "It's an exact statement of the number they counted."

Though statisticians may wonder about the value of an exact Number of People Counted by the Census, even on these tautological terms exactitude is a myth. The estimates, the probabilities, the compromises, the fuzziness that the census publicly abhors have already become an inextricable part of its methodology. Those most familiar with the inner workings of the census describe a machinery freighted with missteps, work-arounds and downright absurdities.

Even the smoothest-running part of the census—the millions of forms properly mailed back and well-enough filled out that no follow-up interviews are conducted—has its problems. For example:

- **Too Many 100-Year-Olds.** Statistically, the census form is like a dartboard. Most people get bull's-eyes, but many manage only to hit the general vicinity. In 1970, the dot to be filled in for those born in "Jan.–Mar." sat next to the dot for "Year of Birth 186-"—with the result that the census reported a wildly large number of centenarians, by some estimates more than 20 times the actual number.

- **Too Many 100-Year-Old Children.** To keep the obvious impossibilities to a minimum, the census has its computers reject answers that seem out of bounds. The 1980 census imposed an upper limit of 112, beyond which no American was allowed to have lived. Yet once again thousands of people chose the wrong century of birth and the final tally of centenarians proved much too large, about double what the bureau and most demographers believe to be the actual number, based on other surveys and on actual records of births and deaths. Why? The computers took care of the 130- and 140- year-olds. "But we had no requirement that children in a household shouldn't be over 100," says Gregory Spencer, chief of the Population Projections branch. "You'd look and find two 112-year-old parents with their 109-year-old child."

- **Sex-Change Procedures.** The bureau's understanding of what constitutes a plausible household makes some arbitrary assumptions. In this year's census, whenever both members of a gay couple fill in the "husband/wife" dot and the "married" dot and the "male" dot, the census computers will automatically choose one of the men at random and "correct" his sex. (The same for two women.) In general, sex is the category best reported by those who respond to the census; even so, in 1980, more than three million people had their sex chosen by computer, Dr. Spencer says.

- **The 1900 Problem.** Too many people think they were born in exactly 1900. Based on past experience, the current census is certain to show a remarkable number of people just turning 90.

- **Teen-Age Widows.** Mispunching errors can create entire categories of nonexistent people. The teen-age widows are one group famous in census lore. "If you have a one-in-a-thousand mispunching, if can create quite a sizable fictitious population," says Dr. Kish of the University of Michigan.

- **Confusion About Relationships.** Filling in the dots under "If a RELATIVE of Person 1," many households glance at their elderly parents and mark "son/daughter" when they should mark "father/mother." Or they look at their husband or wife, who happens to be the father or mother of their children, and mark "father/mother" when they should mark "husband/wife."

Even apart from such errors, the computers must make statistical guesses for the many people about whom census takers know nothing except that they probably exist. More than three million of the Americans enumerated by the 1980 census were not individuals at all, but nameless abstractions, added to the count by a statistical procedure called "sequential hot deck imputation." As the forms run through the machines, the computer keeps a running record of the last 16 plausible-seeming responses to each question. When it stumbles on an implausible-seeming answer—or no answer at all—it substitutes a plausible one from its stack. The process has elements of randomness and of nonrandomness. It is meant to insure that the fabricated records reflect the diversity of the real population. Thus a record may get a new age, a new sex or a whole new identity.

The staff professionals in the Census Bureau have a high reputation among demographers. Though some of their procedures create errors, on the whole they "impute" people and their characteristics for a good reason: field workers often have no way to find out who, if anyone, is living in housing units on their list. Given a choice between declaring the units empty or making a statistical guess, the census chooses to make a statistical guess.

It may as well. Certainty is not to be found door-to-door, either: not on the streets of downtown Los Angeles, where census takers like Arturo Mata have to guess which of the unnumbered doors of a single-room-occupancy hotel represent housing units; not in the farms of rural Arkansas, where Spanish-speaking migrant workers move from place to place picking tomatoes, raising catfish and avoiding Federal agents of all kinds; not in the lobbies of even the most proper Manhattan apartment buildings, where a census taker can sit for weeks, day in and day out, and still not be able to account for certain residents; not in Miami, where an enumerator coping with the successive waves of Cuban, Haitian and Central American refugees tells a reporter that she has been kidnapped by her census crew leader, just as she was kidnapped before and taken to Russia to meet Mitterrand.

When Maurene Miller arrives in the front parlor of a Brooklyn Heights town house, her badge pinned to her shirt, her census briefcase under her arm, she finds a problem. Her computerized address list shows five apartments on this address, but no more than two, she is told, have ever existed. "They just have the numbers so screwed up," Miller says. "They've got the intelligence of a surfboard in the offices."

She fills out the appropriate Deletion Records. Had she instead found new apartments, housing units unrecognized by the census lists, she says, she would simply have passed them by.

"There's no mechanism for that kind of correction," she says. "I'm not looking for new addresses. I'm not looking to say there's a new building there—it's none of my business."

This appalls the census director, Dr. Bryant; she says it is a plain misunderstanding of the enumerator's job. "If anything's missing they are to add it," she says. And indeed, the official Nonresponse Follow-Up Enumerator Instructions state: "If you happen to find a housing unit that is not on the listing page, you will add it, using the Add Page." Unfortunately, the same instructions began: "Your job, as an enumerator, is *not* to canvass each block, looking for housing units that are not on the listing page."

If some census takers are underzealous, others find Americans that don't exist. These "curbstones," in the argot of bureau insiders, inflate the census just as tombstones inflated the voter rolls of the late Mayor Daley's Chicago. Most of the inflation comes from double-counting: an elderly couple fill out a form at their second home in Florida while helpful neighbors vouch for their existence in New

Jersey; a college student gets counted both at home and at school.

If the errors canceled one another, or if they raised or lowered the count uniformly across the country, they would matter only academically. Instead, most studies inside and outside the census show a distinct tilting of the landscape. Those overcounted—by some estimates as many as six million people—tend to be wealthier and more rural than those undercounted. The combination of mail questionnaires and door-to-door counting works best for people well-enough-educated to follow the form's written instructions, and comfortable enough about their place in society to cooperate with Government inquiries. Blacks have been systematically undercounted at a rate about 5 percentage points higher than the rate for whites, a difference that has barely varied in the censuses since 1940, when the bureau first began estimating the undercount.

In poor urban neighborhoods, field workers are often afraid to enter tenements and housing projects. They may not recognize the nonstandard housing units that dot the urban landscape without benefit of mailboxes or electric-company meters. The most persistent census taker will not find every one of the large families living illegally in Los Angeles garages or Chicago subsidized apartments.

Eugene P. Ericksen, a sociologist and statistician at Temple University who has testified for a group of cities that sued the bureau after the 1980 census, did his own comparative count. He assembled a list of New Yorkers from 10 different administrative lists: utility bill payers, people eligible for Medicaid, voters, licensed drivers. He found that the Census Bureau has omitted more than 8 percent of those on his lists. The true rate of omission must be even higher, Ericksen argues, since his lists, too, included only people with connections to the official world. Another check on the accuracy of the census is demographic analysis, which arrives at population figures through an aggregate arithmetic of births, deaths, immigration and emigration.

So far, the watchword of the 1990 census has been "coverage improvement"—a term for the whole range of efforts to squeeze the last drops from the traditional head count. In New York, the bus and subway posters imploring, "Stand Up for Who You Are—Answer the Census," were part of the coverage improvement, as was President Bush's calling on America to "stand up and be counted." Coverage improvement is the bureau's way of battling the law of diminishing returns.

Census experts estimate informally that 90 percent of the cost of the census comes in the last 10 percent of the count. Counting the first 100 million people is easy. The next 100 million are considerably more difficult. And in the end, even if 90 percent of the population were pressed into service to march across the country in a skirmish line, they might not find the other 10 percent.

"Nobody who is watching the disaster that we have in front of us could possibly think that the millions and millions of dollars the census is spending on coverage improvement will work," says Peter L. Zimroth, a former New York City Corporation Counsel and now with Arnold & Porter, who is one of the lawyers representing New York and other localities in a new census lawsuit.

Counting the uncountable is a task that comes up again and again in science. If the United States were a vast lake, with deep, unreachable recesses, populated by 250 million fish with no mailing addresses or telephone numbers, ecologists would know what to do. They routinely employ a technique known as "capture-mark-recapture." A large number of fish, say, are caught, tagged and released back into the lake. Later, a second sample is taken; the ecologists note the proportion of tagged and untagged fish and from there the calcula-

tion is straightforward: if 1 of every 5 fish in the second sample had been caught the first time, then the first sample probably represented one-fifth of the whole population. Though most of the fish are never caught, the laws of probability provide a means of counting them in absentia.

Capture-recapture has its problems. One is the sampling error that arises from sheer chance. Ten identical boats taking samples under identical circumstances will still produce 10 varying counts. Statisticians know how to calculate the expected range of deviation; the larger the sample, the less it will be. The method also produces systematic errors, errors caused by the nature of the selection itself. Some animals are "trap-happy," others "trap-shy." The capture and the recapture have to be far enough apart that the tagged fish can mix randomly through the population, but close enough together that the population has not changed significantly in the meantime.

"This is the hairy part," says Henry Horn, a Princeton ecologist, "making the assumption that all individuals get a chance to mix completely, that the marking process itself has no effect, and that there's no tendency for the marked individuals to be recaptured since they were the easiest to capture in the first place. All those assumptions have to be made, and none of them are true."

For serious counts, the method must be combined with modeling techniques designed to face the selection biases head on, acknowledging them and trying to measure them. To count the 10 billion stars of the Milky Way, astronomers actually count only 100,000 or so. "You have to get basic data, make a model, and understand how your counting depends on the parameters of the model," says Dr. Bahcall of the Institute for Advanced Study. The model is a guide to the galaxy's structure: the ages and compositions of stars, the nature of their clustering, the proportions of hard-to-count blue stars to easy-to-count red stars. Just as the model depends on the raw data produced by telescopes and computers, the accuracy of the count depends in turn on the model. "You try the model on new data, and use the new data to refine the model," Dr. Bahcall says. Though the process is circular, it is effective.

Not that there is an invincible magic in such methods. Some statisticians continue to believe that adjustments through the capture-recapture method could create wild inaccuracies. "You have a big, complicated analytical engine with many parts, many of which to me look shaky," says David Freedman, a statistician at the University of California at Berkeley. "In my opinion a lot of mischief can be done. You can't afford to have an adjustment mechanism prone to errors of 10 percent if you're trying to fix a 1 to 2 percent error."

Ecologists often believe that their civilized-world counterparts, demographers, are unnecessarily uncomfortable with modeling theory. Even so, in planning for the 1990 census, the bureau prepared a statistical program adapting the capture-recapture method to people. A follow-up survey would cover only a small sample of the country but cover it intensively. Methods were developed for confronting selection biases: many people would surely be unwilling to cooperate with any survey; others, having cooperated with the census once, would be unwilling to answer follow-up questions. Many of the bureau's statisticians believed that by checking to see how many people in the follow-up survey had been "captured" in the first count, they would be able to estimate the number of people uncounted in either survey.

In 1980, in response to the many lawsuits seeking a statistical adjustment, the bureau's staff had argued that it did not have enough data to make a valid correction. For the 1990 census, however, the bureau planned to go

ahead with a large scale post-census survey of 300,000 households. "The Census Bureau expects to have the capability to estimate more accurately than ever before the number of people missed in the census," wrote John Keane, President Reagan's Census Bureau director, in a June 1987 report. "We believe that we could improve the official estimates to make some reductions in the differential undercount."

The bureau planned to use nonpolitical technical standards to make a final decision about whether the sampling data should be used. But top officials of the Department of Commerce, the bureau's parent agency, intervened, quietly ordering the bureau to reverse its plans.

The bureau was reduced to "furtive plotting," Barbara A. Bailar, then associate director in charge of statistical research, has said in court papers. "Our task was no longer to present our conclusions to the public, as we had told the public we would do. Rather, it was to conceal those conclusions, and to give the Commerce Department time to contrive a story." That fall, the department announced it had decided to rule out a statistical adjustment. Bailar resigned.

New York and other cities quickly sued again, in 1988, and in an interim court settlement, the Commerce Department agreed to conduct a smaller, 150,000-household survey. That survey, just getting under way in some places, will attempt to sample households scattered across every state and every economic stratum. The department has made clear, however, that it may decide not to use the survey to adjust the count—if, for example, the Secretary of Commerce sees a "potential disruption of the process of the orderly transfer of political representation."

The political pressures are intense. From one to three seats in Congress, and perhaps scores of state legislature seats, could swing to traditionally Democratic city neighborhoods if previously uncounted blacks, Hispanics and illegal aliens are counted. Many Republican legislators have already warned the Administration of potential disruption in their states.

The Commerce Department argues that the technical process of making an adjustment is new and untried. To Michael R. Darby, Under Secretary for Economic and Statistical Administration, whose office has taken active control of the process, the traditional enumeration is the "null hypothesis"—innocent until proven guilty. He and other officials note that even if a statistical adjustment produced a clearly more accurate count at the coarse state-by-state or county-by-county levels, it might not be as reliable at the fine-grained levels of individual census blocks. Such adjustment hasn't worked before, Darby says. "It may work this time. It depends who you believe."

A census that depends on who you believe strikes many officials as a horrible prospect. They wish the count could be free of politics, free of subjectivity, fuzziness and tinkering. There are strong psychological reasons to embrace the idea that a count of every individual is a national event, galvanizing all Americans to work together toward a shared goal. By contrast, however, there seems little value in numbers that are exact but wrong. By scientist standards, the biases of the census are far from subtle. "What they're doing," says Jeremiah P. Ostriker, a Princeton University astrophysicist, "is burying their heads in the sand and saying, 'Look, that's what we counted, don't ask us any other questions.'" These scientists argue that even an imperfect adjustment is an improvement.

Once the heated issues of 1990 are past, the Census Bureau will have an opportunity to integrate statistical sampling more deeply into its methods, rather than trying to augment the street army of hundreds of thousands. A variety of proposals are already on the table, some more ambitious than others. Dr. Kish of the University of Michigan, for example, maintains that the worst distortions of the census come from its instant obsolescence: by the time the data reaches its users, it is already from one to four years out of date. He argues for the "rolling" census, produced from a sequence of weekly surveys, 520 of them every 10 years.

When Bruce Hoadley, a statistician at the Bell Communications Research Company, counts defects in products coming off manufacturers' assembly lines, millions of dollars depend on the accuracy of his methods. The manufacturers need unbiased counts, and they need them fast enough to catch problems in the factories. He counts by taking samples.

"One of our great callings in life is to continually remind people that they're making decisions under uncertainty," he says.

The census, too, he believes, can only improve its count by coming to grips with uncertainty. "The people who say, 'We shouldn't screw around with adjustment because it's known to be subjective,' are being subjective too, in the worst of all possible ways. They know it's wrong. If your adjustment is zero, zero is known to be just about as bad as you can do. Any reasonable methodology is going to do better than zero."

This is the statistician's lot, Hoadley says. "It permeates life—everything is uncertain, and data is very, very expensive."

CHAPTER **10**

Congress

In examining the three branches of the national government, we find that Congress occupies a central role in making public policy. The Founding Fathers considered Congress a major participant in formulating, developing, and approving public policy through the legislative process. In addition to the lawmaking function, which is found in Article I, Section 8, of the Constitution, Congress has several other responsibilities:

1. *The housekeeping function*—control over its own internal procedures;
2. *The fiscal function*—authority over taxation, revenue raising, borrowing, and spending;
3. *The Senate's confirmation role*—approval of presidential appointments and treaties;
4. *The judicial function*—impeachment of civil officers accused of high crimes;
5. *The electoral function*—counting of electoral votes cast for president and vice president, and the House of Representatives selecting the president if no candidate receives a majority of the electoral votes; and
6. *The constitutional role*—proposing amendments to the Constitution.

GETTING ELECTED TO CONGRESS

How are the 100 Senators and 435 House members elected? Senate representation is quite simple. According to the Constitution, Article I, Section 3, each state is guaranteed two senators elected for six-year terms. The Seventeenth Amendment, ratified in 1913, provides for popular election of senators.

House representation is based on four considerations: the total size of the House; allocation of seats to the House from the states; the size of congressional districts within the states; and the shape of House districts. In Article I, Section 2, of the Constitution, House terms are set at two years and members are to be elected by the voters in the states. Each state is guaranteed at least one representative. The total size of the House was fixed in 1911 at 435 members and has remained at that number. Allocation of seats to the states is determined by the results of the national decennial census. Based on the census, some states gain while others lose seats every ten years. This is called reapportionment and consists of the redrawing of congressional district lines following each decennial census. The state legislatures determine the size of House districts. In the 1960s, the Supreme Court ruled that the "one person, one vote" principle applied to the size of House districts. In other words, the states could not malapportion congressional districts to favor rural areas with more representation over urban areas with more population.

The shape of House districts is also determined by state legislatures. A frequent problem is gerrymandering—when a state party majority draws district boundary lines in bizarre ways to help the candidate from that party win an election. Racial gerrymandering has been prohibited by the courts since 1960. Political gerrymandering was a long-established practice of state legislatures until 1986, when the Supreme Court ruled that the courts may nullify election districts when one party consistently degrades the other party's political influence. In the case of *Davis v. Bandemer,* Justice Byron White upheld the Republican redistricting plan, arguing that the Democrats' claim of proportional seats in relation to votes received was not a test of unconstitutional discrimination. The Democrats had received 51.9 percent of the votes in 1982 but only 43 of 100 seats in the Indiana House of Delegates. Future political gerrymanders might be invalidated when there is "evidence of continued frustration of the will of a majority of voters or denial to a minority of voters of a fair chance to influence the political process." Thus the Supreme Court opened the door for future challenges to partisan gerrymandering.

What is the typical profile of a federal legislator? First, incumbents in Congress have an advantage over potential challengers. On the average, fewer than 2 percent of House incumbents are defeated in primary elections and about 93 percent can expect to win in general elections. Senators have only a better-than-even chance of defeating challengers because of their higher visibility on controversial issues. Federal legislators are not very representative of their constituencies. Typically, they are more highly educated, older, wealthier, and have had previous public experience. Congress is a predominantly white male institution. Women, poor people, and racial minorities (especially blacks) are underrepresented in the House and the Senate.

LEGISLATOR-CONSTITUENCY ROLES AND RELATIONSHIPS

How do members of Congress and senators perceive their duties and responsibilities?

First, the elected representative can be an *agent* or delegate of the constituency. Such a role seeks to promote and support the interests, needs, and desires of the people back home. Several important questions arise here: How does the legislator get to know the needs of the constituents? Who does he or she listen to? Does he or she represent all of the constituency, the political party, or special interest groups? How is the legislator's record made known to the voters so they are assured he or she is acting in their best interests?

A second possible role is that of *trustee*—a relatively free actor who is not always bound to constituency demands. This role was suggested by Edmund Burke, the great British politician and philosopher, who, upon his election to Parliament in 1774, claimed that he would not sacrifice his judgment, conscience, or unbiased opinion to his constituents. The problem is that legislative trustees who are not responsive to their district may suffer electoral defeat if they cannot show any tangible results to the voters.

A third legislative response combines the agent and trustee roles. Most legislators do not automatically respond to all constituency demands (which is clearly impossible); neither do they ignore their districts, which is a serious political risk. Rather, they determine their own priorities by responding to issues, selecting those persons with whom they can build a reliable following, and recognizing those pressures that are most persuasive and important.

According to Morris Fiorina (Article 34), congressmen and -women engage in three types of activities: lawmaking, pork-barreling, and casework. The *agent* role is most relevant to serving constituency needs through "pork-barrel" legislation, or the targeting of federal grants and programs to the home district. Visible public works projects are tangible evidence of providing jobs and direct local benefits to constituents, thereby building a strong case for the legislator's reelection prospects.

Fiorina argues that incumbency—the regular reelection of legislators over long periods of time—is a powerful foundation of legislative influence. Some legislators leave Washington voluntarily. This can be attributed to generous pension benefits, but early retirements also result from a variety of other problems, including financial disclosure laws, criticism by journalists, and the tedious treadmill of the job. But most legislators seek reelection regularly. As previously indicated, incumbency re-election rates for the House are about 98 percent.

Casework is an important factor in this ability to get reelected. This is the daily response to the huge volume of requests by the people back home for information, services, and intervention in the federal bureaucracy for favorable actions or decisions. Most legislators try to build good reputations in acting as go-betweens for constituents in cutting bureaucratic red tape.

SENATORIAL ROLES AND FUNCTIONS

How do the roles of senators compare and contrast with House members? Ross Webber[1] has identified five possible senatorial approaches to the job: insider, legislator, ombudsman, public spokesperson, and prospective presidential candidate. The legislator role is similar to the lawmaking in the House, as described by Fiorina. The senator serves on a few key committees, drafts new bills in specific policy areas, and becomes a policy specialist. Also, the ombudsman role is the same as caseworker in the House. The legislator becomes a specialist in constituent services. The other three Senate functions are different from those in the House, although House members may find them useful. The "insider" becomes familiar with how the institution works and tries to become a part of the leadership structure. The "public spokesperson" uses the media and press to publicize issues and educate the public. The "potential presidential candidate" uses the Senate as a forum to prepare for a run at the White House.

THE LEGISLATIVE PROCESS

How does Congress enact legislation? What is the process by which a bill becomes a law? The formal process of enacting legislation is explained in Article 35 by Marjorie Hunter and Tom Bloom. Instructors and students may find it useful to play "The Longest Running Game in Town." Several things should be considered in the legislative game. First, there are differences between the House and the Senate in legal authority, influence, and politics. The House originates many bills and has impeachment authority while the Senate confirms presidential appointments, ratifies treaties, and conducts impeachment trials. Influence is more centralized in the House, which has a hierarchical organizational structure, formal rules and limits on debate, and a more powerful leadership structure. The Senate is less centralized, less formal, and has more flexible rules, particularly in permitting extended debate. There is less policy specialization in the Senate and more influence on foreign affairs. Politically, the Senate is more prestigious, is an arena for grooming potential presidential candidates, and is considered more competitive since the partisan balance of power is more evident than in the House.

The procedural steps for enacting legislation involve considerable overlapping and duplication between the two houses. Bills can be introduced in either chamber; they are usually reviewed separately by subcommittees and committees in both houses, are debated separately on the floor, and require separate voting majorities for approval. Separate two-thirds votes are needed to override presidential vetoes. The principal differences between the House and the Senate involve the critical legislative clearance and scheduling function of the House Rules Committee (which the Senate does not have) and the Senate custom of extended debate. Unlimited debates or filibusters cannot occur in the House due to the time restrictions placed on bills by the Rules Committee.

CONGRESSIONAL POLITICS

How is Congress organized to facilitate the lawmaking process? Two major considerations are the committee system, which disperses and decentralizes decision making, and the party leadership structure, which has a more centralizing impact. Congress does most of its work by committees—due to the volume and technical complexity of bills. There are four types of committees: standing, select, joint, and conference. The standing committees are permanent and most important in shaping bills before they are voted on by the full House or Senate. Select committees are established for specific investigations, for example, Iran-Contra. Joint committees consist of senators and representatives, for example, the Joint Economic Committee. Conference committees between the House and the Senate are needed to resolve differences between bills after House and Senate floor votes. Chairpersons of standing committees are usually selected by party leaders or caucuses on the basis of seniority or longest continuous service on the committee. The congressional caucuses consist of all members of a political party (Democrats or Republicans) who meet to select party leaders or to decide the party's position on proposed legislation.

Party leaders are selected by the majority and minority party members or caucuses at the beginning of each two-year congressional session. The two key leaders are the speaker of the House and the Senate majority leader. Of the two, the speaker has more influence because this leader is a combination of both chief parliamentary officer and political chief, while the Senate majority leader has only the latter role. The speaker presides over the House, recognizes members who wish to speak, and rules on parliamentary and procedural issues. As political leader, the speaker plays a major role in selecting committee members and chairpersons, assigns bills to committees, and appoints or influences the appointment of party legislative leaders and their staffs. Among these aides are the majority leader (chief scheduler of floor votes on bills) and party whips who round up members for crucial floor votes.

The Senate majority leader lacks the speaker's presiding role since the Constitution assigns this function to the vice president, who can only vote to break a deadlock in the Senate. Most vice presidents rarely appear in the Senate except for scheduled votes on anticipated crucial issues.

Consequently, the Senate majority party selects the most senior member to preside as president *pro tem* for each two year session of Congress. This is in reality an honorary position. Actual presiding tasks are rotated among other Senators of the majority party. The Senate majority leader is aided by party whips. Also, the minority parties in both houses have leadership structures similar to the majority parties'.

In the 102d Congress (1990–1991), the Democrats controlled the House 268–167, a 101-seat or 62 percent advantage. The Senate was also controlled by the Democrats, 55–45. The House Speaker was Thomas Foley of Washington and the majority leader was Richard Gephardt of Missouri. David Bonior of Michigan became majority whip in 1991 after William Gray of Pennsylvania resigned from Congress.

The House minority leader was Robert Michel of Illinois. Newt Gingrich of Georgia served as House Republican whip. Representative Jerry Lewis of California served as chair of the House Republican Conference (caucus).

The Senate majority leader was George Mitchell of Maine. Wendell Ford of Kentucky was chief whip; and David Pryor of Arkansas served as secretary of the Democratic Conference (caucus). Robert Dole of Kansas served as Senate minority leader for the Republicans, assisted by Alan Simpson of Wyoming, who was minority whip. Thad Cochran of Mississippi chaired the Senate Republican Conference (caucus).

CONGRESS AND PUBLIC POLICY

How does Congress influence public policy? What is the nature of legislative-executive interaction? Presidential leadership is an important aspect of legislative policy making. Over the past fifty years, the most effective presidential leaders of Congress have been Franklin Roosevelt, Lyndon Johnson, and Ronald Reagan. Roosevelt established many new agencies, rather than delegating tasks to existing departments, in order to create thousands of patronage jobs for congressional constituents and to consolidate his hold on local Democratic party organizations. President Johnson was famous for his direct persuasion with legislators. The Johnson technique included forceful arguments and total familiarity with legislators' backgrounds and district and state needs. Reagan combined the carrot-and-stick approach. He frequently used television as a means of persuading legislators on key issues. He asked legislators what they needed in return for votes on the 1981 budget cuts. Military contracts were awarded to cooperative legislators. He cultivated congressional support by appearing on Capitol Hill and meeting frequently with party leaders and the rank-and-file members. Reagan also threatened to campaign against conservative Democrats who opposed his budget cuts.

As a consequence of strong presidential leadership, Congress was often accused of being a weak second cousin to the chief executive on major legislative initiatives. When it followed presidential advice, Congress was considered a mere rubber stamp of executive will. When Congress opposed the president, it became a convenient scapegoat for the president to blame for not achieving his goals. This situation persisted for nearly twenty-five years after World War II.

The Vietnam War and Watergate changed the environment of executive-legislative relations. Congress became more assertive in restricting the "imperial presidencies" of Lyndon Johnson and Richard Nixon. The 1973 War Powers Act limited presidential commitment of U.S. troops abroad and the House Judiciary Committee voted articles of impeachment leading to President Nixon's resignation in 1974.

According to Kenneth Shepsle in Article 36, Congress has changed dramatically over the past thirty years. Much of this change has occurred through institutional reforms promoted by House Democrats. Congress is no longer balanced between constituencies, committees, and coalitions as it was during the 1940s and 1950s. The earlier textbook model of Congress included powerful committee chairs, a strong seniority rule, and little influence by recently elected members.

This changed particularly in the post-Watergate era of the mid-1970s. House Democrats decentralized power by giving privileges and resources to subcommittees, reduced the power of senior committee chairs, and increased the policy role of the Democratic Caucus. In 1974, Speaker Thomas P. O'Neill gained new authority in appointing committee members and referring bills to committees.

Consequently, the House Democrats' reforms were both decentralizing and centralizing. Influence shifted away from committee chairs to subcommittees and individual members who built their own legislative enterprises. At the same time, more centralized power was conferred on the Speaker and away from powerful committees and senior chairs. Decentralization and collegiality complicate legislative decision making. Arrangements are difficult when the needs of individual legislators must be accommodated with overall policy decisions. Consequently, the legislative process has slowed down considerably and produced a great deal of frustration both within Congress and between the legislative and executive branches.

CONGRESSIONAL ROLES

Congress is increasingly reluctant to tackle controversial issues. This became particularly evident in 1990–91 when President Bush sent U.S. troops abroad to fight in Operation Desert Storm. The president's popularity ratings soared in public opinion polls. George Bush's approach toward congressional Democrats is not one of accommodation, particularly on issues of social policy. Bush engaged in heated battles with Congress over affirmative action, crime and gun control, abortion, and family leave (to require employers with 50 or more employees to provide 12 weeks of unpaid medical leave per year for newborn children or elder care) in 1990–91. He vetoed more legislative bills in his first two years in office than either Jimmy Carter or Ronald Reagan.

In Article 37, John Barry explains that congressional roles are geared more to internal accommodation than challenging the president. The House Democrats are more concerned with protecting institutional power than developing a broad policy agenda. To get ahead in the House, individual members need to be reliable, honest in their voting commitments, and have a knowledge of procedural technicalities.

Barry points out that House Republicans, who have been in the minority since the 1950s, are increasingly rebellious and seek to embarrass the Democrats. Also, House members use lobbyists to achieve individual objectives and build a power base. Getting reelected seems to be the principal goal of most House members. The fear of losing at the polls is a primary motivation to be cautious and not make enemies.

LIMITING CONGRESSIONAL INCUMBENCY

Public support for Congress is particularly low. According to surveys, the proportion of people having confidence in Congress as an institution has declined to the point where it has the least support of any of the three federal branches of government. Interestingly, the same surveys show that citizens often approve of the performance of their own representatives and senators. There is a widespread belief that Congress has difficulties in reaching important policy decisions. The legislative process is considered highly complex and unwieldy. Congress has been a frequent target of presidential criticisms when it does not act on his major initiatives. Also, the job of Congress has been made difficult by the increasing workload in legislative committees and the personal attention required for constituency services. Most senators' offices are not efficiently organized.

Hendrik Hertzberg in Article 38 offers a strong argument to reform Congress by imposing constitutional term limits of twelve years (six two-year House terms, and two six-year Senate terms). In 1991, President Bush endorsed such a proposal as a way of depicting Congress as the source of most of the country's problems.

Thomas Cronin, a political scientist at Colorado College, has offered a series of rebuttals to proponents of congressional term limits.[2] His first argument is that two-thirds of Congress has changed in the past twelve years. Second, Cronin argues that the motives behind the proposal are based more on considerations of power than on fairness or competition. Term limits have been advocated principally by Republicans who have been unable to gain control of the House for decades. Republicans promoted the Twenty-Second Amendment for a two-term limit on the presidency after Franklin D. Roosevelt served four terms. Finally, and most important, Cronin argues that term limits would shift power away from Congress and to lobbyists, political action committees, and experienced executive branch players.

Cronin may be correct that term limits are an "illusory quick-fix for a symptom." In his view, legislative problems are not the result of incumbency, but of "decaying parties, rotten campaign finance arrangements, and gerrymandered and uncompetitive legislative districts."

State and local anti-incumbency fever began to spread in 1990. Oklahoma, California and Colorado voters approved term limits for state officials. Kansas City, Missouri, and San Jose, California, voters did the same for city officials. Legislative bills and ballot initiative petition efforts for term limits began in Massachusetts, Michigan, Ohio, Oregon and Washington.

All of these efforts reflect a basic concern about the effectiveness of state legislatures and local councils. Whether or not anti-incumbency begins to take hold and reaches Congress remains to be seen.

NOTES

1. Ross Webber, "U.S. Senators: See How They Run," *The Wharton Magazine,* vol. 5, No. 2 (1980).
2. Thomas E. Cronin, "Term Limits—A Symptom, Not a Cure," *New York Times,* 23 December 1990, p. E11, col. 1-5.

Legislator—Constituency Roles

34
The Rise of the Washington Establishment
Morris P. Fiorina

Individual legislators face a variety of pressures from their home constituencies, interest groups, the president, and the bureaucracy. What is the relationship between legislators' roles and the various decisions they make? Morris Fiorina argues that representatives and senators are part of the Washington establishment. Their major objective is reelection. This is facilitated by three major activities: lawmaking, pork-barreling, and casework. How do legislators respond to the pressures placed on them? What are the differences between constituency casework and committee responsibilities? What are the most important constituency influences affecting a legislator's record, especially when he or she seeks reelection? In his concluding section, Fiorina reconsiders his earlier findings about legislator-constituency roles and asks: Why is constituency service not the only factor in congressional elections? Why is constituency service not the only explanation for House incumbency advantage?

DRAMATIS PERSONAE

I assume that most people most of the time act in their own self-interest. This is not to say that human beings seek only to amass tangible wealth but rather to say that human beings seek to achieve their own ends—tangible and intangible—rather than the ends of their fellow men. I do not condemn such behavior nor do I condone it (although I rather sympathize with Thoreau's comment that "if I knew for certainty that a man was coming to my house with the conscious design of doing me good, I should run for my life").[1] I only claim that political and economic theories which presume self-interested behavior will prove to be more widely applicable than those which build on more altruistic assumptions.

What does the axiom imply when used in the specific context of this book, a context peopled by congressmen, bureaucrats, and voters? I assume that the primary goal of the typical congressman is reelection. Over and above the $57,000 salary plus "perks" and outside money, the office of congressman carries with it prestige, excitement, and power. It is a seat in the cockpit of government. But in order to retain the status, excitement, and power (not to mention more tangible things) of office, the congressman must win reelection every two years. Even those congressmen genuinely concerned with good public policy must achieve

From Morris P. Fiorina, *Congress: Keystone of the Washington Establishment* (New Haven, Connecticut: Yale University Press, 1989), pp. 37–47, 98–101. Copyright © 1989 by Yale University.

reelection in order to continue their work. Whether narrowly self-serving or more publicly oriented, the individual congressman finds reelection to be at least a necessary condition for the achievement of his goals.

Moreover, there is a kind of natural selection process at work in the electoral arena. On the average, those congressmen who are nonprimarily interested in reelection will not achieve reelection as often as those who are interested. We, the people, help to weed out congressmen whose primary motivation is not reelection. We admire politicians who courageously adopt the aloof role of the disinterested statesman, but we vote for those politicians who follow our wishes and do us favors.

What about the bureaucrats? A specification of their goals is somewhat more controversial—those who speak of appointed officials as public servants obviously take a more benign view than those who speak of them as bureaucrats. The literature provides ample justification for asserting that most bureaucrats wish to protect and nurture their agencies. The typical bureaucrat can be expected to seek to expand his agency in terms of personnel, budget, and mission. One's status in Washington (again, not to mention more tangible things) is roughly proportional to the importance of the operation one oversees. And the sheer size of the operation is taken to be a measure of importance. As with congressmen, the specified goals apply even to those bureaucrats who genuinely believe in their agency's mission. If they believe in the efficacy of their programs, they naturally wish to expand them and add new ones. All of this requires more money and more people. The genuinely committed bureaucrat is just as likely to seek to expand his agency as the proverbial empire-builder.[2]

And what of the third element in the equation, us? What do we, the voters who support the Washington system, strive for? Each of us wishes to receive a maximum of benefits from government for the minimum cost. This goal suggests maximum government efficiency, on the one hand, but it also suggests mutual exploitation on the other. Each of us favors an arrangement in which our fellow citizens pay for our benefits.

With these brief descriptions of the cast of characters in hand, let us proceed.

TAMMANY HALL GOES TO WASHINGTON

What should we expect from a legislative body composed of individuals whose first priority is their continued tenure in office? We should expect, first, that the normal activities of its members are those calculated to enhance their chances of reelection. And we should expect, second, that the members would devise and maintain institutional arrangements which facilitate their electoral activities. . . .

For most of the twentieth century, congressmen have engaged in a mix of three kinds of activities: lawmaking, pork barreling, and casework. Congress is first and foremost a lawmaking body, at least according to constitutional theory. In every postwar session Congress "considers" thousands of bills and resolutions, many hundreds of which are brought to a record vote (over 500 in each chamber in the 93d Congress). Naturally the critical consideration in taking a position for the record is the maximization of approval in the home district. If the district is unaffected by and unconcerned with the matter at hand, the congressman may then take into account the general welfare of the country. (This sounds cynical, but remember that "profiles in courage" are sufficiently rare that their occurrence inspires books and articles.) Abetted by political scientists of the pluralist school, politicians have propounded an ideology which maintains that the good of the country on any given issue is simply what is best for a majority of congressional districts. This ideology provides a philosophical justification for what congressmen do while acting in their own self-interest.

A second activity favored by congressmen consists of efforts to bring home the bacon to their districts. Many popular articles have been written about the pork barrel, a term originally applied to rivers and harbors legislation but now generalized to cover all manner of federal largesse.[3] Congressmen consider new dams, federal buildings, sewage treatment plants, urban renewal projects, etc. as sweet plums to be plucked. Federal projects are highly visible, their economic impact is easily detected by constituents, and sometimes they even produce something of value to the district. The average constituent may have some trouble translating his congressman's vote on some civil rights issue into a change in his personal welfare. But the workers hired and supplies purchased in connection with a big federal project provide benefits that are widely appreciated. The historical importance congressmen attach to the pork barrel is reflected in the rules of the House. That body accords certain classes of legislation "privileged" status: they may come directly to the floor without passing through the Rules Committee, a traditional graveyard for legislation. What kinds of legislation are privileged? Taxing and spending bills, for one: the government's power to raise and spend money must be kept relatively unfettered. But in addition, the omnibus rivers and harbors bills of the Public Works Committee and public lands bills from the Interior Committee share privileged status. The House will allow a civil rights or defense procurement or environmental bill to languish in the Rules Committee, but it takes special precautions to insure that nothing

slows down the approval of dams and irrigation projects.

A third major activity takes up perhaps as much time as the other two combined. Traditionally, constituents appeal to their Congressman for myriad favors and services. Sometimes only information is needed, but often constituents request that their congressman intervene in the internal workings of federal agencies to affect a decision in a favorable way, to reverse an adverse decision, or simply to speed up the glacial bureaucratic process. On the basis of extensive personal interviews with congressmen, Charles Clapp writes:

> Denied a favorable ruling by the bureaucracy on a matter of direct concern to him, puzzled or irked by delays in obtaining a decision, confused by the administrative maze through which he is directed to proceed, or ignorant of whom to write, a constituent may turn to his congressman for help. These letters offer great potential for political benefit to the congressman since they affect the constituent personally. If the legislator can be of assistance, he may gain a firm ally; if he is indifferent, he may even lose votes.[4]

Actually congressmen are in an almost unique position in our system, a position shared only with high-level members of the executive branch. Congressmen possess the power to expedite and influence bureaucratic decisions. This capability flows directly from congressional control over what bureaucrats value most: higher budgets and new program authorizations. In a very real sense each congressman is a monopoly supplier of bureaucratic unsticking services for his district.

Every year the federal budget passes through the appropriations committees of Congress. Generally these committees make perfunctory cuts. But on occasion they vent displeasure on an agency and leave it bleeding all over the Capitol. The most extreme case of which I am aware came when the House committee took away the entire budget of the Division of Labor Standards in 1947 (some of the budget was restored elsewhere in the appropriations process). Deep and serious cuts are made occasionally, and the threat of such cuts keeps most agencies attentive to congressional wishes. Professors Richard Fenno and Aaron Wildavsky have provided extensive documentary and interview evidence of the great respect (and even terror) federal bureaucrats show for the House Appropriations Committee.[5] Moreover, the bureaucracy must keep coming back to Congress to have its old programs reauthorized and new ones added. Again, most such decisions are perfunctory, but exceptions are sufficiently frequent that bureaucrats do not forget the basis of their agencies' existence. For example, the Law Enforcement Assistance Administration (LEAA) and the Food Stamps Program had no easy time of it this last Congress (94th). The bureaucracy needs congressional approval in order to survive, let alone expand. Thus, when a congressman calls about some minor bureaucratic decision or regulation, the bureaucracy considers his accommodation a small price to pay for the goodwill its cooperation will produce, particularly if he has any connection to the substantive committee or the appropriations subcommittee to which it reports.

From the standpoint of capturing voters, the congressman's lawmaking activities differ in two important respects from his pork-barrel and casework activities. First, programmatic actions are inherently controversial. Unless his district is homogeneous, a congressman will find his district divided on many major issues. Thus when he casts a vote, introduces a piece of nontrivial legislation, or makes a speech with policy content he will displease some elements of his district. Some constituents may applaud the congressman's civil rights record, but others believe integration is going too fast. Some support foreign aid, while others believe

it's money poured down a rathole. Some advocate economic equality, others stew over welfare cheaters. On such policy matters the congressman can expect to make friends as well as enemies. Presumably he will behave so as to maximize the excess of the former over the latter, but nevertheless a policy stand will generally make some enemies.

In contrast, the pork barrel and casework are relatively less controversial. New federal projects bring jobs, shiny new facilities, and general economic prosperity, or so people believe. Snipping ribbons at the dedication of a new post office or dam is a much more pleasant pursuit than disposing of a constitutional amendment on abortion. Republicans and Democrats, conservatives and liberals, all generally prefer a richer district to a poorer one. Of course, in recent years the river damming and stream-bed straightening activities of the Army Corps of Engineers have aroused some opposition among environmentalists. Congressmen happily reacted by absorbing the opposition and adding environmentalism to the pork barrel: water treatment plants are currently a hot congressional item.

Casework is even less controversial. Some poor, aggrieved constituent becomes enmeshed in the tentacles of an evil bureaucracy and calls upon Congressman St. George to do battle with the dragon. Again Clapp writes;

> A person who has a reasonable complaint or query is regarded as providing an opportunity rather than as adding an extra burden to an already busy office. The party affiliation of the individual even when known to be different from that of the congressman does not normally act as a deterrent to action. Some legislators have built their reputations and their majorities on a program of service to all constituents irrespective of party. Regularly, voters affiliated with the opposition in other contests lend strong support to the lawmaker whose intervention has helped them in their struggle with the bureaucracy.[6]

Even following the revelation of sexual improprieties, Wayne Hays won his Ohio Democratic primary by a two-to-one margin. According to a *Los Angeles Times* feature story, Hays's constituency base was built on a foundation of personal service to constituents:

> They receive help in speeding up bureaucratic action on various kinds of federal assistance—black lung benefits to disabled miners and their families, Social Security payments, veterans' benefits and passports.
>
> Some constituents still tell with pleasure of how Hays stormed clear to the seventh floor of the State Department and into Secretary of State Dean Rusk's office to demand, successfully, the quick issuance of a passport to an Ohioan.[7]

Practicing politicians will tell you that word of mouth is still the most effective mode of communication. News of favors to constituents gets around and no doubt is embellished in the process.

In sum, when considering the benefits of his programmatic activities, the congressman must tote up gains and losses to arrive at a net profit. Pork barreling and casework, however, are basically pure profit.

A second way in which programmatic activities differ from casework and the pork barrel is the difficulty of assigning responsibility to the former as compared with the latter. No congressman can seriously claim that he is responsible for the 1964 Civil Rights Act, the ABM, or the 1972 Revenue Sharing Act. Most constituents do have some vague notion that their congressman is only one of hundreds and their senator one of an even hundred. Even committee chairmen have a difficult time claiming credit for a piece of major legislation, let alone a rank-and-file congressman. Ah, but casework, and the pork barrel. In dealing with the bureaucracy, the congressman is not merely one vote of 435. Rather, he is a nonpartisan power, someone whose phone calls

snap an office to attention. He is not kept on hold. The constituent who receives aid believes that his congressman and his congressman alone got results. Similarly, congressmen find it easy to claim credit for federal projects awarded their districts. The congressman may have instigated the proposal for the project in the first place, issued regular progress reports, and ultimately announced the award through his office. Maybe he can't claim credit for the 1965 Voting Rights Act, but he can take credit for Littletown's spanking new sewage treatment plant.

Overall then, programmatic activities are dangerous (controversial), on the one hand, and programmatic accomplishments are difficult to claim credit for, on the other. While less exciting, casework and pork barreling are both safe and profitable. For a reelection-oriented congressman the choice is obvious.

The key to the rise of the Washington establishment (and the vanishing marginals) is the following observation: *the growth of an activist federal government has stimulated a change in the mix of congressional activities.* Specifically, a lesser proportion of congressional effort is now going into programmatic activities and a greater proportion into pork-barrel and casework activities. As a result, today's congressmen make relatively fewer enemies and relatively more friends among the people of their districts.

To elaborate, a basic fact of life in the twentieth-century America is the growth of the federal role and its attendant bureaucracy. Bureaucracy is the characteristic mode of delivering public goods and services. Ceteris paribus, the more the government attempts to do for people, the more extensive a bureaucracy it creates. As the scope of government expands, more and more citizens find themselves in direct contact with the federal government. Consider the rise in such contacts upon passage of the Social Security Act, work relief projects and other New Deal programs. Consider the millions of additional citizens touched by the veterans' programs of the post-war period. Consider the untold numbers whom the Great Society and its aftermath brought face to face with the federal government. In 1930 the federal bureaucracy was small and rather distant from the everyday concerns of Americans. By 1975 it was neither small nor distant.

As the years have passed, more and more citizens and groups have found themselves dealing with the federal bureaucracy. They may be seeking positive actions—eligibility for various benefits and awards of government grants. Or they may be seeking relief from the costs imposed by bureaucratic regulations—on working conditions, racial and sexual quotas, market restrictions, and numerous other subjects. While not malevolent, bureaucracies make mistakes, both of commission and omission, and normal attempts at redress often meet with unresponsiveness and inflexibility and sometimes seeming incorrigibility. Whatever the problem, the citizen's congressman is a source of succor. The greater the scope of government activity, the greater the demand for his services.

Private monopolists can regulate the demand for their product by raising or lowering the price. Congressmen have no such (legal) option. When the demand for their services rises, they have no real choice except to meet that demand—to supply more bureaucratic unsticking services—so long as they would rather be elected than unelected. This vulnerability to escalating constituency demands is largely academic, though. I seriously doubt that congressmen resist their gradual transformation from national legislators to errand boy-ombudsmen. As we have noted, casework is all profit. Congressmen have buried proposals to relieve the casework burden by establishing a national ombudsman or Congressman Reuss's proposed Administrative Counsel of the Congress. One of the congressmen interviewed by Clapp stated:

> Before I came to Washington I used to think that it might be nice if the individual states had administrative arms here that would take care of necessary liaison between citizens and the national government. But a congressman running for reelection is interested in building fences by providing personal services. The system is set to reelect incumbents regardless of party, and incumbents wouldn't dream of giving any of this service function away to any subagency. As an elected member I feel the same way.[8]

In fact, it is probable that at least some congressmen deliberately stimulate the demand for their bureaucratic fixit services. . . . Recall that the new Republican in district A travels about his district saying:

> I'm your man in Washington. What are your problems? How can I help you?

And in district B, did the demand for the congressman's services rise so much between 1962 and 1964 that a "regiment" of constituency staff became necessary? Or, having access to the regiment, did the new Democrat stimulate the demand to which he would apply his regiment?

In addition to greatly increased casework, let us not forget that the growth of the federal role has also greatly expanded the federal pork barrel. The creative pork barreler need not limit himself to dams and post offices—rather old-fashioned interests. Today, creative congressmen can cadge LEAA money for the local police, urban renewal and housing money for local politicians, educational program grants for the local education bureaucracy. And there are sewage treatment plants, worker training and retraining programs, health services, and programs for the elderly. The pork barrel is full to overflowing. The conscientious congressman can stimulate applications for federal assistance (the sheer number of programs makes it difficult for local officials to stay current with the possibilities), put in a good word during consideration, and announce favorable decisions amid great fanfare.

In sum, everyday decisions by a large and growing federal bureaucracy bestow significant tangible benefits and impose significant tangible costs. Congressmen can affect these decisions. Ergo, the more decisions the bureaucracy has the opportunity to make, the more opportunities there are for the congressman to build up credits.

The nature of the Washington system is now quite clear. Congressmen (typically the majority Democrats) earn electoral credits by establishing various federal programs (the minority Republicans typically earn credits by fighting the good fight). The legislation is drafted in very general terms, so some agency, existing or newly established, must translate a vague policy mandate into a functioning program, a process that necessitates the promulgation of numerous rules and regulations and, incidentally, the trampling of numerous toes. At the next stage, aggrieved and/or hopeful constituents petition their congressman to intervene in the complex (or at least obscure) decision processes of the bureaucracy. The cycle closes when the congressman lends a sympathetic ear, piously denounces the evils of bureaucracy, intervenes in the latter's decisions, and rides a grateful electorate to ever more impressive electoral showings. Congressmen take credit coming and going. They are the alpha and the omega.

The popular frustration with the permanent government in Washington is partly justified, but to a considerable degree it is misplaced resentment. *Congress is the linchpin of the Washington establishment.* The bureaucracy serves as a convenient light-ning rod for public frustration and a convenient whipping boy for congressmen. But so long as the bureaucracy accommodates congressmen, the latter will oblige with ever larger budgets and grants of authority. Congress does not just react to big government— it creates it. All of Washington prospers. More and more bureaucrats promulgate more and more regulations and dispense more and more money. Fewer and fewer congressmen suffer electoral defeat. Elements of the electorate benefit from government programs, and all of the electorate is eligible for ombudsman services. But the general, long-term welfare of the United States is no more than an incidental by-product of the system.

CONFUSIONS AND CLARIFICATIONS

In public, authors graciously take responsibility for the misunderstandings of readers. In private, they complain about careless reading or even malicious misreading. Over the years I have encountered a number of common misunderstandings of the arguments in *Keystone.* Some of these are primarily the fault of the reader, while others are primarily my fault.

Clarification 1:
Constituency Service Is Not the Only
Factor in Congressional Elections

On several occasions critics have offered examples of elections they believe were determined by presidential coattails, money, issues, a TV commercial, or some other factor than constituency service. Certainly, that is so: many factors affect the voting in House elections. *Keystone* never suggested otherwise. As explained in chapter 1, the average margins of House incumbents rose about 5 percent—from 60 to 65 percent—between the 1950s and the 1970s. I argued that the expansion of constituency service was a likely explanation for that rise, *not* for the entire 65 percent of the vote garnered by the average incumbent. Moreover, chapter 5 reiterated that the actual electoral change we were seeking to explain was "marginal"—about 5 percent, clearly less than 10 percent.

Constituency service is *not* the sole or even the most important factor in House elections. For one thing, party identification still determines more votes than any other single factor. If I were a member of Congress I would surely rather have a district with a 70-30 registration edge for my party than any number of offices and staff.

Nothing just said, however, denigrates the electoral importance of constituency service. Two points should be kept in mind. First, politicians understandably pay disproportionate attention to smaller electoral factors that are under their control—such as constituency service—than to larger electoral factors that are beyond their control—such as the partisan composition of their districts. Second, small electoral differences and changes can have large political consequences. In particular, important things happen in the neighborhood of 50 percent. As margins rise above 50 percent, incumbents become less likely to be swept from office by an electoral triumph for the other party's presidential candidate. When margins rise, incumbents may look that much more formidable to potential primary and general election challengers, some fraction of whom are discouraged from making the race.

In sum, constituency service grew in electoral importance between the 1950s and 1970s, while party and other factors declined. Whether the relative importance of constituency service vis-à-vis other factors increased from, say, 10 to 20 percent of the explanation of the vote, or from 40 to 50 percent, is not a question I addressed. And given the lack of suitable data for the period before the increase, it remains a question without a precise answer.

Clarification 2:
Constituency Service
Is Not the Only Explanation of
the House Incumbency Advantage

The misconception underlying this second clarification is similar to that underlying the first, though I am more to blame here. When *Keystone* was written the advantage of incumbency was believed to be in the range of 5-8 percent. I considered several explanations—advertising, behavioral change by voters, redistricting—and concluded that the evidence failed to support them. Increases in constituency service activities were offered as an alternative explanation. I did not claim that service was the only possible explanation, just that it was the only one still in the race.

While I still believe that increased constituency service can easily account for increases of 5-8 percent in incumbents' margins, additional research has suggested other possible explanations for incumbent strength. Before discussing these, let us note that although redistricting arguments continue to have some adherents, especially among Republicans, careful academic studies continue to find no systematic advantage to incumbents from redistricting. Similarly, there is still no solid evidence that incumbent strength reflects sheer name recognition produced by advertising. Incumbent congressmen are no better known today than they were a generation ago. If it leaves a mark at all, advertising probably does so on the *substance* of voter perceptions.

Three additional sources of incumbent strength have been suggested. First, modern information and communication technology have enhanced the capacity of politicians to track the sentiments of constituents and target specific audiences with suitable messages. While strong parties might constrain the ability of their members to adopt this "every man for himself" strategy, today's parties are less of a constraint than they were even a generation ago. True, the available evidence indicates that only a small minority of constituents have any information on the issue stands of their representatives, but the size of that minority is larger than it was a generation ago, and the influence of issues on its vote is clear. Thus, carefully tailored issue stances probably contribute in some measure to the strength of contemporary incumbents.

A second seemingly obvious source of incumbent strength is money. Congressional races have gotten much more expensive over time, and the gap between incumbent and challenger finances has widened. I will discuss PACs in a later chapter, but two points should be made here. First, the absolute level of challenger spending appears to be more important than the relative differential. Because all incumbents begin with an impressive level of taxpayer-provided resources (staffs, offices, communications technology, and so forth), campaign money appears to have lower marginal benefit for them than for challengers. Indeed, very high levels of incumbent spending can indicate weakness rather than strength: the incumbent goes all out to meet a serious challenge.

Second, whatever the importance of campaign funding today, PACs and the explosion in campaign expenditures are a mid- to late-1970s phenomenon. The changes in congressional elections discussed in *Keystone* were concentrated in the mid- to late-1960s. So, while any discussion of incumbent strength in contemporary elections must deal with money, the importance of money for the arguments I advanced twelve years ago is probably lower.

A third explanation for the advantage of incumbency is different from most of the others in not focusing on incumbents. According to this explanation, challenger weakness not incumbent strength, is the key. The genesis of

this explanation lies in late-1970s research that revealed how poorly challengers were known by constituents, how little money they spent, and how few of them displayed any apparent qualifications for office.[9]

One immediate observation is that challenger weakness at a single point in time—the 1970s—does not explain the *rise* in the advantage of incumbency. Incumbents on average have handily dispatched their opponents throughout the twentieth century. Thus, to support the challenger weakness argument one must show at the least that challenger quality declined *over the same period that incumbent margins increased.* The little data that exists does not support this suggestion. There is a plausible argument why strong challenges may have declined in frequency, though proponents of the challenger weakness argument have not made it. As party organizations declined relative to individual candidate organizations, challengers were left without a natural base of support and resources—the base formerly provided by party organizations. While incumbents were similarly deprived, they were able to vote themselves office, staff, and communications resources to replace whatever they lost from party sources. . . .

A second observation concerns the logical status of the challenger weakness explanation. To some extent challenger strength is endogenous, to use a technical term. What it means is that the strength of challengers is in part determined by the strength of incumbents. An incumbent with a history of comfortable margins, an overflowing war chest, and a reputation for invincibility scares away ambitious prosecutors and state legislators who are natural antagonists. (The image is that of wolves cowering before a grizzly.) In contrast, the incumbent with declining margins, a shortage of funds, and a reputation for ineptitude attracts strong challengers. (The image is that of sharks circling a thrashing presence in the water.) While attempts to verify this argument empirically have been inconclusive, every observer of electoral politics will attest to the prevalence of such beliefs.

NOTES

1. Henry David Thoreau, *Walden* (London: Walter Scott, n.d.), p. 72.
2. For a discussion of the goals of bureaucrats, see William Niskanen, *Bureaucracy and Representative Government* (Chicago: Aldine-Atherton, 1971).
3. The traditional pork barrel is the subject of an excellent treatment by John Ferejohn. See his *Pork Barrel Politics: Rivers and Harbors Legislation, 1947–1968* (Stanford: Stanford University Press, 1974).
4. Charles Clapp, *The Congressman: His Job As He Sees It* (Washington, D.C.: Brookings Institution, 1963), p. 84.
5. Richard Fenno, *The Power of The Purse* (Boston: Little, Brown, 1966); Aaron Wildavsky, *The Politics of the Budgetary Process*, 2d ed. (Boston: Little, Brown, 1974).
6. Clapp, *The Congressman: His Job As He Sees It*, p. 84.
7. "Hays Improves Rapidly from Overdose," *Los Angeles Times*, June 12, 1976, part 1, p. 19.
8. Clapp, *The Congressman: His Job As He Sees It*, p. 94.
9. Barbara Hinckley, "The American Voter in Congressional Elections," *American Political Science Review* 74 (1980): 641–50; Lyn Ragsdale, "Incumbent Popularity, Challenger Invisibility, and Congressional Voters," *Legislative Studies Quarterly* 6 (1981): 201–18.

The Legislative Process

35
The Longest-Running Game in Town
Marjorie Hunter and Tom Bloom

HOW TO PLAY

Enacting legislation is hard work, often frustrating and time-consuming. With the big push now on in the 99th Congress for House and Senate action on a number of major bills, here is a game that shows just how intricate and fraught with pitfalls the legislative process can be.

Some idea of the difficulties can be seen in the fact that in the 98th Congress (1983–84) 12,201 bills were introduced but only 2,670 were adopted by both the Senate and the House. Twenty-four of the bills that made it through both houses were vetoed by the President. Congress was then able to override just two of those vetoes.

To play the game presented here, you need coins for markers and a die. Any number of people may play. Roll the die to determine order of turns.

The game begins with each player choosing a topic and offering a bill for introduction. Then the player with the first turn places a marker on "Start" and rolls the die to determine how many squares to advance. Other players follow in the same manner until someone completes the course.

Sore losers may take their appeals to the House parliamentarian, William Holmes Brown, who vouches for the game's accurate reflection of the difficulties legislation can encounter on Capitol Hill. But he also states that this game provides insight into only basic steps that a bill might go through. There are numerous subtleties and other variables, such as a bill's having to go through two or more committees, as well as a seemingly endless series of points of order that can be raised along the way.

The complexity of it all can best be seen in the fact that the current volume of "Rules of the House," including precedents and refinements, runs to more than a thousand pages, while the Senate rules take up several volumes and many hundreds of pages.

May the lucky player reach the end unscathed. In real life, most legislators don't.

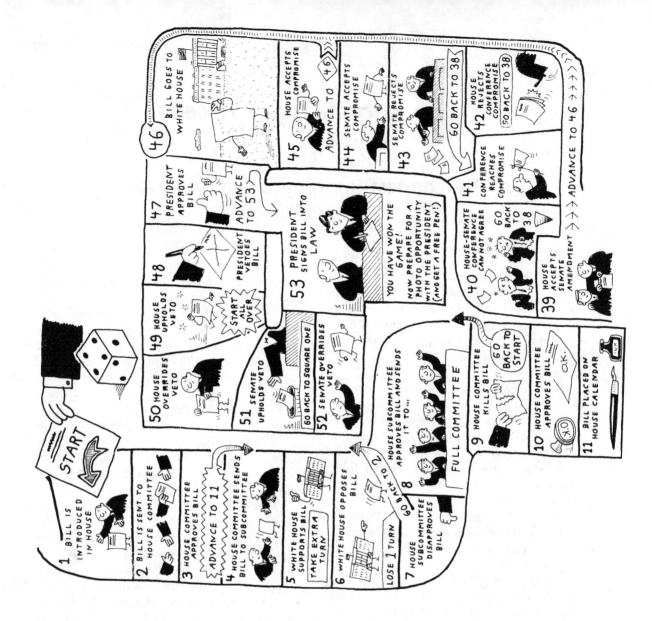

Congressional Politics

36
The Changing Textbook Congress
Kenneth A. Shepsle

Shepsle, from Harvard University, effectively compares and contrasts the Congress of the 1950s and 1960s with the reforms of the post-Watergate era. He argues that the earlier "textbook Congress" was committee-based and had a balance between geography, jurisdiction, and partisanship. How did this model of Congress begin to change in 1958? What does he mean by the "incumbency advantage"? Several reforms were instituted by the House Democrats beginning in the 1970s. Why were the reformers able to bring about these changes? What were the specific reforms made in the House? How was committee power reduced? What were the results of such changes? Shepsle also observes that some of the reforms resulted in recentralizing power. How did this occur? Which four power centers benefit from the 1970 reforms? Considering 1980s developments, what are Shepsle's observations about a new textbook Congress?

When scholars talk about Congress to one another, their students, or the public, they often have a stylized version in mind, a textbook Congress characterized by a few main tendencies and described in broad terms. This is not to say that they are incapable of filling in fine-grained detail, making distinctions, or describing change. But at the core of their descriptions and distinctions are approximations, caricatures, and generalities. They are always incomplete and somewhat inaccurate, but still they consist of robust regularities. This textbook Congress is a specification of equilibrium practices and tendencies; the portrait endures as long as the generalities on which it is based hold true. Major revisions in the textbooks occur when events and practices change the equilibrium and some schol-

ars offer a new vision that more nearly resembles current practice. The new textbook description becomes persuasive when things settle into a new pattern.

The textbook Congress I have in mind is the one that emerged from World War II and the Legislative Reorganization Act of 1946. Its main features persisted until the mid-1960s; its images remained in writings on Congress well into the 1970s. Scholarship on Congress during this period was widely influenced by the behavioral revolution in political science and, more particularly, by the Study of Congress project. Sponsored by the American Political Science Association, the Social Science Research Council, and several other foundations, the project produced a number of descriptive

From John E. Chubb and Paul Peterson, editors, *Can the Government Govern?* (Washington, D.C.: The Brookings Institution, 1989), pp. 238–240; 248–256; 262–266.

studies that formed the core understanding of the textbook Congress.

To illuminate the institutional dynamics of the past forty years, this chapter describes some early signs of change in the textbook Congress in the 1950s, suggests how events of the 1960s and 1970s disrupted the equilibrium, and looks at some of the emerging features of a new textbook Congress, though I am not convinced that a new equilibrium has yet been established. The story I develop here is not a historical tour d'horizon. Rather it addresses theoretical issues of institutional development involving the capacity of Congress and its members to represent their constituencies, to make national policy, and to balance intrinsic tensions between these tasks.

Let me preview my argument. The tensions between constituency representation and national policy making derive from three competing imperatives—geographical, jurisdictional, and partisan. Put differently and more alliteratively, Congress is an arena for constituencies, committees, and coalitions. The textbook Congress of the 1950s represented an equilibrium among these imperatives involving an institutional bargain that gave prominence to committees and the jurisdictional imperative. During these years Congress was a quintessential example of a division of labor. Committees provided a structure for members to realize their ambitions, on the one hand, and poured content into partisan vessels, on the other.

Beginning with the 1958 elections, shocks destroyed this committee-based equilibrium. Members began to give increased attention to their respective geographic constituencies, firming up their electoral bases by redeploying institutional resources to individual electoral purposes. It was during this period that an "incumbency advantage" first began to take on significant proportions.

Tensions between representation and policy making emerged as the now electorally more secure members sought to have greater effect on policy making inside the legislature. These tensions erupted in a fit of institutional reform during the 1970s. Throughout this entire period, parties inside the legislature assumed a residual function while rank-and-file members and committee barons, like two sumo wrestlers, fought for control of the legislature's machinery for setting agendas and making decisions.

As committees were weakened by decentralizing reform, coordination suffered. In response, beginning in the late 1970s and continuing into the 1980s, centralized party institutions were strengthened—the result of increased demand for coordination to fill the void left by the committees and an increased willingness by Democratic politicians to grant partisan institutions the authority to provide this coordination.

The 1950s committee-based legislative equilibrium has thus been radically transformed. The jurisdictional imperative of committees has given way to the imperatives of geography and party. A tenuous balance has been established among legislators with enhanced capabilities, a decentralized subcommittee system, and a recentralized and reinvigorated set of partisan institutions. Is this the new textbook Congress? . . .

THE CHANGING TEXTBOOK CONGRESS: THE 1970S AND 1980S

An idiosyncratic historical factor had an important bearing on the institutional reforms of the 1970s that undermined the textbook Congress. For much of the twentieth century the Democratic party in Congress spoke with a heavy southern accent. In 1948, for example, more than 53 percent of the Democrats in the House and nearly 56 percent of those in the

Senate came from the eleven Confederate states and five border states (Kentucky, Maryland, Missouri, Oklahoma, and West Virginia). These states accounted for only a third of all House and Senate seats. Beginning with the 1958 landslide, however, this distribution changed. In 1960 the same sixteen states accounted for just under 50 percent of Democratically held House seats and 43 percent of Democratically held Senate seats. By 1982 the numbers had fallen to 40 percent and 39 percent respectively, and have held at that level in the One-hundredth Congress. Increasingly, Democrats were winning and holding seats in the North and West and, to a somewhat lesser extent, Republicans were becoming competitive in the South.

The nationalization of the Democratic coalition in Congress, however, was reflected far more slowly at the top of the seniority ladder. Although between 1955 and 1967 the proportion of southern Democrats (border states excluded) in the House had dropped from 43 percent to 35 percent (46 percent to 28 percent in the Senate), the proportion of House committee chairs held by southerners fell from 63 percent to 50 percent, and rose from 53 percent to 56 percent in the Senate. Southerners held two of the three exclusive committee chairs in the House and two of the four in the Senate in 1955; in 1967 they held all of them.

The tension between liberal rank-and-file legislators and conservative southern committee chairs was important in the 1960s but had few institutional repercussions. True, Judge Howard Smith (Democrat of Virginia), the tyrannical chairman of the House Rules Committee, lost in a classic power struggle with Speaker Rayburn in 1961. But the defeat should not be exaggerated. Committees and their chairs maintained both the power to propose legislation and the power to block it in their respective jurisdictions. In 1967 southern Democrats George H. Mahon of Texas, William

M. Colmer of Mississippi, and Wilbur D. Mills of Arkansas chaired the Appropriations, Rules, and Ways and Means committees, respectively, in a manner not very different from that of the incumbents a decade earlier. Although the massive legislative productivity of the Eighty-ninth Congress (1965–66) did much to relieve this tension, it relieved it not so much by changing legislative institutions as by managing to mobilize very large liberal majorities. After the 1966 elections, and with the Vietnam War consuming more and more resources and attention, the Eighty-ninth Congress increasingly seemed like a brief interlude in the committee dominance that stretched back to World War II, if not earlier.

By the end of the 1960s a Democratic president had been chased from office, and the 1968 Democratic convention revealed the tensions created by the war in Vietnam and disagreements over a range of domestic issues. Despite a Democratic landslide in 1964, Republican gains for the decade amounted to thirty-eight seats in the House and eight in the Senate, further accentuating the liberal cast of the Democratic rank and file in Congress. As the 1970s opened, then, liberal Democratic majorities in each chamber confronted a conservative president, conservative Republican minorities in each chamber, and often conservative southern committee chairmen of their own party who together blocked many of their legislative initiatives. The liberals thus turned inward, using the Democratic Caucus to effect dramatic changes in institutional practices, especially in the House.

The Age of Reform
Despite the tensions it caused, the mature committee system had many advantages.[1] The division of labor in the House not only allowed for decisions based on expertise, but perhaps more important, it sorted out and routinized congressional careers. Committees

provided opportunities for political ambitions to be realized, and they did so in a manner that encouraged members to invest in committee careers. In an undifferentiated legislature, or in a committee-based legislature in which the durability of a committee career or the prospects for a committee leadership post depended on the wishes and whims of powerful party leaders (for example, the Speaker in the nineteenth century House), individual legislators have less incentive to invest effort in committee activities. Such investments are put at risk every time the political environment changes. Specialization and careerism are encouraged, however, when rewards depend primarily on individual effort (and luck), and not on the interventions and patronage of others. An important by-product is the encouragement given talented men and women to come to the legislature and to remain there. The slow predictability of career development under a seniority system may repel the impatient, but its inexorability places limits on risks by reducing a member's dependence on arbitrary power and unexpected events.

Even Voltaire's optimistic Dr. Pangloss, however, would recognize another side to this coin. When a committee system that links geography and jurisdiction through the assignment process is combined with an institutional bargain producing deference and reciprocity, it provides the foundation for the distributive politics of interest-group liberalism. But there are no guarantees of success. The legislative process is full of hurdles and veto groups, and occasionally they restrain legislative activism enough to stimulate a reaction. Thus in the 1950s, authorizing committees, frustrated by a stingy House Appropriations Committee, created entitlements as a means of circumventing the normal appropriations process. In the 1960s the Rules Committee became the major obstacle and it, too, was tamed. In the 1970s the Ways and Means Committee, which lacked

an internal division of labor through subcommittees, bottled up many significant legislative proposals; it was dealt with by the Subcommittee Bill of Rights and the Committee Reform Amendments of 1974. The solution in the 1950s had no effect on legislative arrangements. The solution in the 1960s entailed modest structural reform that directly affected only one committee. In the 1970s, however, the committee system itself became the object of tinkering.

The decade of the 1970s was truly an age of legislative reform. In effect, it witnessed a representational revolt against a system that dramatically skewed rewards toward the old and senior who were often out of step with fellow partisans. It is a long story, admirably told in detail elsewhere.[2] Here I shall focus on the way reforms enabled the rise of four power centers that competed, and continue to compete, with the standing committees for political influence.

First, full committees and their chairs steadily lost power to their subcommittees. At least since the Legislative Reorganization Act of 1946, subcommittees have been a significant structural element of the committee system in the House. However, until the 1970s they were principally a tool of senior committee members, especially committee chairmen, who typically determined subcommittee structure, named members, assigned bills, allocated staff resources, and orchestrated the timing and sequence in which the full committee would take up their proposals and forward them to the floor. Because the structures were determined idiosyncratically by individual chairmen, committees could be very different. Ways and Means had no subcommittees. Armed Services had numbered subcommittees with no fixed jurisdictions. Appropriations had rigidly arranged subcommittees. In almost all cases the chairman called the tune, despite an occasional committee revolt.

During the 1970s a series of reforms whittled away at the powers of the committee chairmen. In the 1970s chairmen began to lose some control of their agendas. They could no longer refuse to call meetings; a committee majority could vote to meet anyway with the ranking majority member presiding. Once a rule had been granted for floor consideration of a bill, the chairman could not delay consideration for more than a week; after seven days, a committee majority could move floor consideration.

In 1973 the Democratic members of a House committee were designated as the committee caucus and empowered to choose subcommittee chairs and set subcommittee budgets. During the next two years, committees developed a procedure that allowed members, in order of committee seniority, to bid for subcommittee chairmanships. Also in 1973 the Democratic Caucus passed the Subcommittee Bill of Rights, which mandated that legislation be referred to subcommittees, that subcommittees have full control over their own agendas, and that they be provided with adequate staff and budget.[3] In 1974 the Committee Reform Amendments required that full committees (Budget and Rules excepted) establish at least four subcommittees, an implicit strike against the undifferentiated structure of Ways and Means. In 1976 committee caucuses were given the authority to determine the number of subcommittees and their respective jurisdictions. Finally, in 1977 the selection procedure for committee chairs was changed, allowing the party caucus to elect them by secret ballot.

Full committees and their chairs thus had had their wings clipped. A chair was now beholden to the committee caucus, power had devolved upon subcommittees, and standing committees were rapidly becoming holding companies for their subunits.

Another center of power was created by the growth of member resources. Through House Resolution 5 and Senate Resolution 60, members were able to tap into committee and subcommittee budgets to hire staff to conduct their committee work. Additional resources were available for travel and office support. Budgets for congressional support agencies such as the General Accounting Office, the Congressional Research Service, and the Office of Technology Assessment, which individual members could employ for specific projects, also increased enormously. In short, member enterprises were becoming increasingly self-sufficient.

Committee power was also compromised by increased voting and amendment activity on the floor. The early 1970s marked the virtual end to anonymous floor votes. The secret ballot was never used in floor votes in the House, but voice votes, division votes, and unrecorded teller votes had allowed tallies to be detached from the identity of individual members. This changed as it became increasingly easy to demand a public roll call, a demand greatly facilitated by the advent of electronic voting in 1973. Roll call votes in turn stimulated amendment activity on the floor.[4] In effect, full committees and their chairs, robbed of some of their control of agendas by subcommittees, were now robbed of more control by this change in floor procedure.

Floor activity was further stimulated by the declining frequency with which the Rules Committee was permitted to issue closed rules, which barred floor amendments to legislation. The specific occasion for this change was the debate on retaining the oil depletion allowance. Because this tax break was protected by the Ways and Means Committee, on which the oil-producing states were well represented, efforts to change the policy could only come about through floor amendments. But Ways and Means bills traditionally were protected by a closed rule. The Democratic Caucus devised a policy in which a caucus majority could instruct its members on the Rules Committee to vote specific amendments in order. Applying this strategy to the oil depletion allowance, the caucus in effect ended the tradition of closed-rule protection of committee bills. This encouraged floor amendments and at the same time reduced committee control over final legislation. It also encouraged committees to anticipate floor behavior more carefully when they marked up a bill.[5]

Finally, committee dominance was challenged by the increased power of the Democratic Caucus and the Speaker. For all the delegation of committee operations to subcommittees and individual members, the changes in the congressional landscape were not all of one piece. In particular, before the 1970s the Democratic Caucus was a moribund organization primarily concerned with electing officers and attending to the final stages of committee assignments. After these activities were completed in the first few days of a new Congress, the caucus was rarely heard from. In the 1970s, however, as committees and chairmen were being undermined by subcommittees, there was a parallel movement to strengthen central party leadership and rank-and-file participation.

The first breach came in the seniority system. In 1971 the Democratic Caucus relieved its Committee on Committees—the Democratic members of the Ways and Means Committee—of having to rely on seniority in nominating committee chairs. This had the effect of putting sitting chairs on notice, although none was threatened at the time. In 1974 it became possible for a small number of caucus members to force individual votes on nominees for chairs and later to vote by secret ballot. In 1975 the caucus took upon itself the right to vote on subcommittee chairs of the Appropriations Committee. In that same year

three incumbent chairmen were denied reelection to their posts (a fourth, Wilbur Mills, resigned under pressure).

Next came the democratizing reforms. Members were limited in the number of committee and subcommittee berths they could occupy and the number they could chair. As the constraints became more binding, it was necessary to move further down the ladder of seniority to fill positions. Power thus became more broadly distributed.

But perhaps the most significant reforms were those that strengthened the Speaker and made the position accountable to the caucus. In 1973 House party leaders (Speaker, majority leader, and whip) were included on the Committee on Committees, giving them an increased say in committee assignments. The caucus also established the Steering and Policy Committee with the Speaker as chair. In 1974 Democratic committee assignments were taken away from the party's complement on Ways and Means and given to the new committee. In addition, the Speaker was given the power to appoint and remove a majority of the members of the committee and the Democratic members of the Rules Committee. In 1974 the Speaker also was empowered to refer bills simultaneously or sequentially to several committees, to create ad hoc committees, and, in 1977, to set time limits for their deliberations. Finally, in 1977 Speaker Thomas P. O'Neill started employing task forces to develop and manage particular policy issues. These task forces overlapped but were not coincident with the committees of jurisdiction and, most significant, they were appointed by the Speaker.[6]

The caucus itself became more powerful As mentioned, caucus majorities could instruct the Rules Committee and elect committee chairs and Appropriations subcommittee chairs. Caucus meetings could be called easily, requiring only a small number of signatories to a request, so that party matters could be thoroughly aired. In effect, the caucus became a substitute arena for both the floor and the committee rooms in which issues could be joined and majorities mobilized.

The revolt of the 1970s thus strengthened four power centers. It liberated members and subcommittees, restored to the Speakership an authority it had not known since the days of Joe Cannon, and invigorated the party caucus. Some of the reforms had a decentralizing effect, some a recentralizing effect. Standing committees and their chairs were caught in the middle. Geography and party benefited; the division-of-labor jurisdictions were its victims. . . .

A NEW TEXTBOOK CONGRESS?

The textbook Congress of the 1940s and 1950s reflected an equilibrium of sorts among institutional structure, partisan alignments, and electoral forces. There was a "conspiracy" between jurisdiction and geography. Congressional institutions were organized around policy jurisdictions, and geographic forces were accommodated through an assignment process that ensured representatives would land berths on committees important to their constituents. Reciprocity and deference sealed the bargain. Committees controlled policy formation in their respective jurisdictions. Floor activity was generally dominated by members from the committee of jurisdiction. Members' resources were sufficiently modest that they were devoted chiefly to committee-related activities. Constituencies were sufficiently homogeneous that this limitation did not, for most members, impose much hardship. Coordination was accomplished by senior committee members, each minding his own store. This system was supported by a structure that rewarded specialization, hard work, and waiting one's turn in the queue. Parties hovered in the

background as the institutional means for organizing each chamber and electing leaders. Occasionally they would serve to mobilize majorities for partisan objectives, but these occasions were rare. The parties, especially the Democrats, were heterogeneous holding companies, incapable of cohering around specific policy directions except under unusual circumstances and therefore unwilling to empower their respective leaders or caucuses.

Something happened in the 1960s. The election of an executive and a congressional majority from the same party certainly was one important feature. Policy activism, restrained since the end of World War II, was encouraged. This exacerbated some divisions inside the Democratic coalition, leading to piecemeal institutional tinkering such as the expansion of the Rules Committee and the circumvention of the Appropriations Committee. At the same time the Voting Rights Act, occasioned by the temporarily oversized condition of the majority party in the Eighty-ninth Congress, set into motion political events that, together with demographic and economic trends, altered political alignments in the South. By the 1980s, Democrats from the North and the South were coming into greater agreement on matters of policy.

Thus the underlying conditions supporting the equilibrium among geographical, jurisdictional, and partisan imperatives were overwhelmed during the 1960s. The 1970s witnessed adjustments to these changed conditions that transformed the textbook Congress. Institutional reform was initiated by the Democratic Caucus. Demographic, generational, and political trends, frustrated by the inexorable workings of the seniority system, sought an alternative mode of expression. Majorities in the caucus remade the committee system. With this victimization came less emphasis on specialization, less deference toward committees as the floor became a genuine forum for policy formulation, and a general fraying of the division of labor.

One trend began with the Legislative Reorganization Act of 1946 itself. In the past forty years members have gradually acquired the resources to free themselves from other institutional players. The condition of the contemporary member of Congress has been described as "atomistic individualism" and the members themselves have been called "enterprises."[7] The slow accretion of resources permitted members to respond to the changes in their home districts and encouraged them to cross the boundaries of specialization. These developments began to erode the reciprocity, deference, and division of labor that defined the textbook Congress.

The old equilibrium between geography and jurisdiction, with party hovering in the background, has changed. Geography (as represented by resource-rich member enterprises) has undermined the strictures of jurisdiction. But has the new order liberated party from its former holding-company status? In terms of political power the Democratic Caucus has reached new heights in the past decade. Party leaders have not had so many institutional tools and resources since the days of Boss Cannon. Committee leaders have never in the modern era been weaker or more beholden to party institutions. And, in terms of voting behavior, Democrats and Republicans have not exhibited as much internal cohesion in a good long while. Party, it would seem, is on the rise. But so, too, are the member enterprises.

What, then, has grown up in the vacuum created by the demise of the textbook Congress? I am not convinced that relationships have settled into a regular pattern in anything like the way they were institutionalized in the textbook Congress.

First, too many members of Congress remain too dissatisfied. The aggressive moves by Jim Wright to redefine the Speaker's role are a partial response to this circumstance.[8] Prospective changes in the Senate majority party leadership alignment in the 101st Congress convey a similar signal. The issue at stake is whether central party organs can credibly coordinate activities in Congress, thereby damping the centrifugal tendencies of resource-rich members, or whether leaders will remain, in one scholar's words, "janitors for an untidy chamber."[9]

One possible equilibrium of a new textbook Congress, therefore, would have member enterprises balanced off against party leaders; committees and other manifestations of a specialized division of labor would be relegated to the background. Coordination, formerly achieved in a piecemeal, decentralized fashion by the committee system, would fall heavily on party leaders and their institutional allies, the Rules and Budget committees and the party caucuses. However, unless party leaders can construct a solution to the budgetary mess in Congress—a solution that will entail revising the budget process—the burden of coordination will be more than the leaders can bear.[10] Government by continuing resolutions, reconciliation proposals, and other omnibus mechanisms forms an unstable fulcrum for institutional equilibrium.

Second, any success from the continued strengthening of leadership resources and institutions is highly contingent on the support of the members. Strong leadership institutions have to be seen by the rank and file as solutions to institutional problems. This requires a consensus among majority party members both on the nature of the problems and the desirability of the solutions. A consensus of sorts has existed for several years: demographic and other trends have homogenized the priorities of Democrats; experience with the spate of reforms in the 1970s has convinced many that decentralized ways of doing things severely tax the capacity of Congress to act; and, since 1982, the Reagan presidency has provided a unifying target.

But what happens if the bases for consensus erode? A major issue—trade and currency problems, for instance, or war in Central America or the Middle East—could set region against region within the majority party and reverse the trend toward consensus. Alternatively, the election of a Democratic president could redefine the roles of legislative leaders, possible pitting congressional and presidential factions against one another in a battle for partisan leadership. The point here is that the equilibrium between strong leaders and strong members is vulnerable to perturbations in the circumstances supporting it.

The next few years will be an institutionally messy period during which Speaker Wright and whoever succeeds Senate Majority Leader Robert Byrd have some time to solidify the coordinating power of the central leadership. I would be surprised if the power survived without some major institutional reorganization, perhaps the restoration of some power to committee chairs or the renovation of the budget process. The member enterprises, however, will not go away. Members will never again be as specialized, as deferential, as willing "to go along to get along" as in the textbook Congress of the 1950s. For better or worse, we are stuck with full-service members of Congress. They are incredibly competent at representing the diverse interests that geographic representation has given them. But can they pass a bill or mobilize a coalition? Can they govern?

NOTES

1. For a more detailed discussion, see Kenneth A. Shepsle, "Representation and Governance: The Great Legislative Tradeoff," *Political Science Quarterly,* vol. 103 (Fall 1988), pp. 461-85. Also see Lawrence C. Dodd and Richard L. Schott, *Congress and the Administrative State,* 2d ed. (Macmillan, 1986); and Lawrence C. Dodd, "The Rise of the Technocratic Congress: Congressional Reform in the 1970s," in Richard A. Harris and Sidney M. Milkis, eds., *Remaking American Politics* (Westview, forthcoming).

2. Roger H. Davidson and Walter J. Oleszek, *Congress Against Itself* (Indiana University Press, 1977); Leroy N. Rieselbach, *Congressional Reform: The Policy Impact* (Lexington, 1978); Leroy N. Rieselbach, *Congressional Reform* (CQ Press, 1986); Lawrence C. Dodd and Bruce I. Oppenheimer, "The House in Transition: Partisanship and Opposition," in Dodd and Oppenheimer, eds., *Congress Reconsidered,* 3d ed., pp. 34-64; and James L. Sundquist, *The Decline and Resurgence of Congress* (Brookings, 1981).

3. David W. Rohde, "Committee Reform in the House of Representatives and the Subcommittee Bill of Rights," in Norman J. Ornstein, ed., *Changing Congress: The Committee System* (Philadelphia: American Academy of Political and Social Science, 1974), pp. 39-47.

4. Stanley Bach, "Representatives and Committees on the Floor: Amendments to Appropriations Bills in the House of Representatives, 1963-1982," *Congress and the Presidency,* vol. 13 (Spring 1986), pp. 1-58; and Steven S. Smith, "Revolution in the House: Why Don't We Do It on the Floor?" Governmental Studies discussion paper 5 (Brookings, 1986).

5. Barry R. Weingast, "Floor Behavior in Congress: Committee Power Under the Open Rule," paper prepared for the 1987 annual meeting of the American Political Science Association.

6. Barbara Sinclair, "The Speaker's Task Force in the Post-Reform House of Representatives," *American Political Science Review,* vol. 75 (June 1981), pp. 397-410.

7. Samuel Kernell, *Going Public: New Strategies of Presidential Leadership* (CQ Press,

1986); and Salisbury and Shepsle, "Congressman as Enterprise."

8. Janet Hook, "Jim Wright: Taking Big Risks to Amass Power," *Congressional Quarterly Weekly Report,* vol. 46 (March 12, 1988), pp. 623-26.

9. Roger H. Davidson, "Senate Leaders: Janitors for an Untidy Chamber?" in Dodd and Oppenheimer, *Congress Reconsidered,* 3d ed., pp. 225-52.

10. Kenneth A. Shepsle, "The Congressional Budget Process: Diagnosis, Prescription, Prognosis," in Wander, Hebert, and Copeland, *Congressional Budgeting,* pp. 190-217.

Congressional Roles

37
Games Congressmen Play
John M. Barry

John Barry observed Congress for two years when he did research on his book, The Ambition and the Power, *a profile of former House Speaker Jim Wright. In the following article, Barry identifies several ways that House members get ahead in Congress. In this respect, Barry is describing the Congress of the 1990s, updating Shepsle's observations in Article 36. According to Barry, the three key games in the House are reliability, honesty on one's voting commitment for bills, and understanding of procedure, especially how the House Rules Committee operates. What examples are cited to show how members are punished or ignored if they violate these games? Why were House minority Republicans outraged at Speaker Wright's abuse of the so-called "King of the Mountain" ploy? How has Speaker Foley changed Rules Committee procedures? How are lobbyists involved in the House's inside games? Why are House members of the 1990s motivated by fear? Why have they grown increasingly timid on controversial issues?*

Democratic congressman Charlie Wilson of Texas is tall, lean and as ramrod straight as any movie cowboy. He is also conservative, flamboyant and unpredictable. Through the 1980s, his consuming interest was the Afghan guerrillas: several times he visited them (once trying to take along his friend, a former Miss World; when the Air Force balked, he set out to cut Defense Department appropriations), and his colleagues half-jokingly traded rumors about his firing weapons at Soviet troops. In the House of Representatives, he wanted no assignment more than a seat on the Permanent Select Committee on Intelligence. Several years before Jim Wright became Speaker of the House, Wilson, a longtime Wright loyalist, asked if his fellow Texan would appoint him once he rose to that position.

When Wright did become Speaker and a seat on the committee opened, liberals angrily tried to dissuade him from naming Wilson. They feared that Wilson's conservatism might shift de facto control to the Republicans at a time when the Iran-contra investigation was going on. As the pressure on Wright intensified, Wilson grew desperate and repeatedly pressed a mutual friend for help. Reluctantly, the friend agreed to see the Speaker. In Congress, one's word is one's bond. But all he had actually promised was to see Wright. When he did, he said: "There's no way in hell you can appoint Charlie Wilson to the intelligence committee."

From *New York Times Magazine*, May 13, 1990, pp. 34, 78, 84, 85, 87. Copyright © 1990 by The New York Times Company. Reprinted by permission.

In the end, Wright worked out a compromise. The Republicans agreed to enlarge the committee, allowing Wright to appoint Wilson and another Democrat—Barbara Kennelly, a liberal who could balance Wilson's vote. Thus Democrats did not risk losing control of the committee, and Wright kept Wilson happy. The Speaker then agreed to give the Republicans an extra seat on the Armed Services Committee, which went to Jack Davis, to accommodate the Republican House leader, Robert Michel.

The various morals of the story? In Congress, one's word may be one's bond, but one has to listen very closely to what is said; each party's leadership tries to accommodate the other and anything can be worked out if men (and women) of good will wish to do so.

Welcome to the private world of Congress.

In 1986, a few weeks before Jim Wright became Speaker, I profiled him for this magazine. It was clear even then that Wright wanted to take control of the policy agenda from the White House. I thought a book about his tenure would make an excellent vehicle to explore both how power is exercised in Washington and the inner workings of the Congress. Wright's staff objected, but he agreed to give me daily access to the most private sessions of the Democratic leadership. Other members of Congress, including Wright's nemesis, the Georgia Republican Newt Gingrich, cooperated as well; some of them also allowed me to attend strategy meetings, even when their aim was to defeat Wright. For two years, I was able to observe—as an outsider but from the inside—a very private world.

The House has the feel of fraternity: members punch arms, slap thighs, joke, and those whose families stay in their districts often share houses, like graduate students.

It is, of course, a largely male club; only 28 of the 435 members are women. Only a handful have served long enough to rise to committee chairmanships and attain the power that goes with the job. The senior woman in the House is Patricia Schroeder, Democrat of Colorado, who arrived in 1973.

Schroeder, whose colleagues resent that she is difficult to pin down on votes, has never been accepted in the old boys' network. But even those women who are run into problems. Lynn Martin, an Illinois Republican who plays the inside game, has pointedly never joined the nonpartisan women's caucus in the House. But when she ran for a Republican leadership post at the beginning of this Congress, she lost. A male Republican colleague says, "She's gone about as far as a woman can get here." Now she's running for the Senate.

Members seem like classic extroverts, but they are not. Les Aspin, a Wisconsin Democrat who is as quick to slap a back as anyone in Congress, once defined an extrovert as someone who talks to his neighbor on an airplane and concluded, "Don't you hate that?" Ralph Regula, an Ohio Republican, then said, "I can't think of a single member on my side of the aisle I'd call an extrovert."

Instead, in every encounter, colleagues listen closely to each other, looking for clues that may yield a future advantage, measuring each other. The most important measure is neither ideology nor popularity, but reliability. What one does outside Congress does not matter; only one's behavior inside does.

In the House, it usually takes at least two terms before members win assignments to major committees. During that period, they are being sized up. It took James Cooper, Democrat of Tennessee, the son of a governor and a Rhodes Scholar, four years to win a much desired seat on the Energy and Commerce Committee. Even then, a member of that committee said: "I'm waiting to find out what that Rhodes Scholar business means. I've seen young, smart members who had defects in their character. There's no substitute for character.'' So far, Cooper has passed all the tests.

The first inviolable measure of character is keeping one's word. One who does not is marked forever. More than 10 years ago, John Dingell, a Michigan Democrat and Energy and Commerce chairman, became convinced that James Scheuer, Democrat of New York, was claiming to be an ally on the clean-air act but was in fact meeting with Dingell's opponents. Scheuer is second only to Dingell in seniority on the committee, but Dingell abolished the subcommittee Scheuer headed, making him, in effect, a nonperson. Scheuer has remained so on the committee ever since, even though he could become its next chairman.

Republicans play equally rough. Sherwood Boehlert of New York was once having a drink with Gene Snyder of Kentucky, then the Public Works Committee's senior Republican. Snyder complained about colleagues who voted against their elders and chose to interpret Boehlert's statement of sympathy as a commitment to vote for a dam Snyder favored. Boehlert voted against it. For months afterward, Boehlert could not even get a Federal building in his district renamed for a deceased former Congressman who had been Snyder's friend. When Boehlert asked Snyder why, he replied, ''I don't like the way you vote.'' Boehlert spent days trying to figure out what Snyder was talking about. When he did, Boehlert tried to explain the misunderstanding. It did no good. Finally, Boehlert realized Snyder wanted an apology. He apologized. That afternoon, the committee approved the name change.

In Congress, reliability outweighs personality, and means more than simply keeping a commitment. It includes how hard a colleague works, how much he knows, and how closely one must listen to his words. Members judged to be reliable have influence.

Norm Dicks, Democrat of Washington and a former college linebacker who played in the Rose Bowl, can be as obnoxious as a little boy demanding attention. Once he interrupted a reporter's interview with a colleague—angering the Congressman—to complain that the reporter should be interviewing him instead, even though few of Dicks's Tacoma constituents were regular readers of the reporter's paper, *The Dallas Morning News*. Afterward, the reporter did interview him and Dicks later complained that the story quoted his colleague more often than him.

Yet Dicks has significant influence in Congress because he works hard, knows what he is talking about and deals with his fellow members honestly. One Hill insider says, ''Don't let your judgment of Norm's personality interfere with your judgment of his effectiveness as a member.''

The most important thing in Congress is the next vote, and the true test of reliability comes at vote-counting time. Texas Democrat Jack Brooks says: ''The test is not whether someone votes with you, but whether they tell the truth about it. If you say straight out you're not for something, well, I can't fault you, that's your business. I know where you are.''

Counting votes matters. If a bill lacks the votes to pass, Democrats (but not the minority Republicans) have the power to pull it from the schedule, make accommodations and reschedule it when it can pass. But pinning down a commitment can be tricky. Former Congressman Tony Coelho of California knew this when he ran for House Democratic whip in 1986. Prior to the Congressional election in November, he canvassed and found he had enough votes. After the election, he asked every colleague who had already given him a commitment if they would still vote for him when the actual whip election was held after Congress reconvened. He began with Vic Fazio, his campaign manager. Fazio snorted, "You can't be serious."

"Answer the question," Coelho replied.

A vote-counter asks, and sells, but does not push. Brooks, considered one of the toughest members of Congress, observes: "Flexing muscle is foolishness. Nobody does that. Even Lyndon Johnson said you have to be careful not to unintentionally hurt someone. You never want to ask someone to do something they're really against, or that hurts them in their district. They're the sole judge."

One of the most effective in getting a straight answer is Bob Michel, the House Republican leader. "He has the ability to look you in the eye, man to man, and people have to deal with him straight," says a senior Republican aide.

Power is exercised through the most inside element of the inside game—procedure. In the Senate, the rules are fixed. Members of both parties have an equal chance to master them.

In the House, however, the rules change for each major bill. The House Rules Committee writes a specific "rule" governing procedure on virtually every bill of import. The House must first approve the rule before the bill that it covers comes to the House floor. If the Rules Committee refuses to give a bill a rule, it can prevent it from going to the floor.

John Dingell once told the committee: "If you let me write procedure and I let you write substance, I'll screw you every time."

The most important procedural issue decided by a rule is what amendments can be offered—what issues will be voted on separately. The Rules Committee, for example, can combine a mom-and-apple-pie bill that everyone wants with a piece of unpopular legislation. If a separate vote—on an amendment—is not allowed, to pass the popular bill the

House must also accept the unpopular bill. This gives the Rules Committee enormous power.

All Democrats on the Rules Committee are selected by the Speaker, and on partisan issues they do as he directs. One ploy of the Rules Committee is called "King of the Mountain," which it routinely adopts for budget resolutions and defense authorization bills. "King of the Mountain" means simply that the last amendment to pass knocks off all earlier amendments. If, for example, one amendment passes by 220-200 and the next passes by 211-209, the amendment with 211 votes wins. So the Democratic leadership ordains that its preferred amendment is voted on last.

This maneuver was begun under House Speaker Thomas P. (Tip) O'Neill. His successor was Jim Wright, whose use of procedure created such deep bitterness within the House that it may have ultimately cost him his speakership. His most controversial move came in October 1987. The stock market had just crashed and White House and Congressional officials were in a budget meeting to decide the Government's priorities. Wright wanted to pass a bill, ironically titled "reconciliation," which included tax increases and spending cuts; he believed that passage would give him control over the outcome of the meeting. Failure would give the White House control.

But at the urging of Dan Rostenkowski, the House Ways and Means chairman, Wright included welfare reform in the measure. That meant that by passing this rule, the House would automatically pass a $6 billion bill that would have tremendous impact on American society. It would do so without a single opportunity to amend the proposal. Rules were not supposed to deal with substance at all; though that principle was often honored in the breach, this was a raw power play.

The House rebelled, defeating the rule and preventing the reconciliation bill from reaching the floor. Wright immediately had the Rules Committee strip welfare reform out. But a new rule cannot be voted on the same legislative day that an earlier one has been defeated. Wright, worried that support for the tax bill would disintegrate overnight, adjourned the House at 3:05 P.M. At 3:15, he convened it. Technically, this created a new day, allowing him to bring the rule, and the bill, to a vote. The new rule passed on a party-line vote, but the bill itself passed by only 206–205, after dramatic strong-arm tactics.

It was a Pyrrhic victory. Wright had infuriated Republicans with his tactics. Several months later, another parliamentary maneuver by Wright made Republicans even angrier. Wright's gimmickry prevented Republicans from sending military aid to the contras, but the same power play also led to free elections in Nicaragua, an end to the civil war there and the ouster of the Sandinistas. Immediately after Wright's maneuver, a lobbyist asked Dick Cheney, now Defense Secretary and then in the House Republican leadership, what message he could take to Wright to restore comity. "I'll never forget it," the lobbyist later recalled. "Cheney told me, 'There isn't any message. We want his head.'"

The Rules Committee has changed radically under Speaker Tom Foley who has told it to use only procedures with which Republicans are comfortable. Last year, Republicans voted for a resolution pointedly thanking him.

Gingrich, now the Republican whip says: "O'Neill and Wright were children of the Depression. They had a core hostility to Republicans. Now the Democratic leadership is competent, but they are the children of Eisenhower. It's not Armageddon to them. They live in a democracy and can imagine Republicans being in the majority." Then, talking about Richard Gephardt, the majority leader, Gingrich added: "Gephardt and I have talked about the concept of pleasant partisanship.

We can go one on one but without confrontation."

Not all Democrats are enthusiastic about entirely fair procedures, arguing that when Republicans had working control of the House in 1981, they pioneered some of the same procedures that they now denounce. "Foley will learn," says Dan Glickman, a Democrat from Kansas, "there's a limit to fairness when the White House is controlled by the other party."

In fact, last month, Republicans denounced Foley for using "Jim Wright tactics" on procedures for a child-care vote.

Lobbyists play the inside game, too, primarily through campaign contributions and honoraria, but also in other ways. Money, of course, does matter. In a 1986 study for the Center for Responsive Politics, 20 percent of senators and representatives admitted—anonymously—that campaign contributions influence their votes.

One former Congressman, however, insisted that money is less important than people think. He explained that when he was a member, he wanted "the facts, untwisted. If a lobbyist lies to me just once, I won't see him. I won't answer his phone calls. I won't answer his mail, and I'll tell his clients they're not well represented. The key isn't money. People are naive if they think money buys a vote. The key is to be honest."

Members rely on lobbyists they trust for information, let them write legislative language and grant them direct—very direct—influence on votes. Members vote hundreds of times a year, but unless a vote has national significance or involves their committees or districts, they know little about the issues they are voting on. In the day or two before a vote, staff members may brief them, a colleague directly involved in the issue may say something, or a lobbyist may visit them.

When a vote actually begins, members stream to the Capitol from their offices across the street. The few Congressmen who care about the issue "work the doors"—they stand just inside the chamber as colleagues walk past and try to sum up the argument for their side in a sentence or two. In the hallway outside the chamber, lobbyists form a gauntlet and also make their case—quickly—sometimes just by pointing their thumbs up or down.

And members try to use lobbyists for their own agendas. Tony Coelho, an epileptic, once suggested to the public relations firm of Hill and Knowlton that over a period of years it donate several hundred thousand dollars worth of professional services to a charity campaign for epilepsy. The company refused.

Coelho also used lobbyists to build a power base: his office regularly told lobbyists to arrange honoraria for junior members who lacked the power to command them. These members owed Coelho, not the lobbyist. (Coelho resigned from Congress last year prior to an expected Ethics Committee investigation into a possible violation of House reporting rules involving a $50,000 junk-bond profit. He is now an investment banker.)

Coelho was neither the first nor the last to use this tactic. A member recalls that when the current whip, Bill Gray, ran for another leadership post, "Gray asked for my support and I told him I'd consider it. The next day a lobbyist, a friend of his, offered me $500 to have breakfast with him. Kind of a funny coincidence." The member rejected the invitation.

Effective next year, the House has outlawed honoraria; as yet, the Senate has not. But campaign contributions and other favors serve the same purpose.

Congressional leaders use lobbyists to advance policy agendas as well as personal ones. In 1987, for example, the House Democratic leadership believed the Democratic Party had made a campaign promise to help farmers, which it intended to keep. A meeting was arranged between Agriculture Committee Dem-

ocrats and dozens of interest groups who claimed to represent 100 million people. Farm groups were there, but so were a United Auto Workers lobbyist—the dip in the economy meant that farmers were not buying tractors— and a representative of the Union of American Hebrew Congregations—who worried about "an outburst of anti-Semitism in the Midwest if the economy doesn't improve." As a result of the combined pressure of the leadership and the lobbyists, a reluctant Agriculture Committee passed the Farm Credit Act.

The dominant force in politics is fear. The desire to survive weighs more heavily than the desire to rise. Despite the House's 98 percent incumbency re-election rate in 1988, members fear their districts.

Nothing demonstrates this more than one Democratic "whip meeting" I attended in the last Congress. These meetings occur every Thursday morning, when about 50 House leaders and members gather in Room H-324 in the Capitol to exchange blunt talk.

Colleagues munch doughnuts or muffins, drink coffee and crack jokes. But there are serious undercurrents. Foley calls the meetings "the most important half-hour of the week. If members don't speak their minds at the whip meetings, they'll speak them in small groups in private and then you've got a problem."

At this particular meeting, Tom Foley, then the majority leader, announced that the following week the House would vote on a bill prohibiting unionized construction firms from creating nonunion subsidiaries.

Members exploded. They shouted angrily, spilled their coffee and shook doughnuts in the air. This was a dreaded "labor bill," so named because it was backed by organized labor. Members hate these bills because no matter how they vote it will anger a powerful group, either business or labor.

One Congressman jumped to his feet and shouted: "The two senators from my state can go to the A.F.L.-C.I.O. convention and get a standing ovation, then go across the street to the Chamber of Commerce convention and get a standing ovation. And the reason they can do this is that in the Senate they're smart enough not to schedule these damn labor bills for a vote! Now I want to know why we're doing it!''

His colleagues rocked with laughter. But the point was serious. The member who protested owed his original election in 1974 to union support, and is so strong at home that no Republican has run against him since 1976. Yet even he didn't want to make what is called a "tough vote," and most of his colleagues shared his sentiment.

Members of Congress are more willing to make a tough vote on a bill with a chance to become law but this was certain to be vetoed; members are pragmatists, unattracted to symbolic gestures.

Republicans, frustrated by 36 years in the minority, devise legislative strategies to exploit fear. They often try to get a floor vote on issues for the sole purpose of distorting it for a campaign ad. Californian Jerry Lewis, the third-ranking member of the House minority leadership, once wryly conceded: "We have just enough votes to be irresponsible."

In the last Congress, Republicans included in a package of hundreds of pages dealing with House procedures one sentence making it out of order to call for an increase in income taxes. (They mix procedure and substance, too.) Democrats voted against it, because of the procedural part of the package, enabling future Republican opponents to run a 30-second ad attacking them for supporting an income-tax hike. Even Dick Cheney called the maneuver "a political cheap shot."

Republicans have forced similar votes on everything from the Pledge of Allegiance to drugs. One senior Republican aide says: "I re-

member when liberals used to just stand up and vote. Now they're scared to death."

But Republicans also dodge votes. When the White House asked Wright, at the time the Speaker, to help pass an unpopular bill to raise the debt limit, Wright agreed but asked the White House to get some Republicans to vote for it. James A. Baker 3d, then Treasury Secretary, declined, saying: "It's the responsibility of the majority to govern."

Representative Dan Glickman of Kansas, first elected in 1976, believes his colleagues have grown increasingly timid and speculates that the grass-roots fire-storm Reagan stirred up in 1981 "terrorized" Democrats. (He fails to mention that Democrats terrorized Republicans on Social Security in 1982.)

"There is an absence of risk-taking, both individual and collective," Glickman complains. "Risks become a detour from a nice, safe, permanent job. . . . This job is getting to the point where you feel as if we're incapable of making serious public-policy decisions. We aren't willing to challenge anyone. Every state legislature in the country is making these decisions. Something's wrong."

IS SOMETHING WRONG?

An old political saying goes: The first element of statesmanship is to get elected. This saying reflects a balance between doing what is necessary to win, and doing the right thing.

Recently, this relationship has become unbalanced. Partly, the imbalance comes from distorted, negative 30-second commercials. (Legislation is being discussed to control them.) But the fault lies elsewhere.

In the two years I observed Congress, I learned that most members do care about the public. I learned how to listen, how to count votes, how to interpret polls and how to manipulate the media. I learned about and came to respect the particular kind of honor politicians have. I also learned about much more than policy. I was impressed by the work habits, intelligence and personal integrity of most members of Congress. Yet I think of the comment of the veteran Congressman who wondered about his new colleague: "I've seen young, smart members who had defects in their character. There is no substitute for character."

The 30-second ad may put new pressures on today's politicians, but tough votes are nothing new.

Henry Hyde, Republican of Illinois, recalls that during the Senate impeachment trials of President Andrew Johnson, Thaddeus Stevens, a powerful figure in Congress, warned seven senators that if they supported Johnson they would be defeated. Back then, state legislatures chose senators, and Stevens could back up his threat. All seven defied him, and all seven were defeated.

"Those were real profiles in courage," Hyde says, adding sadly, "I don't think that would happen today."

Limiting Congressional Incumbency

38
Twelve is Enough
Hendrik Hertzberg

Hendrik Hertzberg, who writes for The New Republic *magazine, expands on the fear factor referred to by Barry in the previous article. This refers to each legislator's concern that he or she will not be re-elected to office. The congressional success rate for incumbency has reached 98 percent for House members. Hertzberg believes it is time to amend the Constitution and impose a twelve-year term limit for the House and the Senate. How would this proposal affect the seniority rule? What would be the impact on Congress as an institution? What about the lack of accountability for lame ducks? Why is chronic incumbency a problem? What are the arguments against term limits? What are the chances that such limits will actually be put into effect?*

Before you automatically reject the proposal now making the rounds for a twelve-year limit for members of Congress as a dreadful idea—an anti-democratic, anti-political, mechanistic "reform" that like so many other "reforms" would most likely end up making things worse, a bit of mischievous tinkering with the precious Constitution that has served us so well for 200 years, a misguided gimmick that ignores the *real* problem (PACs, polls, gerrymandering, special interests, negative ads, cowardly politicians, ignorant citizens, whatever) and is probably nothing but a Republican ploy anyway—before you agree with all these dismissals and turn your attention to more pressing matters, consider three numbers.

Number number one: 37.1. Yes, it's a voter turnout figure, the op-ed writer's best friend. This particular figure represents the percentage of American over-eighteens who bestirred themselves to go to the polls in 1986, the last time the citizenry was invited to vote for members of Congress without the added glitz of a presidential contest. Compared with the turnout in any other arguably democratic country—France, Nicaragua, Norway, Hungary, El Salvador, Israel, Turkey, Italy, Lithuania, you name it—this is pathetic. It was the lowest since 1926, not counting 1944, when World War II made voting inconvenient for large numbers of people. And the public's true interest in House elections is even lower. According to *Congressional Quarterly's*

From *The New Republic,* May 14, 1990, pp. 22, 24, 26. Reprinted by permission of *The New Republic,* © 1990, The New Republic, Inc.

Rhodes Cook, if you factor out districts where there was a contest for governor or U.S. senator to lure people out, the turnout was a scandalous 27.6 percent. Only the most perverse elitists argue that this state of affairs is anything but a symptom of extreme political ill health.

Number number two: 98.3. This is the percentage of incumbent members of the House of Representatives who won their "races" for re-election in 1988, up from 98 percent flat in 1966. According to a recent study by David C. Huckabee of the Congressional Research Service of the Library of Congress, this number has remained in the 90s since 1974, and it is currently the highest it has ever been since the middle of President Washington's first term. And because more incumbents now choose to run than ever before, the re-election rate for the House as a whole is now in the 90s, too—92.4 percent last time out, to be exact. In the 19th century, this figure tended to hover somewhere between 40 percent and 70 percent, once dropping to as low as 24 percent (in 1842); it hit the 70s after World War I and has been climbing more or less steadily ever since.

The 98.3 figure actually understates the political stasis of the House. Of the 409 incumbents who ran for re-election, six were defeated in November. But five of these had been tainted by one sort of scandal or another. So the grand total of representatives who lost their seats as a consequence of what we normally think of as politics—that is, a process in which the electorate chooses between competing sets of programs and policies—was exactly one.

Number number three: 36. This is how many years a single party, the Democrats, has controlled the lower house of the national legislature of the United States. By contrast, the British House of Commons has changed hands four times since 1954, the French Chamber of Deputies three times, the West German Bundestag five times, the Canadian House of Commons five times, and the Indian Lok Sabha three times. When it comes to one-party legislative dominance in serious countries, only Japan, Mexico, South Africa, and the Soviet Union are even in our league. And in the last two, unlike in the United States, the ruling party is a pretty good bet to lose the next election. No moral equivalence intended, of course. Or deserved.

In the light of numbers number two and three, the wonder is that number number one is so high. In the overwhelming majority of congressional districts, voting is increasingly an irrational act. Why bother, when 85 percent of the incumbents are getting more than 60 percent of the vote in their districts, when the *average* incumbent is getting 73.5 percent, when sixty-three members are returned with Brezhnevian majorities exceeding 94 percent? Except in the handful of districts where there are open seats or close races, voting may still make sense as a civic sacrament—as a way of refreshing one's soul with a sense of belonging to a democratic community—but it makes no sense as a form of political action. Better to spend the hour or so it takes to vote writing checks and sending them off to candidates in contested districts.

Against this background, the idea of a twelve-year limit begins to acquire a certain logic. Such proposals are neither new nor flakily marginal. A limit on congressional service was considered at the founding constitutional convention (which laid it aside as "entering too much into detail"), and the idea has won the support, over the decades, of a bipartisan list of luminaries including Abraham Lincoln, Harry Truman, Dwight D. Eisenhower, and John F. Kennedy. The current campaign for a constitutional amendment that would limit service to six two-year terms for House members and two six-year terms for senators (with an exemption for the present crew of incumbents, of course) is led by Senators Gordon Humphrey, Republican of New Hampshire, and Dennis DeConcini, Democrat of Arizona. Their ten co-sponsors span the Senate's ideological spectrum, from Jake Garn on the right to Nancy Kassebaum in the center to Tom Daschle on the left.

Even so, truth in packaging compels the admission that the current push is basically a Republican scam. All but three of the Senate co-sponsors are Republicans. The twelve-year limit was endorsed in the 1988 Republican platform. The letterhead pressure group promoting the idea, something called Americans to Limit Congressional Terms, is run out of a Republican political consultant's office and consists mostly of Republican excongressmen and state legislators (though it does include a few Democrats, of whom the most distinguished is former eight-term Representative Donald M. Fraser, now mayor of Minneapolis). Republicans are understandably eager to support any lunatic notion that holds out the promise of helping them break the Democratic stranglehold on Capitol Hill. But this just might be one of those rare cases where the narrow self-interest of the Republican Party is congruent with the public good.

The arguments for the term limit are surprisingly persuasive, especially where the House is concerned. Almost all of them are variations on a single theme: breaking the Gordian knot of entrenched incumbency, which distorts our democracy from the polling place clear up to the Senate and (especially) House chambers. Out in that fabled land beyond the beltway, the term limit would mean that at least once every twelve years (and probably more frequently), every citizen would get a fighting chance to vote in a genuinely *political* congressional election, which is to say one that would turn not on the goodies that good old Congressman Thing has procured for the

district or the Social Security checks he has expedited or the campaign funds he has raised or the newsletters he has franked, but rather on the competing political visions and programs of parties and candidates. But the most interesting, and salutary, effects of the limit would be the ways in which it would change the political ecology of Congress itself.

A twelve-year limit would necessarily bring an end to the much-reformed but still pervasive and undemocratic rule of seniority. The House Speaker, the chairmen of important committees, and the other potentates of Congress have long been elevated by a decades-long, quasi-feudal process of favor-trading, personal alliance-building, ladder-climbing, and "getting along by going along." The term limit would leave Congress little choice but to elect its chiefs democratically, on the basis of the policies and the leadership qualities of the candidates. Like the Speakers of many of our state legislatures, these leaders would tend to be vigorous men and women in their forties and fifties—people in the mold of Bill Gray, Stephen Solarz, and Henry Hyde. The Dingells and Rostenkowskis would remain where they belong, on the back benches or in private life. This would be an important gain. And the frequent turnover of leaders—one who served more than six years would be a rarity—would be a spur both to brisk accomplishment and to attentiveness to the concerns and needs of the country.

The seniority system occasionally produces good leaders as well as bad ones, but there is no denying that it is grossly biased in favor of the most politically sluggish and unchanging parts of the nation. A swing district—one marked by close elections, and the robust debate and clamorous participation that close elections bring—has a hard time keeping somebody in office long enough to survive the glacial process by which congressional power is accumulated. It is precisely such districts that are most likely to elect representatives alive to the cutting-edge problems that most urgently require action. Systematically disempowering these districts and the people representing them, as the current arrangement so efficiently does, is insane.

A Congress invigorated by frequent infusions of new blood would be a more responsive, more democratic, more varied place. So would a Congress whose majority regularly changed from one party to the other, which a term limit would unquestionably promote. However bad this might be for the short-term partisan interests of Democrats like me, it would be good for the long-term interests of the country—and the party, too. Critics of the term limit idea argue that it would "weaken" Congress; and so it would, but in ways that would strengthen both its most useful functions and democratic governance in general. The one-party Congress has become a world unto itself, and the long period of Republican control of the presidency and Democratic control of Congress has produced an insidious mentality on Capitol Hill. The leaders of the Democratic congressional majority, veterans of decades of supremacy in their own little universe, no longer constitute an opposition. They conceive of themselves as ins, not outs— as leaders of one-half of a permanent coalition government. They may imagine that their own fiefdoms are secure, but their party is reaping almost all of the penalties of incumbency and almost none of the benefits. The foundations of Democratic congressional dominance are being relentlessly undermined, and once the structure topples, as eventually it must, rebuilding it will seem as hopeless a task as destroying it does now. A Congress shaped by a term limit would have a different and healthier mentality. During periods when it was controlled by the party that also controls the White House, it would be energetic in pursuit of that party's program; when in opposition, it

would—for a change, and just as energetically—oppose.

The many Americans who deplore the decline of political parties in this country ought especially to welcome the term limit idea. By routinely undermining the totally independent, totally personal power bases that long-serving senators and representatives are able to build and maintain under the current system, and by dramatically increasing the number of elections fought on the basis of national issues, the term limit would enhance the strength and coherence of both national parties.

The term limit would mean that at any given moment something like sixty or seventy representatives, and perhaps half that number of senators, would be ineligible to run again. To critics of the proposal, this is one of its worst features. The lame ducks, say the critics, would be "unaccountable" and unresponsive to their constituents' wishes. But Congress's problem is hardly that its members are insufficiently obsessed with re-election, insufficiently attentive to polling data, and insufficiently ardent in pursuit of district pork barrel. The broader public good could only benefit from having a cohort of comparatively disinterested legislators, relieved from reelection pressures and free to consult their consciences as well as their pollsters and contributors. The critics add that the lame ducks might fall prey to corruption, legal or illegal. This phenomenon is not exactly unknown under present arrangements. But it would not be more likely to happen if most of the departing members are still relatively young and still ambitious. Why should they feather their nests at the cost of their reputations?

It's true, as the critics also say, that the term limit would deprive Congress of the services of legislators whom experience has made wise. This would be a real cost. But it would be a cost worth paying to be rid of the much larger number of timeservers who have learned nothing from longevity in office except cynicism, complacency, and a sense of diminished possibility. And it's not as if the job of being a congressman is so difficult that it takes decades to master. It's easier than being a first-rate schoolteacher, for example, and no harder than such jobs as president, governor, or mayor—all of which are regularly performed very well indeed by people who have had no on-the-job experience at all.

In any case, the senators and representatives obliged to seek other employment after twelve years will not vanish from the face of the earth. They will be available for service in the executive branch, in industry, in advocacy groups, and in the academy. Few will become lobbyists, because the turnover on the Hill will quickly make their contacts obsolete and their influence unpeddlable. Many will run for other public offices. Representatives will run for senator, senators will run for representative, and both will run for president, governor, mayor, and state legislator. The result will be more and better competition for these jobs, too. This would not be such a bad thing. Membership in Congress would no longer be a life calling or a lifetime sinecure, but this would not be such a bad thing either. A shot at Congress would be an attractive option for the young and ambitious, for the old but still energetic, and for men and women in midlife who want something more meaningful than whatever success they have earned elsewhere. There would be no shortage of candidates. Though harder to keep, the job would be easier to get.

A Gallup Poll taken in December found that 70 percent of the American public favors the idea of a term limit. This is uncannily close to the percentages of the public that *(a)* think Congress is doing a lousy job and *(b)* keep on voting to re-elect the same old incumbents. Opponents of the term limit say that if voters are so fed up with Congress, there is a simple way for them to do something about it without tinkering with the Constitution: "Throw the rascals out," as *The Chicago Tribune* suggests. So why don't they? "The explanation," writes my friend Michael Kinsley ("Voters in Chains," TNR, April 2), "is that the voters are lazy hypocrites." Maybe they are, but that's not the explanation. A given voter can vote to throw out a maximum of one rascal—three if you count senators. The problem is not individual incumbents; it's chronic incumbency, and trying to solve it by removing one's own incumbent is like treating tuberculosis with a cough drop. To tell a voter he can solve the problem of chronic incumbency by voting against his own representative is to recommend a particularly fruitless form of single-issue politics. The public's disgust is with Congress as an institution, and defeating one member out of 535 won't revamp Congress any more than firing the Deputy Assistant to the President for Scheduling would revamp the White House.

Thanks to seniority, voting to remove a long-serving congressman necessarily means voting to replace him with someone who will have less power. It therefore means voting to deprive one's district (and oneself) of clout. That's fine if you truly think your representative is a rascal. but what if you simply think he's a mediocrity?

There has to be a better way, and the twelve-year limit just might be it. The movement for it deserves the support of all who think Congress is broke and needs fixing—even those who, unlike me, don't think the limit itself is a particularly good idea. Let's be realistic: the chances a term limit amendment will actually get enacted are pretty remote. Congress, for obvious reasons, is not likely to pass it, and the other route—a constitutional convention called by two-thirds of the state legislatures—has never been successfully traveled. But the movement to impose a limit, if it catches fire, could throw enough of a scare into the Congress we've got to induce it to make changes—in campaign financing, PAC spending, access to television, mandatory campaign debates, and so on—that would accomplish most if not all of the same salutary results. The term limit movement is potentially like the nuclear freeze movement of the early 1980s. As a policy blueprint the freeze proposal left a lot to be desired. But the movement did a world of good by forcing the Reagan administration to offer serious arms control proposals of its own, most of which the Russians eventually accepted. The freeze movement was a cri de coeur. So is the term limit movement. Listen, Congress.

CHAPTER 11

The Supreme Court

The Supreme Court is the nation's highest court of appeals or "court of last resort" in the judicial system. It has played a unique role in shaping and influencing important policy decisions through critical stages of American political development. No other Western democratic government has a high court with powers comparable to those of the Supreme Court in the political process. The Supreme Court is more than the highest appellate court for settling legal disputes. With its special role as constitutional interpreter, the Supreme Court has coequal authority and status with the legislative and executive branches of the national government.

CONSTITUTIONAL FOUNDATIONS

The Framers established judicial powers and authority in Article III of the Constitution. The federal court system consisted of the Supreme Court and other "inferior Courts as Congress may from time to time . . . establish." Article III and the Eleventh Amendment also specified the jurisdiction or scope of judicial authority in particular kinds of cases. The Supreme Court hears cases of original and appellate jurisdiction. Cases of original jurisdiction are decided directly by the Supreme Court without any prior lower court involvement. These involve disputes between two or more states, between the United States and a state, between the United States and foreign ambassadors, and between a state and a citizen of another state. Very few of the more than 4,000 cases considered annually by the Supreme Court—less than one percent—are of original jurisdiction. Most of its cases are by way of appellate jurisdiction, that is, from disputes originating in the lower federal courts or from the highest state courts where a constitutional or "substantial federal question" is involved.

The structure of the federal courts is determined by Congress from the constitutional provision of Article I, Section 8, which gives Congress the right to "constitute Tribunals inferior to the Supreme Court." By the 1890s, Congress had established the basic three-tier system of federal courts which exists today: district courts, courts of appeals, and the U.S. Supreme Court. There are 94 U.S. district courts with nearly 600 federal judges who dealt with 280,000 cases in 1987 involving criminal or civil violations of federal law. Most federal cases begin in the federal district courts. Thirteen U.S. courts of appeals with 168 judges hear appeals from the district courts, independent regulatory commissions, other federal administrative agencies, and various specialized legislative courts that Congress has established. Appeals courts are located geographically in twelve different regions or "circuits" of the country. About 36,000 cases reach these courts each year.

JUDICIAL REVIEW

How did the Supreme Court become a coequal political branch of the federal government? As shown in Article 39, much of the Supreme Court's influence can be traced to the leadership of Chief Justice John Marshall, who established the basis of judicial review in the case of *Marbury v. Madison* (1803). Although the constitutional Framers had not provided for judicial review in Article III of the Constitution—even though Alexander Hamilton argued in *The Federalist,* Number 78, that the Court had such authority—Marshall asserted that the Supreme Court has the right to nullify acts of Congress when such legislation conflicts with the Constitution. Why? The chief justice argued that "It is emphatically the province and duty of the judicial department to say what the law is." Moreover, it is "the very essence of judicial duty" for the Supreme Court to uphold the Constitution when an act of Congress violates the basic charter, because "the Constitution is superior to any ordinary Act of the Legislature," and "the Constitution, and not such ordinary Act, must govern the case to which they both apply."

Judicial review of federal legislation was used rarely during the early course of the nation's development. In fact, the Marshall Court was more involved with state challenges to national authority than with congressional enactments. With the exception of the *Marbury* case, the Supreme Court was more concerned with state laws that conflicted with national constitutional supremacy. The second occasion for judicial review placed the Supreme Court in the political crisis over the slavery issue. In deciding the *Dred Scott* case (1857), Chief Justice Roger Taney struck down the Missouri Compromise, a ruling that contributed to the nation's internal disunity and the Civil War. Since the 1800s, the Supreme Court has declared 900 state laws and 120 federal laws unconstitutional. Four-fifths of federal judicial review has occurred in the twentieth century in cases dealing with civil rights and civil liberties issues.

The most serious clash between judicial and legislative power took place during the 1930s when the Supreme Court used judicial review and statutory interpretation to nullify much of President Roosevelt's New Deal legislation. Roosevelt had attacked the nation's economic crisis with a wide range of reforms, particularly in labor-management relations and controls over industrial production. The Supreme Court viewed these sweeping and comprehensive measures as unconstitutional delegations of power from Congress to the president. This led Roosevelt to propose a "court-packing plan," which would have permitted him to appoint additional justices to the Court to sit alongside those who had reached age 70. Even though Roosevelt had just won a landslide victory in 1936, his court-packing plan was politically unacceptable. The Court ended the crisis by adjusting its internal alignments, and by 1937 a majority of the justices were approving the same economic reforms that only a few months before they had opposed.

The Court's role as constitutional interpreter is buttressed by its authority to determine the meaning of legislation, by the prestige that judges have in the political system, and by the legitimacy and acceptability of judicial decisions granted by other agencies of government. At the same time, the judiciary is limited by public opinion, by various legal and technical checks that delay Court decisions, and by the self-restraint that judges impose on themselves to limit their interference into politically sensitive areas of public policy.

Constitutional Interpretation: Original Intention v. Judicial Activism

Judicial review is one of the Supreme Court's most powerful instruments in maintaining the independence of the courts from the executive and legislative branches. Many presidents have disagreed with the Court's constitutional interpretations. Critics argue that the Supreme Court is the most elite of the three branches and that judicial review effectively nullifies the actions of the popularly elected legislative and executive branches. The Court's power is therefore undemocratic and not controlled at the voting booth or by public opinion.

Are there any checks on judicial power? Congress, the president, and public opinion can restrain the courts. Congress can adopt new laws to replace those nullified by the Supreme Court. It can also deny the courts appellate jurisdiction in certain areas and it has the power to initiate new constitutional amendments that are not subject to judicial review. Presidents can influence the Court by nominating justices. Also, the executive branch can delay or ignore implementation of Supreme Court decisions (such as school desegregation in the 1950s). Public opinion is the most ambiguous constraint, but the Court generally takes into account public sentiment in deciding cases, although it is frequently difficult to resolve competing public attitudes about very controversial issues.

The traditional checks on the Supreme Court usually do not include challenges to its constitutional function and substantive decision-making authority. Presidents and legislators may disagree with Court rulings but they have not criticized the Court's authority to interpret the Constitution. This changed in 1985 when the Reagan administration launched a conservative ideological attack on several of the Court's civil liberties and civil rights decisions. Attorney General Edwin Meese questioned the legitimacy of Supreme Court decisions that disagreed with conservative thinking. In response, Associate Justice William Brennan issued a strong rebuttal in support of judicial activism, arguing that constitutional interpretation involves more than determining the intentions of the constitutional Framers. Brennan called for Supreme Court flexibility and adaptability to changing societal conditions in deciding constitutional issues.

Meese called for a "jurisprudence of original intention" that would require the Supreme Court to interpret the Constitution narrowly, according to what the Framers meant when they drafted it in 1787. The Supreme Court, according to Meese, should avoid any political efforts to depart from the literal provisions of the Constitution. However, Meese did not say what the Framers' intentions were. Instead, he criticized the Supreme Court in specific cases such as applying the Bill of Rights to the states, upholding separation of church and state, and protecting the rights of criminal defendants.

In Article 40, Raymond Polin of St. John's University analyzes the Meese-Brennan debate. He finds merit in both positions. When the Supreme Court decides cases, it takes into account both the original meaning of the Constitution as well as the context and issues of the controversy. The constitutional balance of freedom and authority must be weighed with the specific circumstances of the case.

But Polin sees a political and ideological motivation behind Meese's philosophical arguments. The Reagan administration had an advertised agenda intended to shrink government and to support certain social issues such as school prayer while opposing abortion. In Polin's view, Meese was attempting to restrict the scope of court rulings which conflicted with the Reagan administration's stated policy goals. Polin observes that the Reagan administration's objective was to strengthen executive power at the expense of Congress.

In 1987, the debate over original intent and judicial activism resulted in a bitter debate over President Reagan's nomination of Court of Appeals Judge Robert Bork to replace Justice Lewis Powell on the Supreme Court.

Bork took an uncompromising stand on original intent in his 32 hours of televised testimony before the Senate Judiciary Committee. He opposed the right to privacy and passage of the 1964 Civil Rights Act. He criticized affirmative action.

Following Bork's controversial testimony, the Senate rejected Bork's nomination by a vote of 58–42. This was the widest margin by which a president's Supreme Court nominee had ever been defeated.

JUDICIAL SELECTION CRITERIA

Perhaps the most significant check on judicial authority is the filling of court vacancies. Unlike the president or members of Congress, all federal judges are appointed rather than elected to office. Considering the life tenure of federal judges and the impact they have on the law and public policy, the criteria and standards used to select judges are important. While most states have formal requirements of legal training for judges, this is only an unwritten, although very important, requirement at the federal level.

Prior judicial experience, while always said to be important, has not been an obstacle for some of the most outstanding members of the Supreme Court, including such luminaries as Chief Justice Marshall and Chief Justice Earl Warren. Senatorial courtesy is a political factor in confirming presidential appointments to the lower federal courts. Senatorial courtesy is an unwritten agreement among senators that presidential appointments to the courts will not be approved unless they are acceptable to the senator of the president's party from the state where the judge is located.

According to Henry Abraham, presidents use several criteria in considering Supreme Court nominees: objective merit, political affiliation, ideological consistency, personal attractiveness, and various balancing factors such as religion, race, gender, and geographic location.

The appointment of Sandra Day O'Connor in 1981 provides an interesting application of Abraham's judicial selection criteria. During the 1980 campaign, President Reagan promised to nominate a woman to the Supreme Court. The opportunity became available when Justice Potter Stewart retired from the Court in 1981 after twenty-three years of service. Less than one month later, President Reagan nominated Sandra Day O'Connor to replace Stewart. Her objective merit or previous professional achievements were substantial: she had served on the Arizona State Court of Appeals, was the first woman elected as Republican majority leader of the Arizona State Senate, and had been an assistant state attorney general. Her ideological views were consistent with Reagan's brand of political conservatism. She shared his philosophy of judicial self-restraint and deference to the legislative branch in making law. She was a lifelong Republican. As for personal attractiveness, O'Connor was a close friend of Senator Barry Goldwater, who sponsored her nomination and helped to gain White House support. Finally, the issue of gender was foremost in the nomination process. Reagan was in the position to place the first woman on the Supreme Court. O'Connor easily won confirmation from the Senate in a 99-0 vote.

Governor Mario Cuomo of New York State has suggested additional criteria for high court appointments. Governor Cuomo opposed the Reagan administration's efforts to nominate ideological conservatives to the

Supreme Court. In his view, ideological litmus tests ignore the necessity of identifying men and women who can decide tough and controversial cases.

Cuomo prefers merit criteria for judicial appointments. These include integrity, experience, wisdom, knowledge of the law, judicial temperament, collegiality, and ability to communicate and write effectively.

President Reagan and Attorney General Meese clearly preferred ideological consistency rather than Cuomo's merit criteria in all Supreme Court appointments after Justice O'Connor. The reason was clear. The Court was closely divided on controversial matters such as abortion, specific issues in criminal justice, and various racial and civil rights issues, including affirmative action. The Reagan administration wanted to shift the Court in a permanent conservative direction. It was able to do so because in 1986, five of the nine Court justices were seventy-five years or older.

President Reagan made two key appointments to the Court in 1986. He replaced Chief Justice Warren Burger by elevating Associate Justice William Rehnquist to be the sixteenth Chief Justice. After considerable debate, the Senate confirmed Rehnquist. President Reagan then nominated Antonin Scalia to be associate justice. Scalia was quickly approved by the Senate.

Rehnquist had served on the Court for fifteen years and was well-known as its most conservative member. Scalia was considered to be even more conservative than Rehnquist. He opposed affirmative action, abortion rights for women, and supported strong penalties for persons accused of serious crime.

Following Senate rejection of Robert Bork, President Reagan nominated Appeals Court Judge Douglas Ginsburg to the Supreme Court. At age 41, Ginsburg would have been one of the youngest persons to join the Court in almost fifty years. Unlike Bork, Ginsburg's views on controversial constitutional issues were unknown. After nine days, Ginsburg withdrew his nomination after it became known that he used marijuana as a student and law professor.

Three days later, President Reagan nominated Appeals Court Judge Anthony Kennedy. Kennedy was a low-key, non-controversial conservative. He was quickly confirmed by the Senate.

The Reagan administration's effort to institutionalize a conservative majority on the Supreme Court was completed by President Bush. In 1990, Bush nominated Judge David Souter to replace Justice William Brennan, the Court's senior member and leader of the liberal bloc. Brennan resigned from the Court at age 84.

Souter's nomination came as a complete surprise, for he was unknown, having served for seven years on the New Hampshire Supreme Court and two months on the federal Court of Appeals in Boston. Souter had almost a blank slate on several of the controversial issues before the Supreme Court, particularly the abortion issue.

Souter was unwilling to provide the Senate Judiciary Committee with any clues as to how he might rule on overturning or upholding the controversial *Roe v. Wade* decision of 1973.

The Senate confirmed Souter by a vote of 90-9 with only Democrats voting against confirmation. They were concerned about Souter's lack of a record on civil rights and the right to privacy. President Bush also remained vague on why he nominated Souter, except to state that he was an experienced judge and no litmus test had been applied to him concerning constitutional interpretation.

However, soon after Souter joined the Supreme Court, he began voting consistently with the conservative bloc by opposing affirmative action, abortion rights, and strongly favoring tough restrictions on persons accused of serious crimes.

Justice Thurgood Marshall retired from the Supreme Court in 1991. Marshall had served for many years as the Court's first and only African American, as well as being a consistent voting member of the Court's liberal bloc.

President Bush nominated Judge Clarence Thomas to replace Marshall. Thomas had served as the controversial Director of the Equal Employment Opportunity Commission in the Reagan administration. While he was at the EEOC, Thomas had opposed preferential hiring and promotional employment policies for women and minorities. Thomas also had an extensive written record of conservative activism, including criticisms of many Supreme Court civil rights and civil liberties decisions.

President Bush claimed he nominated Thomas as the best qualified person. Liberal critics argued that the real reason was that Thomas was one of the few conservative blacks available to oppose abortion and affirmative action.

At the Senate Judiciary Committee's confirmation hearings, Thomas portrayed himself as a moderate. He disavowed many of his harsh criticisms of Congress and Supreme Court rulings. Thomas said he would act objectively as a Justice and not be influenced by his own previous statements. He also used David Souter's strategy of refusing to take any stand on the controversial *Roe v. Wade* abortion issue. Most importantly, Thomas effectively portrayed his rise from poverty to national prominence as a self-help role model for other aspiring blacks and minorities.

The Senate Judiciary Committee sent Thomas's nomination to the full Senate without recommendation following a 7 to 7 tie vote. It appeared that Thomas would be confirmed since several Southern Democrats had committed themselves to support him. Then a bombshell dropped when an FBI summary report of allegations of sexual harassment against Judge Thomas was leaked to the press.

The full Senate decided to delay the confirmation vote and directed the Judiciary Committee to reconvene to investigate the allegations. In the full glare of television, the Senators and a nationwide audience became riveted on the testimony of Anita Hill, a former assistant to Thomas. Ms. Hill, a law professor at the University of Oklahoma, testified that Clarence Thomas had made graphic sexual overtures toward her when he was director of the Equal Employment Opportunity Commission.

Judge Thomas then bitterly denied the charges and claimed he was the victim of a "high-tech lynching of an uppity black man." It was impossible for the Senators to know who was telling the truth and who was lying. It was also clear that the Senate confirmation process was severely flawed, since there was considerable bickering and lack of civility among the Senators.

Judge Thomas was subsequently confirmed by the full Senate in a 52–48 vote, with eleven Democrats joining 41 of 43 Republicans. The vote represented one of the narrowest winning margins ever for confirming an associate justice to the Supreme Court.

SUPREME COURT DECISION-MAKING PROCESS

The Supreme Court has a complex decision-making process, parts of which are secret and others which are public. The three key steps of closed decision making are (1) decision to accept or reject cases for review; (2) assigning of opinions; and (3) drafting of written opinions. The open stages are oral argument and formal announcement of opinions.

In selecting cases, the Court was assisted by the 1925 Judges Bill, drafted by Chief Justice Howard Taft and approved by Congress, which reduced the mandatory right of appealing cases to the Supreme Court. The Court could approve or reject cases by a procedure known as *certiorari*. This considerably reduced the volume of cases brought to the Court. Petitions of a *writ of certiorari* could be granted when four of the justices voted affirmatively. This procedure is also called "the rule of four."

In the case-selection procedure, each justice receives copies of *certiorari* petitions and determines whether or not petitions should be granted or denied. The Court receives about 4,000 petitions each year. The Court meets in a private conference every Friday during a term, with the chief justice beginning discussion of each case. After each justice has commented, voting occurs in the reverse order of seniority to determine if four justices agree to hear the case. If so, the petition is granted.

About four months after *certiorari* has been granted, the Court schedules oral argument in public session before the nine justices. Counsel for both sides submit briefs to the court two or three weeks before the argument. Each party is granted thirty minutes to speak. The justices frequently question the attorneys during oral argument. A former justice, John Harlan, suggested four major purposes of oral argument, including selectivity of ideas discussed, simplicity of form and expression, candor or frankness in responding to justices' questions, and flexibility toward the Court. The justices may interject comments during any stage of the oral argument. Consequently, attorneys should not expect to present prepared statements without frequent interruptions.

Following oral argument, the justices return to the Friday conference and discuss cases argued during the week. They follow the same procedure as for certiorari petitions. The chief justice speaks first and voting occurs in the reverse order of seniority. Following the vote, the chief justice assigns preparation of a written decision or opinion or takes the assignment himself if he happens to be in the majority; otherwise, the assignment is made by the senior associate justice who is part of the majority. Draft opinions are then circulated to each justice for his or her comments. Frequently, justices will change their votes on a case during this stage as the final decision is developed. When a final majority of at least five justices agrees on the written decision, the Court is ready to announce it publicly. Unlike the president or Congress, every formal decision of the Supreme Court is part of a permanent record known as the U.S. Reports. The justices may read or excerpt key portions of their decisions in public session. Justices who disagree with Court majorities may file dissenting opinions, stating their reasons for opposition. Other justices who wish to add comments and other personal interpretations of the case may write concurring opinions.

In Article 41, David M. O'Brien discusses how the Supreme Court decides cases and writes opinions. The many direct quotes from various justices give the reader an opportunity to discover what Supreme Court members consider to be the strengths and shortcomings of the decision-making process.

THE SUPREME COURT AND PUBLIC POLICY

In Western democracies the U.S. Supreme Court is unique because of its political function in shaping public policy. Through its great powers of constitutional and statutory interpretation, the Court can affect government in many ways. Over the past thirty years, three chief justices have symbolized different policy roles for the Supreme Court. Under Chief Justice Earl Warren (1954–1969), the Supreme Court was more liberal, activist, and expansive in supporting the Bill of Rights to protect individual rights against state interference in such areas as free speech, religious rights, and procedural protections for persons accused of serious crimes. The Warren Court eliminated racial segregation in public schools in *Brown v. Topeka Board of Education* (1954).

In contrast, President Nixon sought to change the policy direction of the Supreme Court by appointing justices with "law and order" and "strict constructionist" views. Strict construction is a judicial philosophy that favors judicial restraint in interpreting the Constitution. Nixon (as well as

Reagan and Bush) wanted the Supreme Court to avoid judicial activism or "loose construction," which they believed was used excessively by the Warren Court to make liberal interpretations of constitutional protections. The four Nixon appointees—Chief Justice Burger and Associate Justices Blackmun, Powell, and Rehnquist—eroded many of the liberal decisions of the Warren Court. Rather than nullify judgments in school desegregation, civil rights, and civil liberties, the Burger Court changed the scope of such decisions and limited the impact of previous rulings. Most controversial were rulings in such areas as school busing, abortion, and the death penalty in state criminal cases.

The Rehnquist Court, beginning in 1986, became much more conservative than the Burger Court. Since Chief Justice Rehnquist assumed leadership, he has been a judicial partisan for conservative beliefs. These include deference to most federal and state laws. For Rehnquist, conservatism means the Court should avoid ruling positively on civil rights, minority rights, women's issues, or procedural protections for persons accused of serious crimes. Instead, the Court should defer to the wisdom of the president, Congress, and state authority.

Rehnquist's leadership of conservative activism to reverse Warren Court constitutional protections was bolstered by the Reagan and Bush appointments. Justices Scalia, Kennedy, and Souter now vote regularly with Rehnquist, while Justices O'Connor and White are frequent allies. Justices Stevens and Blackmun are now in the minority on most civil rights, abortion, and criminal justice cases.

The Abortion Controversy

No issue has provoked more nationwide controversy than the Supreme Court's *Roe v. Wade* decision of 1973 (Article 42). In that case, Justice Blackmun ruled for the 7-2 majority that abortion was permissible in some situations. He established a trimester framework. During the first three months of pregnancy, abortion was permitted under medical supervision. In the second trimester, states could regulate the conditions and circumstances of abortions to protect a woman's health. In the last three months, the state can prohibit abortion unless it is required to save the mother's life or protect her health.

Blackmun based his decision, which was supported by six other members of the Court, on a constitutional right of privacy.

Roe v. Wade was controversial because the decision required forty-six states to rewrite their anti-abortion laws. The decision was sweeping in its scope and went beyond most public opinion which supported abortion only under circumstances intended to protect a woman's health or life. Most importantly, the decision provoked a continuing political conflict between pro-choice and right to life groups.

Right to life groups argued that abortion is murder of the unborn, a destruction of human life for convenience, and evidence of moral decay. Pro-choice groups responded by arguing for a woman's right to reproductive freedom. They called for religious freedom, civil liberties, and minority rights.

For the next sixteen years, pro-life groups gained increasing support from conservatives in Congress, state legislatures, and appointments to the Supreme Court by Presidents Reagan and Bush. Until 1989, however, the Court rejected the notion that life begins at conception and that states can place obstacles in the path of a woman's right to an abortion. The decisions included nullifying requirements that parental consent was needed for minors; that criminal liabilities could be imposed on physicians; that all abortions must be performed in hospitals; or that doctors must inform pregnant women of the risks and alternatives to abortion.

However, anti-abortion groups were much more successful in Congress. Constitutional amendments to overturn *Roe v. Wade* were regularly introduced. None ever received even a majority vote. More successful were restrictions on government funding of abortions. Henry Hyde (Republican-Illinois) led pro-life forces by achieving a ban on Medicaid funding for abortions except to save the mother's life or in cases of rape or incest. Approved in 1976 by Congress, the Hyde amendment was upheld by the Supreme Court in 1986. Interestingly, however, the restriction on government funding affected only the poorest and mostly minority women requiring Medicaid assistance.

In May 1991, the Supreme Court in the case of *Rust v. Sullivan* upheld federal regulations prohibiting employees of family planning clinics from discussing abortion with their patients. In 1970, Congress provided funding for family planning under Title X of the Public Health Service Act. Until 1988, the Department of Health and Human Services permitted federal funds to be used for counseling about abortion as well as childbirth. In the last years of the Reagan administration, the HHS regulations were changed to prohibit abortion counseling. Planned Parenthood challenged the new regulations, which had previously been upheld by the federal Court of Appeals. In this case, the Supreme Court ruled 5–4 to uphold the 1988 regulation over challenges that restrictions on abortion counseling were a violation of First Amendment free speech protections.

The real focus of anti-abortion groups was a Supreme Court reversal of *Roe v. Wade.* This began to bring results in 1989, when the Court upheld a very restrictive Missouri law, which banned most abortions in state-supported facilities. However, as shown in the Court's *Webster* decision (Article 43), the majority did not specifically overturn *Roe v. Wade.* Four justices implied they were waiting for a better case by which to do so.

Between the *Webster* decision and 1991, several state legislatures began passing restrictive anti-abortion statutes. These were challenged by pro-choice groups and will probably reach the Supreme Court in another year or two.

Three of the strongest state laws were passed in Pennsylvania, Utah, and Louisiana. The Pennsylvania law requires spousal notification, a twenty-four hour waiting period, and counseling about fetal development before abortion is permitted. A federal district court declared this law unconstitutional in 1990.

The Utah law bans most abortions except in cases of serious fetal defects or threats to the mother's health. The Louisiana law, approved over the governor's veto, not only prohibits all abortions except to save the mother's life, but also imposes strict conditions on victims of rape and incest, who must report such crimes to the police. The law also imposes ten years imprisonment and fines up to $100,000 on doctors performing prohibited abortions. A federal district court declared the Louisiana law unconstitutional in 1991.

These state laws go a long way toward prohibiting nearly all abortion rights for pregnant women. If approved by the Supreme Court, there will not be a constitutionally protected right of privacy. In effect, the states would have an unlimited right to establish values, moral practices, and new standards of behavior. Social regulation would replace the constitutional right of privacy.[1]

The abortion issue is an example of how the Supreme Court remains at the center of political controversy. In the 1990s, many civil liberties and civil rights issues cannot be resolved by the president and Congress. Also, the states obviously differ in how they deal with these matters. The Supreme Court has a constitutional obligation to resolve legal disputes which are, in reality, political disagreements between elected executives and legislators who cannot find solutions. Issues such as abortion are so divisive that the popularly elected branches of government find it useful to pass them on to the courts. Supreme Court members do not have to face polarized voters in an election since the justices have life-time appointments.

NOTE

1. Raymond Tatalovich and Byron W. Daynes, eds., *Social Regulatory Policy* (Boulder, Colorado: Westview Press, 1988), 1.

Judicial Review

39
Marbury v. Madison
U.S. Supreme Court

The power of judicial review—the authority of the Supreme Court to declare acts of Congress unconstitutional—is not specifically found in Article III of the Constitution, although Alexander Hamilton argued, in The Federalist, Number 78, that such power was implicit. Judicial review over the constitutionality of state laws was part of the "supremacy clause" of Article VI and included in section 25 of the 1789 Judiciary Act. Chief Justice Marshall's opinion in Marbury v. Madison *(1803) established this doctrine in the context of a bitter political controversy between the Federalist party (which had just lost the presidential election of 1800) and the Jeffersonian Republicans. Just before John Adams left the presidency, he attempted to pack the courts with Federalist appointees, acting under authority of the 1801 Judiciary Act, which was adopted after Jefferson's presidential victory. Marbury, one of these last-ditch appointees, had been selected for a justice of the peace in the District of Columbia. His commission to take office was signed and sealed by John Marshall, then serving as secretary of state as well as chief justice. But Jefferson ordered his new secretary of state, James Madison, to withhold the commission to Marbury. Consequently, Marbury filed suit with the Supreme Court to issue a writ of mandamus under the 1789 Judiciary Act to force Madison to deliver his commission. The case thus involved a dispute between the presidency and the Supreme Court. Marshall knew that the Court could not force the issue since the Jefferson administration would refuse to obey the court order if it was issued. Marshall also knew that he could be severely criticized by the Federalists if he refused to issue the order for Marbury's commission. How did Marshall resolve the dispute? As indicated in the text of the opinion, the solution was to agree that Marbury's commission should be granted but that the Supreme Court could not intervene in the matter because the section of the 1789 Judiciary Act granting such authority to the Court was unconstitutional. Marshall's opinion has been called a masterwork of indirection, that is, a brilliant example of sidestepping danger while seeming to court it, to advance in one direction while his opponents were looking in another. It also should be noted that the Supreme Court is much more inclined to use statutory interpretation rather than judicial review to avoid confrontations with either Congress or the presidency.*

Source: 1 Cranch 137; 2 L. Ed. 60 (1803).

Mr. Chief Justice Marshall delivered the opinion of the Court, saying in part that:

In the order in which the court has viewed this subject, the following questions have been considered and decided.

1st. Has the applicant a right to the commission he demands? . . . [The Court finds that he has.]

2nd. If he has a right, and that right has been violated, do the laws of his country afford him a remedy? . . . [The court finds that they do.]

3rd. If they do afford him a remedy, is it a mandamus issuing from this court? . . .

This, then, is a plain case for a mandamus, either to deliver the commission, or a copy of it from the record; and it only remains to be inquired,

Whether it can issue from this court.

The act to establish the judicial courts of the United States authorizes the Supreme Court "to issue writs of mandamus in cases warranted by the principles and usages of law, to any courts appointed, or persons holding office, under the authority of the United States."

The Secretary of State, being a person holding an office under the authority of the United States, is precisely within the letter of the description, and if this court is not authorized to issue a writ of mandamus to such an officer, it must be because the law is unconstitutional, and therefore absolutely incapable of conferring the authority, and assigning the duties which its words purport to confer and assign.

The Constitution vests the whole judicial power of the United States in one Supreme Court, and such inferior courts as Congress shall, from time to time, ordain and establish. . . .

In the distribution of this power it is declared that "the Supreme Court shall have original jurisdiction in all cases affecting ambassadors, other public ministers and consuls, and those in which a state shall be a party. In all other cases, the Supreme Court shall have appellate jurisdiction." . . .

If it had been intended to leave it in the discretion of the legislature to apportion the judicial power between the supreme and inferior courts according to the will of that body, it would certainly have been useless to have proceeded further than to have defined the judicial power, and the tribunals in which it should be vested. The subsequent part of the section is mere surplusage, is entirely without meanings, . . . the distribution of jurisdiction, made in the Constitution, is form without substance.

It cannot be presumed that any clause in the Constitution is intended to be without effect; and, therefore, such a construction is inadmissible, unless the words require it. . . .

To enable this court, then, to issue a mandamus, it must be shown to be an exercise of appellate jurisdiction, or to be necessary to enable them to exercise appellate jurisdiction. . . .

It is the essential criterion of appellate jurisdiction, that it revises and corrects the proceedings in a cause already instituted, and does not create that cause. Although, therefore, a mandamus may be directed to courts, yet to issue such a writ to an officer for the delivery of a paper, is in effect the same as to sustain an original action for that paper, and, therefore, seems not to belong to appellate but to original jurisdiction. Neither is it necessary in such a case as this to enable the court to exercise its appellate jurisdiction.

The authority, therefore, given to the Supreme Court, by the Act establishing the judicial courts of the United States, to issue writs of mandamus to public officers, appears not to be warranted by the Constitution; and it becomes necessary to inquire whether a jurisdiction so conferred can be exercised.

The question, whether an Act, repugnant to the Constitution can become the law of the land, is a question deeply interesting to the United States; but, happily, not of an intricacy proportioned to its interest. It seems only necessary to recognize certain principles, supposed to have been long and well established, to decide it.

That the people have an original right to establish, for their future government, such principles as, in their opinion, shall most conduce to their own happiness, is the basis on which the whole American fabric has been erected. The exercise of this original right is a very great exertion; nor can it nor ought it to be frequently repeated. The principles, therefore, so established, are deemed fundamental. And as the authority from which they proceed is supreme, and can seldom act, they are designed to be permanent.

This original and supreme will organizes the government, and assigns to different departments their respective powers. It may either stop here, or establish certain limits not to be transcended by those departments.

The government of the United States is of the latter description. The powers of the legislature are defined and limited; and that those limits may not be mistaken, or forgotten, the Constitution is written. To what purpose are powers limited, and to what purpose is that limitation committed to writing, if these limits may, at any time, be passed by those intended to be restrained? The distinction between a government with limited and unlimited powers is abolished, if those limits do not confine the persons on whom they are imposed, and if acts prohibited and acts allowed are of equal obligation. It is a proposition too plain to be contested, that the Constitution controls any legislative Act repugnant to it; or, that the legislature may alter the Constitution by an ordinary Act.

Between these alternatives there is no middle ground. The Constitution is either a superior paramount law, unchangeable by ordinary means, or it is on a level with ordinary legislative Acts, and, like other Acts, is alterable when the legislature shall please to alter it.

If the former part of the alternative be true, then a legislative Act contrary to the Constitution is not law; if the latter part be true, then written constitutions are absurd attempts, on the part of the people, to limit a power in its own nature illimitable.

Certainly all those who have framed written constitutions contemplate them as forming the fundamental and paramount law of the nation, and, consequently, the theory of every such government must be, that an Act of the Legislature, repugnant to the Constitution, is void.

This theory is essentially attached to a written Constitution, and, is consequently, to be considered, by this court, as one of the fundamental principles of our society. It is not therefore to be lost sight of in the further consideration of this subject.

If an Act of the Legislature, repugnant to the Constitution, is void, does it, notwithstanding its invalidity, bind the courts, and oblige them to give it effect? Or, in other words, though it be not law, does it constitute a rule as operative as if it was a law? This would be to overthrow in fact what was established in theory; and would seem, at first view, an absurdity too gross to be insisted on. It shall, however, receive a more attentive consideration.

It is emphatically the province and duty of the judicial department to say what the law is. Those who apply the rule to particular cases, must of necessity expound and interpret that rule. If two laws conflict with each other, the courts must decide on the operation of each.

So if a law be in opposition to the Constitution; if both the law and the Constitution apply to a particular case, so that the court must either decide that case conformably to the law, disregarding the Constitution; or conformably to the Constitution, disregarding the law, the court must determine which of these conflicting rules governs the case. This is of the very essence of judicial duty.

If, then, the courts are to regard the Constitution, and the Constitution is superior to any Act of the Legislature, the Constitution, and not such ordinary Act, must govern the case to which they both apply.

Those, then, who controvert the principle that the Constitution is to be considered, in court, as a paramount law, are reduced to the necessity of maintaining that courts must close their eyes on the Constitution, and see only the law.

This doctrine would subvert the very foundation of all written constitutions. It would declare that an Act which, according to the principles and theory of our government, is entirely void, is yet, in practice, completely obligatory. It would declare that if the legislature shall do what is expressly forbidden, such Act, notwithstanding the express prohibition, is in reality effectual. It would be giving to the legislature a practical and real omnipotence, with the same breath which professes to restrict their powers within narrow limits. It is prescribing limits, and declaring that those limits may be passed at pleasure.

That it thus reduces to nothing what we have deemed the greatest improvement on political institutions, a written constitution, would of itself be sufficient, in America, where written constitutions have been viewed with so much reverence, for rejecting the construction. But the peculiar expressions of the Constitution of the United States furnish additional arguments in favor of its rejection.

The judicial power of the United States is extended to all cases arising under the Constitution.

Could it be the intention of those who gave this power, to say that in using it the Constitution should not be looked into? That a case arising under the Constitution should be decided without examining the instrument under which it arises?

This is too extravagant to be maintained.

In some cases, then, the Constitution must be looked into by the judges. And if they can open it at all, what part of it are they forbidden to read or to obey?

There are many other parts of the Constitution which serve to illustrate this subject.

It is declared that "no tax or duty shall be laid on articles exported from any State." Suppose a duty on the export of cotton, of tobacco, or of flour; and a suit instituted to recover it. Ought judgment to be rendered in such a case? Ought the judges to close their eyes on the Constitution, and see only the law?

The Constitution declares "that no bill of attainder or ex post facto law shall be passed."

If, however, such a bill should be passed, and a person should be prosecuted under it, must the court condemn to death those victims whom the Constitution endeavors to preserve?

"No person," says the Constitution, "shall be convicted of treason unless on the testimony of two witnesses to the same overt act, or on confession in open court."

Here the language of the Constitution is addressed especially to the courts. It prescribes, directly for them, a rule of evidence not to be departed from. If the legislature should change that rule, and declare one witness, or a confession out of court, sufficient for conviction, must the constitutional principle yield to the legislative Act?

From these, and many other selections which might be made, it is apparent, that the framers of the Constitution contemplated that instrument as a rule for the government of courts, as well as of the legislature.

Why otherwise does it direct the judges to take an oath to support it? This oath certainly applies in an especial manner to their conduct in their official character. How immoral to impose it on them, if they were to be used as the instruments, and the knowing instruments, for violating what they swear to support!

The oath of office, too, imposed by the legislature, is completely demonstrative of the legislative opinion on this subject. It is in these words: "I do solemnly swear that I will administer justice without respect to persons, and do equal right to the poor and to the rich; and that I will faithfully and impartially discharge all the duties incumbent on me as _____, according to the best of my abilities and understanding, agreeably to the Constitution and laws of the United States."

Why does a judge swear to discharge his duties agreeably to the Constitution of the United States, if that Constitution forms no rule for his government—if it is closed upon him, and cannot be inspected by him?

If such be the real state of things, this is worse than solemn mockery. To prescribe, or to take this oath, becomes equally a crime.

It is also not entirely unworthy of observation, that in declaring what shall be the supreme law of the land, the Constitution itself is first mentioned; and not the laws of the United States generally, but those only which shall be made in pursuance of the Constitution, that have rank.

Thus, the particular phraseology of the Constitution of the United States confirms and strengthens the principle, supposed to be essential to all written constitutions, that a law repugnant to the Constitution is void; and that courts, as well as other departments, are bound by that instrument.

The rule must be discharged.

Constitutional Interpretation: Original Intention v. Judicial Activism

40
The Supreme Court's Dilemma and Defense
Raymond Polin

During the 1980s, the Reagan administration challenged Supreme Court decisions that did not meet the test of "original intention of the Framers." Raymond Polin, professor of government and politics at St. John's University, analyzes the principal arguments for original intention put forth by former Attorney General Edwin Meese. He also examines the rebuttal to Meese by former Associate Justice William Brennan, who made a case for judicial activism. What are the sources of the original intention viewpoint? Why does Polin support the position that both original intent and judicial activism are considered in all cases before the Supreme Court? In weighing the two positions, which usually has the greater emphasis in Court decisions? Polin sees more than a philosophical debate at issue. Why did the Reagan administration want the Court to accept the original intent viewpoint in deciding cases? According to Polin, what was the real original intention of the Framers? Should executive power be superior to legislative and judicial power?

There is really nothing new insofar as essential legal principle in the dispute over the proper basis of constitutional interpretation that casts Associate Justice William J. Brennan, Jr., and Attorney General Edwin Meese III as rival protagonists. Moreover, it should not be expected that either viewpoint will completely prevail and the other be eliminated from consideration in future cases.

Brennan's position of "judicial activism" and Meese's position of "original intention" are both indispensable to the proper functioning of American constitutionalism. This becomes readily apparent once we recognize that Brennan embraces the need to update constitutional interpretation to keep abreast of constantly changing technology and circumstances, while Meese embraces the need to maintain intact for succeeding generations proven principles of justice and government that were derived from much bitter experience and hard sacrifice. Indeed, the more one ponders this matter, the more it appears that these two positions are different ends of the same stick and require one another for each to have discernible meaning and practicable application. General statements of original intention cannot foresee all particular eventualities, and judicial activism with respect to "current conditions" can be legitimate only if founded on principles derived from constitutional provisions.

The familiar ring of Brennan's argument may be noted in the now classical article by Roscoe Pound on "The Scope and Purpose of Historical Jurisprudence" that appeared in the *Harvard Law Review* in 1912 and stated as its thrust: "The main problem to which sociological jurists are addressing themselves today is to enable and to compel law-making, and also interpretation and application of legal rules, to take more account, and more intelligent account, of the social facts upon which law must proceed and to which it is to be applied." Nor did Pound overlook the import of "a jurisprudence of original intention" that seeks to "resurrect the original meaning of constitutional provisions" espoused by Meese in his speech of July 9, 1985, before the American Bar Association in Washington, D.C. Pound cautioned: "Another point is the importance of reasonable and just solutions of individual causes, too often sacrificed in the immediate past to the attempt to bring out an impossible degree of certainty." Pound again tilted in favor of Brennan's position, as he reported the advocacy of sociological jurists: "They urge that legal precepts are to be regarded more as guides to results which are socially just and less as inflexible molds." This basic coalignment becomes obvious when we examine the keystone passage in Brennan's address at Georgetown University on Oct. 12, 1985:

> We current Justices read the Constitution in the only way we can: as 20th century Americans. We look to the history of the

time of framing and to the intervening history of interpretation. But the ultimate question must be, what do the words of the text mean in our time?

The inescapable conclusion, therefore, is that we are faced by somewhat of a dilemma that can at best be somewhat transformed, but never completely eliminated or avoided. This was apparent especially to Charles Austin Beard, who is still read for his studies of *The Supreme Court and the Constitution* (1912), *An Economic Interpretation of the Constitution* (1913), and *The Economic Basis of Politics* (1922). In the last, Beard laid bare for us a forever-ongoing problem of life and, therefore, of the Court: "In other words, there is no rest for mankind, no final solution of eternal contradictions. Such is the design of the universe. The recognition of this fact is the beginning of wisdom and of statesmanship."

Chief Justice John Marshall was certainly one who showed awareness of dual considerations faced by the Court. Thus, in his *obiter dictum* in *Marbury v. Madison* (1803), Marshall lent support to the importance of Meese's stand in favor of original intention when, in effect, he asked what is the use of having a written constitution as "the supreme Law of the Land" if its provisions can be altered or set aside by Congressional statute? Marshall also affirmed, in *McCulloch v. Maryland* (1819), the claims of original intention when he stated that "This government is acknowledged by all to be one of enumerated powers." Yet, Marshall also saw that original intention, *even when specifically enumerated,* cannot be expected to be fully detected or to cover the whole matter of cases arising later: "But the question respecting the extent of the powers actually granted is perpetually arising, and will probably continue to arise, as long as our system shall exist."

THE NEED FOR ACTUAL CASES

The dispute between original intention and judicial activism with respect to current circumstances cannot be expected ever to go away completely, for both principles should be considered habitually in every case that comes before the Court. They are somewhat reminiscent of the complementary roles played in England by "the fundamental law of the land" and precepts of Equity that "fill up the interstices of the law" to "let justice be done." Which principle should have the superior weight in applying a constitutional provision? That must depend on the facts and issues of each case, and therefore cannot be specified with certitude before judicial examination of them. This sort of approach was set forth with his customary clarity and directness by Associate Justice Wiley Rutledge almost 40 years ago when I asked him why the Supreme Court did not avoid much argumentation, delay, and occasional need-to-undo, by issuing advisory opinions about the constitutionality of pending legislation.

Rutledge replied that there were two cogent reasons why the Court never had, and probably never would, accept such a petition. The first reason was that, if the Court were to issue advisory opinions, it would constantly become embroiled in the political arena and thereby lose its judicial character while causing pileup and even more delay of legislation. He indicated that the Court was strong in its desire to avoid such increased activity and consequent loss of its above-the-political-battle image. The second reason was that one could never be sure how to apply a constitutional provision or general principle of law until a real-world case and its particulars were presented to a court. One could suitably judge the constitutionality of a statute or action only by examining its impact in actual situations and seeing which constitutional provision and

which principle of law should be applied and be determinant.

What Rutledge encapsulated in his response was a description of how the Court has regularly passed upon constitutionality and thereby given continuity to the Constitution's provisions by making them flexible enough to fit various new conditions. Thus, the Commerce Clause was drafted in 1787, when there were no steamboats, railroads, automobiles, trucks, airplanes, or space vehicles, yet it became successfully applicable to operation of all of them.

Accordingly, Brennan was undoubtedly more attuned than Meese to the counsel of Marshall, Beard, Pound, and Rutledge, and to the whole course of development of the opinions of the Supreme Court, when he declared at Georgetown: "For the genius of the Constitution rests not in any static meaning it might have had in a world that is dead and gone, but in the adaptability of its great principles to cope with current problems and current needs."

Thus, if we try to cling to a static stability based too much on the past, we shall be engulfed by the tide of change. Our hope is in a dynamic equilibrium of adaptation to change that requires constant pedaling for constant movement and maintains our constitutional balance of freedom and authority. It is necessary, therefore, to be guided—in respective proper proportion—by the dual principles of original intention and current circumstances, with greater emphasis usually on the latter. Original intention imparts the perspective of the accumulated wisdom of the Founding Fathers and the ages that preceded them, while current circumstances serve as a prism for analyzing contemporary problems and showing lines along which justice may be constitutionally applied and the nation's general welfare promoted.

WHY THE DISPUTE NOW?

Why has the dispute spearheaded by Brennan and Meese broken out anew today? Brennan has been noticeably candid in making known his jurisprudential views, but he has been wont to present them from the bench and in written opinions. Obviously, therefore, he has spoken out away from the bench in reply to Meese and in defense of the Supreme Court against what he perceived as a prominent danger. It is significant that Brennan, a "liberal," was joined by Associate Justice John Paul Stevens, a "centrist," and Associate Justice William H. Rehnquist, a "conservative," in a united defense of the Court in addresses all made away from the bench within the same month.

In a speech before a Federal Bar Association group in Chicago on Oct. 23, 1985, Stevens delivered not only a direct rebuttal of points offered by Meese, but also a public rebuke of him, however politely stated, for a misreading of the Court's position. Stevens took strong issue as well with Meese's characterization of the Court's position of religious neutrality as "bizarre" in the eyes of the founding generation.

Rehnquist, in remarks at the University of Wyoming Law School on Oct. 25, 1985, advised a "hands-off" policy toward the Court. The nub of this question, then, is why Meese seeks to narrow the latitude of judgment of the Court and thus reduce drastically the power exercised by it.

There is certainly nothing hidden about the advertised desire of the Reagan administration to shrink government—except for the nation's security program—and to "get the government off the people's backs and out of their pockets." The more limited role of government in the agricultural age, when the Constitution was drafted, is more consonant with the ideology of the Reagan administration

than it is compatible with the practical requirements of the modern scientific-industrial age of high technology. Also, the Administration has not been as notable as the Court in support of civil and personal rights, especially some which the Court has quite rightly and necessarily protected by the "penumbra principle," as held in *Griswold v. Connecticut* (1965), which it has related to rights explicitly stated in the Constitution.

There are those who mock the Court for holding and so terming the penumbra principle and want the Justices to rely only on express, unmistakably clear provisions in the Constitution, with their limited original intentions. They expect that would achieve their frequent purpose of depriving any court or any agency of government of its jurisdiction or authority to act in matters they want free of government regulation or protection. In effect, they advocate a prescription of governmental inaction that would, at times, negate the slogan of Equity—"let justice be done."

To those who mock the Court and the penumbra principle, the rebuttal should be made that precisely therein lies one of the great functions of the Court. It is in the shadowy areas that the Court is called upon to exercise stronger vision and to "fill in the interstices of the law" according to the light of its understanding, by recognizing in the shape and position of these penumbras the logical outlines cast by constitutional and statutory provisions and other legal sources. It is not in keeping with Article III, Section 2, of the Constitution that, in deciding cases before it, the Court should recognize significant nuances and thereby give vital substance to intentions of the Constitution and pursuant laws and treaties?

However, if the Court could be confined more to judgment in keeping with original intention, it would be stripped of much of its power of logical extension of constitutional and statutory provisions to fit current circumstances and needs and to promote and protect civil and personal rights. Government and the budget—again, except for defense costs—could and would shrink if original intention were to prevail as an almost monistic standard of judgment for the Court.

The timing of the confrontation with the Court fits in patly with the need first to neutralize, deactivate, or convert it if the Reagan administration is soon to achieve its objective of shrinking government. The Court would almost certainly thwart such a purpose if it stayed its historically established course of interpretation of powers assigned respectively to the Congress and to the President. The policy of shrinking government cannot be carried out simply by inducing Congress to cede its constitutionally vested control of the public purse to the President, for a courageous Court has in the past—*e.g.*, in the National Recovery Administration case of *U.S. v. Schechter Brothers* (1935)—voided legislation it regarded as an unconstitutional delegation of legislative power to the President.

The key control the Constitution assigned to the Congress over the operation and policies of the Federal government lies in the power of the purse. Therefore, the crux of the matter is that the passing of the initiative to the Executive Office of the President in drafting of the Federal budget (formalized by the Budget and Accounting Act of 1921) grants insufficient power to the President, in Reagan's view, to shrink the Federal budget and to modify public policies. So, there is an attempted double-play under way to convince the Congress to abdicate in favor of the President essential controls over spending through such a plan as Gramm-Rudman-Hollings and to persuade the Court not to declare it unconstitutional.

The net result would be to diminish—if not in time to destroy—the present constitutional balance that permits the Court and the Congress to serve as effective checks on the President and each other. By any reasonable stretch of the imagination, was it ever the original intention of the Founding Fathers to permit the President to exercise such powers? On this point, we should not expect the Reagan administration to use the argument of original intention.

THE FOUNDING FATHERS' INTENTION

The real original intention of the Founding Fathers was clearly to set up a system of "mixed, balanced government" that gave each branch a proper role and proportion of power, including the power to check one another. They all subscribed to Montesquieu's admonition in *The Spirit of the Laws* (1748) that "Power should be a check to power." It is definitely an insupportable idea that it could have been the original intention of men so suspicious especially of executive tyranny to permit an overconcentration of power in the hands of the President and so little as would be left to the Congress and the Court as Senators Gramm, Rudman, and Hollings and the Attorney General would have it.

It is also essential to correct understanding of the original intentions of the Founding Fathers to appreciate that their purpose in replacing the inadequate Articles of Confederation with the *Federal* Constitution of the U.S. was to set up a supreme national government *endowed with sufficient powers that were specifically enumerated so that they would be known now to be granted to the national government, whereas previously denied to it,* as well as to set limits to its authority. They wanted a more effective government as well as a safe one. The Founding Fathers, in their wisdom, therefore included the "Elastic Clause, the broad general grant of power to the Congress that makes the Constitution workable through logical extension—*i.e.,* the power of the Congress "To make all laws which shall be necessary and proper for carrying into execution the foregoing powers, and all other powers vested by this Constitution in the government of the United States, or in any department or officer thereof." However, this power has been held in *Marbury v. Madison* not to include the power to set aside any express provision of the Constitution.

The conclusion offered here is that there is a lesson of dominant importance that emerges from the entire record of the Supreme Court. It is that the mistakes of interpretation, doctrine, procedure, and application that are occasionally inevitable for any body of humans are only temporary with respect to the holdings and findings of the Court. Ultimately, what remains as received doctrine and standard practice for the Court is what is con-

stitutionally correct and of greater benefit to the American people. Thus, a *Plessy v. Ferguson* (1896), with its specious doctrine of "separate but equal," was in time—although much too slowly—reversed by *Brown v. Topeka Board of Education* (1954), with its correct requirement of "the same facilities at the same time," which will now stand so long as the U.S. endures.

Therefore, we may all adjudge the Court, in the final analysis, as having served us, over all, quite well, and acknowledge that we are beholden to the Justices and their constitutional role. The final point to be made, then, is that the Court is usually—or ultimately—fundamentally correct in how it decides and in the scope of its decisions. Accordingly, it should not be improperly pressured or circumscribed, but left much to its own, independent actions.

Supreme Court Decision-Making Process

41
Deciding Cases and Writing Opinions
David M. O'Brien

The nine members of the U.S. Supreme Court are required to agree (or disagree) on all cases and to write formal opinions indicating their decisions. Unlike the president or Congress, the written opinions of the Court form a permanent record of every major action taken. Supreme Court decision-making, as discussed by David O'Brien, consists of "open" and "closed" phases. The open or public aspects include (1) oral argument and (2) formal announcements of the Court's opinion. How do the justices see the role of oral argument by opposing attorneys? What are some differences among the justices in questioning attorneys? O'Brien also identifies four stages of closed or secret decision-making by the Court: (1) acceptance or rejection of cases for review; (2) conference on the merits; (3) tentative votes; and (4) opinion-writing. What are the different strategies used at the private conference? Why may justices change their votes in deciding a case? How are opinions assigned and circulated among the justices? O'Brien concludes by observing that the Court's opinions are becoming longer and more numerous. What is the impact of the Supreme Court's decisions as consensus becomes more difficult to achieve?

The court grants a full hearing to less than 180 of the more than 5,000 cases on the docket each term. Deciding the merits of those few cases taxes the individual powers of the justices and their capacity for compromise. All the justices agree that they are overworked because they take too many cases. But they cannot agree on what to do about this situation.

When cases are granted full consideration, attorneys for each side submit briefs setting forth their arguments and how they think the case should be decided. The Clerk of the Court circulates the briefs to each chamber and sets a date for the attorneys to argue their views orally before the justices. After hearing oral arguments, the justices in private conference vote on how to decide the issues presented in a case.

Cases are decided by majority rule on the basis of a tally of the justices' votes. But conference votes by no means end the work or

Reprinted from *Storm Center: The Supreme Court in American Politics*, 2nd Ed., by David M. O'Brien, by permission of W. W. Norton & Company, Inc. Copyright © 1990, 1986 by David M. O'Brien.

resolve conflicts. Votes are tentative until an opinion announcing the Court's decision is handed down. After conference, a justice assigned to write the Court's opinion must circulate drafts to all the other justices for their comments and then usually revise the opinion before delivering it in open Court. Justices are free to switch their votes and to write separate opinions concurring in or dissenting from the Court's decision. They thus continue after conference to compete for influence on the final decision and opinion. . . .

"The business of the Court," Potter Stewart said, "is to give institutional opinions for its decisions." The Court's opinion serves to communicate an institutional decision. It should also convey the politically symbolic values of certainty, stability, and impartiality in the law. In most cases, justices therefore try to persuade as many others as possible to join an opinion. Sometimes when the justices cannot agree on an opinion for their decision, or in minor cases, an unsigned (per curiam) opinion is handed down. . . .

THE ROLE OF ORAL ARGUMENT

For those outside the Court, the role of oral argument in deciding cases is vague, if not bewildering. Visitors at the Court must often stand in line for an hour or more before they are seated in the courtroom to hear oral arguments. They are then given only three or four minutes to listen and watch attorneys argue cases, before they are ushered out. Only by special request, and subject to available seats, may members of the public hear entire arguments in a case. There are reserved seats for the press, so it may hear all oral arguments.

The importance of oral argument, Chief Justice Hughes observed, lies in the fact that often "the impression that a judge has at the close of a full oral argument accords with the conviction which controls his final vote." The

justices hold conference and take their initial, usually decisive vote on cases within a day or two after hearing arguments. Oral arguments come at a crucial time. They focus the minds of the justices and present the possibility for fresh perspectives on a case. "Often my idea of how a case shapes up is changed by oral argument," Brennan has noted. "I have had too many occasions when my judgment or a decision has turned on what happened in oral argument." The fact is, Powell said, "that the quality of advocacy—the research, briefing and oral argument of the close and difficult cases—does contribute significantly to the development of precedents." . . .

The Court began cutting back on time for oral arguments in 1848. The 1848 rule allowed eight hours per case—two hours for two counsel on each side. In 1871, the Court cut the amount of time in half, permitting two hours for each side. Subsequently, in 1911, each side got an hour and a half; in 1925, though, time was limited to one hour per side. Finally, in 1970, Burger persuaded the Court to limit arguments to thirty minutes per side.

The Court's current argument calendar permits the hearing of fewer than 180 cases each year. For fourteen weeks each term, from the first Monday in October until the end of April, the Court hears arguments from ten to twelve and from one to three on Monday, Tuesday, and Wednesday about every two weeks. Although the amount of time per case was substantially reduced by the Burger Court, more cases are heard now than thirty years ago. At the turn of the century, the Court heard between 170 and 190 cases. After the Judiciary Act of 1925 enlarged the Court's power to deny cases review, the number of cases accepted for oral argument dropped. During the chief justiceship of Vinson, the Court heard an average of 137 cases each term, and during that of Warren about 138. But by cutting back on time allowed for oral arguments, the

Court increased the number of cases it could hear to about 160 each term. . . .

Oral argument remains the only opportunity for attorneys to communicate directly with the justices. Two basic factors appear to control the relative importance of oral argument. As Wiley Rutledge observed, "One is brevity. The other is the preparation with which the judge comes to it."

Central to preparation and delivery is a bird's-eye view of the case, the issues and facts, and the reasoning behind legal developments. Crisp, concise, and conversational presentations are what the justices want. An attorney must never forget, in Rehnquist's words, that "he is not, after all, presenting his case to some abstract, platonic embodiment of appellate judges as a class, but . . . [to] nine flesh and blood men and women." Oral argument is definitely not a "brief with gestures." . . .

Most justices now come to hear oral arguments armed with bench memos drafted by their law clerks. Bench memos identify the central facts, issues, and possible questions raised by a case. Because of the workload, Scalia explains, "you have to have done all the work you think is necessary for that case before you hear the argument." He no longer thinks, as he did before his appointment, of oral arguments as "a dog and pony show," and he goes over each case with clerks before hearing oral arguments. "Things," he says, "can be put in perspective during oral argument in a way that they can't in a written brief." White adds, "What is going on is also to some extent an exchange of information among the justices themselves. You hear questions of others and see how their minds are working and that stimulates your own thinking."

Justices also vary in their style and approach to the questioning of attorneys during oral arguments. O'Connor and Stevens tend to ask pointed questions, as does White, who appears more blunt and almost combative. Scalia, like Frankfurter before him, has a reputation for outspokenness, which some justices and attorneys find irritating. "He asks far too many questions," claims Blackmun, "and he takes over the whole argument of counsel." During one of Scalia's lengthy questioning of an attorney, Rehnquist finally interrupted to tell the attorney, "You have fifteen minutes remaining. I hope when you're given the opportunity to do so, you'll address some of your remarks to the question on which the Court voted to grant certiorari." Scalia concedes that he is sometimes overbearing in his questioning but explains, "It is the academic in me. I fight against it. The devil makes me do it." Rehnquist, unlike Burger, is much more relaxed in presiding over the courtroom and often interjects his humor into oral arguments. By contrast, Brennan and Blackmun simply tend to sit back and listen, occasionally asking questions to clarify issues and facts in the record. Marshall often sits back listening and saying nothing, but then he'll suddenly fire a battery of involved questions. An often confused attorney will reply, only to receive some comical remark from Marshall, such as "Why didn't you tell me that five minutes ago?" which invariably draws laughter from spectators.

CONFERENCE ON MERITS

The justices hold a private conference on Wednesday afternoons to discuss the merits of the four cases heard on Monday, and then another on Friday to discuss the eight cases they heard on Tuesday and Wednesday. Conference discussions are secret, except for revelations of justices' opinions, off-the-bench communications, or, when available, private papers. "The integrity of decision making would be impaired seriously if we had to reach our judgments in the atmosphere of an ongoing town meeting," Powell asserted. "There must be candid discussion, a willingness to consider arguments advanced by other Justices, and a continuing examination and reexamination of one's own views."

Since the content of conference discussions is not revealed, their importance apart from the voting on cases is difficult to determine. But the significance of conference discussions has certainly changed with the increasing caseload. "Our tasks involve deliberation, reflection and mediation," Douglas observed. Those tasks no longer take place at conference; they now revolve around the activities in and among the chambers before and after conference.

Conference discussions do not play the role that they once did. When the docket was smaller, in the nineteenth century, conferences were integral to the justices' collective deliberations. Cases were discussed in detail and differences hammered out. The justices not only decided how to dispose of cases but also reached agreement on an institutional opinion for the Court. As the caseload grew, conferences became largely symbolic of past collective deliberations. They now serve only to discover consensus. There is no longer time for justices to reach agreement and compromise on opinions for the Court. . . .

Strategies During Conference

Justices vary in the weight they place on conference deliberations. They all come prepared to vote. Some, like Douglas, have little interest in discussions. Others take copious notes. Much depends on a justice's intellectual ability, self-confidence, and style. At conference, some junior justices have been said to experience a so-called freshman effect. That is, since senior justices speak first, newly appointed members may be somewhat circumspect and often have little to say after the others have

spoken. Hughes once observed that "it takes three or four years to get the hang of it, and that so extraordinary an intellect as Brandeis said that it took him four to five years to feel that he understood the jurisdictional problems of the Court." Scalia recalls his "biggest surprise" on arriving at the Court was "the enormity of the workload. I don't think I worked as hard in my life," he adds, "including first-year law school, as I did my first year on the Court." Yet Scalia did not give any indication of experiencing a freshman effect; far from being circumspect, he quickly staked out his sharply conservative positions.

The justices' interaction at conference has been analyzed by the political scientist David Danelski in terms of small-group behavior. He specifically examined the role of the chief justice, distinguishing between two kinds of influence—"task" and "social" leadership. Task leadership relates to the managing of the workload, even at the cost of ignoring personal relations among the justices. By contrast, social leadership addresses the interpersonal relations among the justices that are crucial for a collegial body. Danelski found that some chief justices tend to be either more task or more social leadership-oriented. Few assume both roles, and some fail at both.

Though the chief justice is the titular head of the Court, it by no means follows that he has a monopoly on leadership. Taft was good-humored but, recognizing his own intellectual limitations, relied on Van Devanter for task leadership. Warren, likewise socially oriented, found it useful to consult with Brennan when planning conferences. On the Burger Court, Powell showed considerable task leadership with suggestions for expediting the processing of the Court's caseload.

Any justice may assume task or social leadership. He or she may also assert a third kind of leadership—policy leadership. Justices demonstrate policy leadership by persuading others to vote in ways (in the short and long run) favorable to their policy goals. Some members of the Court deny the possibility of such influence. "It may well be that, since the days of John Marshall, an individual Justice or Chief Justice cannot 'lead,' " Blackmun has noted. "The Court pretty much goes its own way." But all three kinds of influence—task, social, and policy leadership—are intertwined and present various strategies for justices trying to affect the outcome of the Court's decisions. . . .

Tentative Votes

Voting presents each justice with opportunities for negotiating on which issues are finally decided and how. *"Votes* count," one of Black's colleagues reminded him in a note passed at conference. "I vote to reverse, if there were two more of my mind there would be a reversal." But the justices' votes are always tentative until the day the Court hands down its decision and opinion. Before, during, and after conference, justices may use their votes in strategic ways to influence the disposition of a case. "The books on voting are never closed until the decision actually comes down," Harlan explained. "Until then any member of the Court is perfectly free to change his vote, and it is not an unheard of occurrence for a persuasive minority opinion to eventuate as the prevailing opinion."

At conference, a justice may vote with others if they appear to constitute a majority, even though he or she disagrees with their treatment of a case. The justice may then bargain and try to minimize the damage, from his or her policy perspective, of the Court's decision. Alternatively, justices may threaten dissenting opinions or try to form a voting bloc, and thereby influence the final decision and written opinion.

The utility of such voting strategies depends on how the justices line up at conference. They may prove quite useful if the initial vote is five to four or six to three. But their effectiveness also depends on institutional norms and practices. . . .

OPINION-WRITING PROCESS

Opinions justify or explain votes at conference. The opinion for the Court is the most important and most difficult to write because it represents a collective judgment. Writing the Court's opinion, as Holmes put it, requires that a "judge can dance the sword dance; that is he can justify an obvious result without stepping on either blade of opposing fallacies." Holmes in his good-natured way often complained about the compromises he had to make when writing an opinion for the Court. "I am sorry that my moderation," he wrote Chief Justice White, "did not soften your inexorable heart—But I stand like St. Sebastian ready for your arrows."

Since conference votes are tentative, the assignment, drafting, and circulation of opinions are crucial to the Court's rulings. At each stage, justices compete for influence in determining the Court's final decision and opinion.

Opinion Assignment

The power of opinion assignment is perhaps a chief justice's "single most influential function" and, as Tom Clark has emphasized, an exercise in "judicial-political discretion." By tradition, when the chief justice is in the majority, he assigns the Court's opinion. If the chief justice did not vote with the majority, then the senior associate justice who was in the majority either writes the opinion or assigns it to another. . . .

Parity in opinion assignment now generally prevails. But the practice of immediately assigning opinions after conference, as Hughes did, or within a day or two, as Stone did, was gradually abandoned by the end of Vinson's tenure as chief justice. Following Warren and Burger, Rehnquist assigns opinions after each two-week session of oral arguments and conferences. With more assignments to make at any given time, they thus acquired greater flexibility in distributing the workload. Chief justices also enhanced their own opportunities for influencing the final outcome of cases through their assignment of opinions. . . .

Writing and Circulating Opinions

Writing opinions is the justices' most difficult and time-consuming task. As Frankfurter once put it, when appealing to Brennan to suppress a proposed opinion, "psychologically speaking, voting is one thing and expressing views in support of a vote quite another."

Justices differ in their styles and approaches to opinion writing. They now more or less delegate responsibility to their clerks for assistance in the preparation of opinions. . . . But only after a justice is satisfied with an initial draft does the opinion go to the other justices for their reactions.

The circulation of opinions among the chambers added to the Court's workload and changed the process of opinion writing. The practice of circulating draft opinions began around the turn of the century and soon became pivotal in the Court's decision-making process. The circulation of opinions provides more opportunities for the shifting of votes and further coalition building or fragmentation within the Court. Chief Justice Marshall, with his insistence on unanimity and nightly conferences after dinner, achieved unsurpassed unanimity. Unanimity, however, was based on the reading of opinions at conferences. No drafts circulated for other justices' scrutiny. Throughout much of the nineteenth century, when the Court's sessions were shorter and the justices had no law clerks, opinions were drafted in about two weeks and then read at conference.

If at least a majority agreed with the main points, the opinion was approved.

In this century, the practice became that of circulating draft opinions, initially carbon copies and now two photocopies, for each justice's examination and comments. Because they gave more attention to each opinion, the justices found more to debate. The importance of circulating drafts and negotiating language in an opinion was underscored when Jackson announced from the bench, "I myself have changed my opinion after reading the opinions of the members of the Court. And I am as stubborn as most. But I sometimes wind up not voting the way I voted in conference because the reasons of the majority didn't satisfy me." Similarly, Brennan noted, "I converted more than one proposed majority into a dissent before the final decision was announced. I have also, however, had the more satisfying experience of rewriting a dissent as a majority opinion for the Court." In one case, Brennan added, he "circulated 10 printed drafts before one was approved as the Court's opinion."

As the amount of time spent on the considering of proposed opinions grew, so did the workload. More law clerks were needed, and they were also given a greater role in opinion writing. Though clerks are now largely responsible for drafting and commenting on opinions, they remain subordinates when it comes to negotiating opinions for the Court. There are exceptions. Frankfurter often tried to use his clerks as lobbyists within the Court. And Rutledge once found that during his absence "at the request of Justice Black two minor changes were made by [his] staff in the final draft of the opinion, but apparently that draft was not circulated to show those changes." But even if a clerk is delegated or assumes responsibility for working on an opinion, the justice ultimately must account for what is circulated.

How long does opinion writing take? In the average case, Tom Clark observed, about three weeks' work by a justice and his clerks is required before an opinion circulates. "Then the fur begins to fly." The time spent preparing an opinion depends on how fast a justice works, what his style is, how much use of law clerks he makes, and how controversial the assigned case is. Holmes and Cardozo wrote opinions within days after being assigned, with little assistance from law clerks. Even into his eighties, Holmes "thirsted" for opinions. Chief Justice Hughes held back assignments from Cardozo because the justice's law clerk, Melvin Segal, complained that Cardozo would spend his weekends writing his opinions and thus he had little to do during the week. Cardozo later gave his clerk responsibility for checking citations and proofreading drafts. But Cardozo still overworked himself, and Hughes continued to hold back assignments for fear that the bachelor's health would fail. By comparison, Frankfurter relied a great deal on his clerks and was still notoriously slow. As he once said, in apologizing to his brethren for the delay in circulating a proposed opinion, "The elephant's period of gestation is, I believe, eighteen months, but a poor little hot dog has no such excuse." . . .

THE VALUE OF JUDICIAL OPINIONS

Published opinions for the Court are the residue of conflicts and compromises among the justices. But they also reflect changing institutional norms. In historical perspective, changes in judicial norms have affected trends in opinion writing, the value of judicial opinions, and the Court's contributions to public law and policy.

Opinions for the Court

During the nineteenth century and down through the chief justiceship of Hughes, there were few separate, concurring, or dissenting opinions from the opinion for the Court's decision. In the last forty years, however, there has occurred a dramatic increase in the total number of opinions issued each term. . . .

Individual opinions now predominate over institutional opinions for the Court. In keeping with the greater caseload, the Burger and Rehnquist Courts dispose of more cases each term by signed opinion than did the Warren Court, though of about the same number as did the Hughes and Stone Courts. In the last years of the Hughes Court (1937–1940), the justices produced about 144 institutional opinions each term and issued another 35 separate, concurring, or dissenting opinions. By contrast, the Court from 1969 to 1980 averaged 138 institutional opinions and issued another 43 separate opinions, 45 concurring opinions, and 105 dissenting opinions—for a total of 331 opinions each term. When we compare the Court's practice with that of forty years ago, we find ten times the number of concurring opinions, four times more dissenting opinions, and seven times the number of separate opinions in which the justices explain their personal views and why they partially concur in and/or dissent from the Court's opinion. . . .

The justices now care less about reaching a consensus on opinions for the Court. Whereas unanimity remains high on case selection (around 80 percent), unanimity on opinions for the Court drops to around 30 percent. Even though the business of the Court is to give institutional opinions, Stewart observed, "that view has come be that of a minority of the justices." . . .

Not only are members of the Court divided on a larger number of opinions announcing the Court's decisions, but often a bare majority cannot agree on opinions for the Court's rulings. More opinions for the Court now command the support of a mere plurality of the justices. A plurality opinion is an opinion for the Court that fails to command a majority, even though at least five justices agree on the decision. For example, a bare majority may decide a case. But only three justices agree on an opinion announcing the decision. The other two justices in the majority usually file separate concurring opinions, explaining why they think the case was correctly decided but how they disagree with the rationalization in the (plurality) opinion announcing the ruling.

Between 1800 and 1900, there were only 10 opinions that commanded the support of less than a majority of the Court. Between 1901 and the last year of Chief Justice Warren, in 1969, there were 51 cases decided by plurality opinions. By contrast, during the Burger Court years a total of 116 plurality opinions were handed down, more plurality opinions than had been rendered in the entire previous history of the Court. Under Chief Justice Rehnquist, the Court in 1986–1988 handed down only 8 plurality opinions (out of three hundred cases decided by full opinion); in other words, less than 3 percent of all cases decided by opinion failed to command at least a majority.

These trends reflect basic changes in judicial behavior and the value of institutional and individual opinions as well as changes in the Court's composition. Individual opinions are now more highly prized than opinions for the Court. As consensus declines, the Court's rulings and policy-making appear more fragmented, less stable, and less predictable. . . .

Less agreement and more numerous and longer opinions invite uncertainty and confusion about the Court's rulings, interpretation of law, and policy-making. As individual opinions have come to predominate, they have also become more idiosyncratic. "It is a genuine misfortune to have the Court's treatment of the subject to be a virtual Tower of Babel, from which no definite principles can be clearly drawn," Rehnquist lamented in his dissent in *Metromedia v. City of San Diego* (1981), adding, "I regret even more keenly my contribution to this judicial clamor, but find that none of the views expressed in the other opinions written in the case came close enough to mine to warrant the necessary compromise to obtain a Court opinion."

The Abortion Controversy

42
Roe v. Wade
U.S. Supreme Court

One of the most controversial decisions by the Supreme Court occurred in 1973 when a 7–2 majority ruled that abortion was permissible in some situations. Justice Harry Blackmun's majority opinion ruled that a woman had a qualified right to terminate her pregnancy. Jane Roe, a pseudonym for a pregnant single woman, challenged a Texas law which prohibited all abortions except to save the woman's life. The Court overturned the Texas law as a violation of the right to privacy. Where did the Court discover the protection to the right of privacy in the Constitution? The decision also rejected the Texas claim that an unborn child is a "person" constitutionally protected under the Fourteenth Amendment. What did Blackmun's decision say about when life begins? The most controversial feature of the Court's decision related to the trimesters of pregnancy. When is abortion permitted and when is it restricted? On what basis did the Court establish the trimester distinction for permitting or restricting abortion? Why is the majority decision in Roe v. Wade *so controversial?*

Mr. Justice Blackmun delivered the opinion of the Court.

This Texas federal appeal and its Georgia companion, *Doe v. Bolton* . . . present constitutional challenges to state criminal abortion legislation. The Texas statutes under attack here are typical of those that have been in effect in many States for approximately a century. The Georgia statutes, in contrast, have a modern cast and are a legislative product that, to an extent at least, obviously reflects the influences of recent attitudinal change, of advancing medical knowledge and techniques, and of new thinking about an old issue.

We forthwith acknowledge our awareness of the sensitive and emotional nature of the abortion controversy, of the vigorous opposing views, even among physicians, and of the deep and seemingly absolute convictions that the subject inspires. One's philosophy, one's experiences, one's exposure to the raw edges of human existence, one's religious training, one's attitudes toward life and family and their values, and the moral standards one establishes and seeks to observe, are all likely to influence and to color one's thinking and conclusions about abortion.

In addition, population growth, pollution, poverty, and racial overtones tend to complicate and not to simplify the problem.

Our task, of course, is to resolve the issue by constitutional measurement, free

Source: 410 U.S. 113 (1973)

of emotion and of predilection. We seek earnestly to do this, and, because we do, we have inquired into, and in this opinion place some emphasis upon, medical and medical-legal history and what that history reveals about man's attitudes toward the abortion procedure over the centuries. We bear in mind, too, Mr. Justice Holmes' admonition in his now-vindicated dissent in *Lochner v. New York,* 198 U.S. 45, 76 (1905):

"[The Constitution] is made for people of fundamentally differing views, and the accident of our finding certain opinions natural and familiar or novel and even shocking ought not to conclude our judgment upon the question whether statutes embodying them conflict with the Constitution of the United States."

I

The Texas statutes that concern us here are Arts. 1191–1194 and 1196 of the State's Penal Code. These make it a crime to "procure an abortion," as therein defined, or to attempt one, except with respect to "an abortion procured or attempted by medical advice for the purpose of saving the life of the mother." Similar statutes are in existence in a majority of the States.

II

Jane Roe, a single woman who was residing in Dallas County, Texas, instituted this federal action in March 1970 against the District Attorney of the county. She sought a declaratory judgment that the Texas criminal abortion statutes were unconstitutional on their face, and an injunction restraining the defendant from enforcing the statutes.

Roe alleged that she was unmarried and pregnant; that she wished to terminate her pregnancy by an abortion "performed by a competent, licensed physician, under safe, clinical conditions"; that she was unable to get a "legal" abortion in Texas because her life did not appear to be threatened by the continuation of her pregnancy; and that she could not afford to travel to another jurisdiction in order to secure a legal abortion under safe conditions. She claimed that the Texas statutes were unconstitutionally vague and that they abridged her right of personal privacy, protected by the First, Fourth, Fifth, Ninth, and Fourteenth Amendments. By an amendment to her complaint Roe purported to sue "on behalf of herself and all other women" similarly situated.

James Hubert Hallford, a licensed physician, sought and was granted leave to intervene in Roe's action. In his complaint he alleged that he had been arrested previously for violations of the Texas abortion statutes and that two such prosecutions were pending against him. . . .

V

The principal thrust of appellant's attack on the Texas statutes is that they improperly invade a right, said to be possessed by the pregnant woman, to choose to terminate her pregnancy. Appellant would discover this right in the concept of personal "liberty" embodied in the Fourteenth Amendment's Due Process Clause; or in personal, marital, familial, and sexual privacy said to be protected by the Bill of Rights or its penumbras . . . ; or among those rights reserved to the people by the Ninth Amendment, *Griswold v. Connecticut,* 381 U.S., at 486. . . . Before addressing this claim, we feel it desirable briefly to survey, in several aspects, the history of abortion, for such insight as that history may afford us, and then to examine the state purposes and interests behind the criminal abortion laws.

VI

It perhaps is not generally appreciated that the restrictive criminal abortion laws in effect in a majority of States today are of relatively recent vintage. Those laws, generally proscribing abortion or its attempt at any time during pregnancy except when necessary to preserve the pregnant woman's life, are not of ancient or even of common-law origin. Instead, they derive from statutory changes effected, for the most part, in the latter half of the 19th century.

VII

Three reasons have been advanced to explain historically the enactment of criminal abortion laws in the 19th century and to justify their continued existence.

It has been argued occasionally that these laws were the product of a Victorian social concern to discourage illicit sexual conduct. Texas, however, does not advance this justification in the present case, and it appears that no court or commentator has taken the argument seriously. . . .

A second reason is concerned with abortion as a medical procedure. When most criminal abortion laws were first enacted, the procedure was a hazardous one for the woman. This was particularly true prior to the development of antisepsis. Antiseptic techniques, of course, were based on discoveries by Lister, Pasteur, and others first announced in 1867, but were not generally accepted and employed until about the turn of the century. Abortion mortality was high. Even after 1900, and perhaps until as late as the development of antibiotics in the 1940s, standard modern techniques such as dilation and curettage were not nearly so safe as they are today. Thus, it has been argued that a State's real concern in enacting a criminal abortion law was to protect the pregnant woman, that is, to restrain her from submitting to a procedure that placed her life in serious jeopardy.

Modern medical techniques have altered this situation. Appellants and various *amici* refer to medical data indicating that abortion in early pregnancy, that is, prior to the end of the first trimester, although not without its risk, is now relatively safe. Mortality rates for women undergoing early abortions, where the procedure is legal, appear to be as low as or lower than the rates for normal childbirth. . . .

The third reason is the State's interest— some phrase it in terms of duty—in protecting prenatal life. Some of the argument for this justification rests on the theory that a new human life is present from the moment of conception. The State's interest and general obligation to protect life then extends, it is argued, to prenatal life. Only when the life of the pregnant mother herself is at stake, balanced against the life she carries within her, should the interest of the embryo or fetus not prevail. Logically, of course, a legitimate state interest in this area need not stand or fall on acceptance of the belief that life begins at conception or at some other point prior to live birth. In assessing the State's interest, recognition may be given to the less rigid claim that as long as at least *potential* life is involved, the State may assert interests beyond the protection of the pregnant woman alone.

VIII

The Constitution does not explicitly mention any right of privacy. In a line of decisions . . . the Court has recognized that a right of personal privacy, or a guarantee of certain areas or zones of privacy, does exist under the Constitution. In varying contexts, the Court or individual Justices have, indeed, found at least the roots of that right in the First Amendment. . . ; in the Fourth and Fifth Amendments. . . ; in the penumbras of the Bill of Rights, *Griswold* v. *Connecticut*, 381 U.S., . . . in the Ninth Amendment; or in the concept of liberty guaranteed by the first section of the Fourteenth Amendment. . . . These decisions make it clear that only personal rights that can be deemed "fundamental" or "implicit in the concept of ordered liberty," *Palko* v. *Connecticut*, 302 U.S. 319, 325

(1937), are included in this guarantee of personal privacy. They also make it clear that the right has some extension to activities relating to marriage . . . ; procreation . . . ; contraception . . . ; family relationships . . . ; and child rearing and education. . . .

This right of privacy, whether it be founded in the Fourteenth Amendment's concept of personal liberty and restrictions upon state action, as we feel it is, or, as the District Court determined, in the Ninth Amendment's reservation of rights to the people, is broad enough to encompass a woman's decision whether or not to terminate her pregnancy. The detriment that the State would impose upon the pregnant woman by denying this choice altogether is apparent. Specific and direct harm medically diagnosable even in early pregnancy may be involved. Maternity, or additional offspring, may force upon the woman a distressful life and future. Psychological harm may be imminent. Mental and physical health may be taxed by child care. There is also the distress, for all concerned, associated with the unwanted child, and there is the problem of bringing a child into a family already unable, psychologically and otherwise, to care for it. In other cases, as in this one, the additional difficulties and continuing stigma of unwed motherhood may be involved. All these are factors the woman and her responsible physician necessarily will consider in consultation.

On the basis of elements such as these, appellant and some *amici* argue that the woman's right is absolute and that she is entitled to terminate her pregnancy at whatever time, in whatever way, and for whatever reason she alone chooses. With this we do not agree. Appellant's arguments that Texas either has no valid interest at all in regulating the abortion decision, or no interest strong enough to support any limitation upon the woman's sole determination, are unpersuasive.

The Court's decisions recognizing a right of privacy also acknowledge that some state regulation in areas protected by that right is appropriate. As noted above, a State may properly assert important interests in safeguarding health, in maintaining medical standards, and in protecting potential life. At some point in pregnancy, these respective interests become sufficiently compelling to sustain regulation of the factors that govern the abortion decision. The privacy right involved, therefore, cannot be said to be absolute. In fact, it is not clear to us that the claim asserted by some *amici* that one has an unlimited right to do with one's body as one pleases bears a close relationship to the right of privacy previously articulated in the Court's decisions. The Court has refused to recognize an unlimited right of this kind in the past. . . .

We, therefore, conclude that the right of personal privacy includes the abortion decision, but that this right is not unqualified and must be considered against important state interests in regulation.

IX

A.   The appellee and certain *amici* argue that the fetus is a "person" within the language and meaning of the Fourteenth Amendment. In support of this, they outline at length and in detail the well-known facts of fetal development. If this suggestion of personhood is established, the appellant's case, of course, collapses, for the fetus' right to life would then be guaranteed specifically by the Amendment. . . .

The Constitution does not define "person" in so many words. Section 1 of the Fourteenth Amendment contains three references to "person." The first, in defining "citizens," speaks of "persons born or naturalized in the United States." The word also appears both in the Due Process Clause and in the Equal Protection Clause. "Person" is used in other places in the Constitution: in the listing of qualifications for Representatives and Senators . . . ; in the Apportionment Clause. . . ; in the Migration and Importation provision. . . ; in the Emolument Clause. . . ; in the Electors provisions. . . ; in the provision outlining qualifications for the office of President. . . ; in the Extradition provisions . . . and the superseded Fugitive Slave Clause 3; and in the Fifth, Twelfth, and Twenty-second Amendments, as well as in §§ 2 and 3 of the Fourteenth Amendment. But in nearly all these instances, the use of the word is such that it has application only postnatally. None indicates, with any assurance, that it has any possible pre-natal application.

B.   Texas urges that, apart from the Fourteenth Amendment, life begins at conception and is present throughout pregnancy, and that, therefore, the State has a compelling interest in protecting that life from and after conception. We need not resolve the difficult question of when life begins. When those trained in the respective disciplines of medicine, philosophy, and theology are unable to arrive at any consensus, the judiciary, at this point in the development of man's knowledge, is not in a position to speculate as to the answer.

X

In view of all this, we do not agree that, by adopting one theory of life, Texas may override the rights of the pregnant woman that are at stake. We repeat, however, that the State does have an important and legitimate interest in preserving and protecting the health of the pregnant woman, whether she be a resident of the State or a nonresident who seeks medical consultation and treatment there, and that it has still *another* important and legitimate interest in protecting the potentiality of human life. These interests are separate and distinct. Each grows in substantiality as the woman ap-

proaches term and, at a point during pregnancy, each becomes "compelling."

With respect to the State's important and legitimate interest in the health of the mother, the "compelling" point, in the light of present medical knowledge, is at approximately the end of the first trimester. This is so because of the now-established medical fact . . . that until the end of the first trimester mortality in abortion may be less than mortality in normal childbirth. It follows that, from and after this point, a State may regulate the abortion procedure to the extent that the regulation reasonably relates to the preservation and protection of maternal health. Examples of permissible state regulation in this area are requirements as to the qualifications of the person who is to perform the abortion; as to the licensure of that person; as to the facility in which the procedure is to be performed, that is, whether it must be a hospital or may be a clinic or some other place of less-than-hospital status; as to the licensing of the facility; and the like.

This means, on the other hand, that, for the period of pregnancy prior to this "compelling" point, the attending physician, in consultation with his patient, is free to determine, without regulation by the State, that, in his medical judgment, the patient's pregnancy should be terminated. If that decision is reached, the judgment may be effectuated by an abortion free of interference by the State.

With respect to the State's important and legitimate interest in potential life, the "compelling" point is at viability. This is so because the fetus then presumably has the capability of meaningful life outside the mother's womb. State regulation protective of fetal life after viability thus has both logical and biological justifications. If the State is interested in protecting fetal life after viability, it may go so far as to proscribe abortion during that period, except when it is necessary to preserve the life or health of the mother.

Measured against these standards, Art. 1196 of the Texas Penal Code, in restricting legal abortions to those "procured or attempted by medical advice for the purpose of saving the life of the mother," sweeps too broadly. The statute makes no distinction between abortions performed early in pregnancy and those performed later, and it limits to a single reason, "saving" the mother's life, the legal justification for the procedure. The statute, therefore, cannot survive the constitutional attack made upon it here.

XI

To summarize and to repeat:

a.   For the stage prior to approximately the end of the first trimester, the abortion decision and its effectuation must be left to the medical judgment of the pregnant woman's attending physician.

b.   For the stage subsequent to approximately the end of the first trimester, the State, in promoting its interest in the health of the mother, may, if it chooses, regulate the abortion procedure in ways that are reasonably related to maternal health.

c.   For the stage subsequent to viability, the State in promoting its interest in the potentiality of human life may, if it chooses, regulate, and even proscribe, abortion except where it is necessary, in appropriate medical judgment, for the preservation of the life or health of the mother.

43
Webster v. Reproductive Health Services
U.S. Supreme Court

Sixteen years after Roe v. Wade, *a narrow 5–4 Supreme Court majority up-held a very restrictive Missouri anti-abortion law. Four justices indicated they were ready to overrule* Roe v. Wade. *The Missouri law was challenged by a group of physicians and an abortion clinic. They won in the lower federal courts which declared the state law unconstitutional in most respects. The Supreme Court reversed the earlier rulings and upheld all provisions of the law, including a ban on abortions in public hospitals and other tax-supported facilities; a prohibition against public employees, including doc-tors, nurses, and other health care providers, from performing abortions not required to save the mother's life; prohibiting abortion counseling; and re-quiring physicians to perform viability tests on fetuses at twenty weeks or more. How did the Court rule on the preamble of the state law, which defined life beginning at conception? What was the Court majority's justifi-cation for upholding the Missouri law? In his dissent, Justice Blackmun bit-terly criticized the majority opinion. How did Blackmun view the reversal of* Roe's *trimester framework? What would be the result of overruling* Roe v. Wade, *according to Justice Blackmun?*

FROM THE OPINION
By Chief Justice Rehnquist

This appeal concerns the constitutionality of a Missouri statute regulating the performance of abortions. The United States Court of Appeals for the Eighth Circuit struck down several pro-visions of the statute on the ground that they violated this Court's decision in *Roe v. Wade,* 410 U.S. 113 (1973), and cases following it. We noted probable jurisdiction, and now reverse.

I

In June 1986, the Governor of Missouri signed into law Missouri Senate Committee Substitute for House Bill No. 1596 (hereinafter Act or statute), which amended existing state law

concerning unborn children and abortions. The Act consisted of 20 provisions, 5 of which are now before the Court. The first provision, or preamble, contains "findings" by the state legislature that "[t]he life of each human being begins at conception," and that "un-born children have protectable interests in life, health, and well-being." . . . The Act fur-ther requires that all Missouri laws be inter-preted to provide unborn children with the same rights enjoyed by other persons, subject to the Federal Constitution and this Court's precedents. . . . Among its other provisions, the Act requires that, prior to performing an abortion on any woman whom a physician has reason to believe is 20 or more weeks preg-nant, the physician ascertain whether the fetus

Source: 109 S. Ct. 3040 (1989).

is viable by performing "such medical examinations and tests as are necessary to make a finding of the gestational age, weight, and lung maturity of the unborn child." . . . The Act also prohibits the use of public employees and facilities to perform or assist abortions not necessary to save the mother's life, and it prohibits the use of public funds, employees, or facilities for the purpose of "encouraging or counseling" a woman to have an abortion not necessary to save her life.

II

Decision of this case requires us to address four sections of the Missouri Act: (a) the preamble; (b) the prohibition of the use of public facilities or employees to perform abortions; (c) the prohibition on public funding of abortion counseling, and (d) the requirement that physicians conduct viability tests prior to performing abortions. We address these *seriatim*.

A

The Act's preamble . . . sets forth "findings" by the Missouri legislature that "[t]he life of each human being begins at conception," and that "[u]nborn children have protectable interests in life, health, and well-being." The Act then mandates that state laws be interpreted to provide unborn children with "all the rights, privileges and immunities available to other persons, citizens and residents of this state," subject to the Constitution and this Court's precedents. In invalidating the preamble, the Court of Appeals relied on this Court's dictum that "a state may not adopt one theory of when life begins to justify its regulation of abortions." . . . It rejected Missouri's claim that the preamble was "abortion-neutral," and "merely determine[d] when life begins in a nonabortion context, a traditional state prerogative." . . .

The State contends that the preamble itself is prefatory and imposes no substantive restrictions on abortions, and that appellees

therefore do not have standing to challenge it. Appellees, on the other hand, insist that the preamble is an operative part of the Act intended to guide the interpretation of other provisions of the Act. They maintain, for example, that the preamble's definition of life may prevent physicians in public hospitals from dispensing certain forms of contraceptives, such as the intrauterine device. . . .

Certainly, the preamble does not by its terms regulate abortion or any other aspect of appellees' medical practice. The Court has emphasized that *Roe v. Wade* "implies no limitation on the authority of a state to make a value judgment favoring childbirth over abortion." The preamble can be read simply to express that sort of value judgment.

Protections to Unborn Children

We think the extent to which the preamble's language might be used to interpret other state statutes or regulations is something that only the courts of Missouri can definitively decide. State law has offered protections to unborn children in tort and probate law, . . . and Section 1.205.2 can be interpreted to do no more than that. . . . It will be time enough for Federal courts to address the meaning of the preamble should it be applied to restrict the activities of appellees in some concrete way.

Until then, this Court "is not empowered to decide . . . abstract propositions, or to declare, for the government of future cases, principles or rules of law which cannot affect the result as to the thing in issue in the case before it." . . . We therefore need not pass on the constitutionality of the Act's preamble.

B

Section 188.210 provides that "[i]t shall be unlawful for any public employee within the scope of his employment to perform or assist an abortion, not necessary to save the life of the mother," while Section 188.215 makes it "unlawful for any public facility to be used for the purpose of performing or assisting an abortion not necessary to save the life of the mother." The Court of Appeals held that these provisions contravened this Court's abortion decisions. We take the contrary view.

As we said earlier this term in *DeShaney v. Winnebago County Dept. of Social Services,* "our cases have recognized that the due process clauses generally confer no affirmative right to governmental aid, even where such aid may be necessary to secure life, liberty or property interests of which the government itself may not deprive the individual."

In *Maher v. Roe* (1977), the Court upheld a Connecticut welfare regulation under which Medicaid recipients received payments for medical services related to childbirth, but not for nontherapeutic abortions. The Court rejected the claim that this unequal subsidization of childbirth and abortion was impermissible under *Roe v. Wade.* . . .

Just as Congress' refusal to fund abortions in *McRae* left "an indigent woman with at least the same range of choice in deciding whether to obtain a medically necessary abortion as she would have had if Congress had chosen to subsidize no health care costs at all," Missouri's refusal to allow public employees to perform abortions in public hospitals leaves a pregnant woman with the same choices as if the State had chosen not to operate any public hospitals at all.

Allocation of Public Resources

The challenged provisions only restrict a woman's ability to obtain an abortion to the extent that she chooses to use a physician affiliated with a public hospital. This circumstance is more easily remedied, and thus considerably less burdensome, than indigency, which "may make it difficult—and in some cases, perhaps, impossible—for some women to have abortions" without public funding.

Having held that the State's refusal to fund abortions does not violate *Roe v. Wade,* it strains logic to reach a contrary result for the use of public facilities and employees. If the State may "make a value judgment favoring childbirth over abortion and . . . implement that judgment by the allocation of public funds," surely it may do so through the allocation of other public resources, such as hospitals and medical staff.

C

The Missouri Act contains three provisions relating to "encouraging or counseling a woman to have an abortion not necessary to save her life." Section 188.205 states that no public funds can be used for this purpose; § 188.210 states that public employees cannot, within the scope of their employment, engage in such speech; and § 188.215 forbids such speech in public facilities. The Court of Appeals did not consider § 188.205 separately from § 188.210 and 188.215. It held that all three of these provisions were unconstitutionally vague, and that "the ban on using public funds, employees, and facilities to encourage or counsel a woman to have an abortion is an unacceptable infringement of the woman's fourteenth amendment right to choose an abortion after receiving the medical information necessary to exercise the right knowingly and intelligently." . . .

Missouri has chosen only to appeal the Court of Appeals' invalidation of the public funding provision, § 188.205. . . . A threshold question is whether this provision reaches primary conduct, or whether it is simply an instruction to the State's fiscal officers not to allocate funds for abortion counseling. We accept, for purposes of decision, the State's claim that § 188.205 "is not directed at the conduct of any physician or health care provider, private or public," but "is directed solely at those persons responsible for expending public funds." . . .

D

[This section was joined by only Justices Byron R. White and Anthony M. Kennedy, and therefore is a plurality, not the majority, opinion.]

Section 188.029 of the Missouri Act provides:

"Before a physician performs an abortion on a woman he has reason to believe is carrying an unborn child of 20 or more weeks gestational age, the physician shall first determine if the unborn child is viable by using and exercising that degree of care, skill and proficiency commonly exercised by the ordinarily skillful, careful and prudent physician engaged in similar practice under the same or similar conditions. In making this determination of viability, the physician shall perform or cause to be performed such medical examinations and tests as are necessary to make a finding of the gestational age, weight and lung maturity of the unborn child and shall enter such findings and determination of viability in the medical record of the mother."

Viability-Testing Provision

As with the preamble, the parties disagree over the meaning of this statutory provision. The State emphasizes the language of the first sentence, which speaks in terms of the physician's determination of viability being made by the standards of ordinary skill in the medical profession. Appellees stress the language of the second sentence, which prescribes such "tests as are necessary" to make a finding of gestational age, fetal weight and lung maturity.

The Court of Appeals read Section 188.029 as requiring that after 20 weeks "doctors *must* perform tests to find gestational age, fetal weight and lung maturity." The court indicated that the tests needed to determine fetal weight at 20 weeks are "unreliable and inaccurate" and would add $125 to $250 to the cost of an abortion.

It also stated that "amniocentesis, the only method available to determine lung maturity, is contrary to accepted medical practice until 28–30 weeks of gestation, expensive, and imposes significant health risks for both the pregnant woman and the fetus."

We must first determine the meaning of Section 188.029 under Missouri law. Our usual practice is to defer to the lower court's construction of a state statute, but we believe the Court of Appeals has "fallen into plain error" in this case. . . .

We think the viability-testing provision makes sense only if the second sentence is read to require only those tests that are useful to making subsidiary findings as to viability. . . .

The viability-testing provision of the Missouri Act is concerned with promoting the State's interest in potential human life rather than in maternal health. Section 188.029 creates what is essentially a presumption of viability at 20 weeks, which the physician must rebut with tests indicating that the fetus is not viable prior to performing an abortion. It also directs the physician's determination as to viability by specifying consideration, if feasible, of gestational age, fetal weight and lung capacity.

Testing at 20 Weeks Supported

The District Court found that "the medical evidence is uncontradicted that a 20-week fetus is *not* viable," and that "23 1/2 to 24 weeks gestation is the earliest point in pregnancy where a reasonable possibility of viability exists." But it also found that there may be a 4-week error in estimating gestational age, which supports testing at 20 weeks.

In *Roe v. Wade*, the Court recognized that the State has "important and legitimate" interests in protecting maternal health and in the potentiality of human life. During the second trimester, the State "may, if it chooses, regulate the abortion procedure in ways that are reasonably related to maternal health." After viability, when the State's interest in potential human life was held to become compelling, the State "may, if it chooses, regulate, and even proscribe, abortion except where it is necessary, in appropriate medical judgment, for the preservation of the life or health of the mother."

In *Colautti v. Franklin* (1979), upon which appellees rely, the Court held that a Pennsylvania statute regulating the standard of care to be used by a physician performing an abortion of a possibly viable fetus was void for vagueness. But in the course of reaching that conclusion, the Court reaffirmed its earlier statement in *Planned Parenthood of Central Missouri v. Danforth,* that " 'the determination of whether a particular fetus is viable is, and must be, a matter of the judgement of the responsible attending physician.' "

To the extent that Section 188.029 regulates the method for determining viability, it undoubtedly does superimpose state regulation on the medical determination of whether a particular fetus is viable. The Court of Appeals and the District Court thought it unconstitutional for this reason. . . .

We think that the doubt cast upon the Missouri statute by these cases is not so much a flaw in the statute as it is a reflection of the fact that the rigid trimester analysis of the course of a pregnancy enunciated in *Roe* has resulted in subsequent cases like *Colautti* and *Akron* making constitutional law in this area a virtual Procrustean bed. . . .

Stare decisis is a cornerstone of our legal system, but it has less power in constitutional cases, where, save for constitutional amendments, this Court is the only body able to make needed changes. . . . We have not refrained from reconsideration of a prior construction of the Constitution that has proved "unsound in principle and unworkable in practice." . . . We think the *Roe* trimester framework falls into that category.

In the first place, the rigid *Roe* framework is hardly consistent with the notion of a Constitution case in general terms, as ours is, and usually speaking in general principles, as ours does. The key elements of the *Roe* framework—trimester and viability—are not found in the text of the Constitution or in any place else one would expect to find a constitutional principle. Since the bounds of the inquiry are essentially indeterminate, the result has been a web of legal rules that have become increasingly intricate, resembling a code of regulations rather than a body of constitutional doctrine. As Justice White has put it, the trimester framework has left this Court to serve as the country's "*ex officio* medical board with powers to approve or disapprove medical and operative practices and standards throughout the United States." . . .

In the second place, we do not see why the state's interest in protecting potential human life should come into existence only at the point of viability, and that there should therefore be a rigid line allowing state regulation after viability but prohibiting it before viability. . . .

The tests that Section 188.029 requires the physician to perform are designed to determine viability. The State here has chosen viability as the point at which its interest in potential human life must be safeguarded. . . . It is true that the tests in question increase the expense of abortion and regulate the discretion of the physician in determining the viability of the fetus. Since the tests will undoubtedly show in many cases that the fetus is not viable, the tests will have been performed for what were in fact second-trimester abortions. But we are satisfied that the requirement of these tests permissibly furthers the State's interest in protecting potential human life, and we therefore believe Section 188.029 to be constitutional.

The dissent . . . accuses us . . . of cowardice and illegitimacy in dealing with "the most politically divisive domestic legal issue of our time." . . . There is no doubt that our holding today will allow some governmental regulation of abortion that would have been prohibited under the language of cases such as *Colautti v. Franklin* . . . and *Akron v. Akron Center for Reproductive Health Inc.* (1983). But the goal of constitutional adjudication is surely not to remove inexorably "politically divisive" issues from the ambit of the legislative process, whereby the people through their elected representatives deal with matters of concern to them. The goal of constitutional adjudication is to hold true the balance between that which the Constitution puts beyond the reach of the democratic process and that which it does not. We think we have done that today. The dissent's suggestion . . . that legislative bodies, in a nation where more than half of our population is women, will treat our decision today as an invitation to enact abortion regulation reminiscent of the dark ages not only misreads our views but does scant justice to those who serve in such bodies and the people who elect them.

Both appellants and the United States as *Amicus Curiae* have urged that we overrule our decision in *Roe v. Wade.* . . . The facts of the present case, however, differ from those at issue in *Roe.* Here, Missouri has determined that viability is the point at which its interest in potential human life must be safeguarded. In *Roe,* on the other hand, the Texas statute criminalized the performance of all abortions, except when the mother's life was at stake. . . . This case therefore affords us no occasion to revisit the holding of *Roe,* which was that the Texas statute unconstitutionally infringed the right to an abortion deprived from the Due Process Clause. . . . and we leave it undisturbed. To the extent indicated in our opinion, we would modify and narrow *Roe* and succeeding cases.

Because none of the challenged provisions of the Missouri Act properly before us conflict with the Constitution, the judgment of the Court of Appeals is *reversed.*

[*Justice Blackmun, with whom Justice Brennan and Justice Marshall join, concurring in part and dissenting in part.*]

Today, *Roe v. Wade,* and the fundamental constitutional right of women to decide whether to terminate a pregnancy, survive but are not secure. Although the Court extricates itself from this case without making a single, even incremental, change in the law of abortion, the plurality and Justice Scalia would overrule *Roe* '(the first silently, the other explicitly) and would return to the states virtually unfettered authority to control the quintessentially intimate, personal and life-directing decision whether to carry a fetus to term.

Although today, no less than yesterday, the Constitution and the decisions of this Court prohibit a state from enacting laws that inhibit women from the meaningful exercise of that right, a plurality of this Court implicitly invites every state legislature to enact more and more restrictive abortion regulations in order to provoke more and more test cases, in the hope that sometime down the line the Court will return the law of procreative freedom to the severe limitations that generally prevailed in this country before January 22, 1973. Never in my memory has a plurality announced a judgment of this Court that so foments disregard for the law and for our standing decisions.

Nor in my memory has plurality gone about its business in such a deceptive fashion. At every level of its review, from its effort to read the real meaning out of the Missouri statute to its intended evisceration of precedents and its deafening silence about the constitutional protections that it would jettison, the plurality obscures the portent of its analysis. With feigned restraint, the plurality announces that its analysis leaves *Roe* "undisturbed," albeit "modif[ied] and narrow[ed]." But this disclaimer is totally meaningless.

Winks, Nods and Knowing Glances

The plurality opinion is filled with winks and nods and knowing glances to those who would do away with *Roe* explicitly, but turns a stone face to anyone in search of what the plurality conceives as the scope of a woman's right under the due process clause to terminate a pregnancy free from the coercive and brooding influence of the State. The simple truth is that *Roe* would not survive the plurality's analysis, and that the plurality provides no substitute for *Roe's* protective umbrella.

I fear for the future. I fear for the liberty and equality of the millions of women who have lived and come of age in the 16 years since *Roe* was decided. I fear for the integrity of, and public esteem for, this court.

I dissent.

In the plurality's view, the viability-testing provision imposes a burden on second-trimester abortions as a way of furthering the State's interest in protecting the potential life of the fetus. Since under the *Roe* framework, the State may not fully regulate abortion in the interest of potential life (as opposed to maternal health) until the third trimester, the plurality finds it necessary, in order to save the Missouri testing provision, to throw out *Roe's* trimester framework.

In flat contradiction to *Roe*, the plurality concludes that the State's interest in potential life is compelling before viability, and upholds the testing provision because it "permissibly furthers" that state interest.

At the onset, I note that in its haste to limit abortion rights the plurality compounds the errors of its analysis by needlessly reaching out to address constitutional questions that are not actually presented. The conflict between Section 188.029 and *Roe's* trimester framework, which purportedly drives the plurality to reconsider our past decisions, is a contrived conflict: the product of an aggressive misreading of the viability-testing requirement and a needlessly wooden application of the *Roe* framework.

Had the plurality read the statute as written, it would have had no cause to reconsider the *Roe* framework. As properly construed, the viability-testing provision does not pass constitutional muster under even a rational-basis standard, the least restrictive level of review applied by this Court.

By mandating tests to determine fetal weight and lung maturity for every fetus thought to be more than 20 weeks of gestational age, the statute requires physicians to undertake procedures, such as amniocentesis, that, in the situation presented, have no medical justification, impose significant additional health risks on both the pregnant woman and the fetus, and bear no rational relation to the State's interest in protecting fetal life.

As written, Section 188.029 is an arbitrary imposition of discomfort, risk and expense, furthering no discernible interest except to make the procurement of an abortion as arduous and difficult as possible. Thus, were it not for the plurality's tortured effort to avoid the plain import of Section 188.029, it could have struck down the testing provision as patently irrational irrespective of the *Roe* framework.

'Dramatic Retrenchment' Is Charged

The plurality eschews this straightforward resolution in the hope of precipitating a constitutional crisis. Far from avoiding constitutional difficulty, the plurality attempts to

engineer a dramatic retrenchment in our jurisprudence by exaggerating the conflict between
its untenable construction of Section 188.029
and the *Roe* trimester framework.

No one contests that under the *Roe* framework the State, in order to promote its interest in potential human life, may regulate and
even proscribe non-therapeutic abortions once
the fetus becomes viable.

If, as the plurality appears to hold, the
testing provision simply requires a physician
to use appropriate and medically sound tests
to determine whether the fetus is actually viable when the estimated gestational age is
greater than 20 weeks (and therefore within
what the District Court found to be the margin of error for viability), then I see little or
no conflict with *Roe*. Nothing in *Roe,* or any
of its progeny, holds that a state may not ef-
fectuate its compelling interest in the potential
life of a viable fetus by seeking to insure that
no viable fetus is mistakenly aborted because
of the inherent lack of precision in estimates
of gestational age.

A requirement that a physician make a
finding of viability, one way or the other, for
every fetus that falls within the range of possible viability, does no more than preserve the
State's recognized authority. Although as the
plurality correctly points out, such a testing requirement would have the effect of imposing
additional costs on second-trimester abortions
where the tests indicated that the fetus was
not viable, these costs would be merely incidental to, and a necessary accommodation
of, the State's unquestioned right to prohibit non-therapeutic abortions after the
point of viability.

In short, the testing provision, as construed by the plurality, is consistent with the
Roe framework and could be upheld effort-
lessly under current doctrine.

A Deeper Constitutional Thicket

How ironic it is, then, and disingenuous, that
the plurality scolds the Court of Appeals for
adopting a construction of the statute that fails
to avoid constitutional difficulties. By distorting the statute, the plurality manages to avoid
invalidating the testing provision on what
should have been noncontroversial constitutional grounds; having done so, however, the
plurality rushes headlong into a much deeper
constitutional thicket, brushing past an obvious basis for upholding Section 188.029 in
search of a pretext for scuttling the trimester
framework.

Evidently, from the plurality's perspective,
the real problem with the Court of Appeals'
construction of Section 188.029 is not that it
raised a constitutional difficulty, but that it
raised the wrong constitutional difficulty—one
not implicating *Roe*. The plurality has remedied that, traditional canons of construction
and judicial forbearance notwithstanding. . . .

The Fundamental Right to Privacy

With respect to the *Roe* framework, the general constitutional principle—indeed, the fundamental constitutional right—for which it
was developed is the right to privacy. See,
e.g., *Griswold v. Connecticut* (1965), a species of "liberty" protected by the due process
clause, which under our past decisions safeguards the right of women to exercise some
control over their own role in procreation.

As we recently reaffirmed in *Thornburg v.
American College of Obstetricians and Gyne-
cologists,* 476 U.S. 747 (1986), few decisions
are "more basic to individual dignity and
autonomy" or more appropriate to that "certain private sphere of individual liberty" that
the Constitution reserves from the intrusive
reach of government than the right to make the
uniquely personal, intimate and self-defining
decision whether to end a pregnancy. It is this
general principle, the " 'moral fact that a

person belongs to himself and not others nor to society as a whole,'" that is found in the Constitution.

The trimester framework simply defines and limits that right to privacy in the abortion context to accommodate, not destroy, a state's legitimate interest in protecting the health of pregnant women and in preserving potential human life. Fashioning such accommodations between individual rights and the legitimate interests of government, establishing benchmarks and standards with which to evaluate the competing claims of individuals and government, lies at the very heart of constitutional adjudication.

To the extent that the trimester framework is useful in this enterprise, it is not only consistent with constitutional interpretation, but necessary to the wise and just exercise of this Court's paramount authority to define the scope of constitutional rights.

The plurality next alleges that the result of the trimester framework has "been a web of legal rules that have become increasingly intricate, resembling a code of regulations rather than a body of constitutional doctrine." Again, if this were a true and genuine concern, we would have to abandon vast areas of our constitutional jurisprudence. . . .

Back-Alley Abortions Feared

The plurality would clear the way once again for government to force upon women the physical labor and specific and direct medical and psychological harms that may accompany carrying a fetus to term. The plurality would clear the way again for the State to conscript a woman's body and to force upon her a "distressful life and future."

The result, as we know from experience, would be that every year hundreds of thousands of women, in desperation, would defy the law and place their health and safety in the unclean and unsympathetic hands of back-alley abortionists, or they would attempt to perform abortions upon themselves, with disastrous results. Every year many women, especially poor and minority women, would die or suffer debilitating physical trauma, all in the name of enforced morality or religious dictates or lack of compassion, as it may be.

Of the aspirations and settled understandings of American women, of the inevitable and brutal consequences of what it is doing, the tough-approach plurality utters not a word. This silence is callous. It is also profoundly destructive of this Court as an institution.

To overturn a constitutional decision is a rare and grave undertaking. To overturn a constitutional decision that secured a fundamental personal liberty to millions of persons would be unprecedented in our 200 years of constitutional history.

For today, at least, the law of abortion stands undisturbed. For today, the women of this Nation still retain the liberty to control their destinies. But the signs are evident and very ominous, and a chill wind blows.

I dissent.

The Outputs of Government

CHAPTER **12**

Public Policy

Public policy is the productive output of government in response to external and internal political pressures. Governmental policy making includes a variety of actors who may initiate, formulate, approve, or administer different kinds of program objectives. The actors may represent either broad or narrow interests. Their involvement and intensity of participation in the policy process will depend on the range of issues, the demands for action, different priorities, timing of decisions, available resources, and the necessity to reach satisfactory compromises over conflicting goals.

POLICY PROCESSES

Public-policy processes can be analyzed by identifying policy actors, the sources of their power and influence, their institutional roles, bargaining activity, and interaction that lead to various kinds of policy decisions and actions. Elitism, pluralism, and group theory are frequently-cited explanations of how the public-policy process works.

Elitism and pluralism are useful ways of explaining what happens in American government. They help to identify the formal elective and appointive actors in executive, legislative, and administrative agencies who act on public policy. Elitism assumes that public policy reflects the actions of small groups of decision makers. Pluralism shows the formation of coalitions and the nature of bargaining, negotiation, and compromise in the policy process. For example, the development of the American Constitution has competing elite or pluralist interpretations. The Supreme Court is an elite institution of nine appointed justices with life tenure, but the Court's decisions on social policy and criminal procedures cause a great deal of pluralist controversy between liberals and conservatives. Competition and cooperation between the national government and the states can be used to show how the federal system developed. The president and Congress engage in considerable bargaining, negotiation, and compromise in the legislative process. Congress has many procedural problems resulting from defects in its pluralistic decision-making structure. The federal bureaucracy is a vastly diverse pluralistic system having considerable influence on public-policy development and administration.

Group theory considers that the struggle between contending participants produces public policy. Individuals with common interests and goals join together to bring their demands to the attention of government. For example, the National Rifle Association has been highly effective in preventing federal gun control legislation, while Common Cause has been successful in achieving federal campaign-finance reform. *The Federalist*, Numbers 10 and 51, contained early warnings about the dangers of "factions" that could hinder popular control of government. According to James Madison, the system of separation of powers and checks and balances was necessary to overcome the power of majority or minority factions. The development of political parties competing for the presidency led to the formation of the two-party system. The electoral college is a highly complex mechanism intended to balance popular votes with state influence in electing the president. Group formation occurs when presidential candidates seek to develop winning combinations in election campaigns. Following elections, there is a continuing group struggle over obtaining federal funds for state and local programs. The president tries to maintain group support from electoral mandates and favorable ratings in public-opinion polls. Group combinations by lobbies, legislators, and bureaucrats often control specific areas of public policy with iron triangles.

How does public policy emerge from elite influence, pluralism, or the group struggle? One approach is to identify the different stages of the policy-making process: problem identification, policy formulation, policy adoption, policy implementation, and policy evaluation.

Problem Identification

Problem identification can be defined as certain public needs, conditions, or dissatisfactions which require relief for large groups of affected people. Public officials address such problems when they reach the government agenda. How do identified problems get on the government agenda? Among several possibilities are public demonstrations, natural catastrophes, failure of technologies, or changes in population composition or conditions.

Major participants in this initial stage of policy making include the media, interest groups, government administrators, and legislators. Typically, the president with the aid of the White House staff promotes the top policy agenda through speeches, press conferences, the State of the Union Address, the budget message, and other requests to Congress.

John Kingdon provides an effective summary of the connection between identified public problems and the government agenda-setting process.[1] Problems are addressed by government when they begin to flow in policies and political streams. In the policies stream, specialists develop solutions for agenda issues. The political stream includes changes in public opinion, election results, and shifts in party composition of Congress and party control of the presidency. When the problems, policies, and political streams flow together and converge, a window of opportunity is present for government to address the problems society is most concerned with.

Article 44 by Kevin Phillips identifies several consequences of problems facing American government and society today, resulting from Reagan administration policies of the 1980s. These include economic recession, debt, reduced revenue for government, and large budget deficits. According to Phillips, Reagan administration policies favored the rich over the middle class and the poor. Policies aimed at reducing income taxes, large-scale domestic and foreign borrowing, and deregulation produced the savings and loan crisis. Foreign investors held large amounts of U.S. debt resulting from the devalued dollar. President Bush's main tax objective was to reduce the capital gains rate which would benefit the wealthiest Americans.

Similarly, E. J. Dionne, Jr., in Article 47 is critical of both liberal and conservative policies that have antagonized many American voters. Liberal policies, in Dionne's view, worked against values like self-reliance, family stability and hard work. Conservative policies benefitted those who sought instant wealth, fame and luxury.

Problem identification and agenda-setting are facilitated more quickly in foreign policy when there is a perceived threat to American interests. In Operation Desert Storm (Article 45), President Bush considered Saddam Hussein's invasion of Kuwait a threat to the "new world order." Plans were quickly developed to remove Iraqi forces from Kuwait by economic sanctions, U.N. resolutions, and military force.

Bil Gilbert tells us in Article 46 that the environmental movement achieved government agenda status in 1970. The problem of environmental protection was galvanized by such natural disasters as the 1969 Santa Barbara oil spill, which was widely reported in the media, and the first celebration of Earth Day.

Policy Formulation

After public problems have been identified and placed on the government agenda, policymakers next deal with developing solutions to those problems. This is called policy formulation. It involves developing a course of action on a policy problem by examining and evaluating alternative solutions. Policy formulation usually involves information (getting the facts); analysis (assessing the facts); resources (determining the costs and benefits of various options); and identifying the option that will best solve the problem.

The president, Congress, and interest groups are frequently involved in policy formulation. The president calls on the White House staff and the bureaucracy to develop solutions to policy problems (see Chapter 9). Congress can request the Congressional Budget Office, the General Accounting Office, and the Congressional Research Office to assist in legislative formulation. Legislative formulation includes drafting bills, conducting investigations, confirming presidential appointments, and dealing with the budget and appropriations.

Interest groups try to influence executive and legislative officials in formulating policy proposals. They may even develop their own solutions and try to get government officials to use them. Foundations, think tanks, and universities frequently are a source of policy proposals which government officials may use.

The articles by Drew (Article 45) and Gilbert (Article 46) demonstrate how solutions were developed to policy problems. In Operation Desert Storm, the solution was clear-cut. First, President Bush gave clear warnings to Saddam Hussein. When Saddam did not respond to economic sanctions, U.N. resolutions, and threats of military force, President Bush decided to use military force directly to remove Iraqi troops from Kuwait.

Bil Gilbert tells us that the Nixon administration and Congress responded to environmental concerns in 1970 with the National Environmental Policy Act, Environmental Impact Statements, the Environmental Protection Agency, and several air and water pollution control measures and legislative enactments. Environmental interest groups, universities, the executive branch, Congress, and the bureaucracy were all involved in formulating these policy solutions.

Policy Adoption

Policy adoption involves the legitimation or approval of formulated policy proposals. It is the process by which policy proposals are approved, modified, or rejected.

Policy adoption can occur in several ways. Congress can approve a bill through various subcommittee, committee, floor, and conference votes (see Chapter 10). The president can issue self-executing orders. Administrative agencies may issue rules or regulations to implement laws approved by Congress and the president. Courts may issue orders to carry out decisions such as school desegregation or to reduce prison overcrowding. Interest groups, of course, use direct lobbying to influence the policy adoption process, particularly in Congress (see Chapters 5 and 10).

Policy formulation and adoption moved together simultaneously in Operation Desert Storm (Article 45) since President Bush controlled all decisions relating to the Persian Gulf crisis. Elizabeth Drew points out that many members of Congress, who supported the air war, initially opposed using ground troops. President Bush, however, finally issued a deadline for

Saddam's Iraqi troops to get out of Kuwait. This coincided with Bush's approval of General Schwarzkopf's plan to start the ground war.

Policies approved to protect the environment included legislative enactment of NEPA and various air, water, endangered species, and resource recovery measures by large bipartisan congressional majorities. The EPA issued regulations to implement these measures. Environmental interest groups supported stronger legislation and enforcement by the federal government.

Policy Implementation

Policy implementation consists of government activities that put legitimated policies into effect. The introduction to Chapter 9 explained how policy implementation works as it relates to the bureaucracy and executive-administrative relationships. Implementation usually includes considerable interpretation of laws and discretion by administrators. The president, Congress, courts, and interest groups are also involved.

Policy implementation is discussed in all four selections in this chapter. Both Kevin Phillips (Article 44) and E. J. Dionne, Jr. (Article 47) refer to the failures of administrative deregulation contributing to the savings and loan crisis. Elizabeth Drew (Article 45) tells us that Operation Desert Storm succeeded militarily in the four day ground war and quickly achieved the removal of Iraqi troops from Kuwait. The EPA was the principal federal agency designated to implement anti-pollution policies. Federal agencies were required to file Environmental Impact Statements to NEPA for all of their programs and projects affecting the environment. Interest groups and attorneys gained federal court support for holding agencies accountable for the content of impact statements monitored by the Council on Environmental Quality (Article 46).

Policy Evaluation

The last stage of the policy-making process concerns the assessment of how well the public policy has achieved its intended results. The introduction to Chapter 9 also discussed this policy stage. Policy evaluation is not only considered in this chapter but in many articles throughout the book. All students of American government can become policy evaluators. To be an effective evaluator, you need to determine the goals of the policy, its consequences, achievements, benefits, and costs. An evaluator also needs to develop and specify a clear method of evaluation analysis. Depending upon the results of the evaluation, the public policy may be revised, modified, changed, or terminated.

Kevin Phillips (Article 44) uses two methods of evaluation, economic and political, to criticize Reagan administration policies of the 1980s. He argues that the consequences of these policies were to shift resources and political power to the wealthiest members of American society. The middle class and the poor were the victims of this "capitalist blowout." Phillips bases his evaluation on political-electoral cycles of Republican party dominance, the latest of which began in 1968.

E. J. Dionne, Jr., is also a critical evaluator of American public policy in Article 47. Dionne observes that Americans hate politics because of the excesses and failures of ideological liberals and conservatives. He calls for a new politics of the center which will restore the values of American democracy and republicanism.

Elizabeth Drew (Article 45) considers the military objectives of Operation Desert Storm successful. The war was over quickly and U.S. casualties were quite low. But the unstated objective of removing Saddam Hussein was not achieved and it is doubtful that peace has been established in the Middle East.

The most positive evaluation is offered by Bil Gilbert in Article 46. Since 1970, the environmental movement has grown and government has responded. While much remains to be done, air pollution and water pollution are less serious today then twenty years ago. A number of poisonous compounds have been regulated or banned. More parks and conservation areas have been established. Environmental protection still faces many challenges, but environmental awareness is now a global phenomenon. The environmental movement, in Gilbert's view, has had an enormous impact in making most people aware of the fragile nature that we occupy.

NOTE

1. John W. Kingdon, *Agendas, Alternatives, and Public Policies* (Boston: Little, Brown, 1984), Chapter 8.

The Politics of Rich and Poor

44
Reagan's America: A Capital Offense
Kevin P. Phillips

The early 1990s witnessed a prolonged economic recession which neither Washington nor the states could address. Why were there no political solutions to these economic woes? Kevin P. Phillips, one of the nation's foremost political analysts, identifies the problems of the 1990s resulting from the excessive greed, wealth, and money politics of the Reagan years in the 1980s. America is now facing the debts of capitalist overdrive. Who benefitted from Republican policies of the 1980s? Who suffered financial distress? Phillips identifies four specific federal government policies which redistributed wealth to the richest individuals and corporations. What were these policies? How did foreign investors increase their resources in the United States? Phillips also discusses cycles of Republican dominance in American politics. Why haven't the Democrats challenged Republican power effectively? How is President Bush addressing the economic problems of the 1990s?

The 1980s were the triumph of upper America—an ostentatious celebration of wealth, the political ascendancy of the rich and a glorification of capitalism, free markets and finance. Not only did the concentration of wealth quietly intensify, but the sums involved took a megaleap. The definition of who's rich—and who's no longer rich—changed as radically during the Reagan era as it did during the great nouveaux riches eras of the late 19th century and the 1920s, periods whose excesses preceded the great reformist upheavals of the Progressive era and the New Deal.

But while money, greed and luxury became the stuff of popular culture, few people asked why such great wealth had concentrated at the top and whether this was the result of public policy. Political leaders, even those who professed to care about the armies of homeless sleeping on grates and other sad evidence of a polarized economy, had little to say about the Republican Party's historical role: to revitalize capitalism but also to tilt power, Government largess, more wealth and income toward the richest portion of the population.

The public, however, understood and worried about this Republican bias, if we can trust late 80's opinion polls; nevertheless, the Demo-crats largely shunned the issue in the '88 election, a reluctance their predecessors also displayed during Republican booms of the Gilded Age of the late 19th century and the Roaring Twenties.

As the decade ended, too many stretch limousines in Manhattan, too many yacht jams off Newport Beach and too many fur coats in Aspen foreshadowed a significant shift of mood. Only for so long would strung-out $35,000-a-year families enjoy magazine articles about the hundred most successful business-men in Dallas, or television shows about greed and glitz. Class structures may be weak in the United States, but populist sentiments run high. The political pendulum has swung in the past, and may be ready to swing again.

Indeed, money politics—be it avarice of fi-nanciers or the question of who will pay for the binges of the 80s—is shaping up as a prime theme for the 1990s. As we shall see, there is a historical cycle to such shifts: When-ever Republicans are in power long enough to transform economic policy from a middle-class orientation to capitalist overdrive, the rich get so far ahead that a popular reaction inevitably follows, with the Democrats usually tagging along, rather than leading.

But this time, the nature of the reaction against excess is likely to be different. The previous gilded ages occurred when America was on the economic rise in the world. The 1980s, on the other hand, turned into an era of paper entrepreneurialism, reflecting a na-tion consuming, rearranging and borrowing more than it built. For the next generation of populists who would like to rearrange Ameri-can wealth, the bad news is that a large amount of it has already been redistributed—to Japan, West Germany and to the other countries that took Reagan-era I.O.U.'s and credit slips.

Society matrons, Wall Street arbitrageurs, Palm Beach real-estate agents and other money-conscious Americans picking up USA Today on May 22, 1987, must have been at first bewildered and then amused by the top story. In describing a Harris survey of the atti-tudes of upper-bracket citizens, the article summed up the typical respondents as "rich. Very. He's part of the thinnest economic upper crust: households with incomes of more than $100,000 a year."

A surprising number of 1980's polls and commentaries contributed to this naïve percep-tion—that "rich" somehow started at $50,000 or $100,000 a year, and that gradations above that were somehow less important. The truth is that the critical concentration of wealth in the United States was developing at higher levels—decamillionaires, centimillionaires, half-billionaires and billionaires. Garden-variety American mil-lionaires had become so common that there were about 1.5 million of them by 1989.

In fact, even many families with what seemed like good incomes—$50,000 a year, say, in Wichita, Kan., or $90,000 a year in New York City (almost enough to qualify as "rich," according to USA Today)—found it hard to make ends meet because of the com-bined burden of Federal income and Social Se-curity taxes, plus the soaring costs of state taxes, housing, health care and children's edu-cation. What few understood was that real economic status and leisure-class purchasing power had moved higher up the ladder, to groups whose emergence and relative afflu-ence Middle America could scarcely compre-hend.

No parallel upsurge of riches had been seen since the late 19th century, the era of the Vanderbilts, Morgans and Rockefellers. It was the truly wealthy, more than anyone else, who flourished under Reagan. Calculations in a Brookings Institution study found that the share of national income going to the wealthi-est 1 percent rose from 8.1 percent in 1981 to 14.7 percent in 1986. Between 1981 and 1989, the net worth of the Forbes 400 richest Americans nearly tripled. At the same time, the division between them and the rest of the country became a yawning gap. In 1980, corporate chief executive officers, for example, made roughly 40 times the income of average factory workers. By 1989, C.E.O.'s were making *93 times as much.*

Finance alone built few billion-dollar fortunes in the 1980s relative to service industries like real estate and communications, but it is hard to overstate Wall Street's role during the decade, partly because Federal monetary and fiscal policies favored financial assets and because deregulation promoted new debt techniques and corporate restructuring.

Selling stock to retail clients, investment management firms or mutual funds paid well; repackaging, remortgaging or dismantling a Fortune 500 company paid magnificently. In 1981, analysts estimate, the financial community's dozen biggest earners made $5 million to $20 million a year. In 1988, despite the stock-market collapse the October before, the dozen top earners made $50 million to $200 million.

The redistribution of American wealth raised questions not just about polarization, but also about trivialization. Less and less wealth was going to people who produced something. Services were ascendant—from fast food to legal advice, investment vehicles to data bases. It is one thing for new technologies to reduce demand for obsolescent professions, enabling society to concentrate more resources in emerging sectors like health and leisure. But the distortion lies in the disproportionate rewards to society's economic, legal and cultural manipulators—from lawyers and financial advisers to advertising executives, merchandisers, media magnates and entertainers.

A related boom and distortion occurred in nonfinancial assets—art and homes, in particular. Art and antiques appreciated fourfold in the Reagan era, to the principal benefit of the richest 200,000 or 300,000 families. Similar if lesser explosions in art prices took place in the Gilded Age and in the 1920s. While the top one-half of 1 percent of Americans rolled in money, the luxuries they craved—from Picassos and 18th-century English furniture to Malibu beach houses—soared in markets virtually auxiliary to those in finance.

Meanwhile, everyone knew there was pain in society's lower ranks, from laid-off steelworkers to foreclosed farmers. A disproportionate number of female, black, Hispanic and young Americans lost ground in the 1980s, despite the progress of upscale minorities in each category. According to one study, for example, the inflation-adjusted income for families with children headed by an adult under 30 collapsed by roughly one-fourth between 1973 and 1986.

Even on an overall basis, median family and household incomes showed only small inflation-adjusted gains between 1980 and 1988. Middle America was quietly hurting too.

While corporate presidents and chairmen feasted in the 1980s, as many as 1.5 million midlevel management jobs are estimated to have been lost during those years. Blue-collar America paid a larger price, but suburbia, where fathers rushed to catch the 8:10 train to the city, was counting its casualties, too. "Middle managers have become insecure," observed Peter F. Drucker in September 1988, "and they feel unbelievably hurt. They feel like slaves on an auction block."

American transitions of the magnitude of the capitalist blowout of the 1980s have usually coincided with a whole new range of national economic attitudes. Evolving government policies—from tax cuts to high interest rates—seem distinct, but they are actually linked.

Whether in the late 19th century, the 1920s or the 1980s, the country has witnessed conservative politics, a reduced role for government, entrepreneurialism and admiration of business, corporate restructuring and mergers, tax reduction, declining inflation, pain in states that rely on commodities like oil and wheat, rising inequality and concentration of wealth, and a buildup of debt and speculation. The scope of these trends has been impressive—and so has their repetition, though the two periods of the 20th century have involved increasingly more paper manipulation and less of the raw vigor typical of the late 19th-century railroad and factory expansion.

Federal policy from 1981 to 1988 enormously affected investment, speculation and the creation and distribution of wealth and income, just as in the past.

The reduction or elimination of Federal income taxes was a goal in previous capitalist heydays. But it was a personal preoccupation for Ronald Reagan, whose antipathy toward income taxes dated back to his high-earning Hollywood days, when a top tax bracket of 91 percent in the 40s made it foolish to work beyond a certain point. Under him, the top personal tax bracket would drop from 70 percent to 28 percent in only seven years. For the first time since the era of Franklin D. Roosevelt, tax policy was fundamentally rearranging its class loyalties.

Reaganite theorists reminded the country that the Harding-Coolidge income-tax cuts—from a top rate of 73 percent in 1920 to 25 percent in 1925—helped create the boom of the 20s. Back then, just as in the 80s, the prime beneficiaries were the top 5 percent of Americans, people who rode the cutting edge of the new technology of autos, radios and the like, emerging service industries, including new practices like advertising and consumer finance, a booming stock market and unprecedented real-estate development. Disposable income soared for the rich, and with it, conspicuous consumption and financial speculation. After the 1929 crash and the advent of

the New Deal, tax rates rose again; the top rate reached 79 percent by 1936 and 91 percent right after the war. In 1964, the rate fell in two stages, to 77 percent and then to 70 percent.

Under Reagan, Federal budget policy, like tax changes, became a factor in the realignment of wealth, especially after the 1981-82 recession sent the deficit soaring. The slack was made up by money borrowed at home and abroad at high cost. The first effect lay in who received more Government funds. Republican constituencies—military producers and installations, agribusiness, bondholders and the elderly—clearly benefited, while decreases in social programs hurt Democratic interests and constituencies: the poor, big cities, housing, education. Equally to the point, the huge payments of high-interest charges on the growing national debt enriched the wealthy, who bought the bonds that kept Government afloat.

Prosperous individuals and financial institutions were beneficiaries of Government policies in other ways. Starting in the Carter years, Congress began to deregulate the financial industry; but the leap came in the early 1980s, when deposit and loan interest ceilings were removed. To attract deposits, financial institutions raised their interest rates, which rose and even exceeded record postwar levels. The small saver profited, but the much larger gain, predictably, went to the wealthy. (The benefits of high interest were intensified, of course, by the declining maximum tax rate on dividend and interest income. The explosion of after-tax unearned income for the top 1 percent of Americans was just that—an explosion.)

The savings and loan crisis now weighing on American taxpayers also had roots in deregulation. Before 1982, savings and loan associations were required to place almost all their loans in home mortgages, a relatively safe and stable class of assets. But in 1982, after soaring interest rates turned millions of low-interest mortgages into undesirable assets, a new law allowed savings and loans to invest their funds more freely—100 percent in commercial real-estate ventures if they so desired. Like banks in the 1920s, many thrifts proceeded to gamble with their deposits, and by 1988, many had lost. Gamblers and speculators enriched themselves even as they stuck other Americans with the tab.

Reagan's permissiveness toward mergers, antitrust enforcement and new forms of speculative finance was likewise typical of Republican go-go conservatism. Unnerving parallels were made between the Wall Street raiders of the 1980s—Ivan Boesky and T. Boone Pickens—and the takeover pools of the 1920s, when high-powered operators would combine to "boom" a particular stock. For a small group of Americans at the top, the pickings were enormous.

An egregious misperception of late 20th-century politics is to associate only Democrats with extremes of public debt. Before 1933, conservatives—Federalists, Whigs and Republicans alike—sponsored Government indebtedness and used high-interest payments to redistribute wealth upward.

In addition, Republican eras were noted for a huge expansion of private debt. In the 1920s, individual, consumer and corporate debt kept setting record levels, aided by new techniques like installment purchases and margin debt for purchasing securities. In the kindred 80s, total private and public debt grew from $4.2 trillion to more than $10 trillion. And just as they had 60 years earlier, new varieties of debt became an art form.

Government fiscal strategists were equally loose. In part to avoid the deficit-reduction mandates of the Gramm-Rudman-Hollings Act, they allowed Federal credit programs, including student and housing loans, to balloon from $300 billion in 1984 to $500 billion in 1989.

In contrast to previous capitalist blowouts, the fast-and-loose Federal debt strategies of the 80s did not simply rearrange assets within the country but served to transfer large amounts of the nation's wealth overseas as well. America's share of global wealth expanded in the Gilded Age and again in the 1920s. The late 1980s, however, marked a significant downward movement: one calculation, by the Japanese newspaper *Nihon Keizai Shimbun,* had Japan overtaking the United States, with estimated comparative assets of $43.7 trillion in 1987 for Japan, versus $36.2 trillion for the United States.

The United States was losing relative purchasing power on a grand scale. There might be more wealthy Americans than ever before, but foreigners commanded greater resources. On the 1989 *Forbes* list of the world's billionaires, the top 12, with the exception of one American, were all foreigners—from Japan, Europe, Canada and South Korea. Dollar millionaires, once the envy of the world, were becoming an outdated elite.

This shift partly reflected the ebb of America's postwar pre-eminence. Yet the same Reagan policies that moved riches internally also accelerated the shift of world wealth, beginning with the budget deficits of the early 1980s but intensifying after the ensuing devaluation of the dollar from 1985 to 1988.

If the devalued dollar made the Japanese, French and Germans relatively richer, it also increased their purchasing power in the United States, turning the country into a bargain basement for overseas buyers. This is the explanation for the surging foreign acquisition of properties, from Fortune 500 companies to Rockefeller Center in Manhattan and a large share of the office buildings in downtown Los Angeles.

The dollar's decline also pushed per capita gross national product and comparative wages in the United States below those of a number of Western European nations. The economist Lester C. Thurow summed up the predicament: "When it comes to wealth, we can argue about domestic purchasing power. But, in terms of international purchasing power, the United States is now only the ninth wealthiest country in the world in terms of per capita G.N.P. We have been surpassed by Austria, Switzerland, the Netherlands, West Germany, Denmark, Sweden, Norway and Japan."

Not everyone looked askance at foreign wealth and investment. American cities and states welcomed it. From the textile towns of South Carolina to the rolling hills of Ohio, foreigners were helping declining regions to reverse their fate. Yet as Warren Buffett, the investor, said: "We are much like a wealthy family that annually sells acreage so that it can sustain a life style unwarranted by its current output. Until the plantation is gone, it's all pleasure and no pain. In the end, however, the family will have traded the life of an owner for the life of a tenant farmer."

Nowhere was Japanese investment more obvious than in Hawaii, where real-estate moguls from Tokyo pronounced the property they were grabbing up "almost free." An economist at a Hawaiian bank warned that the state was "a kind of test lab for what's facing the whole country." Indeed, in 1988, broader foreign ambitions were apparent. The author Daniel Burstein quoted Masaaki Kurokawa, then head of Japan's Nomura Securities International, who raised with American dinner guests the possibility of turning California into a joint U.S.-Japanese economic community.

Public concern over America's international weakness had been a factor in Ronald Reagan's election back in 1980. Voters had wanted a more aggressive leader than Jimmy Carter. For various reasons, the great things promised were not delivered. Reagan could recreate a sense of military prowess with his attacks on Grenada and Libya. But in the global economy he took a country that had been the world's biggest creditor in 1980 and turned it into the world's largest debtor. Despite opinion polls documenting public concern about this erosion, surprisingly little was made of the issue in the 1988 Presidential campaign, possibly because the Democrats could not develop a coherent domestic and international alternative.

Much of the new emphasis in the 1980s on tax reduction and the aggressive accumulation of wealth reflected the Republican Party's long record of support for unabashed capitalism. It was no fluke that three important Republican supremacies coincided with and helped generate the Gilded Age, the Roaring Twenties and the Reagan-Bush years.

Part of the reason survival-of-the-fittest periods are so relentless, however, rests on the performance of the Democrats as history's secondmost enthusiastic capitalist party. They do not interfere with capitalist momentum, but wait for excesses and the inevitable popular reaction.

In the United States, elections arguably play a more important cultural and economic role than in other lands. Because we lack a hereditary aristocracy or Establishment, our leadership elites and the alignment of wealth are more the product of political cycles than they are elsewhere. Capitalism is maneuvered more easily in the United States, pushed in new regional and sectoral directions. As a result, the genius of American politics—failing only in the Civil War—has been to manage through ballot boxes the problems that less-fluid societies resolve with barricades and with party structures geared to class warfare.

Because we are a mobile society, Americans tolerate one of the largest disparities in the industrial world between top and bottom incomes, as people from the middle move to the top, and vice versa. Opportunity has counted more than equality.

But if circulating elites are a reality, electoral politics is an important traffic controller. From the time of Thomas Jefferson, the nation has undulated in 28- to 36-year waves as each watershed election puts a new dominant region, culture, ideology or economic interest (or combination) into the White House, changing the country's direction. But after a decade or two, the new forces lose touch with the public, excessively empower their own elites and become a target for a new round of populist reform. Only the United States among major nations reveals such recurrent electoral behavior over two centuries.

The Republicans rode such a wave into office in 1968, as a middle-class, anti-elite correction, successfully squelching the social permissiveness and disorder of the 60s. Significantly, each Republican coalition—from Lincoln's to Nixon's—began by emphasizing national themes and unity symbols, while subordinating commercial and financial interests.

But it is the second stage—dynamic capitalism, market economics and the concentration of wealth—that the Republican Party is all about. When Republicans are in power long enough, they ultimately find themselves embracing limited government, less regulation of business, reduced taxation, disinflation and high real interest rates. During America's first two centuries, these policies shaped the three periods that would incubate the biggest growth of American millionaires (or, by the 1980s, billionaires). History suggests that it takes a decade or more for the Republican Party to shift from broad middle-class nationalism into capitalist overdrive, and the lapse of 12 years between the first Nixon inauguration in 1969 and the first Reagan inauguration repeats this transformation.

Nixon, like the previous Republican nationalist Presidents Abraham Lincoln and William McKinley, was altogether middle class, as was his "new majority" Republicanism. He had no interest in unbridled capitalism during his 1969-74 Presidency.

In fact, many of the new adherents recruited for the Republican coalition in 1968 and 1972 were wooed with the party's populist attacks on inflation, big government, social engineering and the Liberal Establishment. Many Republican voters of that era embraced outsider and anti-elite values, and like similar participants in previous Republican national coalitions, they would become uneasy in the 1980s as Reagan or Bush Republicanism embraced Beverly Hills or Yale culture and the economics of leveraged buyouts, not of Main Street.

Besides this uneasiness, reflected in opinion polls, a second sign that a conservative cycle is moving toward its climax has been the extent to which Democratic politics has been cooperative: when wealth is in fashion, Democrats go along. The solitary Democratic President of the Gilded Age, Grover Cleveland, was a conservative with close Wall Street connections. In the 20s, the Democratic Presidential nominees in both 1920 (James Cox, an Ohio publisher) and 1924 (John W. Davis, a corporate lawyer) were in the Cleveland mold. Alfred E. Smith, who ran in 1928, would eventually oppose Roosevelt and the New Deal. In the 20s, Congressional Democrats competed with Republicans to cut upper-bracket and corporate taxes.

Fifty years later, Jimmy Carter, the only Democratic President to interrupt the long Republican hegemony after 1968, was accused by the historian Arthur M. Schlesinger, Jr., of an "eccentric effort to carry the Democratic Party back to Grover Cleveland." Despite his support for substantial new Federal regulation, Carter clearly deviated from his party's larger post-New Deal norm. He built foundations that would become conservative architecture under Reagan: economic deregulation; capital-gains tax reduction and the tight-money policies of the Federal Reserve. (The Fed's chairman, Paul A. Volcker, was a Carter appointee.) Congressional Democrats even echoed their policies of the 1920s by colluding in the bipartisan tax-bracket changes of 1981 and 1986.

Thus, the Democrats could hardly criticize Reagan's tax reductions. For the most part, they laid little groundwork for an election-year critique in 1988, leaving the issue to Jesse Jackson, whose appeal was limited by his race and third-world rhetoric, and to noncandidates like Mario M. Cuomo. Michael S. Dukakis was obviously uncomfortable with populist politics. Though several consultants and economists urged him to pick up the theme of economic inequality, Dukakis made competence, not ideology, his initial campaign issue. Only in late October, with his campaign crumbling, did the Democratic candidate reluctantly convert to a more traditional party line. It came too late.

Republican strategists could hardly believe their luck. Said Lee Atwater, Bush's campaign manager, after the election: "The way to win a Presidential race against the Republicans is to develop the class-warfare issue, as Dukakis did at the end—to divide up the haves and have-nots and to try to reinvigorate the New Deal coalition and to attack."

On the surface, this was a missed Democratic opportunity. But the lesson of history is that the party of Cleveland, Carter and Dukakis has rarely rushed its anti-elite corrective role. There would be no rush again in 1988—nor, indeed, in 1989.

Early in his presidency, George Bush replaced the Coolidge portrait hung by Ronald Reagan in the White House with one of Theodore Roosevelt, reflecting Bush's belief in T. R.'s commitment to conservation, patrician reform and somewhat greater regulatory involvement.

Yet there has not been too much evidence of a kinder, gentler America beyond softer, more conciliatory rhetoric. The budget remained unkind to any major expansion of domestic programs, and Bush's main tax objective was a reduction in the capital gains rate, a shift that critics said would continue to concentrate benefits among the top 1 percent of Americans.

By spring 1990, Washington politicians confronted the most serious debt- and credit-related problems since the bank failures, collapsed stock prices, farm foreclosures and European war debt defaults of the Great Depression. From the savings and loan associations bailout to junk bonds, from soaring bankruptcies and shaky real-estate markets to Japanese influence in the bond market, Federal policy makers were forced to realize that a crucial task—and peril—of the 1990s would involve cleaning up after the previous decade's credit-card parties and speculative distortions.

In May, the facade of successful deficit reduction crumbled as Administration officials confessed that bailing out insolvent savings and loans could cost as much as a half-trillion dollars. It became clear that taxes would have to rise. In California, where the anti-tax revolt began more than a decade ago, the approval by the state's voters earlier this month of an increase in the gasoline tax was seen by many as a sign of public willingness to come to grips with the fiscal deficiencies of the 1980s.

Even some Democrats who previously collaborated with Republican economics have begun to argue that the rich who had made so much money in the 80s should bear a larger share of the new burdens of the 90s. A number of Republicans share this disquiet. The Senate minority leader, Bob Dole of Russell,

Kan., insisted in late 1989 that if the White House wanted to cut capital-gains taxes for the prosperous, it should also raise the minimum wage for the poor. Last month, the House Republican leader, Robert H. Michael of Peoria, Ill., was reported to favor an increase in the tax rate for the top 1 percent of Americans, from 28 percent to 33 percent. The second-ranking Republican leader in the House, Newt Gingrich of Georgia, suggested in April that conservatives, too, had to develop some ideas for economic redistribution.

Meanwhile, opinion poll after opinion poll has shown lopsided voter support for raising the income-tax rate for people making more than $80,000, $100,000 or $200,000. The 1990s seem ready to reflect a new anti-Wall Street, anticorporate and antigreed outlook set forth in books (and coming movies) like "Bonfire of the Vanities," "Liar's Poker" and "Barbarians at the Gate."

Nor was the changing mood apparent only in the United States. Kindred psychologies and political analyses could also be seen in other countries like Britain, Japan and Canada, where 1980s financial and real-estate booms likewise concentrated wealth in the hands of the very rich and increased economic inequity. A headline last month in the *Financial Times* of London could have been written in the United States: "The Rich Get Nervous."

Whether the populist reactions that followed past boom periods recur in the 90s no one can know. But there could be no doubt that the last decade ended as it had begun: with a raising imperative for a new political and economic philosophy, and growing odds that the 1990s will be a very different chapter than the 1980s in the annals of American wealth and power.

The Persian Gulf War

45
Operation Desert Storm
Elizabeth Drew

In the previous article, Kevin Phillips mentioned that presidents can divert attention from domestic problems by pursuing foreign military actions. President Bush launched Operation Desert Storm to force Iraqi troops out of Kuwait in January 1991. Elizabeth Drew, a reporter for The New Yorker *magazine, argues that the Bush administration also wanted Saddam Hussein removed from power. What were the sources of this unstated objective? When Hussein could not be removed, what did U.S. military and political strategy seek to accomplish? How was the decision made to begin the allied forces' ground war? Why did U.S. officials oppose Soviet efforts to negotiate an end to the war? How did Saddam miss opportunities to prevent the war? The ground war lasted only four days. Why? Which U.S. military leaders gained in stature and reputation as a result of the war? What was the nature of President Bush's leadership? Drew suggests several impacts of the Persian Gulf War. What occurred after the war ended to assess it as a success? Did the Persian Gulf conflict produce additional problems at home and in the Middle East?*

The swift collapse of the Iraqi Army took almost all of Washington by surprise. Even Administration officials who had expected the ground war to go well and quickly were surprised. Though the ground war went well from the beginning, we had learned that Iraq keeps surprising us, and were reluctant to allow ourselves to think that events were now predictable. But by Monday, two days after the ground war began, the question was whether there would be any remaining substantial difficulties, and by Tuesday morning, after Saddam Hussein had said on Baghdad radio that Iraqi troops were withdrawing—a luxury President Bush wasn't willing to give them—the question was when, exactly, the war would come to an end and what would happen next. By that time, the Bush Administration and some of its key allies had become determined not to give Hussein any easy out.

Actually, that determination had been reached much earlier than is generally thought; it's not so much that, as many believe, the war aims grew as the war went on as that they became more explicit. War creates its own logic. The goal had for some time been not just the liberation of Kuwait and the removal of Iraq's weapons of mass destruction but the removal of Saddam Hussein and his regime from power—indirectly, if necessary.

From *The New Yorker,* March 11, 1991, pp. 83-87. Reprinted by permission; © 1991 Elizabeth Drew. Originally in *The New Yorker.*

The only thing that could have diverted us and our key allies from this goal (not all of them shared it) would have been a cleverness on Hussein's part that he never exhibited. By the time, two weeks ago, that Hussein began to show signs he wished to wriggle out of Kuwait, but on terms that were unacceptable on the face of it, the Bush Administration and most of its key allies in the coalition had long been committed to not allowing him to do so. Thus the ground war became an inevitability.

When our bombs failed to find Hussein and the Iraqis didn't oblige by overthrowing him, the next priority was to destroy as much of his military machinery as possible and force a humiliating loss on him. The systematic bombing if Iraq's infrastructure had the dual purpose of eliminating what we could that might help Hussein militarily and encouraging domestic rage against him for putting his people through such an ordeal. The thinking was that even if Hussein was alive at the end of the war he wouldn't be in power, or alive, for long. At some point, Bush's rhetoric had also made the elimination of Hussein a political necessity. In recent weeks, two senators who had opposed going to war have told me that the overwhelming majority of their constituents want Saddam Hussein removed from office. Bush's demonizing of him had its own results—both in his mind and in the minds of his listeners. A senator who had opposed the war said to me recently, "My people say that if Saddam Hussein is Hitler, how can we end the war leaving Hitler in power?"

The real aim of getting rid of Hussein had to remain unstated—if obvious—a senior official told me a couple of weeks ago, because to declare his demise an explicit goal would make him a hero every day that he remained alive, and would make him a martyr if he were killed under such circumstances. Though seeking the demise of Saddam Hussein's regime isn't specifically mentioned in the United Nations resolutions, the authority for working toward it lies in an expansive view of that portion of the U.N. resolution (Resolution 678) authorizing the use of force to implement *all* of the U.N. resolutions—not just the one calling for an Iraqi withdrawal from Kuwait—and also calling for a restoration of "international peace and security in the area." When this resolution was adopted by the U.N., at the end of November, all the attention was on the part that authorized the use of "all necessary means" to implement the resolutions, but the other section was put there with the deliberate aim of enabling the allies to make severe postwar demands on Iraq if Saddam Hussein was still in charge—and drive him from office. An allied diplomat says that when Resolution 678 was drafted, negotiated, and finally adopted "everyone knew what we were talking about. We put in a sentence that could cover a wide range of things. One was that he must not be a threat to his neighbors—and how could he not be a threat to his neighbors if he has four thousand tanks? When we adopted 678, we were thinking then that once we engaged with this man we were going to win clear-cut—it had to end in his total defeat." Administration officials also say that the second part of Resolution 678 was written in a way to grant us wide latitude, backed by the U.N., in defining how the war should end—especially if Saddam Hussein was still around. Going on to Baghdad wasn't politically feasible. Prince Bandar bin Sultan, the Saudi Ambassador to the United States and one of our more hawkish, and influential, allies, said to me recently, "We can't drive to Baghdad. We want to make the liberation of Kuwait so expensive that his people will question the wisdom of what he did, and we leave the rest to them." For some time, the President and others have said publicly that they wouldn't be terribly sorry if he were gone, and some officials privately confirm that our bombers searched for him. Not long ago, a Pentagon official said to me, "We can't find the guy—that's the big problem." It was also out of concern that we wouldn't be able to find him (we had had enough trouble with Qaddafi and Noriega) that high military officials urged that we not make finding him a stated goal. So when officials were asked in formal interviews whether the goals of the war had expanded to include the demise of Hussein and his regime, they answered, almost uniformly, that getting rid of Hussein was "not a war aim."

But it had become a political aim, and an indirect war aim. When Bush two weeks ago called on the Iraqi people to overthrow Hussein, he was basing his request more on hope than on information, but officials now flatly state privately that they don't expect Hussein to remain in power very long after the end of the war. He will have lost two major wars and the bulk of his military wherewithal, and his country is in ruins. An allied diplomat says, "I think we've done everything to facilitate and hasten" his end. If Saddam Hussein would still be in power at the end of the war (as the intelligence agencies were telling Bush), it followed that he must be further disarmed, and revolt against him must be encouraged, by demanding that his military in Kuwait lay down their arms and by issuing tough demands at the end of the war. The trick, of course, is to see to it that Iraqi rage is directed against Hussein, not us. Not only has the President felt strongly that Hussein must be disarmed and, if possible, removed but so do such key allies as the Saudis and the British, as well as the Kuwaitis. The Egyptians feel less strongly about this, in part because they don't share a border with Iraq. Once it became clear that Hussein might still be standing at the end of the war, the policy became explicit that his must be a humiliating defeat. Therefore, he couldn't be allowed to withdraw from Kuwait with whatever he had left, and therefore the Soviet Union's effort last week to negotiate a withdrawal was a nuisance. There were some people in the government, even high in the military, who felt that the air war had done such damage to Iraq's war machine that his withdrawing from Kuwait with whatever was left posed no further danger to the region. But this wasn't enough for Bush and for some of our allies.

As Administration officials told it later, the decision to go to a ground war had already been made by the time Cheney and Colin Powell, the chairman of the Joint Chiefs of Staff, went to Saudi Arabia to meet with General Norman Schwarzkopf over the second weekend in February. Schwarzkopf was invited to suggest a "window" of time during which he thought the ground war should commence. During that "window," the tremendous logistical feat of moving about three hundred thousand troops, and sixty days' supplies, far to the west, in a flanking maneuver to surprise Saddam Hussein, was to be completed, and the battlefield and the troops were to be made ready. Policymakers here could plan. Then Schwarzkopf was to pick a date within that window for beginning the ground war, and to proceed unless he was stopped by his superiors for any reason. Schwarzkopf's suggestion that the window open during the last week of February was conveyed to the President upon Cheney and Powell's return. So, as many of us thought, when the President told the public that "we're not talking about dates" he was purposely—and, given the subject matter, justifiably—misleading us.

Officials also insist that Schwarzkopf picked February 23rd for the beginning of the ground war *before* the slight hitch of the Soviet intervention occurred, and therefore the ground war wasn't held up by that, but others aren't so sure. The twenty-third was actually Schwarzkopf's second date; his first choice was set aside, an official says, so that troop movement could be completed. The factors in the timing for beginning the ground war, a senior Defense Department official says, were that all the needed troops were in place, with their needed supplies, and ready; the battlefield had been "shaped" (that is, a fair amount of Iraq's artillery in Kuwait, including that which might fire chemical weapons, had been removed by force; the weather, the moon, and the tides were about right. (It turned out that all the talk of an amphibious landing on Kuwait was a feint.) Also, some of our Arab allies (as well as the French) were arguing that the continued bombing of Iraq was causing anger to rise in the region, so best to get the whole thing over with soon. The Saudis wanted the war over before Ramadan, the monthlong religious fasting period that begins in mid-March—not, as many had thought, because they would be offended by fighting during that holiday (Arabs had started the 1973 Yom Kippur war during Ramadan) but because of the sensitivities that would be stirred by their having to help feed a half million foreign troops at that time, and because Saudi leaders thought that Ramadan would be a propitious time to get everyone to calm down after the war.

Though it seems hard to remember now, Bush actually began the ground war against substantial political resistance. A number of key members of Congress, in both parties, had publicly and privately urged that he continue the air war without bringing the ground troops into it—at least for some time. When Schwarzkopf said in an interview with the Los Angeles *Times,* on February 19th, that the Iraqi troops were "on the verge of collapse," a number of people here took that as evidence that there need be no ground war, except, perhaps, as a mopping-up exercise. Though that's close to what the ground war turned out to be, Congress had no way of

foreseeing that. One senior Pentagon official said to me later that Schwarzkopf "got a little carried away," and in the official briefings here stressed that, as Lieutenant General Thomas Kelly put it a week ago Wednesday, "it's not going to be a snap." Actually, the field commanders couldn't know how strong an Iraqi force they would encounter until they actually encountered it, and all along the Defense Intelligence Agency estimates of the damage to Iraqi forces had been more conservative than those of the field commanders. But Schwarzkopf was closer to the truth.

Though Administration officials, starting with the President, said that they "appreciated" the Soviet efforts, before the ground war began, to negotiate an end to the war, they weren't at all appreciative. There was, however, a difference of view within the Administration; some State Department officials were more interested in seeing whether anything could be made of the Soviet negotiations with Iraq than were their counterparts on the staff of the National Security Council or Cheney. (Washington loves splits between the N.S.C. and the State Department, and last week's sudden spate of stories saying that Brent Scowcroft, the national-security adviser, and his deputy, Robert Gates, had gained the upper hand on Gulf and Soviet policy from James Baker, the Secretary of State and close friend of the President, set off a fair amount of gossip here. These two men, joined by Cheney and Vice-President Dan Quayle, had been more hawkish than Baker through much of the Gulf crisis, and take a more skeptical view of the Soviet Union. Baker had once suppressed a skeptical speech by Gates. There had been enough incidents—an earlier press story portraying Baker as the restraining hand on Bush in Gulf policy, the mysterious joint United States-Soviet Union statement on ending the Gulf war, an unusual public row between Baker and the Israeli Ambassador here, into which Baker, overriding the judgment of certain White House officials, dragged the President—to spawn some attacks on Baker by his antagonists through the press. There was some speculation that potential rivalries in 1992, or 1996, were at play here. Whatever the President really thought—he was said by an adviser to be "very upset" about the stories—he quite visibly took Baker off with him to Camp David last weekend.)

In any event, on Tuesday, February 19th, the President, with the full agreement of most of his key coalition allies, dismissed the first Soviet proposal, saying, "It falls well short of what would be required." The proposal, which wasn't made public, was deemed too vague, since it lacked timetables and deadlines, and it stated that the Soviet Union would try to guarantee the security of Hussein and the territorial integrity of Iraq—but maintaining Saddam Hussein in power was exactly what we didn't want. A senior Administration official said to me at the time, "The Soviet bottom line is different from ours." And if Hussein was permitted to withdraw—as the Soviets proposed—without having to face continued economic and military sanctions, one of the levers for forcing him from office would be removed. (In an appearance at a military base in early February, a pumped-up Bush said, "And when we win . . . we will have taught a dangerous dictator . . . that what we say goes.") One reason the President and other officials remained so polite about the Soviet Union's efforts is that its cooperation will be needed in the postwar period, especially as the U.N. considers continued sanctions, or other long-term arrangements. Still, most officials were miffed that the Soviets had got into the act at all—not to mention that they didn't tell us beforehand about their proposal—since the upshot might have been something that got in the way of the Administration's determination to prosecute the war to the point where Saddam Hussein would be left with few troops and weapons, and have to comply with all the U.N. resolutions. In the words of one allied diplomat, "The problem was how you say no without looking like you don't want a peaceful resolution." Therefore, Baker sent a long letter to his Soviet counterpart, Aleksandr Bessmertnykh, suggesting revisions in the proposal—including a four-day withdrawal timetable, a requirement that the weapons be left behind, and observance of all the U.N. resolutions. Almost no one expected Saddam Hussein to accept this.

When, last Thursday, the Soviets came forth with yet another proposal—one that called for withdrawal "within a fixed time frame," to be specified later, and still called for a lifting of the other U.N. resolutions—the Administration and its major allies decided that it was time to get hold of the process by setting their own terms. Since they were planning to launch the ground war, they couldn't wait around while Iraq dickered over withdrawal terms, and they needed to regain control. Ideas for how to spell out a ceasefire had been in the works since even before the war began: the thought was that at some point a third country would come up with a ceasefire proposal, or the Iraqis would announce a withdrawal or request a ceasefire, and we should be ready. Earlier in the week, there had been conversations among the major allies about coming forward with their own plan, so as to take the game away from the Soviets. This is what led to Bush's ultimatum last Friday, accompanied by tough withdrawal terms—which, it appears, no one in the Administration expected Hussein to accept. Saddam Hussein was faced with two stark alternatives: withdraw quickly, within a week (the four days was too brief for some of our allies) and without his weapons, and face the other U.N. resolutions or lose the war and his weapons and face the other U.N. resolutions.

All along, Bush didn't make it easy for Saddam Hussein to back down from his invasion of Kuwait, but all along Hussein missed opportunities to do so. All along, Bush's demands were absolute—no "face-saving," no negotiating the withdrawal. But Hussein let pass opportunities, before the war began, to accept offers by other (the French, the U.N.) that would have let him get out with a little face-saving, such as the Middle East peace conference he said meant so much to him—until late last week, when it was dropped from the Soviet-Iraqi proposal. Had he accepted one of these proposals, even though we deemed it unacceptable we would have had difficulty starting the war. Administration officials were worried about this possibility. Even up to last weekend, Hussein could have simply started withdrawing, making it difficult for us to launch the ground war. The principle behind setting this deadline was, a senior Administration official explains, the same as that behind the January 15th deadline: at some point, it's time to call a halt to diplomatic efforts and bring matters to a head.

The new deadline—noon on Saturday, February 23rd—coincided with Schwarzkopf's date and time for starting the ground war. (Setting a noon deadline allowed the allied forces to commence operations that night, whereas the midnight deadline on January 15th forced a delay until the next day.) On Friday, the Soviets came up with yet another proposal—this one calling for a withdrawal within three weeks, along with lifting other U.N. resolutions—but the Administration still wasn't interested.

When the ground war began, on Saturday night, there was no surprise here; we had come to know that on this subject Bush meant what he said. There was also little outcry. Few members of Congress were in town: most were taking the long Washington's Birthday weekend off. So, except for some nervous private conversations, most members of Congress were essentially mute when the ground war began. Most were waiting to see how it turned out. On Sunday, when we saw on television the long lines of Iraqi soldiers giving up, we began to get the idea that this phase of the war might indeed go quickly, but Pentagon officials, though privately optimistic, tried to tamp down public expectations—just as they had done after the air war began. By Tuesday, we knew that it was over.

Meanwhile, Saddam Hussein continued to try to "withdraw"—on terms more acceptable to him than what we had in mind—and each of his proposals was swiftly batted down by the White House. The idea was that he shouldn't be able, at this late date and in such dire circumstances, to set the terms of his defeat, or to "withdraw," claiming some sort of victory, rather than surrender. Besides, some units of the Republican Guard, Iraq's best troops and the backbone of Hussein's power, were still in fighting form. Most of them were stationed in southern Iraq, and while Hussein was attempting to withdraw, the allied forces were moving to encircle them, preventing their escape. On Tuesday, the encirclement was complete, but tank battles against the Guard took place on Tuesday and Wednesday, ending in the defeat of most of the Guard. On Wednesday, allied forces were in Kuwait City; in keeping with the delicate politics with which the coalition was formed and the war was waged, Arab forces were allowed to be the first to enter it. The Marines followed close behind. The exultation of the Kuwaiti citizens made many people here who had dismissed their plight feel guilty. (The stories of atrocities are still being sorted out, and Kuwait City is darkened by the smoke from oil fires.) By Wednesday afternoon, Bush and his advisers decided that enough was enough—that others might attempt to broker a ceasefire and we might look vengeful, so it was time, once again, to get command of the process. Also, word seeped out that Iraq was ready to accept all the U.N. resolutions. Therefore, that night the President went on television to announce, "Kuwait is liberated." He announced his intention to "suspend offensive combat operations" at midnight—setting forth the procedures for reaching a formal ceasefire. The ground war, Bush said, would have gone on for "exactly one hundred hours." This time, Iraq accepted, and said it was willing to abide by all the U.N. resolutions.

Also on Wednesday, Schwarzkopf's bravura briefing on the war capped his reputation as one of the most interesting military men we'd seen in a long time. At once forceful and sensitive, and obviously very smart, Schwarzkopf is now a major figure. If we needed people to look up to, this war has provided them, and if we needed to overcome some of the lingering bitterness about Vietnam, this war helped do that. Whatever we thought about the necessity of this war, it gave us, in Powell and Schwarzkopf, military leaders who gave us confidence. Even the fact that none of our military leaders seemed crazy was a relief. Cheney came across as he is—steady, tough, calm. (The Administration should strike a medal for Senate Armed Services Committee chairman Sam Nunn for having made sure that John Tower didn't become Secretary of Defense.) The low casualty figures for the Americans gave the end of the war a triumphal air. The military leaders have avoided talking about Iraqi deaths, which were high and by some accounts may have reached about a hundred thousand. And there was heavy bombing of Baghdad on Wednesday, though by then it was hard to know why. (The military aren't certain why Iraq didn't use chemical weapons. The theories are that the allies took out many of them when they attacked its artillery, and didn't stay stationary long enough to be targeted. Also, Iraq didn't

have the capability of delivering chemicals by airplanes, as it had done in the past. Our military never ruled out that Iraq had the capability of putting chemicals on Scuds.) Our generals were smart, but they were also lucky; the Iraqi troops' vaunted dug-inness (combined with our cutting off their supply lines) doomed them. As Schwarzkopf pointed out, Saddam Hussein wasn't an impressive military strategist. The success of this war has made it all the more politically popular, and some wrong conclusions may be drawn from it. We can never know whether there was a viable alternative; history doesn't grant us such knowledge.

Bush's aides argue that the traits we saw in him during this crisis were always there—that the "wimp" charge had never been accurate. In any event, in the course of this crisis we saw in Bush a focussed, in the main steady (once he calmed down and stopped calling Hussein names), skillful leader. He knew where he wanted to go, and he took the country there—even when a large portion of the political establishment, including former military officials, was doubtful about his course. He showed impressive diplomatic skills. He took risks, but we pay Presidents to take risks—we just prefer that they be sensible ones. Now more people think that Bush's risk was more sensible.

Most people here are aware that what had just happened may have been simple compared to what is ahead. The war has created both problems and opportunities in the Middle East, and it will be a long time before we know which are the greater. The brilliance of a Schwarzkopf or a Powell and the weapons at their command don't apply to our domestic problems. Some brutal politics lie ahead; Republicans have made it clear they will show no mercy to Democrats who opposed the war. Some Democrats who might have run for the Presidency may be reconsidering, and the considerable number of Democrats who have been hanging around this town waiting for big government roles are glum. Some Democrats point out that the election is more than a year away, and suggest that the economy might just be bad enough by then to help them; others foresee, with mixed feelings, an economic recovery by then. Many people here are just beginning to feel released from the grip and the pall that the war had put on their lives. We know that many complexities lie ahead, but, even if just for a little while, we would prefer not to think about it.

Environmental Protection: An Assessment

46
Earth Day Plus 20, and Counting
Bil Gilbert

Bil Gilbert, who has been writing about conservation matters for more than thirty years, assesses the progress of enviromental protection in the following article from a special anniversary issue of Smithsonian magazine. Gilbert claims that the environmental movement is one of the three great national reform efforts since World War II. In his view, it has had the greatest psychic and material impact on society when compared with civil rights and the sexual revolution. Do you agree or disagree? What evidence does Gilbert offer to make this claim? What were the origins of environmentalism in the 1970s? What were the impacts of NEPA on federal natural resources programs? Gilbert identifies a "tough, interlocking mesh of law" to regulate and protect the environment. What does this include? Which nongovernmental organizations and interest groups are most involved in environmental protection? Why is pessimism the hallmark of the environmental movement? What do public opinion polls say about environmental problems and the environmental movement?

Strickly construed, "environment" refers to everything everywhere, but the word and its derivatives are seldom employed in this sense. For example, few if any think of "environmentalist" as meaning a Renaissance sort with universal interests. In practice, such vague terms mean more or less what their users think they do. Therefore they must be individually defined to avoid confusion and deceit. To make a start, my understanding of "environmentalist" is based on the following observations and opinions.

In this country, environmentalists are—with all exceptions granted—commonly Caucasians who possess more than the average means, education and leisure, and are found in relatively attractive and comfortable circumstances. They are distinguished from others who share these attributes by a set of strongly held, fairly homogeneous convictions. They believe:

- The world is divided into two disparate, often conflicting spheres. One comprises humans and their works. Everything else is the "environment," or nature.
- The manner in which humans have encroached upon, despoiled and otherwise

From *Smithsonian*, Vol. 21, No. 1 (April 1990), pp. 47–52. Reprinted by permission of the author.

abused nature is the cause of virtually all environmental problems.

- Nevertheless, what is left of nature still operates so efficiently, is so beautiful and benign that any major changes in it will probably be for the worse. For example, it is estimated that there are between 10 million and 30 million species of plants and animals now living in this world. Environmentalists are convinced that this, whatever the exact number, is about how many there should be. If the total were to be substantially altered by, say, extinction, mutation or genetic engineering, the consequences would be catastrophic.

- With strong views about what nature and our relationship to it should be, environmentalists feel obliged to instruct the ignorant, inspire the apathetic and confront nonbelievers in regard to these matters. "Clearly, Man has become an unnatural force in the world," says Jay Hair, the president of the National Wildlife Federation, which with 5,600,000 members is the nation's largest environmental organization. "To be an environmentalist now, it is no longer enough to enjoy or study nature passively. We are activists engaged in promoting the wiser use and protection of our global natural resources."

There have been environmentalists among us since at least the Eisenhower era, which is when I began reporting on them and their concerns. However, there was not, or was not generally perceived to be, an environmental movement until about 1970. To the extent the origins of any complicated phenomenon can be traced to a single event, the first Earth Day happenings in the spring of that year were catalysts that transformed a fairly specialized interest into a pervasive, popular one.

Gaylord Nelson, then a U.S. senator from Wisconsin, is sometimes referred to as the father of Earth Day because he was instrumental in getting it off the ground. He's now counselor of the Wilderness Society. When we talked in his office recently about the circumstances and events of 20 years ago, he could recall only five other senators who were concerned with environmental issues in 1963, the year he began serving his first term in office. "The number increased somewhat in the next decade," he reflected. "But Earth Day—as was intended—demonstrated to the Washington Establishment and the public that there *was* an environmental movement. The principal and lasting effect was to make environmental concerns a permanent part of the political dialogue in this country. Obviously not all members of Congress are now what I would call environmentalists, but almost without exception they are sensitive to environmental issues—because they have to address them while campaigning—and they have at least one staff member who is knowledgeable about them."

Nelson's claims about the impact of the movement that Earth Day triggered are probably too narrow and modest. In the past two decades, environmental concerns have substantially changed, among other things, our habits of work, travel and play, our diets, dress and architecture. Many of these effects (more about some of them later) have been very material and quantifiable. But to my mind the most extraordinary accomplishment of environmentalists—and the one largely responsible for their present economic, social and political influence—has been essentially psychic. In a few decades they have radically altered the image of nature and the opinions that had popularly prevailed for many centuries about how society should treat it.

According to ancient artifacts and records, people everywhere have almost always personified nature as female. She has been previously known as the Maker of Life itself, the passionate White Goddess, a nurturing mother and a vengeful hag. At times she could be magnificent, but the "grandeurs" of Nature, like the charms of a Valkyrie, were awesome and intimidating. Sophisticates and esthetes might venture forth to ogle her and commune with her briefly, but continued intimacy was apt to addle mortals and make them bestial. Whatever else she might be, Nature was always a brawny, powerful, strong-willed being, quick to punish those who showed impudence or disrespect. She worked in her own ways for purposes that sometimes proved contrary to the short-term ambitions of humans.

The Nature that Europeans brought to North America had been fashioned by centuries of Christian theological investigation and sacerdotal science. She was as formidable as the pagan goddesses but more hostile—the savage mistress of the wicked wilderness; the evil witch-queen and implacable enemy of civilization, the spread of which was God's cherished design. Fences, highways, walls, cities and other works were thrown up to keep Nature at bay, but sometimes it was necessary to enter her domains because she also happened to be an immensely rich storekeeper. In this guise Nature was a jealous miser who guarded her hoard like a dragon. Needy men had to wrest what they could from her by trickery and force. Successes in doing so were counted as "triumphs of Man over Nature" and as demonstrations of human industry and ingenuity.

The new, environmental-age Nature bears little resemblance to previous versions. She is a slight, frail being, prone to vapors, fainting fits and many other debilitating ailments. The new Nature is not so intimidating, does not have the sort of grandeur that the old one did, but she is still very beautiful, though now somewhat in the style of an anorexic fashion model. Also she is very good—much better than the old one—for people. In fact, there is a widespread conviction that frequent congress with Nature is the ultimate therapy for mortal bodies and souls; thus, natural foods, fibers, medicines, exercises and gardens.

The new Nature may be even richer than the old, but she is not strong enough or aggressive enough to defend her treasures against rapacious humans. Environmentalists find this passive Nature even more frightening than the combative ones of yore. Their basic premise is that unless we quickly mend our ways she will certainly become comatose and fade away. We will then not only be very sorry but also, in short order, defunct. Biochemist and biophysicist Jessica Tuchman Mathews, a former environmental adviser to President Jimmy Carter and a member of the National Security Council, is now a vice president of the World Resources Institute. Speaking in 1988 of the prospects of her 3-year-old son, she said: "If we are talking about 75 years from now and things don't change, I think he will inherit an unlivable planet."

A NATION OF ENVIRONMENTALISTS?

An anthology of recent opinion surveys gives some indication of the public's reaction to such warnings. The pollsters conclude that a majority—on most questions, a large one—of Americans believe that the poor quality of the environment is one of our most serious national problems, of more magnitude than, for example, homelessness and unemployment. If it will protect the environment, the majority favor, among other things, limiting economic development, changing consumptive habits, increasing government regulations and raising taxes. They say they will support politicians who support such measures.

All the environmentalists I know contend that these sentiments flow inevitably from reality; that they themselves have not been, in the usual manipulative sense, molders of opinion or imagemakers. Their role, they insist, has been only that of objective observers who have collected and passed along facts that led rational, public-spirited people to the inescapable conclusion that Nature can no longer protect herself against us, and therefore we must protect her against ourselves. Whatever or whoever is responsible, the defenseless image of the new Nature has, during the past 20 years, come to be generally accepted as a true one. In direct consequence, it seems to me, the environmental movement has prospered, and environmental works have multiplied at an astonishing rate.

With the possible exception of the abolitionists, no reform group in our history has used federal law so effectively—or created more of it—than environmentalists have. Though it was not immediately recognized, the first great legislative leap forward was made in the 1969-70 Congressional sessions. Galvanized by eco-disasters, such as the 1969 Santa Barbara oil spill, and attuned to the ongoing Earth Day preparations, the staff of the late Senator Henry (Scoop) Jackson, assisted by Indiana University professor Lynton K. Caldwell, wrote most of what became the National Environmental Protection Act (NEPA). A curious provision of it stated that before leaping into any development projects involving federal lands or funds, public agencies and private entrepreneurs would henceforth have to look at the likely environmental consequences. Environmental Impact Statements (the frequently despised EISes, as they came to be known) would be monitored by a newly created federal advisory body, the Council on Environmental Quality.

Since this council had no enforcement powers, the legislation was generally thought to be innocuous—essentially a statement of good principles on the order of those that speak well of mothers and apple pie. During the next few years, however, environmental activists took NEPA and ran with it to the courts. There, to summarize a number of cases, it was decreed that the EISes had to be substantial documents that considered such things as the effects of the planned works on soil, water, wildlife and recreation.

Once an EIS was completed, public agencies were expected to treat it seriously. An EIS had to be made available for public study and comment. As it turned out, this provision put some very sharp teeth in NEPA, since it gave environmentalists a chance to put intense pressure on agencies to respect EIS findings.

Initially, many public land managers and would-be private developers fiercely resisted the EIS process on the grounds that it was impractical, inconvenient and economically ruinous. After a number of adverse legal rulings, however, most of them concluded that NEPA was a slippery crevice that was best avoided by planning projects and filing EISes that did not bring down the wrath and lawyers of the environmentalists.

NEPA SAID: LOOK BEFORE YOU LEAP

NEPA revolutionized the federal natural-resource business, which is a very considerable one. In addition to overseeing highway construction, irrigation plans, flood control, erosion control, military projects and many other public works, federal agencies own nearly a third of the United States. These holdings include many of the nation's most valuable coal, oil, gas, hard mineral and grazing lands. Since 1971 very little has been done on any of them without some kind of environmental review.

Before the impact of NEPA was fully appreciated, Congress passed, without much technical study or debate, a number of other substantial pieces of proenvironmental legislation. The Endangered Species Act became law during, and generally with the approval of, the Nixon Administration. So did revisions of federal air and water legislation known as the Clean Air Act and the Clean Water Act. As Gaylord Nelson and others have observed, there were then not many true environmental believers in Congress and fewer still in the executive branch.

In 1970 William Ruckelshaus, an assistant attorney general in the Justice Department, was appointed as the first head of the newly created Environmental Protection Agency. Looking back on that time recently, Ruckelshaus told me: "After about 90 days at EPA, I decided the laws we were expected to administer were poorly conceived and in many instances unworkable. Congress mandated that we do the impossible—create a permanently perfect environment."

In Ruckelshaus' opinion, unreasonable expectations about what the EPA—which is slated to receive full Cabinet status this year—could and should do inclined activists to blame the agency for all environmental imperfections. As a result, the environmental community has come to regard the EPA not as an ally—as, for example, the Commerce Department is regarded as an ally of the business community—but as a major federal enemy. This antagonism, Ruckelshaus thinks, has often curtailed support and funds for doable projects that could have alleviated, if not eliminated, many environmental problems.

The Endangered Species, Clean Air and Clean Water acts complemented and strengthened NEPA by increasing the number of natural phenomena and federal regulations that had to be considered by anyone preparing an EIS. A number of other statutes—for instance, the Resource Conservation and Recovery Act—were passed to require even more progress. Whatever else it has or has not done,

this tough, interlocking mesh of law created what can be described as the environmental-protection industrial establishment, which has come to have a very direct, material impact on the lives of a sizable number of Americans and indirect influences on those of nearly everyone.

This enterprise has become so large and complex that it is difficult to quantify, but the EPA and other sources roughly estimate that public agencies and private firms are now spending about $100 billion a year on pollution control. A decade ago this figure was about $50 billion. All authorities who follow trends in this industry are certain that during the next decades it will grow at least as rapidly as it has in the past.

Environmental protectionists now work on many problems that were ignored or not recognized 20 years ago, and they try to solve them with strategies and devices that did not exist then. In consequence, the industry has created new trades and professions, particularly in the pollution-control and waste-disposal lines. It has also enlarged and upgraded opportunities in a number of traditional vocations. For example, the government agencies that administer EISes, and the private contractors that must abide by them, now employ biologists, ecologists and assorted other terrestrial, aquatic and atmospheric professionals.

The legal profession, which acted somewhat as a midwife at the birth of the environmental movement, has certainly benefited from its growth. Records and recollections are hazy, but there were probably only a few hundred attorneys specializing in this field in the 1960s. Today, there may be as many as 20,000. In 1971 a summary of federal environmental law in the *Environmental Law Reporter* occupied 33 pages. Last year the *ELR* published more than 3,500 pages to cover current developments in the field.

Another group of people whose lives surely would be much different if there were no environmental movement: the cadres who earn their keep and make their mark working for environmental organizations. The National Wildlife Federation annually publishes a directory of conservation-oriented groups. In 1975 there were approximately 200 of them, with a combined membership of 4 million. In 1990 there are 350 or so, with more than 12 million members. They range from Accord Associates ("founded to act as an intermediary in environmental disputes") to Zero Population Growth ("which works to achieve a balance among people, resources and environment by advocating population stabilization"). They vary greatly in size and resources, but I cannot think of any that do not now have more staff, publications and areas of concern than they did.

If the number of new environmental groups is impressive, the changes during the past 20 years in the older ones is more so. Many of the largest and most influential organizations were founded before anyone had heard or thought of an environmental movement. As their names—National Audubon Society, World Wildlife Fund, Izaak Walton League, the Nature Conservancy, the Wilderness Society—suggest, many were established principally as sporting, nature appreciation or nature preservation associations. The "new" environmentalists of 20 years ago spoke somewhat disparagingly of the "old-line conservationists" and tended to mock them for having timid and excessively narrow interests. However, not a few of the activists, after the first Earth Day shouting and tumult had subsided, joined the old conservationists (whose numbers gave them political clout) or went to work for them (because they offered paying jobs). As time passed, the activists raised the environmental consciousness of the conservation organizations, and modernized their management

and promotional practices. In symbiotic return, the conservationists gave the activists strong operating bases.

In considering this evolutionary process, one element is seldom given the credit it probably deserves. This is (or was) James Watt, Ronald Reagan's Secretary of the Interior. Virtually all environmentalists and conservationists despised the man or, more to the point, his policies. Doing something about him brought the movement together and marvelously energized it. Probably no other individual has done so much to popularize the cause, recruit members and raise money.

And so what difference has it all made—the manifestos, legislation, impact statements, money and work? In one of the aforementioned opinion polls, people were asked about the quality of their personal environments (as distinct from those elsewhere that they had read or heard about). Half of them said they thought things were about the same or better than they had been before, and 20 percent thought they might be a bit worse. If the respondents were right, this represents no mean feat of environmental protection. Between 1970 and 1988, the population increased by 40 million; the gross national product, a rough measure of consumptive activity, expanded dramatically. Between 1968 and 1984, the number of cars in the country grew by 60 million vehicles. In short, things from which the environment needs to be protected have so increased that had the effort not been made, its quality would almost certainly have declined drastically.

BY SOME MEASURES, DISCERNIBLE PROGRESS

Here and there, we have even made progress or, more accurately, retaken some ground. In 1970, for example, 200 million tons of sulfur dioxide, carbon monoxide and soot were spewed into the air as gaseous waste. Though we now generate more of these contaminants, their flow into the atmosphere has been reduced by more than 30 percent, with the result that, by some measures, the air is clearer and less noxious. This has been accomplished mainly by adding contaminant-trapping devices to industrial plants and automobiles, or changing the composition of fuels, or both.

The quantity of raw or inadequately treated domestic sewage that is dumped into surface waters has been reduced substantially. Over the past ten years, the number of people served at least by secondary sewage treatment facilities has increased by 72 percent. In the early 1970s it was generally thought that Lake Erie was dying and certainly by this time would be dead—that is, would not support any aquatic flora or fauna. Presently its waters appear to be relatively wholesome and support a thriving commercial and sport fishing industry, though scientists warn that the lake continues to be threatened by toxic chemcials. Similarly a number of other lakes and rivers are now, contrary to earlier predictions, fairly lively places biologically, reasonably safe and attractive for swimming, boating and other recreational uses.

The use of a number of poisonous compounds has been severely regulated or absolutely banned. Like the names of distant battlegrounds where it once seemed the fate of the Republic might be decided, even the designations of many of the most notorious substances are becoming hazy: 1080; asbestos; DDT; Diazinon; Alar. We have been less successful in dealing with many other toxins. Government agencies have yet to regulate—or even study in detail—thousands of chemicals used at work and in the home. But we have become more sophisticated about identifying them, and we are increasingly wary about how they are produced, employed and disposed of.

A NUMBER OF CREATURES ARE BETTER OFF

Since 1970 eight national parks have been established, and the wilderness system has been expanded by 80 million acres. An untotaled amount of land has been set aside for natural preserves by state and local governments, private individuals and organizations. Many highway berms and medians that were formerly seeded and mowed as turf are now planted with species of the native flora. As a result of a 1985 federal law, 34 million acres of farmland particularly vulnerable to erosion have been withdrawn from production and placed in a ten-year "conservation reserve."

It has often been observed that the condition of wildlife is a good measure of general environmental quality. That the status of many creatures was poor and seemed to be worsening rapidly was an argument used with good effect in the 1970s by activists seeking new land and water regulations. Subsequently (and again because the protectionists achieved some successes) the fortunes of a number of species have improved. Among others, alligators, antelope, badgers, bald eagles, bighorn sheep, pelicans, peregrine falcons and turkeys have multiplied or at least are in stronger survival positions than they were. In almost every instance, species have recovered because people have been taught or required to protect their habitats and to stop poisoning, preying on or otherwise molesting them.

Some species—beavers, Canada geese, crows, deer, gray squirrels, raccoons, redtailed hawks, several sparrows and woodchucks, among others—have proved particularly adaptable in the face of human encroachment. In their cases we have not simply protected habitats but have inadvertently created new ecological niches, which they have exploited with alacrity.

Those who are most involved in its affairs tend to be the least impressed with the accomplishments of the environmental movement. Activists point out, for instance, that while we may have cut down a bit on the sulfur dioxide in the air, we are discharging chlorofluorocarbons (chemicals used in such products as refrigerants and aerosol propellants), and generating carbon dioxide as we burn fossil fuels, at a prodigious rate. Unless we reverse this trend, these compounds will probably, within the next 50 years, alter the climate and cause problems that will make all previous ones seem trivial.

Pessimism is a hallmark of the environmental movement. The movement has grown and prospered by being ever ready to point out new crises just around the corner. Consequently, environmentalists are sometimes accused of being merchants of gloom and doom who push the prospect of imminent catastrophes to recruit members, raise money and increase their political clout. Since they deal with the future, most of these indictments remain to be proved. However, in the immediate past and present, environmentalists have been extraordinarily persuasive.

The majority of Americans who look favorably on the environmental movement do not live in circumstances where endangered species, soil erosion, acid rain, the timbering of rain forests, desertification, and the quality of the air, water and land are immediate personal problems. The catastrophic consequences of a hole in the ozone layer, global warming trends and environmental disease must largely be accepted on faith. As the opinion surveys make clear, they have been.

Jay Hair, of the National Wildlife Federation, thinks the charges that, for reasons of self-interest, environmentalists try to frighten people with predictions of coming disaster are false and cynical. Their role has been more like that of a passer-by who, seeing smoke curl out of a window, warns the occupants that their house may be on fire. Nevertheless, Hair feels that while this approach continues to be necessary, the time may have come to reinforce it with more positive ones. "We are facing enormous problems," he says, ticking off the usual ones. "But I am optimistic that, if we make a global effort, we can create a sustainable environment. Essentially the problems have been created by how we live, and the solutions require that we change how we live. I think we can, while in the long term raising rather than lowering our standards of living. However, I don't think this can be mandated from above by government regulations and treaties. It has to come about because the people themselves *want* to make changes."

Many other environmentalists agree. Their notions about creating a sustainable global environment by greatly altering the global lifestyle may strike some as being wildly impractical, even ludicrous. But so did many of the proposals that were made in 1970.

Since World War II there have been three great national reform movements—those having to do with racial, sexual and environmental relations. For some of the reasons given above, a good case can be made for claiming that the latter has had the greatest impact, psychic and material, on society. Whether environmentalists can keep up the pace remains to be seen. But because of their impressive record, the possibility that they will cannot be lightly dismissed.

The Future of American Politics, Policies, and Priorities

47
The Politics of the Restive Majority
E. J. Dionne, Jr.

The following selection by E. J. Dionne, Jr., a reporter for the Washington Post, is from his provocative book, Why Americans Hate Politics. *Dionne tells us why most American voters have rejected the extremes of liberalism and conservatism. He says that voters want to change the status quo without risking too much. How do they achieve this? Why have many voters given up on government? Dionne contends that voter confidence in politics needs to be restored. Which public policy changes will achieve this goal? How does the Savings and Loan crisis illustrate the dangers of "an incoherent approach to regulation"? Dionne concludes by focusing on U.S. foreign and military policy. He discusses the Persian Gulf War and the death of communism in the Soviet Union and Eastern Europe. What were the lessons of the Gulf War in terms of the "new world order" proclaimed by President Bush? Why is promoting economic growth in the Third World and Eastern Europe an "economic imperative" for the U.S.? In the final section, Dionne refers to the underlying principles of American democracy as a source for strengthening politics, policies, and priorities for the future. He argues that America is a democratic republic. What are the values of republicanism that can revitalize the political center in American politics?*

America has traveled a long way from the days of the late 1940s when Arthur Schlesinger, Jr., proclaimed his *Vital Center* and from the 1950s, when Daniel Bell declared *The End of Ideology.* The old Vital Center was destroyed, partly by events—notably the Vietnam War—and partly because of its arrogant dismissal of challenges from both the left and the right. *The End of Ideology* was proclaimed a bit too early. America, it turned out, had a lot of fighting to do over the fundamentals, from war and peace to race and feminism.

But America's restive middle class is weary of a politics of confrontation that seems to have so little to do with the challenges the nation faces to its standard of living and with its uncertainty about the role it will play in a world without communism. Given the choices on offer for the last two decades, the American electorate has uneasily split the difference, looking to Republicans to set broad policy in the White House and to Democrats in Congress for protection against Republican excess. It is an ungainly sort of compromise, and voters have come to dislike the results, even as they see few alternatives. Thus do voters increasingly look for ways to protest the *status quo* without risking too much change. Thus the success in 1990 of measures to limit legislative terms, of two Independents seeking governorships, of an independent socialist in Vermont and of a poorly financed but appealingly eccentric left-wing professor in Minnesota. Thus the rout of incumbent governors of both parties in state after state.

What all this represents is an inchoate demand for a new center that will draw on the lessons and achievements of the last thirty years by way of moving the country forward—and ending, as Vigilante would have it, the "screaming." It is a demand for an end to ideological confrontations that are largely irrelevant to the 1990s. It is a demand for steadiness, for social peace, for broad tolerance, for more egalitarian economic policies, for economic growth. It is the politics of the restive majority, the great American middle.

This great American middle felt cheated by our politics for most of the last thirty years. In liberalism it saw a creed that demeaned its values; in conservatism it saw a doctrine that shortchanged its interests. To reengage members of this broad middle, liberals must show more respect for their values, and conservatives must pay more heed to their interests.

For liberals, the preeminent tasks are to achieve greater equity in American economic life and to preserve the social and racial tolerance that is one of the greatest legacies of the 1960s. The liberal project went off track in part because so many voters in the middle stopped believing that government programs were operating in their interests. Indeed, they stopped believing that government could work

at all. And when it did act, government, to those in the middle, seemed to work against values like self-reliance, responsibility, family stability and hard work.

Conservatives have long paid homage to these values. But by allowing the standard of living of so many Americans in the middle to deteriorate, partly through regressive tax policies, the Reagan and Bush administrations and the culture they promoted have sent exactly the opposite message. For the last decade we have given honor of place not to those who labored daily for wages and salaries or who built businesses through long-term, painstaking effort, but to those who reached instant wealth, instant fame, and instant luxury. If the hardworking middle felt that its devotion to the work ethic went unappreciated in the years of liberal dominance, it felt insufficiently rewarded in the years of conservative triumph.

And while all this was going on, politics focused on abstract ideological questions to the exclusion of the basics. When government was seen to fail on the basics—educating children, delivering health care, building roads and mass transit, fighting crime—the broad American middle gave up on government. This message was misread by conservatives as a demand for less government when, in fact, it was a demand for better government.

The basic flaw in the Reagan supply-side vision was that it saw the "supply side" as only the private sector; the government could only be a drain on the society, not a contributor. This led the supply-siders to a disastrous fiscal assumption: it would be easy to cut taxes because it would be easy to cut government spending. Of course it was not easy, because while the government *as an institution* has become unpopular, many government functions remain broadly popular and extremely hard to cut. One result was our foolish and entirely unnecessary budget disaster. Another result is drastic underinvestment in those aspects of government that *promote* growth: Education, research and development, job training, roads and bridges, and mass transit. The country is prepared to pay for those aspects of government it believes are necessary—provided it also believes that the government actually has a chance of accomplishing what it sets out to do.

For the moment, this faith is frayed. Thus, another aspect of a politics of a new center must be experimentation. If the American people are tired of an ideological approach to divisive social issues, so also are they unhappy with placing ideological straitjackets on programs. To restore popular faith in the possibilities of government, government must be shown to work. And it must also be shown that government intervention need not be either intrusive or excessively bureaucratic.

In fact, many good policy ideas defy ideological classification. Vouchers are thought of as a conservative idea, but one of the most successful voucher programs—food stamps—was a creation of Lyndon Johnson's Great Society. The earned-income tax credit, which essentially subsidizes the wages of poor people who work, is popular among liberals, who like it because it redistributes income, and among conservatives because it is efficient and promotes work. And some policy ideas can actually be quite simple. The country would go a long way toward solving its problems with day care for children over the age of five simply by keeping public schools open until 6 P.M.

Much of the pressure for experimentation in social programming is now coming from the right, which wants to dismantle government bureaucracies. But liberals should welcome the reengagement of conservatives with social policy and simply insist that if conservatives are serious about alternative ways of helping the middle class and the poor, they

will have to find money to finance their social experiments.

The restive majority is also seeking a more stable economy in which a new balance is found among the competing values of opportunity, security, and responsibility. The emphasis during the 1980s on entrepreneurship, though in many ways healthy, also distorted our view of how wealth is created. If Marx's labor theory of value oversimplified the economic process, so, too, does what might be called the "capital theory of value" espoused by many on the right. Economics in the 1980s so romanticized the brave, risk-taking souls who provide investment capital that it overlooked the much larger group that ultimately makes a company successful: the people who work for it. In our economic life, no less than in our political life, we have forgotten the old values of loyalty, hard work, and craftsmanship. If any one aspect of the economic changes of the 1980s threatened the social fabric, it was the growing loss of faith on the part of long-time employees in the companies they thought they had served faithfully. The 1980s pattern of corporate restructurings sent the message that the interests of investors nearly always took precedence over the interests of employees. At a time when Americans were wondering why Japanese workers worked harder or more loyally for their companies than Americans, here was part of the answer. The United States does not need to copy Japanese management styles to become competitive. The idea of shared responsibility is surely as American as it is Japanese.

Thus, a central theme of a politics that will restore popular confidence must be: Reward the work performed by the vast American middle. There is a widening consensus over some of the steps required to do this.

First, the tax system must be made less onerous to the middle class and the poor, and the burdens must be reduced especially for parents, both single and married. Any future tax changes must be aimed at making the tax system more progressive, starting with cuts in the payroll tax and increases in the exemptions accorded to parents with young children. Money for this purpose could be freed up by levying social security taxes on a higher proportion of the income of the wealthy, and by limiting government benefits—including tax breaks—that flow to the well-to-do. Even relatively wealthy people who get most of their income from salaries have an interest in tax fairness: Tax avoidance and evasion is far higher on income from capital than on income from salaries.

The first step to welfare reform must be to increase the benefits that go to the working poor. They live by all the rules society claims to believe in, but reap few rewards. A good first step was taken in 1990 when the earned-income tax credit was expanded. It should be expanded further, and all who work should be guaranteed medical insurance. At the same time, the children of the very poor must be allowed to enter the working mainstream. That means expanding health, nutrition, and education programs for preschool children, especially those who live in impoverished and broken families. Such programs have a proven record; the money that flows to them can genuinely be seen as a prudent investment. And everyone should be encouraged to invest in himself or herself. This means expanding access to college, to midcareer education and retraining programs, and to apprenticeship programs that prepare young people for the work force.

Finally, the bonds among our citizens would be strengthened if young people were encouraged to pay back student loans and other government benefits not with *money* but with *time*— a few years devoted to teaching or police work, to the military, or to providing health care for the needy. Such programs could also strengthen the morale of government agencies by providing them with a regular transfusion of young talent and idealism. And some among the young might thereby be encouraged to devote their lives to public service, surely a good thing in a society that provides few incentives for such dedication.

This short list is meant only to be illustrative. It represents back-to-basics priorities, a kind of GI Bill for the 1990s. It emphasizes the things we know that government knows how to do. It is built around the idea that when budgets are strained, new spending should be aimed at helping individuals prosper in a world economy that puts an ever higher premium on education and creativity. The broader point is that the key to successful government in the 1990s will be to find ways of combining compassion and self-reliance, rights and obligations, equity and achievement—in short, to find ways of making peace between the values of the sixties and the values of the eighties. Liberal talk about social justice need not contradict conservative talk about "choice" and "empowerment." Indeed, if conservatives are serious about empowerment, they are talking about social justice.

But voters will not look to government for such initiatives until they are convinced that the government can behave responsibly. The savings-and-loan crisis is a good example of why Americans have come to hate politics so. If there is one area in which antigovernment libertarians have made a powerful contribution, it is in pointing out that government subsidies and regulations are often established in ways that enrich private interests without benefiting the public interest. This, of course, is an old story—remember the railroad subsidies of the 1870s? But it becomes an especially important story in an era when economic regulation is so complex and widespread.

The dangers of an incoherent approach to regulation became manifest in the savings-and-loan scandal. The deregulation of the savings and loans combined with an increase in the amount of savings covered by deposit insurance created the monstrosity of capitalism without risk. The profits were private, the risks were socialized, members of Congress and presidential candidates received substantial campaign contributions—and the taxpayers were left with a very large bill. The politics of a new center will thus be centrally concerned with reconnecting government subsidies and regulations with public purposes. Cleaning up the election process would make it much easier for Congress to take steps toward doing this.

Underlying the majority's restiveness is worry over what the coming decades will mean for American power in the world and for the American standard of living at home. Before the collapse of communism, Paul Kennedy and other scholars began promoting the idea that America faced a period of economic decline fostered by a kind of "imperial overreach" and too much emphasis on military spending. Ultimately, this economic decline would foster political decline as well, no matter how many weapons America had in its arsenals.

The collapse of communism, which followed almost immediately after the wave of "declinist" talk, was by any measure a victory for forty years of American foreign policy. Foes of declinism noted with some glee that with the Soviet Union's collapse, the United States was the only nation in the world that could claim to be simultaneously militarily powerful and economically robust—in short, the only real superpower. The war in the Gulf, fought under American leadership and with all the sophisticated weaponry in the great arsenal built in the Reagan years, underscored the continuing importance of American

power. Germany and Japan, it was said, could produce marvelous consumer goods, but they still lacked America's arsenal, its influence, and its will.

Yet the death of communism and the Persian Gulf War also raised many questions about the future of American power and world stability. If there was one great advantage to the United States in the old bipolar world, it was that it gave the U.S. and the U.S.S.R. enormous influence over events around the globe. To the extent that the world was organized around East-West competition, the two superpowers could shape the behavior of scores of nations.

Iraq's invasion of Kuwait and the war that followed proved that the post-Communist world could be far more disorderly than the old. To be sure, Bush's bold moves and the strength of American arms suggested to many on the right that the United States had, at last, transcended the Vietnam syndrome. It would, once again, be possible to use American power. At the very least, conservatives and interventionist liberals could argue that the antiwar left had manifestly lost many of its most compelling arguments. It could simply not be argued that Saddam Hussein was "on the right side of history." The extraordinary levels of public support Bush enjoyed during the war showed that given a particularly odious enemy and military success, the slogan "No more Vietnams" might finally be nearing the end of its useful life as an argument against all forms of intervention.

Still, in the wake of war, Americans had to face the fact that a decade of fiscal irresponsibility had left the United States in a position of nearly begging for foreign contributions to the war effort. And the war also showed how costly maintaining a "new world order" could be. How often will Americans be willing to mount such a vast and all-consuming operation? The Persian Gulf War may mark the end of the post-Vietnam Era, but that only means the beginning of a new, and, one hopes, more promising argument about the proper use of American power. Military tactics, even when dazzling, do not make a foreign policy.

The most valuable lessons of the war are almost certainly those that relate to our domestic, civic life. As a nation, our political discontent grows from a nagging worry that we lost our sense of common citizenship. Divided by bitter debates over values, torn by growing inequalities among classes and races, Americans have become increasingly skeptical about whether public engagement could ever produce much of value. A nation whose people perform brilliantly as individuals, we questioned whether we could also respond to crises collectively.

War, as libertarians remind us, may be the ultimate expression of what is wrong with collective action. Yet one could not help but be struck by the fact that after a decade widely derided as self-indulgent, there were still hundreds of thousands of Americans willing to sacrifice their lives in the service of their country. Were there not also peaceful ways of tapping this civic potential? After a period in which all government was derided as ineffectual, the combination of government money and private endeavor had produced truly ingenious weapons of mass destruction. The United States, after all, did know how to produce things. Did America's genius have to be confined to weapons of war? Did the government's ability to finance research and development have to be limited to the military sphere?

Yet the country also faced the disturbing fact that the sacrifices of war had been born in a wildly inequitable way. Many commented on the disproportionate number of black Americans who serve in the Gulf. But there were other inequities as well, notably the fact that tens of thousands of reservists had their lives and careers abruptly interrupted while Americans exactly like them went on as if nothing had happened. Polls suggest that the United States is not ready to restore the draft. But the aftermath of this war demands that the country rethink its approach to civic obligation and shared sacrifice. This is a debate that must be nurtured both by conservative ideas about service and obligation, and liberal ideas about fairness.

The aftermath of war will also lead to debate over the meaning of President Bush's "new world order." What has been missing so far is much talk about that order's political content and economic implications. As both a moral and practical matter, promoting democracy around the world is in the long-term interest of the United States, if only because democracies tend to be less threatening than dictatorships and less prone to war. Yet if the United States is serious about promoting democracy, the success of that endeavor will depend in large part on whether the United States and the other wealthy democracies pursue economic policies that will allow new democracies in Eastern Europe and the Third World enough prosperity to maintain that democratic faith. Already, there are signs in Central Europe of disaffection with democracy as economies continue to stagnate. Economic catastrophe is now threatening to strangle democracy in the Soviet Union before it is even fully realized. It would be a profound tragedy if the Revolution of 1989 yielded not new democracies but a series of sullen, authoritarian states.

Promoting economic growth in the Third World and Eastern Europe is by no means a purely altruistic act. It is an economic imperative for the United States itself. The United States could make some economic progress in the medium term by striking better trade bargains with its wealthiest competitors, notably Japan and the European community. But in the long run, real economic growth at home will depend on a far more buoyant world economy. Americans will be able to maintain their high standard of living only by helping to lift the standard of living in the rest of the world. This is a complicated task. But it is essential, and requires a seriousness of national purpose that our recent approaches to politics seems unlikely to produce. One can only hope that the tragedy of war will at least help us find a sober and intelligent politics that has eluded us for so long. . . .

II

The 1990s are daunting, but they also offer an opportunity for creative political thinking not seen since the industrial revolution ushered in new intellectual systems that we now call Marxism and capitalism.

The decline of Soviet-style socialism creates an enormous opening for American social and political thought since Americans were never much taken with the capitalist-socialist debate. The relative efficiency of markets over bureaucracies was never really questioned here. When Americans made the case for social reform, they did so using a presocialist language of democracy, community, and republicanism. That is precisely the language that is most relevant in the postcommunist world. It also offers an approach that could rescue American politics from its current impasse.

Taken together, the economic collapse of communism and the affluence of Western market societies would seem to prove conclusively that the choice between rigid state economic control and largely unregulated economic activity is, in truth, no choice at all. When it is market against bureaucracy, market wins.

This comes as a surprise to almost no one—and certainly not to most American liberals or European social democrats, who have always accepted the efficiency of markets. But the argument that the Eastern European experience proves that all bureaucracies and all governments are doomed to the same kinds of inefficiencies is simply wrong. This view, now popular on the right, assumes that all governments and all bureaucracies are more or less the same, and that public endeavor is always inferior to private endeavor.

There is a dangerous moral equivalence at work here that misses the primary difference between the Western societies and communist regimes: Western governments were *democratic*. Our bureaucracies, though at times inefficient and unresponsive, were the creations and creatures of the popular will. Communism's biggest crime was not economic failure or inefficiency but tyranny. Communism was both inefficient *and* repressive.

As Vaclav Havel has reminded us so eloquently, political repression robbed Eastern European nations of a healthy civic life and decent public institutions. Eastern Europe is in trouble today not simply because of a shortage of private investment, but because all the *public* structures, ranging from phones and roads to schools and, yes, the bureaucracy itself, are in such a state of disrepair.

The antisocial nature of the sort of socialism created in the East is most glaring in the way communist regimes treated the environment. Their environmental crimes are almost as outrageous as their crimes against human rights. It is true that the environment is cleaner in the West in part because the West had the money available to clean things up. But the *primary* cause of the West's environmental consciousness is democracy, not the market. A cleaner environment is the product of *public life*. The bureaucrats who ran industry in Eastern Europe had no fear of popular democratic pressure; the capitalists and managers who ran the economies of the West did. If you want to know the difference between communist dictatorship and democracy, it is this: In the East, government officials, *free from public pressure,* nearly destroyed the environment; in the West, government officials, *responding to public pressure,* cleaned up the environment. In the East, bureaucrats were the polluters. In the West, bureaucrats—the people at the environmental protection agencies—were the foes of pollution.

The point here is that government and public life are not abstractions; they are what we make them. The lesson from Eastern Europe is not that we must fear government and public engagement, but that we need a *democratic* public life built on a sensible theory of public engagement. The communists were thoroughly wrong in seeing capitalist democracies as doomed to collapsing into dictatorships of the rich. But they were wrong not only because they underestimated capitalism's productive capacities but also because they underestimated democracy's gift for self-correction. It was democracy that fostered the growth of social movements that called attention to those aspects of capitalism that didn't work. Such movements—New Dealism in the United States, democratic socialism and social democracy in Western Europe—insisted on a broad definition of democratic citizenship. In T. H. Marshall's famous formulation, citizenship in a free society consisted not only in civil and legal rights, not only in political rights, but also in social rights. Marshall's insight was that citizens could not fully exercise their basic civil rights and civil liberties without a degree of economic security. The struggle for Marshall's social rights produced the West's social insurance systems, which preserve tens of millions from lives of desperation.

It would be tragic indeed if the welcomed collapse of communist dictatorships were to teach us that the struggle for such "social rights" has become unnecessary. The demo-cratic idea for which the United States and the other Western nations waged a cold war for forty years includes a recognition of both political *and* social rights. The truth is that the progress of the West has depended on the friendly rivalry between the capitalists's insistence on individual initiative and the communitarians's insistence on the broadest possible definition of citizenship and the most inclusive view of the national community. The capitalist and the democratic communitarian needed each other before communism collapsed, and they need each other now.

What is required to end America's hatred of politics is an organizing idea that simultaneously accepts the efficiencies of markets and the importance of a vigorous public life. The American political tradition contains such an idea, an idea that reaches back to the noblest traditions of Western culture. The idea is what the Founding Fathers called republicanism, before there was a political party bearing that name. At the heart of republicanism is the belief that self-government is not a drab necessity but a joy to be treasured. It is the view that politics is not simply a grubby confrontation of competing interests but an arena in which citizens can learn from each other and discover an "enlightened self-interest" in common. Republicanism is based on the realistic hope that, as the political philosopher Michael Sandel has put it, "when politics goes well, we can know a good in common that we cannot know alone."

Republicanism can sound foolishly utopian. When unchecked by the libertarian impulse, republicanism can be oppressive. Rousseau's declaration that "the better the constitution of a state is, the more do public affairs encroach on private in the minds of the citizens" sends a chill up our spines at the thought of republican mind-control.

But we are a very long way from such dangers and face instead the dangers of too little faith in the possibilities of politics. Citizens in a free, democratic republic need to accept that there will always be a healthy tension among liberty, virtue, equality, and community. It is an ancient but still valid idea that liberty without virtue will collapse, and that virtue without liberty will become despotic. And without a sense of community and equity, free citizens will be unwilling to come to the aid and defense of each other's liberty. These notions are broadly accepted by Americans—notably by the restive middle class. Our current political dialogue fails us and leads us to hate politics because it insists on stifling yes/no, either/or approaches that ignore the elements that must come together to create a successful and democratic civic culture. Democracy is built on constant struggle among competing goods, not on an absolute certainty about which goods are paramount. This must be the central theme of a new political center.

In our efforts to find our way toward a new world role, we would do well to review what made us a special nation long before we became the world's leading military and economic power—our republican tradition that nurtured free citizens who eagerly embraced the responsibilities and pleasures of self-government. With democracy on the march outside our borders, our first responsibility is to ensure that the United States becomes a model for what self-government should be and not an example of what happens to free nations when they lose interest in public life. A nation that hates politics will not long survive as a democracy.

Appendix

The Declaration of Independence

The 1976 bicentennial of the Declaration of Independence drew nation-wide attention to one of the fundamental documents of American government. John Adams, one of the founders of the nation, had prescribed the Fourth of July celebration as a "great anniversary Festival . . . with pomp and parade, with shows, games, sports, guns, bells, bonfires, and illuminations, from one end of the continent to the other, from this time foreward, forevermore." The major events in the chronology of the Declaration included: (1) Richard Henry Lee's resolution in the Continental Congress on June 7, 1776, which was referred to a committee of five to draft a declaration; (2) the drafting of the declaration by Thomas Jefferson; (3) revision of Jefferson's draft by the committee and presentation to Congress on June 28th; (4) adoption of the Lee-Adams resolution of independence on July 2nd by a vote of twelve colonies in favor, none against, and New York abstaining; (5) discussion of the Declaration with revisions and editing, with approval of the final document on July 4th by a vote of 12-0, New York again abstaining; and (6) printing of the Declaration and signing by 55 delegates, presided over by President John Hancock on July 19th, with the signing completed by August 2nd. The Declaration consisted of three parts: the preamble and philosophical statement, the list of grievances or causes, and the actual declaration itself, which incorporated the Lee-Adams resolution of independence passed on July 2.

IN CONGRESS, JULY 4, 1776

The Unanimous Declaration of the Thirteen United States of America

When in the Course of human events, it becomes necessary for one people to dissolve the political bands which have connected them with another, and to assume among the Powers of the earth, the separate and equal station to which the Laws of Nature and of Nature's God entitle them, a decent respect to the opinions of mankind requires that they should declare the causes which impel them to the separation.

We hold these truths to be self-evident, that all men are created equal, that they are endowed by their Creator with certain unalienable Rights, that among these are Life, Liberty and the pursuit of Happiness. That to secure these rights, Governments are instituted among Men, deriving their just powers from the consent of the governed, That whenever any Form of Government becomes destructive of these ends, it is the Right of the People to alter or to abolish it, and to institute new Government, laying its foundation on such principles and organizing its powers in such form, as to them shall seem most likely to effect their Safety and Happiness. Prudence, indeed, will dictate that Governments long established should not be changed for light and transient causes; and accordingly all experience hath shown, that mankind are more disposed to suffer, while evils are sufferable, than to right themselves by abolishing the forms to which they are accustomed. But when a long train of abuses and usurpations, pursuing invariably the same Object evinces a design to reduce them under absolute Despotism, it is their right, it is their duty, to throw off such Government, and to provide new Guards for their future security.—Such has been the patient sufferance of these Colonies; and such is now the necessity which constrains them to alter their former Systems of Government. The history of the present King of Great Britain is a history of repeated injuries and usurpations, all having in direct object the establishment of an absolute Tyranny over these States. To prove this, let Facts be submitted to a candid world.

He has refused his Assent to Laws, the most wholesome and necessary for the public good.

He has forbidden his Governors to pass Laws of immediate and pressing importance, unless suspended in their operation till his Assent should be obtained; and when so suspended, he has utterly neglected to attend to them.

He has refused to pass other Laws for the accommodation of large districts of people, unless those people would relinquish the right of Representation in the Legislature, a right inestimable to them and formidable to tyrants only.

He has called together legislative bodies at places unusual, uncomfortable, and distant from the depository of their public Records, for the sole purpose of fatiguing them into compliance with his measures.

He has dissolved Representative Houses repeatedly, for opposing with manly firmness his invasions on the rights of the people.

He has refused for a long time, after such dissolutions, to cause others to be elected; whereby the Legislative Powers, incapable of Annihilation, have returned to the People at large for their exercise; the State remaining in the mean time exposed to all the dangers of invasion from without, and convulsions within.

He has endeavored to prevent the population of these States; for that purpose obstructing the Laws for Naturalization of Foreigners; refusing to pass others to encourage their migrations hither, and raising the conditions of new Appropriations of Lands.

He has obstructed the Administration of Justice, by refusing his Assent to Laws for establishing Judiciary Powers.

He has made Judges dependent on his Will alone, for the tenure of their offices, and the amount and payment of their salaries.

He has erected a multitude of New Offices, and sent hither swarms of Officers to harass our people, and eat out their substance.

He has kept among us, in times of peace, Standing Armies without the Consent of our legislatures.

He has affected to render the Military independent of and superior to the Civil Power.

He has combined with others to subject us to a jurisdiction foreign to our constitution, and unacknowledged by our laws; giving his Assent to their acts of pretended Legislation:

For quartering large bodies of armed troops among us:

For protecting them, by a mock Trial, from Punishment for any Murders which they should commit on the Inhabitants of these States:

For cutting off our Trade with all parts of the world:

For imposing taxes on us without our Consent:

For depriving us in many cases, of the benefits of Trial by Jury:

For transporting us beyond Seas to be tried for pretended offences:

For abolishing the free System of English Laws in a neighbouring Province, establishing therein an Arbitrary government, and enlarging its Boundaries so as to render it at once an example and fit instrument for introducing the same absolute rule into these Colonies:

For taking away our Charters, abolishing our most valuable Laws, and altering fundamentally the Forms of our Governments:

For suspending our own Legislatures, and declaring themselves invested with Power to legislate for us in all cases whatsoever.

He has abdicated Government here, by declaring us out of his Protection and waging War against us.

He has plundered our seas, ravaged our Coasts, burnt our towns, and destroyed the lives of our people.

He is at this time transporting large armies of foreign mercenaries to compleat the works of death, desolation and tyranny, already begun with circumstances of Cruelty & perfidy scarcely parralled in the most barbarous ages, and totally unworthy the Head of a civilized nation.

He has constrained our fellow Citizens taken Captive on the high Seas to bear Arms against their Country, to become the executioners of their friends and Brethren, or to fall themselves by their Hands.

He has excited domestic insurrections amongst us, and has endeavored to bring on the inhabitants of our frontiers, the merciless Indian Savages, whose known rule of warfare, is an undistinguished destruction of all ages, sexes and conditions.

In every stage of these Oppressions We have Petitioned for Redress in the most humble terms: Our repeated Petitions have been answered only by repeated injury. A Prince, whose character is thus marked by every act which may define a Tyrant, is unfit to be the ruler of a free people.

Nor have We been wanting to attentions to our British brethren. We have warned them from time to time of attempts by their legislature to extend an unwarrantable jurisdiction over us. We have reminded them of the circumstances of our emigration and settlement here. We have appealed to their native justice and magnanimity, and we have conjured them by the ties of our common kindred to disavow these usurpations which would inevitably interrupt our connections and correspondence. They too have been deaf to the voice of justice and of consanguinity. We must, therefore, acquiesce in the necessity, which denounces our Separation, and hold them, as we hold the rest of mankind, Enemies in War, in Peace Friends.

We, therefore, the Representatives of the United States of America, in General Congress, Assembled, appealing to the Supreme Judge of the world for the rectitude of our intentions, do, in the Name, and by authority of the good People of these Colonies, solemnly publish and declare, That these United Colonies are, and of Right ought to be Free and Independent States; that they are Absolved from all allegiance to the British Crown, and that all political connection between them and the State of Great Britain, is and ought to be totally dissolved; and that as Free and Independent States, they have full power to levy War, conclude Peace, contract Alliances, establish Commerce, and to do all other Acts and Things which Independent States may of right do. And for the support of this Declaration, with a firm reliance on the Protection of Divine Providence, we mutually pledge to each other our Lives, our Fortunes and our sacred Honor.

The Constitution of the United States

The Constitution, framed to replace the Articles of Confederation, is the fundamental legal charter of American government. The relatively plain language of Article I, Sections 2 and 3, conceals the intensive struggles in the convention to reach agreement over the structure of legislative representation. Article I, Section 8, discusses the delegated powers of Congress (see Chapter 10) which were considerably strengthened by Chief Justice Marshall's interpretation of the "necessary and proper" clause in *McCulloch v. Maryland* (see Chapter 4). Article II specifies the powers of the president. The Framers were most concerned with the manner of electing the president and designed the rather curious system of the electoral college in Section 1 (see Chapter 7). Section 2 is the source of the president's foreign policy and national defense authority. Section 3 provides the chief executive's legislative power (see Chapters 8 and 10). Article III deals with the Supreme Court and the federal judiciary. Notice the omission of "judicial review" as a power of the Supreme Court, although Hamilton, in *The Federalist*, Number 78, implied such power from Article VI and Marshall incorporated it in *Marbury v. Madison* (see Chapter 11). The Constitution also includes the Bill of Rights—the first ten amendments which were considerably strengthened by the Warren Court (see Chapter 3). Additional amendments reflect various changes made since the Constitution went into effect on March 4, 1789. Particularly important for the cause of civil rights were amendments 13, 14, and 15, which were adopted after the Civil War.

PREAMBLE

We, the People of the United States, in Order to form a more perfect Union, establish Justice, insure domestic Tranquility, provide for the common defence, promote the general Welfare, and secure the Blessings of Liberty to ourselves and our Posterity, do ordain and establish this Constitution for the United States of America.

ARTICLE I*

Legislative Branch

Section 1. *Legislative power; in whom vested.* All legislative powers herein granted shall be vested in a Congress of the United States, which shall consist of a Senate and House of Representatives.

*Note: Parts of the Constitution no longer in effect are printed in italics.

Section 2. *House of Representatives, how chosen, qualifications. Impeachment power.* The House of Representatives shall be composed of members chosen every second year by the people of the several states, and the electors in each state shall have the qualifications requisite for electors of the most numerous branch of the state legislature.

No person shall be a representative who shall not have attained to the age of twenty-five years, and been seven years a citizen of the United States, and who shall not, when elected, be an inhabitant of that state in which he shall be chosen.

Representatives and direct taxes shall be apportioned among the several states which may be included within this union, according to their respective numbers, *which shall be determined by adding to the whole number of free persons, including those bound to service for a term of years, and excluding Indians not taxed, three-fifths of all other persons.*[1] The actual enumeration shall be made within three years after the first meeting of the Congress of the United States, and within every subsequent term of ten years, in such manner as they shall by law direct. The number of representatives shall not exceed one for every 30,000, but each state shall have at least one representative; *and until such enumeration shall be made, the state of New Hampshire shall be entitled to choose three, Massachusetts eight, Rhode Island and Providence Plantations one, Connecticut five, New York six, New Jersey four, Pennsylvania eight, Delaware one, Maryland six, Virginia ten, North Carolina five, South Carolina five, and Georgia three.*[2]

When vacancies happen in the representation from any state, the executive authority thereof shall issue writs of election to fill such vacancies.

The House of Representatives shall choose their speaker and other officers; and shall have the sole power of impeachment.

Section 3. *Senators; how chosen, classified; Qualifications; Power to try impeachments.* The Senate of the United States shall be composed of two senators from each state, *chosen by the legislature thereof,*[3] for six years; and each senator shall have one vote.

Immediately after they shall be assembled in consequence of the first election, they shall be divided as equally as may be into three classes. The seats of the senators of the first class shall be vacated at the expiration of the second year, of the second class at the expiration of the fourth year, and of the third class at the expiration of the sixth year, so that one-third may be chosen every second year; and if vacancies happen by resignation, or otherwise, during the recess of the legislature of any state, the executive thereof may make temporary appointments until the next meeting of the legislature, which shall then fill such vacancies.[4]

No person shall be a senator who shall not have attained to the age of thirty years, and been nine years a citizen of the United States, and who shall not, when elected, be an inhabitant of that state for which he shall be chosen.

The Vice President of the United States shall be president of the Senate, but shall have no vote, unless they be equally divided.

The Senate shall choose their other officers, and also a president pro tempore, in the absence of the Vice President, or when he shall exercise the office of President of the United States.

The Senate shall have the sole power to try all impeachments. When sitting for that purpose, they shall be on oath or affirmation. When the President of the United States is tried, the chief justice shall preside: And no person shall be convicted without the concurrence of two-thirds of the members present.

Judgment in cases of impeachment shall not extend further than to removal from office, and disqualification to hold and enjoy any office of honor, trust or profit under the United States; but the party convicted shall nevertheless be liable and subject to indictment, trial, judgment and punishment, according to law.

Section 4. *Times and manner of holding elections.* The Times, Places and Manner of holding Elections for Senators and Representatives, shall be prescribed in each State by the Legislature thereof; but the Congress may at any time by Law make or alter such Regulations, except as to the Places of choosing Senators.

The Congress shall assemble at least once in every year, and such meeting *shall be on the first Monday in December,*[5] unless they shall by law appoint a different day.

Section 5. *Membership, quorum, rules, power to punish or expel.* Each house shall be the judge of the elections, returns and qualifications of its own members, and a majority of each shall constitute a quorum to do business; but a smaller number may adjourn from day to day, and may be authorized to compel the attendance of absent members, in such manner, and under such penalties as each house may provide.

Each house may determine the rules of its proceedings, punish its members for disorderly behavior, and, with the concurrence of two-thirds, expel a member.

Each house shall keep a journal of its proceedings, and from time to time publish the same, excepting such parts as may, in their judgment, require secrecy; and the yeas and nays of the members of either house on any question, shall, at the desire of one-fifth of those present, be entered on the journal.

Neither house, during the session of Congress, shall, without the consent of the other, adjourn for more than three days, nor to any other place than that in which the two houses shall be sitting.

Section 6. *Compensation, privileges, disqualifications.* The Senators and Representatives shall receive a Compensation for their Services, to be ascertained by Law, and paid out of the Treasury of the United States. They shall in all Cases, except Treason, Felony and Breach of the Peace, be privileged from Arrest during their Attendance at the Session of their respective Houses, and in going to and returning from the same; and for any Speech or Debate in either House, they shall not be questioned in any other Place.

No Senator or Representative shall, during the Time for which he was elected, be appointed to any civil Office under the Authority of the United States, which shall have been created, or the Emoluments whereof shall have been increased during such time; and no Person holding any Office under the United States, shall be a Member of either House during his Continuance in Office.

Section 7. *Revenue bills. Vetoes. Orders, resolutions.* All Bills for raising Revenue shall originate in the House of Representatives; but the Senate may propose or concur with Amendments as on other Bills.

Every Bill which shall have passed the House of Representatives and the Senate, shall, before it become a Law, be presented to the President of the United States; if he approve he shall sign it, but if not he shall return it, with his Objection to that House in which it shall have originated, who shall enter the Objections at large on their Journal, and proceed to reconsider it. If after such Reconsideration two thirds of that House shall agree to pass the Bill, it shall be sent, together with the Objections, to the other House, by which it shall likewise be reconsidered, and if approved by two thirds of that House, it shall become a Law. But in all such Cases the Votes of both Houses shall be determined by Yeas and Nays, and the Names of Persons voting for and against the Bill shall be entered on the Journal of each House respectively. If any Bill shall not be returned by the President within ten Days (Sundays excepted) after it shall have been presented to him, the Same shall be a Law, in like Manner as if he has signed it, unless the Congress by their Adjournment prevent its Return, in which Case it shall not be Law.

Every Order, Resolution, or Vote to which the Concurrence of the Senate and House of Representatives may be necessary (except on a question of Adjournment) shall be presented to the President of the United States; and before the Same shall take Effect, shall be approved by him, or being disapproved by him, shall be repassed by two thirds of the Senate and House of Representatives, according to the Rules and Limitations prescribed in the Case of a Bill.

Section 8. *Powers of Congress.* The Congress shall have Power to lay and collect Taxes, Duties, Imposts and Excises, to pay the Debts and provide for the common Defence and general Welfare of the United States; but all Duties, Imposts and Excises shall be uniform throughout the United States;

To borrow money on the credit of the United States;

To regulate Commerce with foreign Nations, and among the several States, and with the Indian Tribes;

To establish an uniform Rule of Naturalization, and uniform Laws on the subject of Bankruptcies throughout the United States;

To coin Money, regulate the Value thereof, and of foreign Coin, and fix the Standard of Weights and Measures;

To provide for the Punishment of counterfeiting the Securities and current Coin of the United States;

To Establish Post Offices and post Roads;

To promote the Progress of Science and useful Arts, by securing for limited Times to Authors and Inventors the exclusive Right to their respective Writings and Discoveries;

To constitute Tribunals inferior to the Supreme Court;

To define and punish Piracies and Felonies committed on the high Seas, and Offenses against the Law of Nations;

To declare War, grant Letters of Marque and Reprisal, and make Rules concerning Captures on Land and Water;

To raise and support Armies, but no Appropriation of Money to that Use shall be for a longer Term than two Years;

To provide and maintain a Navy;

To make Rules for the Government and Regulation of the land and naval Forces;

To provide for calling forth the Militia to execute the Laws of the Union, suppress Insurrections and repel Invasions;

To provide for organizing, arming, and disciplining the Militia, and for governing such Part of them as may be employed in the Service of the United States, reserving to the States respectively, the Appointment of the Officers, and the Authority of training the Militia according to the discipline prescribed by Congress.

To exercise exclusive Legislation in all Cases whatsoever, over such District (not exceeding ten Miles square) as may, by Cession of particular States, and the acceptance of Congress, become the Seat of the Government of the United States, and to exercise like Authority over all Places purchased by the Consent of the Legislature of the State in which the Same shall be, for the Erection of Forts, Magazines, Arsenals, dock-Yards, and other needful Buildings;—And

To make Laws which shall be necessary and proper for carrying into Execution the foregoing Powers, and all other Powers vested by this Constitution in the Government of the United States, or in any Department or Officer thereof.

Section 9.   *Immigration, habeas corpus, bills of attainder. Taxes, apportionment. How money shall be drawn from Treasury. Ban on titled nobility. The migration or importation of such persons as any of the states now existing shall think proper to admit, shall not be prohibited by the Congress prior to the year 1808, but a tax or duty may be imposed on such importations, not exceeding ten dollars for each person.*[6]

The privilege of the Writ of Habeas Corpus shall not be suspended, unless when in Cases of Rebellion or Invasion the public Safety may require it.

No Bill of Attainder or ex post facto Law shall be passed.

No capitation, or other direct, Tax shall be laid, unless in Proportion to the Census or Enumeration herein before directed to be taken.[7]

No Tax or Duty shall be laid on Articles exported from any State.

No preference shall be given by any Regulation of Commerce or Revenue to the Ports of one State over those of another: nor shall Vessels bound to, or from, one State be obliged to enter, clear, or pay Duties in another.

No money shall be drawn from the Treasury, but in Consequence of Appropriations made by Law; and a regular Statement and Account of the Receipts and Expenditures of all public Money shall be published from time to time.

No Title of Nobility shall be granted by the United States: And no Person holding any Office of Profit or Trust under them, shall, without the Consent of the Congress, accept of any present, Emolument, Office, or Title, of any kind whatever, from any King, Prince, or foreign State.

Section 10.   *Powers prohibited the States.* No State shall enter into any Treaty, Alliance, or Confederation; grant Letters of Marque and Reprisal; coin Money; emit Bills of Credit; make any Thing but gold and silver Coin a Tender in Payment of Debts; pass any Bill of Attainer, ex post facto Law, or Law impairing the Obligation of Contracts, or grant any Title of Nobility.

No State shall, without the Consent of the Congress, lay any Imposts or Duties on Imports or Exports, except what may be absolutely necessary for executing its inspection Laws; and the net Produce of all Duties and Imposts, laid by any State on Imports or Exports, shall be for the Use of the Treasury of the United States; and all such Laws shall be subject to the Revision and Control of the Congress.

No State shall, without the Consent of Congress, lay any duty of Tonnage, keep Troops, or Ships of War in time of Peace, enter into any Agreement of Compact with another State, or with a foreign Power, or engage in War, unless actually invaded, or in such imminent Danger as will not admit of delay.

ARTICLE II

The Executive

Section 1.   *The President, term, electors, qualification, death or removal, compensation, oath.* The executive Power shall be vested in a President of the United States of

America. He shall hold his Office during the Term of four Years,[8] and, together with the Vice-President, chosen for the same Term, be elected as follows:

Each State[9] shall appoint, in such Manner as the Legislature thereof may direct, a Number of Electors, equal to the whole Number of Senators and Representatives to which the State may be entitled in the Congress: but no Senator or Representative, or Person holding an Office of Trust or Profit under the United States, shall be appointed an Elector.

The electors shall meet in their respective states, and vote by ballot for two persons, of whom one at least shall not be an inhabitant of the same state with themselves. And they shall make a list of all the persons voted for, and of the number of votes for each; which list they shall sign and certify, and transmit sealed to the seat of the government of the United States, directed to the president of the Senate. The president of the Senate shall, in the presence of the Senate and House of Representatives, open all the certificates and the votes shall then be counted. The person having the greatest number of votes shall be the President, if such number be a majority of the whole number of electors appointed; and if there be more than one who have such majority, and have an equal number of votes, then the House of Representatives shall immediately choose by ballot one of them for President; and if no person have a majority, then from the five highest on the list, the said House shall, in like manner, choose the President. But in choosing the President, the votes shall be taken by states, the representation from each state having one vote; a quorum for this purpose shall consist of a member or members from two-thirds of the states, and a majority of all the states shall be necessary to a choice. In every case, after the choice of the President, the person having the greatest

number of votes of the electors shall be the Vice President. But if there should remain two or more who have equal votes, the Senate shall choose from them by ballot the Vice President.[10]

The Congress may determine the time of choosing the electors, and the day on which they shall give their votes; which day shall be the same throughout the United States.

No person except a natural born citizen, *or a citizen of the United States, at the time of the adoption of this Constitution,* shall be eligible to the office of President; neither shall any person be eligible to that office, who shall not have attained to the age of thirty-five years, and been fourteen years a resident within the United States.[11]

In the case of the removal of the President from office, or of his death, resignation, or inability to discharge the powers and duties of the said office, the same shall devolve on the Vice President, and the Congress may by law provide for the case of removal, death, resignation, or inability, both of the President and Vice President, declaring what officer shall then act as President, and such officer shall act accordingly, until the disability be removed, or a President shall be elected.[12]

The President shall, at stated times, receive for his services, a compensation, which shall neither be increased nor diminished during the Period for which he shall have been elected, and he shall not receive within that Period any other Emolument from the United States, or any of them.

Before he enter on the Execution of his Office, he shall take the following Oath or Affirmation: "I do solemnly swear (or affirm) that I will faithfully execute the Office of President of the United States, and will to the best of my ability, preserve, protect, and defend the Constitution of the United States."

Section 2. *President as Commander-in-Chief; role of cabinet; power to pardon and make treaties.* The President shall be Commander-in-Chief of the Army and Navy of the United States, and of the Militia of the several States, when called into the actual Service of the United States; he may require the Opinion, in writing, of the principal Officer in each of the executive Departments, upon any subject relating to the Duties of their respective Offices, and he shall have Power to grant Reprieves and Pardons for Offenses against the United States, except in Cases of Impeachment.

He shall have power, by and with the Advice and Consent of the Senate, to make Treaties, provided two thirds of the Senators present concur; and he shall nominate, and by and with the Advice and Consent of the Senate, shall appoint Ambassadors, other public Ministers and Consuls, Judges of the supreme Court, and all other Officers of the United States, whose Appointments are not herein otherwise provided for, and which shall be established by Law; but the Congress may by Law vest the Appointment of such inferior Officers, as they think proper, in the President alone, in the Courts of Law, or in the Heads of Departments.

The President shall have Power to fill up all Vacancies that may happen during the Recess of the Senate, by granting Commission which shall expire at the End of their next Session.

Section 3. *Presidential powers re Congress; to receive ambassadors, execute laws, commission officers.* He shall from time to time give to the Congress Information on the State of the Union, and recommended to their Consideration such Measures as he shall judge expedient; he may, on extraordinary Occasions, convene both Houses, or either of them, and in Case of Disagreement between

them, with Respect to the Time of Adjournment, he may adjourn them to such Time as he shall think proper; he shall receive Ambassadors and other public Ministers; he shall take Care that the Laws be faithfully executed, and shall Commission all the Officers of the United States.

Section 4. *Forfeiture of office.* The President, Vice President, and all civil Officers of the United States, shall be removed from Office on Impeachment for, and Conviction of, Treason, Bribery, or other high Crimes and Misdemeanors.

ARTICLE III
The Judiciary

Section 1. *Judicial powers, tenure, compensation.* The judicial Power of the United States, shall be vested in one supreme Court, and in such inferior Courts as the Congress may from time to time ordain and establish. The Judges, both of the supreme and inferior Courts, shall hold their Offices during good Behaviour, and shall, at stated Times, receive for their Services a Compensation which shall not be diminished during their Continuance in Office.

Section 2. *Scope of judicial power.* The judicial Power shall extend to all Cases, in Law and Equity, arising under the Constitution, the Laws of the United States, and Treaties made, or which shall be made, under their Authority;—to all Cases affecting Ambassadors, other public Ministers and Consuls;—to all Cases of admiralty and maritime Jurisdiction;—to Controversies to which the United States shall be a Party;—to Controversies between two or more States;—*between a State and Citizen of another State;*—between Citizens of different states;—between Citizens of the same State claiming Lands under Grants of different States, and between a State, or the Citizens thereof, and foreign States, *Citizens or Subject.*[13]

In all Cases affecting Ambassadors, other public Ministers and Consuls, and those in which a State shall be Party, the supreme Court shall have original Jurisdiction. In all the other Cases before mentioned, the supreme Court shall have appellate Jurisdiction, both as to Law and Fact, with such Exceptions, and under such Regulation as the Congress shall make.

The trial of all Crimes, except in Cases of Impeachment, shall be by Jury; and such Trial shall be held in the State where the said Crimes shall have been committed; but when not committed within any State, the Trial shall be at such Place or Places as the Congress may by Law have directed.

Section 3.   *Treason.* Treason against the United States, shall consist only in levying War against them, or, in adhering to their Enemies, giving them Aid and Comfort. No Person shall be convicted of Treason unless on the Testimony of two Witnesses to the same overt Act, or on Confession in open Court.

The Congress shall have power to declare the Punishment of Treason, but no Attainder of Treason shall work Corruption of Blood, or Forfeiture except during the Life of the Person attained.

ARTICLE IV
The States

Section 1.   *Full faith and credit.* Full faith and Credit shall be given in each State to the pubic Acts, Records, and judicial Proceedings of every other State. And the Congress may by general Laws prescribe the Manner in which such Acts, Records and Proceedings shall be proved, and the Effect thereof.

Section 2.   *Privileges of citizens of each State.* The Citizens of each State shall be entitled to all Privileges and Immunities of Citizens in the several States.

A Person charged in any State with Treason, Felony, or other Crime, who shall flee from Justice, and be found in another State, shall on demand of the executive Authority of the State from which he fled, be delivered up, to be removed to the State having Jurisdiction of the Crime.

No person held to service or labor in one state, under the laws thereof, escaping into another, shall, in consequence of any law or regulation therein, be discharged from such service or labor, but shall be delivered up on claim of the party to whom such service or labor may be due.[14]

Section 3.   *Admission of new States.* New States may be admitted by the Congress into this union; but no new State shall be formed or erected within the Jurisdiction of any other State, nor any State be formed by the Junction of two or more States, or parts of States, without the Consent of the Legislatures of the States concerned as well as of the Congress.

The Congress shall have Power to dispose of and make all needful Rules and Regulations respecting the Territory or other Property belonging to the United States; and nothing in this Constitution shall be so construed as to Prejudice any Claims of the United States, or of any particular State.[15]

Section 4.   *Republican form of government guaranteed.* The United States shall guarantee to every State in this Union a Republican Form of Government, and shall protect each of them against Invasion, and on

Application of the Legislature, or of the Executive (when the Legislature cannot be convened) against domestic Violence.

ARTICLE V

Amendment of Constitution

The Congress, whenever two-thirds of both Houses shall deem it necessary, shall propose Amendments to this Constitution, or, on the Application of the Legislatures of two-thirds of the several States, shall call a Convention for proposing Amendments, which, in either Case, shall be valid to all Intents and Purposes, as part of this Constitution, when ratified by the Legislatures of three-fourths of the several States, or by Conventions in three-fourths thereof, as the one or the other Mode of Ratification may be proposed by the Congress; Provided that *no Amendment which may be made prior to the Year One thousand eight hundred and eight shall in any Manner affect the first and fourth Clauses in the Ninth Section of the first Article; and that*[16] no State, without its Consent, shall be deprived of its equal Suffrage in the Senate.

ARTICLE VI

Supremacy of Constitution

All Debts contracted and Engagements entered into, before the Adoption of this Constitution shall be as valid against the United States under this Constitution, as under the Confederation.

This Constitution, and the Laws of the United States which shall be made in Pursuance thereof; and all Treaties made, or which shall be made under the Authority of the United States, shall be the supreme Law of the Land; and the Judges in every State shall be bound thereby, any Thing in the Constitution or Laws of any State to the Contrary notwithstanding.

The Senators and Representatives before mentioned, and the Members of the several State Legislatures, and all executive and judicial Officers, both of the United States and of the several States shall be bound by Oath or Affirmation, to support this Constitution; but no religious Test shall ever be required as a Qualification to any Office or public Trust under the United States.

ARTICLE VII

Ratification

The Ratification of the Conventions of nine States shall be sufficient for the Establishment of this Constitution between the States so ratifying the Same.

DONE in convention by the unanimous consent of the states present, the 17th day of September, in the year of our Lord 1787, and of the Independence of the United States of America the 12th. In witness whereof we have hereunto subscribed our names.

—George Washington, *President,
and Deputy from Virginia*

Attest:
  William Jackson, *Secretary*
New Hampshire
  John Langdon
  Nicholas Gilman
Massachusetts
  Nathaniel Gorham
  Rufus King
New Jersey
  William Livingston
  David Brearley
  William Paterson
  Jonathan Dayton
Pennsylvania
  Benjamin Franklin
  Thomas Mifflin
  Robert Morris
  George Clymer
  Thomas FitzSimons
  Jared Ingersoll
  James Wilson
  Gouverneur Morris
Delaware
  George Read
  Gunning Bedford, Jr.
  John Dickinson
  Richard Bassett
  Jacob Broom

Maryland
  James McHenry
  Daniel of St. Thomas
    Jenifer
  Daniel Carroll
Connecticut
  William Samuel
    Johnson
  Roger Sherman
New York
  Alexander Hamilton
Virginia
  John Blair
  James Madison, Jr.
North Carolina
  William Blount
  Richard Dobbs
    Spaight
  Hugh Williamson
South Carolina
  John Rutledge
  Charles Cotesworth
    Pinckney
  Charles Pinckney
  Pierce Butler
Georgia
  William Few
  Abraham Baldwin

Dates of Ratification by States

The Constitution was ratified by the thirteen original states in the following order.

Delaware, *December 7, 1787*

Pennsylvania, *December 12, 1787*

New Jersey, *December 18, 1787*

Georgia, *January 2, 1788*

Connecticut, *January 9, 1788*

Massachusetts, *February 6, 1788*

Maryland, *April 28, 1788*

South Carolina, *May 23, 1788*

New Hampshire, *June 21, 1788*

Virginia, *June 25, 1788*

New York, *July 26, 1788*

North Carolina, *November 21, 1789*

Rhode Island, *May 29, 1790*

Vermont, by convention, ratified January 10, 1791; and Congress, February 18, 1791, admitted that State into the Union.

[The Continental Congress on September 13, 1788, proclaimed the ratification by nine states, and ordered the convening of the new government on March 4, 1789.]

THE FIRST TEN AMENDMENTS— THE BILL OF RIGHTS

Note: The first ten amendments, usually called the Bill of Rights, went into effect December 15, 1791.

ARTICLE I.

Freedom of Speech, Press, Religion, Petition

Congress shall make no law respecting an establishment of religion, or prohibiting the free exercise thereof, or abridging the freedom of speech, or of the press; or the right of the people peaceably to assemble, and to petition the Government for a redress of grievances.

ARTICLE II.

Right to Keep and Bear Arms

A well-regulated militia, being necessary to the security of a free State, the right of the people to keep and bear arms, shall not be infringed.

ARTICLE III.

Quartering of Soldiers

No soldier shall, in time of peace be quartered in any house, without the consent of the owner, nor in time of war, but in a manner to be prescribed by law.

ARTICLE IV.

Search and Seizure, Warrants

The right of the people to be secure in their persons, houses, papers, and effects, against unreasonable searches and seizures, shall not be violated, and no warrants shall issue, but upon probable cause, supported by oath or affirmation, and particularly describing the place to be searched, and the persons or things to be seized.

ARTICLE V.

Provisions Concerning Prosecution, Trial and Punishment, Double Jeopardy, Due Process, Self-Incrimination

No person shall be held to answer for a capital, or otherwise infamous crime, unless on a presentment or indictment of a Grand Jury, except in cases arising in the land or naval forces, or in the militia, when in actual service in time of war or public danger; nor shall any person be subject for the same offense to be twice put in jeopardy of life or limb; nor shall be compelled in any criminal case to be a witness himself, nor be deprived of life, liberty, or property, without due process of law; nor shall private property be taken for public use without just compensation.

ARTICLE VI.

Right to Speedy Trial, Witnesses, Counsel

In all criminal prosecution, the accused shall enjoy the right to a speedy and public trial, by an impartial jury of the State and district wherein the crime shall have been committed, which district shall have been previously ascertained by law, and to be informed of the nature and cause of the accusation; to be confronted with the witnesses against him; to have compulsory process for obtaining witnesses in his favor, and to have the assistance of counsel for his defense.

ARTICLE VII.

Right of Trial by Jury

In suits at common law, where the value in controversy shall exceed twenty dollars, the right of trial by jury shall be preserved, and no fact tried by a jury shall be otherwise re-examined in any court of the United States, than according to the rules of the common law.

ARTICLE VIII.

Excessive Bail or Fines, Cruel Punishment

Excessive bail shall not be required, nor excessive fines imposed, nor cruel and unusual punishments inflicted.

ARTICLE IX.

Rule of Constitutional Construction

The enumeration in the Constitution, of certain rights, shall not be construed to deny or disparage others retained by the people.

ARTICLE X.

Rights of States Under Constitution

The powers not delegated to the United States by the Constitution, nor prohibited by it to the States, are reserved to the States respectively, or to the people.

AMENDMENTS SINCE THE BILL OF RIGHTS

ARTICLE XI.

Judicial Powers Construed

The judicial power of the United States shall not be construed to extend to any suit in law or equity, commenced or prosecuted against one of the United States by citizens of another State, or by citizens or subjects of any foreign state.

(Proposed by Congress in March 1794; declared to have been ratified January 8, 1798.)

ARTICLE XII.

Manner of Choosing President and Vice President

The Electors shall meet in their respective States[17] and vote by ballot for President and Vice-President, one of whom, at least, shall not be an inhabitant of the same State with themselves; they shall name in their ballots the person voted for as President, and in distinct ballots the person voted for as Vice-President, and they shall make distinct lists of all persons voted for as President, and of all persons voted for as Vice-President, and of the number of votes for each, which lists they shall sign and certify, and transmit sealed to the seat of Government of the United States, directed to the President of the Senate; the President of the Senate shall, in the presence of the Senate and House of Representatives, open all the certificates and the votes shall then be counted;—The person having the greatest number of votes for President, shall be the President, if such number be a majority of the whole number of Electors appointed; and if no person have such majority, then from the persons having the highest numbers not exceeding three on the list of those voted for as President, the House of Representatives shall choose immediately, by ballot, the President. But in choosing the President, the votes shall be taken by States the representation from each State having one vote; a quorum for this purpose shall consist of a member or members from two-thirds of the states, and a majority of all the States shall be necessary to a choice. And if the House of Representatives shall not choose a President whenever the right of choice shall devolve upon them, before *the fourth day of March*[18] next following, then the Vice-President shall act as President, as in case of the death or other constitutional disability of the President. The person having the greatest number of votes as Vice-President shall be the Vice-President, if such number be a majority of the whole number of electors appointed, and if no person have a majority, then from the two highest numbers on the list, the Senate shall choose the Vice-President; a quorum for the purpose shall consist of two-thirds of the whole number of Senators, and a majority of the whole number shall be necessary to a choice. But no person constitutionally ineligible to the office of President shall be eligible to that of Vice-President of the United States.

(Proposed December 1803; ratification completed June 15, 1804.)

ARTICLE XIII.
Abolition of Slavery

1. Neither slavery nor involuntary servitude, except as punishment for crime whereof the party shall have been duly convicted, shall exist within the United States, or any place subject to their jurisdiction.

2. Congress shall have power to enforce this article by appropriate legislation.

(Proposed January 1865; ratification completed December 6, 1896.)

ARTICLE XIV.
Citizenship Rights; Apportionment of Representatives; Validity of Public Debt

1. All persons born or naturalized in the United States, and subject to the jurisdiction thereof are citizens of the United States and of the State wherein they reside. No State shall make or enforce any law which shall abridge the privileges of immunities of citizens of the United States; nor shall any State deprive any person of life, liberty, of property, without due process of law; nor deny to any person within its jurisdiction the equal protection of the laws.

2. Representatives shall be apportioned among the several States according to their respective numbers, counting the whole number of persons in each State, *excluding Indians not taxed.*[19] But when the right to vote at any election for the choice of Electors for President and Vice-President of the United States,

Representatives in Congress, the executive and judicial officers of a State, or the members of the Legislature thereof, is denied to any of the male inhabitants of such State, being twenty-one years of age, and citizens of the United States, or any way abridged, except for participation in rebellion, or other crime, the basis of representation therein shall be reduced in the proportion which the number of such male citizens shall bear to the whole number of male citizens twenty-one years of age in such State.[20]

3.   No person shall be a Senator or Representative in Congress, or Elector of President and Vice-President, or hold any office, civil or military, under the United States, or under any State, who, having previously taken an oath, as a member of Congress, or as an officer of the United States, or as a member of any State Legislature, or as an executive or judicial officer of any State, to support the constitution of the United States, shall have engaged in insurrection or rebellion against the same, or given aid or comfort to the enemies thereof. But Congress may by a vote of two-thirds of each House, remove such disability.

4.   The validity of the public debt of the United States, authorized by law, including debts incurred for payment of pensions and bounties for services in suppressing insurrection or rebellion, shall not be questioned. But neither the United States, nor any State shall assume or pay any debt or obligation incurred in aid of insurrection or rebellion against the United States, or any claim for the loss or emancipation of any slave; but all such debts, obligations and claims shall be held illegal and void.

5.   The Congress shall have power to enforce, by appropriate legislation, the provisions of this article.

(Proposed June 1866; declared to have been ratified in July 1868.)

ARTICLE XV.

Equal Voting Rights for White and Colored Citizens

1.   The right of citizens of the United States to vote shall not be denied or abridged by the United States or by any State on account of race, color, or previous condition of servitude.

2.   The Congress shall have power to enforce this article by appropriate legislation.

(Proposed February 1869; declared to have been ratified on March 30, 1870.)

ARTICLE XVI.

Income Taxes Authorized

The Congress shall have power to lay and collect taxes on incomes, from whatever sources derived, without apportionment among the several States, and without regard to any census or enumeration.

(Proposed July 1909; ratification completed February 3, 1913.)

ARTICLE XVII.

Direct Election of U.S. Senators

1.   The Senate of the United States shall be composed of two Senators from each State, elected by the people thereof, for six years; and each Senator shall have one vote. The electors in each State shall have the qualifications requisite for electors of the most numerous branch of the State Legislatures.

2.   When vacancies happen in the representation of any State in the Senate, the executive authority of such State shall issue writs of

election to fill such vacancies: Provided, That the Legislature of any State may empower the Executive thereof to make temporary appointments until the people fill the vacancies by election as the Legislature may direct.

3.   This amendment shall not be so construed as to affect the election or term of any Senator chosen before it becomes valid as part of the Constitution.

(Proposed May 1912; ratification completed April 8, 1913.)

ARTICLE XVIII.

Liquor Prohibition

1.   After one year from the ratification of this article the manufacture, sale, or transportation of intoxicating liquors within, the importation thereof into, or exportation thereof from the United States and all territory subject to the jurisdiction thereof, for beverage purposes is hereby prohibited.

2.   The Congress and the several states shall have concurrent power to enforce this article by appropriate legislation.

3.   This article shall be inoperative unless it shall have been ratified as an amendment to the Constitution by the legislatures of the several states, as provided in the Constitution, within seven years from the date of submission hereof to the states by the Congress.

(Proposed December 1917; ratification completed January 16, 1919. Amendment repealed by Article XXI, effective December 5, 1933.)

ARTICLE XIX.

Nationwide Suffrage for Women

1.   The right of citizens of the United States to vote shall not be denied or abridged by the United States or by any State on account of sex.

2.   Congress shall have power to enforce this Article by appropriate legislation.

(Proposed June 1919; ratification certified August 26, 1920.)

ARTICLE XX.

Beginning Date of Terms of President, Vice President, Members of Congress

1.   The terms of the President and Vice President shall end at noon on the 20th day of January and the terms of Senators and Representatives at noon on the 3rd day of January, of the years in which terms would have ended if this article had not been ratified, and the terms of their successors shall then begin.

2.   The Congress shall assemble at least once in every year, and such meeting shall begin at noon on the 3rd day of January, unless they shall by law appoint a different day.

3.   If, at the time fixed for the beginning of the term of the President, the President elect shall have died, the Vice President elect shall become President. If the President shall not have been chosen before the time fixed for the beginning of his term, or if the President elect shall have failed to qualify, then the Vice-President elect shall act as President until a President shall have qualified, and the Congress may by law provide for the case wherein neither a President elect nor a Vice-President shall have qualified, declaring who shall then act as President, or the manner in which one who is to act shall be selected, and such person shall act accordingly until a President or Vice-President shall have qualified.[21]

4.   The Congress may by law provide for the case of the death of any of the persons

from whom the House of Representatives may choose a President whenever the right of choice shall have devolved upon them, and for the case of the death of any of the persons from whom the Senate may choose a Vice-President whenever the right of choice shall have devolved upon them.

5.   Sections 1 and 2 shall take effect on the 15th day of October following the ratification of this article [Oct. 1933].

6.   This article shall be inoperative unless it shall have been ratified as an amendment to the Constitution by the Legislatures of three-fourths of the several States within seven years from the date of its submission.

(Proposed March 1932; ratification completed January 23, 1933.)

ARTICLE XXI.

Repeal of Eighteenth Amendment

1.   The eighteenth article of amendment to the Constitution of the United States is hereby repealed.

2.   The transportation or importation into any State, Territory, or Possession of the United States for delivery or use therein of intoxicating liquors, in violation of the laws thereof, is hereby prohibited.

3.   This article shall be inoperative unless it shall have been ratified as an amendment to the Constitution by conventions in the several States, as provided in the Constitution, within seven years from the date of the submission hereof to the States by the Congress.

(Proposed February 1933; ratification completed December 5, 1933, by State conventions rather than legislative bodies.)

ARTICLE XXII.

Limit on Number of Presidential Terms

1.   No person shall be elected to the office of the President more than twice, and no person who has held the office of President, or acted as President, for more than two years of a term to which some other person was elected President shall be elected to the office of the President more than once. But this Article shall not apply to any person holding the office of President when this Article was proposed by the Congress, and shall not prevent any person who may be holding the office of President, or acting as President, during the term within which this Article becomes operative from holding the office of President or acting as President during the remainder of such term.

2.   This article shall be inoperative unless it shall have been ratified as an amendment to the Constitution by the Legislatures of three-fourths of the several States within seven years from the date of its submission to the States by the Congress.

(Proposed March 1947; ratification completed February 27, 1951.)

ARTICLE XXIII.

Presidential Vote for Residents of the District of Columbia

1.   The District constituting the seat of Government of the United States shall appoint in such manner as the Congress may direct:

A number of electors of President and Vice President equal to the whole number of Senators and Representatives in Congress to which the District would be entitled if it were a State, but in no event more than the least populous State; they shall be in addition to those appointed by the States, but they shall be considered, for the purposes of the election of President and Vice President, to be electors appointed by a State; and they shall meet in the District and perform such duties as provided by the twelfth article of amendment.

2.   The Congress shall have power to enforce this article by appropriate legislation.

(Proposed June 1960; ratification completed March 29, 1961.)

ARTICLE XXIV.

Prohibition of Poll Tax in Federal Elections

1.   The right of citizens of the United States to vote in any primary or other election for President or Vice President, for electors for President or Vice President, or for Senator or Representative in Congress, shall not be denied or abridged by the United States or any State by reason of failure to pay any poll tax or other tax.

2.   The Congress shall have power to enforce this article by appropriate legislation.

(Proposed August 1962; ratification completed January 23, 1964.)

ARTICLE XXV.

Presidential Inability and Succession

1.   In case of the removal of the President from office or of his death or resignation, the Vice President shall become President.

2.   Whenever there is a vacancy in the office of the Vice President, the President shall nominate a Vice President who shall take office upon confirmation by a majority vote of both houses of Congress.

3.   Whenever the President transmits to the President pro tempore of the Senate and the Speaker of the House of Representatives his written declaration that he is unable to discharge the powers and duties of his office, and until he transmits to them a written declaration to the contrary, such powers and duties shall be discharged by the Vice President as Acting President.

4.   Whenever the Vice President and a majority of either the principal officers of the executive departments of such other body as Congress may by law provide, transmit to the President pro tempore of the Senate and the Speaker of the House of Representatives their written declaration that the President is unable to discharge the powers and duties of his office, the Vice President shall immediately assume the powers and duties of the office as Acting President.

Thereafter, when the President transmits to the President pro tempore of the Senate and the Speaker of the House of Representatives his written declaration that no inability exists, he shall resume the powers and duties of his office unless the Vice President and a majority of either the principal officers of the executive department or of such other body as Congress may by law provide, transmit within four days to the President pro tempore of the Senate and the Speaker of the House of Representatives their written declaration that the President is unable to discharge the powers and duties of his office. Thereupon Congress shall decide the issue, assembling within forty-eight hours for that purpose if not in session. If the Congress, within twenty-one days after receipt of the latter written declaration, or, if Congress is not in session, within twenty-one days after Congress is required to assemble, determines by two-thirds vote of both houses that the President is unable to discharge the powers and duties of his office, the Vice President shall continue to discharge the same as Acting President; otherwise, the President shall resume the powers and duties of his office.

(Proposed July 1965; ratification completed February 10, 1967.)

ARTICLE XXVI.

Lowering Voting Age to 18 Years

1. The right of citizens of the United States, who are 18 years of age or older, to vote shall not be denied or abridged by the United States or any state on account of age.

2. The Congress shall have power to enforce this article by appropriate legislation.

(Proposed March 1971; ratification completed June 30, 1971.)

NOTES

1. Changed by Amendment XIV, Section 2, "counting the whole number of persons in each State." The "other persons" were slaves, and all Indians are now subject to federal taxation.
2. A temporary provision, superseded by Congressional reapportionments based on each decennial Census.
3. Changed by Amendment XVII, paragraph 1, "elected by the people thereof."
4. Filing of vacancies modified by Amendment XVII, paragraph 2.
5. Changed by Amendment XX, Section 2; "shall begin at noon on the 3rd day of January."
6. Made obsolete January 1, 1808, when Congress prohibited all further importation of slaves.
7. Amendment XVI exempts the federal income tax from this provision.
8. Amendment XXII limits a President to two terms.
9. Extended by Amendment XXIII.
10. This whole paragraph is superseded by Amendment XII.
11. See Amendment XII: "But no person constitutionally ineligible to the office of President shall be eligible to that of Vice President of the United States."
12. Extended by Amendment XX, Sections 3 and 4.
13. These two italicized passages are limited by Amendment XI.
14. Made obsolete as to slaves by Amendment XIII.
15. Relating to unsettled boundaries at the time of adoption of the Constitution.
16. A temporary provision protecting the slave trade until 1808.
17. Extended by Amendment XXIII.
18. Changed by Amendment XX, Section 1, "at noon on the 20th day of January."
19. All Indians are now subject to federal taxation.
20. This provision has never been enforced.
21. The Presidential Succession Act of 1886, as amended in 1947, fixes the order of succession as follows: Speaker of the House, President of the Senate, Secretary of State, of Treasury, of Defense, Attorney-General, Postmaster-General, Secretary of Interior, of Agriculture, of Commerce, of Labor, and of Health and Human Services.

Index

A

Aberback, J. D., 328
Abortion, and U.S. Supreme
    Court, 398-400, 420-25
Abraham, Henry, 393
Accountability, 321-22
Accused, protections for, 91-101
Acheson, Dean, 23
Achievement, 5, 15
Action, political. *See* Political
    action
Adamany, David, 250
Adams, John, 183, 317
Adams, John Quincy, 35, 46
Administration, and presidency,
    329-30
Advertising, and negative
    television ads, 230-31,
    253-58, 260-61
Advisory Commission on
    Intergovernmental
    Relations, 57
Affirmative action, 66-70
AFL-CIO, 144
Age Discrimination in
    Employment Act, 61
Agency, government. *See*
    Government
Agent, 343
Agranoff, Robert, 219
Agrarianism, 120
Aid to Families with Dependent
    Children, 109
AIPAC. *See* American Israeli
    Public Affairs Committee
    (AIPAC)
Alexander, Lamar, 134-35
Alien and Sedition Acts, 46

Amendments, 31-33, 73-78,
    489-98
First, 51, 59, 62, 63, 75-76,
    79, 82, 100
Fourth, 60, 70, 71, 76, 96, 97
Fifth, 60, 70, 71, 86, 99,
    100, 101
Sixth, 60, 70, 71, 76
Seventh, 492
Eighth, 60, 70, 492
Ninth, 77, 85-86, 492
Tenth, 47, 103, 104, 113, 492
Eleventh, 35, 50, 492
Twelfth, 492-93
Thirteenth, 31, 105, 493
Fourteenth, 51, 59, 60, 64,
    65, 70, 72, 77, 88-90,
    105, 420-25, 493-94
Fifteenth, 31, 105, 225, 494
Sixteenth, 494
Seventeenth, 47, 494-95
Eighteenth, 32, 495
Nineteenth, 31, 105, 225, 495
Twentieth, 495-96
Twenty-first, 32, 496
Twenty-second, 275, 277, 496
Twenty-third, 31, 496-97
Twenty-fourth, 105, 497
Twenty-fifth, 497-98
Twenty-sixth, 31, 105, 225,
    498
See also Bill of Rights *and*
    Constitution
American Bankers Association,
    178
American Broadcasting
    Corporation (ABC), 25
American Civil Liberties Union
    (ACLU), 61, 78

American Creed, 13
American Enterprise Institute
    for Public Policy
    Research, 166
American government,
    foundations of, 1-137. *See
    also* Government
American Israeli Public Affairs
    Committee (AIPAC), 166,
    167
American Law Institute, 97
American Medical Association
    (AMA), 145
American Municipal Association,
    133
American Nazi Party. *See* Nazis
American Partnership, The, 114
American Political Creed, The,
    12-17
"American Polity, The," 54
American Progress, 191
American Socialist Party, 62
American Society of Public
    Administration, 134
Amtrak, 313
Andrews, Thomas H., 177
Anonymity, 322
Appendix, 477-98
Appleby, Joyce, 86
Area and Power, 117
Areson, Todd W., 294-99
Arizona v. Fulmuinante, 72
Armed Forces and Society, 306
Arnold & Porter, 337
Articles of Confederation,
    28-29, 52, 86, 103, 104,
    274
*Art of Presidential Persuasion,
    The,* 294-99

B

Bahcall, John, 333, 337
Bailar, Barbara A., 338
Baker, Howard, 164, 311
Baker, James, 310
Baker, James Jay, 176-77
Bakke, Allan, 66
Balances, checks and. *See*
    Checks and balances
Barber, Benjamin, 4, 8-11
Barber, James David, 270
Barrett, Edward, 97
Barry, John M., 348, 374-81
Barthelemy, Sidney, 133, 135
Beard, 156
Becker, Carl, 86
Beliefs, and political culture,
    5-6, 57-58
Bennett, Wallace, 169
Berg, Alan, 174
Berlin Wall, 5, 18, 19
Bernstein, Carl, 262
Bias, mobilization of, 155-62
Biden, Joseph, 213
Bigness, and federalism, 129-30
Bill of Rights, 31-33, 49, 50, 51,
    59, 60, 61, 64, 70, 71, 72,
    73-78, 79, 85, 98, 492
    and Constitutional change,
    31-33
    and minorities and
    dissenters, 61-62, 73-78,
    79-84, 85-91
    See also Amendments *and*
    Constitution
*Bill of Rights: Protector of
    Minorities and
    Dissenters, The,* 73-78
Black, Hugo, 74
Black, Manafort, Stone, and
    Kelly, 167
Blackmun, Harry, 398, 431-34
Bloom, Tom, 344, 361-63
Boggs, Hale, 164
Boggs, Lindy, 164
Boggs, Tommy, 164, 166
Bolling v. Sharpe, 88
Boos v. Barry, 80, 81

Bork, Robert, 392, 394
Borut, Donald J., 135, 136, 137
Boulware, Sandra, 95
Bradley, Bill, 57
Brady, James, 147, 170-79
Brady, Sarah, 147, 170-79
Brandeis, Louis, 75
Brandenburg, Clarence, 63
Brandenburg v. Ohio, 63
Brennan, William Joseph, Jr.,
    64, 68, 79-82, 94, 96,
    392, 394, 406, 431-34
Brewer, David Josiah, 89
Broder, David, 224, 290
Brown, George E., Jr., 177
*Brown v. Board of Education
    of Topeka,* 65, 77, 89, 90,
    397
Bryant, Barbara Everitt, 333, 336
Buck v. Bell, 89
Bureaucracy
    and executive branch, 309-39
    growth and expansion,
    313-16
    implementation and action,
    314-16, 332-39
    management of, 314, 326-31
Bureau of Alcohol, Tobacco,
    and Firearms, 171
Burger, Warren, 65, 90, 394, 398
Burke, Edmund, 343
Burns, James MacGregor, 54,
    56, 203, 277
Bush, George, 3, 19, 23, 24, 25,
    60, 63, 64, 69, 70, 71, 72,
    107, 109, 133, 147, 171,
    230, 253, 272, 311, 394,
    395, 399, 452-59
Busing, 65

C

Cahn, Edmund, 16
Calhoun, John C., 46, 113
California Law Review, 97
Camden, Lord, 97
Campaigns, 6, 181
    changing, 257-58

and finance, 227-28, 244-52
and interest groups, 170-79
*Can Democracy Survive the
    Media in the 1990s?,*
    259-63
Carter, Jimmy, 106, 107, 123,
    164, 283
Casework, 343-44
Caucus, 204
Ceausescu, Nicolae, 5
*Census: Why We Can't Count,
    The,* 332-39
Central Intelligence Agency
    (CIA), 269, 278
Centralism, 120
Centralization, 107, 110, 119-30
Certiorari, 396
Chaplinsky v. New Hampshire,
    80
Charles II, 97
Checks and balances, 41-44
Cheney, Richard, 57, 320, 454
Chisolm v. Georgia, 34, 50
*Choosing Presidential
    Candidates: Why the Best
    Man Doesn't Necessarily
    Win,* 209-15
Chrysler Corporation, 168
Churchill, Winston, 9
Civil liberties
    and civil rights, 59-72
    current status, 72
    government in, 60-62
Civil rights
    and civil liberties, 59-72
    current status, 72
    government in, 60-62
Civil Rights Act, 60, 61, 66, 68,
    69, 88
Civil Rights Cases, 89
Civil Rights Commission, 60, 61
Civil War, 3, 17, 25, 46, 53, 64,
    113, 114, 183, 211, 268,
    390
Clarity, 296
Clark, William, 310
Clay, Henry, 25, 183
Cleveland, Grover, 183-84

Cleveland Firefighters case, 68
Clifford, Clark, 55, 164
Close, Glenn, 94
Cochran, Tom, 132, 133, 134, 135
Coelho, Tony, 166
Coercive cooperation, 121
Cohen, David, 169
Cohens v. Virginia, 52
Cold War, 3, 77, 100
Colorado College, 348
Columbia Broadcasting System (CBS), 63
Columbia University, 98
Committee for the Study of the American Electorate, 223, 236
Committee on Constitutional Development, 32
Committee on the Constitutional System, 54, 56
Common Cause, 168, 438
Communications, 126, 188, 216-24
  elections and intermediary functions, 220
  and public and private balance, 221-24
  and voters, 216-21
  and voting, elections, and media, 225-63
Communism, 3, 5, 18, 62, 75, 100
Community Development Block Grants, 108, 136
Comprehensive Employment Training Act, 132
Compromise, 283
Concentrated cooperation, 121
Conflict, socialization of, 155
Congress, 277, 341-87
  and elections, 341-42
  incumbency limitations, 348-49, 382-87
  and politics, 345-46, 364-73
  and public policy, 346-47, 364-73

and roles, 347-48, 374-81
Congressional Quarterly, 304
Connally, John, 174
Connecticut Compromise, 29
Connor, Bull, 78
Consensus, 24
Constanza, Midge, 322
Constituency, and legislators, 343-44, 350-59
Constitution, 27-58, 481-98
  Amendments. *See* Amendments
  Bill of Rights. *See* Bill of Rights
  changing, 31-33
  endurance of, 45-52
  and equality, 64
  evolution of constitutional protection, 73-78, 79-84
  foundations, 104-5
  and free expression, 75-76
  interpretation of, 391-92
  and James Wilson, 34-40
  and presidency, 267-68, 274-80
  protection of unpopular political expression, 79-84
  and reform, 32, 53-58
  and U.S. Supreme Court. *See* United States Supreme Court
Constitutional Convention, 3, 4, 29-30, 53
Constitutional Equality, 85-91
Construction Construed and Constitutions Vindicated, 114
Cooperation, 106-8, 121
Cooperative federalism, 114-15
Cooperative theories, 114-17
Copeland, R. M., 328
County News, 133
Cox, Archibald, 90
Crawford, William, 210
Creative federalism, 115
Creed, 13
Crime, and due process, 70-72, 86

Crisis-oriented centralism, 120
Cronin, Thomas E., 55, 229, 270-71, 281-93, 348
Cruikshank, Nelson, 322
Culture, 5-6, 12-17
Cuomo, Mario, 258, 393-94
Cutler, Lloyd N., 54
Cutright, 218

D

Dahl, 156
Danforth, John, 69
Darman, Richard, 297
Davis v. Bandemer, 342
Deaver, Michael, 223, 310
Decentralization, 107, 110, 115, 119-30, 185-86
Deciding Cases and Writing Opinions, 412-19
Decision-making process, and U.S. Supreme Court, 396-97, 412-19
Declaration of Independence, 9, 14, 28, 34, 477-80
De facto segregation, 65
De jure segregation, 65
Democracy, 17
  and American political system, 3-26
  contemporary, 6-7, 18-26
  direct and indirect, 4-5
  and media, 259-63
  and participatory democracy, 17
  and responsiveness to people's needs, 7
  and substantive democracy, 5
  and values origins, 8-11
Democracy in America?, 18-26
Dewey, Thomas E., 211
Dickenson, Mollie, 173
Dickinson, John, 34, 47
Dilemmas, and values, 12-17
Dine, Tom, 166
Dionne, E. J., Jr., 439, 441, 442, 468-76
Direct democracy, 4-5

Disclosure, and finance, 250-52

Discrimination, and reverse discrimination, 66-70

Dissenters, and Bill of Rights, 61-62, 73-78, 79-84

Dole, Robert, 69, 253

Domestic policy, 300-308

Dorsen, Norman, 61, 62, 73-78

Douglas, Chuck, 177

Dred Scott case, 88, 390

Drew, Elizabeth, 440, 441, 442, 452-59

Dual federalism, 114, 119

Due process, 70-72, 86

Dukakis, Michael, 226, 230, 253, 254

Duke, David, 25, 69, 70

Dye, Thomas R., 143, 144

E

Eagle Entangled, 302

Eastern Europe, 5, 6, 18

Eisenhower, Dwight D., 64, 164, 276

Eizenstat, Stuart, 324

Elazar, Daniel J., 103, 105, 110, 114, 119-30

Elections
and Congress, 341-42
key intermediary function in, 220
and media and politics, 231-32, 259-63
and presidency, 229-30
and voting and media, 225-63

Electoral College, 38, 209

Electorate, remobilization of, 233-43

Elitism, 143-44, 305, 437

Ellender, Allen, 169

Ellsworth, Oliver, 37

Emery, David F., 178

Empowerment, 37

Entitlement programs, 107-8

Entrenchment, 120

Environmental Protection Agency (EPA), 312, 460-67

Equal Employment Opportunity Commission (EEOC), 60, 61, 66

Equality, 5, 14-15, 64, 77, 85-91

Equal Pay Act, 61

Ericksen, Eugene P., 336

Espionage Act, 62

Essence of White House Service, The, 317-25

Ethics, 322-23

Ethics in Government Act, 33

Executive branch, 74, 309-39, 485-87

Executive management, 309-12

Executive Office of the President (EXOP), 309

Executive Reorganization Act, 310

F

Face the Nation, 19

Factions, 141-44, 149-54

Fahrenkopf, Frank, 248

Federal Communications Commission (FCC), 222

Federal Deposit Insurance Corporation (FDIC), 313

Federal Election Campaign Act (FECA), 227, 248, 251, 256, 258

Federal Election Commission (FEC), 227, 248, 251, 256, 258

Federal Firearms Act, 170

Federalism
and bigness, 129-30
and cooperative federalism, 114-15
and creative federalism, 115
and dual federalism, 114, 119
and federal-state relations, 119-30
and intergovernmental relations, 103-37
and nation-centered federalism, 112-13
New. *See* New Federalism

phases of, 106
and political process, 111-18
and state-centered federalism, 113-14
and twentieth-century patterns of American federalism, 120-21

Federalism and Theory, 111-18

Federalist, The, 30, 37, 41-44, 48, 49, 50, 112, 113, 141, 149-54, 183-84, 199-202, 267, 268, 274-80, 390, 438

Federal Trade Commission, 312-13

Few Parchment Pages Two Hundred Years Later, A, 45-52

Field Research Corporation, 288

Final Days, The, 262

Finance, and campaigns, 227-28, 244-52

Fiorina, Morris P., 343, 344, 350-59

Firearms, 170-79

Firefighters Local Union 1784 v. Stotts, 67

Fischer, Raymond L., 227, 230-31, 253-58

Fitch, John, 51

Flag burning, 63-64, 75, 79-84

Flag Protection Act. *See* Flag burning

Foley, Thomas S., 178

Ford, Gerald R., 211, 283

Ford Foundation, 110

Foreign policy, 300-308

Forrest, Nathan Bedford, 211

Franklin, Benjamin, 36, 37

Freedman, David, 338

Freedom, 5, 9-10, 62-65

Free expression, 75-76

Friendly, Henry, 99

Frontiero v. Richardson, 90

Fullilove v. Klutznick, 67

G

Gallup Polls, 189–97
Gans, Curtis B., 226, 227, 233–43
Garcia v. San Antonio Metropolitan Transit Authority, 122, 124
Gardner, John, 58, 323
Garin-Hart Strategic Research, 192
Garment, Leonard, 262
Garn, Jake, 169
General revenue sharing, 108
General Services Administration, 312
Gephardt, Richard, 212
Gerry, Elbridge, 200
Gerrymandering, 342
Gilbert, Bil, 439, 440, 441, 442, 460–67
Ginsburg, Douglas, 394
Glasnost, 5, 10, 259
Gleick, James, 315, 332–39
Goals, and policy, 294–99
Goddard, Terry, 132, 133, 136
Goldwater, Barry, 393
Gong Lum v. Rice, 89
Goodpaster, Andrew J., 324
Gorbachev, Mikhail, 5, 18
Gore, Al, 212
Governance, 242–43
Government, 242–43
    agency types, 312–13
    and aid to local governments, 131–37
    and aid to states, 131–37
    American. *See* American government
    and civil rights and civil liberties, 60–62
    and federal-state relations, 119–30
    and fiscal cooperation, 106–8
    and intergovernmental relations, 103–37
    and intergovernmental system, 277
    local. *See* Local government

outputs of, 435–76
and political action and government machinery, 265–434
Graham, Bob, 55
Graham, Katherine, 174
Gramm-Rudman-Hollings law, 133, 280
Gray, Robert, 164
Great Compromise, 47
Great Depression, 53, 56, 198, 276, 313
Great Society, 277
Greeks, 4, 8–9
Greeley, Horace, 217
Greenstein, Fred, 56
Greider, William, 165
Grodzins, Morton, 107, 111, 114, 115
Groups, interest. *See* Interest groups
Group theories of politics, 159–62
Gun Control Act, 171
Gun lobby, 170–79
Gunther, John, 164

H

Haggerty v. United States, 64
Hague, Frank, 78
Hale, Matthew, 97
Halpert, Leon, 302
Hamilton, Alexander, 30, 49, 50, 51, 53, 275, 276, 323, 390
Hamilton, Lee, 257–58
Hand, Learned, 25
Handgun Control, Inc., 171
Harkin, Tom, 177
Harlan, John, 75, 396
Harrison, William Henry, 217, 254
Hart, Gary, 219
Harvard University, 115, 216
Hatch, Orrin, 169
Herson, Lawrence J. R., 5, 6, 12–17

Hertzberg, Hendrik, 348, 382–87
Hettinger, Steve, 135
Hickman-Maslin Research, 195
Hill, Anita, 396
Hinckley, John, 147
Hinkley, John, 170
Hiroshima, 57
Hoadley, Bruce, 339
Hobbes, Thomas, 9–10
Holmes, Oliver Wendell, 62, 75, 89
Hook, Janet, 304
Hoover, Herbert, 285
Hoover, J. Edgar, 321
Hope, 296
Horton, Willie, 230
Housing and Community Development Act, 108
How Washington Really Works, 167
Hudgins v. Wrights, 87
Humphrey, Hubert, 211
Hunter, Marjorie, 344, 361–63
Huntington, Samual, 291
Hussein, Saddam, 3, 21, 452–59
Hustler Magazine, Inc. v. Falwell, 82
Hyde, Henry, 399

I

Idealists, 9
Implied powers, 105–6
Incumbency, limiting, 348–49, 382–87
Indirect democracy, 4–5
Industrial Revolution, 128
Influence
    and persuasion, 294–99
    and political participation, 139–263
Innovation, 110, 284–85
Institutions, 241
Interest groups, 141–79, 276–77
    and campaigning, 170–79
    pros and cons, 147–48
Intergovernmental fiscal cooperation, 106–8

Intergovernmental relations, and federalism, 103-37
Intergovernmental system, 277
Internationalism, 305
Interstate Commerce Commission, 312
Interviews, and polls, 194
Interview with a Founding Father, 34-40
Invention, 284-85
Involvement, 243
Iran-Contra Affair, 33, 272, 278, 279

J

Jackson, Andrew, 46, 276
Jackson, Jesse, 212
Jagged Edge, The, 94
James v. Illinois, 71
Jaworski, Leon, 269
Jay, John, 30, 49, 50
Jefferson, Thomas, 9, 17, 27-28, 34, 85, 86, 87, 95, 113, 225, 276
Jennings, Kent, 304
Jensen, Merrill, 86
Jim Crow laws, 64
Johnson, Andrew, 69
Johnson, Lyndon B., 60, 115, 134, 164, 276, 277, 281
Johnson v. Transportation Agency, 68-69
Jones, Charles D., 333
Jones, Tom, 132
Joyce, Diane, 69
Judgment, 84
Judicial branch, 74
Judicial guardians, 77-78
Judicial review, 390-92, 401-5
Judiciary, 487-88
Judiciary Act, 52
Justice, 5, 15-16

K

Kaiser Aluminum Company, 66
Kames, Lord, 35

Katz, Stanley N., 64, 65, 85-91
Keane, John, 338
Kennedy, Anthony, 394, 398
Kennedy, John F., 24, 56, 171, 233, 276, 277, 303
Kenney, Charles, 181, 189-97
Kerry, John, 177
King, Martin Luther, Jr., 61
King, Wayne, 147, 170-79
King Caucus, 204
Kingdon, John, 438
Kish, Leslie, 332, 339
KISS theory, 295-96
Korematsu case, 90
Korologis, Tom, 169
Kramer, Gerald, 218
Ku Klux Klan, 62, 63, 69, 75
Kuwait, 452-59

L

Ladd, Everett Carll, 54
Lamm, Richard, 58
Lapham, Lewis H., 6, 7, 18-26
Laski, Harold, 156, 286
Latham, 156, 159
Latimer, George, 132, 134, 135
Laws
    Jim Crow, 64
    and Special Prosecutor, 33
    See also Rule of law *and specific laws*
Lazarus, Edward H., 192
Leach, Richard H., 106, 111-18
Leadership
    and policy, 300-308
    and presidency, 268-73, 281-93
Leadership Conference on Civil Rights, 61
League of Women Voters, 159, 238
Legislative branch, 74
Legislative process, 344-45, 361-63
Legislators, and constituency, 343-44, 350-59

Lehnert v. Ferris Faculty Association, 71
Leiserson, 156
Lend Lease Act, 269
Levellers, 99-100
Lever Act, 269
Liberalism, 86-88
Liberty, 5, 14-15. *See also* Civil liberties
Lierman, Terry, 166
Lilburne, John, 100
Lincoln, Abraham, 46, 52, 88, 112, 183, 268, 276
Lindblom, 156
Literary Digest, 189-97
Lobbying
    and guns, 170-79
    strategies and tactics, 144-47, 163-69
Lobbying for the Good Old Days, 131-37
Local government, federal aid to, 131-37
Localism, 5, 17
Locke, John, 27-28, 73, 87
Log Cabin, 217
Long, Russell, 169
Longest-Running Game in Town, The, 344, 361-63
Louisiana Railroad Accommodation Law, 64

M

McCarthy, Joseph, 77, 100
McClure, James A., 170
McClure-Volkmer bill, 170
McConnell, Grant, 17
McCulloch v. Maryland, 104, 105-6, 111, 112
McCullough, Dale R., 332
McDonald, Forrest, 275, 277
McGovern, George, 283
McNamara, Robert, 301, 302
"MacNeil-Lehrer News Hour," 231, 255, 259

Madison, James, 29, 30-31, 32, 36, 41-44, 46, 48, 49, 50, 53, 59, 77-78, 141, 149-54, 199-202, 274-80, 438
Madison, John, 113
Magnuson, Warren, 169
Management
    and executive branch, 309-12
    and federal bureaucracy, 314, 326-31
Mandelbaum, Michael, 302
Mapp v. Obio, 96, 97
Marble-cake federalism, 107
Marbury v. Madison, 74, 390, 401-5
Market Opinion Research, 196
Marshall, John, 35, 50, 52, 74, 105, 106, 111, 112, 390, 393, 401-5
Marshall, Thurgood, 96, 395, 431-34
Martin, Seymour, 15
Martin v. Wilks, 69
Mason, George, 48
Mathematica Policy Research, 334
Mathias, Charles McC., Jr., 55
Matthews, Christopher, 164, 165
Mayer, William G., 188, 216-24
Media, 242
    and political parties, 187-88, 216-24
    and politics and elections, 231-32, 259-63
    and presidency, 298
    and voting and elections, 225-63
Medicaid, 109
Meese, Edwin, 49, 60, 67, 99, 164, 310, 392, 394, 406
Megatrends, 125
Mencken, H. L., 26
Mercer, John, 136, 137
Metcalf, Charles E., 334
Michigan v. Sitz, 71
Mill, John Stuart, 95
Miller, Maurene, 336

Miller, Warren, 304
Mills, C. Wright, 143
Minorities, and Bill of Rights, 61-62, 73-78, 85-91
Minority Business Enterprises, 67
Miranda, Ernesto, 98-99
Miranda v. Arizona, 70, 71, 98-99, 100-101
Mobilization, of electorate, 233-43
Mondale, Walter F., 226, 253, 291
Monoghan, Henry, 98
Mooney, Jim, 169
Morris, Richard B., 32, 45-52
Morris, Robert, 45
Morrison v. Olson, 33
Mosbacher, Robert, 315, 316
Murphy v. Waterfront Commission, 101
Muskie, Edmund, 211
Myrdal, Gunnar, 13, 14

N

Nader, Ralph, 168, 247
Nagasaki, 57
Naisbit, John, 125
Nast, Thomas, 163
National Association for the Advancement of Colored People (NAACP), 61, 65, 77, 159
National Association of Counties, 132, 134, 137
National Association of State Budget Officers, 133
National Conference of State Legislatures, 131
National Firearms Act, 170
National Governors' Association, 109, 115, 131, 133, 134
National Law Journal, 91
National League of Cities, 131, 132, 135, 136
National League of Cities v. Usery, 124

National Organization of Women (NOW), 61
National parties, and presidency, 186-87, 209-15
National Rail and Passenger Corporation (Amtrak), 313
National Rifle Association (NRA), 146-47, 167, 170-79, 247, 438
National Security Council (NSC), 278
Nation-centered federalism, 112-13
Nation's Cities Weekly, 133
Nazis, 69, 75, 78
Negative 1988 Presidential Campaign, The, 253-58
Negative television ads, 230-31, 253-58, 260-61
Neodualism, 121
Neustadt, Richard, 55, 56, 321
New Deal, 3, 31, 128
New Federalism, 106, 108-10, 124-25
New Jersey Plan, 29
New Republic, The, 24
Newsweek, 19
New York Times, 19, 63, 116, 181, 262, 263
Next American Frontier, 125
Nightline, 19
"Nightline," 255
Nixon, Richard, 107, 115, 134, 164, 262, 269, 278, 279, 281, 397-98
Noncentralism restoration, 121
Nonpartisan, 24
Non-voting, and voting, 225-27, 233-43
Noriega, General, 3
Normalized entrenchment, 120
North, Oliver, 279
Northrop, Alana, 314, 326-31
Northwestern University, 30
Nuclear Regulatory Commission, 312

O

O'Brien, David M., 397, 412-19
O'Connor, Sandra Day, 68, 393, 394, 398
Office of Personnel Management, 312
Old-Breed and New-Breed Lobbying, 163-69
Oldfield, Duane M., 272, 300-308
O'Malley, Peter, 95, 96
Omnibus Crime Control and Safe Streets Act, 108
O'Neill, Thomas P., 164, 165, 283
Opening the Third Century of American Federalism: Issues and Prospects, 119-30
Operation Desert Storm, 452-59
Opinion, public. *See* Public opinion
Optimism, 296
Orasin, Charles J., 171
Ornstein, Norm, 166
Orren, Gary R., 188, 216-24
Ostriker, Jeremiah P., 339
Oswald, Lee Harvey, 171

P

PAC. *See* Political action committee (PAC)
Park, Tongsun, 165
Parrington, Vernon, 13, 14
Participation, political. *See* Political participation
Participatory democracy, 17
Parties in Transition, 304
Partnership for Health Act, 108
Paster, Howard, 168
Paterson, William, 36
Patterson, Bradley H., Jr., 317-25
Patterson, Thomas, 224
Pennsylvania v. Muniz, 71
Perestroika, 5, 10
Persian Gulf War, 272, 452-59

Persuasion, and influence, 294-99
Peters, Charles, 167
Phillips, Kevin P., 439, 441, 443-51
Pierce, Samuel, 327
Pitt, William (the Elder), 76
Plessy, Homer, 64
Plessy v. Ferguson, 64, 65, 89
Pluralism, 143, 437
Policy, 239-40
   and adoption, 440-41
   domestic, 300-308
   and evaluation, 441
   foreign, 300-308
   and formulation, 439-40
   future of, 468-76
   goal achievement, 294-99
   and implementation, 441
   and leadership, 300-308
   and processes, 437-42
   public. *See* Public policy
Polin, Raymond, 392, 406-11
Political action, and government machinery, 265-434
Political action committee (PAC), 146, 148, 206, 227-28, 244-52
Political culture, 5, 12-17
Political participation, 139-263
Political parties, 181, 182, 240-41
   decentralization, 185
   development, 183-84
   fragmentation and prospects of reform, 185-86, 198-208
   and Madisonian model, 199-202
   and media, 187-88, 216-24
   and presidency, 186-87, 209-15
   and responsible-party model, 201-2
   traditional roles declining, 184-85
Political survey research, and polls, 189-97

Political system, and democracy, 3-26
Politics
   and American creed, 13-14
   and Congress, 345-46, 364-73
   future of, 468-76
   group theories of, 159-62
   and media and elections, 231-32, 259-63
   process and federalism, 111-18
   and rich and poor, 443-51
Politics of Ideas: Political Theory and American Public Policy, The, 12
Politics of the Restive Majority, The, 468-76
Polities, states as, 123-24
Polls
   a layman's guide, 192-93
   making of, 193-95
   and political survey research, 189-97
   uses of, 195-96
Polsby, Nelson, 57
Poor, and politics, 443-51
Positive freedom, 5
Pound, Bill, 135
Powell, Colin, 454
Powell, Jody, 174
Powell, Lewis, 392, 398
Powell v. Alabama, 76
Power Elite, The, 143
Power Game: How Washington Works, The, 163
Powers, separation of. *See* Separation of powers
Precedent, 5, 16
Prerogative, 39
Presidency, 267-308
   and administration, 329-30
   and Constitution, 267-68, 274-80
   and elections, 229-30
   executive branch and bureaucracy, 309-39

and leadership, 268-73,
281-93
and media, 298
and national parties, 186-87,
209-15
and persuasion and
influence, 294-99
*Presidency and Its Paradoxes,
The,* 281-93
*President and the
Bureaucracy: Enemies,
Helpmates, or
Noncontenders?,* 326-31
Presidential Character, The, 270
Pressure system, 155-62
Priorities, 296, 468-76
Private, and communications,
221-24
Private property, 16-17
Privilege, 39
Progressive agrarianism, 120
Property, 16-17
Protection, constitutional. *See*
Constitution
Protections, for accused, 91-101
Public
and communications, 221-24
and finance proposals,
249-50
Public Administration
Clearinghouse, 131
Public opinion, 181-82, 189-97
Public policy, 437-76
and adoption, 440-41
and Congress, 346-47,
364-73
and evaluation, 441-42
future of, 468-76
and implementation, 441
and policy formulation,
439-40
and policy processes, 437-42
and problem identification,
438-39
and U.S. Supreme Court,
397-400
See also Policy

Public Works Employment Act,
67
Publius, 30, 44, 154

Q

Questionnaire, 193-94
Quotas, 66-70

R

Rainmakers, 165
Randolph, Edmund, 46
Ranney, Austin, 221
Ratification, 489-91
Reagan, Nancy, 168
Reagan, Ronald, 19, 20, 23, 33,
57, 60, 61, 68, 69, 72,
106, 107, 108-10, 119,
124-25, 147, 164, 167,
170, 226, 272, 277, 279,
297-98, 310, 393, 394,
399
*Reagan's America: A Capital
Offense,* 443-51
*Real and Imagined Corruption
in Campaign Financing,*
244-52
Realists, 9
*Reconsidering the Two
Presidencies,* 300-308
Reconstruction Era, 51
Reedy, George, 269
Reform
and campaign financing,
248-52
and Constitution, 32, 53-58
of political parties, 185-86,
198-208
Regan, Donald, 311, 312, 317,
329
*Regents of the University of
California v. Bakke,* 66,
67
Rehnquist, William, 394, 398,
426-31
Reich, Robert, 125
Reid, Ira, 158

Religious freedom, 76
*Remobilizing the American
Electorate,* 233-43
Republicanism, 86
Research, and surveys, 189-97
Resolution Trust Corporation
(RTA), 313
Responsible-party model, 201-2
Responsiveness, of democracy, 7
Restatement of Torts, 97
Restoration, 121
Reverse discrimination, 66-70
Revolutionary War, 28
Reynolds, Nancy, 168
Reynolds, William Bradford, 67
Rich, and politics, 443-51
*Richmond, Virginia v. Croson
Company,* 68
Rights, civil. *See* Civil rights
*Rise of the Washington
Establishment, The,*
350-59
Riverside v. McLaughlin, 72
Robertson, Pat, 253
Rockefeller, Nelson, 115
Rockman, B. A., 306, 328
Roe v. Wade, 395, 398, 399,
420-25
Roosevelt, Franklin D., 56, 77,
133, 184, 269, 276, 310
Roosevelt, Theodore, 268, 276
Rossi, 218
Rostenkowski, Danny, 168
Rousseau, Jean Jacques, 9-10,
37, 38, 91
Rule of four, 396
Rule of law, 5, 16
Russert, Timothy J., 224, 231,
232
Rust v. Sullivan, 399
Rutledge, John, 37

S

Sabato, Larry, 227, 228, 244-52
Saikowski, Charlotte, 53-58
St. John's University, 392
SALT, 57

Samples, and polls, 194
Sarah and James Brady, Target: The Gun Lobby, 170-79
Savimbi, Jonas, 167
Savoy, Paul, 71, 91-101
Scalia, 398
Schattschneider, E. E., 143
Schenck, Charles, 62
Schenck v. United States, 62
Scheppach, Ray, 135
Schlesinger, Arthur M., Jr., 55, 57, 269, 278
Schneider, William, 302
Schwarzkopf, Norman, 454
Scope and Bias of the Pressure System, The, 155-62
Scott, Dred, 88, 390
Sears, John P., III, 57
Second Treatise, Of Civil Government, 27
Secord, Richard, 279
Segregation, 65
Self-government, 22-23
Senator, roles and functions, 344
Sensationalism, 6
Separate but equal, 64, 65
Separation of powers, 41-44
Sexual harassment, 395, 396
Shafroth, Frank, 135
Shank, Alan, 268, 274-80
Shannon, John, 57
Shapiro, Martin, 56
Sharpton, Al, 25
Sheet Metal Workers case, 68
Sheppard, Osborne, 95, 96
Shepsle, Kenneth A., 347, 364-73
Simon, Paul, 177
Sinclair, Upton, 163
Slaughterhouse Cases, 89
Slavery, 31, 48, 85, 86
Smith, Edgar, 93
Smith, Hedrick, 146, 147, 163-69
Smith Act, 62
Snyder, John M., 177
Socialization of conflict, 155

Sorensen, Theodore, 321
Souter, David, 71, 394, 395, 398
South Carolina v. Baker, 122
Southern Christian Leadership Conference (SCLC), 61
Soviet Union, 3, 5
Special Prosecutor law, 33
Spence v. Washington, 81
Staff, of White House, 317-25
Stare decisis, 16, 84
State action, control of, 76-77
State-centered federalism, 113-14
States, 128-29, 488-89
   federal aid to, 131-37
   and federal-state relations, 119-30
   reassertion as polities, 123-24
Stennis, John, 169
Stephenson, D. Grier, Jr., 187, 209-15
Stevens, John Paul, 64, 82-84, 398
Stevenson, Adlai, 283, 291
Stewart, Potter, 393
Strategic Defense Initiative (SDI), 301
Strategy, of lobbying, 144-47, 163-69
Strauss, Robert, 164
Strengthening the National Parties, 198-208
Struggle for Democracy, The, 8-11
Substantive democracy, 5
Suffrage, 31
Sundquist, James L., 198-208
Sununu, John, 19
Super Tuesday, 212, 213, 214
Supreme Court. *See* United States Supreme Court
Supreme Court's Dilemma and Defense, The, 406-11
Surveys, and research, 189-97
Swann v. Charlott-Mecklenburg Board of Education, 65
Swett, Richard, 177

T
Tactics, of lobbying, 144-47, 163-69
Taft, William Howard, 268, 396
Taney, Roger, 88, 112, 114, 390
Tarmac politics, 213
Taylor, John, 114
Team lobbying, 168
Teeter, Robert, 196
Teflon president, 297-98
Television, 187-88, 216-24, 230-31, 253-58, 260-61
Temple University, 119
Tennessee Valley Authority (TVA), 313
Terminiello v. Chicago, 82
Texas v. Johnson, 63, 79, 80, 81, 82, 83, 84
Texas v. White, 46, 112
Theory
   competitive, 112-14
   and cooperative theories, 114-17
   and federalism, 111-18
   group theories of politics, 159-62
   and KISS, 295-96
Thevnot, Wayne, 166
They've Got Your Number, 189-97
Thomas, Clarence, 395, 396
Thomas, John, 134, 137
Thumbs Up, 173
Tiananmen Square, 18
Timberg, Robert, 251
Time, 21
Times Mirror Center for the People and the Press, 21, 26, 181
Timmons, Bill, 168
Timmons and Company, 168
Tocqueville, Alexis de, 15, 17
Transition, 120
Trivialization, 6
True Believer, 94
Truman, Harry, 23, 156, 164, 276, 289
Trustee, 343

Tucker, St. George, 87
Twilight of the Presidency, 269
Tyranny, and democracy, 3

U

Udall, Morris, 57, 283
United Automobile Workers
    (UAW), 144, 168
United States Chamber of
    Commerce, 144
United States Postal Service, 313
United States Supreme Court,
    33, 34, 35, 49, 50, 52, 56,
    389-434
and abortion, 398-400,
    420-25, 426-34
and centralization and
    decentralization, 121-22
and civil liberties and civil
    rights, 59-72
and constitutional
    foundations, 389-90,
    401-5
and constitutional
    interpretation, 391-92,
    406-11
and decision-making process,
    396-97, 412-19
and evolution of
    constitutional protections,
    73-78
and gerrymandering, 342
and judicial review, 390-92,
    401-5
and judicial selection criteria,
    393-96
and presidency, 272
and protecting minorities,
    85-91
and protecting the accused,
    91-101
and protecting unpopular
    political expression, 79-84
and public policy, 397-400
United States v. Curtiss Wright,
    272
United States v. Eichman, 64,
    79
United States v. Haggerty, 79
United States v. Miller, 176
United States v. O'Brien, 80
*United Steelworkers of
    America v. Weber,* 66, 67
University of California at
    Berkeley, 338
University of California at Davis,
    97
University of Michigan, 218, 332
University of Oklahoma, 396
Unpopular political expression,
    protection of, 79-84
Unsoeld, Jolene, 178
Urban Development Action
    Grants, 132
U.S. Mayor, 133

V

Values
    and dilemmas, 12-17
    origin of, 8-11
    and political culture, 5-6,
        57-58
Van Buren, Martin, 210
Vanguards, 68
Velasquez, Willie, 243
Veto power, 69
Vidal, Gore, 26
Vietnam War, 75, 278, 281
Vinson, Fred, 62
Virginia Commonwealth
    University, 294
Virginia Plan, 29, 30, 48
Volgy, Thomas, 136
Volkmer, Harold L., 170
Voters
    communicating with, 216-21
    and remobilization of
        electorate, 233-43
Voting
    and elections and media,
        225-63
    and non-voting, 225-27,
        233-43

Voting Rights Act, 60, 61, 166

W

Walker, Charls, 164, 169
Walters, Jonathan, 110, 131-37
Wards Cove v. Atonio, 69
War of 1812, 53
War Powers Resolution, 272,
    279
Warren, Earl, 60, 64, 70, 90, 93,
    96, 99, 123, 393, 397
Washington, George, 34, 36, 37,
    46, 50, 51, 53, 59, 104,
    112, 489
Washington Post, 25, 165, 258
Watergate, 33, 123, 262, 269,
    278, 281
Watson, Patrick, 4, 8-11
Webber, Ross, 344
Weber, Brian, 66
Webster, Daniel, 25, 46, 183
*Webster v. Reproductive Health
    Services,* 399, 400, 426-34
*West Virginia Board of
    Education v. Barnette,* 82
Wexler, Anne, 164, 168
Wexler, Reynolds, Harrison &
    Schule, 168
*When Criminal Rights Go
    Wrong,* 91-101
Whicker, Marcia Lynn, 294-99
White, Byron, 67, 94, 96, 101,
    342, 398
White, William Allen, 285
White House, staff of, 317-25
Wildavsky, Aaron, 272, 300-308
Wilkes, John, 97
Will, George, 254
Wills, Gary, 30, 34-40, 91
Wilson, James, 30, 34-40, 46, 48
Wilson, Woodrow, 77, 184
Wirtz, Willard, 321
Wolfinger, Raymond, 227
Wolter, Kirk M., 334
Woodruff, Judy, 227, 231,
    259-63
Woods, James, 94

Woodward, Bob, 262
*World's Most Stable
    Democracy, The,* 53-58
World War I, 53, 62, 75
World War II, 31, 53, 77
Wright, Jim, 56
Writ of *certiorari,* 396

*Wygant v. Jackson Board of
    Education,* 67
Wythe, George, 87

Y

Ylvisaker, Paul, 117

Z

Zeigler, L. Harmon, 144
Zielinski, Vickie, 93
Zimroth, Peter L., 337